ACTIVE SERVER PAGES HOW-TO

THE DEFINITIVE ACTIVE SERVER PAGES PROBLEM-SOLVER

Nathan Wallace

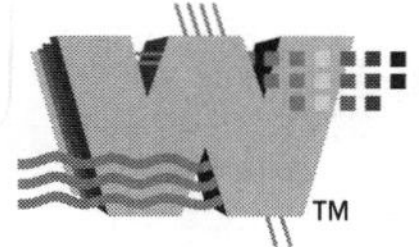

Waite Group Press™
A Division of
Macmillan Computer Publishing
Corte Madera, CA

Publisher: Mitchell Waite
Associate Publisher: Charles Drucker

Acquisitions Manager: Susan Walton

Project Editor: Andrea Rosenberg
Content Editor: Russ Jacobs
Technical Editor: Amy Sticksel
Production Editor: Colleen Williams
Copy Editor: Deirdre Greene/Creative Solutions
Managing Editor: Brice Gosnell
Indexing Manager: Johnna L. VanHoose
Indexer: Cheryl Jackson
Resource Coordinators: Deborah Frisby and Charlotte Clapp
Editorial Assistant: Carmela Carvajal
Software Specialist: Dan Scherf
Director of Marketing: Kelli S. Spencer
Product Marketing Manager: Wendy Gilbride
Marketing Coordinator: Linda B. Beckwith

Production Manager: Cecile Kaufman
Production Team Supervisor: Andrew Stone
Book Designer: Jean Bisesi
Production: Elizabeth Deeter, Shawn Ring, Ian A. Smith

Published by Waite Group Press™, 200 Tamal Plaza, Corte Madera, CA 94925.

Waite Group Press™ is a division of Macmillan Computer Publishing.

Printed in the United States of America
97 98 99 • 10 9 8 7 6 5 4 3 2 1

ISBN 1-57169-116-2

DEDICATION

To Eve. Second in number, first in my heart, and always my favorite police-woman. The only reason I can still smile is I know you're waiting for me.

—Nathan Wallace

ABOUT THE AUTHOR

Nathan Wallace has been developing computer programs since the days of the Apple IIe, in AppleSoft Basic and Turbo Basic from Borland, before moving to Visual Basic for Windows. He has been authoring best-selling computer books since 1994, including the very popular Delphi titles *Borland Delphi How-To* and *Delphi 2 Developer's Solutions* both from Waite Group Press. He has two undergraduate degrees, one in biochemistry and history, and the other in artificial intelligence. He has done graduate work in neural network design to simulate living brain computational models, and has published several papers on hypertext and hypermedia during his undergraduate studies. His computer company, CIUPKC Software, consulted on the C-17 project for MacDonald Douglas, and has supplied the VISA/PLUS GlobalLocator software to InfoNow corporation. He is currently developing Internet Commander, a breakthrough Internet and WWW application using the new Internet Client SDK from Microsoft.

TABLE OF CONTENTS

CONTENTS

ACKNOWLEDGMENTS

Like most worthwhile endeavors, this book is really the work of many people. I'd like to thank Susan Walton, the Acquisitions Manager at Waite Group Press who proposed the whole idea, for support and assistance throughout the whole process. A special thank you goes to Andrea Rosenberg, my Project Editor, who has as always shepherded my tome through the intricate process of creating a modern technical book. A tip of the authorial hat to Dan Scherf, the Waite Group Software Specialist, who created the CD and has been the liaison for all those ugly but essential technical production details. And a special thank you to Russ Jacobs, my Content Editor, and Amy Sticksel, my Technical Reviewer, for all their help in making this book the best it could be. And of course, a final word of appreciation for Mitchell Waite, who started the whole process for me in 1995.

Due for some kudos as well are all those Microsoft programmers who have developed ASP, ActiveX, and all the other elements of the modern Active Internet. A special thank you must also be extended to all those folks on the Microsoft Mailing Lists who help out whenever any of us hit a brick wall with the technology!

Also, I'd like, as always, to extend personal thanks to Alex Champion and Laura Welch, the two dearest people in my life; their tolerance of my "life in byteland" makes books like this possible!

INTRODUCTION

What This Book Is All About (C++ Is the Answer, Not Scripts!)

This book is slightly misnamed; it really should be called *The Active Platform How-To*. It is called *Active Server Pages How-To* because ASP is the glue that holds the rest of the Active Platform together. But make no mistake: There is a lot more here than just Active Server Pages scripts! While most of the How-To's here use ASP in some form, they also focus on the other four technologies that make up the Active Platform: ActiveX controls, Active Server Pages components, ISAPI Extensions and Filters, and ActiveX data objects and OLE DB Interfaces. And unlike most other ASP books, this book concentrates on the C++ programming needed to make Active Platform applications work. Get ready to take C++ programming onto the Information Superhighway!

ActiveX Controls

ActiveX controls are what started the whole Active Platform revolution, and they remain its cornerstone. Designed to provide sophisticated capabilities which their competition (Java Applets) could not, ActiveX controls have matured into a powerful mechanism for packaging user interface functionality to be used not only on the WWW, but also in cross-language environments (such as Delphi, Visual Basic, and Visual J++). *Active Server Pages How-To* provides three chapters that start at the very beginning of ActiveX, proceed through its core technology, and end up on its cutting edge.

Active Server Pages Scripts and Components

Although ASP is the namesake of this book, most people associate it with simple but powerful scripts that add features to HTML pages. The three chapters dedicated to ASP technology provide a clearer picture of this amazing technology, with details not only on all the range of scripting possibilities, but also on using ASP components provided with the system, and creating C++ ASP components that interface with the ASP system.

ISAPI Extensions and Filters

ISAPI stands for Internet Server Application Programming Interface, and it works with PWS (Personal Web Server and Peer Web Services) as well as its big brother IIS (Internet Information Server.) Extensions are the equivalent of CGI scripts, and provide similar features such as responding to form inputs, outputting formatted HTML code, and even sending back image or binary data. Filters are additions to the IIS/PWS system itself, and provide much more power at a corresponding level of risk, including the capability to redirect page requests based on browser type, and add custom HTML to all pages passing through the server. Each technology has its own chapter.

ActiveX Data Objects

ActiveX data objects (ADO) are the way that ASP scripts interact with ODBC databases in the creation of dynamic HTML pages. Provided as an ASP component, ADO encapsulates the functionality of the OLE DB API, and permits ASP scripts to open ODBC databases, create cursors, browse recordsets, and update data from user input. ADO has its own chapter, and is covered in many How-To's in other chapters.

OLE DB Interfaces (ActiveX Data Objects in C++)

OLE DB is a little-known project from Microsoft that has all the power of an atomic bomb in database programming: it allows nondatabase data sources (like a directory of e-mail message files) to be accessed as a database, using SQL and ODBC techniques. The ADO system, which accesses ODBC in ASP scripting, can also be used directly in C++ programs, and thus added to any other Active Platform element. The last chapter covers this new and breakthrough technology.

Cross-Technology: Lacing Up The Seams

Although ASP is the glue that binds the Active Platform's five technologies together, there are some gaping seams left over! How do you connect an ActiveX control with an ASP script? What is the technique to use an ASP component from an ALX HTML Layout control? Which is the best way to interface ActiveX data objects with ISAPI Extensions? And how do OLE DB Interfaces work with ISAPI Filters? If you have had to deal with any of these questions, or others like them, each chapter of this book has something for you! Every chapter has at least one cross-technology How-To, and a number have three or four or even five technology elements. Look for special icons next to How-To's that have this feature.

Icons used in *Active Server Pages How-To*

ICON	DESCRIPTION
ADO-AXC	ActiveX Data Objects-ActiveX Controls
ADO-ASPC	ActiveX Data Objects-Active Server Pages Components
ADO-IEXT	ActiveX Data Objects-ISAPI Extensions
IFIL-ADO-ASP	ISAPI Filters-ActiveX Data Objects-Active Server Pages Scripts
AX-ASP	ActiveX Controls-Active Server Pages Scripts
ADO-ASP	ActiveX Data Objects-Active Server Pages Scripts
ISAPI-ASP	ISAPI Extensions-Active Server Pages Scripts
IFIL-IEXT	ISAPI Filters-ISAPI Extensions

Question and Answer Format (Plus More!)

The "question and answer format" is the one Mitchell Waite developed many years ago, and it remains one of the best ways to learn complicated and arcane information. This book uses the How-To technique with special emphasis on cross-technology coverage. When you have to merge two, three, four, or five different functionalities that were not even developed by the same programmers, a How-To is definitely the way to go!

Source Code, Pictures, and Goodies!

The CD contains all the source code and projects from the book, as well as a directory of all the screen captures from the book (we make them in color, and they are rather attractive, but unfortunately the book must be grayscale), and a number of useful SDK and freeware/shareware programming tools for ASP and Active Platform development. The Installation section in the back of the book explains how to use the WISE installation utility that allows you to copy the CD files to your hard drive.

Expected Level of Reader

You need to understand three things to use this book: how to program in C++, how to use a word processor like Notepad, and how to use Visual C++ 5.0. You don't need to know a thing about the Internet, ActiveX, HTML, ISAPI, or ASP. The book is broken into Beginning, Intermediate, and Advanced How-To's that build on one another, so that you can learn enough from each one to do the next. If you are experienced in any of the Active Platform technologies (or all of them), you can use this book as either a reference to the ones you know, or to how to get them to work together!

What You Need To Use This Book

You need a copy of Visual C++ 5.0, professional edition, to use this book because most of its programming projects use this version of the Microsoft compiler and development environment. You also will need to have Active Server Pages running on your computer (see the next section for installing and using ASP). And if you wish to use the last chapter, you will need to download the OLE DB SDK onto your computer and install it. You will also need to have Internet Explorer 3.02 or 4.0 installed, and either ActiveX Control Pad or FrontPad installed as well.

Installing and Using Active Server Pages

Active Server Pages is not a standalone technology. Instead, it lives on top of two other technologies: Internet Information Server and Internet Explorer. You can obtain the whole suite in one of the following ways.

If you are using Windows NT Server 4.0, you already have IIS installed. If you have an earlier version, you must either upgrade to 4.0 or install a Service Pack. Go to the NT Web site at Microsoft and locate the IIS pages; they will give you exact directions on what you need to install IIS. Then download the latest version of IIS and install it; ASP will be installed automatically. Finally, obtain either Internet Explorer 3.*x* or 4.0, from Microsoft's Web site and install it, and you are ready to go!

If you are using Windows NT Workstation 4.0, you have Peer Web Services already installed; it will allow ASP to work for a small intranet or one computer. Go to the Microsoft NT Web site and locate the IIS pages; find the download pages and locate the ASP installation file and download it. Then install it by running the executable; it will configure your system and make ASP functionality available. Finally, obtain either Internet Explorer 3.*x* or 4.0, from Microsoft's Web Site and install it, and you are ready to go!

If you are using Windows 95, you need to acquire Personal Web Server. There are several ways to do this: Obtain the latest version, which is still in beta testing as of this writing, which includes ASP, and download and install it on your computer (you can obtain it at the Windows NT Web site's IIS pages); or obtain a copy of the older PWS either as part of the FrontPage 97 product or the Visual InterDev product. If you choose the latter method, you need to go to the IIS pages on the Windows NT Web site at Microsoft, locate the ASP download file, download it, and run the self-installing executable to place ASP on your system. Finally, obtain either Internet Explorer 3.*x* or 4.0, from Microsoft's Web site and install it, and you are ready to go!

Once you have ASP on your system, you need to create "virtual directories" to be able to use ASP scripts in HTML pages. The process to do this is described in detail in the appropriate How-To's for Personal Web Server. For Peer Web Services or Internet Information Server, please check out the online help for administering the server in question. Each directory that is to contain ASP scripts must have its "execute" permissions set or the scripts will not be interpreted.

How This Book Is Organized

This book is broken into 10 chapters, each of which has 10 How-To's. Each How-To has an introduction, then a set of steps which outline how to create a project or Web page, followed by an explanation of what is going on once the result is obtained, and a comment on side issues raised in the process.

Chapter 1—Basic ActiveX: Starting Out on the World Wide Web

This chapter starts you out with both ActiveX and the Internet and World Wide Web. Its 10 How-To's show you how to make an ActiveX control using Visual C++ 5.0 without writing a single line of code, and how to create an upgraded Windows control that is usable as an ActiveX control. It also demonstrates adding `.LIC` license file support to control developer usage of freely downloadable controls, and how to obtain and use Authenticode Software Protection Certificates to make users comfortable with your software over the Internet. Finally, the chapter demonstrates placing an ActiveX control on the World Wide Web, creating an LPK file to control its access and usage, and adding client and server scripts to enhance its functionality. When you finish this chapter, you're up to speed on ActiveX and the Internet!

Chapter 2—Intermediate ActiveX: Creating Customized ActiveX Controls

This chapter moves into the core of ActiveX control development in Visual C++ 5.0. It focuses on using the various wizards to create properties, methods, and events for customized ActiveX controls. The capabilities covered include stock and ambient properties, standard and custom methods and events, and text and font support. Also included are using custom images, property persistence, ActiveX scripting and ASP scripting of the custom properties, methods, and events. This chapter leaves you ready to create any standard ActiveX control you like!

Chapter 3—Advanced ActiveX: Special Features, Control Containers, ActiveX Documents, and VBScript 2.0

This chapter covers the high end of ActiveX control development. Topics include creating and using property pages, adding custom font and image support with property pages, and using advanced optimizations including transparency and nonrectangular controls. Further advanced ActiveX topics covered are nonvisual controls, using ActiveX controls in C++ applications, and creating ActiveX document servers and containers. Finally, the process of creating ActiveX controls using HTML pages dynamically at runtime and the power of the VBScript 2 TextStream object are outlined. This chapter leaves you with an expertise in ActiveX controls that approaches guru level!

Chapter 4—Basic ASP: Server- and Client-Side Scripting

This is the first of the three Active Server Pages chapters, and it allows even the most basic beginner to easily come up to speed with this exciting new technology! The early How-To's cover basic ASP scripts using <%%> syntax, conditional script output, and user interaction. More advanced How-To's include information on obtaining user information via the Request Object, and sending data back with the Response Object (objects are ASP components included with the ASP system). The final How-To's bring in RUNAT script syntax, mixing ASP and ActiveX (client-side) scripting, and using ActiveX data objects (ADO) in ASP scripts. Even if you aren't sure what ASP stands for, when you finish this chapter you will be writing awesome ASP scripts for your HTML pages!

Chapter 5—Intermediate ASP: Active Server Components

Once you've learned what ASP is and how to use its basic functionality, this chapter moves you towards the fast lane with How To's that cover creating ASP applications via virtual directories, using `GLOBAL.ASA` to handle startup and shutdown tasks, and interacting with multiple users via application locking. It then speeds up even faster with information on the potent Server and Session ASP Component objects, and examples of the AdRotator and BrowsCap ASP Components. Finally, the chapter brings in the more exotic "trails" capabilities, TextStream input and output capabilities, and ODBC Connection Pooling. This chapter will leave you breathing hard and users of your increasingly powerful Web pages breathing even harder!

Chapter 6—Advanced ASP: Creating ASP Components with Visual C++ 5.0

The underlying power of ASP scripts are the ASP component objects, and this chapter shows you how to add your own objects to the system! It starts out with a simple ASP component Visual C++ 5.0 project, and then enhances it with events, the `IScriptingContext` interface, and direct HTML output. The custom ASP component development tutorial then continues with coverage of HTML forms input capabilities, using the `Session` and `Server` objects from a C++ ASP component, and accessing the Cookies system. Finally, using HTML scripts with ASP scripts and a custom ASP component object, and using a custom ASP component with ActiveX data objects are explained. This chapter ends direct coverage of Active Server Pages, leaving you ready and eager to add all their power to your Web applications!

Chapter 7—ActiveX Data Objects: OLE DB Made Easy

Databases are an increasingly important element in the Internet and World Wide Web, and the Active Platform has an exciting way to add their information to its capabilities: the ActiveX data object (ADO). This chapter covers using ADO with ASP scripts and allowing users to interact with ODBC databases accessed via ADO. Further How-To's illustrate connecting ADO with ASP components and allowing user navigation and updates directly via ADO recordsets and cursors. Advanced features are covered with How-To's on adding client-side scripting to ADO ASP pages, and using ActiveX controls and HTML layouts with ADO capabilities. Finally, ADO interactions with both ISAPI Extensions and ISAPI Filters are covered. This chapter will leave you ready to unleash the full power of ODBC databases on your ASP pages!

Chapter 8—ISAPI Extensions: Using ActiveX DLL's to Replace CGI

ISAPI Extensions are the IIS equivalent of Common Gateway Interface (CGI) scripts and applications. This chapter starts out with a basic ISAPI Extension project in Visual C++ 5.0, then adds server information acquisition and parse map functionality to the Extension, allowing it to duplicate basic CGI capabilities. The more powerful features of ISAPI are then displayed with additional How-To's including customized header output to send binary files from form requests, direct HTML output, error handling, and browser redirection. Finally three cross-technology How-To's cover adding ActiveX control interactions to ISAPI Extensions, using ASP scripts with ISAPI Extensions, and linking ADO objects with ISAPI Extensions. This chapter will enable either an old-style CGI programmer or a new IIS developer to unlock and use all the power of ISAPI in his Web projects!

Chapter 9—ISAPI Filters: Customizing Internet Information Server

ISAPI Extensions behave like CGI scripts, but ISAPI Filters are somewhat unique: they add to the capabilities of the Server itself. While CGI scripts could duplicate some Filter functionality, many Filter features are unique to IIS. This chapter covers creating a basic Filter, and using it to implement a Web site counter, do virtual URL redirection, and send a customized HTML page based on the accessing browser. The How-To's then move beyond CGI capabilities to cover custom HTML addition and modification for all Web pages accessed on a server. Finally, four cross-technology How-To's cover interactions between ISAPI Filters and ISAPI Extensions, ActiveX controls, and client and server scripting and ADO functionality. This chapter leaves you with unprecedented command over the IIS Web server on your Web site!

Chapter 10—OLE DB: ActiveX Data Objects in Visual C++ 5.0

ActiveX data objects (ADO) are actually a wrapper around the OLE DB system, one of the most powerful and least-known of the new Microsoft Active Platform technologies. This chapter provides unique and cutting edge information on using ADO with C++ (which is of course quite different from using the ADO components in ASP scripts). This process is complicated by the fact that there is currently no documentation on using ADO in C++, only in Visual Basic. The How-To's start with creating a simple ADO project, which is an ActiveX control, then add features to it including user navigation, user updates, record finding, and record addition and deletion. Then the same technology is transferred to an ASP Component, an ISAPI Extension, and an ISAPI Filter. Server- and client-side scripting capabilities are added, and the final How-To is a capstone technology demonstrator that uses all five core Active Platform technologies to create a virtual directory system that uses URL and user inputs to allow access to restricted database information entirely over the WWW! This chapter leaves you ready for the twenty-first century and armed for all the WWW can throw at you!

Last Minute Changes: Read the `README`!

Despite our best efforts, this book has a flaw or two. There are still areas where the five Active Platform technologies don't interact well or even at all! To help deal with this problem in the press of modern fast-paced technical book development, it is essential that you, the reader, consult three sources: the `README.TXT` file on the CD distributed with this book, which holds last minute revisions to the text and changes to the code printed in the the book; the `README.TXT` files in each directory on the CD, which will explain whether significant changes have been made to the code on the CD after the book was printed; and the `README.TXT` file on the Waite Group Press Web site (`http://www.waite.com/`), which contains last minute changes that came in too late to get on the CD.

This Book on the Internet

Finally, I maintain my own Web site for this book at `http://www.tde.com/~ciupkc/books/aspht/default.htm`. Please look here for the very latest `README.TXT`, as well as bug fixes, code updates, and any number of useful goodies for ASP development.

Also, be sure and check out the Microsoft Active Platform mailing lists. These are moderated (relatively) email-based discussion groups similar to Usenet newsgroups but without all the posting about dirty pictures and get rich quick schemes. Point your brower to `http://www.microsoft.com/sitebuilder/resource/mail-faq.asp` to get started with them; you'll be extremely glad you did! I regularly post to these lists, and will be happy to answer questions about this book or any other Active Platform topic there.

And last but not least, feel free to drop me a line at `kilgalen@tde.com`. Please put "ASP How-To" in the subject line somewhere so my mail sorter can put your message in the right inbox, or it might not get read for several weeks! I'm especially interested in either bugs you've found (and hopefully fixed!) or inaccuracies you've noticed in the text. Either will be immediately fixed and the update will be posted to the Web resources for the book.

Thanks for buying *Active Server Pages How-To*, and happy Active coding!

CHAPTER 1

BASIC ACTIVEX: STARTING OUT ON THE WORLD WIDE WEB

1

BASIC ACTIVEX: STARTING OUT ON THE WORLD WIDE WEB

How do I...

1.1 Create an ActiveX control with Visual C++ 5.0?

1.2 Put the functions of a standard Windows control in an ActiveX control?

1.3 Control how other developers can use my ActiveX control with LIC registration files?

1.4 Create a CAB (Cabinet) compressed archive to distribute my ActiveX control with reduced size and greater speed?

1.5 Obtain an Authenticode™ Software Protection Certificate to allow secure use of my ActiveX control on the World Wide Web?

1.6 Use Authenticode code signing to protect my ActiveX control on the Web?

1.7 Put my ActiveX control on a Web page?

1.8 Prevent unauthorized use of my ActiveX control on Web pages?

1.9 Interact with my ActiveX control using ActiveX Scripting?

1.10 Link my ActiveX control with an Active Server Pages script?

ActiveX controls are the latest incarnation of object linking and embedding (OLE) technology from the days of Windows 3.1 and later, optimized for use over the Internet and on World Wide Web Hypertext Markup Language (HTML) pages. This chapter will get you up to speed on creating these powerful programming tools with Visual C++ 5.0, both from scratch and as an extension of an existing Windows control. But there is more involved than just whipping out clean code in C++; many technologies come together now to create Active Server Pages (ASP)! How-To's in this chapter illustrate using CAB (Cabinet) technology to produce ZIP-like compression of ActiveX controls while downloading. Other How-To's show the mechanics of LIC and LPK licensing and SPC code signing that give developers control and safety on the electronic frontier. The last How-To's demonstrate creation of HTML, ALX, and ASP files that permit ActiveX controls to be downloaded and viewed on the World Wide Web using ActiveX and Active Server Pages scripting to produce dynamic and exciting user interaction capabilities! Although this chapter is rated as beginning in complexity, there is plenty of information here for even the most advanced programmer. So fire up your computer and move ahead into the active World Wide Web with these 10 sections.

1.1 Create an ActiveX Control with Visual C++ 5.0

Visual C++ 5.0 has been redesigned to automate almost the entire process of ActiveX control creation. This How-To guides you through all the steps of creating and testing your first ActiveX control.

1.2 Put the Functions of a Standard Windows Control in an ActiveX Control

Many Windows controls would be very useful in a Web page. This How-To illustrates the steps needed to create an ActiveX control in Visual C++ 5.0 that uses a standard Windows control as its basis.

1.3 Control how Other Developers Can Use My ActiveX Control with LIC Registration Files

Because ActiveX is designed for unlimited distribution of working, uncrippled code modules over the Internet and World Wide Web, some mechanism is needed to allow developers to receive payment for their control. Microsoft has provided this capability with ActiveX Registration and `.LIC` files; this How-To illustrates the exact steps needed to modify an ActiveX control to use LIC protection for design while allowing end users free access to the control.

1.4 Create a CAB (Cabinet) Compressed Archive to Distribute My ActiveX Control with Reduced Size and Greater Speed

Large controls, or groups of controls might take significant time to download over the Internet and consume space on Web server computers. To remedy these problems, Microsoft has released its internal compression system, Cabinet (`.CAB`) files. This How-To explains how to obtain the Cabinet Software Development Kits (SDKs) from Microsoft free and how to use them to compress an OCX or DLL file into a CAB file.

1.5 Obtain an Authenticode Software Protection Certificate to Allow Secure Use of My ActiveX Control on the World Wide Web

The problem inherent in downloading and executing unknown code over the Internet is the risk of destructive behavior, such as viruses and Trojan Horses. To combat this problem, Microsoft has developed the Authenticode technology in conjunction with the VeriSign Corporation. This How-To shows you the complete process needed to acquire a Software Protection Certificate (SPC) that allows the Internet Explorer browser and other browsers that support Authenticode to use your ActiveX controls safely without requiring user interactions, regardless of their security settings.

1.6 Use Authenticode Code Signing to Protect My ActiveX Control on the Web

Aside from the need to reassure users that your ActiveX control is safe, once the control is distributed on the World Wide Web, others gain access to the binary code of your control and could maliciously alter it by inserting viruses or even rewriting it completely! To prevent this, Microsoft Authenticode allows you to digitally "sign" your control or other binary file (such as a CAB file) so that tampering is not possible without alerting users. This How-To shows all the steps to acquire the ActiveX SDK, which contains the Authenticode system, and use it to protect your Web binaries.

1.7 Put My ActiveX Control on a Web Page

Now you have your shiny new ActiveX control and would like to use it on a World Wide Web page and show it off to others. This How-To introduces you to the ActiveX Control Pad and demonstrates placing your control on an HTML layout and then into an HTML file, uploading it to your Web server, and displaying it on Internet Explorer.

1.8 Prevent Unauthorized Use of My ActiveX Control on Web Pages

In some cases, you might want to prevent the use of an ActiveX control on the Web without a license being purchased. Microsoft has built the capability to do this into ActiveX, and this How-To demonstrates using it via HTML tags and LPK files.

1.9 Interact with My ActiveX Control Using ActiveX Scripting

Although it's fun to stare at your lovely new ActiveX control on the Web page, it's even more fun to make it do something! This How-To gives a quick lesson in using ActiveX Scripting inside an HTML page to control the behavior of an ActiveX control on the client's machine.

1.10 Link My ActiveX Control with an Active Server Pages Script

Although ActiveX Scripting will allow some nice operations once an HTML page is downloaded, being able to control what is displayed prior to a page being downloaded is even more powerful, and that is what ASP does! This How-To gives a simple but effective example of linking an ActiveX control to an ASP script to produce dynamic responses to user input without requiring complex Common Gateway Interface (CGI) scripting.

1.1 How do I… Create an ActiveX control with Visual C++ 5.0?

Problem

I need to create a simple ActiveX control fast! Can Visual C++'s wizard system help me out here?

Technique

Version 5.0 of Visual C++ (VC 5) upgraded its wizard functionality specifically for ActiveX control generation. This How-To guides you through the steps of creating a simple but fully functional ActiveX control with VC 5. Although the directions here start from scratch, you can find the entire project on the CD under `\CH01\HT01\ASPHT0101\`.

Steps

1. Start Visual C++ 5.0. If there is an active workspace, close it and all document windows. Then choose File|New... from the menu and select the MFC ActiveX ControlWizard entry, as shown in Figure 1-1. Enter a new path for the project on your computer and name the project `aspht0101`. Then click the OK button.

2. The MFC ActiveX ControlWizard dialog's first page will appear, as shown in Figure 1-2. Leave all the options set to their defaults for this first project and press the Next button.

3. The second page of the MFC ActiveX ControlWizard will appear as shown in Figure 1-3. Again leave all the options set to their defaults, and press the Finish button. A final confirmation dialog will appear showing the previous choices. Press the OK button, and the VC workspace will be created automatically.

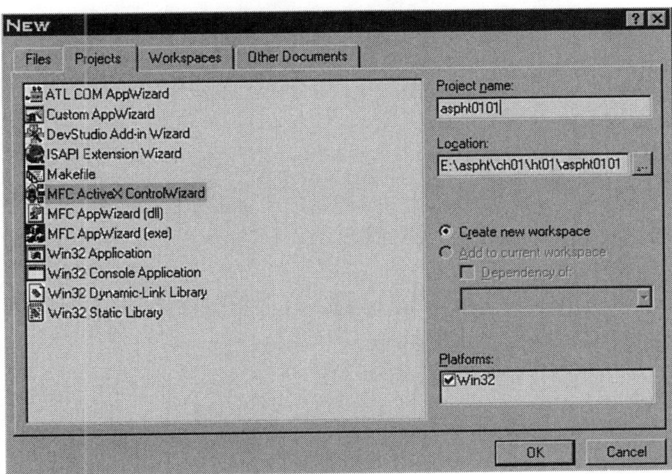

Figure 1-1 The VC 5 New Projects dialog

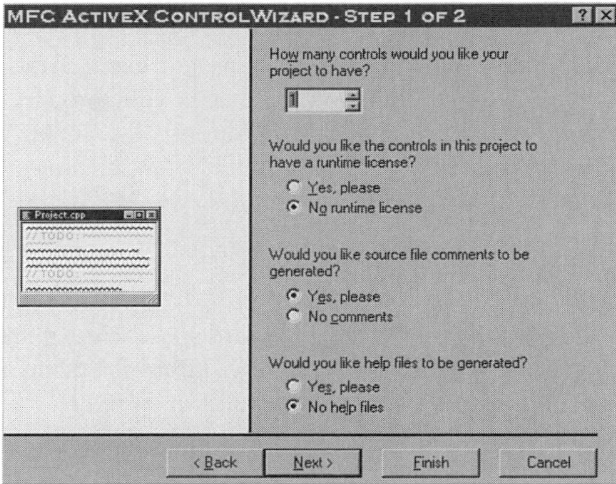

Figure 1-2 The VC 5 MFC ActiveX ControlWizard dialog first page

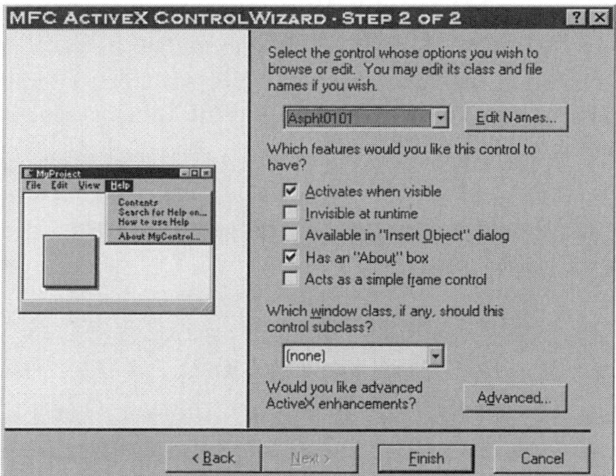

Figure 1-3 The VC 5 MFC ActiveX ControlWizard dialog second page

4. After the project has been created, select the Files pane of the project viewer and expand the various files in the project. Then double-click on the `ASPHT0101.ODL` entry. It will be displayed in the source window, producing a display similar to that shown in Figure 1-4. Spend a few minutes browsing the source code created by the system but do not make any changes at this time.

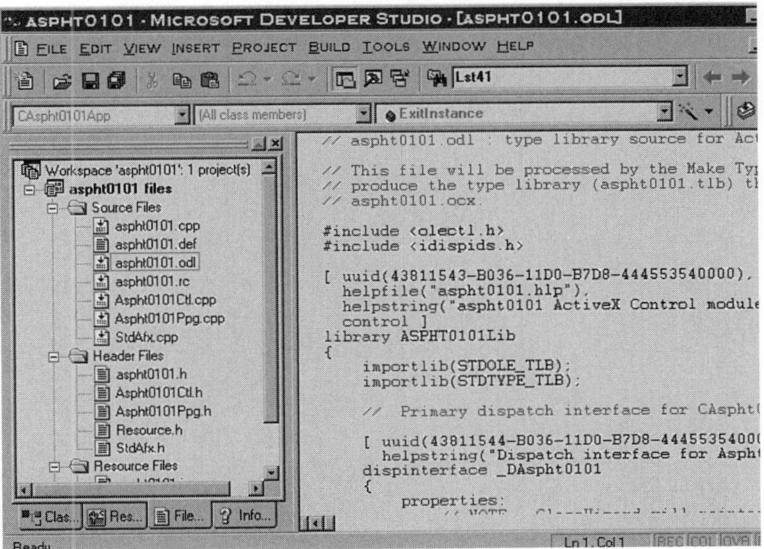

Figure 1-4 The `ASPHT0101.ODL` file in the Developer Studio environment, along with the various files created for the project

5. Next, select the Build|Compile ASPHT0101.ODL menu option as shown in Figure 1-5. The Developer Studio environment will activate the MIDL compiler to create the type library TLB file needed by the system for the ActiveX control, as shown in Figure 1-6.

NOTE

You do not have to do this step unless you need the TLB file for something before you compile the OCX; building the OCX will automatically generate the TLB file.

6. Now choose the Build|Build ASPHT0101.OCX menu option, which is just below the previously selected one. The Developer Studio environment will compile all the appropriate files and register the ActiveX control, as shown in Figure 1-7.

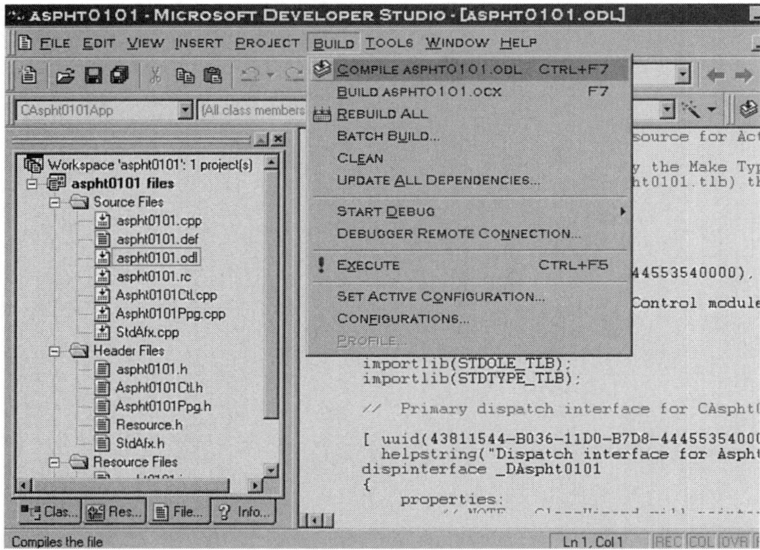

Figure 1-5 The menu option to create the TLB file from ASPHT0101.ODL

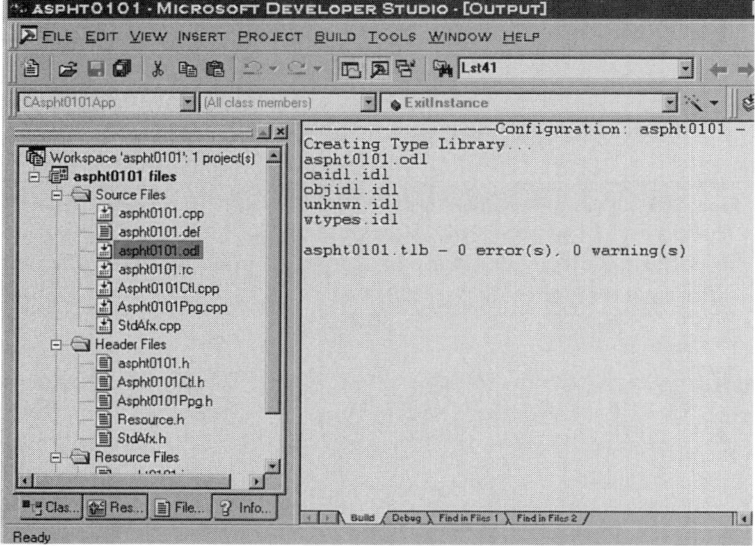

Figure 1-6 The output from the MIDL compiler started by Developer Studio on ASPHI0101.ODL

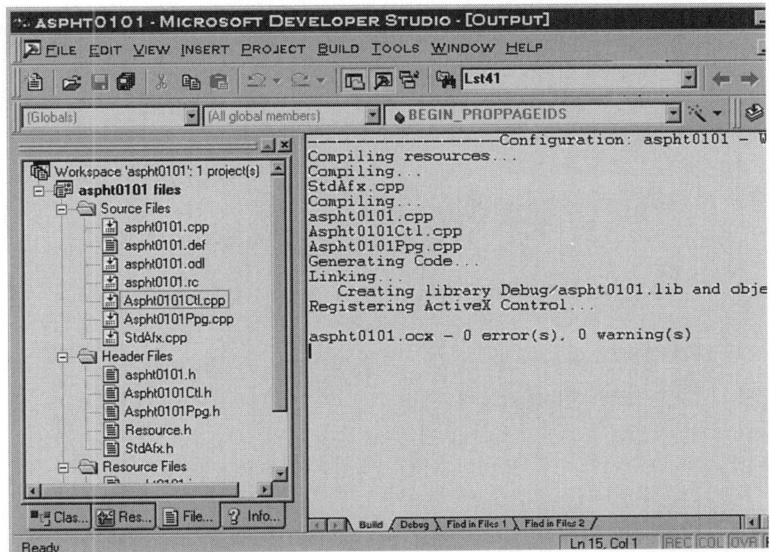

Figure 1-7 **The `ASPHT0101.OCX` project being compiled and registered by the Developer Studio environment**

7. Next, choose the Tools|ActiveX Control Test Container menu option. A new application will start the ActiveX Control Test Container (as expected!). Press the leftmost speed button, and the Insert OLE Control dialog will appear. Scroll down if needed to the `ASPHT0101` control and select it, as shown in Figure 1-8. Press OK.

8. The newly created control, which draws an ellipse inside its bounding rectangle, will appear on the display surface surrounded by hatching and grab handles. Move it and resize it to a larger area, and it will respond just as expected, producing a display similar to that shown in Figure 1-9. Congratulations! You have just created your first ActiveX control!

How It Works

ActiveX is a new name for OCX controls, which are in turn an extension of OLE 2 functionality. MFC has added increasing support for OCX over the last two releases of Visual C++ in Developer Studio; now in version 5.0, the support is complete. You created a complete, fully functioning ActiveX control without writing a single line of code!

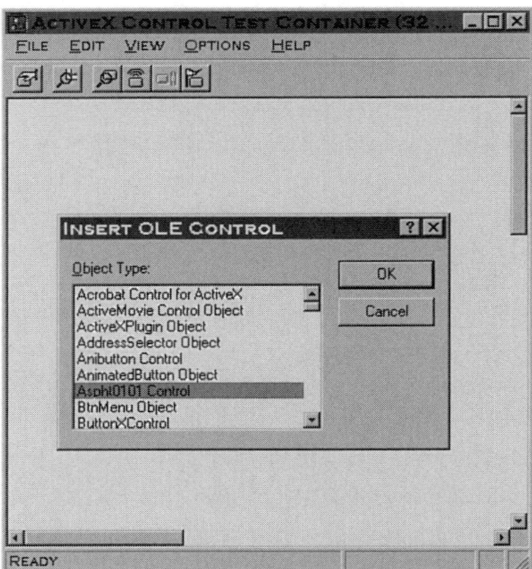

Figure 1-8 The Insert OLE Control dialog of the ActiveX Test Container application, showing the newly created `ASPHT0101` control

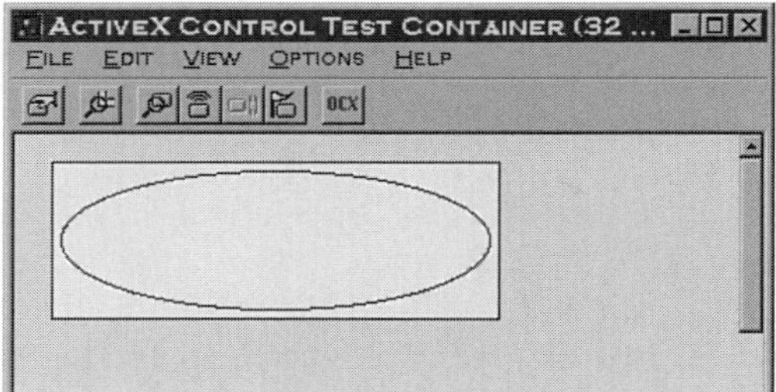

Figure 1-9 `ASPHT0101.OCX`, displayed in the ActiveX test container after resizing and moving

Before moving on, it is worth spending a few minutes examining the code created by the system as an example of what is required to create and use an ActiveX control. First, notice the ODL file created for the project; this type of file is not needed by a normal application and is used to create the type library (TLB) required by the OLE 2 system to allow other applications (such as Internet Explorer and the ActiveX control test container) to know what the features and capabilities of an ActiveX control are. Listing 1-1 shows the contents of this file.

Listing 1-1 ASPHT0101.ODL type library source code

```
// aspht0101.odl : type library source for ActiveX Control project.

// This file will be processed by the Make Type Library (mktyplib) tool to
// produce the type library (aspht0101.tlb) that will become a resource in
// aspht0101.ocx.

#include <olectl.h>
#include <idispids.h>

[ uuid(43811543-B036-11D0-B7D8-444553540000), version(1.0),
  helpfile("aspht0101.hlp"),
  helpstring("aspht0101 ActiveX Control module"),
  control ]
library ASPHT0101Lib
{
importlib(STDOLE_TLB);
importlib(STDTYPE_TLB);

//  Primary dispatch interface for CAspht0101Ctrl

[ uuid(43811544-B036-11D0-B7D8-444553540000),
helpstring("Dispatch interface for Aspht0101 Control"), hidden ]
dispinterface _DAspht0101
{
properties:
// NOTE - ClassWizard will maintain property information here.
//    Use extreme caution when editing this section.
//{{AFX_ODL_PROP(CAspht0101Ctrl)
//}}AFX_ODL_PROP

methods:
// NOTE - ClassWizard will maintain method information here.
//    Use extreme caution when editing this section.
//{{AFX_ODL_METHOD(CAspht0101Ctrl)
//}}AFX_ODL_METHOD

[id(DISPID_ABOUTBOX)] void AboutBox();
};

//  Event dispatch interface for CAspht0101Ctrl

[ uuid(43811545-B036-11D0-B7D8-444553540000),
helpstring("Event interface for Aspht0101 Control") ]
dispinterface _DAspht0101Events
{
properties:
//  Event interface has no properties

methods:
// NOTE - ClassWizard will maintain event information here.
//    Use extreme caution when editing this section.
//{{AFX_ODL_EVENT(CAspht0101Ctrl)
//}}AFX_ODL_EVENT
};
```

continued on next page

continued from previous page

```
//  Class information for CAspht0101Ctrl

[ uuid(43811546-B036-11D0-B7D8-444553540000),
helpstring("Aspht0101 Control"), control ]
coclass Aspht0101
{
[default] dispinterface _DAspht0101;
[default, source] dispinterface _DAspht0101Events;
};


//{{AFX_APPEND_ODL}}
//}}AFX_APPEND_ODL}}
};
```

This file lists all the interfaces supported by the control, gives its UUIDs (Universal Unique IDs), and lists all its properties and events. As you create more complex ActiveX controls in future How-To's, you will notice that significant additions occur to this file to tell the system about the features of your control.

Next, take a look at the ASPHT0101.CPP file, which is shown in Listing 1-2.

Listing 1-2 ASPHT0101.CPP base project source code

```
// aspht0101.cpp : Implementation of CAspht0101App and DLL registration.

#include "stdafx.h"
#include "aspht0101.h"

#ifdef _DEBUG
#define new DEBUG_NEW
#undef THIS_FILE
static char THIS_FILE[] = __FILE__;
#endif


CAspht0101App NEAR theApp;

const GUID CDECL BASED_CODE _tlid =
{ 0x43811543, 0xb036, 0x11d0, { 0xb7, 0xd8, 0x44, 0x45, 0x53, 0x54, 0, 0 } };
const WORD _wVerMajor = 1;
const WORD _wVerMinor = 0;


////////////////////////////////////////////////////////////////////////////
// CAspht0101App::InitInstance - DLL initialization

BOOL CAspht0101App::InitInstance()
{
BOOL bInit = COleControlModule::InitInstance();

if (bInit)
{
// TODO: Add your own module initialization code here.
}
```

```
return bInit;
}


/////////////////////////////////////////////////////////////////////////////
// CAspht0101App::ExitInstance - DLL termination

int CAspht0101App::ExitInstance()
{
// TODO: Add your own module termination code here.

return COleControlModule::ExitInstance();
}


/////////////////////////////////////////////////////////////////////////////
// DllRegisterServer - Adds entries to the system registry

STDAPI DllRegisterServer(void)
{
AFX_MANAGE_STATE(_afxModuleAddrThis);

if (!AfxOleRegisterTypeLib(AfxGetInstanceHandle(), _tlid))
return ResultFromScode(SELFREG_E_TYPELIB);

if (!COleObjectFactoryEx::UpdateRegistryAll(TRUE))
return ResultFromScode(SELFREG_E_CLASS);

return NOERROR;
}


/////////////////////////////////////////////////////////////////////////////
// DllUnregisterServer - Removes entries from the system registry

STDAPI DllUnregisterServer(void)
{
AFX_MANAGE_STATE(_afxModuleAddrThis);

if (!AfxOleUnregisterTypeLib(_tlid, _wVerMajor, _wVerMinor))
return ResultFromScode(SELFREG_E_TYPELIB);

if (!COleObjectFactoryEx::UpdateRegistryAll(FALSE))
return ResultFromScode(SELFREG_E_CLASS);

return NOERROR;
```

Notice a number of macros unique to the MFC ActiveX system, such as `AFX_MANAGE_STATE`. These are inserted by the wizards to save space in the source code and produce all the complex code features needed to handle ActiveX interactions. Either they should not be edited at all or, if they are edited by hand, changes should be made *very* carefully! Also notice the **`ResultFromScode`** function; this function converts the **`HRESULT`** values returned by ActiveX functions in the 32-bit environment into more useful values.

Finally, take a glance at the **`ASPHT0101CTL.CPP`** file in Listing 1-3. It contains the implementations of the various methods and classes of the control.

Listing 1-3 ASPHT0101CTL.CPP control implementation source code

```
// Aspht0101Ctl.cpp : Implementation of the CAspht0101Ctrl ActiveX Control class.

#include "stdafx.h"
#include "aspht0101.h"
#include "Aspht0101Ctl.h"
#include "Aspht0101Ppg.h"


#ifdef _DEBUG
#define new DEBUG_NEW
#undef THIS_FILE
static char THIS_FILE[] = __FILE__;
#endif


IMPLEMENT_DYNCREATE(CAspht0101Ctrl, COleControl)


/////////////////////////////////////////////////////////////////////////////
// Message map

BEGIN_MESSAGE_MAP(CAspht0101Ctrl, COleControl)
//{{AFX_MSG_MAP(CAspht0101Ctrl)
// NOTE - ClassWizard will add and remove message map entries
//    DO NOT EDIT what you see in these blocks of generated code !
//}}AFX_MSG_MAP
ON_OLEVERB(AFX_IDS_VERB_PROPERTIES, OnProperties)
END_MESSAGE_MAP()


/////////////////////////////////////////////////////////////////////////////
// Dispatch map

BEGIN_DISPATCH_MAP(CAspht0101Ctrl, COleControl)
//{{AFX_DISPATCH_MAP(CAspht0101Ctrl)
// NOTE - ClassWizard will add and remove dispatch map entries
//    DO NOT EDIT what you see in these blocks of generated code !
//}}AFX_DISPATCH_MAP
DISP_FUNCTION_ID(CAspht0101Ctrl, "AboutBox", DISPID_ABOUTBOX, AboutBox, ⇐
VT_EMPTY, VTS_NONE)
END_DISPATCH_MAP()


/////////////////////////////////////////////////////////////////////////////
// Event map

BEGIN_EVENT_MAP(CAspht0101Ctrl, COleControl)
//{{AFX_EVENT_MAP(CAspht0101Ctrl)
// NOTE - ClassWizard will add and remove event map entries
//    DO NOT EDIT what you see in these blocks of generated code !
//}}AFX_EVENT_MAP
END_EVENT_MAP()


/////////////////////////////////////////////////////////////////////////////
// Property pages
```

```
// TODO: Add more property pages as needed.  Remember to increase the count!
BEGIN_PROPPAGEIDS(CAspht0101Ctrl, 1)
PROPPAGEID(CAspht0101PropPage::guid)
END_PROPPAGEIDS(CAspht0101Ctrl)


/////////////////////////////////////////////////////////////////////////////
// Initialize class factory and guid

IMPLEMENT_OLECREATE_EX(CAspht0101Ctrl, "ASPHT0101.Aspht0101Ctrl.1",
0x43811546, 0xb036, 0x11d0, 0xb7, 0xd8, 0x44, 0x45, 0x53, 0x54, 0, 0)


/////////////////////////////////////////////////////////////////////////////
// Type library ID and version

IMPLEMENT_OLETYPELIB(CAspht0101Ctrl, _tlid, _wVerMajor, _wVerMinor)


/////////////////////////////////////////////////////////////////////////////
// Interface IDs

const IID BASED_CODE IID_DAspht0101 =
{ 0x43811544, 0xb036, 0x11d0, { 0xb7, 0xd8, 0x44, 0x45, 0x53, 0x54, 0, 0 } };
const IID BASED_CODE IID_DAspht0101Events =
{ 0x43811545, 0xb036, 0x11d0, { 0xb7, 0xd8, 0x44, 0x45, 0x53, 0x54, 0, 0 } };


/////////////////////////////////////////////////////////////////////////////
// Control type information

static const DWORD BASED_CODE _dwAspht0101OleMisc =
OLEMISC_ACTIVATEWHENVISIBLE |
OLEMISC_SETCLIENTSITEFIRST |
OLEMISC_INSIDEOUT |
OLEMISC_CANTLINKINSIDE |
OLEMISC_RECOMPOSEONRESIZE;

IMPLEMENT_OLECTLTYPE(CAspht0101Ctrl, IDS_ASPHT0101, _dwAspht0101OleMisc)


/////////////////////////////////////////////////////////////////////////////
// CAspht0101Ctrl::CAspht0101CtrlFactory::UpdateRegistry -
// Adds or removes system registry entries for CAspht0101Ctrl

BOOL CAspht0101Ctrl::CAspht0101CtrlFactory::UpdateRegistry(BOOL bRegister)
{
// TODO: Verify that your control follows apartment-model threading rules.
// Refer to MFC TechNote 64 for more information.
// If your control does not conform to the apartment-model rules, then
// you must modify the code below, changing the 6th parameter from
// afxRegApartmentThreading to 0.

if (bRegister)
return AfxOleRegisterControlClass(
AfxGetInstanceHandle(),
```

continued on next page

continued from previous page

```
m_clsid,
m_lpszProgID,
IDS_ASPHT0101,
IDB_ASPHT0101,
afxRegApartmentThreading,
dwAspht0101OleMisc,
tlid,
wVerMajor,
wVerMinor);
else
return AfxOleUnregisterClass(m_clsid, m_lpszProgID);
}


/////////////////////////////////////////////////////////////////////////////
// CAspht0101Ctrl::CAspht0101Ctrl - Constructor

CAspht0101Ctrl::CAspht0101Ctrl()
{
InitializeIIDs(&IID_DAspht0101, &IID_DAspht0101Events);

// TODO: Initialize your control's instance data here.
}


/////////////////////////////////////////////////////////////////////////////
// CAspht0101Ctrl::~CAspht0101Ctrl - Destructor

CAspht0101Ctrl::~CAspht0101Ctrl()
{
// TODO: Cleanup your control's instance data here.
}


/////////////////////////////////////////////////////////////////////////////
// CAspht0101Ctrl::OnDraw - Drawing function

void CAspht0101Ctrl::OnDraw(
CDC* pdc, const CRect& rcBounds, const CRect& rcInvalid)
{
// TODO: Replace the following code with your own drawing code.
pdc->FillRect(rcBounds, CBrush::FromHandle((HBRUSH)GetStockObject(WHITE_BRUSH)));
pdc->Ellipse(rcBounds);
}


/////////////////////////////////////////////////////////////////////////////
// CAspht0101Ctrl::DoPropExchange - Persistence support

void CAspht0101Ctrl::DoPropExchange(CPropExchange* pPX)
{
ExchangeVersion(pPX, MAKELONG(_wVerMinor, _wVerMajor));
```

```
COleControl::DoPropExchange(pPX);

// TODO: Call PX_ functions for each persistent custom property.

}


/////////////////////////////////////////////////////////////////////////////
// CAspht0101Ctrl::OnResetState - Reset control to default state

void CAspht0101Ctrl::OnResetState()
{
COleControl::OnResetState();  // Resets defaults found in DoPropExchange

// TODO: Reset any other control state here.
}


/////////////////////////////////////////////////////////////////////////////
// CAspht0101Ctrl::AboutBox - Display an "About" box to the user

void CAspht0101Ctrl::AboutBox()
{
CDialog dlgAbout(IDD_ABOUTBOX_ASPHT0101);
dlgAbout.DoModal();
}
/////////////////////////////////////////////////////////////////////////////
```

The most important portion of this code is the `OnDraw` method. It is passed a pointer to a device context object (`pdc`) and a `rect` structure that is the current display area of the control in appropriate coordinates (`rcBounds`). Any normal GDI (Graphics Device Interface) drawing function supported by the CDC object can be invoked at this point to draw the visible representation of the control. The default code simply fills the rectangle with white and draws a black ellipse. How-To's in Chapters 2, "Intermediate ActiveX: Creating Customized ActiveX Controls," and 3, "Advanced ActiveX: Special Features, Control Containers, ActiveX Documents, and VBScript 2.0," demonstrate modifying this code to create much more effective displays!

Comments

The purpose of this and How-To 1.2 is to get your feet wet using MFC and Visual C++ to create an ActiveX control. The remainder of this chapter will cover issues related to using ActiveX controls; Chapters 2 and 3 return to the internal details of writing ActiveX controls in C++.

1.2 How do I... Put the functions of a standard Windows control in an ActiveX control?

Problem

I'd really like to use a standard Windows control's functionality in my ActiveX control. Do I have to rewrite all that code from scratch?

Technique

No! For several of the most basic Windows controls, VC 5 includes the capability to use its functions as part of the basis of a new ActiveX control. This How-To will demonstrate all the steps needed to use this powerful enhancement capability. Although the directions here start from scratch, you can find the entire project on the book CD under `\CH01\HT02\ASPHT0102\`.

Steps

1. Start Visual C++ 5.0. If there is an active workspace, close it and all document windows. Then choose File|New... from the menu and select the MFC ActiveX ControlWizard entry as you did in How-To 1.1. Enter a new path for the project and name it `ASPHT0102`. Proceed through the wizard's steps to the second dialog page. On that page, activate the combo box below the `SubClass` label and choose BUTTON, as shown in Figure 1-10. Continue with the creation process as in How-To 1.1 and the new project files will be created.

2. Follow the steps outlined in How-To 1.1 to compile the ODL file and build the OCX. Then activate the ActiveX Control Test Container application and select the `ASPHT0102` control from its Insert OLE Control dialog box. The control, without you adding a single line of code, displays a default Windows button, as shown in Figure 1-11. Notice that it responds to mouse clicks just like the standard control! Your command of ActiveX controls has now increased to include creating an ActiveX control that works just like a Windows control.

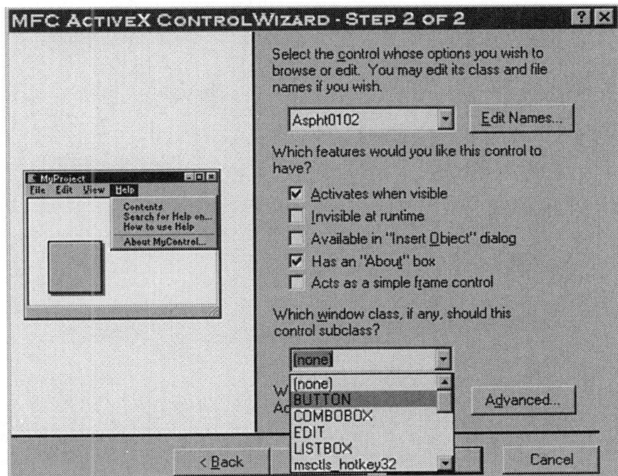

Figure 1-10 Using the Button window's control for an ActiveX control base class during wizard generation

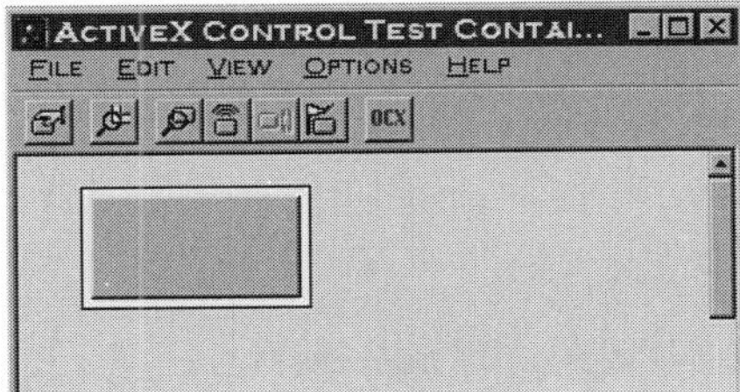

Figure 1-11 ASPHT0102 control displaying button functionality in ActiveX control test container

How It Works

The technique here is sometimes called *subclassing*, because you are creating a descendant class from an existing one and borrowing most or all of the existing class's functionality. The important differences between this control and the one created in How-To 1.1 can be seen by examining the **ASPHT0102CTL.CPP** file, which is shown in Listing 1-4.

Listing 1-4 ASPHT0102CTL.CPP control implementation source code

```
// Aspht0102Ctl.cpp : Implementation of the CAspht0102Ctrl ActiveX Control class.

#include "stdafx.h"
#include "aspht0102.h"
```

continued on next page

continued from previous page

```
#include "Aspht0102Ctl.h"
#include "Aspht0102Ppg.h"


#ifdef _DEBUG
#define new DEBUG_NEW
#undef THIS_FILE
static char THIS_FILE[] = __FILE__;
#endif


IMPLEMENT_DYNCREATE(CAspht0102Ctrl, COleControl)


/////////////////////////////////////////////////////////////////////////////
// Message map

BEGIN_MESSAGE_MAP(CAspht0102Ctrl, COleControl)
//{{AFX_MSG_MAP(CAspht0102Ctrl)
// NOTE - ClassWizard will add and remove message map entries
//    DO NOT EDIT what you see in these blocks of generated code !
//}}AFX_MSG_MAP
ON_MESSAGE(OCM_COMMAND, OnOcmCommand)
ON_OLEVERB(AFX_IDS_VERB_PROPERTIES, OnProperties)
END_MESSAGE_MAP()


/////////////////////////////////////////////////////////////////////////////
// Dispatch map

BEGIN_DISPATCH_MAP(CAspht0102Ctrl, COleControl)
//{{AFX_DISPATCH_MAP(CAspht0102Ctrl)
// NOTE - ClassWizard will add and remove dispatch map entries
//    DO NOT EDIT what you see in these blocks of generated code !
//}}AFX_DISPATCH_MAP
DISP_FUNCTION_ID(CAspht0102Ctrl, "AboutBox", DISPID_ABOUTBOX, AboutBox,⇐
VT_EMPTY, VTS_NONE)
END_DISPATCH_MAP()


/////////////////////////////////////////////////////////////////////////////
// Event map

BEGIN_EVENT_MAP(CAspht0102Ctrl, COleControl)
//{{AFX_EVENT_MAP(CAspht0102Ctrl)
// NOTE - ClassWizard will add and remove event map entries
//    DO NOT EDIT what you see in these blocks of generated code !
//}}AFX_EVENT_MAP
END_EVENT_MAP()


/////////////////////////////////////////////////////////////////////////////
// Property pages

// TODO: Add more property pages as needed.  Remember to increase the count!
BEGIN_PROPPAGEIDS(CAspht0102Ctrl, 1)
```

```
PROPPAGEID(CAspht0102PropPage::guid)
END_PROPPAGEIDS(CAspht0102Ctrl)


/////////////////////////////////////////////////////////////////////////////
// Initialize class factory and guid

IMPLEMENT_OLECREATE_EX(CAspht0102Ctrl, "ASPHT0102.Aspht0102Ctrl.1",
0xc17f94e6, 0xb03a, 0x11d0, 0xb7, 0xd8, 0x44, 0x45, 0x53, 0x54, 0, 0)


/////////////////////////////////////////////////////////////////////////////
// Type library ID and version

IMPLEMENT_OLETYPELIB(CAspht0102Ctrl, _tlid, _wVerMajor, _wVerMinor)


/////////////////////////////////////////////////////////////////////////////
// Interface IDs

const IID BASED_CODE IID_DAspht0102 =
{ 0xc17f94e4, 0xb03a, 0x11d0, { 0xb7, 0xd8, 0x44, 0x45, 0x53, 0x54, 0, 0 } };
const IID BASED_CODE IID_DAspht0102Events =
{ 0xc17f94e5, 0xb03a, 0x11d0, { 0xb7, 0xd8, 0x44, 0x45, 0x53, 0x54, 0, 0 } };


/////////////////////////////////////////////////////////////////////////////
// Control type information

static const DWORD BASED_CODE _dwAspht0102OleMisc =
OLEMISC_ACTIVATEWHENVISIBLE ¦
OLEMISC_SETCLIENTSITEFIRST ¦
OLEMISC_INSIDEOUT ¦
OLEMISC_CANTLINKINSIDE ¦
OLEMISC_RECOMPOSEONRESIZE;

IMPLEMENT_OLECTLTYPE(CAspht0102Ctrl, IDS_ASPHT0102, _dwAspht0102OleMisc)


/////////////////////////////////////////////////////////////////////////////
// CAspht0102Ctrl::CAspht0102CtrlFactory::UpdateRegistry -
// Adds or removes system registry entries for CAspht0102Ctrl

BOOL CAspht0102Ctrl::CAspht0102CtrlFactory::UpdateRegistry(BOOL bRegister)
{
// TODO: Verify that your control follows apartment-model threading rules.
// Refer to MFC TechNote 64 for more information.
// If your control does not conform to the apartment-model rules, then
// you must modify the code below, changing the 6th parameter from
// afxRegApartmentThreading to 0.

if (bRegister)
return AfxOleRegisterControlClass(
AfxGetInstanceHandle(),
m_clsid,
m_lpszProgID,
```

continued on next page

continued from previous page

```
IDS_ASPHT0102,
IDB_ASPHT0102,
afxRegApartmentThreading,
dwAspht0102OleMisc,
tlid,
wVerMajor,
wVerMinor);
else
return AfxOleUnregisterClass(m_clsid, m_lpszProgID);
}


/////////////////////////////////////////////////////////////////////////////
// CAspht0102Ctrl::CAspht0102Ctrl - Constructor

CAspht0102Ctrl::CAspht0102Ctrl()
{
InitializeIIDs(&IID_DAspht0102, &IID_DAspht0102Events);

// TODO: Initialize your control's instance data here.
}


/////////////////////////////////////////////////////////////////////////////
// CAspht0102Ctrl::~CAspht0102Ctrl - Destructor

CAspht0102Ctrl::~CAspht0102Ctrl()
{
// TODO: Cleanup your control's instance data here.
}


/////////////////////////////////////////////////////////////////////////////
// CAspht0102Ctrl::OnDraw - Drawing function

void CAspht0102Ctrl::OnDraw(
CDC* pdc, const CRect& rcBounds, const CRect& rcInvalid)
{
DoSuperclassPaint(pdc, rcBounds);
}


/////////////////////////////////////////////////////////////////////////////
// CAspht0102Ctrl::DoPropExchange - Persistence support

void CAspht0102Ctrl::DoPropExchange(CPropExchange* pPX)
{
ExchangeVersion(pPX, MAKELONG(_wVerMinor, _wVerMajor));
COleControl::DoPropExchange(pPX);

// TODO: Call PX_ functions for each persistent custom property.

}


/////////////////////////////////////////////////////////////////////////////
```

```
// CAspht0102Ctrl::OnResetState - Reset control to default state

void CAspht0102Ctrl::OnResetState()
{
COleControl::OnResetState();  // Resets defaults found in DoPropExchange

// TODO: Reset any other control state here.
}


///////////////////////////////////////////////////////////////////////////
// CAspht0102Ctrl::AboutBox - Display an "About" box to the user

void CAspht0102Ctrl::AboutBox()
{
CDialog dlgAbout(IDD_ABOUTBOX_ASPHT0102);
dlgAbout.DoModal();
}


///////////////////////////////////////////////////////////////////////////
// CAspht0102Ctrl::PreCreateWindow - Modify parameters for CreateWindowEx

BOOL CAspht0102Ctrl::PreCreateWindow(CREATESTRUCT& cs)
{
cs.lpszClass = _T("BUTTON");
return COleControl::PreCreateWindow(cs);
}


///////////////////////////////////////////////////////////////////////////
// CAspht0102Ctrl::IsSubclassedControl - This is a subclassed control

BOOL CAspht0102Ctrl::IsSubclassedControl()
{
return TRUE;
}


///////////////////////////////////////////////////////////////////////////
// CAspht0102Ctrl::OnOcmCommand - Handle command messages

LRESULT CAspht0102Ctrl::OnOcmCommand(WPARAM wParam, LPARAM lParam)
{
#ifdef _WIN32
WORD wNotifyCode = HIWORD(wParam);
#else
WORD wNotifyCode = HIWORD(lParam);
#endif

// TODO: Switch on wNotifyCode here.

return 0;
}


///////////////////////////////////////////////////////////////////////////
// CAspht0102Ctrl message handlers
```

First, notice the `OnDraw` method. It now calls the MFC function `DoSuperClassPaint`. Because the control is a subclass of the Button control, this has the effect of causing the `button paint` code to be executed. Next, observe the `onOcmCommand` method. This method takes in the message codes sent through interactions with the control and creates a notification code variable (`wNotifyCode`) from them. This is where response code is placed to respond to mouse actions on the control.

Comments

You can use this technique to subclass any of the available Windows controls in the drop-down list on the Wizard page.

COMPLEXITY
BEGINNING

1.3 How do I… Control how other developers can use my ActiveX control with LIC registration files?

Problem

I've spent considerable time and money creating my ActiveX control for use on the Web, and now I discover that everyone gets to use it for free! Is there a way for me to make sure I've been paid when other developers use my control?

Technique

Yes! Microsoft included the new Registration Application Programming Interface (API) calls to the OCX 96 specification, which are supported by LIC registration files. This How-To directs you along the path needed to include and use LPK files with your code in Visual C++ 5.0. Although the directions here start from scratch, you can find the entire project on the CD under `\CH01\HT03\ASPHT0103\`.

Steps

1. Start Visual C++ 5.0. If there is an active workspace, close it and all document windows. Then, choose File|New… from the menu and select the MFC ActiveX ControlWizard entry as you did in How-To 1.2, except choose the Edit control to subclass rather than the Button control, for variety. Enter a new path for the project and name it `ASPHT0103`. On the first wizard page, change the license support radio button to `Yes, please`, as shown in Figure 1-12. Continue with the creation process as in How-To 1.1 and the new project files will be created.

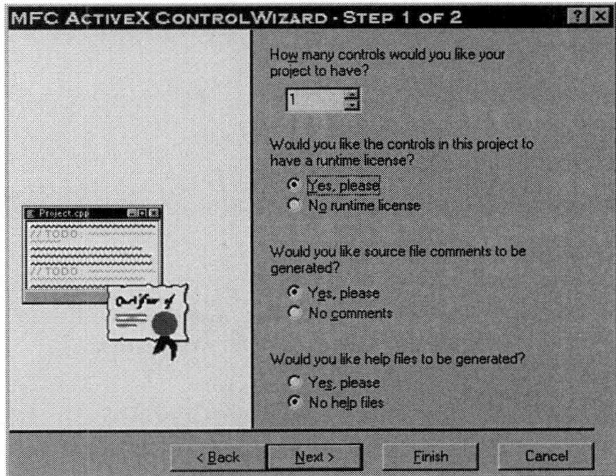

Figure 1-12 Adding license support to an ActiveX control during wizard generation

2. Follow the steps outlined in How-To 1.1 to compile the ODL file and build the OCX. Then activate the ActiveX Control Test Container application and select the `ASPHT0103` control from its Insert OLE Control dialog box. The control will be displayed normally. Then, temporarily remove the `ASPHT0103.LIC` file from the directory with the OCX and try again to insert the control. An error dialog will appear, indicating that the control cannot be created (it does not give the lack of a license file as the reason, unfortunately). You have taken the next major step in basic ActiveX development: protecting your ActiveX control with a LIC license file.

How It Works

The critical changes to the code to support licensing are found in the `ASPHT0103CTL.CPP` file, which is shown in Listing 1-5.

Listing 1-5 ASPHT0103CTL.CPP control implementation source code

```
// Aspht0103Ctl.cpp : Implementation of the CAspht0103Ctrl ActiveX Control class.

#include "stdafx.h"
#include "aspht0103.h"
#include "Aspht0103Ctl.h"
#include "Aspht0103Ppg.h"


#ifdef _DEBUG
#define new DEBUG_NEW
#undef THIS_FILE
static char THIS_FILE[] = __FILE__;
```

continued on next page

continued from previous page

```
#endif


IMPLEMENT_DYNCREATE(CAspht0103Ctrl, COleControl)


/////////////////////////////////////////////////////////////////////////////
// Message map

BEGIN_MESSAGE_MAP(CAspht0103Ctrl, COleControl)
//{{AFX_MSG_MAP(CAspht0103Ctrl)
// NOTE - ClassWizard will add and remove message map entries
//    DO NOT EDIT what you see in these blocks of generated code !
//}}AFX_MSG_MAP
ON_MESSAGE(OCM_COMMAND, OnOcmCommand)
ON_OLEVERB(AFX_IDS_VERB_PROPERTIES, OnProperties)
END_MESSAGE_MAP()


/////////////////////////////////////////////////////////////////////////////
// Dispatch map

BEGIN_DISPATCH_MAP(CAspht0103Ctrl, COleControl)
//{{AFX_DISPATCH_MAP(CAspht0103Ctrl)
// NOTE - ClassWizard will add and remove dispatch map entries
//    DO NOT EDIT what you see in these blocks of generated code !
//}}AFX_DISPATCH_MAP
DISP_FUNCTION_ID(CAspht0103Ctrl, "AboutBox", DISPID_ABOUTBOX, AboutBox,⇐
VT_EMPTY, VTS_NONE)
END_DISPATCH_MAP()


/////////////////////////////////////////////////////////////////////////////
// Event map

BEGIN_EVENT_MAP(CAspht0103Ctrl, COleControl)
//{{AFX_EVENT_MAP(CAspht0103Ctrl)
// NOTE - ClassWizard will add and remove event map entries
//    DO NOT EDIT what you see in these blocks of generated code !
//}}AFX_EVENT_MAP
END_EVENT_MAP()


/////////////////////////////////////////////////////////////////////////////
// Property pages

// TODO: Add more property pages as needed.  Remember to increase the count!
BEGIN_PROPPAGEIDS(CAspht0103Ctrl, 1)
PROPPAGEID(CAspht0103PropPage::guid)
END_PROPPAGEIDS(CAspht0103Ctrl)


/////////////////////////////////////////////////////////////////////////////
// Initialize class factory and guid

IMPLEMENT_OLECREATE_EX(CAspht0103Ctrl, "ASPHT0103.Aspht0103Ctrl.1",
```

```
0xc17f94fd, 0xb03a, 0x11d0, 0xb7, 0xd8, 0x44, 0x45, 0x53, 0x54, 0, 0)


///////////////////////////////////////////////////////////////////////////
// Type library ID and version

IMPLEMENT_OLETYPELIB(CAspht0103Ctrl, _tlid, _wVerMajor, _wVerMinor)


///////////////////////////////////////////////////////////////////////////
// Interface IDs

const IID BASED_CODE IID_DAspht0103 =
{ 0xc17f94fb, 0xb03a, 0x11d0, { 0xb7, 0xd8, 0x44, 0x45, 0x53, 0x54, 0, 0 } };
const IID BASED_CODE IID_DAspht0103Events =
{ 0xc17f94fc, 0xb03a, 0x11d0, { 0xb7, 0xd8, 0x44, 0x45, 0x53, 0x54, 0, 0 } };


///////////////////////////////////////////////////////////////////////////
// Control type information

static const DWORD BASED_CODE _dwAspht0103OleMisc =
OLEMISC_ACTIVATEWHENVISIBLE |
OLEMISC_SETCLIENTSITEFIRST |
OLEMISC_INSIDEOUT |
OLEMISC_CANTLINKINSIDE |
OLEMISC_RECOMPOSEONRESIZE;

IMPLEMENT_OLECTLTYPE(CAspht0103Ctrl, IDS_ASPHT0103, _dwAspht0103OleMisc)


///////////////////////////////////////////////////////////////////////////
// CAspht0103Ctrl::CAspht0103CtrlFactory::UpdateRegistry -
// Adds or removes system registry entries for CAspht0103Ctrl

BOOL CAspht0103Ctrl::CAspht0103CtrlFactory::UpdateRegistry(BOOL bRegister)
{
// TODO: Verify that your control follows apartment-model threading rules.
// Refer to MFC TechNote 64 for more information.
// If your control does not conform to the apartment-model rules, then
// you must modify the code below, changing the 6th parameter from
// afxRegApartmentThreading to 0.

if (bRegister)
return AfxOleRegisterControlClass(
AfxGetInstanceHandle(),
m_clsid,
m_lpszProgID,
IDS_ASPHT0103,
IDB_ASPHT0103,
afxRegApartmentThreading,
dwAspht0103OleMisc,
tlid,
wVerMajor,
wVerMinor);
else
```

continued on next page

continued from previous page

```
return AfxOleUnregisterClass(m_clsid, m_lpszProgID);
}


/////////////////////////////////////////////////////////////////////////////
// Licensing strings

static const TCHAR BASED_CODE _szLicFileName[] = _T("aspht0103.lic");

static const WCHAR BASED_CODE _szLicString[] =
L"Copyright (c) 1997 CIUPKC Software";


/////////////////////////////////////////////////////////////////////////////
// CAspht0103Ctrl::CAspht0103CtrlFactory::VerifyUserLicense -
// Checks for existence of a user license

BOOL CAspht0103Ctrl::CAspht0103CtrlFactory::VerifyUserLicense()
{
return AfxVerifyLicFile(AfxGetInstanceHandle(), _szLicFileName,
szLicString);
}


/////////////////////////////////////////////////////////////////////////////
// CAspht0103Ctrl::CAspht0103CtrlFactory::GetLicenseKey -
// Returns a runtime licensing key

BOOL CAspht0103Ctrl::CAspht0103CtrlFactory::GetLicenseKey(DWORD dwReserved,
BSTR FAR* pbstrKey)
{
if (pbstrKey == NULL)
return FALSE;

*pbstrKey = SysAllocString(_szLicString);
return (*pbstrKey != NULL);
}


/////////////////////////////////////////////////////////////////////////////
// CAspht0103Ctrl::CAspht0103Ctrl - Constructor

CAspht0103Ctrl::CAspht0103Ctrl()
{
InitializeIIDs(&IID_DAspht0103, &IID_DAspht0103Events);

// TODO: Initialize your control's instance data here.
}


/////////////////////////////////////////////////////////////////////////////
// CAspht0103Ctrl::~CAspht0103Ctrl - Destructor

CAspht0103Ctrl::~CAspht0103Ctrl()
{
// TODO: Cleanup your control's instance data here.
```

```
}


////////////////////////////////////////////////////////////////////////////
// CAspht0103Ctrl::OnDraw - Drawing function

void CAspht0103Ctrl::OnDraw(
CDC* pdc, const CRect& rcBounds, const CRect& rcInvalid)
{
DoSuperclassPaint(pdc, rcBounds);
}


////////////////////////////////////////////////////////////////////////////
// CAspht0103Ctrl::DoPropExchange - Persistence support

void CAspht0103Ctrl::DoPropExchange(CPropExchange* pPX)
{
ExchangeVersion(pPX, MAKELONG(_wVerMinor, _wVerMajor));
COleControl::DoPropExchange(pPX);

// TODO: Call PX_ functions for each persistent custom property.

}


////////////////////////////////////////////////////////////////////////////
// CAspht0103Ctrl::OnResetState - Reset control to default state

void CAspht0103Ctrl::OnResetState()
{
COleControl::OnResetState();  // Resets defaults found in DoPropExchange

// TODO: Reset any other control state here.
}


////////////////////////////////////////////////////////////////////////////
// CAspht0103Ctrl::AboutBox - Display an "About" box to the user

void CAspht0103Ctrl::AboutBox()
{
CDialog dlgAbout(IDD_ABOUTBOX_ASPHT0103);
dlgAbout.DoModal();
}


////////////////////////////////////////////////////////////////////////////
// CAspht0103Ctrl::PreCreateWindow - Modify parameters for CreateWindowEx

BOOL CAspht0103Ctrl::PreCreateWindow(CREATESTRUCT& cs)
{
cs.lpszClass = _T("EDIT");
return COleControl::PreCreateWindow(cs);
}
```

continued on next page

continued from previous page

```
/////////////////////////////////////////////////////////////////////////////
// CAspht0103Ctrl::IsSubclassedControl - This is a subclassed control

BOOL CAspht0103Ctrl::IsSubclassedControl()
{
return TRUE;
}


/////////////////////////////////////////////////////////////////////////////
// CAspht0103Ctrl::OnOcmCommand - Handle command messages

LRESULT CAspht0103Ctrl::OnOcmCommand(WPARAM wParam, LPARAM lParam)
{
#ifdef _WIN32
WORD wNotifyCode = HIWORD(wParam);
#else
WORD wNotifyCode = HIWORD(lParam);
#endif

// TODO: Switch on wNotifyCode here.

return 0;
}


/////////////////////////////////////////////////////////////////////////////
// CAspht0103Ctrl message handlers
```

First, notice these lines of code:

```
static const TCHAR BASED_CODE _szLicFileName[] = _T("aspht0103.lic");
static const WCHAR BASED_CODE _szLicString[] =
L"Copyright (c) 1997 CIUPKC Software";
```

They create two strings that hold a default filename for the license file, including its path, and the string to represent the license itself, which in this case is a copyright notice for the company name with which you have registered your copy of VC 5. If you wanted to have your license file elsewhere, such as in the Windows system directory, you would modify the `szLicFileName` constant appropriately. Next, these lines of code determine if the license file is on the computer trying to create the control and if the file has the correct information.

```
// CAspht0103Ctrl::CAspht0103CtrlFactory::VerifyUserLicense -
// Checks for existence of a user license

BOOL CAspht0103Ctrl::CAspht0103CtrlFactory::VerifyUserLicense()
{
return AfxVerifyLicFile(AfxGetInstanceHandle(), _szLicFileName,
szLicString);
}
```

The `AfxVerifyLicFile` function will return `true` if the license file exists at the named location and if it has the valid string as its first line. Otherwise, it returns `false` and an error will be generated if the control is in design mode. If the control is in display mode, however, this code takes over:

```
/////////////////////////////////////////////////////////////////////////////
// CAspht0103Ctrl::CAspht0103CtrlFactory::GetLicenseKey -
// Returns a runtime licensing key

BOOL CAspht0103Ctrl::CAspht0103CtrlFactory::GetLicenseKey(DWORD dwReserved,
BSTR FAR* pbstrKey)
{
if (pbstrKey == NULL)
return FALSE;

*pbstrKey = SysAllocString(_szLicString);
return (*pbstrKey != NULL);
}
```

It creates its own copy of the string to allow display of the control even without a LIC file, because the system assumes that registration is aimed mainly at developers, as opposed to end users, on the Internet.

Comments

The string used as the actual license key is entirely arbitrary. An alternative method employed by Borland's Delphi product creates a separate GUID (Globally Unique ID) for the license key and stores it instead!

1.4 How do I… Create a CAB (Cabinet) compressed archive to distribute my ActiveX control with reduced size and greater speed?

Problem

My ActiveX control is somewhat large, and I'm concerned about the time it takes to download it over the Web. When compressed into a ZIP file, the control is quite small, but ActiveX doesn't seem to support ZIP files! Is there a way to get ZIP compression with my OCX file on the Web?

Technique

Microsoft has used cabinet (`.CAB`) files for years in its own distribution system. Now it has made the CAB API available via a Software Development Kit (SDK) available for free from Microsoft's Web site. This How-To guides you through the process of downloading and installing the two SDKs and using their tools to turn your monster OCX file into a tiny CAB archive. (Note: This and the following How-To's use the `MyPanelXControl` ActiveX control, which is supplied on the CD with this book under the `CH01\HT04\` subdirectory. It is a much flashier control than can be created at this level of difficulty, but is better for illustrating display behaviors.)

Steps

1. Activate Internet Explorer and navigate to the following URL: `http://www.microsoft.com/workshop/prog/cab/`. Click on the `CAB_SDK` link and, in the changed center page, click on each of the download links to obtain the two SDK files for the CABinet Development Kit. Figure 1-13 shows the Web page for this URL with the download in progress.

NOTE

Microsoft's Web pages change like smoke in a wind tunnel! Please see the `README.TXT` file on the CD under "Last-Minute URL Changes" for the most recent URL for the `CABDEV SDK`.

2. In Windows Explorer (or an equivalent file manager utility), double-click each of the executable files you just downloaded. They will self-install, prompting you for a directory for each one; don't install both of them into

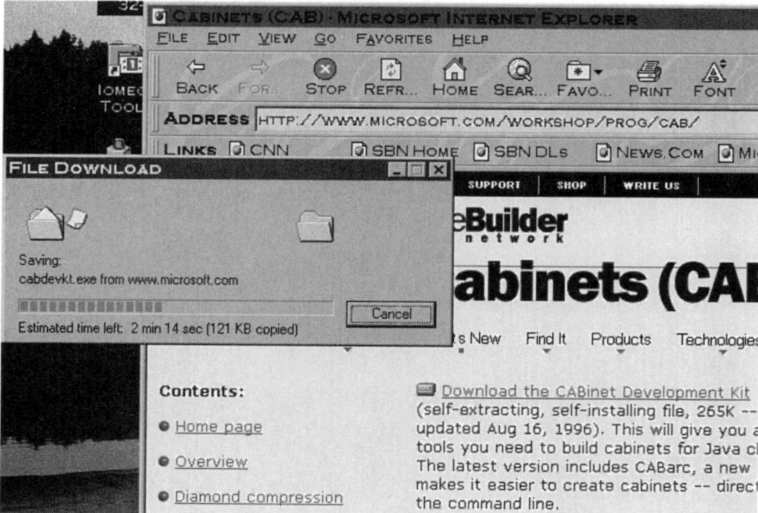

Figure 1-13 Downloading the CABinet Development Kit

the same directory, however! Spend a few minutes reading the `README` files with each kit; pay particular attention to the `CABARC.EXE` utility in the CABinet Development Kit.

3. Open an MS-DOS window and navigate to the directory where you did the CD installation for How-To 1.4; if you did the default, it is in `\ASPHT\CH01\HT04\`. Copy the OCX file there to `\ASPHT\CH01\HT05\`. Then move to that directory and type in the following DOS command line exactly: `cabarc -s 6144 n mpcx.cab *.ocx`, and press Return. You will see several status messages; if you receive an error, make sure you typed what is above exactly. Once you have successfully created the CAB file, type `DIR` to determine how much it was compressed. The results you see should be similar to those shown in Figure 1-14. You now know how to create compressed CAB files containing ActiveX controls for use on the Internet.

How It Works

The key to this How-To is the `CABARC.EXE` utility from the Microsoft CABinet Development Kit. It is an MS-DOS utility that accepts a number of command line parameters for the creation and use of Cabinet files. The `CABARC` command line has the following structure:

```
CABARC [<options>] <command> <cabfile> [<filelist>] [destdir]
```

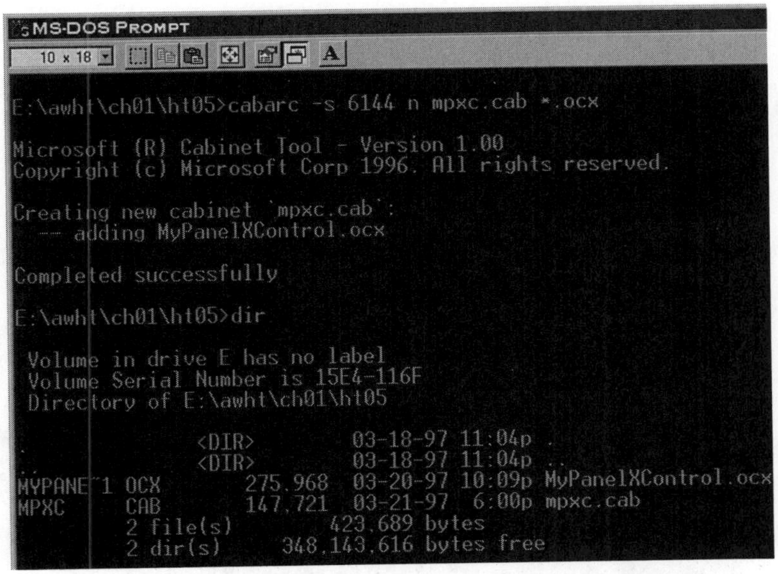

```
MS-DOS Prompt
E:\awht\ch01\ht05>cabarc -s 6144 n mpxc.cab *.ocx

Microsoft (R) Cabinet Tool - Version 1.00
Copyright (c) Microsoft Corp 1996. All rights reserved.

Creating new cabinet `mpxc.cab':
  -- adding MyPanelXControl.ocx

Completed successfully

E:\awht\ch01\ht05>dir

 Volume in drive E has no label
 Volume Serial Number is 15E4-116F
 Directory of E:\awht\ch01\ht05

.              <DIR>        03-18-97 11:04p .
..             <DIR>        03-18-97 11:04p ..
MYPANE~1 OCX       275,968  03-20-97 10:09p MyPanelXControl.ocx
MPXC     CAB       147,721  03-21-97  6:00p mpxc.cab
         2 file(s)         423,689 bytes
         2 dir(s)      348,143,616 bytes free
```

Figure 1-14 Running the CABARC.EXE utility from MS-DOS

Portions of the command line inside [] are optional; those inside <> are required. The <command> portion is either N to create a new archive (an old one is erased), L to list the contents of an existing archive, or X to extract from an existing archive. The <cabfile> portion can be a filename or a fully or partially qualified path. If no <filelist> is found, all files in the current directory are added to the archive; multiple filenames and wildcards are separated with spaces. [destdir] is used only during extraction and must end in a backslash.

The options and their functions are summarized in Table 1-1.

Table 1-1 Command line options for CABARC.EXE

OPTION	FOLLOWING PARAM	USAGE
-c		Confirms each file operation.
-o		Silently overwrites during extract.
-m	MZIP¦NONE	Compression algorithm; MZIP default.
-p		Preserves relative paths (only).
-P		Strips out relative paths if present.
-r		Recurses into subdirectories when adding.
-s	Number of bytes	Adds number of bytes for signing.
-i	Integer number	Cabinet ID value (creation only).
--		Disables further option parsing.

Comments

CAB files are being considered here only in the context of using them with automatic ActiveX control downloads by Internet Explorer. However, included with the CABinet Development and Resource Kits are C libraries and header files to use Cabinet API calls in C++ programs, and the DIAMOND.EXE utility that uses DDF and INF files and is a full-featured installation program. Extensive documentation for DIAMOND.EXE and INF file formats is included with the SDK downloaded in this How-To.

1.5 How do I... Obtain an Authenticode Software Protection Certificate to allow secure use of my ActiveX control on the World Wide Web?

Problem

A friend of mine had his system trashed by an unsigned ActiveX control he downloaded! Now I have my browser set to accept only ActiveX controls that have been verified by Authenticode, and I want to be able to add this capability to my new ActiveX control. The documentation tells me I need to obtain a file called an SPC; how do I get this information?

Technique

The process is easy to do and works in combination with email and the World Wide Web. This How-To will guide you through all the steps needed to obtain a Class 2 Individual Software Protection Certificate (SPC) from VeriSign, the company authorized by Microsoft to offer this service.

Steps

1. Create a directory on a removable disk (a floppy, jaz, jet, or bernoulli) to hold the license information as it is created for your SPC. (Although you are permitted to use your hard drive, it is strongly discouraged for security reasons.)
2. Activate Internet Explorer and navigate to the following URL: `http://digitalid.verisign.com/`. You should see a display similar to that shown in Figure 1-15. This is the home page of the VeriSign Corporation, which currently is the only issuer of SPCs.
3. Click on the Request a Digital ID image button. You should see a display similar to that shown in Figure 1-16 after the browser has navigated to the new page. These are the various kinds of SPCs available from VeriSign.

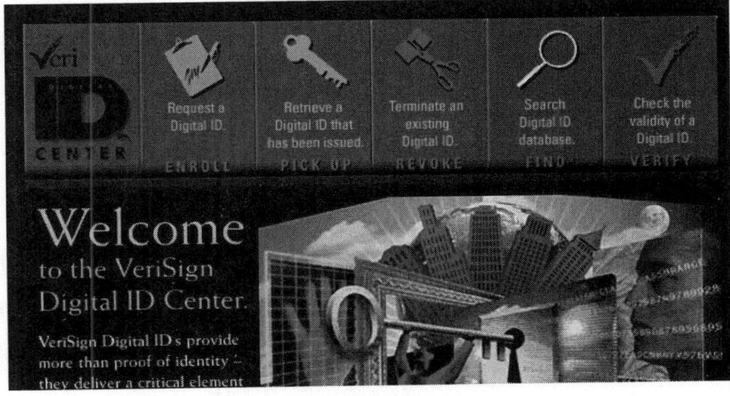

Figure 1-15 The VeriSign home page

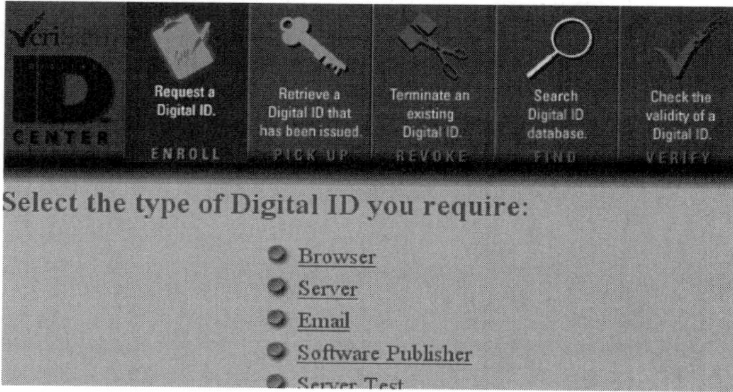

Figure 1-16 The VeriSign SPC services page

4. Click on the `Software Publisher` link. After the navigation is complete, you should see a display similar to Figure 1-17. Two types of software publisher SPCs are currently available, both of which are explained here. (Note that to use either service, a valid credit card with at least $20.00 credit is required. Also, Class 2 SPCs are available at this time only to U.S. residents.)

5. If you are an individual or a small business, click the `Class 2` link or image. If you are a large business, click the `Class 3` link or image. The following steps are for the Class 2 SPC, but the Class 3 steps are very similar. You will see a display similar to Figure 1-18, which is the initial data entry screen for the SPC.

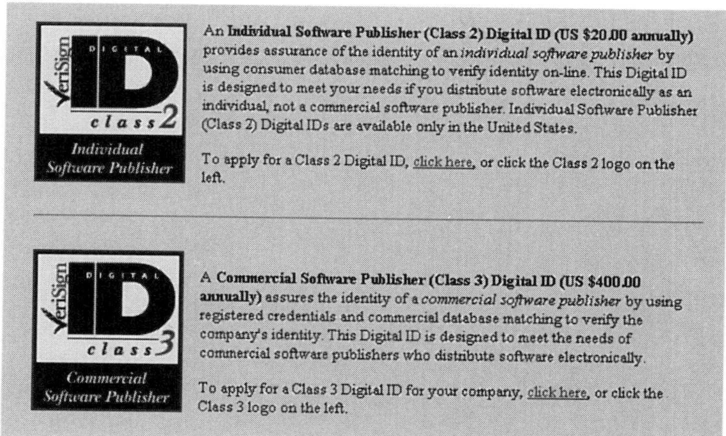

Figure 1-17 The VeriSign software publisher SPC classes page

Digital ID Application Information

This information is used to create your Digital ID. You must enter information in all of these fields. You can choose whether to include your home address in your Digital ID.

Digital ID Class **Class 2**
E-mail Address kilgalen@tde.com
First Name nathan Middle Initial f
Last Name wallace Suffix no suffix
Mailing Address: Street and Number 530 Meadowlark Drive If your mailing address is a P.O. Box, enter it Street Address field. For example, Box 438.
Apartment or Unit Number City Lakewood
State or Province co ZIP Code or Postal Code 80226

Figure 1-18 Initial data entry screen for the Class 2 VeriSign SPC

6. Fill out the data entry form very carefully. Obtaining the Class 2 SPC requires that your information be completely accurate and up to date! When you are finished, press the Submit image at the bottom of the page. You will then see a display similar to Figure 1-19, the pledge agreement required to obtain the SPC.

7. The pledge agreement is an absolute requirement to obtaining the SPC; it legally binds you to behave responsibly with whatever software is encoded using your SPC. After reading and agreeing with it, press the Accept image at the bottom of the page. You will then see a display similar to Figure 1-20, which is the display page to begin the actual process of obtaining your SPC.

SUBSCRIBER AGREEMENT

YOU MUST READ THIS SUBSCRIBER AGREEMENT BEFORE APPLYING FOR, ACCEPTING, OR USING A DIGITAL ID/CERTIFICATE. IF YOU DO NOT AGREE TO THE TERMS OF THIS SUBSCRIBER AGREEMENT, DO NOT APPLY FOR, ACCEPT, OR USE THE DIGITAL ID (CERTIFICATE).

THIS SUBSCRIBER AGREEMENT will become effective on the date you submit the certificate application to the designated issuing authority (IA).By submitting this Subscriber Agreement (and certificate application) you are requesting that the IA issue a Digital ID (certificate) to you and are expressing your agreement to the terms of this Subscriber Agreement. VeriSign's Public Certification Services are governed by VeriSign's Certification Practice Statement (the "CPS"), which is incorporated by reference into this Subscriber Agreement. The CPS is published on the Internet in VeriSign's repository at https://www.verisign.com and ftp://ftp.verisign.com/repository/CPS, and is available via E-mail from: **CPS-requests@verisign.com**.

YOU AGREE TO USE THE DIGITAL ID (CERTIFICATE) AND ANY RELATED IA SERVICES ONLY IN ACCORDANCE WITH THE CPS. AS STATED IN THE CPS, THE IA DISCLAIMS CERTAIN IMPLIED AND EXPRESS WARRANTIES, INCLUDING WARRANTIES OF MERCHANTABILITY OR FITNESS FOR A PARTICULAR PURPOSE, PLACES LIMITS ON ITS LIABILITY UNDER THIS AGREEMENT AND REFUSES ALL LIABILITY FOR CONSEQUENTIAL AND PUNITIVE DAMAGES. SEE THE CPS FOR

Figure 1-19 SPC pledge agreement page

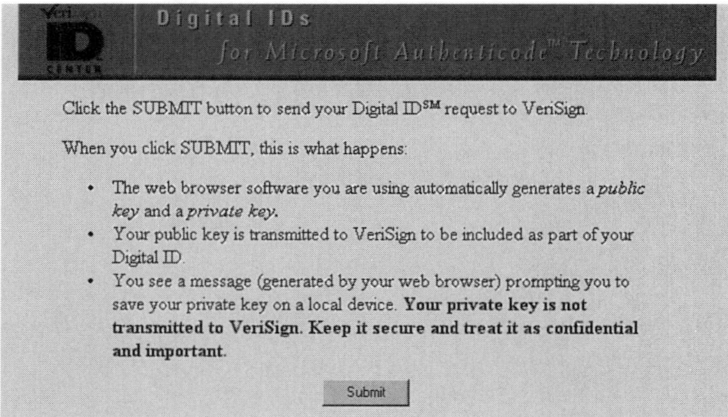

Figure 1-20 SPC submission start screen

8. Make sure there is a removable disk with about 500 K of space in whatever device you previously set up to hold your license files. Then press the Submit button. The browser will begin to display a series of wizard dialog boxes, the first of which is shown in Figure 1-21. These wizards guide you through the automated process of acquiring your private portion of the SPC.

9. Press the Next button on the first wizard dialog box and you will see a data entry dialog similar to that shown in Figure 1-22. It is used to enter the location of the removable media device you will use to store your private key (PVK) file for use in digitally signing files.

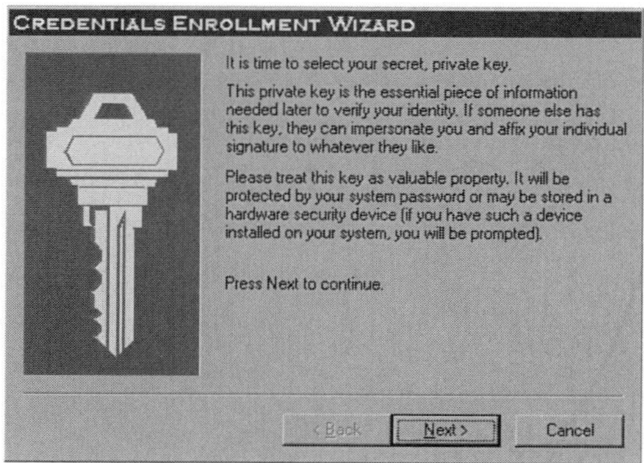

Figure 1-21 Initial PVK Wizard display dialog

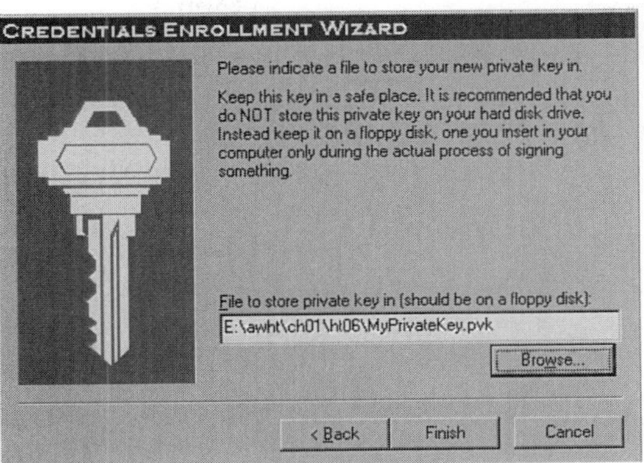

Figure 1-22 Path Entry dialog for the PVK file

10. Use the Browse button to navigate to the drive and directory where you plan to store your PVK and SPC files. Then press Finish. The PVK file will be created and stored, and you will see a display similar to Figure 1-23, giving you the URL to return and obtain your SPC file.

11. At this point there will be a delay; if you are obtaining a Class 2 SPC it will be only a few moments, but if you are obtaining a Class 3 SPC, it may be several days. Eventually you will receive an email message similar to that shown in Figure 1-24, indicating you have been awarded the SPC you requested or explaining why it was not awarded and giving you the steps to follow to correct the problem.

12. At this point, you should reactivate your copy of Internet Explorer and navigate to the URL `http://digitalid.verisign.com/msgetiscs.htm`, seeing a display similar to that shown in Figure 1-25, which is a form to allow entry of your PIN to retrieve the SPC file.

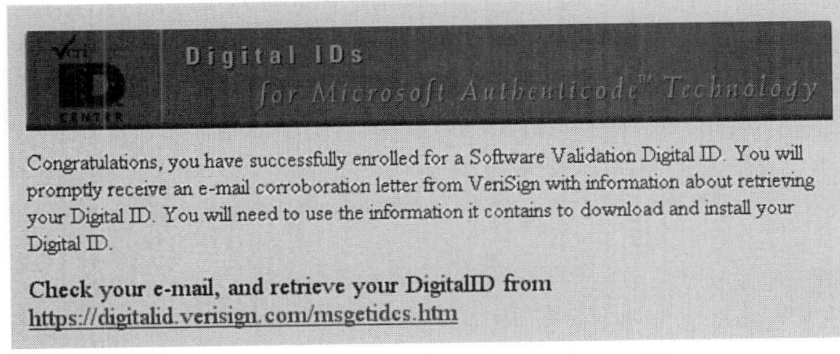

Figure 1-23 URL display for retrieval of SPC file

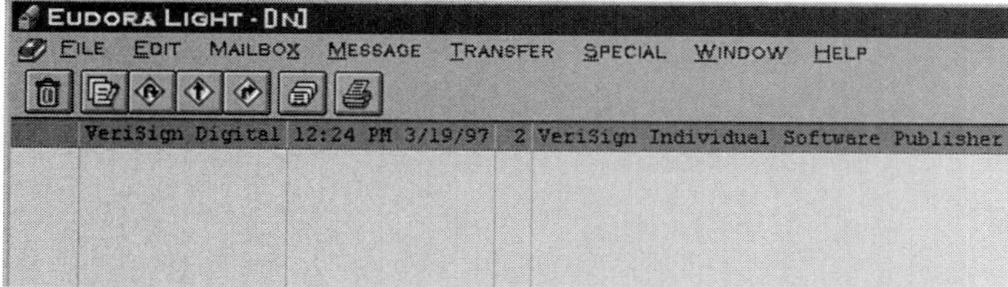

Figure 1-24 Email displaying VeriSign confirmation message

Important: Make sure that you are using the same computer that you used to enroll for your Digital ID. The private key that was generated during the enrollment process must match the public key included in your Digital ID.

Enter your Digital ID personal identification number (PIN), then select the SUBMIT button to download and install your Digital ID.

Your Digital ID PIN is listed in the confirmation letter you received from VeriSign.

For Class 1 Digital IDs: After you select the SUBMIT button, your certificate will be delivered to you momentarily. Do not interrupt your browser until you get a response.

For Class 2 and 3 Digital IDs: After you select the SUBMIT button, generating your Digital ID will take up to three minutes. Do not interrupt your browser until you get a response.

Digital ID PIN

SUBMIT

Figure 1-25 VeriSign SPC PIN entry form

13. The PIN is in the email message from step 11. Enter it in the text box and press the Submit button. There will be a pause of up to several minutes while secured information is exchanged between VeriSign and your copy of Internet Explorer. Eventually you will see a display similar to Figure 1-26, unless a problem is encountered. In the latter case, you will be given a phone number to call and will be able to clear up the matter and resubmit your PIN. The display indicates that the SPC file is ready to be placed on your removable media device.

14. Pressing the INSTALL button on the display will bring up the Credentials Enrollment Wizard dialog box shown in Figure 1-27. Make sure the removable disk with your PVK file is available to the system, and enter the same path for the SPC file.

15. Press Finish, and in a few moments you will see the dialog box shown in Figure 1-28. Congratulations! You have now acquired a Class 2 or Class 3 VeriSign Software Protection Certificate!

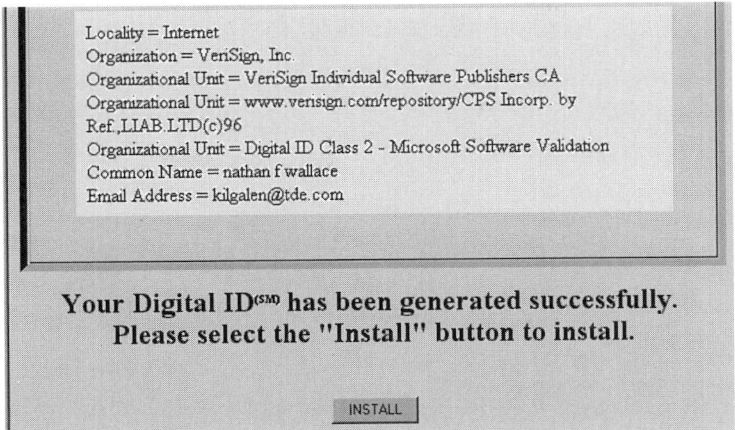

Locality = Internet
Organization = VeriSign, Inc.
Organizational Unit = VeriSign Individual Software Publishers CA
Organizational Unit = www.verisign.com/repository/CPS Incorp. by
Ref.,LIAB.LTD(c)96
Organizational Unit = Digital ID Class 2 - Microsoft Software Validation
Common Name = nathan f wallace
Email Address = kilgalen@tde.com
Your Digital ID(SM) has been generated successfully.
Please select the "Install" button to install.
INSTALL

Figure 1-26 SPC installation preparation screen

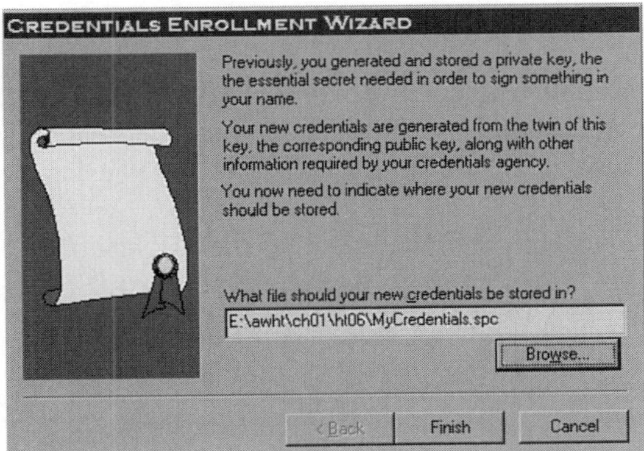

Figure 1-27 Credentials Enrollment Wizard dialog box

How It Works

VeriSign uses various commercial databases to verify that the person submitting the request for an SPC actually lives at the address submitted and has done so for at least 2 years without evidence of criminal activities or software misdeeds. For a Class 3 license, additional proof of financial stability is required. Once the information has been verified, the SPC file is created using encryption technology that is part of Internet Explorer. This technology will be discussed in more detail in the next How-To.

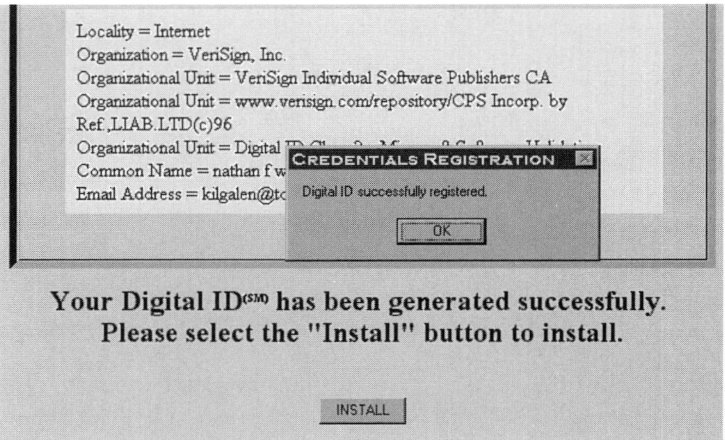

Figure 1-28 SPC installation success dialog box

Comments

It is very important *never* to distribute the PVK and SPC files you receive in this process! Doing so could make you liable to civil and perhaps even criminal penalties if someone uses your SPC to perform malicious or destructive actions with their computer code using your digital signature.

Version 2 of the Authenticode system that uses SPCs has been released; see the "Authenticode Version 2" section of `README.TXT` on the CD for more details.

1.6 How do I... Use Authenticode code signing to protect my ActiveX control on the Web?

Problem

Now that I've obtained my SPC, how do I "sign" my ActiveX control so that Internet Explorer allows it through safely?

Technique

Microsoft includes the Authenticode Code Signing SDK as part of the larger ActiveX SDK. Although it eventually will only be available to Microsoft Developer Network subscribers, it is currently available for free from the

Microsoft Web site. This How-To takes you through the process of downloading the SDK, installing it, and using its tools to sign your ActiveX control's CAB file using your VeriSign SPC.

NOTE

This How-To requires that you have obtained a valid Software Protection Certificate (SPC) from VeriSign as outlined in How-To 1.6. The steps below will fail without both the SPC and PVK files obtained in How-To 1.6. It also assumes you have created the CAB file explained in How-To 1.5.

Steps

1. Activate Internet Explorer and navigate to the URL `http://www.microsoft.com/workshop/prog/sdk`. This site is shown in Figure 1-29. It is the home page for obtaining the ActiveX SDK.
2. Click on the `Download` link. This moves the browser to a page that at its bottom has a combo box control with the names of several software packages in it, as shown in Figure 1-30. Select ActiveX SDK Core Components for Windows 95 & NT 4 and press the Go to Download button.
3. You will move to a page with numerous FTP download links. Select one and it will put up a dialog box to confirm saving the file and obtaining a path and filename. Once you have confirmed and selected, the download will begin and you will have a progress dialog shown, similar to that in Figure 1-31. Wait until the download is finished, which will take anywhere from 1 to 4 hours, depending on the speed of your modem, unless you are on a high-speed ISDN or T1 line.

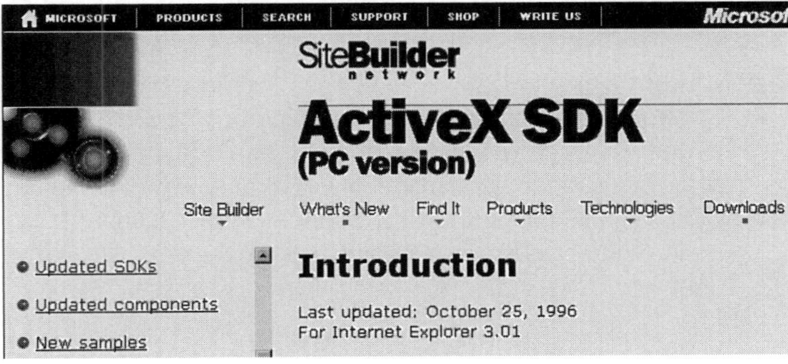

Figure 1-29 ActiveX SDK home page at Microsoft

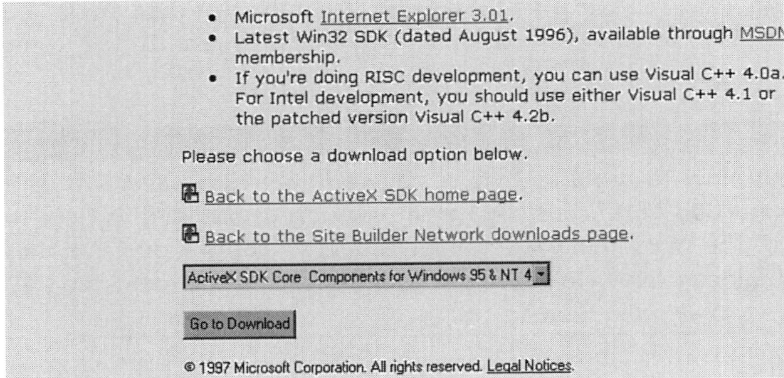

Figure 1-30 ActiveX SDK Download selection page

Figure 1-31 SDK download progress dialog

4. Once the download is complete, activate the EXE file and it will self-install, prompting you for directory information. When you are finished, you should see a directory structure similar to that shown in Figure 1-32. Navigate to the `\INETSDK\BIN\` directory and select a subdirectory that matches your machine architecture; for Intel machines, use `I386\`.

5. Now bring up an MS-DOS window in the directory `INETSDK\BIN\I386\` (or the one appropriate to your architecture). Type in `SIGNCODE` and press Return. Although you are running a DOS-mode program, a set of wizard dialog boxes will appear to guide you through the code signing process, with the initial dialog shown in Figure 1-33. (`SIGNCODE.EXE` can also be used from the DOS command line; see the ActiveX SDK documentation for details.)

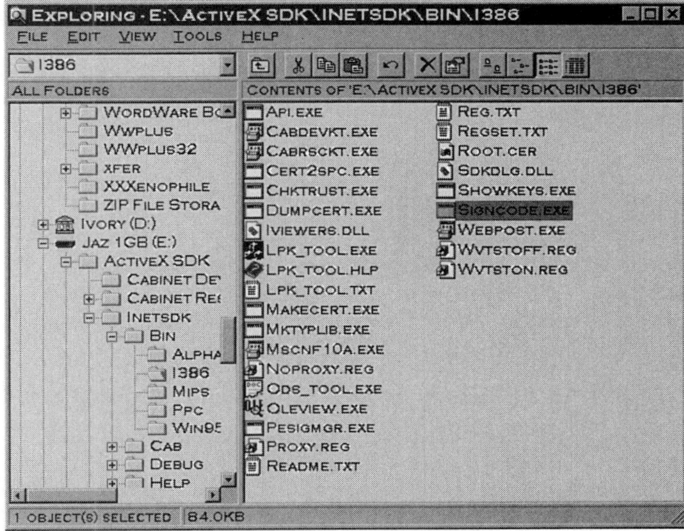

Figure 1-32 ActiveX SDK directory structure after installation

Figure 1-33 SIGNCODE Code Signing Wizard initial dialog

6. Press Next on the initial dialog box. A new wizard dialog appears, as shown in Figure 1-34. Fill in the top text entry control with the path and name of the CAB file created in How-To 1.5. Give it a descriptive name in the middle text control of this wizard dialog. Finally, enter a URL for your Web site or a README filename on the local drive.

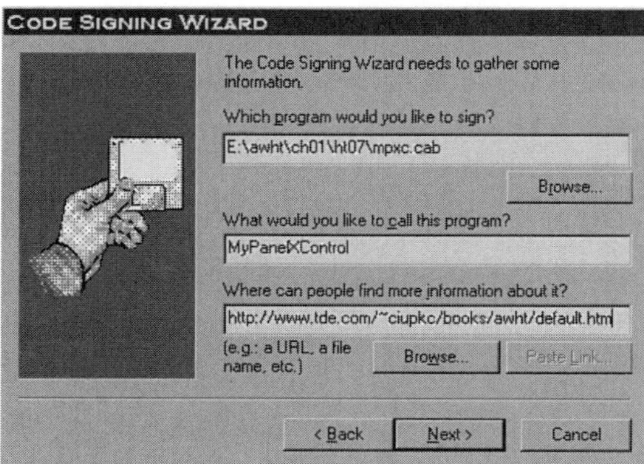

Figure 1-34 Code Signing Wizard initial data acquisition dialog

7. Press Next and the wizard dialog shown in Figure 1-35 will appear. It has two text controls that should already be filled in with the names and paths to the PVK and SPC files created in How-To 1.6. If they are not, it is probably because you have not inserted the removable disk in the drive containing them; do so and use the Browse buttons to obtain the paths and filenames for your PVK and SPC files.

8. Pressing Next after completing the PVK and SPC file entry will bring up the dialog shown in Figure 1-36. It is a confirmation dialog that allows you to go back if needed and change parts of the code-signing data.

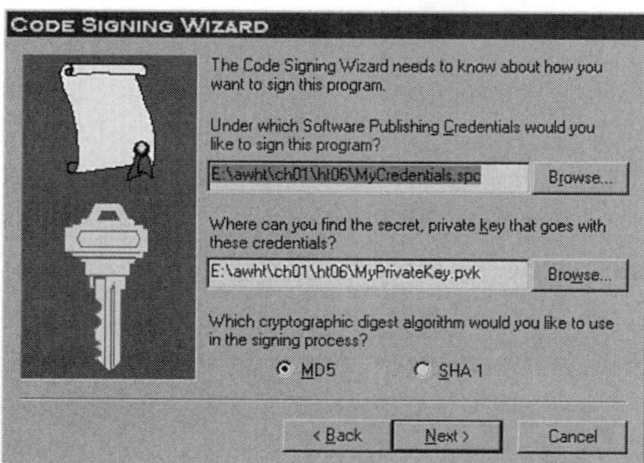

Figure 1-35 Code Signing Wizard PVK/SPC path entry dialog

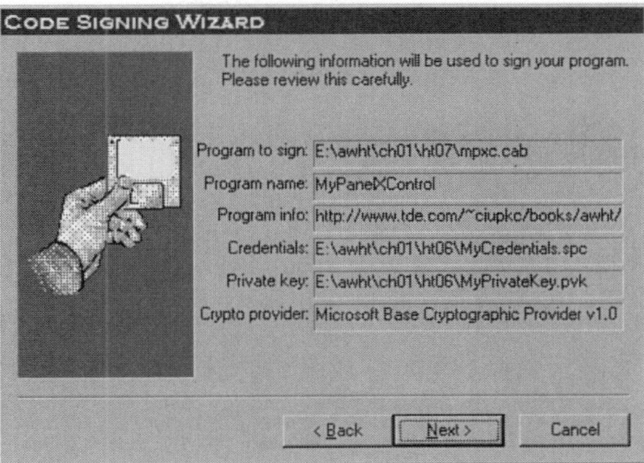

Figure 1-36 Code Signing Wizard data confirmation dialog

9. Pressing Next moves you to the dialog shown in Figure 1-37. It is the final gateway prior to activating the code-signing process; if for some reason you do not wish to continue the process, press Cancel; if you remember a needed data change, press Back. Otherwise press Sign to sign your code.

10. Once the signing process is complete, you will see a dialog similar to that shown in Figure 1-38. It indicates that the file has been digitally signed and is ready for secure Internet, intranet, or World Wide Web use. If for any reason you recompile or re-create the file, however, you must repeat the entire signing process! If the code-signing process fails for any reason, an explanatory dialog box will appear; consult the ActiveX SDK documentation files for directions as to fixing the problem. (It is usually either an invalid SPC or PVK file or a problem with locating the file to be signed or the PVK or SPC files.)

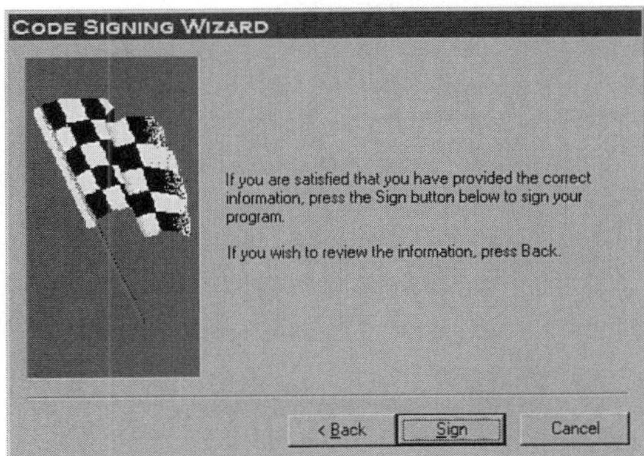

Figure 1-37 Code Signing Wizard final confirmation dialog

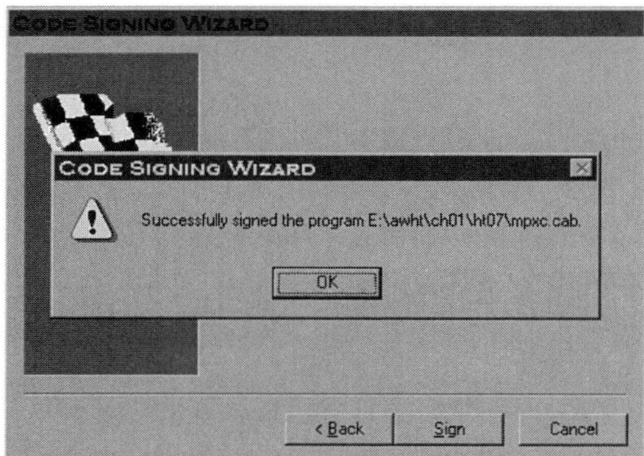

Figure 1-38 Code Signing Wizard success dialog

11. Once a file has been digitally signed, Microsoft provides a way to check the file prior to using it over the networks. This utility is called `CHKTRUST`, and it is another MS-DOS utility in the same directory as `SIGNCODE`. Activate another MS-DOS window, move to the `\INETSDK\BIN\` directory, and type in `CHKTRUST -C E:\ASPHT\CH01\HT07\MPXC.CAB`, replacing the path for the `MPXC.CAB` file with the one for your installation of the CD files. After a moment you should see a certificate displayed similar to that shown in Figure 1-39 except using your name and the distinctive name you gave the control in step 6. If this dialog does not appear, make sure you have the added `-C` and the correct filename and path on the command line for `CHKTRUST`. Congratulations! You now have a signed, guaranteed safe CAB file with an ActiveX control ready to be distributed over the World Wide Web!

How It Works

The key to the code-signing process is a technique called *hashing*. Hashing is an algorithm that takes certain combinations of data values and manipulates them mathematically to come up with unique values. Although it is normally used to find information quickly in large databases, it also has the property of uniquely identifying a set of data. This property enables determining if a binary file has been tampered with after its encryption. Code signing works in the following way.

First, two sets of encryption keys are produced. One is public and will be transmitted with all encrypted documents. The other is private and guarantees that only the authorized signer can sign documents with his or her digital signature. This process is the creation of the PVK and SPC files from How-To 1.6.

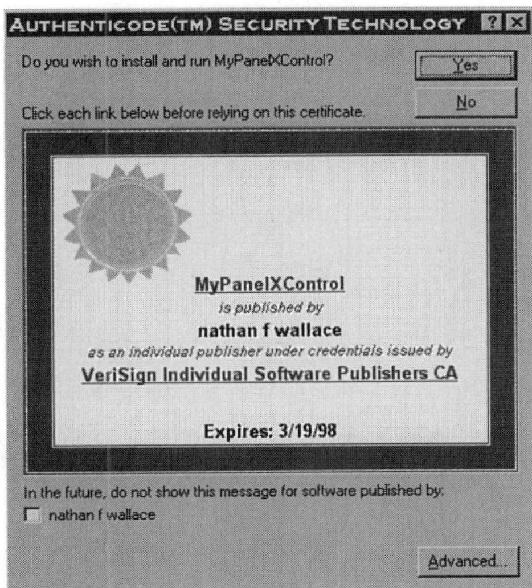

Figure 1-39 Confirmation dialog, showing code-signing certificate

Next, the binary document to be signed is hashed using an agreed-on algorithm. As you might have noticed in the Code Signing Wizard dialogs, Authenticode supports two hashing algorithms. This produces a numerical value that is then encrypted with the private key on the signing person's computer. This set of numbers is added to the file being signed (thus the need for the 6144 byte "space" in the CAB file in How-To 1.5. The public key needed to decrypt the signature is also included in the signed file and transmitted to its destination.

Once the public key reaches its destination, the Authenticode technology removes the signing information and extracts a hash value, signing information, and encryption key. It then rehashes the binary file, producing a numerical value. This value is then encrypted using the public key transmitted with the file, and if the file has not been tampered with, the value obtained from the new encryption matches the one transmitted with the signed file to authenticate it. If the binary structure of the file has been altered either by substituting a new file of the same name or by adding malicious or unauthorized code, the newly encrypted hash value will not match the transmitted hash signature and authentication will fail. In either case, unless the file has been completely corrupted, the ID and name of the signing person can be viewed and he or she can be contacted.

Comments

Although in theory Authenticode is foolproof, in practice it has several holes, not in its encryption scheme but rather in the way Windows keeps track of who is doing what internally so that a malicious ActiveX control can have its author penalized properly; this is known as a *black widow attack*. A URL to check for more information on the topic is `http://www.news.com/`; do a search on `black widow` and `activex security`.

1.7 How do I… Put my ActiveX control on a Web page?

Problem

Okay, I have my signed, licensed, and compressed ActiveX control. Now how do I get it to appear on my World Wide Web page? Visual C++ doesn't have a wizard for this.

Technique

For good reason, you don't use C++ for this task! Instead, you use the ActiveX Control Pad, a free downloadable utility from Microsoft that makes placing ActiveX controls on WWW pages a snap! This How-To shows you just how to obtain and install the ActiveX Control Pad and how to use it to create the HTML file that downloads your control's CAB archive and installs it after checking its VeriSign Authenticode certificate. Finally, the process to upload the CAB and HTML files to your Web server is explained and demonstrated.

Steps

1. The best way to put ActiveX controls on the World Wide Web at present is a free utility from Microsoft called the ActiveX Control Pad. It can be downloaded from the following URL: `http://www.microsoft.com/workshop/author/cpad/`. Navigate with Internet Explorer to this URL and download the self-extracting executable file containing the program. Then execute it and it will install ActiveX Control Pad on your system.

2. Start ActiveX Control Pad. It will display a minimal HTML page already created for you. Select the Edit menu and the option Insert ActiveX Control. You will then see a display similar to that shown in Figure 1-40. Select the `MyPanelXControl` ActiveX control and press the OK button.

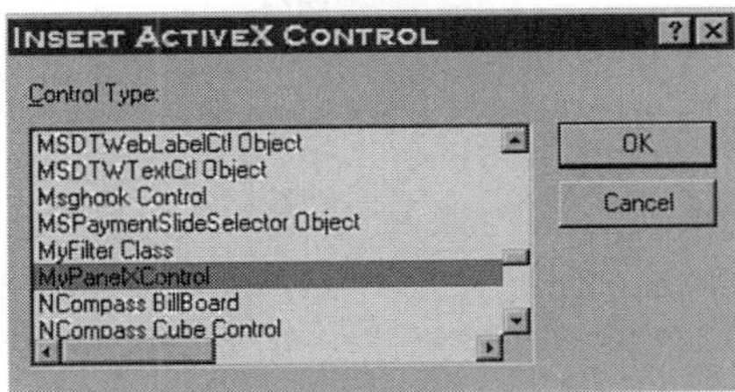

Figure 1-40 ActiveX Control Pad inserting ActiveX control into an HTML page

NOTE

See the section "Installing All OCX and DLL Files" in the `README.TXT` file to make sure `MyPanelXControl` is registered on your system.

3. There will be a considerable delay while the program searches the Registry and creates the control and displays it. A workspace dialog will appear, along with an editable copy of the control. Drag it to a desired size with the mouse. Then right-click on it to bring up a shortcut menu. From the menu, select Properties. This will bring up a dialog box that permits changing the properties of the control. Set its `BevelInner` property to `vbLowered`, its `BevelWidth` and `BorderWidth` properties to 5 pixels, and its `caption` to `This is MyPanelXContol!`. (To set a property, click on it with the mouse; edit its value in the upper text entry control, combo box, or similar control; and then press the Apply button.) Choose the `Color` property and press the button to the right of the edit box. This will bring up the color editor dialog box shown in Figure 1-41. Select a nice green color and press OK and Apply, and the displayed panel will turn green! Then set the `CODEBASE` property of the control to whatever directory you wish to keep it on your Web provider plus `mpxc.cab`; I used `http://www.tde.com/~ciupic/cabs/mpxc.cab`. This is particularly important because it is the only way the system can load the control onto a new user's machine.

4. To save the configuration of the ActiveX control to the HTML file, press the Close button on the main editor dialog. This will cause a varying amount of data and parameters to be written into the HTML page, as shown in Figure 1-42. Press the Save speed button or use the File|Save menu option to save the file as `TESTMPXC.HTM`.

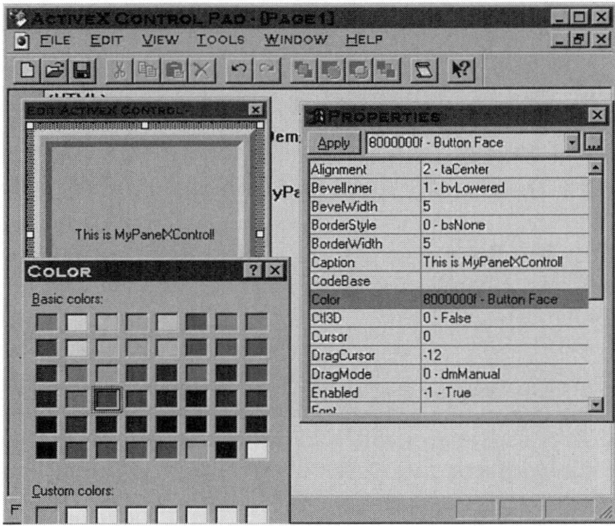

Figure 1-41 ActiveX Control Pad visually editing ActiveX control and `Color` property

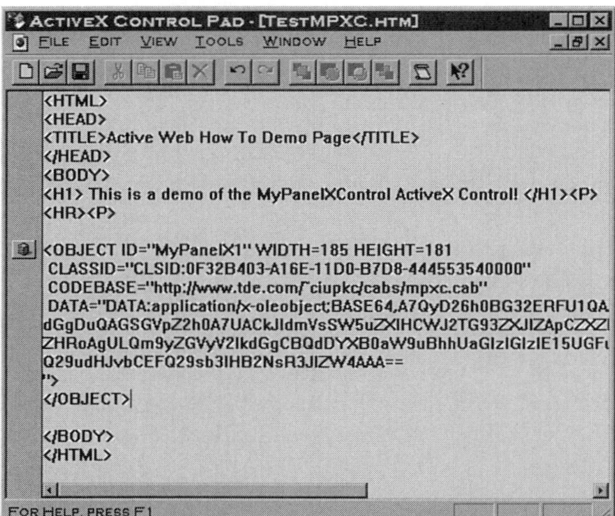

Figure 1-42 ActiveX Control Pad showing the inserted HTML code and data for the ActiveX control

5. Now locate the File Transfer Protocol (FTP) utility you have available on your system. (If you don't have one, point your browser to `http://www.shareware.com` and do a search on `ws_ftp`; this site will give you a dozen locations in a second! Unzip `ws_ftp` and run its setup program.) Use it to connect to your Web site provider and log into your account there. (If you are unclear on how to do this, read the documentation with your FTP program and consult your Web site provider.) Once you are logged in, use the FTP client to navigate on the site to the directory where you wish to keep CAB files. If you need to create a new directory, do so using the FTP client, as shown in Figure 1-43.

6. Once you have created or located the directory to store your CAB file(s) in, use the FTP client's binary upload function to move the signed CAB file created in the earlier How-To's to your Web site, as shown in Figure 1-44. Do the same with the `TESTMPXC.HTM` file created in steps 1 through 4.

7. To simulate a new user downloading your ActiveX control for the first time, you can take one of two steps here. One is to move to a computer other than the one you used to develop `MyPanelXControl` and enter the URL for your `TESTMPXC.HTM` page on your Web site. The other is to use `REGEDIT.EXE` on your development system and do a search on `MyPanelXControl`; the program will show you the entry in the Registry containing the control. Delete it and save the Registry. Then enter the URL for `TESTMPXC.HTM` into the Internet Explorer browser and watch as it downloads and installs the new control from the CAB file, as shown in Figure 1-45.

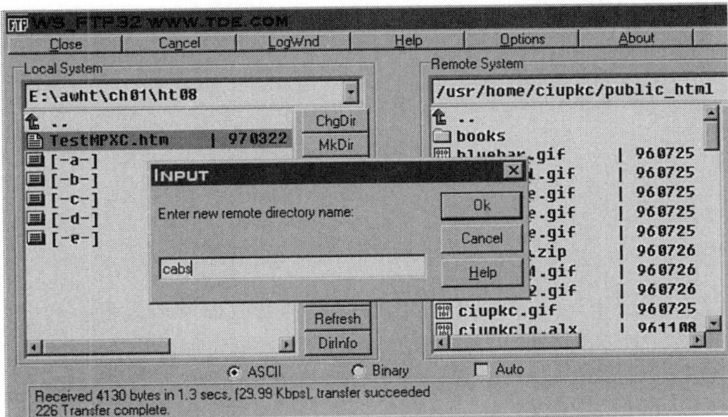

Figure 1-43 Using an FTP client to create a new directory at your Web site to store CAB files

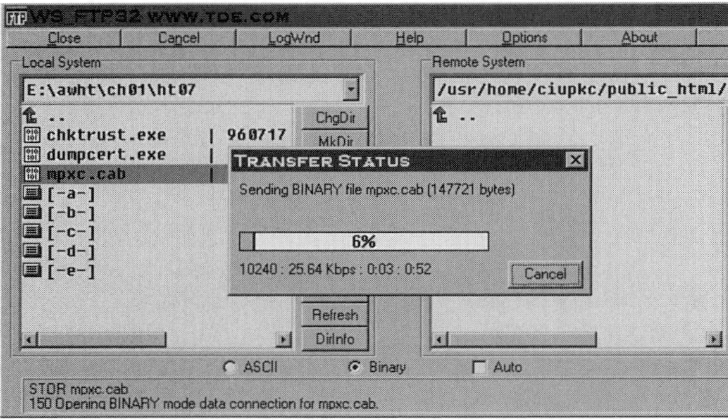

Figure 1-44 Using the FTP client to upload a binary CAB file to the Web site

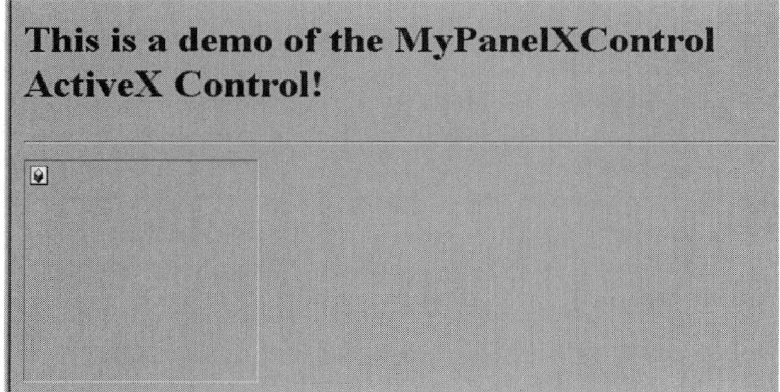

Figure 1-45 Internet Explorer downloaded and installing a new ActiveX control from a CAB file at a remote Web site

8. When the download and opening of the CAB file by Internet Explorer are complete, but prior to installing and running the new ActiveX control, the Authenticode system in Internet Explorer will check for the SPC in the new control and display it, as shown in Figure 1-46. (Note that this will happen only if you have your copy of Internet Explorer's security settings on the High or Medium setting, and if you have not already installed a control with your own SPC on it and checked the Do not show check box on the SPC dialog box when it displayed your certificate.)

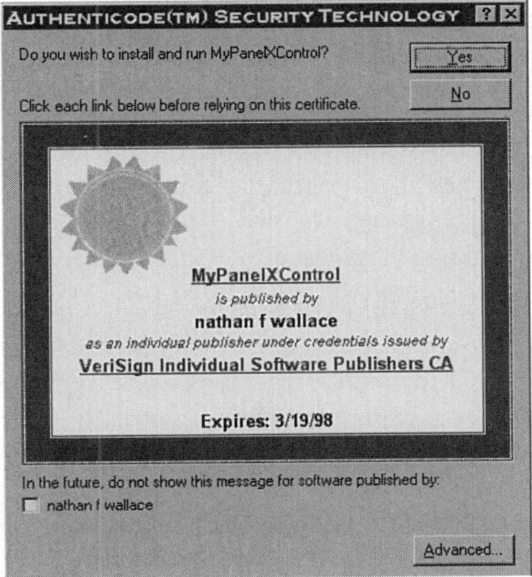

Figure 1-46 Internet Explorer showing the SPC from the ActiveX control in the `MPXC.CAB` file it just downloaded

9. Notice that there are two links on the display. One is to the VeriSign home page; the other is to whatever file or HTML page you specified when you signed your ActiveX control. Clicking on the link will open the page or file. This assures the user of your control that you exist, are benign, and generally are an okay person to provide active content. A broken link here may cause the person NOT to install your control!

10. Press the Yes button on the certificate (assuming you trust yourself!). This will allow Internet Explorer to install, register, and display the new ActiveX control. Your level of ActiveX mastery now includes placing your ActiveX control on a WWW server and downloading and displaying it on a remote Web page!

How It Works

This How-To uses three key pieces of functionality: ActiveX Control Pad, an FTP client program, and Internet Explorer.

ActiveX Control Pad is a simple text editor very much like Notepad (hence the name, perhaps?) that has been augmented with three critical pieces of functionality. First, it can search the Windows Registry and automatically locate all registered ActiveX controls on a machine or network. Then, once a control has been located, it can contact the OLE system and create an editable copy of the control to allow interactive setting of its properties using the mouse and keyboard as well as dialog boxes. Finally, it can write out HTML code that allows Internet Explorer to download the control, install it, and display it with the settings entered in its editor environment. Doing all these tasks by hand is certainly possible, but the Control Pad makes it a breeze, and after all, it's free!

Notice this line of code in the HTML page created by the Control Pad:

```
<OBJECT ID="MyPanelX1" WIDTH=185 HEIGHT=181
 CLASSID="CLSID:0F32B403-A16E-11D0-B7D8-444553540000"
```

This "CLASSID=" number is a GUID, which is assigned to an ActiveX control when Developer Studio creates its skeleton code. The program has obtained it from the Windows Registry and, by adding it to the OBJECT tag, allows Internet Explorer to know which unique control is being referenced.

FTP is one of the foundation stones of the Internet and the World Wide Web, and details about it are beyond the scope of this book. FTP is required by most Web sites as the tool to upload files to them and move files around on them prior to using the site on the WWW itself. To make your ActiveX controls available to other users via HTML pages, the OCX or CAB file containing the control(s) must be moved to a Web server computer where users can obtain it.

Finally, Internet Explorer must be used to download the page containing the <OBJECT> tag and its reference to your new control. First, Internet Explorer will search the Registry of its host computer for the GUID in the tag. If it finds it, it will create and display the control normally. If it does not find it, it looks for that CODEBASE parameter you added earlier:

```
<OBJECT ID="MyPanelX1" WIDTH=185 HEIGHT=181
 CLASSID="CLSID:0F32B403-A16E-11D0-B7D8-444553540000"
CODEBASE="http://www.tde.com/~ciupkc/cabs/mpxc.cab"
```

This parameter is essential because it is the only way that Internet Explorer can locate a control that is not already installed on a user's system! The reference can point to a DLL, an OCX, or a CAB file; Internet Explorer will download all types and check them for an SPC (if it is not on Low security). If the SPC is found, it is checked to ensure the code has not been altered, and either the SPC or a warning message is shown. Then the new control is extracted if needed and registered with the system, and a copy is created on the Web page. *Voilá*!

Comments

The strange characters in the HTML <OBJECT> tag are called *Multipurpose Internet Mail Extension (MIME)*, a way the World Wide Web sends binary data as text. It is very important not to alter the data in any way, or the control will not display property on its page, or even at all!

If you would like a nice tutorial on using ActiveX Control Pad and creating active content from the user's perspective, you might try *Learn ActiveX Scripting with Internet Explorer 4.0* by Nathan Wallace, from WordWare Publishing.

1.8 How do I… Prevent unauthorized use of my ActiveX control on Web pages?

Problem

Now that I can put my control on the Web, I just realized everyone can use it for free! How do I prevent this?

Technique

In addition to requiring a LIC file for use in a design environment, the ActiveX system also has the capability to require a license in a Web page via the LPK system. This How-To shows you the steps needed to use LPK files in a Web page to protect your ActiveX controls from unauthorized use.

Steps

1. Activate the ActiveX Control Pad application as outlined in How-To 1.7. Then enter the HTML code in Listing 1-6 and save the page as ASPHT0108.HTM.

Listing 1-6 ASPHT0108.HTM HTML source code

```
<HTML>
<HEAD>
<TITLE>LPK Test Page</TITLE>
</HEAD>
<BODY>
<OBJECT
CLASSID="clsid:5220cb21-c88d-11cf-b347-00aa00a28331"
>
<PARAM NAME="LPKPath" VALUE="aspht0108.lpk">
</OBJECT>

<OBJECT ID="Aspht01031" WIDTH=100 HEIGHT=51
 CLASSID="CLSID:C17F94FD-B03A-11D0-B7D8-444553540000">
    <PARAM NAME="_Version" VALUE="65536">
    <PARAM NAME="_ExtentX" VALUE="2646">
    <PARAM NAME="_ExtentY" VALUE="1323">
    <PARAM NAME="_StockProps" VALUE="0">
</OBJECT>
</BODY>
</HTML>
```

2. Activate the `LPKTOOL.EXE` utility that shipped with the ActiveX SDK you used earlier. (Note: If you placed the SDK on a different drive than the one containing the `WINDOWS` directory of your system, the `LKPTOOL` will incorrectly report that you have not registered your license manager OCX file, which was installed automatically with Internet Explorer. If this happens, copy the `LPKTOOL.EXE` file to your `WINDOWS` directory and the problem will be resolved.) Select the `ASPHT0103.OCX` control and place it in the LPK file with the Add button. Then press the Save and Exit button; a dialog box will appear for a filename; enter `ASPHT0108.LPK`, as shown in Figure 1-47, saving the file to the same directory as the `ASPHT0108.HTM` file (this is very important!). The application will create the LPK file and terminate.

3. Bring up `ASPHT0108.HTM` in Internet Explorer. It will display the control correctly, as shown in Figure 1-48.

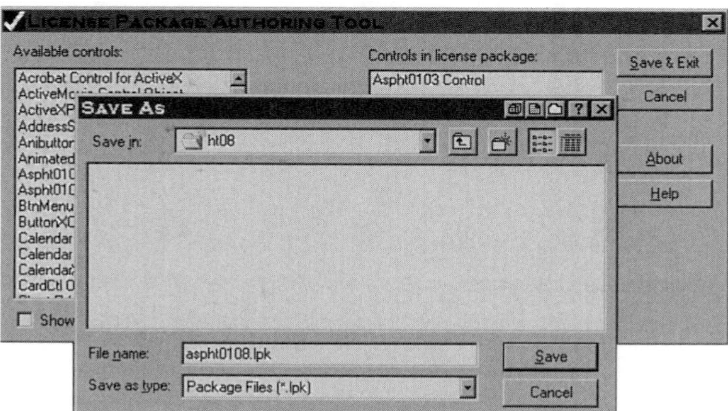

Figure 1-47 LPKTOOL, showing its LPK file creation dialog

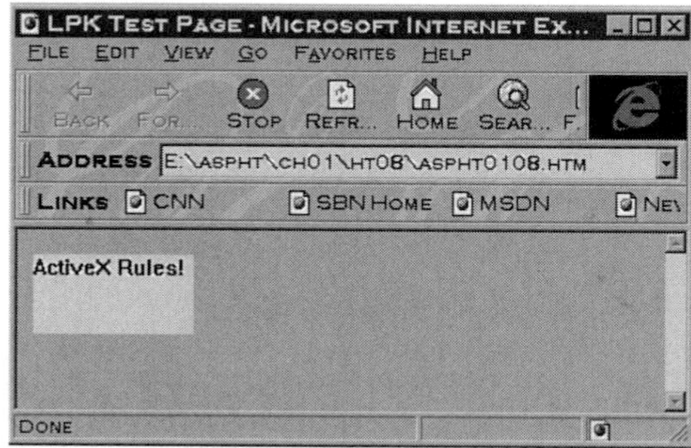

Figure 1-48 IE showing `ASPHT0108.HTM` with its licensed control

4. Now move the LPK file to a different directory, and make sure the LIC file is moved to a different location than the control expects. Close IE and reload the `ASPHT0108.HTM` file (do not just refresh the display, because this does not recheck the LPK file). Now the ActiveX control does not load. Congratulations! You have now protected your ActiveX control from unauthorized Web page use.

How It Works

To use LPK licensing, first a copy of the `Licensing Manager` object must be activated; this line of code does that in the HTML file:

```
<OBJECT
CLASSID="clsid:5220cb21-c88d-11cf-b347-00aa00a28331"
>
<PARAM NAME="LPKPath" VALUE="aspht0108.lpk">
</OBJECT>
```

It takes the filename of the LPK file to check for all controls on the page. It is important to note that a complete URL is not permitted for the LPK file; this prevents downloading the LPK file from another location on the Web, perhaps without authorization. By making the location relative to the base URL for the HTML file, the licensing system makes it easier to provide the LPK file when one has been acquired but still requires deliberate alteration of the system to use the control without permission.

The LPK file itself is simply a copy of the LIC file that has been encoded for security. Listing 1-7 shows the contents of `ASPHT0108.LPK`.

Listing 1-7 `ASPHT0108.LPK`-encoded Internet license file

```
LPK License Package

//////////////////////////////////////////////////////////////////////////////

//  WARNING:  The information in this file is protected by copyright law    //

//  and international treaty provisions. Unauthorized reproduction or       //

//  distribution of this file, or any portion of it, may result in severe   //

//  criminal and civil penalties, and will be prosecuted to the maximum     //

//  extent possible under the law.  Further, you may not reverse engineer,  //

//  decompile, or disassemble the file.                                     //

//////////////////////////////////////////////////////////////////////////////

{3d25aba1-caec-11cf-b34a-00aa00a28331}
```

continued on next page

continued from previous page


```
4dYxOdOw0BG32ERFU1QAAA=


AQAAAA=


/ZR/wTqw0BG32ERFU1QAACIAAAB

DAG8AcAB5AHIAaQBnAGgAdAAgACgAYwApACAAMQA5ADkANwAgAEMASQBVAFAASwBD

ACAAUwBvAGYAdAB3AGEAcgBlAA=
```


Notice the `LPK License Package` first line; it is what is checked to determine that the file is indeed an LPK file. After this is the GUID of the control being licensed, and following that is a set of uuencoded (via MIME syntax) text, which is the license file.

Comments

Microsoft has taken the position that licensing is important but should not be used to strangle distribution of ActiveX controls. In general, it recommends using LIC files at design time rather than LPK files at display time.

1.9 How do I... Interact with my ActiveX control using ActiveX Scripting?

Problem

My ActiveX control looks really nice on its Web page, but I've put a lot of interactive features into it that work fine in my C++ application and I'd like the Web version to work similarly. Is there a way to invoke my control's properties and methods from a Web page?

Technique

Absolutely! This is one-third of the active platform picture, the ability to control ActiveX controls while they are on the Web page. The capability to do this is called *ActiveX Scripting*, and it is used with ActiveX Control Pad. This How-To demonstrates precisely how to use VBScript to control an ActiveX control on the Web page created in the last How-To.

Steps

1. Activate ActiveX Control Pad (obtained in How-To 1.7; if you aren't reading these in order, look there for download instructions). Choose File|New HTML Layout from the menu and after a number of minutes you will see a display similar to Figure 1-49. The Toolbox dialog is used to display many of the ActiveX controls on your system but not all. Right-click on it to bring up the shortcut menu shown in the figure and select the Additional Controls option.

2. A dialog box will appear, showing all the ActiveX controls registered on your system, as well as some OLE servers that can function as ActiveX controls in some cases. The list is alphabetical by name of control, so scroll down to the `MyPanelXControl` listing and check its check box as shown in Figure 1-50. Press OK; after a delay, the control will be added to the end of the list on the Standard tab of the toolbox.

NOTE

See the section "Installing All OCX and DLL Files" in the `README.TXT` file to make sure `MyPanelXControl` is registered on your system.

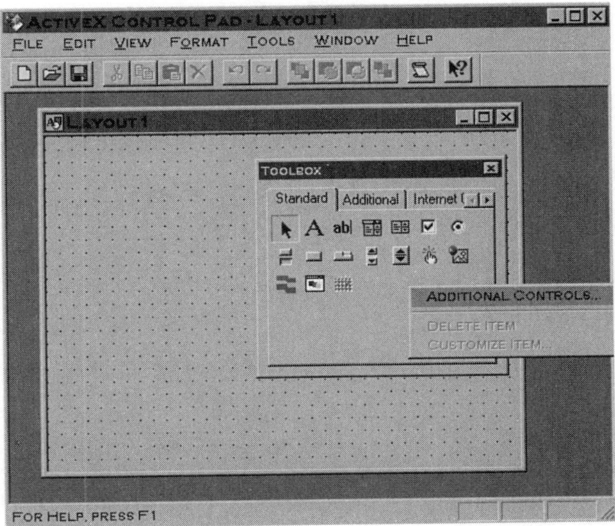

Figure 1-49 ActiveX Control Pad displaying its HTML layout editor, controls toolbox dialog, and shortcut menu.

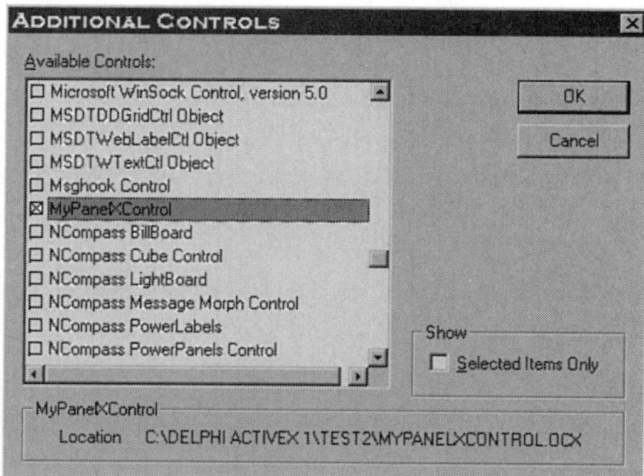

Figure 1-50 Adding the `MyPanelXControl` ActiveX Control to the HTML layout editor toolbox dialog

3. Click on the end of the list of small images on the toolbox dialog, then click and drag on the HTML layout editor and a new `MyPanelXControl` will be created. Set its properties to those in How-To 1.8. Then use the same technique to place a `TextBox` control (symbolized by the two letters and a cursor picture) below it, and a `CommandButton` control (symbolized by a single sculptured button) below it. Click inside the command button and a cursor will appear; delete the name and type in `Press To Change Panel Caption` and click outside the button; the text will remain as the button's new caption. At this point you should see a display similar to Figure 1-51.

Figure 1-51 Visually editing `MyPanelXControl` on an HTML layout

4. Now click on the small scroll icon on the speed bar for the Control Pad. This brings up a script editor dialog similar to that shown in Figure 1-52. In the upper-left pane, click to open the `CommandButton1` element, and then click on its `Click` event. A subroutine in VBScript will appear in the code panel below (if the pane is in List View mode, set it to Code View mode with the radio button below it). In the upper-right pane, find the `MyPanelX1` entry and click to open it, then double-click on its `Caption` property; notice that a text reference appears in the code pane. Type an equal sign (=) after the reference, then locate the `TextBox1` entry in the upper-right pane and click to open it. Scroll down to its `Text` property and double-click; a reference to it will appear in the code window after the = sign, as shown in Figure 1-52. Press OK to add this script command to your layout.

5. Select the File|Save As... menu option, and save the layout as `Layout1.ALX`. Then close the layout editor by clicking the Close box. Create a new HTML file in the Control Pad, and enter the HTML code in Listing 1-8. Then position your cursor between the two `<HR>` tags and select the Edit|Insert HTML Layout menu option. From the dialog box, select `Layout1.ALX`, and the source code to include the HTML layout will be included, as shown in Figure 1-53. Save this HTML file as `TESTASXC.HTM` and close the Control Pad.

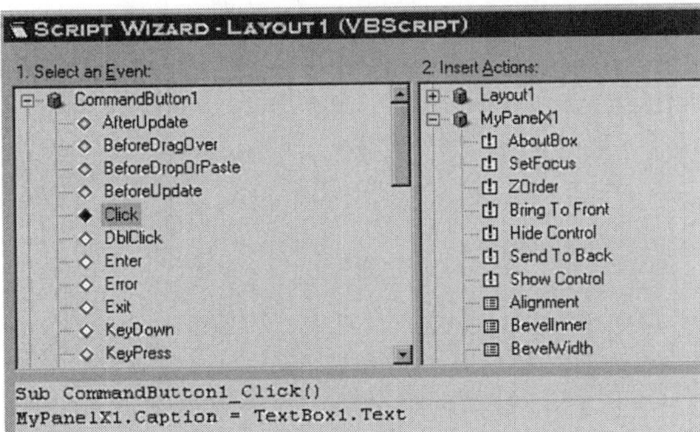

Figure 1-52 The Script Wizard dialog box, shown adding a script command to the command button's `Click` event.

Listing 1-8 TESTAXSC.HTM HTML source code

```
<HTML>
<HEAD>
<TITLE>ActiveX Scripting Test Page</TITLE>
</HEAD>
<BODY>
<H1>This is a demo of ActiveX Scripting!</H1>
<HR>
<HR>
</BODY>
</HTML>
```

6. Using the same techniques as explained in How-To 1.8, step 5, move the `TESTAXSC.HTM` and `LAYOUT1.ALX` files to your Web site. Then enter its URL into your copy of Internet Explorer, and after the page downloads, you should see a display similar to that shown in Figure 1-54. Notice how precisely the positioning of the `Panel`, `TextBox`, and `CommandButton` controls are maintained, just as you placed them on the editor window! Now type a string into the text box control and press the command button; the string will become the caption of the panel without requiring a new copy of the page to be downloaded. You can now use ActiveX Scripting to control the functionality of your ActiveX control on a Web page!

How It Works

This How-To is based on two separate but interlinked pieces of the active platform: the HTML `Layout` control and ActiveX scripting.

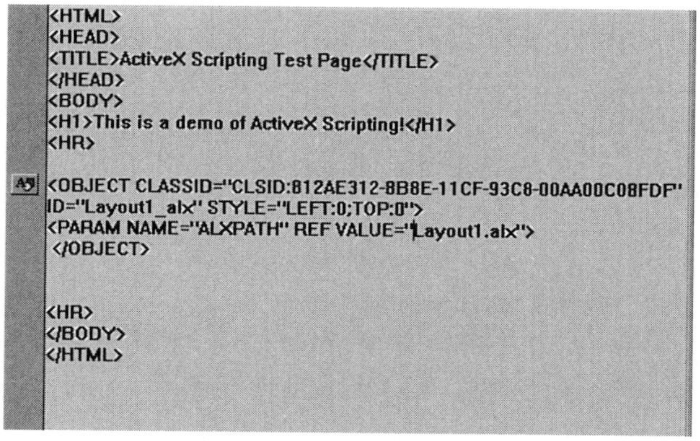

```
<HTML>
<HEAD>
<TITLE>ActiveX Scripting Test Page</TITLE>
</HEAD>
<BODY>
<H1>This is a demo of ActiveX Scripting!</H1>
<HR>

<OBJECT CLASSID="CLSID:812AE312-8B8E-11CF-93C8-00AA00C08FDF"
ID="Layout1_alx" STYLE="LEFT:0;TOP:0">
<PARAM NAME="ALXPATH" REF VALUE="Layout1.alx">
 </OBJECT>


<HR>
</BODY>
</HTML>
```

Figure 1-53 The HTML file showing an HTML layout entry

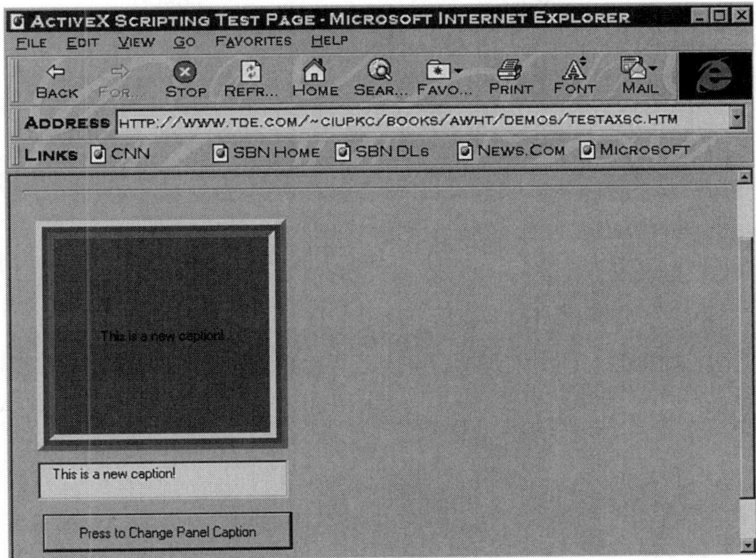

Figure 1-54 Internet Explorer showing the HTML layout with `MyPanelXContol` from the WWW

The HTML `Layout` control is an ActiveX control that serves as a *control container*, much like Internet Explorer itself. However, unlike IE, which does its containing based on HTML syntax, the HTML `Layout` container uses exact pixel-based two-dimensional coordinates to place its controls, thus permitting the same sophisticated displays possible in application programs. If you are a C++ programmer and say "so what?," just ask a Web designer friend about it and prepare to be yelled at, because this capability has been the Holy Grail of Web page creators for four years—only now is it finally available! The positioning of the three ActiveX controls on the `Layout` control you created in the editor has been faithfully reproduced on the Web page, and this cannot be done in HTML!

ActiveX Scripting is Microsoft's version of JavaScript, a hybrid system supporting JScript (Microsoft's dialect of JavaScript) and VBScript (Microsoft's own scripting language). The purpose of scripting is to allow code to be embedded in HTML pages and run by the Web browser so that it can be controlled like a small program on the client's machine. The Control Pad's Script Wizard uses the scripting object model to display events and properties of the HTML layout and Web page HTML and place script statements in them so that the desired behavior is obtained.

Once the page is downloaded by Internet Explorer, its script statements are processed and wait for a user action to trigger them. When the command button is pressed by the viewer of the HTML page containing it, the script is run by IE and the text in the `TextBox` ActiveX control is taken by the browser and used to change the caption of the `MyPanelXControl` ActiveX control. The browser then redisplays itself automatically to show the new information.

Scripting is a very complex topic, and due to space limitations, it cannot be considered here further. The book *Learn ActiveX Scripting with Internet Explorer 4.0* by Nathan Wallace from WordWare Publishing is an excellent resource for this complex but amazingly powerful feature of the active platform.

Comments

The ALX file you uploaded is the HTML text used to create and display the HTML `Layout` control. It is kept in another file format because at present only IE and the `Layout` control understand it, and so it would not be appropriate for it to be part of an HTML file that other browsers could not read.

AX-ASP

1.10 How do I... Link my ActiveX control with an Active Server Pages script?

Problem

My Web service provider has just started using the Internet Information Server (IIS) from Microsoft, and tells me that my Web site can now use Active Server Pages (ASP) to enhance its functionality. How can my ActiveX control take advantage of the new ASP technology?

Technique

Active Server Pages is a fantastic new capability available to IIS Web sites that allows dynamic interactions using simple scripts very much like ActiveX Scripting, but that executes on the server rather than the client computer. This How-To illustrates a simple but powerful example of using ASP with the previously created ActiveX control and scripted HTML page to customize the page for its user.

NOTE

This is the first "cross technology" How-To. The icon beside it indicates that it is a combination of ActiveX and Active Server Pages. Look for other combination How-To icons in the remainder of the book!

Steps

1. Activate your copy of ActiveX Control Pad. Start a new HTML file and add the code in Listing 1-9. Then save the file as `ACTIVEXASP.ASP` (choose All Files in the Type combo box to prevent adding `.HTM` to the filename.)

Listing 1-9 `ACTIVEXASP.ASP` Active Server Pages script file

```
<%@ LANGUAGE = VBScript %>
<HTML>
<HEAD>
<TITLE>ActiveX and ASP Demo Page</TITLE>
</HEAD>
<BODY>
<% Set OBJbrowser = Server.CreateObject("MSWC.BrowserType") %>
<% If OBJbrowser.ActiveXControls = "True" Then %>
<% Else %>
<%= "You are only seeing this if your browser doesn't support ActiveX! Get a Real
Browser!"%>
<% End If %>
</BODY>
</HTML>
```

2. Place the cursor in front of the `<%else%>` line and choose Edit|Insert ActiveX Control. Add another copy of the `MyPanelXControl` from the previous How-To's. Make sure to set its `CODEBASE` property to your Web site's CAB file, as arranged in How-To 1.8. Then close the ActiveX control editor and delete the line from the resulting HTML that contains the `CLASSID` for the control. You should see a display similar to Figure 1-55.

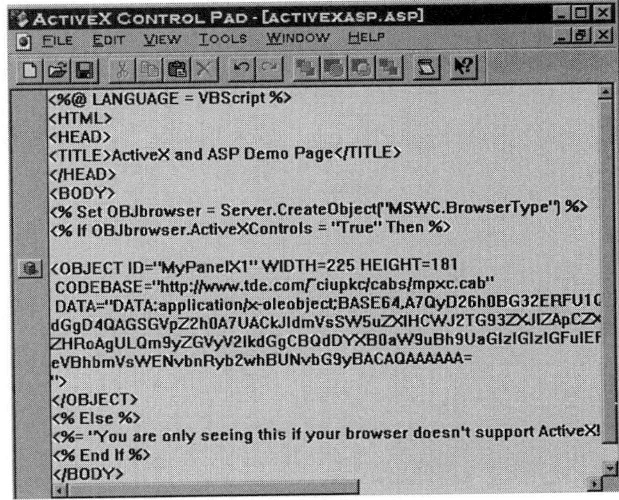

Figure 1-55 The ASP file with an ActiveX control `<OBJECT>` tag without a `CLASSID` parameter

3. Save the ASP file and close ActiveX Control Pad. At this point, this How-To assumes you have downloaded and installed either the IIS (Internet Information Server) or PWS (Personal Web Server) software from Microsoft. If you have not, please see the `README.TXT` file section "Getting IIS/PWS" for directions on how to obtain and install these products, which are currently free (at least in their beta versions). The following directions are for PWS for Windows 95; for the corresponding actions in IIS, please consult your IIS documentation. On the lower-right corner of your task bar are the tray icons of background processes. Right-click on the one for the PWS and select Administrate from the shortcut menu. It will start Internet Explorer set to the default administration page for PWS, as shown in Figure 1-56.

4. Click on the Directories tab of the display; when it changes to the directory display, move down to the `Add` link, as shown in Figure 1-57. Click on this link to bring up the Directory Add page.

5. In the directory text control, type in the drive and directory where you are keeping the files for this How-To on your computer. In the text box for the virtual directory, give the directory a meaningful alias. Make sure the Execute check box is checked, as shown in Figure 1-58. Then press the OK button and return to the main administration page.

6. Carefully type this URL into the address bar of Internet Explorer, replacing the `[myserver]` and `[myalias]` portions with the server name your system is using (`default` is the most common) and the alias you used in step 5 for the directory (`http://[myserver]/[myalias]/activexasp.asp`). The ASP file will then bring up the page shown in Figure 1-59, creating the ActiveX control from the information in the `CODEBASE` parameter and displaying it.

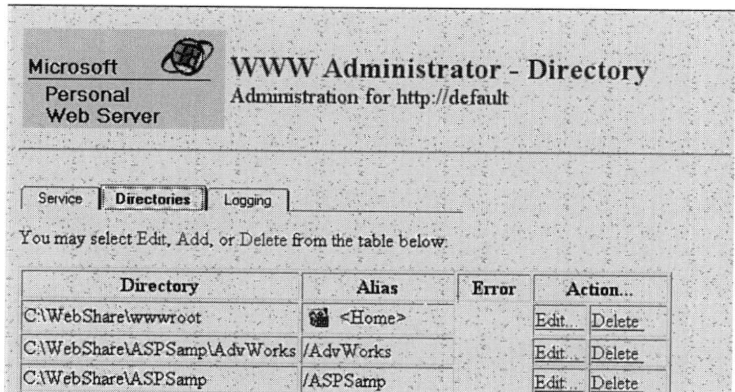

Figure 1-56 Bringing up the administration page for the PWS

C:\WebShare\ASPSamp	/ASPSamp	Edit...	Delete
e:\awht\ch01\ht10	/awht1	Edit...	Delete
C:\Program Files\WebSvr\Docs	/Docs	Edit...	Delete
C:\Program Files\WebSvr\Htmla	/Htmla	Edit...	Delete
C:\Program Files\WebSvr\Htmlascr	/HtmlaScripts	Edit...	Delete
C:\Program Files\WebSvr\Docs	/IASDocs	Edit...	Delete
C:\WebShare\scripts	/Scripts	Edit...	Delete
			Add...

Enable Default Document
Default Document : Default.htm

Directory Browsing Allowed

Figure 1-57 The Add link on the directories administration page for PWS

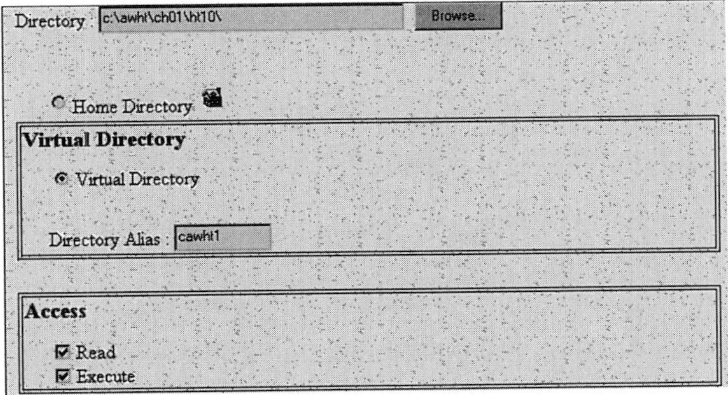

Figure 1-58 The PWS directory permissions and aliases addition page

7. If you have a copy of another browser on your system, such as Netscape Navigator or NCSA Mosaic, use it to bring up the same page. You will see only one line of text, as shown in Figure 1-60, rather than an error when the browser cannot display the ActiveX control. You have just merged an ActiveX control's functionality with the power of Active Server Pages and taken your first big step into the complex and powerful world of the active platform!

How It Works

Even though this book is titled *Active Server Pages How-To*, this is the first How-To on ASP! It uses aspects of both Active Server Pages and ActiveX to work its

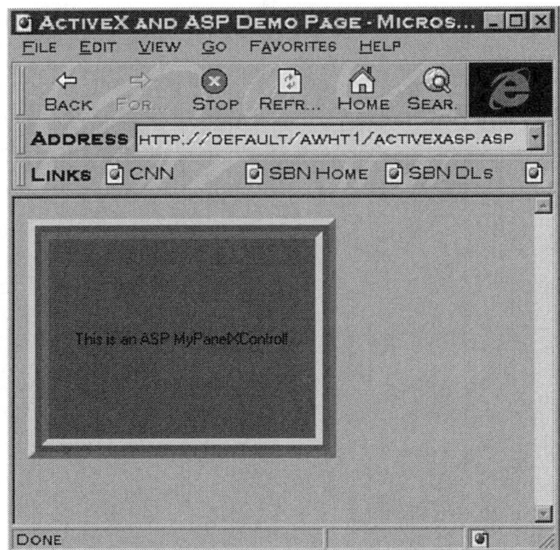

Figure 1-59 Internet Explorer displaying the ASP page with its ActiveX control

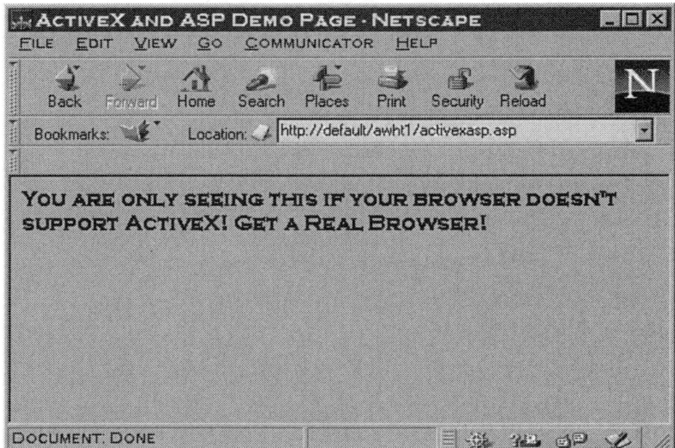

Figure 1-60 A non–ActiveX-capable browser displaying the alternate text and no error for the ASP file

magic. (If you are completely unfamiliar with how ASP works, you should read Chapter 4, "Basic ASP: Server-and Client-Side Scripting," first, before trying this How-To.) ASP uses the ASP component technology, whereas ActiveX uses an unadvertised functionality of the `<OBJECT>` tag in Internet Explorer.

This line of code in the ASP file creates an ASP component on the server:

```
<% Set OBJbrowser = Server.CreateObject("MSWC.BrowserType") %>
```

This component (BrowserType) is a system object that is able to interact with the browser requesting the page and determine what its capabilities are. This next line calls a function of the object that returns true if the browser can display ActiveX controls, and false if not:

```
<% If OBJbrowser.ActiveXControls = "True" Then %>
<% Else %>
<%= "You are only seeing this if your browser doesn't support ActiveX! Get a⇐
Real Browser!"%>
```

Based on this information, the ASP page writes out an <OBJECT> tag with the data needed to display MyPanelXControl or a simple line of text warning that the browser is inadequate. This completes the ASP end of the picture.

The ASP <OBJECT> tag does not include a CLASSID parameter. According to the documentation, this should cause the <OBJECT> tag reference to fail. However, if a CODEBASE parameter is included with only one ActiveX control in the file, Internet Explorer will figure out on its own which control is needed, download and install it, and display a working copy!

Comments

One might wonder why the “back door” for ActiveX components exists in IE. One reason could be that writers of ASP pages might not have access to the CLASSID of a control, due to inexperience with programming syntax and behaviors, but would know the control's parameters and the OCX or CAB file containing it from other Web pages or ASP files. This simpler syntax will permit a control to be used even by inexperienced developers!

CHAPTER 2

INTERMEDIATE ACTIVEX: CREATING CUSTOMIZED ACTIVEX CONTROLS

2

INTERMEDIATE ACTIVEX: CREATING CUSTOMIZED ACTIVEX CONTROLS

How do I…

2.1 Use ambient properties with my ActiveX control in Visual C++ 5.0?

2.2 Handle standard events with my ActiveX control using Visual C++ 5.0?

2.3 Create custom properties for my ActiveX control in Visual C++ 5.0?

2.4 Define and handle custom events with my ActiveX control in Visual C++ 5.0?

2.5 Include custom methods with my ActiveX control in Visual C++ 5.0?

2.6 Add text and font support to my ActiveX control with Visual C++ 5.0?

2.7 Add custom graphics to my ActiveX control using Visual C++ 5.0?

2.8 Make my ActiveX control's custom properties persistent using Visual C++ 5.0?

2.9 Interact with my ActiveX control's custom events, properties, and methods using ActiveX Scripting?

2.10 Keep track of user-set custom properties on my custom ActiveX control with an Active Server Pages script?

Now that you have mastered the basics of creating an MFC (Microsoft Foundation Classes) ActiveX control, protecting it with licensing, compressing it with CAB, and downloading and controlling it with Internet Explorer, it is time to make your ActiveX controls do something useful! In this chapter, you will learn how to use properties, events, and methods in your custom control, both those provided by the object linking and embedding (OLE) system and those you write yourself. You will also understand how to control your control's fonts and how to add exciting graphics to its display. Finally, you'll come up to speed on making your control's properties persistent and controlling the custom behaviors of your control with scripting and Active Server Pages. So flex your fingers, fire up Visual C++ 5.0, and take control over ActiveX with these ten sections.

2.1 Use Ambient Properties with My ActiveX Control in Visual C++ 5.0

The ActiveX system provides a number of standard or *ambient* properties that an ActiveX control can implement. This How-To shows you the methods needed to access and use ambient ActiveX properties with an MFC ActiveX control in Visual C++ 5.0.

2.2 Handle Standard Events with My ActiveX Control Using Visual C++ 5.0

Along with ambient properties, MFC ActiveX controls automatically support a number of standard events. However, a control may still implement actions in response to the events. This How-To illustrates acquiring event notifications with an MFC ActiveX control in Visual C++ 5.0 and responding effectively to them.

2.3 Create Custom Properties for My ActiveX Control in Visual C++ 5.0

Properties are the way ActiveX controls expose their data elements to other programs such as Visual Basic and Internet Explorer. This How-To lays out the procedures in Visual C++ 5.0 to add your own properties to an MFC ActiveX control so that any other program or environment can access them.

2.4 Define and Handle Custom Events with My ActiveX Control in Visual C++ 5.0

Events are the mechanism used to communicate among an ActiveX control, its hosting environment, and the user; a useful control must be able to define its own events and handle them. This How-To includes all the details for adding and responding to custom events for an MFC ActiveX control in Visual C++ 5.0.

2.5 Include Custom Methods With My ActiveX Control in Visual C++ 5.0

Methods are the procedures and functions that expose capabilities beyond the visual display of an ActiveX control to calling programs and environments. This How-To teaches you the steps needed to add custom methods to your MFC ActiveX control in Visual C++ 5.0.

2.6 Add Text and Font Support to My ActiveX Control with Visual C++ 5.0

Fonts are one of the most powerful display features of Windows controls, but they are also one of the hardest to manage. MFC ActiveX controls in Visual C++ 5.0 have special support for controlling their font environment, and this How-To outlines how you can take advantage of this capability in your own ActiveX control.

2.7 Add Custom Graphics to My ActiveX Control Using Visual C++ 5.0

Although ActiveX isn't just another pretty face, it doesn't hurt to add a nice graphical element to a control. This How-To lays out the precise steps needed to enhance your MFC ActiveX control in Visual C++ 5.0 with a resource icon and bitmap, using code that can be generalized to output any sort of graphical image.

2.8 Make My ActiveX Control's Custom Properties Persistent Using Visual C++ 5.0

It may surprise you to learn that the nifty way in which ActiveX control properties are saved and restored by development environments such as Visual Basic and Visual C++ is not a function of those environments. Instead, the control itself must implement the saving and restoring of its property values; this is called *persistence* in the OLE 2 system. This How-To shows you the steps required to add this vital feature to your own MFC ActiveX controls in Visual C++ 5.0.

2.9 Interact with My ActiveX Control's Custom Events, Properties, and Methods Using ActiveX Scripting

Now that you have a really spiffy ActiveX control with custom properties, events, and methods, you would like to try it out on a Web page, but are not sure how to access all those new features in ActiveX Scripting. This How-To remedies that problem by giving a complete example of creating and using an ActiveX-scripted Web page with a custom MFC ActiveX control.

2.10 Keep Track of User-Set Custom Properties on My Custom ActiveX Control with an Active Server Pages Script

Cookies are a way to persist user information over time. This How-To illustrates using ASP to create a complete, scripted HTML page using a custom ActiveX control and how to set its properties via cookie information on the client computer.

COMPLEXITY
INTERMEDIATE

2.1 How do I… Use ambient properties with my ActiveX control in Visual C++ 5.0?

Problem

I have my extremely basic ActiveX control created with MFC. I notice that in Internet Explorer there is a `Background Color` property for my control, but I didn't add it and it doesn't work. Can I activate this phantom property for my own control?

Technique

These "phantom" properties are called *ambient properties* by the ActiveX specification; they represent standard functionality provided and maintained by the container application. However, these ambient properties will have no effect on a custom ActiveX control unless it accesses them and makes use of their data. This How-To shows you the way to create an MFC ActiveX control and have it use the `BackColor` and `ForeColor` ambient properties, as well as adding two other properties for later. Although the directions here start from scratch, you can find the entire project on the CD under `\CH02\HT01\ASPHT0201\`.

Steps

1. Start Visual C++ 5.0. If there is an active workspace, close it and all document windows. Then choose File|New… from the menu and select the MFC ActiveX ControlWizard entry. Enter a new path for the project on your computer and name the project **aspht0201**. Then press the OK button.

2. Select all the default options for the project and press Finish. The environment will create all the needed files for the workspace. Save it using the Save All menu option.

3. Now select ClassWizard from the View menu, as shown in Figure 2-1. When the wizard dialog comes up, select the Automation tab, as shown in Figure 2-2. Then press the Add Property... button.

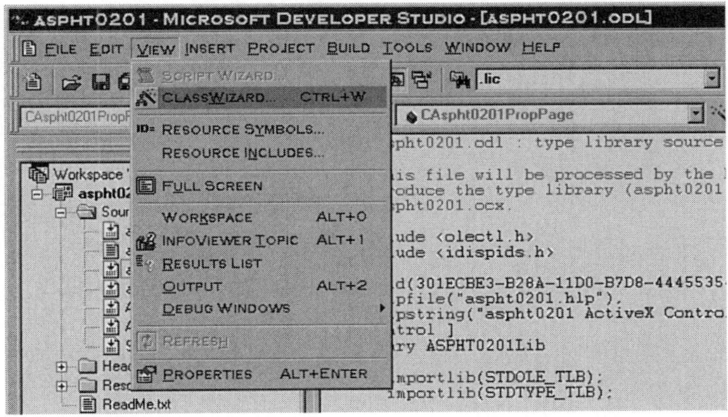

Figure 2-1 Activating ClassWizard from the View menu in Visual C++ 5.0

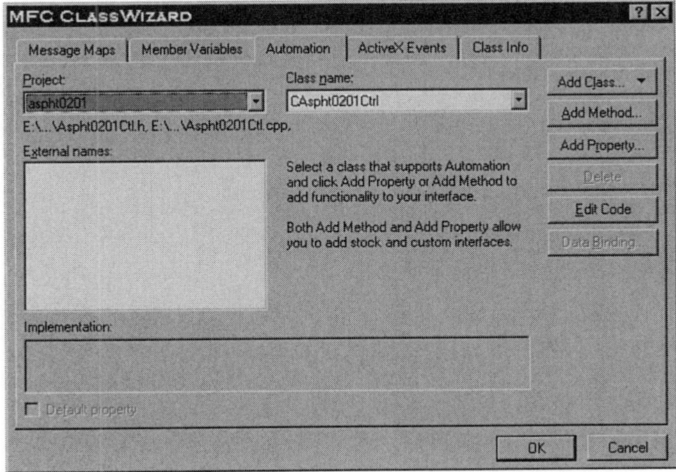

Figure 2-2 The Automation tab of the ClassWizard dialog

4. Select `BackColor` from the External name drop-down list, producing the display shown in Figure 2-3. Press OK to add this stock property to the control. Perform the same action to add the `ForeColor`, `Font`, and `Caption` properties to the control. Select Caption in the properties list and click the Default check box to make it the default property for the control. When you are done, the wizard dialog should look very similar to Figure 2-4. Click OK to write your changes into the project's files, then choose Save All to write the changes to disk.

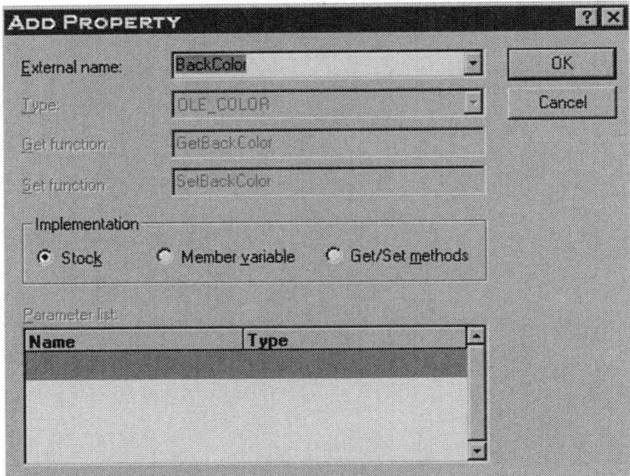

Figure 2-3 Selecting the `BackColor` stock property to add

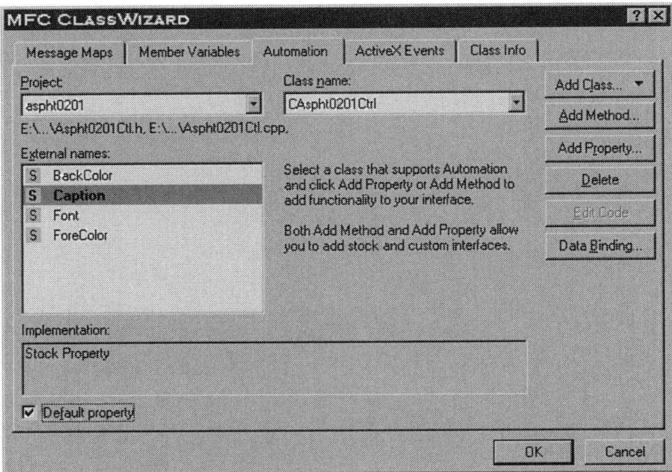

Figure 2-4 Results of adding `ForeColor`, `BackColor`, `Font`, and `Caption` stock properties to the control

5. Open the ASPHT0201CTL.CPP file in the text editor. Find the OnDraw function and enter text so that it contains the code in Listing 2-1. Save the workspace.

Listing 2-1 ASPHT0201CTL.CPP OnDraw function source code

```
/////////////////////////////////////////////////////////////////////////////
// CAspht0201Ctrl::OnDraw - Drawing function

void CAspht0201Ctrl::OnDraw(
CDC* pdc, const CRect& rcBounds, const CRect& rcInvalid)
{
CBrush cbBackBrush( TranslateColor( GetBackColor()));
CBrush cbForeBrush( TranslateColor( GetForeColor()));
pdc->FillRect( rcBounds, &cbBackBrush );
CPen pForePen(PS_SOLID, 1, TranslateColor( GetForeColor()));
CPen *pOldPen = pdc->SelectObject( &pForePen );
CBrush *pOldBrush = pdc->SelectObject( &cbForeBrush );
pdc->Ellipse(rcBounds);
pdc->SelectObject(pOldPen);
pdc->SelectObject(pOldBrush);
}
```

6. Compile the ODL file of the project by selecting it in the text viewer and choosing the Compile ASPHT0201.ODL menu option. Then choose the Build ASPHT0201.OCX menu option. The OCX control will be compiled and registered.

7. Activate the ActiveX Control Pad. Add the HTML code in Listing 2-2. Place the cursor in front of the second <HR> tag, then select the Edit|Insert ActiveX control menu option. From the dialog box, choose the ASPHT0201 control. When it appears in the editor window, set its BackColor property to a shade of green and its ForeColor property to a shade of yellow, as shown in Figure 2-5. Notice that the control immediately responds to the choices from the Properties dialog! Close the ActiveX control editor window and save the file as ASPHT0201.HTM.

Listing 2-2 ASPHT0201.HTM HTML source code

```
<HTML>
<HEAD>
<TITLE>Chapter Two Test Page 1</TITLE>
</HEAD>
<BODY>
<H1>ASPHT0201 ActiveX Control Test Page One</H1>
<HR>
<HR>
</BODY>
</HTML>
```

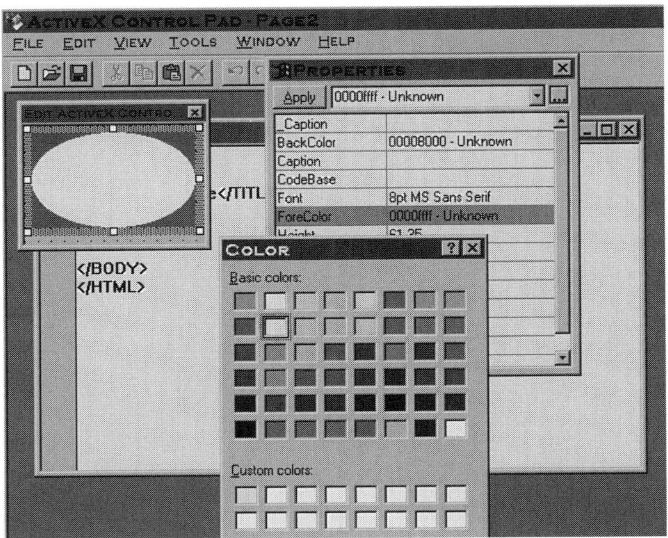

Figure 2-5 The new ActiveX control responding to stock properties in ActiveX Control Pad

8. Open the `ASPHT0201.HTM` file in Internet Explorer. The control should load and display normally with the proper color settings, as shown in Figure 2-6. Congratulations! You have created a custom ActiveX control that responds correctly to ambient stock properties.

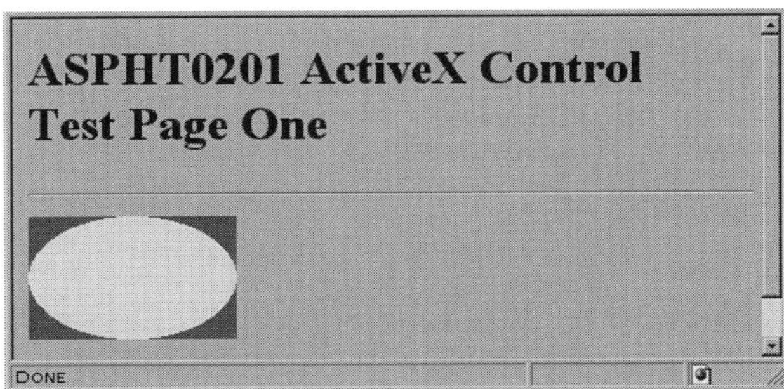

Figure 2-6 The `ASPHT0201` ActiveX control showing correct new colors in Internet Explorer on an HTML page

How It Works

The Class Wizard made changes to two files when you added stock properties to the control project. Listing 2-3 shows the first changed file, ASPHT0201.ODL.

Listing 2-3 ASPHT0201.ODL type library source code

```
//{{AFX_APPEND_ODL}}
// aspht0201.odl : type library source for ActiveX Control project.

// This file will be processed by the Make Type Library (mktyplib) tool to
// produce the type library (aspht0201.tlb) that will become a resource in
// aspht0201.ocx.

#include <olectl.h>
#include <idispids.h>

[ uuid(301ECBE3-B28A-11D0-B7D8-444553540000), version(1.0),
  helpfile("aspht0201.hlp"),
  helpstring("aspht0201 ActiveX Control module"),
  control ]
library ASPHT0201Lib
{
importlib(STDOLE_TLB);
importlib(STDTYPE_TLB);

//  Primary dispatch interface for CAspht0201Ctrl

[ uuid(301ECBE4-B28A-11D0-B7D8-444553540000),
 helpstring("Dispatch interface for Aspht0201 Control"), hidden ]
dispinterface _DAspht0201
{
properties:
// NOTE - ClassWizard will maintain property information here.
//    Use extreme caution when editing this section.
//{{AFX_ODL_PROP(CAspht0201Ctrl)
[id(DISPID_BACKCOLOR), bindable, requestedit] OLE_COLOR BackColor;
[id(DISPID_CAPTION), bindable, requestedit] BSTR Caption;
[id(DISPID_FONT), bindable] IFontDisp* Font;
[id(DISPID_FORECOLOR), bindable, requestedit] OLE_COLOR ForeColor;
[id(0)] BSTR _Caption;
//}}AFX_ODL_PROP

methods:
// NOTE - ClassWizard will maintain method information here.
//    Use extreme caution when editing this section.
//{{AFX_ODL_METHOD(CAspht0201Ctrl)
//}}AFX_ODL_METHOD

[id(DISPID_ABOUTBOX)] void AboutBox();
};

//  Event dispatch interface for CAspht0201Ctrl

[ uuid(301ECBE5-B28A-11D0-B7D8-444553540000),
helpstring("Event interface for Aspht0201 Control") ]
```

continued on next page

continued from previous page

```
dispinterface _DAspht0201Events
{
properties:
//  Event interface has no properties

methods:
// NOTE - ClassWizard will maintain event information here.
//    Use extreme caution when editing this section.
//{{AFX_ODL_EVENT(CAspht0201Ctrl)
//}}AFX_ODL_EVENT
};

//  Class information for CAspht0201Ctrl

[ uuid(301ECBE6-B28A-11D0-B7D8-444553540000),
helpstring("Aspht0201 Control"), control ]
coclass Aspht0201
{
[default] dispinterface _DAspht0201;
[default, source] dispinterface _DAspht0201Events;
};


//{{AFX_APPEND_ODL}}
//}}AFX_APPEND_ODL}}
};
```

Notice these critical lines that were changed:

```
properties:
// NOTE - ClassWizard will maintain property information here.
//    Use extreme caution when editing this section.
//{{AFX_ODL_PROP(CAspht0201Ctrl)
[id(DISPID_BACKCOLOR), bindable, requestedit] OLE_COLOR BackColor;
[id(DISPID_CAPTION), bindable, requestedit] BSTR Caption;
[id(DISPID_FONT), bindable] IFontDisp* Font;
[id(DISPID_FORECOLOR), bindable, requestedit] OLE_COLOR ForeColor;
[id(0)] BSTR _Caption;
//}}AFX_ODL_PROP
```

These lines maintain the new properties in the type library so that other programs such as Visual Basic, ActiveX Control Pad, and Internet Explorer can read and use them with the control. Pay particular attention to the heavy use of macros here; the new support for ActiveX in VC 5 is extremely macro-dependent, so be paranoid before removing any of them! Also note that system-defined constants for the **DISPID** values (unique values required by the OLE system for internal identification) are already available for all the stock properties.

The **bindable** and **requestedit** attributes are discussed in more detail in Chapter 3, "Advanced ActiveX: Special Features, Control Containers, ActiveX Documents, and VBScript 2.0," and involve communication between the container application and the control. The type values for the properties are excellent examples of the changes made to standard C++ types by the ActiveX system. Colors are no longer RGB but become **OLE_COLOR**, and strings become **BSTR**s. Both these changes allow exporting these values across process and even machine boundaries. The repeat entry for the **Caption** property is due to its being selected as the default property for the control.

The other important changes took place in ASPHT0201CTL.CPP, which is shown in Listing 2-4.

Listing 2-4 ASPHT0201CTL.CPP module source code

```
//}}AFX_APPEND_ODL}}
// Aspht0201Ctl.cpp : Implementation of the CAspht0201Ctrl ActiveX Control class.

#include "stdafx.h"
#include "aspht0201.h"
#include "Aspht0201Ctl.h"
#include "Aspht0201Ppg.h"


#ifdef _DEBUG
#define new DEBUG_NEW
#undef THIS_FILE
static char THIS_FILE[] = __FILE__;
#endif


IMPLEMENT_DYNCREATE(CAspht0201Ctrl, COleControl)


/////////////////////////////////////////////////////////////////////////////
// Message map

BEGIN_MESSAGE_MAP(CAspht0201Ctrl, COleControl)
//{{AFX_MSG_MAP(CAspht0201Ctrl)
// NOTE - ClassWizard will add and remove message map entries
//    DO NOT EDIT what you see in these blocks of generated code !
//}}AFX_MSG_MAP
ON_OLEVERB(AFX_IDS_VERB_PROPERTIES, OnProperties)
END_MESSAGE_MAP()


/////////////////////////////////////////////////////////////////////////////
// Dispatch map

BEGIN_DISPATCH_MAP(CAspht0201Ctrl, COleControl)
//{{AFX_DISPATCH_MAP(CAspht0201Ctrl)
DISP_DEFVALUE(CAspht0201Ctrl, "Caption")
DISP_STOCKPROP_BACKCOLOR()
DISP_STOCKPROP_CAPTION()
DISP_STOCKPROP_FONT()
DISP_STOCKPROP_FORECOLOR()
//}}AFX_DISPATCH_MAP
DISP_FUNCTION_ID(CAspht0201Ctrl, "AboutBox", DISPID_ABOUTBOX, AboutBox,⇐
VT_EMPTY, VTS_NONE)
END_DISPATCH_MAP()


/////////////////////////////////////////////////////////////////////////////
// Event map
```

continued on next page

continued from previous page

```
BEGIN_EVENT_MAP(CAspht0201Ctrl, COleControl)
//{{AFX_EVENT_MAP(CAspht0201Ctrl)
// NOTE - ClassWizard will add and remove event map entries
//    DO NOT EDIT what you see in these blocks of generated code !
//}}AFX_EVENT_MAP
END_EVENT_MAP()


/////////////////////////////////////////////////////////////////////////////
// Property pages

// TODO: Add more property pages as needed.  Remember to increase the count!
BEGIN_PROPPAGEIDS(CAspht0201Ctrl, 1)
PROPPAGEID(CAspht0201PropPage::guid)
END_PROPPAGEIDS(CAspht0201Ctrl)


/////////////////////////////////////////////////////////////////////////////
// Initialize class factory and guid

IMPLEMENT_OLECREATE_EX(CAspht0201Ctrl, "ASPHT0201.Aspht0201Ctrl.1",
0x301ecbe6, 0xb28a, 0x11d0, 0xb7, 0xd8, 0x44, 0x45, 0x53, 0x54, 0, 0)


/////////////////////////////////////////////////////////////////////////////
// Type library ID and version

IMPLEMENT_OLETYPELIB(CAspht0201Ctrl, _tlid, _wVerMajor, _wVerMinor)


/////////////////////////////////////////////////////////////////////////////
// Interface IDs

const IID BASED_CODE IID_DAspht0201 =
{ 0x301ecbe4, 0xb28a, 0x11d0, { 0xb7, 0xd8, 0x44, 0x45, 0x53, 0x54, 0, 0 } };
const IID BASED_CODE IID_DAspht0201Events =
{ 0x301ecbe5, 0xb28a, 0x11d0, { 0xb7, 0xd8, 0x44, 0x45, 0x53, 0x54, 0, 0 } };


/////////////////////////////////////////////////////////////////////////////
// Control type information

static const DWORD BASED_CODE _dwAspht0201OleMisc =
OLEMISC_ACTIVATEWHENVISIBLE ¦
OLEMISC_SETCLIENTSITEFIRST ¦
OLEMISC_INSIDEOUT ¦
OLEMISC_CANTLINKINSIDE ¦
OLEMISC_RECOMPOSEONRESIZE;

IMPLEMENT_OLECTLTYPE(CAspht0201Ctrl, IDS_ASPHT0201, _dwAspht0201OleMisc)


/////////////////////////////////////////////////////////////////////////////
// CAspht0201Ctrl::CAspht0201CtrlFactory::UpdateRegistry -
// Adds or removes system registry entries for CAspht0201Ctrl

BOOL CAspht0201Ctrl::CAspht0201CtrlFactory::UpdateRegistry(BOOL bRegister)
{
```

```
// TODO: Verify that your control follows apartment-model threading rules.
// Refer to MFC TechNote 64 for more information.
// If your control does not conform to the apartment-model rules, then
// you must modify the code below, changing the 6th parameter from
// afxRegApartmentThreading to 0.

if (bRegister)
return AfxOleRegisterControlClass(
AfxGetInstanceHandle(),
m_clsid,
m_lpszProgID,
IDS_ASPHT0201,
IDB_ASPHT0201,
afxRegApartmentThreading,
dwAspht0201OleMisc,
tlid,
wVerMajor,
wVerMinor);
else
return AfxOleUnregisterClass(m_clsid, m_lpszProgID);
}


/////////////////////////////////////////////////////////////////////////////
// CAspht0201Ctrl::CAspht0201Ctrl - Constructor

CAspht0201Ctrl::CAspht0201Ctrl()
{
InitializeIIDs(&IID_DAspht0201, &IID_DAspht0201Events);

// TODO: Initialize your control's instance data here.
}


/////////////////////////////////////////////////////////////////////////////
// CAspht0201Ctrl::~CAspht0201Ctrl - Destructor

CAspht0201Ctrl::~CAspht0201Ctrl()
{
// TODO: Cleanup your control's instance data here.
}


/////////////////////////////////////////////////////////////////////////////
// CAspht0201Ctrl::OnDraw - Drawing function

void CAspht0201Ctrl::OnDraw(
CDC* pdc, const CRect& rcBounds, const CRect& rcInvalid)
{
CBrush cbBackBrush( TranslateColor( GetBackColor()));
CBrush cbForeBrush( TranslateColor( GetForeColor()));
pdc->FillRect( rcBounds, &cbBackBrush );
CPen pForePen(PS_SOLID, 1, TranslateColor( GetForeColor()));
CPen *pOldPen = pdc->SelectObject( &pForePen );
CBrush *pOldBrush = pdc->SelectObject( &cbForeBrush );
pdc->Ellipse(rcBounds);
```

continued on next page

continued from previous page

```
pdc->SelectObject(pOldPen);
pdc->SelectObject(pOldBrush);
}


/////////////////////////////////////////////////////////////////////////////
// CAspht0201Ctrl::DoPropExchange - Persistence support

void CAspht0201Ctrl::DoPropExchange(CPropExchange* pPX)
{
ExchangeVersion(pPX, MAKELONG(_wVerMinor, _wVerMajor));
COleControl::DoPropExchange(pPX);

// TODO: Call PX_ functions for each persistent custom property.

}


/////////////////////////////////////////////////////////////////////////////
// CAspht0201Ctrl::OnResetState - Reset control to default state

void CAspht0201Ctrl::OnResetState()
{
COleControl::OnResetState();  // Resets defaults found in DoPropExchange

// TODO: Reset any other control state here.
}


/////////////////////////////////////////////////////////////////////////////
// CAspht0201Ctrl::AboutBox - Display an "About" box to the user

void CAspht0201Ctrl::AboutBox()
{
CDialog dlgAbout(IDD_ABOUTBOX_ASPHT0201);
dlgAbout.DoModal();
}


/////////////////////////////////////////////////////////////////////////////
// CAspht0201Ctrl message handlers
```

The changes made to this file are in the `Dispatch map` code:

```
/////////////////////////////////////////////////////////////////////////////
// Dispatch map

BEGIN_DISPATCH_MAP(CAspht0201Ctrl, COleControl)
//{{AFX_DISPATCH_MAP(CAspht0201Ctrl)
DISP_DEFVALUE(CAspht0201Ctrl, "Caption")
DISP_STOCKPROP_BACKCOLOR()
DISP_STOCKPROP_CAPTION()
DISP_STOCKPROP_FONT()
DISP_STOCKPROP_FORECOLOR()
//}}AFX_DISPATCH_MAP
DISP_FUNCTION_ID(CAspht0201Ctrl, "AboutBox", DISPID_ABOUTBOX, AboutBox, VT⇐
_EMPTY, VTS_NONE)
END_DISPATCH_MAP()
```

These changes are macros that map interface requests for the stock properties to the underlying MFC code, thus avoiding the need for you to write any code at all to take advantage of these ambient properties!

Comments

The power released in this How-To cannot be overstated! This How-To simultaneously demonstrates how to customize the drawing functionality of the control and how to interact with containers such as Visual Basic and ActiveX Control Pad; this capability can be upgraded to make a very powerful control with the addition of a relatively small amount of code.

(For a list of all the ambient properties that Visual C++ 5.0 supports for ActiveX controls, select Add Property as explained in step 3 and examine the External name drop-down list; each of these entries represents an available ambient property.)

2.2 How do I… Handle standard events with my ActiveX control using Visual C++ 5.0?

Problem

Okay, I can use ambient properties correctly with my custom ActiveX control now. But nothing happens when I click on it with the mouse! I know this a standard Windows event, so how can I get my control to respond to it?

Technique

ActiveX controls created with MFC do indeed receive many standard Windows event messages, but the trick is to tell the control how to react to them. This How-To implements mouse click events for the control created in How-To 2.1. The CD contains an already created workspace with a new name but all the previous code and settings in place in `CH02\HT02\ASPHT0202\`. The complete control is in `CH02\HT02\FINAL\ASPHT0202\`.

Steps

1. Activate Visual C++ 5.0 and load the `ASPHT0202` workspace, which as noted above contains all the code and settings from How-To 2.1. Choose ClassWizard from the View menu and click on the ActiveX Events tab, as shown in Figure 2-7. Press the Add Event… button.

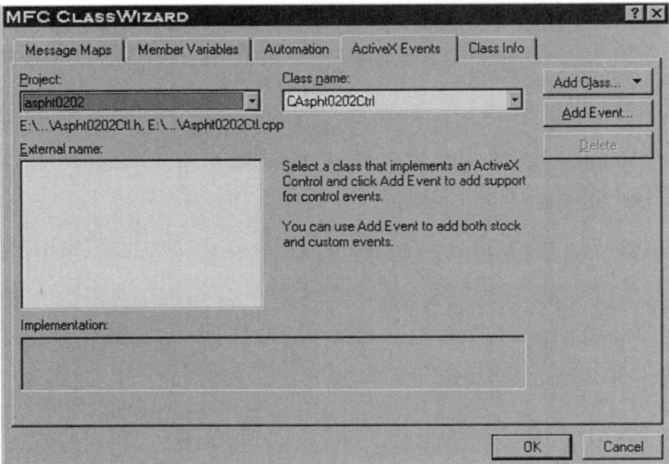

Figure 2-7 The ActiveX Events tab of the ClassWizard

2. Select the `Click` event from the drop-down list, producing a display similar to Figure 2-8. Click OK on the Add Event dialog and OK on the ClassWizard and the system will update your code.

3. Compile the `ASPHT0202.ODL` file. Then build the `ASPHT0202.OCX` control. Once the registration is complete, activate the ActiveX Control Pad and start a new HTML page. Enter the HTML source code in Listing 2-5. Then use the Edit|Insert ActiveX Control menu option and add an `ASPHT0202` control, setting its background color to green and foreground color to yellow. Save the file as `ASPHT0202.HTM`.

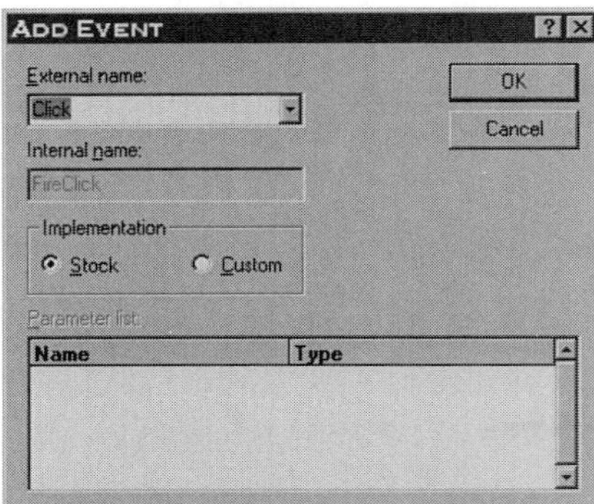

Figure 2-8 Adding a stock event to the ActiveX Events tab

Listing 2-5 ASPHT0202.HTM HTML source code

```
<HTML>
<HEAD>
<TITLE>Chapter Two Test Page 2</TITLE>
</HEAD>
<BODY>
<H1>ASPHT0202 ActiveX Control Test Page One</H1>
<HR>
<HR>
</BODY>
</HTML>
```

4. Click on the small scroll icon on the speed bar, or use the Tools|Script Wizard menu option to bring up the ActiveX Control Pad Script Wizard dialog. In the upper-left pane, open the events available under the `ASPHT0202` control and click on `Click`. In the code pane below, enter `Alert("Hello, I am a Stock CLICK Event!")`, as shown in Figure 2-9. Press the OK button and save the HTML file.

5. Activate the `ASPHT0202.HTM` file in Internet Explorer, then click on the colored area of the ActiveX control. A dialog box will appear displaying the script text you entered in ActiveX Control Pad's Script Wizard, as shown in Figure 2-10. Your skills with custom ActiveX control have increased to include responding to stock events.

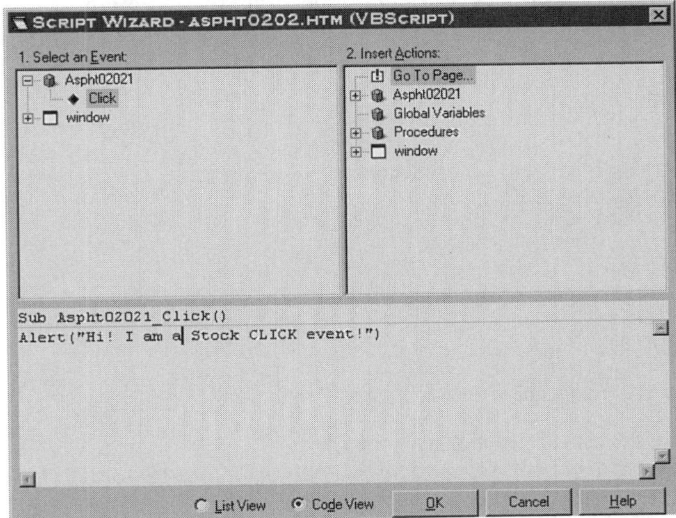

Figure 2-9 The Script Wizard of ActiveX Control Pad writing a script for the `Click` event of the custom ActiveX control

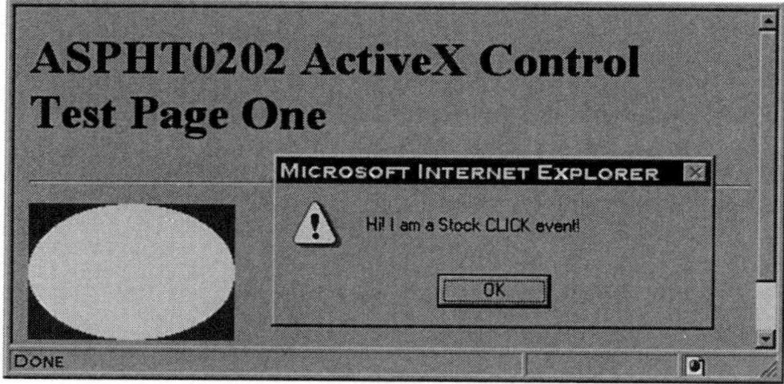

Figure 2-10 The custom ActiveX control in IE responding to a mouse click with a custom ActiveX Scripting message

How It Works

Wow! With a few quick clicks of the mouse, your custom ActiveX control just became scriptable! Examine the ODL file shown in Listing 2-6 first and notice the change the ClassWizard made.

Listing 2-6 ASPHT0202.ODL type library file source code

```
// aspht0202.odl : type library source for ActiveX Control project.

// This file will be processed by the Make Type Library (mktyplib) tool to
// produce the type library (aspht0202.tlb) that will become a resource in
// aspht0202.ocx.

#include <olectl.h>
#include <idispids.h>

[ uuid(EB30397E-B4B9-11D0-B7D8-444553540000), version(1.0),
  helpfile("aspht0202.hlp"),
  helpstring("aspht0202 ActiveX Control module"),
  control ]
library ASPHT0202Lib
{
importlib(STDOLE_TLB);
importlib(STDTYPE_TLB);

//  Primary dispatch interface for CAspht0202Ctrl

[ uuid(EB30397F-B4B9-11D0-B7D8-444553540000),
helpstring("Dispatch interface for Aspht0202 Control"), hidden ]
dispinterface _DAspht0202
{
properties:
// NOTE - ClassWizard will maintain property information here.
//    Use extreme caution when editing this section.
//{{AFX_ODL_PROP(CAspht0202Ctrl)
[id(DISPID_BACKCOLOR), bindable, requestedit] OLE_COLOR BackColor;
```

```
[id(DISPID_CAPTION), bindable, requestedit] BSTR Caption;
[id(DISPID_FONT), bindable] IFontDisp* Font;
[id(DISPID_FORECOLOR), bindable, requestedit] OLE_COLOR ForeColor;
[id(0)] BSTR _Caption;
//}}AFX_ODL_PROP

methods:
// NOTE - ClassWizard will maintain method information here.
//    Use extreme caution when editing this section.
//{{AFX_ODL_METHOD(CAspht0202Ctrl)
//}}AFX_ODL_METHOD

[id(DISPID_ABOUTBOX)] void AboutBox();
};

//  Event dispatch interface for CAspht0202Ctrl

[ uuid(EB303980-B4B9-11D0-B7D8-444553540000),
 helpstring("Event interface for Aspht0202 Control") ]
dispinterface _DAspht0202Events
{
properties:
//  Event interface has no properties

methods:
// NOTE - ClassWizard will maintain event information here.
//    Use extreme caution when editing this section.
//{{AFX_ODL_EVENT(CAspht0202Ctrl)
[id(DISPID_CLICK)] void Click();
//}}AFX_ODL_EVENT
};

//  Class information for CAspht0202Ctrl

[ uuid(EB303981-B4B9-11D0-B7D8-444553540000),
helpstring("Aspht0202 Control"), control ]
coclass Aspht0202
{
[default] dispinterface _DAspht0202;
[default, source] dispinterface _DAspht0202Events;
};


//{{AFX_APPEND_ODL}}
//}}AFX_APPEND_ODL}}
};
```

Now the ODL file includes this code:

```
//  Event dispatch interface for CAspht0202Ctrl

[ uuid(EB303980-B4B9-11D0-B7D8-444553540000),
 helpstring("Event interface for Aspht0202 Control") ]
dispinterface _DAspht0202Events
{
properties:
//  Event interface has no properties
```

continued on next page

continued from previous page

```
methods:
// NOTE - ClassWizard will maintain event information here.
//    Use extreme caution when editing this section.
//{{AFX_ODL_EVENT(CAspht0202Ctrl)
[id(DISPID_CLICK)] void Click();
//}}AFX_ODL_EVENT
};
```

These lines create an interface for the stock `Click` event so that other programs will know that the control can respond to it. Again note the use of the `AFX_ODL_EVENT` macros and the `DISPID_CLICK` predefined GUID (Globally Unique ID) for the event.

Now examine the source code for `ASPHT0202CTL.CPP`, shown in Listing 2-7.

Listing 2-7 ASPHT0202CTL.CPP module source code

```
//}}AFX_APPEND_ODL}}
// Aspht0202Ctl.cpp : Implementation of the CAspht0202Ctrl ActiveX Control class.

#include "stdafx.h"
#include "aspht0202.h"
#include "Aspht0202Ctl.h"
#include "Aspht0202Ppg.h"


#ifdef _DEBUG
#define new DEBUG_NEW
#undef THIS_FILE
static char THIS_FILE[] = __FILE__;
#endif


IMPLEMENT_DYNCREATE(CAspht0202Ctrl, COleControl)


/////////////////////////////////////////////////////////////////////////////
// Message map

BEGIN_MESSAGE_MAP(CAspht0202Ctrl, COleControl)
//{{AFX_MSG_MAP(CAspht0202Ctrl)
// NOTE - ClassWizard will add and remove message map entries
//    DO NOT EDIT what you see in these blocks of generated code !
//}}AFX_MSG_MAP
ON_OLEVERB(AFX_IDS_VERB_PROPERTIES, OnProperties)
END_MESSAGE_MAP()


/////////////////////////////////////////////////////////////////////////////
// Dispatch map

BEGIN_DISPATCH_MAP(CAspht0202Ctrl, COleControl)
//{{AFX_DISPATCH_MAP(CAspht0202Ctrl)
DISP_DEFVALUE(CAspht0202Ctrl, "Caption")
DISP_STOCKPROP_BACKCOLOR()
DISP_STOCKPROP_CAPTION()
```

```
DISP_STOCKPROP_FONT()
DISP_STOCKPROP_FORECOLOR()
//}}AFX_DISPATCH_MAP
DISP_FUNCTION_ID(CAspht0202Ctrl, "AboutBox", DISPID_ABOUTBOX, AboutBox,⇐
VT_EMPTY, VTS_NONE)
END_DISPATCH_MAP()


/////////////////////////////////////////////////////////////////////////////
// Event map

BEGIN_EVENT_MAP(CAspht0202Ctrl, COleControl)
//{{AFX_EVENT_MAP(CAspht0202Ctrl)
EVENT_STOCK_CLICK()
//}}AFX_EVENT_MAP
END_EVENT_MAP()


/////////////////////////////////////////////////////////////////////////////
// Property pages

// TODO: Add more property pages as needed.  Remember to increase the count!
BEGIN_PROPPAGEIDS(CAspht0202Ctrl, 1)
PROPPAGEID(CAspht0202PropPage::guid)
END_PROPPAGEIDS(CAspht0202Ctrl)


/////////////////////////////////////////////////////////////////////////////
// Initialize class factory and guid

IMPLEMENT_OLECREATE_EX(CAspht0202Ctrl, "ASPHT0202.Aspht0202Ctrl.1",
0xeb303981, 0xb4b9, 0x11d0, 0xb7, 0xd8, 0x44, 0x45, 0x53, 0x54, 0, 0)


/////////////////////////////////////////////////////////////////////////////
// Type library ID and version

IMPLEMENT_OLETYPELIB(CAspht0202Ctrl, _tlid, _wVerMajor, _wVerMinor)


/////////////////////////////////////////////////////////////////////////////
// Interface IDs

const IID BASED_CODE IID_DAspht0202 =
{ 0xeb30397f, 0xb4b9, 0x11d0, { 0xb7, 0xd8, 0x44, 0x45, 0x53, 0x54, 0, 0 } };
const IID BASED_CODE IID_DAspht0202Events =
{ 0xeb303980, 0xb4b9, 0x11d0, { 0xb7, 0xd8, 0x44, 0x45, 0x53, 0x54, 0, 0 } };


/////////////////////////////////////////////////////////////////////////////
// Control type information

static const DWORD BASED_CODE _dwAspht0202OleMisc =
OLEMISC_ACTIVATEWHENVISIBLE ¦
OLEMISC_SETCLIENTSITEFIRST ¦
OLEMISC_INSIDEOUT ¦
```

continued on next page

continued from previous page

```
OLEMISC_CANTLINKINSIDE |
OLEMISC_RECOMPOSEONRESIZE;

IMPLEMENT_OLECTLTYPE(CAspht0202Ctrl, IDS_ASPHT0202, _dwAspht0202OleMisc)


/////////////////////////////////////////////////////////////////////////////
// CAspht0202Ctrl::CAspht0202CtrlFactory::UpdateRegistry -
// Adds or removes system registry entries for CAspht0202Ctrl

BOOL CAspht0202Ctrl::CAspht0202CtrlFactory::UpdateRegistry(BOOL bRegister)
{
// TODO: Verify that your control follows apartment-model threading rules.
// Refer to MFC TechNote 64 for more information.
// If your control does not conform to the apartment-model rules, then
// you must modify the code below, changing the 6th parameter from
// afxRegApartmentThreading to 0.

if (bRegister)
return AfxOleRegisterControlClass(
AfxGetInstanceHandle(),
m_clsid,
m_lpszProgID,
IDS_ASPHT0202,
IDB_ASPHT0202,
afxRegApartmentThreading,
dwAspht0202OleMisc,
tlid,
wVerMajor,
wVerMinor);
else
return AfxOleUnregisterClass(m_clsid, m_lpszProgID);
}


/////////////////////////////////////////////////////////////////////////////
// CAspht0202Ctrl::CAspht0202Ctrl - Constructor

CAspht0202Ctrl::CAspht0202Ctrl()
{
InitializeIIDs(&IID_DAspht0202, &IID_DAspht0202Events);

// TODO: Initialize your control's instance data here.
}


/////////////////////////////////////////////////////////////////////////////
// CAspht0202Ctrl::~CAspht0202Ctrl - Destructor

CAspht0202Ctrl::~CAspht0202Ctrl()
{
// TODO: Cleanup your control's instance data here.
}
```

```
/////////////////////////////////////////////////////////////////////////////
// CAspht0202Ctrl::OnDraw - Drawing function

void CAspht0202Ctrl::OnDraw(
CDC* pdc, const CRect& rcBounds, const CRect& rcInvalid)
{
CBrush cbBackBrush( TranslateColor( GetBackColor()));
CBrush cbForeBrush( TranslateColor( GetForeColor()));
pdc->FillRect( rcBounds, &cbBackBrush );
CPen pForePen(PS_SOLID, 1, TranslateColor( GetForeColor()));
CPen *pOldPen = pdc->SelectObject( &pForePen );
CBrush *pOldBrush = pdc->SelectObject( &cbForeBrush );
pdc->Ellipse(rcBounds);
pdc->SelectObject(pOldPen);
pdc->SelectObject(pOldBrush);
}

/////////////////////////////////////////////////////////////////////////////
// CAspht0202Ctrl::DoPropExchange - Persistence support

void CAspht0202Ctrl::DoPropExchange(CPropExchange* pPX)
{
ExchangeVersion(pPX, MAKELONG(_wVerMinor, _wVerMajor));
COleControl::DoPropExchange(pPX);

// TODO: Call PX_ functions for each persistent custom property.

}

/////////////////////////////////////////////////////////////////////////////
// CAspht0202Ctrl::OnResetState - Reset control to default state

void CAspht0202Ctrl::OnResetState()
{
COleControl::OnResetState();  // Resets defaults found in DoPropExchange

// TODO: Reset any other control state here.
}

/////////////////////////////////////////////////////////////////////////////
// CAspht0202Ctrl::AboutBox - Display an "About" box to the user

void CAspht0202Ctrl::AboutBox()
{
CDialog dlgAbout(IDD_ABOUTBOX_ASPHT0202);
dlgAbout.DoModal();
}

/////////////////////////////////////////////////////////////////////////////
// CAspht0202Ctrl message handlers
```

The change that enables the **Click** event is in this code:

```
/////////////////////////////////////////////////////////////////////////////
// Event map

BEGIN_EVENT_MAP(CAspht0202Ctrl, COleControl)
//{{AFX_EVENT_MAP(CAspht0202Ctrl)
EVENT_STOCK_CLICK()
//}}AFX_EVENT_MAP
END_EVENT_MAP()
```

This code creates code with macros (`AFT_EVENT_MAP`, `EVENT_STOCK_CLICK`) that expand into calls to the ActiveX system encapsulated inside MFC. A method called `FireClick` is created that can be invoked by other methods and event handlers, as well as being automatically called by the ActiveX system whenever the container application needs to do so.

Comments

It is worth noting that you did not have to write any special code to have your custom ActiveX control respond to a scripting statement on a mouse click. The sophisticated integration of the various parts of the ActiveX system in the other applications with the MFC encapsulation code gave it all to you for free!

COMPLEXITY
INTERMEDIATE

2.3 How do I... Create custom properties for my ActiveX control in Visual C++ 5.0?

Problem

Now I'm up to speed on the standard properties and events. But how do I add a new property to my custom MFC ActiveX control?

Technique

MFC supports a set of special mechanisms for adding custom properties to ActiveX controls. This How-To takes you through the steps to add custom color properties to the control created and modified in the first two How-To's in this chapter. The CD contains an already created workspace with a new name but all the previous code and settings in place under `CH02\HT03\ASPHT0203\`. The complete control is under `CH02\HT03\FINAL\ASPHT0203\`.

Steps

1. Activate Visual C++ 5.0 and load the **ASPHT0203** workspace, which as noted above contains all the code and settings from How-To 2.2. Choose ClassWizard from the View menu and click on the Automation tab, then press the Add Property... button. In the Add Property dialog box, select the Get/Set methods radio button, then choose **OLE_COLOR** as the type for the property. Finally, type in **HighlightColor** as the external name, and the **Get** and **Set** function name controls will fill in automatically, as shown in Figure 2-11. Press OK to accept the new property.

2. Perform the same steps to add three additional properties: **PanelColor**, **BorderWidth** (which should have a type of **short**), and **ShadowColor**. When you are finished, the ClassWizard Automation tab should look very similar to the one shown in Figure 2-12. Press OK to add these changes to your files and then save all files.

3. Bring up the **ASPHT0203CTL.H** file in the text editor. Enter the highlighted text in Listing 2-8 to add four private member variables to the control's class.

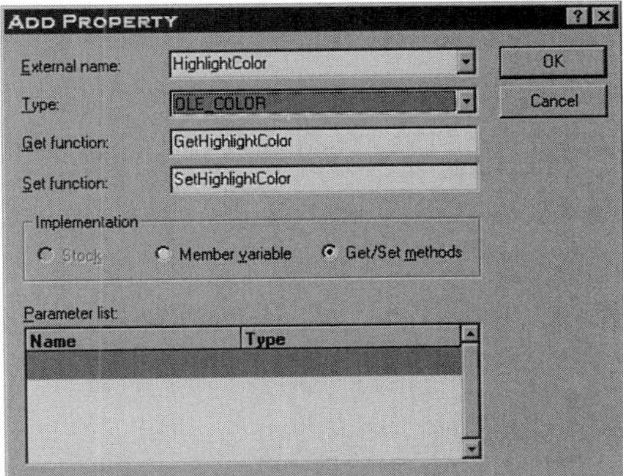

Figure 2-11 The Add Property dialog of the ClassWizard is shown adding a custom ActiveX property

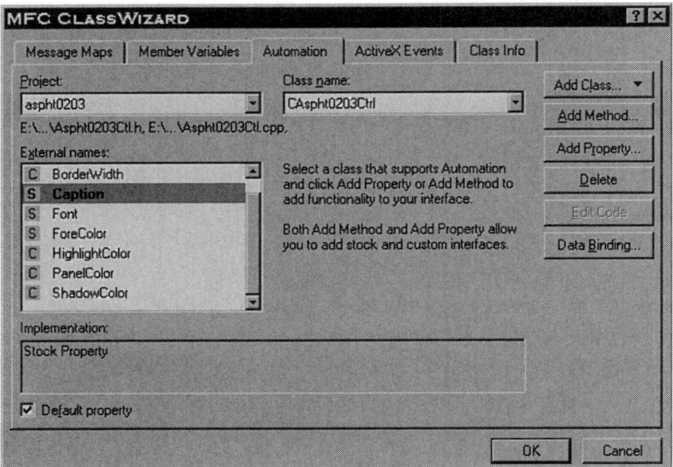

Figure 2-12 The ClassWizard Automation tab, showing three custom properties added

Listing 2-8 ASPHT0203CTL.H header file source code

```
#if !defined(AFX_ASPHT0203CTL_H__EB3039BD_B4B9_11D0_B7D8_444553540000__INCLUDED_)
#define AFX_ASPHT0203CTL_H__EB3039BD_B4B9_11D0_B7D8_444553540000__INCLUDED_

#if _MSC_VER >= 1000
#pragma once
#endif // _MSC_VER >= 1000

// Aspht0203Ctl.h : Declaration of the CAspht0203Ctrl ActiveX Control class.

/////////////////////////////////////////////////////////////////////////////
// CAspht0203Ctrl : See Aspht0203Ctl.cpp for implementation.

class CAspht0203Ctrl : public COleControl
{
DECLARE_DYNCREATE(CAspht0203Ctrl)

// Constructor
public:
CAspht0203Ctrl();

// Overrides
// ClassWizard generated virtual function overrides
//{{AFX_VIRTUAL(CAspht0203Ctrl)
public:
virtual void OnDraw(CDC* pdc, const CRect& rcBounds, const CRect& rcInvalid);
virtual void DoPropExchange(CPropExchange* pPX);
virtual void OnResetState();
//}}AFX_VIRTUAL

// Implementation
protected:
```

```
~CAspht0203Ctrl();

DECLARE_OLECREATE_EX(CAspht0203Ctrl)     // Class factory and guid
DECLARE_OLETYPELIB(CAspht0203Ctrl)       // GetTypeInfo
DECLARE_PROPPAGEIDS(CAspht0203Ctrl)      // Property page IDs
DECLARE_OLECTLTYPE(CAspht0203Ctrl)       // Type name and misc status

// Message maps
//{{AFX_MSG(CAspht0203Ctrl)
// NOTE - ClassWizard will add and remove member functions here.
//    DO NOT EDIT what you see in these blocks of generated code !
//}}AFX_MSG
DECLARE_MESSAGE_MAP()

// Dispatch maps
//{{AFX_DISPATCH(CAspht0203Ctrl)
afx_msg OLE_COLOR GetHighlightColor();
afx_msg void SetHighlightColor(OLE_COLOR nNewValue);
afx_msg OLE_COLOR GetShadowColor();
afx_msg void SetShadowColor(OLE_COLOR nNewValue);
afx_msg OLE_COLOR GetPanelColor();
afx_msg void SetPanelColor(OLE_COLOR nNewValue);
afx_msg short GetBorderWidth();
afx_msg void SetBorderWidth(short nNewValue);
//}}AFX_DISPATCH
DECLARE_DISPATCH_MAP()

afx_msg void AboutBox();

// Event maps
//{{AFX_EVENT(CAspht0203Ctrl)
//}}AFX_EVENT
DECLARE_EVENT_MAP()

// Dispatch and event IDs
public:
enum {
//{{AFX_DISP_ID(CAspht0203Ctrl)
dispidHighlightColor = 1L,
dispidShadowColor = 2L,
dispidPanelColor = 3L,
dispidBorderWidth = 4L,
//}}AFX_DISP_ID
};
private:
OLE_COLOR m_HighlightColor;
OLE_COLOR m_PanelColor;
OLE_COLOR m_ShadowColor;
short m_BorderWidth;
};

//{{AFX_INSERT_LOCATION}}
// Microsoft Developer Studio will insert additional declarations immediately
//before the previous line.

#endif //
!defined(AFX_ASPHT0203CTL_H__EB3039BD_B4B9_11D0_B7D8_444553540000__INCLUDED)
```

4. Bring up the `ASPHT0203CTL.CPP` file in the text editor. Enter the highlighted text in Listing 2-9 to add code to the various functions of the control to use the custom properties.

Listing 2-9 ASPHT0203CTL.CPP module source code

```
// Microsoft Developer Studio will insert additional declarations immediately
//before the previous line.

// Aspht0203Ctl.cpp : Implementation of the CAspht0203Ctrl ActiveX Control class.

#include "stdafx.h"
#include "aspht0203.h"
#include "Aspht0203Ctl.h"
#include "Aspht0203Ppg.h"


#ifdef _DEBUG
#define new DEBUG_NEW
#undef THIS_FILE
static char THIS_FILE[] = __FILE__;
#endif


IMPLEMENT_DYNCREATE(CAspht0203Ctrl, COleControl)


/////////////////////////////////////////////////////////////////////////////
// Message map

BEGIN_MESSAGE_MAP(CAspht0203Ctrl, COleControl)
//{{AFX_MSG_MAP(CAspht0203Ctrl)
// NOTE - ClassWizard will add and remove message map entries
//    DO NOT EDIT what you see in these blocks of generated code !
//}}AFX_MSG_MAP
ON_OLEVERB(AFX_IDS_VERB_PROPERTIES, OnProperties)
END_MESSAGE_MAP()


/////////////////////////////////////////////////////////////////////////////
// Dispatch map

BEGIN_DISPATCH_MAP(CAspht0203Ctrl, COleControl)
//{{AFX_DISPATCH_MAP(CAspht0203Ctrl)
DISP_PROPERTY_EX(CAspht0203Ctrl, "HighlightColor", GetHighlightColor,⇐
SetHighlightColor, VT_COLOR)
DISP_PROPERTY_EX(CAspht0203Ctrl, "ShadowColor", GetShadowColor, SetShadowColor,⇐
VT_COLOR)
DISP_PROPERTY_EX(CAspht0203Ctrl, "PanelColor", GetPanelColor, SetPanelColor,⇐
VT_COLOR)
DISP_PROPERTY_EX(CAspht0203Ctrl, "BorderWidth", GetBorderWidth, SetBorderWidth,⇐
VT_I2)
DISP_DEFVALUE(CAspht0203Ctrl, "Caption")
DISP_STOCKPROP_BACKCOLOR()
DISP_STOCKPROP_CAPTION()
DISP_STOCKPROP_FONT()
DISP_STOCKPROP_FORECOLOR()
```

```
//}}AFX_DISPATCH_MAP
DISP_FUNCTION_ID(CAspht0203Ctrl, "AboutBox", DISPID_ABOUTBOX, AboutBox,⇐
VT_EMPTY, VTS_NONE)
END_DISPATCH_MAP()


/////////////////////////////////////////////////////////////////////////////
// Event map

BEGIN_EVENT_MAP(CAspht0203Ctrl, COleControl)
//{{AFX_EVENT_MAP(CAspht0203Ctrl)
EVENT_STOCK_CLICK()
//}}AFX_EVENT_MAP
END_EVENT_MAP()


/////////////////////////////////////////////////////////////////////////////
// Property pages

// TODO: Add more property pages as needed.  Remember to increase the count!
BEGIN_PROPPAGEIDS(CAspht0203Ctrl, 1)
PROPPAGEID(CAspht0203PropPage::guid)
END_PROPPAGEIDS(CAspht0203Ctrl)


/////////////////////////////////////////////////////////////////////////////
// Initialize class factory and guid

IMPLEMENT_OLECREATE_EX(CAspht0203Ctrl, "ASPHT0203.Aspht0203Ctrl.1",
0xeb3039af, 0xb4b9, 0x11d0, 0xb7, 0xd8, 0x44, 0x45, 0x53, 0x54, 0, 0)


/////////////////////////////////////////////////////////////////////////////
// Type library ID and version

IMPLEMENT_OLETYPELIB(CAspht0203Ctrl, _tlid, _wVerMajor, _wVerMinor)


/////////////////////////////////////////////////////////////////////////////
// Interface IDs

const IID BASED_CODE IID_DAspht0203 =
{ 0xeb3039ad, 0xb4b9, 0x11d0, { 0xb7, 0xd8, 0x44, 0x45, 0x53, 0x54, 0, 0 } };
const IID BASED_CODE IID_DAspht0203Events =
{ 0xeb3039ae, 0xb4b9, 0x11d0, { 0xb7, 0xd8, 0x44, 0x45, 0x53, 0x54, 0, 0 } };


/////////////////////////////////////////////////////////////////////////////
// Control type information

static const DWORD BASED_CODE _dwAspht0203OleMisc =
OLEMISC_ACTIVATEWHENVISIBLE ¦
OLEMISC_SETCLIENTSITEFIRST ¦
OLEMISC_INSIDEOUT ¦
OLEMISC_CANTLINKINSIDE ¦
OLEMISC_RECOMPOSEONRESIZE;
```

continued on next page

continued from previous page

```
IMPLEMENT_OLECTLTYPE(CAspht0203Ctrl, IDS_ASPHT0203, _dwAspht0203OleMisc)


/////////////////////////////////////////////////////////////////////////////
// CAspht0203Ctrl::CAspht0203CtrlFactory::UpdateRegistry -
// Adds or removes system registry entries for CAspht0203Ctrl

BOOL CAspht0203Ctrl::CAspht0203CtrlFactory::UpdateRegistry(BOOL bRegister)
{
// TODO: Verify that your control follows apartment-model threading rules.
// Refer to MFC TechNote 64 for more information.
// If your control does not conform to the apartment-model rules, then
// you must modify the code below, changing the 6th parameter from
// afxRegApartmentThreading to 0

if (bRegister)
return AfxOleRegisterControlClass(
AfxGetInstanceHandle(),
m_clsid,
m_lpszProgID,
IDS_ASPHT0203,
IDB_ASPHT0203,
afxRegApartmentThreading,
dwAspht0203OleMisc,
tlid,
wVerMajor,
wVerMinor);
else
return AfxOleUnregisterClass(m_clsid, m_lpszProgID);
}


/////////////////////////////////////////////////////////////////////////////
// CAspht0203Ctrl::CAspht0203Ctrl - Constructor

CAspht0203Ctrl::CAspht0203Ctrl()
{
InitializeIIDs(&IID_DAspht0203, &IID_DAspht0203Events);

// TODO: Initialize your control's instance data here.
SetPanelColor( (OLE_COLOR) RGB( 0 , 128 , 0 )) ;
SetHighlightColor( (OLE_COLOR) RGB( 0 , 255 , 0 ));
SetShadowColor( (OLE_COLOR) RGB( 0 , 64 , 0 ));
SetBorderWidth(10);
}


/////////////////////////////////////////////////////////////////////////////
// CAspht0203Ctrl::~CAspht0203Ctrl - Destructor

CAspht0203Ctrl::~CAspht0203Ctrl()
{
// TODO: Cleanup your control's instance data here.
}


/////////////////////////////////////////////////////////////////////////////
```

```
// CAspht0203Ctrl::OnDraw - Drawing function

void CAspht0203Ctrl::OnDraw(
CDC* pdc, const CRect& rcBounds, const CRect& rcInvalid)
{
CBrush cbPanelBrush( TranslateColor( m_PanelColor ));
pdc->FillRect( rcBounds, &cbPanelBrush );
CPen pHiLitePen(PS_SOLID, 2, TranslateColor( GetHighlightColor() ));
CPen pShadowPen(PS_SOLID, 2, TranslateColor( GetShadowColor() ));
CPen *pOldPen = pdc->SelectObject( &pHiLitePen );
pdc->MoveTo(rcBounds.left + 2 , rcBounds.top + 2);
pdc->LineTo(rcBounds.right - 2 , rcBounds.top + 2 );
pdc->MoveTo(rcBounds.left + 2 , rcBounds.top + 2 );
pdc->LineTo(rcBounds.left + 2 , rcBounds.bottom - 2);
pdc->SelectObject( &pShadowPen );
pdc->MoveTo(rcBounds.right - 2 , rcBounds.bottom - 2 );
pdc->LineTo(rcBounds.right - 2 , rcBounds.top + 2);
pdc->MoveTo(rcBounds.right - 2 , rcBounds.bottom - 2);
pdc->LineTo(rcBounds.left + 2  , rcBounds.bottom - 2);
pdc->MoveTo(rcBounds.left + m_BorderWidth + 4 , rcBounds.top + m_BorderWidth + 4);
pdc->LineTo(rcBounds.right - m_BorderWidth - 4 , rcBounds.top + m_BorderWidth +⇐
4);
pdc->MoveTo(rcBounds.left + m_BorderWidth + 4 , rcBounds.top + m_BorderWidth + 4);
pdc->LineTo(rcBounds.left + m_BorderWidth + 4 , rcBounds.bottom - m_BorderWidth⇐
 - 4);
pdc->SelectObject( &pHiLitePen );
pdc->MoveTo(rcBounds.right - m_BorderWidth - 4 , rcBounds.bottom - m_BorderWidth⇐
- 4);
pdc->LineTo(rcBounds.right - m_BorderWidth - 4 , rcBounds.top + m_BorderWidth +⇐
4);
pdc->MoveTo(rcBounds.right - m_BorderWidth - 4 , rcBounds.bottom - m_BorderWidth⇐
- 4);
pdc->LineTo(rcBounds.left + m_BorderWidth + 4, rcBounds.bottom - m_BorderWidth⇐
- 4);
pdc->SelectObject(pOldPen);
}


/////////////////////////////////////////////////////////////////////////////
// CAspht0203Ctrl::DoPropExchange - Persistence support

void CAspht0203Ctrl::DoPropExchange(CPropExchange* pPX)
{
ExchangeVersion(pPX, MAKELONG(_wVerMinor, _wVerMajor));
COleControl::DoPropExchange(pPX);

// TODO: Call PX_ functions for each persistent custom property.
}


/////////////////////////////////////////////////////////////////////////////
// CAspht0203Ctrl::OnResetState - Reset control to default state

void CAspht0203Ctrl::OnResetState()
{
COleControl::OnResetState();  // Resets defaults found in DoPropExchange
```

continued on next page

continued from previous page

```
// TODO: Reset any other control state here.
}


/////////////////////////////////////////////////////////////////////////////
// CAspht0203Ctrl::AboutBox - Display an "About" box to the user

void CAspht0203Ctrl::AboutBox()
{
CDialog dlgAbout(IDD_ABOUTBOX_ASPHT0203);
dlgAbout.DoModal();
}


/////////////////////////////////////////////////////////////////////////////
// CAspht0203Ctrl message handlers

OLE_COLOR CAspht0203Ctrl::GetHighlightColor()
{
// TODO: Add your property handler here

return m_HighlightColor;
}

void CAspht0203Ctrl::SetHighlightColor(OLE_COLOR nNewValue)
{
// TODO: Add your property handler here

SetModifiedFlag();
m_HighlightColor = nNewValue;
}

OLE_COLOR CAspht0203Ctrl::GetShadowColor()
{
// TODO: Add your property handler here

return m_ShadowColor;
}

void CAspht0203Ctrl::SetShadowColor(OLE_COLOR nNewValue)
{
// TODO: Add your property handler here

SetModifiedFlag();
m_ShadowColor = nNewValue;
}

OLE_COLOR CAspht0203Ctrl::GetPanelColor()
{
// TODO: Add your property handler here

return m_PanelColor;
}
```

```
void CAspht0203Ctrl::SetPanelColor(OLE_COLOR nNewValue)
{
// TODO: Add your property handler here

SetModifiedFlag();
m_PanelColor = nNewValue;
}

short CAspht0203Ctrl::GetBorderWidth()
{
// TODO: Add your property handler here

return m_BorderWidth;
}

void CAspht0203Ctrl::SetBorderWidth(short nNewValue)
{
// TODO: Add your property handler here

SetModifiedFlag();
m_BorderWidth = nNewValue;
}
```

5. Compile the ODL file and build the OCX. Then activate ActiveX Control Pad and create the HTML file shown in Listing 2-10. Save it as `ASPHT0203.HTM`. Place the cursor in front of the second `<HR>` tag and choose the Edit|Insert ActiveX Control menu option. In the dialog box choose `ASPHT0203` as the control. When it appears in the ActiveX editor window, you will see a display similar to Figure 2-13.

Listing 2-10 ASPHT0203.HTM HTML source code

```
<HTML>
<HEAD>
<TITLE>Chapter Two Test Page 3</TITLE>
</HEAD>
<SCRIPT LANGUAGE="VBScript">
<!--
Sub Aspht02031_Click()
Alert("I look better, don't I?")
end sub
-->
    </SCRIPT>
<BODY>
<H1>ASPHT0203 ActiveX Control Test Page One</H1>
<HR>
<HR>
</BODY>
</HTML>
```

6. Select the `PanelColor` property in the Properties dialog. Clear the old entry text, type in `000000af`, and press Apply. Then click outside the control to force it to repaint. You will see a display similar to Figure 2-14.

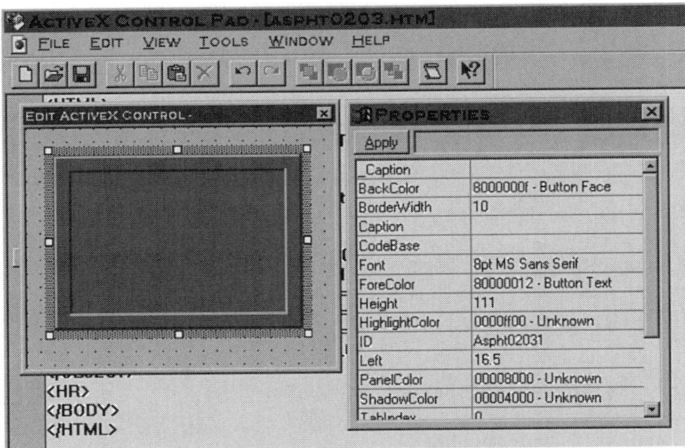

Figure 2-13 The ASPHT0203 OCX control showing its new display in ActiveX Control Pad

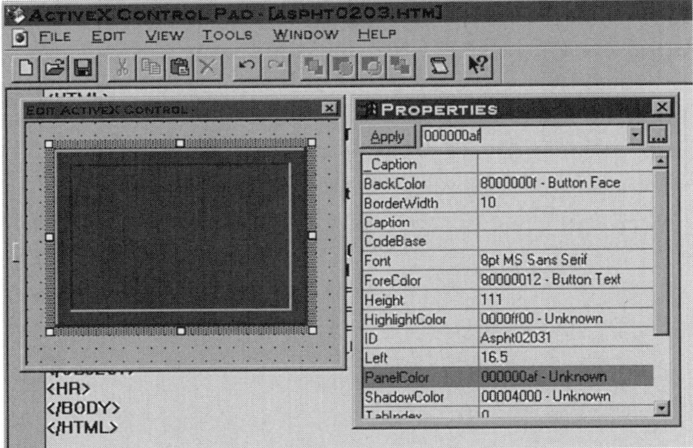

Figure 2-14 The ASPHT0203 OCX control responding to the custom property setting in the Control Pad

7. Select the `HighlightColor` and `ShadowColor` properties in the Properties dialog. Clear the old entry text and type in **`000000ff`** and **`00000077`** and press Apply. Then select the `BorderWidth` property and change it to **`20`**. Click outside the control to force it to repaint. You will see a display similar to Figure 2-15.

8. Close the ActiveX editor window and save the HTML file. Then open the HTML file in Internet Explorer. You will see a display similar to Figure 2-16. You will notice that the custom property settings have reverted to

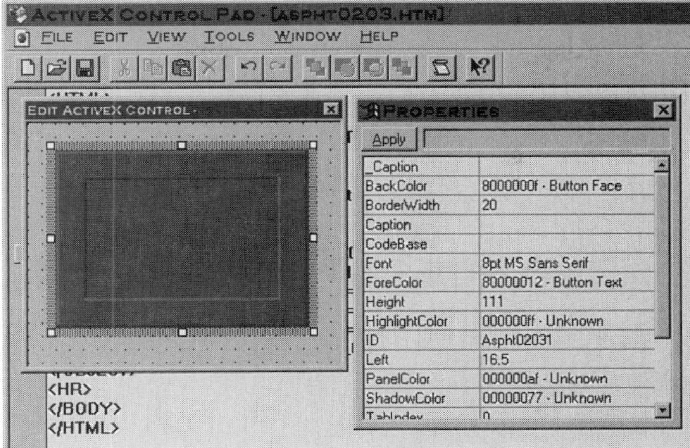

Figure 2-15 The ASPHT0203 OCX control responding to all the custom property settings in the Control Pad

their defaults; this is explained in the Comments section. You have added custom properties to your custom ActiveX control, taking a major step forward in designing your own useful controls.

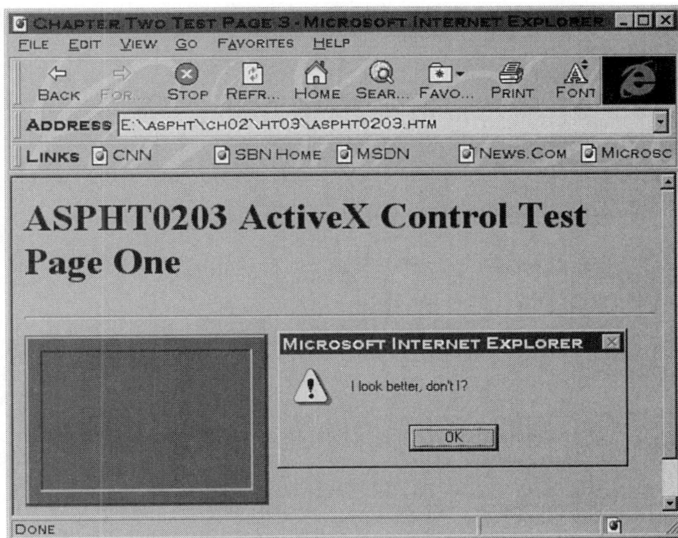

Figure 2-16 The ASPHT0203 OCX control in Internet Explorer, reverted to its default settings

How It Works

Notice this fragment of code from the ASPHT0203CTL.CPP file:

```
/////////////////////////////////////////////////////////////////////////////
// Dispatch map

BEGIN_DISPATCH_MAP(CAspht0203Ctrl, COleControl)
//{{AFX_DISPATCH_MAP(CAspht0203Ctrl)
DISP_PROPERTY_EX(CAspht0203Ctrl, "HighlightColor", GetHighlightColor,⇐
SetHighlightColor, VT_COLOR)
DISP_PROPERTY_EX(CAspht0203Ctrl, "ShadowColor", GetShadowColor, SetShadowColor,⇐
VT_COLOR)
DISP_PROPERTY_EX(CAspht0203Ctrl, "PanelColor", GetPanelColor, SetPanelColor,⇐
VT_COLOR)
DISP_PROPERTY_EX(CAspht0203Ctrl, "BorderWidth", GetBorderWidth, SetBorderWidth,⇐
VT_I2)
DISP_DEFVALUE(CAspht0203Ctrl, "Caption")
DISP_STOCKPROP_BACKCOLOR()
DISP_STOCKPROP_CAPTION()
DISP_STOCKPROP_FONT()
DISP_STOCKPROP_FORECOLOR()
//}}AFX_DISPATCH_MAP
DISP_FUNCTION_ID(CAspht0203Ctrl, "AboutBox", DISPID_ABOUTBOX, AboutBox, VT⇐
_EMPTY, VTS_NONE)
END_DISPATCH_MAP()
```

In it, the ClassWizard has added a dispatch map for all the new custom properties. Along with the initialization, data retrieval and storage, and drawing code, this is three-quarters of the code needed to add the custom properties and make them work. The remainder is in Listing 2-11, the ASPHT0203.ODL file.

Listing 2-11 ASPHT0203.ODL type library source code

```
</HTML>
// aspht0203.odl : type library source for ActiveX Control project.

// This file will be processed by the Make Type Library (mktyplib) tool to
// produce the type library (aspht0203.tlb) that will become a resource in
// aspht0203.ocx.

#include <olectl.h>
#include <idispids.h>

[ uuid(EB3039AC-B4B9-11D0-B7D8-444553540000), version(1.0),
  helpfile("aspht0203.hlp"),
  helpstring("aspht0203 ActiveX Control module"),
  control ]
library ASPHT0203Lib
{
importlib(STDOLE_TLB);
importlib(STDTYPE_TLB);

//  Primary dispatch interface for CAspht0203Ctrl

[ uuid(EB3039AD-B4B9-11D0-B7D8-444553540000),
```

```
helpstring("Dispatch interface for Aspht0203 Control"), hidden ]
dispinterface _DAspht0203
{
properties:
// NOTE - ClassWizard will maintain property information here.
//    Use extreme caution when editing this section.
//{{AFX_ODL_PROP(CAspht0203Ctrl)
[id(DISPID_BACKCOLOR), bindable, requestedit] OLE_COLOR BackColor;
[id(DISPID_CAPTION), bindable, requestEdit] BSTR Caption;
[id(DISPID_FONT), bindable] IFontDisp* Font;
[id(DISPID_FORECOLOR), bindable, requestedit] OLE_COLOR ForeColor;
[id(1)] OLE_COLOR HighlightColor;
[id(2)] OLE_COLOR ShadowColor;
[id(3)] OLE_COLOR PanelColor;
[id(0)] BSTR _Caption;
[id(4)] short BorderWidth;
//}}AFX_ODL_PROP

methods:
// NOTE - ClassWizard will maintain method information here.
//    Use extreme caution when editing this section.
//{{AFX_ODL_METHOD(CAspht0203Ctrl)
//}}AFX_ODL_METHOD

[id(DISPID_ABOUTBOX)] void AboutBox();
};

//  Event dispatch interface for CAspht0203Ctrl

[ uuid(EB3039AE-B4B9-11D0-B7D8-444553540000),
helpstring("Event interface for Aspht0203 Control") ]
dispinterface _DAspht0203Events
{
properties:
//  Event interface has no properties

methods:
// NOTE - ClassWizard will maintain event information here.
//    Use extreme caution when editing this section.
//{{AFX_ODL_EVENT(CAspht0203Ctrl)
[id(DISPID_CLICK)] void Click();
//}}AFX_ODL_EVENT
};

//  Class information for CAspht0203Ctrl

[ uuid(EB3039AF-B4B9-11D0-B7D8-444553540000),
helpstring("Aspht0203 Control"), control ]
coclass Aspht0203
{
[default] dispinterface _DAspht0203;
[default, source] dispinterface _DAspht0203Events;
};


//{{AFX_APPEND_ODL}}
```

continued on next page

continued from previous page

```
//}}AFX_APPEND_ODL}}
};
```

Notice this fragment from the file:

```
//  Primary dispatch interface for CAspht0203Ctrl

[ uuid(EB3039AD-B4B9-11D0-B7D8-444553540000),
helpstring("Dispatch interface for Aspht0203 Control"), hidden ]
dispinterface _DAspht0203
{
properties:
// NOTE - ClassWizard will maintain property information here.
//    Use extreme caution when editing this section.
//{{AFX_ODL_PROP(CAspht0203Ctrl)
[id(DISPID_BACKCOLOR), bindable, requestedit] OLE_COLOR BackColor;
[id(DISPID_CAPTION), bindable, requestEdit] BSTR Caption;
[id(DISPID_FONT), bindable] IFontDisp* Font;
[id(DISPID_FORECOLOR), bindable, requestedit] OLE_COLOR ForeColor;
[id(1)] OLE_COLOR HighlightColor;
[id(2)] OLE_COLOR ShadowColor;
[id(3)] OLE_COLOR PanelColor;
[id(0)] BSTR _Caption;
[id(4)] short BorderWidth;
//}}AFX_ODL_PROP
```

In it, the ClassWizard has added all the interfaces needed to connect to the custom properties from outside. Notice that unlike the stock properties, which have defined constants, the custom interfaces all use positive numbers starting at `1` (`0` is reserved for the default property, which is `Caption`).

Comments

The reason the custom properties did not appear in the HTML file and thus were not saved for use in Internet Explorer is that they were not set up to be "serialized" or stored using the OLE system. This detail is discussed in How-To 2.8.

COMPLEXITY
INTERMEDIATE

2.4 How do I... Define and handle custom events with my ActiveX control in Visual C++ 5.0?

Problem

Wow! Now that I have custom properties for my ActiveX control, how hard will it be to add custom event handlers to it?

Technique

Actually, not that hard! MFC has special macros and features to aid in adding and managing custom events in ActiveX controls. This How-To demonstrates adding events to invert and reinvert the drawing bevels of the control implemented in How-To's 2.1, 2.2., and 2.3 when the mouse clicks on it, simulating a button pushing in and out. The CD contains an already created workspace with a new name but all the previous code and settings in place under `CH02\HT04\ASPHT0204\`. The complete control is under `CH02\HT04\FINAL\ASPHT0204\`.

Steps

1. Activate Visual C++ 5.0 and load the `ASPHT0204` workspace, which as noted above contains all the code and settings from the previous How-To. Choose the ClassWizard from the View menu and click on the ActiveX Events tab, then press the Add Event... button. In the Add Event dialog box, fill in the value `InvertColors` as the external name. Then add a parameter named `ColorsToInvert`, of type `short`, as shown in Figure 2-17. Press OK to accept the new event.

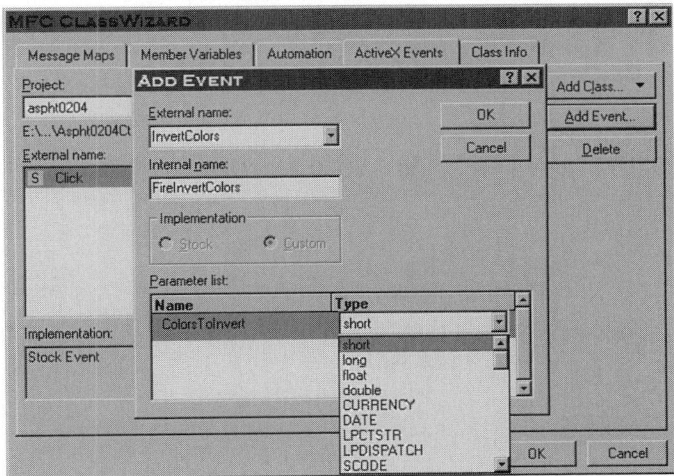

Figure 2-17 The Add Event dialog of the Class Wizard is shown adding a custom ActiveX event

2. The new event will be added to the events list of the ActiveX Events tab as shown in Figure 2-18. Press OK to write the event into the appropriate files. Because you intend this event initially only for use by external containers, go ahead and build `ASPHT0204.OCX`.

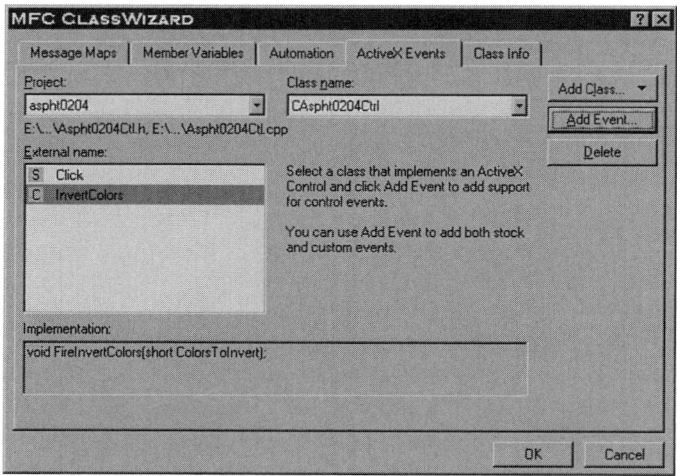

Figure 2-18 The ClassWizard dialog showing the custom event added to ASPHT0204.OCX

3. Activate ActiveX Control Pad. Create a new HTML file and enter the code in Listing 2-12. Save it as **ASPHT0204.HTM**. Insert a copy of the **ASPHT0204** ActiveX control before the second **<HR>** tag. Save the file. Then bring up the Script Wizard and add the script code shown in Listing 2-13 to the OnLoad, Click, and InvertColors events, creating a display similar to that shown in Figure 2-19. Close the Script Wizard and save the file.

Listing 2-12 ASPHT0204.HTM HTML source code

```
<HTML>
<HEAD>
<TITLE>Chapter Two Test Page 4</TITLE>
</HEAD>
<BODY>
<H1>ASPHT0204 ActiveX Control Test Page One</H1>
<HR>
<HR>
</BODY>
</HTML>
```

Listing 2-13 ASPHT0204.HTM script events source code

```
<SCRIPT LANGUAGE="VBScript">
<!--
Sub window_onLoad()
Aspht02041.PanelColor = &H000000AF
```

```
Aspht02041.HighlightColor = &H000000FF
Aspht02041.ShadowColor = &H00000077
CycleVar = 0
end sub
-->
    </SCRIPT>
    <SCRIPT LANGUAGE="VBScript">
<!--
dim HC1

dim HC2

dim CycleVar

-->
    </SCRIPT>
<SCRIPT LANGUAGE="VBScript">
<!--
Sub Aspht02041_InvertColors(ColorsToInvert)
select case ColorsToInvert
  case 0
    Alert("Storing Values!")
    HC1 = Aspht02041.ShadowColor
    HC2 = Aspht02041.HighlightColor
  case 1
    Alert("Inverting!")
    Aspht02041.ShadowColor = HC2
    Aspht02041.HighlightColor = HC1
  case 2
    Alert("Reverting!")
    Aspht02041.ShadowColor = HC1
    Aspht02041.HighlightColor = HC2
end select
end sub
Sub Aspht02041_Click()
select case CycleVar
  case 0
     CycleVar = 1
     Aspht02041_InvertColors(0)
  case 1
     CycleVar = 2
     Aspht02041_InvertColors(1)
  case 2
     CycleVar = 0
     Aspht02041_InvertColors(2)
end select
end sub
-->
    </SCRIPT>
```

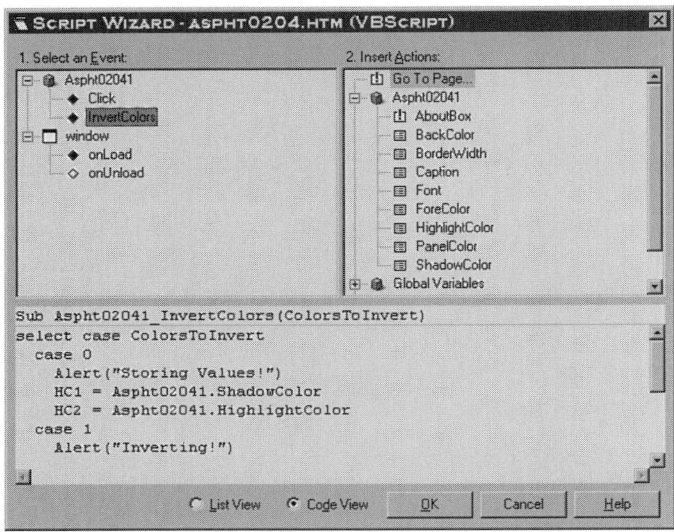

Figure 2-19 The ClassWizard dialog, showing the custom event added to ASPHT0204.OCX

4. Bring up the **ASPHT0204.HTM** file in Internet Explorer. You will probably be surprised to see that initially the control is still its default green colors. Minimize IE and restore it *without* reloading the page, and you will immediately see that the display now takes on the scripted red colors. Click on the control and you will see a message box informing you of the variable storage action as the first **InvertColors** event fires. Click again and a second message box will appear, as shown in Figure 2-20, but no initial inversion will be seen. Minimize and restore the IE window again, however, and you will see the inversion, as shown in Figure 2-21. Clicking and redisplaying again will return to the initial display with a final message box. You now know how to add a custom event to your custom ActiveX control.

NOTE

The greyscale images in the book may not do justice to this particular effect, but try it on an actual computer and it is quite striking!

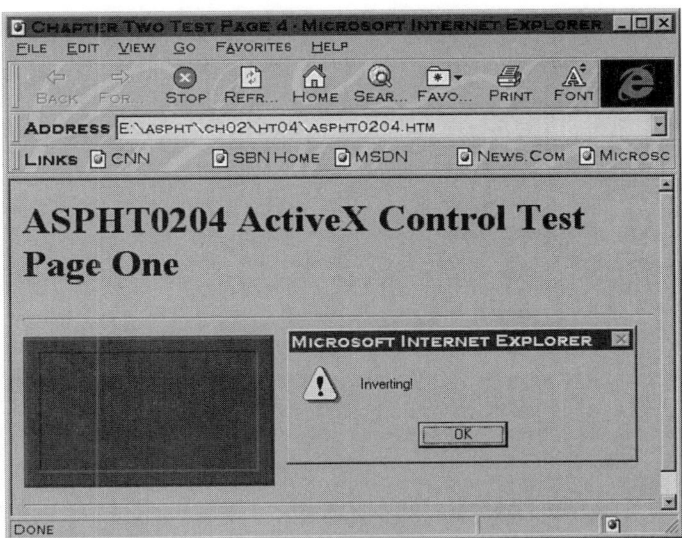

Figure 2-20 The script-altered colors of `ASPHT0204.OCX` on an HTML page

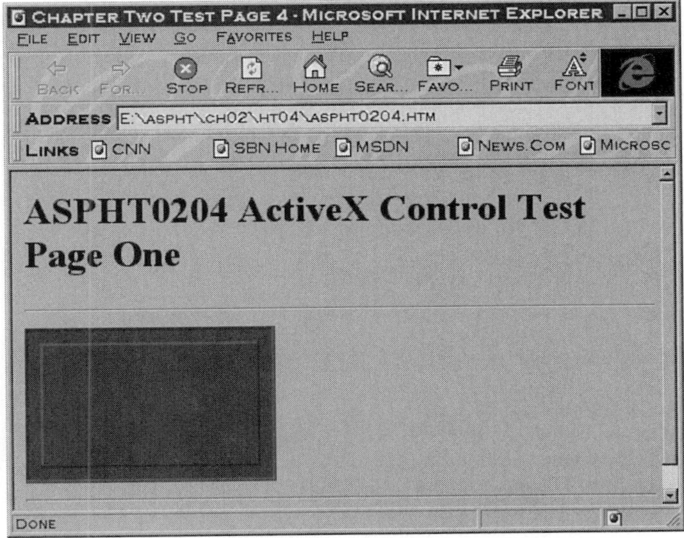

Figure 2-21 `ASPHT0204` showing the results of the `InvertColors` event

How It Works

The following code fragment from the ASPHT0204.ODL file shows the change made there by the ClassWizard:

```
<SCRIPT LANGUAGE="VBScript">
//  Event dispatch interface for CAspht0204Ctrl

[ uuid(EB3039DC-B4B9-11D0-B7D8-444553540000),
helpstring("Event interface for Aspht0204 Control") ]
dispinterface _DAspht0204Events
{
properties:
//  Event interface has no properties

methods:
// NOTE - ClassWizard will maintain event information here.
//    Use extreme caution when editing this section.
//{{AFX_ODL_EVENT(CAspht0204Ctrl)
[id(DISPID_CLICK)] void Click();
[id(1)] void InvertColors(short ColorsToInvert);
//}}AFX_ODL_EVENT
};
<!--
```

Here the InvertColors event is added to the ODL_EVENT section of the type library with its short parameter. Even though the event is never called inside the control itself, external controls can reference it and use it like any normal event.

This fragment of code in the main ASPHT0204CTL.CPP file was also created by the ClassWizard:

```
/////////////////////////////////////////////////////////////////////////////
// Event map

BEGIN_EVENT_MAP(CAspht0204Ctrl, COleControl)
//{{AFX_EVENT_MAP(CAspht0204Ctrl)
EVENT_CUSTOM("InvertColors", FireInvertColors, VTS_I2)
EVENT_STOCK_CLICK()
//}}AFX_EVENT_MAP
END_EVENT_MAP()
```

The EVENT_CUSTOM macro adds the code to create an externally accessible method of the class that can be called with a single short parameter. Although you did not use the FireInvertColors method in the control's source code at this time, the method is nonetheless available for use.

Comments

The reason for the song and dance needed to get the control to redisplay itself after its values change is because the control presently has no way to notify the container that it needs to be repainted. The following How-To rectifies that problem.

2.5 How do I... Include custom methods with my ActiveX control in Visual C++ 5.0?

Problem

I would really like to have one of my control's functions available to the programs that use it. How can I export my ActiveX control's internal functionality to other environments?

Technique

The functionality to do this is called a *method*; it is a function call made available through the ActiveX system to the program hosting the control. MFC supports custom methods fully, and this How-To demonstrates this support by implementing a custom method to encapsulate inverting the colors of the control developed in the previous How-To's. The CD contains an already created workspace with a new name but all the previous code and settings in place under `CH02\HT05\ASPHT0205\`. The complete control is under `CH02\HT05\FINAL\ASPHT0205\`.

Steps

1. Activate Visual C++ 5.0 and load the `ASPHT0205` workspace, which as noted above contains all the code and settings from the previous How-To. Choose the ClassWizard from the View menu and click on the Automation tab, then press the Add Method... button. In the Add Method dialog box, select Refresh from the drop-down list as the external name, as shown in Figure 2-22. Press OK to accept the new method.

2. Repeat the process, but this time type `FlipColors` as the external name and add a return type of `void` and a single parameter named `DoUpdate` of type `BOOL`, as shown in Figure 2-23. Press OK. The new methods will be added to the list of the Automation tab, as shown in Figure 2-24. Press OK to write the methods into the appropriate files.

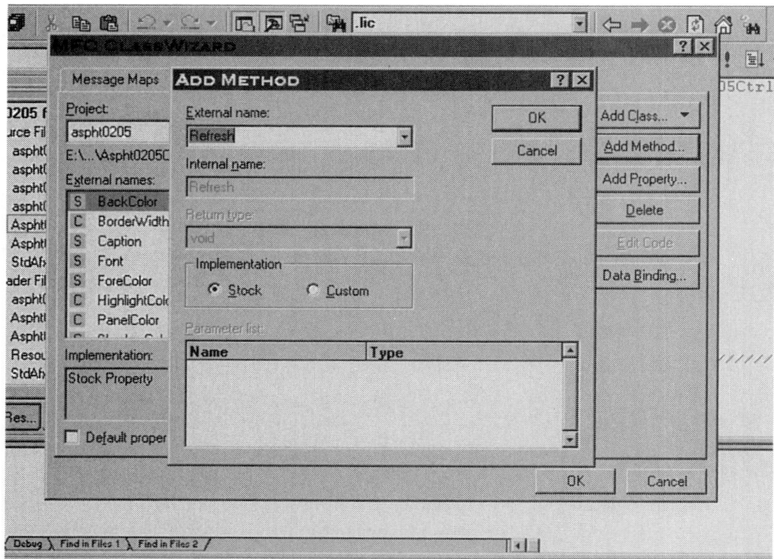

Figure 2-22 The Add Method dialog of the ClassWizard shown adding a stock ActiveX method

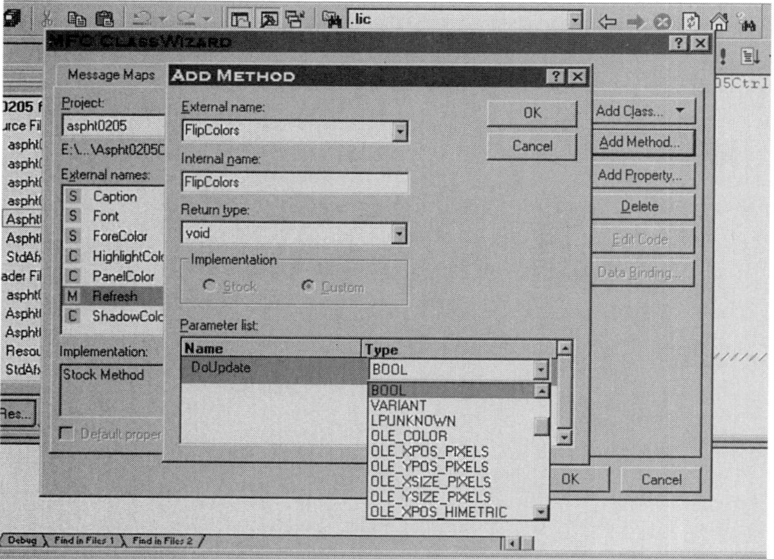

Figure 2-23 The Add Method dialog showing the custom method added to `ASPHT0205.OCX`

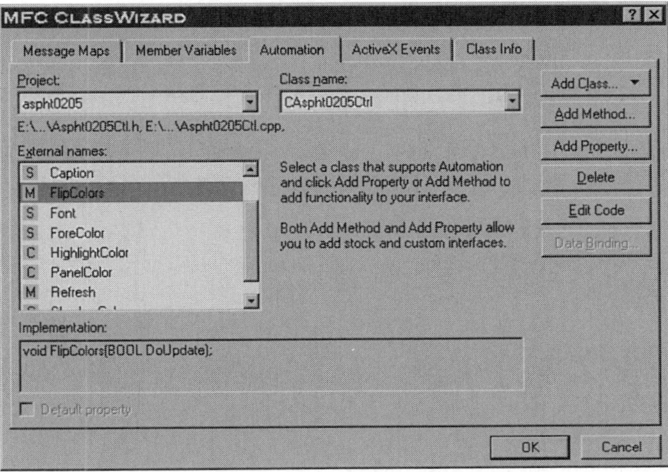

Figure 2-24 The ClassWizard dialog showing the stock and custom methods added to `ASPHT0205.OCX`

3. Bring up the **`ASPHT0205CTL.CPP`** file in the text editor. Move down to the bottom and the **`FlipColors`** method definition. Add the code in Listing 2-14 to the definition and save the file. Build **`ASPHT0205.OCX`**.

Listing 2-14 `ASPHT0205CTL.CPP` module source code fragment

```
void CAspht0205Ctrl::FlipColors(BOOL DoUpdate)
{
// TODO: Add your dispatch handler code here
OLE_COLOR holdcolor = GetShadowColor();
SetShadowColor( GetHighlightColor() );
SetHighlightColor( holdcolor );
if ( DoUpdate != 0 )
{
Refresh();
}
```

4. Activate ActiveX Control Pad. Create a new HTML file and enter the nonscript code in Listing 2-15. Use the Edit|Insert ActiveX Control menu option to insert an **`ASPHT0205`** control with default values beside the second `<HR>` tag. Save the file as **`ASPHT0205.HTM`**. Then activate the Script Wizard and enter the script code in Listing 2-15 to the **`OnLoad`**, **`Click`**, and **`InvertColors`** events, resulting in a display similar to Figure 2-25. Press OK and save the file.

Listing 2-15 `ASPHT0205.HTM` HTML and script source code

```
<HTML>
<HEAD>
    <SCRIPT LANGUAGE="VBScript">
```

continued on next page

continued from previous page

```
<!--
Sub window_onLoad()
Aspht02051.PanelColor = &H000000AF
Aspht02051.HighlightColor = &H000000FF
Aspht02051.ShadowColor = &H00000077
call Aspht02051.Refresh()
end sub
-->
    </SCRIPT>
<TITLE>Chapter Two Test Page 5</TITLE>
</HEAD>
<BODY>
<H1>ASPHT0205 ActiveX Control Test Page One</H1>
<HR>
    <SCRIPT LANGUAGE="VBScript">
<!--
Sub Aspht02051_Click()
Aspht02051_InvertColors(1)
end sub
Sub Aspht02051_InvertColors(ColorsToInvert)
call Aspht02051.FlipColors(ColorsToInvert)
end sub
-->
    </SCRIPT>
<HR>
</BODY>
</HTML>
```

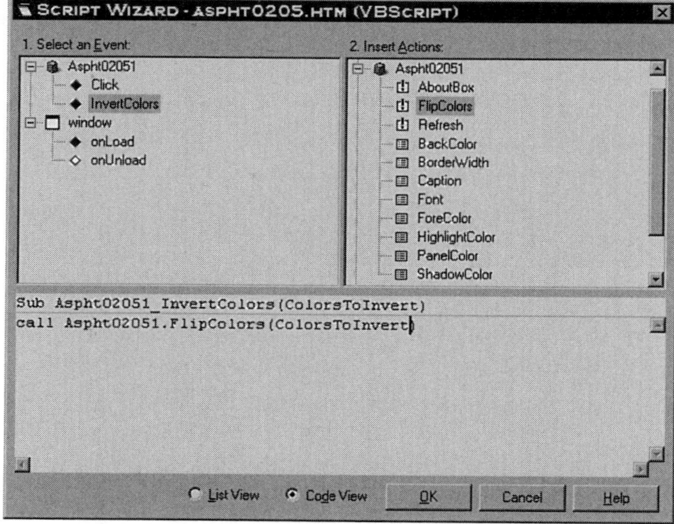

Figure 2-25 The Script Wizard dialog showing the new `FlipColors` and `Refresh` methods available to `ASPHT0205.OCX`

5. Bring up the HTML file in Internet Explorer. Notice that the new colors take effect immediately after the page loads as the `OnLoad` event's `Refresh` call is made. Click on the control and observe how it instantly inverts and reverts its colors, as shown in Figure 2-26. You have added stock and custom methods to your custom ActiveX control, giving it access to full programmatic power at runtime.

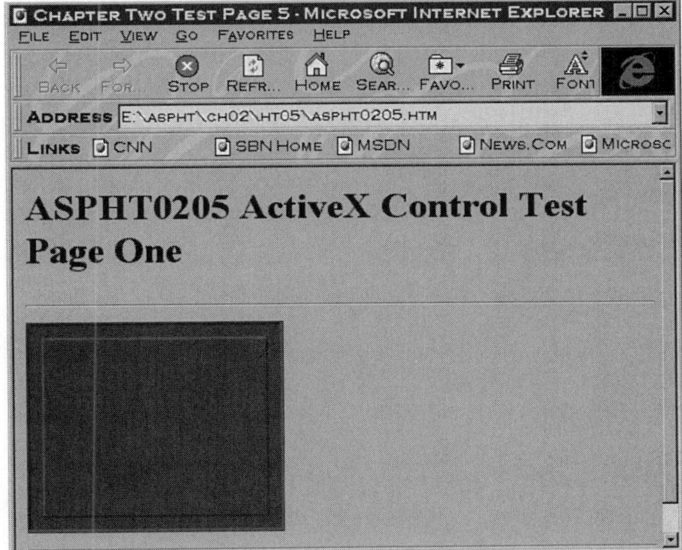

Figure 2-26 `ASPHT0205.HTM` in Internet Explorer, demonstrating the much simpler color inversion effect

How It Works

Notice this code section from the `ASPHT0205.ODL` file. It is part of the primary dispatch interface of the control:

```
dispinterface _DAspht0205
{
...
methods:
// NOTE - ClassWizard will maintain method information here.
//    Use extreme caution when editing this section.
//{{AFX_ODL_METHOD(CAspht0205Ctrl)
[id(DISPID_REFRESH)] void Refresh();
[id(5)] void FlipColors(boolean DoUpdate);
//}}AFX_ODL_METHOD

[id(DISPID_ABOUTBOX)] void AboutBox();
};
```

The AFX_ODL_METHOD macros here generate the code needed to include both the stock method Refresh with its name constant DispID and the custom method FlipColors with its numbered DispID (which, please note, continues the sequence started with the previous properties) in the type library for external program usage.

Now look at this code fragment from ASPHT0205CTL.CPP:

```
</BODY>
/////////////////////////////////////////////////////////////////////////////
// Dispatch map

BEGIN_DISPATCH_MAP(CAspht0205Ctrl, COleControl)
//{{AFX_DISPATCH_MAP(CAspht0205Ctrl)
DISP_PROPERTY_EX(CAspht0205Ctrl, "BorderWidth", GetBorderWidth, SetBorderWidth,⇐
VT_I2)
DISP_PROPERTY_EX(CAspht0205Ctrl, "HighlightColor", GetHighlightColor,⇐
SetHighlightColor, VT_COLOR)
DISP_PROPERTY_EX(CAspht0205Ctrl, "PanelColor", GetPanelColor, SetPanelColor,⇐
VT_COLOR)
DISP_PROPERTY_EX(CAspht0205Ctrl, "ShadowColor", GetShadowColor, SetShadowColor,⇐
VT_COLOR)
DISP_FUNCTION(CAspht0205Ctrl, "FlipColors", FlipColors, VT_EMPTY, VTS_BOOL)
DISP_STOCKFUNC_REFRESH()
DISP_STOCKPROP_BACKCOLOR()
DISP_STOCKPROP_CAPTION()
DISP_STOCKPROP_FONT()
DISP_STOCKPROP_FORECOLOR()
//}}AFX_DISPATCH_MAP
DISP_FUNCTION_ID(CAspht0205Ctrl, "AboutBox", DISPID_ABOUTBOX, AboutBox, ⇐
VT_EMPTY, VTS_NONE)
END_DISPATCH_MAP()
</HTML>
```

The DISP_FUNCTION and DISP_STOCKFUNC macros expand to create the required OLE 2 code to interface the methods with the ActiveX system. Notice that the return and parameter types are VT variants rather than their underlying C++ types!

Comments

At this point you have a fully working ActiveX control and the skills needed to enhance it to virtually any simple capability you might like. Play around with the code, try things out! (And if things break, keep reading…!)

COMPLEXITY
INTERMEDIATE

2.6 How do I... Add text and font support to my ActiveX control with Visual C++ 5.0?

Problem

Now that I have the basic drawing stuff down pat, I'd like to add some text and font support to my control. Can I do this?

Technique

MFC-based ActiveX controls can take advantage of special font and text capabilities. This How-To shows you how to do this by adding a caption with a user-configured font to the control developed in previous How-To's in this chapter. The CD contains an already created workspace with a new name but all the previous code and settings in place under `CH02\HT06\ASPHT0206\`. The complete control is under `CH02\HT06\FINAL\ASPHT0206\`.

Steps

1. Activate Visual C++ 5.0 and load the `ASPHT0206` workspace, which as noted above contains all the code and settings from the previous How-To. Bring up the `ASPHT0206CTL.CPP` file in the text editor. Locate the `OnDraw` method and add the boldfaced code in Listing 2-16. Save the file and build `ASPHT0206.OCX`.

Listing 2-16 `ASPHT0206CTL.CPP` `OnDraw` function source code

```
//////////////////////////////////////////////////////////////////////////////
// CAspht0206Ctrl::OnDraw - Drawing function

void CAspht0206Ctrl::OnDraw(
CDC* pdc, const CRect& rcBounds, const CRect& rcInvalid)
{
CBrush cbPanelBrush( TranslateColor( m_PanelColor ));
pdc->FillRect( rcBounds, &cbPanelBrush );
CPen pHiLitePen(PS_SOLID, 2, TranslateColor( GetHighlightColor() ));
CPen pShadowPen(PS_SOLID, 2, TranslateColor( GetShadowColor() ));
CPen *pOldPen = pdc->SelectObject( &pHiLitePen );
```

continued on next page

continued from previous page

```
pdc->MoveTo(rcBounds.left + 2 , rcBounds.top + 2);
pdc->LineTo(rcBounds.right - 2 , rcBounds.top + 2 );
pdc->MoveTo(rcBounds.left + 2 , rcBounds.top + 2 );
pdc->LineTo(rcBounds.left + 2 , rcBounds.bottom - 2);
pdc->SelectObject( &pShadowPen );
pdc->MoveTo(rcBounds.right - 2 , rcBounds.bottom - 2 );
pdc->LineTo(rcBounds.right - 2 , rcBounds.top + 2);
pdc->MoveTo(rcBounds.right - 2 , rcBounds.bottom - 2);
pdc->LineTo(rcBounds.left + 2  , rcBounds.bottom - 2);
pdc->MoveTo(rcBounds.left + m_BorderWidth + 4 , rcBounds.top + m_BorderWidth + 4);
pdc->LineTo(rcBounds.right - m_BorderWidth - 4 , rcBounds.top + m_BorderWidth +⇐
4);
pdc->MoveTo(rcBounds.left + m_BorderWidth + 4 , rcBounds.top + m_BorderWidth + 4);
pdc->LineTo(rcBounds.left + m_BorderWidth + 4 , rcBounds.bottom - m_BorderWidth⇐
- 4);
pdc->SelectObject( &pHiLitePen );
pdc->MoveTo(rcBounds.right - m_BorderWidth - 4 , rcBounds.bottom - m_BorderWidth⇐
- 4);
pdc->LineTo(rcBounds.right - m_BorderWidth - 4 , rcBounds.top + m_BorderWidth +⇐
4);
pdc->MoveTo(rcBounds.right - m_BorderWidth - 4 , rcBounds.bottom - m_BorderWidth⇐
- 4);
pdc->LineTo(rcBounds.left + m_BorderWidth + 4, rcBounds.bottom - m_BorderWidth⇐
- 4);
pdc->SelectObject(pOldPen);
CFont *hfOldFont = SelectStockFont( pdc);
pdc->SetTextColor( TranslateColor( GetForeColor()));
pdc->SetBkMode( TRANSPARENT);
RECT rcHolder = rcBounds;
pdc->DrawText( InternalGetText() , -1 , &rcHolder , DT_SINGLELINE | DT_CENTER |
DT_VCENTER );
pdc->SelectObject( hfOldFont );
```

2. Activate ActiveX Control Pad. Start a new HTML file and enter the code in Listing 2-17. Then insert a copy of `ASPHT0206.OCX` into the file before the second `<HR>` tag. Add a caption of `ActiveX is Cool!` and set the font to Copperplate Gothic Bold, 16 Points, Bold. The control immediately detects the font changes and caption value as shown in Figure 2-27. Close the ActiveX editor window and save the file as `ASPHT0206.HTM`.

Listing 2-17 `ASPHT0206.HTM` HTML source code

```
<HTML>
<HEAD>
 <TITLE>Chapter Two Test Page 6</TITLE>
</HEAD>
<BODY>
<H1>ASPHT0206 ActiveX Control Test Page One</H1>
<HR>
<HR>
</BODY>
</HTML>
```

3. Bring up `ASPHT0206.HTM` in Internet Explorer and you will see a display similar to Figure 2-28. You have added font and text output capabilities to your custom ActiveX control.

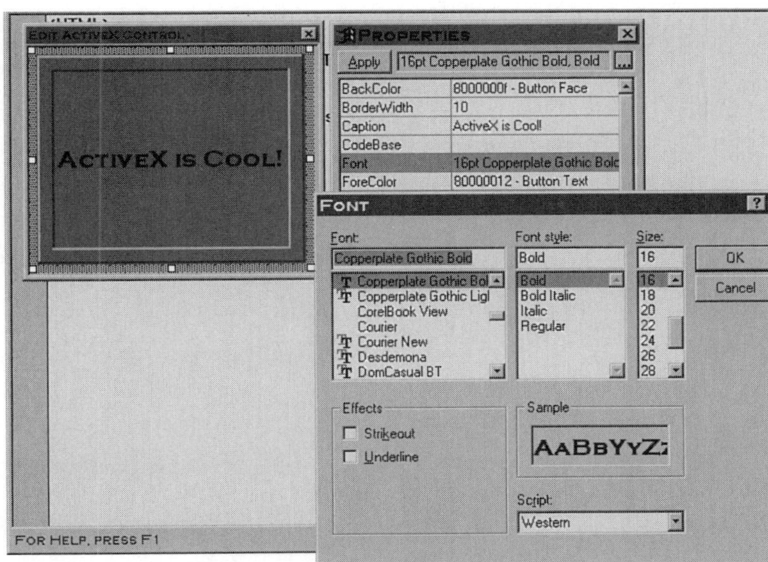

Figure 2-27 ActiveX Control Pad's ActiveX window showing `ASPHT0206.OCX` responding to `Font` and `Caption` properties

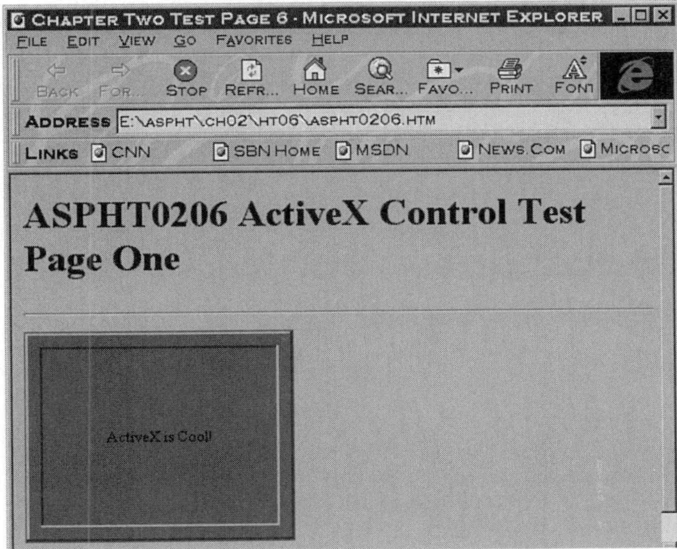

Figure 2-28 `ASPHT0206.HTM` in Internet Explorer showing the `Caption` and `Font` properties

How It Works

Two key lines of code in the `OnDraw` function interface the control with the ActiveX font and text system. The first is

```
CFont *hfOldFont = SelectStockFont( pdc);
```

The `SelectStockFont` function obtains the currently set font for the system and selects the device context object. This allows any change made to the current display font to be detected instantly and used by your control.

The other key line of code is

```
pdc->DrawText( InternalGetText() , -1 , &rcHolder , DT_SINGLELINE ¦ DT_CENTER ¦⇐
DT_VCENTER );
```

The `InternalGetText` function call obtains the `Caption` property for the control and outputs it in the correct format for the `DrawText` function. That is really all there is to it!

Comments

At first you might think that there is a mistake here, because although the custom font selection shows up just fine in the ActiveX editor window, it does not display on the Web page in Internet Explorer! There is actually no bug in the ActiveX control, but rather a flaw in ActiveX Control Pad; it does not *serialize* (store to disk) stock font property settings. Visual Basic 5.0, however, does serialize stock font settings. To see this for yourself, either run the `ACTIVEXFONTTESTPROJECT.EXE` file in the `CH02\HT06\` subdirectory or open the `ACTIVEXFONTTESTPROJECT.VBP` project in Visual Basic 5.0 if you have a copy.

COMPLEXITY
INTERMEDIATE

2.7 How do I… Add custom graphics to my ActiveX control using Visual C++ 5.0?

Problem

All right, let's go for broke! I want to display an icon *and* a bitmap in my ActiveX control. How bad is this going to hurt?

Technique

You won't even need a bandage! Thanks to the MFC support for pictures and internal resources, you can include sophisticated graphical display functionality for your ActiveX control very easily. This How-To demonstrates the needed steps by adding an identifying icon and bitmap to the control created in previous How-To's in this chapter. The CD contains an already created workspace with a new name but all the previous code and settings in place under **CH02\HT07\ASPHT0207**. The complete control is under **CH02\HT07\FINAL\ASPHT0207**.

Steps

1. Activate Visual C++ 5.0 and load the **ASPHT0207** workspace, which as noted above contains all the code and settings from the previous How-To. Bring up the **ASPHT0207CTL.CPP** file in the text editor. Locate the **OnDraw** method and add the boldfaced code in Listing 2-18. Save the file. Build ASPHT0207.OCX.

Listing 2-18 ASPHT0207CTL.CPP OnDraw function source code

```
</BODY>
/////////////////////////////////////////////////////////////////////////////
// CAspht0207Ctrl::OnDraw - Drawing function

void CAspht0207Ctrl::OnDraw(
CDC* pdc, const CRect& rcBounds, const CRect& rcInvalid)
{
CBrush cbPanelBrush( TranslateColor( m_PanelColor ));
pdc->FillRect( rcBounds, &cbPanelBrush );
CPen pHiLitePen(PS_SOLID, 2, TranslateColor( GetHighlightColor() ));
CPen pShadowPen(PS_SOLID, 2, TranslateColor( GetShadowColor() ));
CPen *pOldPen = pdc->SelectObject( &pHiLitePen );
pdc->MoveTo(rcBounds.left + 2 , rcBounds.top + 2);
pdc->LineTo(rcBounds.right - 2 , rcBounds.top + 2 );
pdc->MoveTo(rcBounds.left + 2 , rcBounds.top + 2 );
pdc->LineTo(rcBounds.left + 2 , rcBounds.bottom - 2);
pdc->SelectObject( &pShadowPen );
pdc->MoveTo(rcBounds.right - 2 , rcBounds.bottom - 2 );
pdc->LineTo(rcBounds.right - 2 , rcBounds.top + 2);
pdc->MoveTo(rcBounds.right - 2 , rcBounds.bottom - 2);
pdc->LineTo(rcBounds.left + 2  , rcBounds.bottom - 2);
pdc->MoveTo(rcBounds.left + m_BorderWidth + 4 , rcBounds.top + m_BorderWidth + 4);
pdc->LineTo(rcBounds.right - m_BorderWidth - 4 , rcBounds.top + m_BorderWidth +⇐
4);
pdc->MoveTo(rcBounds.left + m_BorderWidth + 4 , rcBounds.top + m_BorderWidth + 4);
pdc->LineTo(rcBounds.left + m_BorderWidth + 4 , rcBounds.bottom - m_BorderWidth⇐
- 4);
pdc->SelectObject( &pHiLitePen );
pdc->MoveTo(rcBounds.right - m_BorderWidth - 4 , rcBounds.bottom - m_BorderWidth⇐
- 4);
pdc->LineTo(rcBounds.right - m_BorderWidth - 4 , rcBounds.top + m_BorderWidth +⇐
4);
```

continued on next page

continued from previous page

```
pdc->MoveTo(rcBounds.right - m_BorderWidth - 4 , rcBounds.bottom - m_BorderWidth⇐
- 4);
pdc->LineTo(rcBounds.left + m_BorderWidth + 4, rcBounds.bottom - m_BorderWidth⇐
- 4);
pdc->SelectObject(pOldPen);
CFont *hfOldFont = SelectStockFont( pdc);
pdc->SetTextColor( TranslateColor( GetForeColor()));
pdc->SetBkMode( TRANSPARENT);
RECT rcHolder = rcBounds;
pdc->DrawText( InternalGetText() , -1 , &rcHolder , DT_SINGLELINE ¦ DT_CENTER ¦⇐
DT_VCENTER );
pdc->SelectObject( hfOldFont );
HICON hIc = LoadIcon(  AfxGetInstanceHandle() , MAKEINTRESOURCE( IDI_ABOUTDLL ) );
HBITMAP hBmp = LoadBitmap( AfxGetInstanceHandle() , MAKEINTRESOURCE( IDB⇐
_ASPHT0207 ) );
int iOldMM = pdc->SetMapMode( MM_TEXT );
pdc->DrawIcon( rcBounds.left + m_BorderWidth + 8 , rcBounds.top + m_BorderWidth⇐
+ 8 , hIc );
pdc->SetMapMode( iOldMM );
CDC dcMem;
dcMem.CreateCompatibleDC( pdc );
CBitmap* pOldBMP = (CBitmap*) dcMem.SelectObject( hBmp );
pdc->BitBlt( rcBounds.left + m_BorderWidth + 8 , rcBounds.bottom - m_BorderWidth⇐
- 24 ,
16, 16 , &dcMem , 0 , 0 , SRCCOPY );
}
```

2. Activate ActiveX Control Pad and create a new HTML file with the source code in Listing 2-19. Save the file as `ASPHT0207.HTM`. Then create a new HTML layout and insert a copy of `ASPHT0207.OCX` in it. Add a caption value such as `Graphics are cooler!`. Save the file as `ASPHT0207LO.ALX`. Back in your HTM file, use the Edit|Insert HTML Layout menu option to place the ALX file inside the `<HR>` tags and save the file. Bring up the page in Internet Explorer and you will see the icon proudly displayed above the caption and the bitmap below it, as shown in Figure 2-29. Congratulations! You have added icon and bitmap image display capabilities to your custom ActiveX control.

Listing 2-19 `ASPHT0207.HTM` HTML source code

```
<HTML>
<HEAD>
 <TITLE>Chapter Two Test Page 7</TITLE>
</HEAD>
<BODY>
<H1>ASPHT0207 ActiveX Control Test Page One</H1>
<HR>
<HR>
</BODY>
</HTML>
```

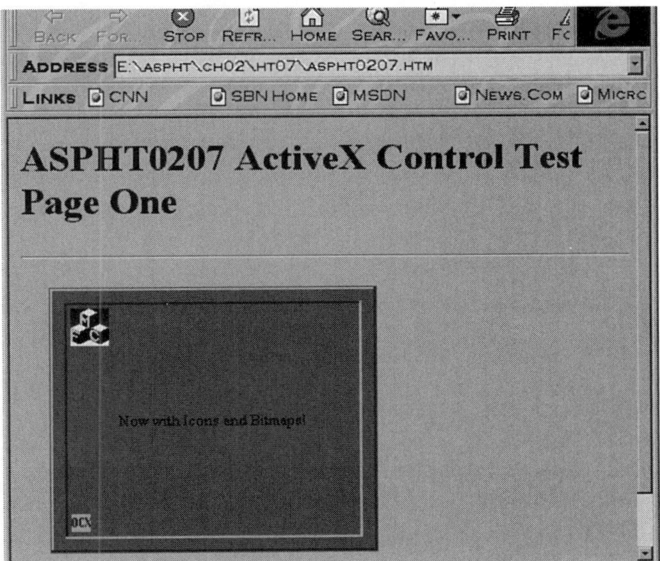

Figure 2-29 `ASPHT0207.HTM` in Internet Explorer showing the custom icon and bitmap

How It Works

The key point this How-To illustrates is very simple: The PDC imported into the `OnDraw` function is a completely functional CDC object, with all the functionality it would have in a standard MFC executable. All the drawing tricks you have learned over the years with MFC work just fine in ActiveX. There is one important change, though. Notice this code fragment:

```
HICON hIc = LoadIcon(  AfxGetInstanceHandle() , MAKEINTRESOURCE( IDI_ABOUTDLL ) );
```

Here, the special `AfxGetInstanceHandle` function is needed to get an `HINSTANCE` application handle, because the code is running inside a dynamic link library rather than an application.

Comments

This How-To demonstrates using resource icons and bitmaps. You can also use file-based bitmaps and icons with the `LoadImage` API function in virtually the same way.

COMPLEXITY
INTERMEDIATE

2.8 How do I... Make my ActiveX control's custom properties persistent using Visual C++ 5.0?

Problem

I just tried to use the ActiveX control created in this chapter with Visual Basic and discovered that none of my custom properties are being saved by the form file! Has my control broken VB, or did I miss something?

Technique

You didn't miss anything, and VB is not broken. Instead, you need to implement a special ActiveX feature called *persistence*, which allows controls to "save their state" to the disk when their container saves them as OLE 2 objects. This How-To illustrates the steps needed to implement persistence on an MFC ActiveX control by adding it to the custom control developed in the preceding How-To's. The CD contains an already created workspace with a new name but all the previous code and settings in place under CH02\HT08\ASPHT0208\. The complete control is under CH02\HT08\FINAL\ASPHT0208\.

Steps

1. Activate Visual C++ 5.0 and load the ASPHT0208 workspace, which as noted above contains all the code and settings from the previous How-To. Bring up the ASPHT0208CTL.CPP file in the text editor. Locate the DoPropExchange method and add the boldfaced code in Listing 2-20. Save the file and build ASPHT0208.OCX.

Listing 2-20 ASPHT0208CTL.CPP DoPropExchange source code

```
/////////////////////////////////////////////////////////////////////////////
// CAspht0208Ctrl::DoPropExchange - Persistence support

void CAspht0208Ctrl::DoPropExchange(CPropExchange* pPX)
{
ExchangeVersion(pPX, MAKELONG(_wVerMinor, _wVerMajor));
COleControl::DoPropExchange(pPX);

// TODO: Call PX_ functions for each persistent custom property.
PX_Color( pPX , _T("PanelColor"), m_PanelColor );
PX_Color( pPX , _T("HighlightColor"), m_HighlightColor );
PX_Color( pPX , _T("ShadowColor"), m_ShadowColor );
```

```
PX_Short( pPX , _T("BorderWidth"), m_BorderWidth );

}
```

2. Activate ActiveX Control Pad and create a new HTML file with the source code in Listing 2-21. Insert a copy of `ASPHT0208.OCX` before the second `<HR>` tag. Add a caption value such as `I'm Finished!` and set all four of the custom properties to appropriate values. Save the file as `ASPHT0208.HTM`. Bring up the page in Internet Explorer and you will see that all the settings you made in ActiveX Control Pad are now preserved, even custom properties, as shown in Figure 2-30. Congratulations! You have added custom property persistence capabilities to your custom ActiveX control and completed the intermediate phase.

Listing 2-21 ASPHT0208.HTM HTML source code

```
<HTML>
<HEAD>
 <TITLE>Chapter Two Test Page 8</TITLE>
</HEAD>
<BODY>
<H1>ASPHT0208 ActiveX Control Test Page One</H1>
<HR>
<HR>
</BODY>
</HTML>
```

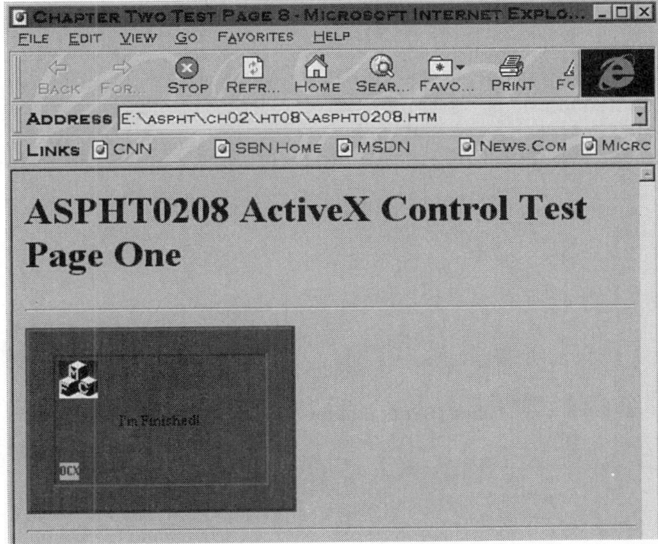

Figure 2-30 ASPHT0208.HTM in Internet Explorer showing custom properties maintained via persistence from ActiveX Control Pad

How It Works

The key to persistence is the PX_ functions, as illustrated by these lines of code:

```
PX_Color( pPX , _T("ShadowColor"), m_ShadowColor );
PX_Short( pPX , _T("BorderWidth"), m_BorderWidth );
```

When DoPropExchange is called, it calls OLE 2 functions inside MFC that find out whether to read or write the properties and how. This behavior is hidden inside the PX_ functions. There is one for each OLE 2 data type supported by the system; check the online help under PX for the list. The first parameter is the exchange structure used to keep track of everything internally; it is passed in to the function. Next is a string used to display the name of the property, cast into the Unicode environment with the _T macro. Next is the name of the member variable to be used to store and supply the actual data to be written or read. An optional final parameter holds a default value in case invalid data is found in the persistence stream.

Comments

Notice the way in which the names of the persistent properties (ShadowColor, BorderWidth) become parameters in the <OBJECT> HTML tag:

```
<OBJECT ID="Aspht02081" WIDTH=209 HEIGHT=165
     CLASSID="CLSID:EB303AA2-B4B9-11D0-B7D8-444553540000">
        <PARAM NAME="_Version" VALUE="65536">
        <PARAM NAME="_ExtentX" VALUE="5530">
        <PARAM NAME="_ExtentY" VALUE="4366">
        <PARAM NAME="_StockProps" VALUE="15">
        <PARAM NAME="Caption" VALUE="Script Me!">
        <PARAM NAME="ForeColor" VALUE="65535">
        <PARAM NAME="PanelColor" VALUE="255">
        <PARAM NAME="HighlightColor" VALUE="8421631">
        <PARAM NAME="ShadowColor" VALUE="4194432">
        <PARAM NAME="BorderWidth" VALUE="10">
    </OBJECT>
```

COMPLEXITY
INTERMEDIATE

2.9 How do I… Interact with my ActiveX control's custom events, properties, and methods using ActiveX Scripting?

Problem

Now that I have my shiny new ActiveX control, how do I interact with all these custom properties, events, and methods on a Web page?

Technique

Actually, you use much the same techniques you used in the last chapter for a standard ActiveX control, but apply them to the custom properties, methods, and events you've added! This How-To demonstrates this by controlling all the custom features of the new ActiveX control developed in this chapter with scripting on an HTML page. Although the directions here create the project by hand, you can find the entire project on the CD under `\CH02\HT09\`.

Steps

1. Activate ActiveX Control Pad. Choose File|New HTML from the menu. Enter the HTML code in Listing 2-22 except for the `<OBJECT>` tag and parameters. Save the file as `ASPHT0209.HTM`.

Listing 2-22 ASPHT0209LO.ALX HTML source code

```
<HTML>
<HEAD>
<TITLE>Chapter Two Demo Page 9</TITLE>
</HEAD>
<BODY>
<H1>ASPHT0209 Demo Page One</H1>
<SCRIPT LANGUAGE="VBScript">
<!--
Sub Aspht02081_Click()
call Aspht02081.FlipColors(1)
end sub
-->
    </SCRIPT>
<HR>
    <OBJECT ID="Aspht02081" WIDTH=209 HEIGHT=165
     CLASSID="CLSID:EB303AA2-B4B9-11D0-B7D8-444553540000">
        <PARAM NAME="_Version" VALUE="65536">
        <PARAM NAME="_ExtentX" VALUE="5530">
        <PARAM NAME="_ExtentY" VALUE="4366">
        <PARAM NAME="_StockProps" VALUE="15">
        <PARAM NAME="Caption" VALUE="Script Me!">
        <PARAM NAME="ForeColor" VALUE="65535">
        <PARAM NAME="PanelColor" VALUE="255">
        <PARAM NAME="HighlightColor" VALUE="8421631">
        <PARAM NAME="ShadowColor" VALUE="4194432">
        <PARAM NAME="BorderWidth" VALUE="10">
    </OBJECT>
<HR>
    <FORM NAME="Form1">
        <INPUT TYPE=TEXT NAME="Text1">
        <INPUT LANGUAGE="VBScript" TYPE=BUTTON VALUE="Set BorderWidth"⇐
ONCLICK="Aspht02081.BorderWidth = Document.Form1.Text1.value
call Aspht02081.Refresh()"
         NAME="Button1">
<P>
        <INPUT TYPE=TEXT NAME="Text2">
```

continued on next page

continued from previous page

```
        <INPUT LANGUAGE="VBScript" TYPE=BUTTON VALUE="Set Caption"⇐
ONCLICK="Aspht02081.Caption = Document.Form1.Text2.value
call Aspht02081.Refresh()"
         NAME="Button2">
<P>
        <INPUT TYPE=TEXT NAME="Text3">
        <INPUT LANGUAGE="VBScript" TYPE=BUTTON VALUE="Set Panel Color in Hex"
         ONCLICK="Aspht02081.PanelColor = Document.Form1.Text3.value
call Aspht02081.Refresh()"
         NAME="Button3">
        <INPUT LANGUAGE="VBScript" TYPE=BUTTON VALUE="Set HiLite Color in Hex"
         ONCLICK="Aspht02081.HighlightColor = Document.Form1.Text3.value
call Aspht02081.Refresh()"
         NAME="Button4">
        <INPUT LANGUAGE="VBScript" TYPE=BUTTON VALUE="Set Shadow Color in Hex"
         ONCLICK="Aspht02081.ShadowColor = Document.Form1.Text3.value
call Aspht02081.Refresh()"
         NAME="Button5">
<P>
    </FORM>
<HR>
</BODY>
</HTML>
```

2. Add an `ASPHT0208.OCX` ActiveX control to the page between the first two `<HR>` tags. Set its custom properties to interesting values such as those given in Listing 2-22. Save the file.

3. Bring up `ASPHT0209.HTM` in Internet Explorer and experiment with the controls. After some changes you might see a display similar to Figure 2-31, as you find you can alter all the custom properties of the control with the HTML page scripts. Congratulations! You have learned to control all your custom ActiveX control's custom properties, events, and methods fully via ActiveX Scripting.

How It Works

The key to this How-To is that as far as ActiveX Scripting is concerned, a property is a property. ActiveX doesn't know or care which properties you wrote and which ones MFC wrote! Thus, once you have written a property, method, or event using MFC and have it correctly implemented inside your control, you automatically can script it for free! What a deal.

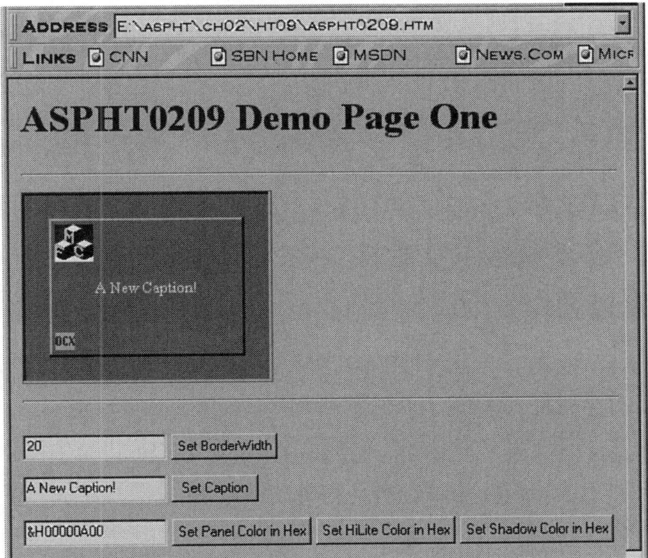

Figure 2-31 `ASPHT0209.HTM` in Internet Explorer

There are pitfalls, however! Look at this script fragment:

```
<INPUT TYPE=TEXT NAME="Text1">
        <INPUT LANGUAGE="VBScript" TYPE=BUTTON VALUE="Set BorderWidth"⇐
ONCLICK="Aspht02081.BorderWidth = Document.Form1.Text1.value
call Aspht02081.Refresh()"
         NAME="Button1">
```

Here you use the `Value` property of the `TEXT` element of `FORM`. This property does an internal conversion to match the variable to which it is being assigned. There is an alternative property, `Text`, but it would have returned a string that would have required a typecast `CInt` call prior to assigning it to the underlying `Short` property.

Comments

There are still glitches in the system. You may have noticed that the lovely color entry dialogs in ActiveX Control Pad do not work with the color properties. Microsoft is still shaking out a few bugs here. Please check the `README.TXT` file on the CD under "ActiveX Control Pad Bugs" for any last-minute information.

AX-ASP

2.10 How do I… Keep track of user-set custom properties on my custom ActiveX control with an Active Server Pages script?

Problem

I would like to be able to use ASP with my custom ActiveX control, specifically to keep track of previous custom property settings on the page when the user jumps to another page. How do I do this?

Technique

The solution you need is the ASP cookie! This How-To shows you the way to create complete, scripted HTML pages using custom ActiveX controls via ASP scripts and how to customize them using stored cookies properties on the client's machine. Although the directions here create the project by hand, you can find the entire project on the CD under \CH02\HT10\.

Steps

1. Activate your copy of ActiveX Control Pad. Start a new HTML file and add the code in Listing 2-23. Then save the file as ACTIVEXASP2.ASP (choose All Files in the type combo box to prevent adding .HTM to the filename.)

Listing 2-24 ACTIVEXASP2.ASP Active Server Pages script file

```
<%@ LANGUAGE = VBScript %>
<%
      if IsEmpty( Request("Text1")) then
        Response.Cookies("ASPHT0208")("BorderWidth") = "10"
      else
        Response.Cookies("ASPHT0208")("BorderWidth") = Request("Text1")
      end if
      if IsEmpty( Request("Text2")) then
        Response.Cookies("ASPHT0208")("Caption") = "ActiveX is Cool!"
      else
        Response.Cookies("ASPHT0208")("Caption") = Request("Text2")
      end if
      if IsEmpty( Request("Text3")) then
```

```
        Response.Cookies("ASPHT0208")("PanelColor") = "&H0000AF00"
      else
        Response.Cookies("ASPHT0208")("PanelColor") = Request("Text3")
      end if
      if IsEmpty( Request("Text4")) then
        Response.Cookies("ASPHT0208")("HighlightColor") = "&H0000FF00"
      else
        Response.Cookies("ASPHT0208")("HighlightColor") = Request("Text4")
      end if
      if IsEmpty( Request("Text5")) then
        Response.Cookies("ASPHT0208")("ShadowColor") = "&H00000A00"
      else
        Response.Cookies("ASPHT0208")("ShadowColor") = Request("Text5")
      end if
%>
<HTML>
<HEAD>
 <TITLE>ActiveX and ASP Cookies Demo Page</TITLE>
</HEAD>
<BODY>
<HTML>
<HEAD>
<TITLE>Chapter Two Demo Page 10</TITLE>
</HEAD>
<BODY>
<H1>ASPHT0210 Demo Page One</H1>
<HR>
    <SCRIPT LANGUAGE="VBScript">
<!--
Sub Aspht02081_Click()
call Aspht02081.FlipColors(1)
end sub
-->
    </SCRIPT>
<HR>
    <FORM ACTION="http://default/ASPExec/activexasp2.asp" METHOD="POST"
     ONSUBMIT="Document.Form1.Text1.value = Aspht02081.BorderWidth
Document.Form1.Text2.value = Aspht02081.Caption
Document.Form1.Text3.value = Aspht02081.PanelColor
Document.Form1.Text4.value = Aspht02081.HighlightColor
Document.Form1.Text5.value = Aspht02081.ShadowColor"
     NAME="Form1">
        <INPUT TYPE=TEXT NAME="Text1">
        <INPUT LANGUAGE="VBScript" TYPE=BUTTON VALUE="Set BorderWidth"⇐
ONCLICK="Aspht02081.BorderWidth = Document.Form1.Text1.value
call Aspht02081.Refresh()"
         NAME="Button1">
<P>
        <INPUT TYPE=TEXT NAME="Text2">
        <INPUT LANGUAGE="VBScript" TYPE=BUTTON VALUE="Set Caption"⇐
ONCLICK="Aspht02081.Caption = Document.Form1.Text2.value
call Aspht02081.Refresh()"
         NAME="Button2">
<P>
```

continued on next page

continued from previous page

```
        <INPUT TYPE=TEXT NAME="Text3">
        <INPUT LANGUAGE="VBScript" TYPE=BUTTON VALUE="Set Panel Color in Hex"
         ONCLICK="Aspht02081.PanelColor = Document.Form1.Text3.value
call Aspht02081.Refresh()"
         NAME="Button3">
<P>
        <INPUT TYPE=TEXT NAME="Text4">
        <INPUT LANGUAGE="VBScript" TYPE=BUTTON VALUE="Set HiLite Color in Hex"
         ONCLICK="Aspht02081.HighlightColor = Document.Form1.Text4.value
call Aspht02081.Refresh()"
         NAME="Button4">
<P>
        <INPUT TYPE=TEXT NAME="Text5">
        <INPUT LANGUAGE="VBScript" TYPE=BUTTON VALUE="Set Shadow Color in Hex"
         ONCLICK="Aspht02081.ShadowColor = Document.Form1.Text5.value
call Aspht02081.Refresh()"
         NAME="Button5">
<P>
<HR>
        <INPUT TYPE=SUBMIT VALUE="Press to Store Custom Settings!" NAME="Submit1">
    </FORM>
<HR>
<SCRIPT LANGUAGE="VBSCRIPT">
dim HoldBW
dim HoldCap
dim HoldPC
dim HoldHC
dim HoldSC
<%

   if IsEmpty( Request.Cookies("ASPHT0208")("BorderWidth") ) then
     Response.Write "HoldBW = 10"
   else
     Response.Write "HoldBW = " & CInt(Request.Cookies("ASPHT0208")⇐
("BorderWidth"))
   end if
%>
   Aspht02081.BorderWidth = HoldBW
   Document.Form1.Text1.Value = holdBW
<%
   AString = "10"
   QuoteString = chr( 34 )
   if IsEmpty( Request.Cookies("ASPHT0208")("Caption") ) then
     Response.Write "HoldCap = " & QuoteString & "A Default Value" & QuoteString
   else
     Response.Write "HoldCap = " & QuoteString & Request.Cookies("ASPHT0208")⇐
("Caption") & QuoteString
   end if
%>
   Aspht02081.Caption = HoldCap
   Document.Form1.Text2.Value = HoldCap
```

```
<%
   if IsEmpty( Request.Cookies("ASPHT0208")("PanelColor") ) then
     Response.Write "HoldPC = &H0000AF00"
   else
     Response.Write "HoldPC = " & CLng(Request.Cookies("ASPHT0208")("PanelColor"))
   end if
%>
   Aspht02081.PanelColor = HoldPC
  Document.Form1.Text3.Value = HoldPC
<%
   if IsEmpty( Request.Cookies("ASPHT0208")("HighlightColor") ) then
     Response.Write "HoldHC = &H0000FF00"
   else
     Response.Write "HoldHC = " & CLng(Request.Cookies("ASPHT0208")⇐
("HighlightColor"))
   end if
%>
   Aspht02081.HighlightColor = HoldHC
   Document.Form1.Text4.Value = HoldHC
<%
   if IsEmpty( Request.Cookies("ASPHT0208")("ShadowColor") ) then
     Response.Write "HoldSC = &H00000A00"
   else
     Response.Write "HoldSC = " & CLng(Request.Cookies("ASPHT0208")⇐
("ShadowColor"))
   end if
%>
   Aspht02081.ShadowColor = HoldSC
   Document.Form1.Text5.Value = HoldSC
</SCRIPT>
</BODY>
</HTML>
```

2. Use the Control Pad to insert a copy of `ASPHT0208.OCX` into the ASP page just above the `<HR>` tag above the `<FORM>` statement. Be sure to create some initial custom property settings! Save the file.

3. Activate Internet Explorer. In the address field, type in `HTTP://DEFAULT/ASPEXEC/ACTIVEXASP2.ASP` and press Return. The page will initially display using the settings you gave it in ActiveX Control Pad. Use the text and button controls to change all the settings to new values, then press the Press to Store Custom Settings! button. The page will refresh and you will see that your settings are not lost. Navigate to another page or two and return to `ACTIVEXASP2.ASP`. Instead of coming up with the default settings from ActiveX Control Pad again, the file displays the custom settings you entered last time, as shown in Figure 2-32. You have learned to use ASP to store custom ActiveX Control properties settings.

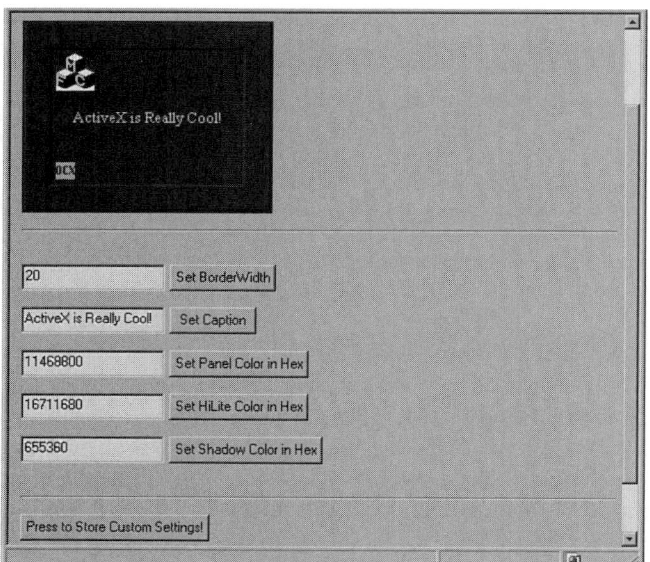

Figure 2-32 ACTIVEXASP2.ASP in Internet Explorer showing custom property settings maintained between pages via cookies

How It Works

Be warned, what you are about to learn may sprain your brain; it nearly did mine!

Some of you may remember Edgar Allan Poe's famous line about the world being "a dream within a dream." Well, to achieve the effect I wanted for this How-To, ASP had to become a "script within a script!" There are two separate and vital parts to this How-To. First, check out these lines of ASP script:

```
<%
if IsEmpty( Request("Text1")) then
  Response.Cookies("ASPHT0208")("BorderWidth") = "10"
else
  Response.Cookies("ASPHT0208")("BorderWidth") = Request("Text1")
end if
if IsEmpty( Request("Text2")) then
  Response.Cookies("ASPHT0208")("Caption") = "ActiveX is Cool!"
else
  Response.Cookies("ASPHT0208")("Caption") = Request("Text2")
end if
if IsEmpty( Request("Text3")) then
  Response.Cookies("ASPHT0208")("PanelColor") = "&H0000AF00"
else
  Response.Cookies("ASPHT0208")("PanelColor") = Request("Text3")
end if
if IsEmpty( Request("Text4")) then
  Response.Cookies("ASPHT0208")("HighlightColor") = "&H0000FF00"
```

```
      else
        Response.Cookies("ASPHT0208")("HighlightColor") = Request("Text4")
      end if
      if IsEmpty( Request("Text5")) then
        Response.Cookies("ASPHT0208")("ShadowColor") = "&H00000A00"
      else
        Response.Cookies("ASPHT0208")("ShadowColor") = Request("Text5")
      end if
%>
```

Notice that they are placed in the header of the HTML page. This is important; if you try to place them anywhere else, you will get an ASP error because they write header information and that can be done only prior to sending the HTML body from the server. Their functionality involves using the `Request` object, which encapsulates all the information about the page and client computer currently available to the server. Each block of code checks to see if one of the text elements from the `FORM` block has sent its information using its name; if there is no data for that `FORM` element in the response, the server returns a variable of type `Empty`, which will evaluate to `true` on the `IsEmpty` function and trigger the first statement; otherwise it will return the value from `FORM` and that will be nonempty and trigger the second statement. In either case, the `Response` object's `Cookies` property is invoked with a double-keyed entry on the name of the custom control and a property name and either a default value or the value from the `FORM` object. It is important to note that none of this is ever seen by the HTML page; it all takes place on the server.

Now check out the second major ASP script block:

```
<SCRIPT LANGUAGE="VBSCRIPT">
dim HoldBW
dim HoldCap
dim HoldPC
dim HoldHC
dim HoldSC
<%

   if IsEmpty( Request.Cookies("ASPHT0208")("BorderWidth") ) then
     Response.Write "HoldBW = 10"
   else
     Response.Write "HoldBW = " & CInt( Request.Cookies("ASPHT0208")⇐
("BorderWidth"))
   end if
%>
   Aspht02081.BorderWidth = HoldBW
   Document.Form1.Text1.Value = holdBW
<%
   AString = "10"
   QuoteString = chr( 34 )
   if IsEmpty( Request.Cookies("ASPHT0208")("Caption") ) then
     Response.Write "HoldCap = " & QuoteString & "A Default Value" & QuoteString
   else
     Response.Write "HoldCap = " & QuoteString & Request.Cookies("ASPHT0208")⇐
("Caption") & QuoteString
   end if
```

```
%>
   Aspht02081.Caption = HoldCap
   Document.Form1.Text2.Value = HoldCap
<%
   if IsEmpty( Request.Cookies("ASPHT0208")("PanelColor") ) then
     Response.Write "HoldPC = &H0000AF00"
   else
     Response.Write "HoldPC = " & CLng(Request.Cookies("ASPHT0208")("PanelColor"))
   end if
%>
   Aspht02081.PanelColor = HoldPC
  Document.Form1.Text3.Value = HoldPC
<%
   if IsEmpty( Request.Cookies("ASPHT0208")("HighlightColor") ) then
     Response.Write "HoldHC = &H0000FF00"
   else
     Response.Write "HoldHC = " & CLng(Request.Cookies("ASPHT0208")⇐
("HighlightColor"))
   end if
%>
   Aspht02081.HighlightColor = HoldHC
   Document.Form1.Text4.Value = HoldHC
<%
   if IsEmpty( Request.Cookies("ASPHT0208")("ShadowColor") ) then
     Response.Write "HoldSC = &H00000A00"
   else
     Response.Write "HoldSC = " & CLng(Request.Cookies("ASPHT0208")⇐
("ShadowColor"))
   end if
%>
   Aspht02081.ShadowColor = HoldSC
   Document.Form1.Text5.Value = HoldSC
</SCRIPT>
```

This is where the nested scripting is required. It is vital to understand when using ASP that ASP scripts are never seen by the HTML page, even though they can refer to objects on that page. If all the interaction takes place inside the `<%%>` tags, the net effect on the HTML result is zero! To cause effects from ASP scripts on the HTML page, you need a combination of explicit `<SCRIPT>` tags in the HTML and `Response.write` statements in ASP Scripting. Notice this particular fragment of ASP wizardry:

```
<%
   AString = "10"
   QuoteString = chr( 34 )
   if IsEmpty( Request.Cookies("ASPHT0208")("Caption") ) then
     Response.Write "HoldCap = " & QuoteString & "A Default Value" & QuoteString
   else
     Response.Write "HoldCap = " & QuoteString &⇐
Request.Cookies("ASPHT0208")("Caption") & QuoteString
   end if
%>
```

In these lines, a string is written into the HTML page, either as a default value or as the value held in the **Cookies** object. Try this using **"** or **""** and you will get errors out the wazoo! Instead, the script tricks the entire system by using the **CHR** function to create a string variable holding a single quote. What HTML gets written to the page depends on the values found in the **Request.Cookies** object property. In either case, however, the ASP script itself has zero effect on the final user display. Instead, the HTML scripting statements must be parsed and displayed by Internet Explorer to set the custom properties of the custom ActiveX control at runtime! Whew!

As a final example, check out the actual HTML created by the above ASP page shown in Listing 2-24, after some custom values were entered into the cookies.

Listing 2-24 Actual HTML source code sent to the browser by ACTIVEXASP2.ASP

```
<HTML>
<HEAD>
 <TITLE>ActiveX and ASP Cookies Demo Page</TITLE>
</HEAD>
<BODY>
<HTML>
<HEAD>
<TITLE>Chapter Two Demo Page 10</TITLE>
</HEAD>
<BODY>
<H1>ASPHT0210 Demo Page One</H1>
<HR>
    <SCRIPT LANGUAGE="VBScript">
<!--
Sub Aspht02081_Click()
call Aspht02081.FlipColors(1)
end sub
-->
    </SCRIPT>
    <OBJECT ID="Aspht02081" WIDTH=209 HEIGHT=165
     CLASSID="CLSID:EB303AA2-B4B9-11D0-B7D8-444553540000">
        <PARAM NAME="_Version" VALUE="65536">
        <PARAM NAME="_ExtentX" VALUE="5530">
        <PARAM NAME="_ExtentY" VALUE="4366">
        <PARAM NAME="_StockProps" VALUE="15">
        <PARAM NAME="Caption" VALUE="Script Me!">
        <PARAM NAME="ForeColor" VALUE="65535">
        <PARAM NAME="PanelColor" VALUE="255">
        <PARAM NAME="HighlightColor" VALUE="8421631">
        <PARAM NAME="ShadowColor" VALUE="4194432">
        <PARAM NAME="BorderWidth" VALUE="10">
    </OBJECT>
<HR>
    <FORM ACTION="http://default/ASPExec/activexasp2.asp" METHOD="POST"
     ONSUBMIT="Document.Form1.Text1.value = Aspht02081.BorderWidth
Document.Form1.Text2.value = Aspht02081.Caption
Document.Form1.Text3.value = Aspht02081.PanelColor
```

continued on next page

continued from previous page

```
Document.Form1.Text4.value = Aspht02081.HighlightColor
Document.Form1.Text5.value = Aspht02081.ShadowColor"
     NAME="Form1">
        <INPUT TYPE=TEXT NAME="Text1">
        <INPUT LANGUAGE="VBScript" TYPE=BUTTON VALUE="Set BorderWidth"⇐
ONCLICK="Aspht02081.BorderWidth = Document.Form1.Text1.value
call Aspht02081.Refresh()"
         NAME="Button1">
<P>
        <INPUT TYPE=TEXT NAME="Text2">
        <INPUT LANGUAGE="VBScript" TYPE=BUTTON VALUE="Set Caption"⇐
ONCLICK="Aspht02081.Caption = Document.Form1.Text2.value
call Aspht02081.Refresh()"
         NAME="Button2">
<P>
        <INPUT TYPE=TEXT NAME="Text3">
        <INPUT LANGUAGE="VBScript" TYPE=BUTTON VALUE="Set Panel Color in Hex"
         ONCLICK="Aspht02081.PanelColor = Document.Form1.Text3.value
call Aspht02081.Refresh()"
         NAME="Button3">
<P>
        <INPUT TYPE=TEXT NAME="Text4">
        <INPUT LANGUAGE="VBScript" TYPE=BUTTON VALUE="Set HiLite Color in Hex"
         ONCLICK="Aspht02081.HighlightColor = Document.Form1.Text4.value
call Aspht02081.Refresh()"
         NAME="Button4">
<P>
        <INPUT TYPE=TEXT NAME="Text5">
        <INPUT LANGUAGE="VBScript" TYPE=BUTTON VALUE="Set Shadow Color in Hex"
         ONCLICK="Aspht02081.ShadowColor = Document.Form1.Text5.value
call Aspht02081.Refresh()"
         NAME="Button5">
<P>
<HR>
        <INPUT TYPE=SUBMIT VALUE="Press to Store Custom Settings!" NAME="Submit1">
    </FORM>
<HR>
<SCRIPT LANGUAGE="VBSCRIPT">
dim HoldBW
dim HoldCap
dim HoldPC
dim HoldHC
dim HoldSC
HoldBW = 20
   Aspht02081.BorderWidth = HoldBW
   Document.Form1.Text1.Value = holdBW
HoldCap = "ActiveX is Really Cool!"
   Aspht02081.Caption = HoldCap
   Document.Form1.Text2.Value = HoldCap
HoldPC = 11468800
   Aspht02081.PanelColor = HoldPC
  Document.Form1.Text3.Value = HoldPC
HoldHC = 16711680
```

```
   Aspht02081.HighlightColor = HoldHC
   Document.Form1.Text4.Value = HoldHC
HoldSC = 655360
   Aspht02081.ShadowColor = HoldSC
   Document.Form1.Text5.Value = HoldSC
</SCRIPT>
</BODY>
</HTML>
```

Now *that's* power. All the final script block was dynamically created; imagine the possibilities that capability unleashes!

Comments

It is important to note that starting a new session (that is, closing and restarting Internet Explorer) will destroy the `Cookies` values because they have no expiration date. Although you can set cookies to last beyond a single user session, many people consider this a breach of privacy. Cookies and their uses remain one of the hottest topics on the WWW today.

CHAPTER 3

ADVANCED ACTIVEX: SPECIAL FEATURES, CONTROL CONTAINERS, ACTIVEX DOCUMENTS, AND VBSCRIPT 2.0

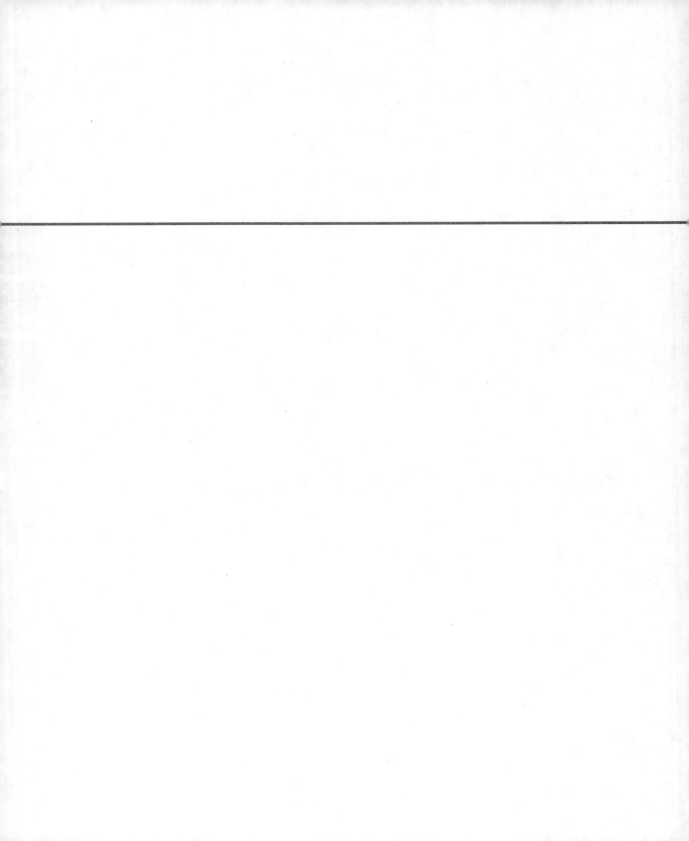

3

ADVANCED ACTIVEX: SPECIAL FEATURES, CONTROL CONTAINERS, ACTIVEX DOCUMENTS, AND VBSCRIPT 2.0

How do I...

3.4 Create a transparent custom ActiveX control with advanced optimization features using Visual C++ 5.0?

3.5 Create a nonvisual ActiveX control in Visual C++ 5.0?

3.6 Create an application that can use ActiveX controls at runtime with Visual C++ 5.0?

3.7 Create an ActiveX document server using Visual C++ 5.0?

3.8 Create an ActiveX document container using Visual C++ 5.0?

3.9 Create ActiveX documents on an HTML page entirely at runtime with VBScript 2.0?

3.10 Use Active Server Pages with the VBScript 2.0 `TextStream` object to produce cookies that last between sessions?

At this point, you know how to create and use very powerful custom ActiveX controls, but there are plenty of powerful, advanced features of the ActiveX system you have not yet tapped! In this chapter, you will learn how to use property pages, both stock and custom, to allow visual input of your control's data. Fonts and images will come under your control, as will a number of subtle but powerful advanced features and optimization options. Then you will learn how to create the two remaining special types of ActiveX controls not yet covered: those that are invisible at runtime (such as a Timer control) and those that can accept and display new ActiveX controls at runtime (Control Container controls). Then the older OLE system reappears as the new and potent ActiveX `document` class, which you will learn to both create and use in a new document type How-To and document server How-To. Last but not least, two of the very useful features of VBScript 2.0 are covered: runtime ActiveX document object creation and `TextStream` objects. It is time to start up Visual C++ 5.0 and become an ActiveX master!

3.1 Use Stock and Custom Property Pages with My ActiveX Control in Visual C++ 5.0

Windows 95 and NT provide a slick mechanism for entering the values of groups of settings at the same time: the Property Page dialog. This How-To explains just how to use both stock and custom property pages with your custom MFC ActiveX control from How-To 2.8.

3.2 Use Custom Font Features with My ActiveX Control Using Visual C++ 5.0

Because there are some problems with the stock `Font` property, this How-To gives precise instructions on adding a custom `Font` property to your MFC ActiveX control from How-To 3.1, including hooking it up to the font property page.

3.3 Use Custom Images with My ActiveX Control with Visual C++ 5.0

Users often like to customize image-oriented ActiveX controls with their own graphics files. This How-To shows you all the steps needed to implement a custom image property for the MFC ActiveX control developed in the previous How-To and how to include it in a stock picture property page.

3.4 Create a Transparent Custom ActiveX Control with Advanced Optimization Features Using Visual C++ 5.0

A number of advanced and optimization features are available to MFC ActiveX controls in Visual C++ 5.0, including transparency and fast drawing. This How-To explains how to include these features in the two versions of the ActiveX control from the previous How-To.

3.5 Create a Nonvisual ActiveX Control in Visual C++ 5.0

Some days you just don't feel like being seen, and the same is true of your ActiveX controls! This How-To illustrates how to implement a Timer control in MFC using Visual C++ 5.0.

3.6 Create an Application that Can Use ActiveX Controls at Runtime with Visual C++ 5.0

The type of executable that can host ActiveX controls at runtime is called a Control Container application. This How-To shows you the steps to create a simple but effective container application that uses one of the previous How-To's ActiveX control.

3.7 Create an ActiveX Document Server Using Visual C++ 5.0

OLE isn't dead, it's just changed its name! Now OLE documents (DocObjects) are called ActiveX documents, and servers for them can be created directly in MFC with help from the Class Wizard. This How-To implements a very simple mouse-based pen document type and its server.

3.8 Create an ActiveX Document Container Using Visual C++ 5.0

Now that you can create your own types of ActiveX document files, it would be even nicer to include them in an application! This How-To shows the steps required to include support for an ActiveX document container in an MFC application.

3.9 Create ActiveX Documents on an HTML Page Entirely at Runtime with VBScript 2.0

Although it is nice to use a helper environment such as ActiveX Control Pad, sometimes you have to create HTML pages entirely at runtime. This How-To shows how the new VBScript 2.0 runtime object creation syntax permits this needed flexibility.

3.10 Use Active Server Pages with the VBScript 2.0 `TextStream` Object to Produce Cookies that Last Between Sessions

The main drawback of cookies is that they go away between sessions unless they are given an expiration date, and many users consider that intrusive. This How-To uses the VBScript 2.0 `TextStream` object with Active Server Pages (ASP) to create a "server cookie" that stores settings between sessions.

3.1 How do I...
Use stock and custom property pages with my ActiveX control in Visual C++ 5.0?

Problem

I just noticed the slick way some commercial ActiveX controls let users modify their properties, using a tabbed dialog box. Can I do this with my custom ActiveX control?

Technique

That clever tabbed dialog box is really just a Windows 95/NT Applications Programming Interface (API) facility called a *property page*. This How-To builds on the ActiveX control created in How-To 2.8 to add MFC's built-in support for property pages for both custom and stock properties. The CD contains an already created workspace with a new name but all the previous code and settings in place under `CH03\HT01\ASPHT0301\`. The complete control is under `CH03\HT01\FINAL\ASPHT0301\`.

Steps

1. Activate Visual C++ 5.0 and load the `ASPHT0301` workspace, which as noted above contains all the code and settings from the How-To 2.8. Open the `ASPHT0301CTL.CPP` file and find the code section marked `Property Pages` in the comments. Enter the boldfaced code in Listing 3-1 to add a stock color property page to the control's default property page.

Listing 3-1 ASPHT0301CTL.CPP property pages source code

```
/////////////////////////////////////////////////////////////////////////////
// Property pages

// TODO: Add more property pages as needed.  Remember to increase the count!
BEGIN_PROPPAGEIDS(CAspht0301Ctrl, 2)
PROPPAGEID(CAspht0301PropPage::guid)
PROPPAGEID( CLSID_CColorPropPage )
END_PROPPAGEIDS(CAspht0301Ctrl)
```

2. Activate the Resource tab in the Project viewer pane; once it has compiled the project's resources, open the Dialog entry. Then choose Insert|Resource... from the menu. In the dialog box, select the Dialog|IDD_OLE_PROPPAGE_SMALL entry and press New, as shown in Figure 3-1.

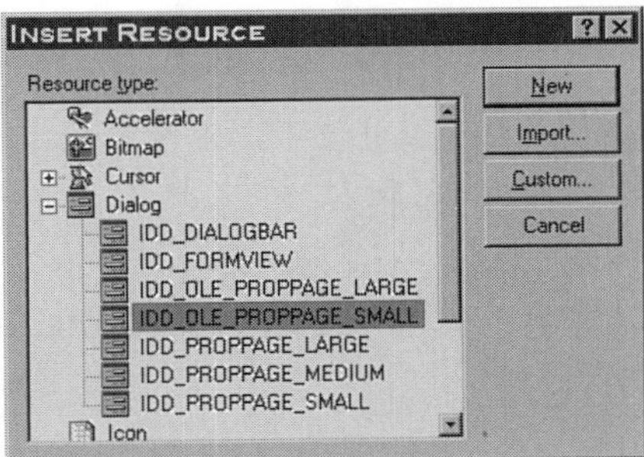

Figure 3-1 Inserting a new OLE property page resource dialog in Visual C++ 5.0

3. After the system creates the new resource, the resource will appear in the resource editor window of the C++ integrated development environment (IDE). From the View menu, select Properties. Then click on the Styles tab and you will see a display similar to Figure 3-2. Notice that the styles are set to no border and no title bar. Dismiss the properties dialog.

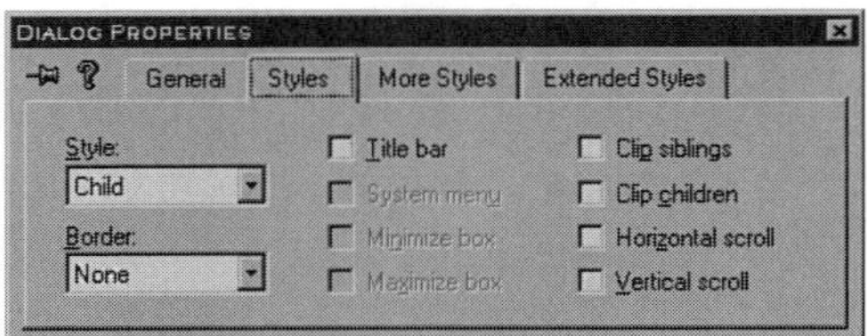

Figure 3-2 The properties dialog for the OLE Property Page dialog in the C++ IDE resource editor

4. Double-click on the surface of the dialog in the resource editor window; this will bring up the Class Wizard dialog and a confirmation dialog to create a new class for the dialog, as shown in Figure 3-3. Click OK. The New Class dialog will appear; select `COlePropertyPage` as the base class for the dialog, and enter `CCustColorPropPage` as its name. Your display should look very similar to that shown in Figure 3-4. Press OK on both dialogs to add the new class to your project.

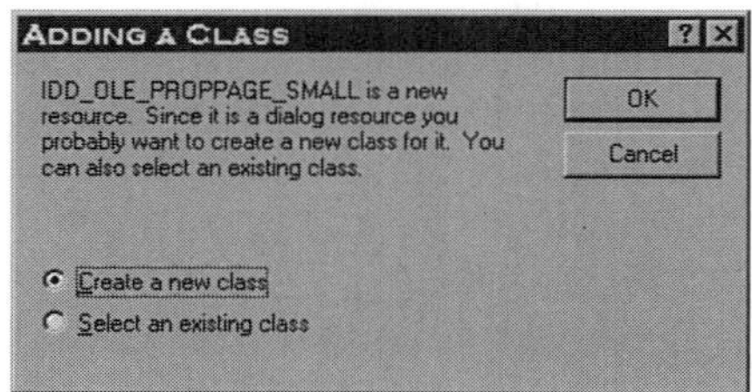

Figure 3-3 Confirming creation of a new class for the dialog property page

5. Open the `ASPHT0301CTL.CPP` file in the text editor again. Find the Property Pages macro and enter the boldfaced changes in Listing 3-2. Save the workspace.

Listing 3-2 `ASPHT0301CTL.CPP` property pages source code

```
/////////////////////////////////////////////////////////////////////////////
// Property pages

// TODO: Add more property pages as needed.  Remember to increase the count!
BEGIN_PROPPAGEIDS(CAspht0301Ctrl, 3)
PROPPAGEID(CAspht0301PropPage::guid)
PROPPAGEID( CLSID_CColorPropPage )
PROPPAGEID(CCustColorPropPage::guid)
END_PROPPAGEIDS(CAspht0301Ctrl)
```

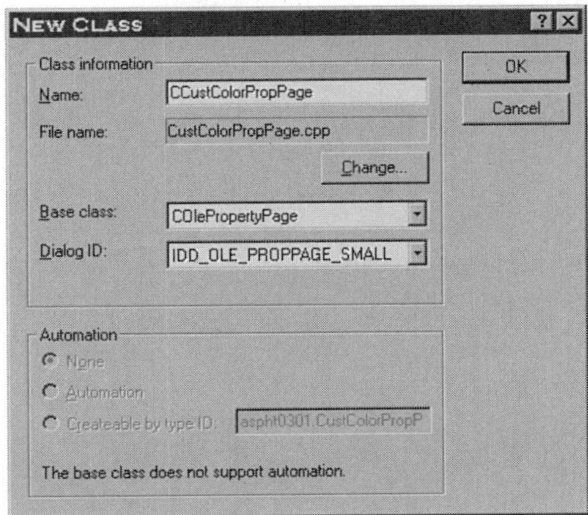

Figure 3-4 New class information entered in the New Class dialog

6. Still in `ASPHT0301CTL.CPP`, move up to the top of the file and enter Listing 3-3 to include the header file for the new dialog class.

Listing 3-3 `ASPHT0301CTL.CPP` header file includes source code

```
// Aspht0301Ctl.cpp : Implementation of the CAspht0301Ctrl ActiveX Control class.
#include "stdafx.h"
#include "aspht0301.h"
#include "Aspht0301Ctl.h"
#include "Aspht0301Ppg.h"
#include "CustColorPropPage.h"
```

7. Move back to the Resource tab in the Project pane and activate the String Table resource in the editor window. Select the blank last line and begin typing; this will bring up the Properties dialog for the entry. Give it a caption of `Custom Color Property Page` and an ID of `IDS_CUSTOM_COLOR_PPG`. Repeat this procedure for another entry with a caption of `Custom 3D Colors` and an ID of `IDS_CUSTOM_COLOR_PPG_CAPTION`, as shown in Figure 3-5. Save the workspace files.

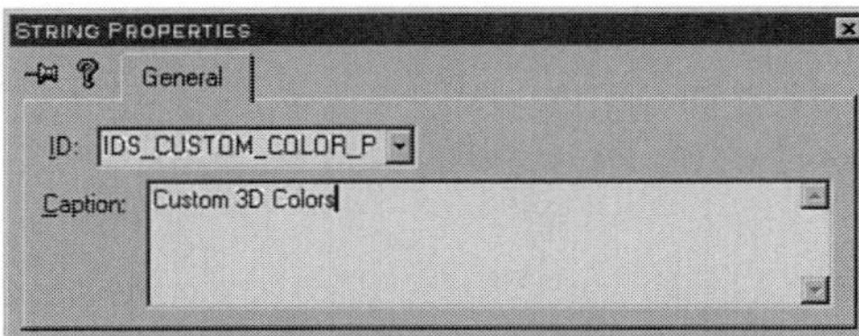

Figure 3-5 Entering new String Table resources for the new property page dialog

8. Open the `CUSTCOLORPROPPAGE.CPP` file in the text editor. Locate the code in Listing 3-4 and make the boldfaced changes. Save the workspace.

Listing 3-4 CUSTCOLORPROPPAGE.CPP source code

```
/////////////////////////////////////////////////////////////////////////////
// CCustColorPropPage::CCustColorPropPageFactory::UpdateRegistry -
// Adds or removes system registry entries for CCustColorPropPage

BOOL CCustColorPropPage::CCustColorPropPageFactory::UpdateRegistry(BOOL bRegister)
{
// TODO: Define string resource for page type; replace '0' below with ID.

if (bRegister)
return AfxOleRegisterPropertyPageClass(AfxGetInstanceHandle(),
m_clsid, IDS_CUSTOM_COLOR_PPG);
else
return AfxOleUnregisterClass(m_clsid, NULL);
}


/////////////////////////////////////////////////////////////////////////////
// CCustColorPropPage::CCustColorPropPage - Constructor

// TODO: Define string resource for page caption; replace '0' below with ID.

CCustColorPropPage::CCustColorPropPage() :
COlePropertyPage(IDD, IDS_CUSTOM_COLOR_PPG_CAPTION)
{
//{{AFX_DATA_INIT(CCustColorPropPage)
// NOTE: ClassWizard will add member initialization here
//    DO NOT EDIT what you see in these blocks of generated code !
//}}AFX_DATA_INIT
}
```

9. Open the `IDD_PROPPAGE_ASPHT0301` Dialog resource in the resource editor window of the IDE. Add two static Text controls and two Edit controls in the approximate layout shown in Figure 3-6. Bring up the Properties dialog for each control; give the top Static control an ID of `IDC_CAPTION_TEXT` and a caption of `Caption Text:`; give the bottom Static control an ID of `IDC_BORDER_WIDTH` and a caption of `Border Width:`; give the top Edit control an ID of `IDC_CAPTION_EDIT` and the bottom Edit control an ID of `IDC_BORDER_WIDTH_EDIT`. Save the workspace.

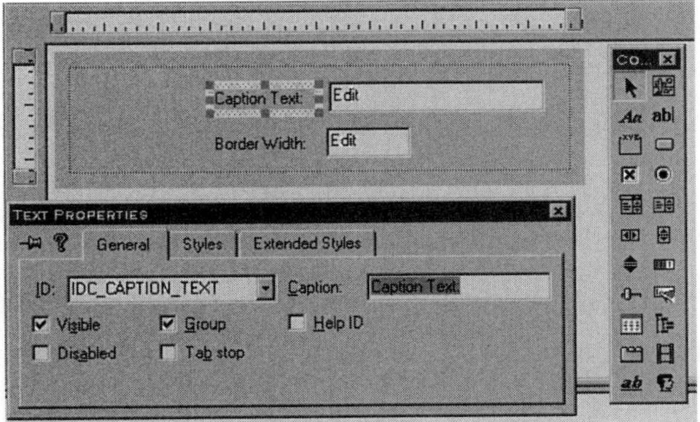

Figure 3-6 Layout of the controls on the standard property page supplied with MFC ActiveX controls

10. Press CTRL and double-click the upper Edit control. The MFC Class Wizard Add Member Variable dialog box appears. Set its properties to a member variable name of `m_Caption`, a category of `Value`, a variable type of `CString`, and an optional property name of `Caption`. Your finished dialog box should appear very similar to that shown in Figure 3-7. Press OK. Do the same for the other Edit control, giving it a member variable name of `m_BorderWidth`, a category of `Value`, a variable type of `short`, and an optional property name of `BorderStyle`. (Don't worry that this seems wrong; you'll fix it in a moment! By including a property name now, even an incorrect one, you make sure the wizard includes the proper entries in its generated code, a trick useful in other circumstances.) Save the workspace.

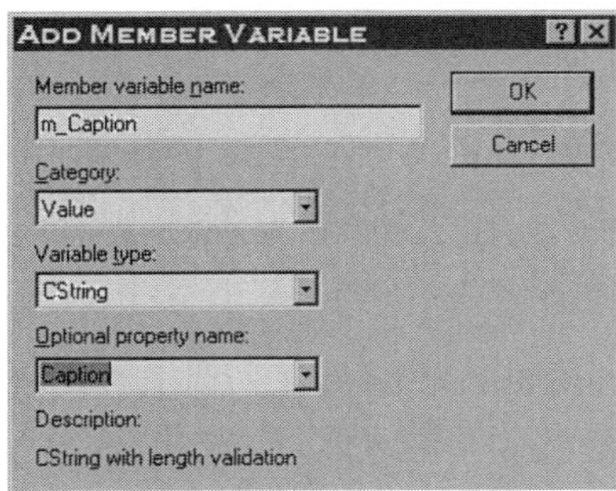

Figure 3-7 Adding a member variable to connect the Edit controls with data elements

11. In a similar fashion, open the Custom Colors Property Page dialog in the resource editor window of the IDE and position three Caption and three Edit controls on it in a layout similar to that shown in Figure 3-8. Give the three static controls IDs of `IDC_STATIC1`, `IDC_STATIC2`, and `IDC_STATIC3` (left to right) and the Edit controls IDs of `IDC_EDIT3`, `IDC_EDIT4`, and `IDC_EDIT5` (left to right). Give the leftmost Static control a caption of `Panel Color (Dec):`, the middle Static control a caption of `Highlight Color (Dec):`, and the rightmost Static control a caption of `Shadow Color (Dec):`. Use the CTRL-double-click method to add three member variables to the dialog class linked to the Edit controls with member variable names of `m_PanelColor` for `IDC_EDIT3`, `m_HighlightColor` for `IDC_EDIT4`, and `m_ShadowColor` for `IDC_EDIT5`. Give each a variable type of `DWORD`, a category of `Value`, and an optional property of `BackColor`. (Again, don't be concerned that this isn't right; it will be fixed next!) Save the project.

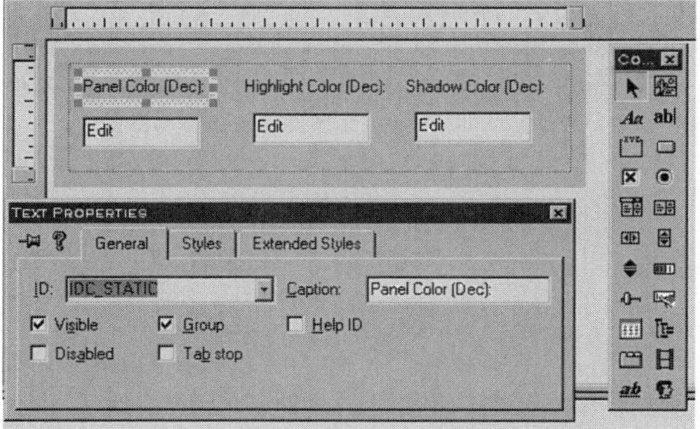

Figure 3-8 The layout of the Custom Colors Property Page dialog

12. Open the `ASPHT0301PPG.CPP` file in the text editor. Locate the `DoDataExchange` method and enter the boldfaced code in Listing 3-5, changing the information placed by the wizard to connect the Edit control to the correct property of the ActiveX control. Save the workspace.

Listing 3-5 ASPHT0301PPG.CPP source code

```
//////////////////////////////////////////////////////////////////////////////
// CAspht0301PropPage::DoDataExchange - Moves data between page and properties

void CAspht0301PropPage::DoDataExchange(CDataExchange* pDX)
{
//{{AFX_DATA_MAP(CAspht0301PropPage)
DDP_Text(pDX, IDC_CAPTION_EDIT, m_Caption, _T("Caption") );
DDP_Text(pDX, IDC_BORDER_WIDTH_EDIT, m_BorderWidth, _T("BorderWidth") );
DDX_Text(pDX, IDC_CAPTION_EDIT, m_Caption);
DDX_Text(pDX, IDC_BORDER_WIDTH_EDIT, m_BorderWidth);
//}}AFX_DATA_MAP
DDP_PostProcessing(pDX);
}
```

13. Open the `CUSTCOLORPROPPAGE.CPP` file in the text editor. Locate the `DoDataExchange` method and enter the boldfaced code in Listing 3-6, changing the information placed by the wizard to connect the Edit controls to the correct properties of the ActiveX control. Save the workspace.

Listing 3-6 CUSTCOLORPROPPAGE.CPP source code

```
//////////////////////////////////////////////////////////////////////////////
void CCustColorPropPage::DoDataExchange(CDataExchange* pDX)
{
// NOTE: ClassWizard will add DDP, DDX, and DDV calls here
//    DO NOT EDIT what you see in these blocks of generated code !
//{{AFX_DATA_MAP(CCustColorPropPage)
DDP_Text(pDX, IDC_EDIT3, m_PanelColor, _T("PanelColor") );
DDX_Text(pDX, IDC_EDIT3, m_PanelColor);
DDP_Text(pDX, IDC_EDIT4, m_HighlightColor, _T("HighlightColor") );
DDX_Text(pDX, IDC_EDIT4, m_HighlightColor);
DDP_Text(pDX, IDC_EDIT5, m_ShadowColor, _T("ShadowColor") );
DDX_Text(pDX, IDC_EDIT5, m_ShadowColor);
//}}AFX_DATA_MAP
DDP_PostProcessing(pDX);
}
```

14. Build `ASPHT0301.OCX`. Then activate the ActiveX Control Test Container tool, press the Insert OLE Control button, and from the dialog box select `ASPHT0301`. Resize the control to a comfortable size, then press the Properties button and push the Invoke Properties Verb button. You will see that the newly created property pages are now linked to their properties of the running ActiveX control. Now press the Colors tab and you will see the stock property page for colors, as shown in Figure 3-9. Try setting the caption, border width, and three custom color properties using only the property pages; you will find they work correctly and produce a custom display similar to that shown in Figure 3-10. Congratulations! You have mastered adding fully functioning custom property pages to your custom ActiveX control.

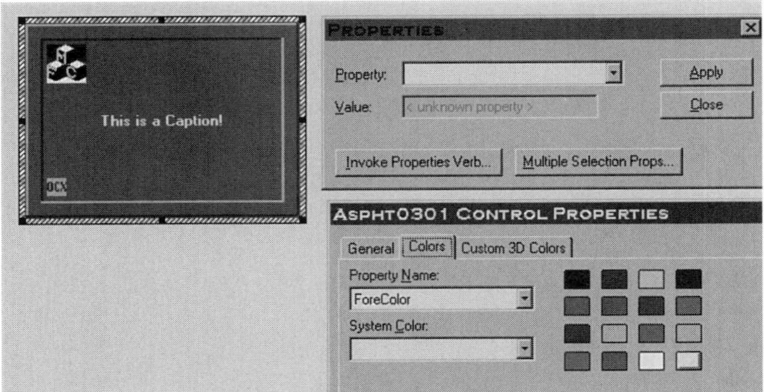

Figure 3-9 The stock colors property page for the custom ActiveX control in the ActiveX Control Test Container tool

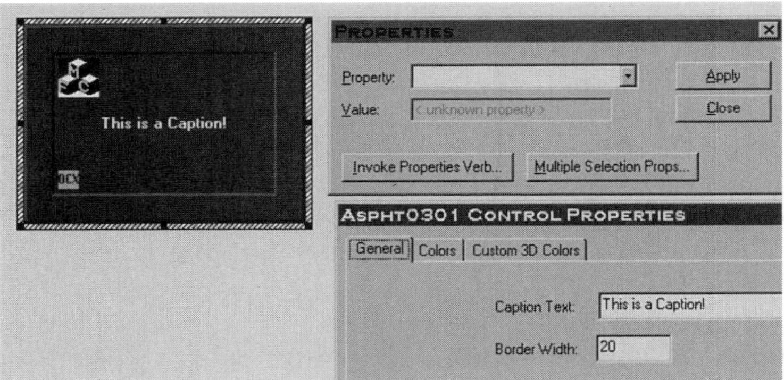

Figure 3-10 Custom property pages at work with the custom ActiveX control

How It Works

Whew! These advanced How-To's contain a lot of material, or some very complex material, or both; this one fits into the third category! Four separate major processes are required to accomplish the functionality of this How-To: stock property pages, custom dialog resources, custom string table resources, and dialog box control messaging macros. Each is explained in its own section.

Notice this code fragment from step 1:

```
BEGIN_PROPPAGEIDS(CAspht0301Ctrl, 2)
PROPPAGEID(CAspht0301PropPage::guid)
PROPPAGEID( CLSID_CColorPropPage )
END_PROPPAGEIDS(CAspht0301Ctrl)
```

There are two factors at work here. The first is the **PROPPAGEID** macro, which contains the stock property page identifier **CLSID_CColorPropPage**, and the other is the increase in the total page count number, which is the second parameter of the **BEGIN_PROPPAGEIDS** macro. This technique can be used to add any of the three stock property pages, as will be seen in the next two How-To's. No other code is required; the pages hook up automatically to all properties of the control that support their data type.

The next element is the complex process needed to insert and connect the new Dialog Box resource to serve as the new custom property page. Although technically any Dialog Box resource type would have worked, using the OLE type produces automatic settings that fit the OLE system; this is a new feature of VC 5. The new page must be descended from **COlePropertyPage** so that it will respond properly in the OLE environment. Now notice the way that the custom property page is added to the **PROPPAGEID** macros:

```
BEGIN_PROPPAGEIDS(CAspht0301Ctrl, 3)
PROPPAGEID(CAspht0301PropPage::guid)
PROPPAGEID( CLSID_CColorPropPage )
PROPPAGEID(CCustColorPropPage::guid)
END_PROPPAGEIDS(CAspht0301Ctrl)
```

The syntax is critical here, because both the dialog class name and its **::guid** member are required to link the code from the dialog box into the property page at runtime correctly. A different dialog class would use its name, but keep the **::guid** the same. Again, be sure to increment the total page count or things will go to heck fast!

Two small weaknesses in the otherwise excellent automatic code generation are the need to insert the header file reference for the dialog box class file manually and the requirement to add both the String Table resources for the ID and caption for the new dialog box and their IDs in the OLE registration and constructor code manually. Do not forget these steps!

The final step in the process is to add the controls desired to the dialogs of the property pages (both the default one created with the MFC project and the custom one) and then to connect them to class member variables. This is done via the Add Member Variable Wizard dialog, but again a small glitch appears! Although the process works fine for stock properties, it cannot (obviously) know about custom ones. Therefore, a default stock property must be selected for each new member variable so that a proper entry is written into the data exchange function. Now notice the following code fragment:

```
DDP_Text(pDX, IDC_EDIT3, m_PanelColor, _T("PanelColor") );
DDX_Text(pDX, IDC_EDIT3, m_PanelColor);
DDP_Text(pDX, IDC_EDIT4, m_HighlightColor, _T("HighlightColor") );
DDX_Text(pDX, IDC_EDIT4, m_HighlightColor);
```

continued on next page

continued from previous page

```
DDP_Text(pDX, IDC_EDIT5, m_ShadowColor, _T("ShadowColor") );
DDX_Text(pDX, IDC_EDIT5, m_ShadowColor);
```

Here we committed the cardinal sin of editing automatically generated code, but we have a good excuse: We know what we are doing! The only change is to replace the default property value string in the `DDP_Text` macros with the correct one. (Remember that the `DDX` macros connect the raw data in the controls with their member variables, and the `DDP` macros export them to OLE properties, and vice versa.)

Comments

Although this is a somewhat "grungy" How-To, with lots of different parts and some fairly ugly code hacking, it illustrates that even with all the firepower in VC 5, you still have to get your fingernails dirty now and then!

COMPLEXITY
ADVANCED

3.2 How do I... Use custom font features with my ActiveX control using Visual C++ 5.0?

Problem

My users are having trouble with the stock `Font` property. Can I work around this by including a custom `Font` property and adding it to the property pages without hiring the CalTech Class of 97 to do it?

Technique

Fortunately, MFC ActiveX controls can count on several useful capabilities in the font wars! This How-To implements a custom `Font` property and property page for the `Caption` property. The CD contains an already created workspace with a new name but all the previous code and settings in place under `CH03\HT02\ASPHT0302\`. The complete control is under `CH03\HT02\FINAL\ASPHT0302\`.

Steps

1. Activate Visual C++ 5.0 and load the `ASPHT0302` workspace, which as noted above contains all the code and settings from the previous How-To. Select the View|ClassWizard menu option; make sure the `Aspht0302ctl` object is selected and go to the Automation tab. Click on the Add Property button. In the dialog box, click Get/Set Methods and make its name

CaptionFont and its type LPFONTDISP. When you are finished, your dialog box should appear very similar to Figure 3-11. Press OK twice to add the new property to the project, and save the workspace.

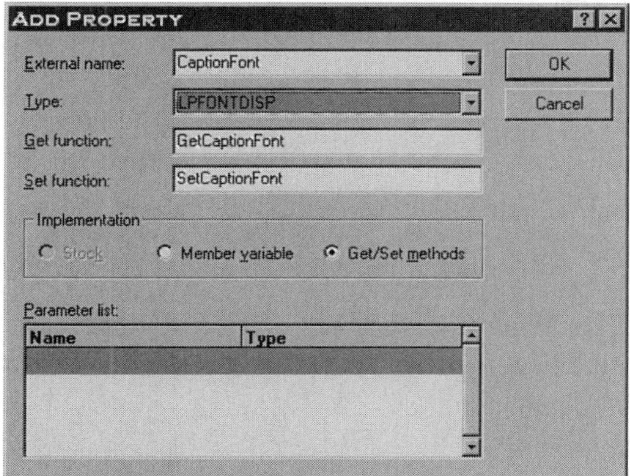

Figure 3-11 Adding the custom Font property

2. Bring up the ASPHT0302CTL.H file in the text editor. Locate the "protected" section and add the boldfaced code in Listing 3-7 to include a member variable that can hold a font DISPINTERFACE. Save the file.

Listing 3-7 ASPHT0302CTL.H source code

```
// Implementation
protected:
~CAspht0302Ctrl();
CFontHolder m_fontCaption;

DECLARE_OLECREATE_EX(CAspht0302Ctrl)     // Class factory and guid
DECLARE_OLETYPELIB(CAspht0302Ctrl)       // GetTypeInfo
DECLARE_PROPPAGEIDS(CAspht0302Ctrl)      // Property page IDs
DECLARE_OLECTLTYPE(CAspht0302Ctrl)       // Type name and misc status
```

3. Bring up the ASPHT0302CTL.CPP file and find the constructor code shown in Listing 3-8. Add the boldfaced code to link initialization of the font member variable to startup of the control. Save the workspace.

Listing 3-8 ASPHT0302CTL.CPP constructor source code

```
/////////////////////////////////////////////////////////////////////////////
// CAspht0302Ctrl::CAspht0302Ctrl - Constructor

CAspht0302Ctrl::CAspht0302Ctrl() : m_fontCaption( &m_xFontNotification )
{
InitializeIIDs(&IID_DAspht0302, &IID_DAspht0302Events);
```

continued on next page

continued from previous page

```
// TODO: Initialize your control's instance data here.
SetPanelColor( (OLE_COLOR) RGB( 0 , 128 , 0 )) ;
SetHighlightColor( (OLE_COLOR) RGB( 0 , 255 , 0 ));
SetShadowColor( (OLE_COLOR) RGB( 0 , 64 , 0 ));
SetBorderWidth(10);
}
```

4. Move up in the code to just above the `OLECTLTYPE` macro and enter the boldfaced code in Listing 3-9 to implement the type holder for font information. Save the workspace.

Listing 3-9 ASPHT0302CTL.CPP FONTDESC source code

```
/////////////////////////////////////////////////////////
// Custom Font Information

static const FONTDESC _fontdescCaption =
{ sizeof( FONTDESC ), OLESTR("MS Sans Serif"), FONTSIZE(12), FW_BOLD ,
  ANSI_CHARSET , FALSE, FALSE, FALSE };
```

5. Move down to the `DoPropExchange` function and enter the boldfaced line of code in Listing 3-10 to serialize the custom `Font` property. Save the workspace.

Listing 3-10 ASPHT0302CTL.CPP DoPropExchange Source code

```
void CAspht0302Ctrl::DoPropExchange(CPropExchange* pPX)
{
ExchangeVersion(pPX, MAKELONG(_wVerMinor, _wVerMajor));
COleControl::DoPropExchange(pPX);

// TODO: Call PX_ functions for each persistent custom property.

PX_Color( pPX , _T("PanelColor"), m_PanelColor );
PX_Color( pPX , _T("HighlightColor"), m_HighlightColor );
PX_Color( pPX , _T("ShadowColor"), m_ShadowColor );
PX_Short( pPX , _T("BorderWidth"), m_BorderWidth );
PX_Font(  pPX , _T("CaptionFont"), m_fontCaption , &_fontdescCaption );
}
```

6. Move down to the end of the file where the two dispatch handlers for the `Get` and `Set` methods are waiting. Fill in the boldfaced code in Listing 3-11 to implement reading and writing the `Font` property. Save the workspace.

Listing 3-11 ASPHT0302CTL.CPP font Get/Set methods source code

```
LPFONTDISP CAspht0302Ctrl::GetCaptionFont()
{
// TODO: Add your property handler here

return m_fontCaption.GetFontDispatch();
}
```

```
void CAspht0302Ctrl::SetCaptionFont(LPFONTDISP newValue)
{
// TODO: Add your property handler here

SetModifiedFlag();
m_fontCaption.InitializeFont( &_fontdescCaption, newValue);
OnFontChanged();
}
```

7. Move back up to the `OnDraw` function and change the boldfaced code in Listing 3-12 to use the new custom font instead of the stock font. Save the workspace.

Listing 3-12 ASPHT0302CTL.CPP OnDraw source code

```
/////////////////////////////////////////////////////////////////////////////
// CAspht0302Ctrl::OnDraw - Drawing function

void CAspht0302Ctrl::OnDraw(
CDC* pdc, const CRect& rcBounds, const CRect& rcInvalid)
{
CBrush cbPanelBrush( TranslateColor( m_PanelColor ));
pdc->FillRect( rcBounds, &cbPanelBrush );
CPen pHiLitePen(PS_SOLID, 2, TranslateColor( GetHighlightColor() ));
CPen pShadowPen(PS_SOLID, 2, TranslateColor( GetShadowColor() ));
CPen *pOldPen = pdc->SelectObject( &pHiLitePen );
pdc->MoveTo(rcBounds.left + 2 , rcBounds.top + 2);
pdc->LineTo(rcBounds.right - 2 , rcBounds.top + 2 );
pdc->MoveTo(rcBounds.left + 2 , rcBounds.top + 2 );
pdc->LineTo(rcBounds.left + 2 , rcBounds.bottom - 2);
pdc->SelectObject( &pShadowPen );
pdc->MoveTo(rcBounds.right - 2 , rcBounds.bottom - 2 );
pdc->LineTo(rcBounds.right - 2 , rcBounds.top + 2);
pdc->MoveTo(rcBounds.right - 2 , rcBounds.bottom - 2);
pdc->LineTo(rcBounds.left + 2  , rcBounds.bottom - 2);
pdc->MoveTo(rcBounds.left + m_BorderWidth + 4 , rcBounds.top + m_BorderWidth + 4);
pdc->LineTo(rcBounds.right - m_BorderWidth - 4 , rcBounds.top + m_BorderWidth +⇐
4);
pdc->MoveTo(rcBounds.left + m_BorderWidth + 4 , rcBounds.top + m_BorderWidth + 4);
pdc->LineTo(rcBounds.left + m_BorderWidth + 4 , rcBounds.bottom - m_BorderWidth⇐
- 4);
pdc->SelectObject( &pHiLitePen );
pdc->MoveTo(rcBounds.right - m_BorderWidth - 4 , rcBounds.bottom - m_BorderWidth⇐
- 4);
pdc->LineTo(rcBounds.right - m_BorderWidth - 4 , rcBounds.top + m_BorderWidth +⇐
4);
pdc->MoveTo(rcBounds.right - m_BorderWidth - 4 , rcBounds.bottom - m_BorderWidth⇐
- 4);
pdc->LineTo(rcBounds.left + m_BorderWidth + 4, rcBounds.bottom - m_BorderWidth -⇐
4);
pdc->SelectObject(pOldPen);
CFont* pOldCaptionFont;
pOldCaptionFont = SelectFontObject( pdc, m_fontCaption );
```

continued on next page

continued from previous page

```
pdc->SetTextColor( TranslateColor( GetForeColor()));
pdc->SetBkMode( TRANSPARENT);
RECT rcHolder = rcBounds;
pdc->DrawText( InternalGetText() , -1 , &rcHolder , DT_SINGLELINE ¦ DT_CENTER ¦⇐
DT_VCENTER );
pdc->SelectObject( pOldCaptionFont );
HICON hIc = LoadIcon(  AfxGetInstanceHandle() , MAKEINTRESOURCE( IDI_ABOUTDLL ) );
HBITMAP hBmp = LoadBitmap( AfxGetInstanceHandle() , MAKEINTRESOURCE⇐
( IDB_ASPHT0302 ) );
int iOldMM = pdc->SetMapMode( MM_TEXT );
pdc->DrawIcon( rcBounds.left + m_BorderWidth + 8 , rcBounds.top + m_BorderWidth⇐
+ 8 , hIc );
pdc->SetMapMode( iOldMM );
CDC dcMem;
dcMem.CreateCompatibleDC( pdc );
CBitmap* pOldBMP = (CBitmap*) dcMem.SelectObject( hBmp );
pdc->BitBlt( rcBounds.left + m_BorderWidth + 8 , rcBounds.bottom - m_BorderWidth⇐
- 24 ,
16, 16 , &dcMem , 0 , 0 , SRCCOPY );
}
```

8. Move back up to the `PROPPAGEID` macros. Add the boldfaced code in Listing 3-13 to add the Stock Font page for setting the custom `Font` property. Save the workspace.

Listing 3-13 `ASPHT0302CTL.CPP PROPPAGEID` source code

```
/////////////////////////////////////////////////////////////////////////////
// Property pages

// TODO: Add more property pages as needed.  Remember to increase the count!
BEGIN_PROPPAGEIDS(CAspht0302Ctrl, 4)
PROPPAGEID(CAspht0302PropPage::guid)
PROPPAGEID( CLSID_CColorPropPage )
PROPPAGEID(CCustColorPropPage::guid)
PROPPAGEID( CLSID_CFontPropPage )
END_PROPPAGEIDS(CAspht0302Ctrl)
```

9. Build `ASPHT0302.OCX`. Then activate the ActiveX Control Test Container tool and load a copy of `ASPHT0302`. Bring up its property pages and you will see that a Font tab has been added. Select it and change the font to something interesting, then add a caption and some custom colors, and you will have a display similar to Figure 3-12. Your ActiveX arsenal now includes the capability to add and manipulate custom `Font` properties in your custom ActiveX control.

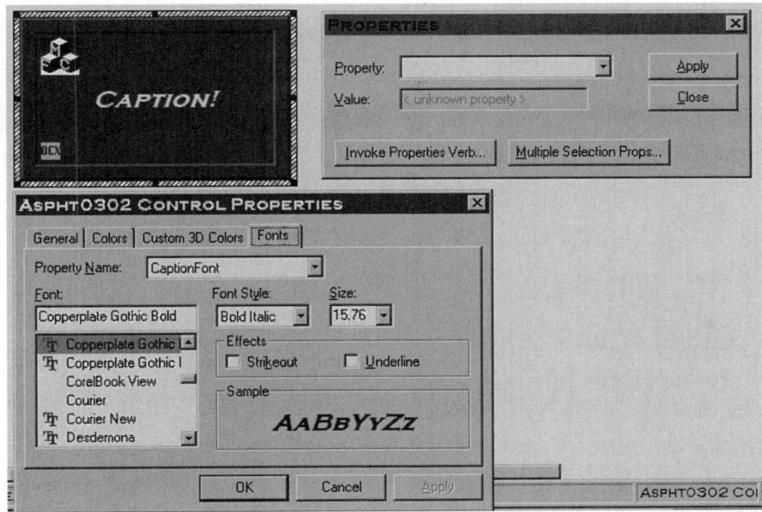

Figure 3-12 The custom `Font` property at work

How It Works

A lot of pieces come together in this How-To. First, of course, is the ubiquitous Class Wizard, which adds the basic code for the new property. Then comes the usual hard-coding, with the addition of the protected member variable and the various initialization, serialization, and **Get/Set** methods. The more arcane parts of the code, though, deserve further explanation. Notice this code fragment:

```
CAspht0302Ctrl::CAspht0302Ctrl() : m_fontCaption( &m_xFontNotification )
```

This line is a special link that ties the `m_fontCaption` member variable to the notification messages sent through the OLE system whenever a font is changed.

The other noteworthy point is the unusual code in the **Get/Set** methods. Notice this fragment from the **Get** method

```
return m_fontCaption.GetFontDispatch();
```

It does not return the `m_fontCaption` directly the way other **Get** methods do; instead it calls a function! The reason for this is that `m_fontCaption` is actually a **DISPINTERFACE** and needs to call the internal OLE functions to return its pointer in a valid way. Likewise, this fragment from the **Set** method

```
m_fontCaption.InitializeFont( &_fontdescCaption, newValue);
```

shows the `m_fontCaption` being set via an **Initialize** call rather than directly, again because it is a **DISPINTERFACE** rather than a standard variable!

Comments

The bad news is some applications, such as ActiveX Control Pad, don't recognize the stock font and color property pages or this custom `Font` property. This lack of support is a major hole in Microsoft's current Web tools; please check the `README.TXT` file on the CD under "ActiveX Control Pad Bugs" for possible fixes!

COMPLEXITY
ADVANCED

3.3 How do I...
Use custom images with my ActiveX control with Visual C++ 5.0?

Problem

I need to allow my users to enter a graphics filename for display at runtime. These How-To's cover only resource images. How much harder is it to use a file-based image with an ActiveX control?

Technique

Actually, it isn't hard at all! This How-To implements a file-based image property that can be set at runtime with a stock property page. The CD contains an already created workspace with a new name but all the previous code and settings in place under `CH03\HT03\ASPHT0302\`. The complete control is under `CH03\HT03\FINAL\ASPHT0302\`. (Because the control has gotten large enough that retyping it under a new name for each project is burdensome, we will use the same control with updated functionality for the remaining How-To's in this chapter.)

Steps

1. Activate Visual C++ 5.0 and load the `ASPHT0302` workspace from its new directory, which as noted above contains all the code and settings from the previous How-To. Select the View|ClassWizard menu option; make sure the `Aspht0302ctl` object is selected and go to the Automation tab. Click on the Add Property button. In the dialog box, click Get/Set Methods and make its name `BackgroundImage` and its type `LPPICTUREDISP`. When you are finished, your dialog box should appear very similar to Figure 3-13. Press OK twice to add the new property to the project and save the workspace.

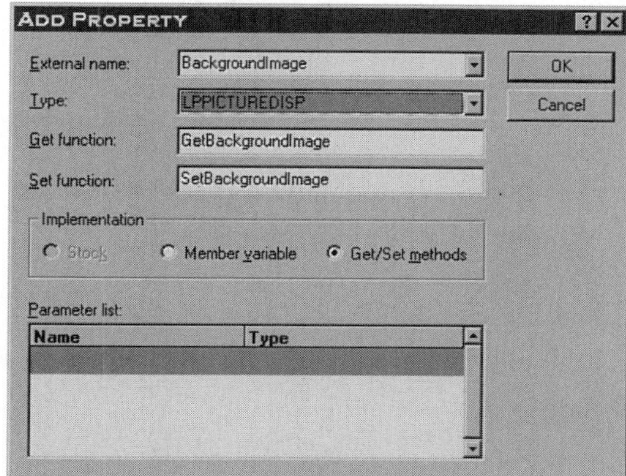

Figure 3-13 Adding the custom `Image` property

2. Bring up the `ASPHT0302CTL.H` file in the text editor. Locate the `protected` section and add the boldfaced code in Listing 3-14. Save the file.

Listing 3-14 `ASPHT0302CTL.H` source code

```
// Implementation
protected:
~CAspht0302Ctrl();
CFontHolder m_fontCaption;
CPictureHolder m_pictureBackground;

DECLARE_OLECREATE_EX(CAspht0302Ctrl)     // Class factory and guid
DECLARE_OLETYPELIB(CAspht0302Ctrl)       // GetTypeInfo
DECLARE_PROPPAGEIDS(CAspht0302Ctrl)      // Property page IDs
DECLARE_OLECTLTYPE(CAspht0302Ctrl)       // Type name and misc status
```

3. Bring up the `ASPHT0302CTL.CPP` file and find the `OnResetState` function code shown in Listing 3-15. Add the boldfaced code to create a blank image at startup of the control. Save the workspace.

Listing 3-15 `ASPHT0302CTL.CPP OnResetState` source code

```
/////////////////////////////////////////////////////////////////////////////
// CAspht0302Ctrl::OnResetState - Reset control to default state

void CAspht0302Ctrl::OnResetState()
{
COleControl::OnResetState();  // Resets defaults found in DoPropExchange

// TODO: Reset any other control state here.
m_pictureBackground.CreateEmpty();
}
```

4. Move down to the `DoPropExchange` function and enter the code in Listing 3-16 to serialize the custom picture property. Save the workspace.

Listing 3-16 `ASPHT0302CTL.CPP DoPropExchange` source code

```
void CAspht0302Ctrl::DoPropExchange(CPropExchange* pPX)
{
ExchangeVersion(pPX, MAKELONG(_wVerMinor, _wVerMajor));
COleControl::DoPropExchange(pPX);

// TODO: Call PX_ functions for each persistent custom property.

PX_Color( pPX , _T("PanelColor"), m_PanelColor );
PX_Color( pPX , _T("HighlightColor"), m_HighlightColor );
PX_Color( pPX , _T("ShadowColor"), m_ShadowColor );
PX_Short( pPX , _T("BorderWidth"), m_BorderWidth );
PX_Font(  pPX , _T("CaptionFont"), m_fontCaption , &_fontdescCaption );
PX_Picture( pPX, _T("BackgroundImage"), m_pictureBackground );
}
```

5. Move down to the end of the file where the two dispatch handlers for the `Get` and `Set` methods are waiting. Fill in the boldfaced code in Listing 3-17 to implement reading and writing the `Picture` property. Save the workspace.

Listing 3-17 `ASPHT0302CTL.CPP` picture `Get/Set` methods source code

```
{
LPPICTUREDISP CAspht0302Ctrl::GetBackgroundImage()
{
// TODO: Add your property handler here
return m_pictureBackground.GetPictureDispatch();
}

void CAspht0302Ctrl::SetBackgroundImage(LPPICTUREDISP newValue)
{
// TODO: Add your property handler here
SetModifiedFlag();
m_pictureBackground.SetPictureDispatch(newValue);
InvalidateControl();
}
```

6. Move back up to the `OnDraw` function and change the boldfaced code in Listing 3-18 to use the new custom picture instead of the resource images. Save the workspace.

Listing 3-18 ASPHT0302CTL.CPP OnDraw source code

```
/////////////////////////////////////////////////////////////////////////////
// CAspht0302Ctrl::OnDraw - Drawing function

void CAspht0302Ctrl::OnDraw(
CDC* pdc, const CRect& rcBounds, const CRect& rcInvalid)
{
CBrush cbPanelBrush( TranslateColor( m_PanelColor ));
pdc->FillRect( rcBounds, &cbPanelBrush );
CPen pHiLitePen(PS_SOLID, 2, TranslateColor( GetHighlightColor() ));
CPen pShadowPen(PS_SOLID, 2, TranslateColor( GetShadowColor() ));
CPen *pOldPen = pdc->SelectObject( &pHiLitePen );
pdc->MoveTo(rcBounds.left + 2 , rcBounds.top + 2);
pdc->LineTo(rcBounds.right - 2 , rcBounds.top + 2 );
pdc->MoveTo(rcBounds.left + 2 , rcBounds.top + 2 );
pdc->LineTo(rcBounds.left + 2 , rcBounds.bottom - 2);
pdc->SelectObject( &pShadowPen );
pdc->MoveTo(rcBounds.right - 2 , rcBounds.bottom - 2 );
pdc->LineTo(rcBounds.right - 2 , rcBounds.top + 2);
pdc->MoveTo(rcBounds.right - 2 , rcBounds.bottom - 2);
pdc->LineTo(rcBounds.left + 2  , rcBounds.bottom - 2);
pdc->MoveTo(rcBounds.left + m_BorderWidth + 4 , rcBounds.top + m_BorderWidth + 4);
pdc->LineTo(rcBounds.right - m_BorderWidth - 4 , rcBounds.top + m_BorderWidth +⇐
4);
pdc->MoveTo(rcBounds.left + m_BorderWidth + 4 , rcBounds.top + m_BorderWidth + 4);
pdc->LineTo(rcBounds.left + m_BorderWidth + 4 , rcBounds.bottom - m_BorderWidth⇐
- 4);
pdc->SelectObject( &pHiLitePen );
pdc->MoveTo(rcBounds.right - m_BorderWidth - 4 , rcBounds.bottom - m_BorderWidth⇐
- 4);
pdc->LineTo(rcBounds.right - m_BorderWidth - 4 , rcBounds.top + m_BorderWidth +⇐
4);
pdc->MoveTo(rcBounds.right - m_BorderWidth - 4 , rcBounds.bottom - m_BorderWidth⇐
- 4);
pdc->LineTo(rcBounds.left + m_BorderWidth + 4, rcBounds.bottom - m_BorderWidth -⇐
4);
pdc->SelectObject(pOldPen);
RECT rcPicBounds = rcBounds;
rcPicBounds.left += ( m_BorderWidth + 8 );
rcPicBounds.right -= ( m_BorderWidth + 10 );
rcPicBounds.top += ( m_BorderWidth + 8 );
rcPicBounds.bottom -= ( m_BorderWidth + 10 );
m_pictureBackground.Render( pdc, rcPicBounds , rcBounds );CFont* pOldCaptionFont;
pOldCaptionFont = SelectFontObject( pdc, m_fontCaption );
pdc->SetTextColor( TranslateColor( GetForeColor()));
pdc->SetBkMode( TRANSPARENT);
RECT rcHolder = rcBounds;
pdc->DrawText( InternalGetText() , -1 , &rcHolder , DT_SINGLELINE ¦ DT_CENTER ¦
DT_VCENTER );
pdc->SelectObject( pOldCaptionFont );
}
```

7. Move back up to the `PROPPAGEID` macros. Add the boldfaced code in Listing 3-19 to add the stock picture page for setting the custom `Picture` property. Save the workspace.

Listing 3-19 ASPHT0302CTL.CPP PROPPAGEID source code

```
////////////////////////////////////////////////////////////////////////////
// Property pages

// TODO: Add more property pages as needed.  Remember to increase the count!
BEGIN_PROPPAGEIDS(CAspht0302Ctrl, 5)
PROPPAGEID(CAspht0302PropPage::guid)
PROPPAGEID( CLSID_CColorPropPage )
PROPPAGEID(CCustColorPropPage::guid)
PROPPAGEID( CLSID_CFontPropPage )
PROPPAGEID( CLSID_CPicturePropPage )
END_PROPPAGEIDS(CAspht0302Ctrl)
```

8. Build `ASPHT0302.OCX`. Then activate the ActiveX Control Test Container tool and load a copy of `ASPHT0302`. Bring up its property pages and you will see that a Picture tab has been added. Select it and choose an available bitmap from your system, then add a caption and some custom colors, and you will have a display similar to Figure 3-14. You can now add and manipulate custom file-based picture properties in your custom ActiveX control.

Figure 3-14 The custom `Picture` property at work

How It Works

This How-To is pretty much a mirror of How-To 3.2, except for the use of the `LPPICTUREDISP` type and some different drawing code. The only other noteworthy points are the use of the `OnResetState` method instead of the constructor to initialize the picture, and the lack of a notification message because the picture can be changed only via the property page or similar functionality.

Comments

Unfortunately, this property is not available in ActiveX Control Pad. Please check the `README.TXT` file on the CD under "ActiveX Control Pad Bugs" for a possible fix.

3.4 How do I... Create a transparent custom ActiveX control with advanced optimization features using Visual C++ 5.0?

Problem

I need to create a transparent custom ActiveX control that draws as quickly as possible. Can any of the advanced optimization options on the MFC ActiveX Control Wizard help me here?

Technique

Several advanced features can create transparent and fast-drawing custom MFC ActiveX controls! This How-To illustrates creating a fast-drawing custom MFC ActiveX control and then a transparent version of the same control. The CD contains already created workspaces under `CH03\HT04\ASPHT0304a\` and `CH03\HT04\ASPHT0304b\`.

Steps

1. Activate Visual C++ 5.0. Choose the File|New... menu option and select MFC ActiveX Control Wizard. Enter `ASPHT0304a` for the project name. Press OK. Move to the second page of the wizard dialog. Uncheck the Activates when visible check box on the features list on the second dialog page, as shown in Figure 3-15.

2. Press the Advanced... button to bring up the Optimization Options dialog. Check the Unclipped device context, Flicker-free activation, Mouse pointer notifications when inactive, and Optimized drawing code check boxes. When you are finished, the display should look very much like the one shown in Figure 3-16. Press OK and Finish and OK to accept the new ActiveX control and let the wizard create the skeleton project.

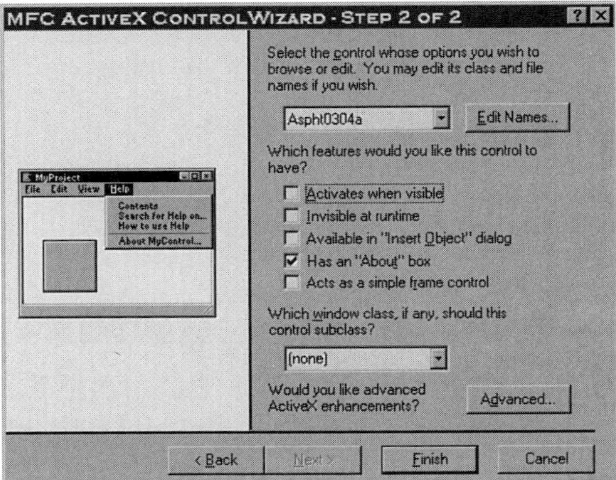

Figure 3-15 Unchecking the Activates when visible check box on the MFC Control Wizard dialog page

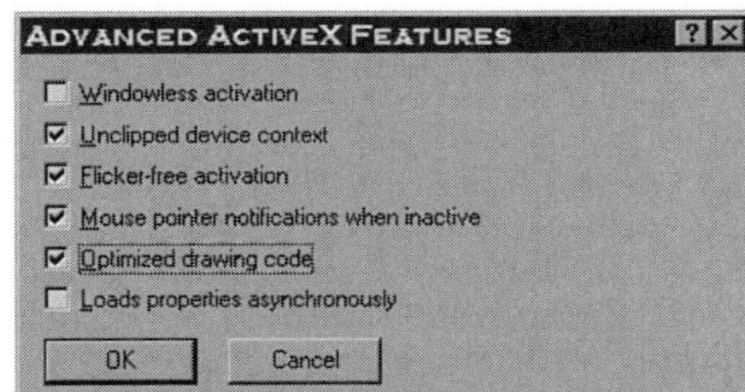

Figure 3-16 Activating advanced ActiveX features in the MFC Class Wizard

3. Bring up `ASPHT0304aCTL.H` in the text editor. Locate the end of the class declaration and enter the boldfaced code in Listing 3-20 to add private member variables to the class. Save the workspace.

Listing 3-20 `ASPHT0304aCTL.H` header file source code

```
// Dispatch and event IDs
public:
enum {
//{{AFX_DISP_ID(CAspht0304aCtrl)
// NOTE: ClassWizard will add and remove enumeration elements here.
//    DO NOT EDIT what you see in these blocks of generated code !
//}}AFX_DISP_ID
};
```

```
private
OLE_COLOR m_HighlightColor;
OLE_COLOR m_PanelColor;
OLE_COLOR m_ShadowColor;
short m_BorderWidth;
CPen m_highlightpen;
CPen m_shadowpen;
CPen m_forepen;
CBrush m_backbrush;
};

//{{AFX_INSERT_LOCATION}}
// Microsoft Developer Studio will insert additional declarations immediately
before the previous line.
```

4. Select View|ClassWizard from the menu. Press the Automation tab and add the `ForeColor` and `BackColor` stock properties. Add a custom `BorderWidth` short property with `Get/Set` methods, and three custom `OLE_COLOR` properties—`PanelColor`, `HighlightColor`, and `ShadowColor`—with `Get/Set` methods. Press OK and save the workspace.

5. Bring up `ASPHT0304aCTL.CPP` in the text editor. Find the constructor function and add the boldfaced code in Listing 3-21 to initialize the custom properties. Save the workspace.

Listing 3-21 ASPHT0304aCTL.CPP constructor source code

```
/////////////////////////////////////////////////////////////////////////////
// CAspht0304aCtrl::CAspht0304aCtrl - Constructor

CAspht0304aCtrl::CAspht0304aCtrl()
{
InitializeIIDs(&IID_DAspht0304a, &IID_DAspht0304aEvents);

// TODO: Initialize your control's instance data here.
SetPanelColor( (OLE_COLOR) RGB( 0 , 128 , 0 )) ;
SetHighlightColor( (OLE_COLOR) RGB( 0 , 255 , 0 ));
SetShadowColor( (OLE_COLOR) RGB( 0 , 64 , 0 ));
SetBorderWidth(10);
}
```

6. Move down to the `OnDraw` function and enter the boldfaced code in Listing 3-22 to draw the control on the screen. Save the workspace.

Listing 3-22 ASPHT0304aCTL.CPP OnDraw source code

```
/
/////////////////////////////////////////////////////////////////////////////
// CAspht0304aCtrl::OnDraw - Drawing function

void CAspht0304aCtrl::OnDraw(
CDC* pdc, const CRect& rcBounds, const CRect& rcInvalid)
{
CBrush cbPanelBrush( TranslateColor( GetPanelColor() ));
```

continued on next page

continued from previous page

```
pdc->FillRect( rcBounds, &cbPanelBrush );
if (m_highlightpen.m_hObject == NULL)
m_highlightpen.CreatePen( PS_SOLID , 2 , TranslateColor( GetHighlightColor() ));
if (m_shadowpen.m_hObject == NULL)
m_shadowpen.CreatePen( PS_SOLID , 2 , TranslateColor( GetShadowColor() ));
CPen *pOldPen = pdc->SelectObject( &m_highlightpen );
pdc->MoveTo(rcBounds.left + 2 , rcBounds.top + 2);
pdc->LineTo(rcBounds.right - 2 , rcBounds.top + 2 );
pdc->MoveTo(rcBounds.left + 2 , rcBounds.top + 2 );
pdc->LineTo(rcBounds.left + 2 , rcBounds.bottom - 2);
pdc->SelectObject( &m_shadowpen );
pdc->MoveTo(rcBounds.right - 2 , rcBounds.bottom - 2 );
pdc->LineTo(rcBounds.right - 2 , rcBounds.top + 2);
pdc->MoveTo(rcBounds.right - 2 , rcBounds.bottom - 2);
pdc->LineTo(rcBounds.left + 2  , rcBounds.bottom - 2);
pdc->MoveTo(rcBounds.left + m_BorderWidth + 4 , rcBounds.top + m_BorderWidth + 4);
pdc->LineTo(rcBounds.right - m_BorderWidth - 4 , rcBounds.top + m_BorderWidth +⇐
4);
pdc->MoveTo(rcBounds.left + m_BorderWidth + 4 , rcBounds.top + m_BorderWidth + 4);
pdc->LineTo(rcBounds.left + m_BorderWidth + 4 , rcBounds.bottom - m_BorderWidth⇐
- 4);
pdc->SelectObject( &m_highlightpen );
pdc->MoveTo(rcBounds.right - m_BorderWidth - 4 , rcBounds.bottom - m_BorderWidth⇐
- 4);
pdc->LineTo(rcBounds.right - m_BorderWidth - 4 , rcBounds.top + m_BorderWidth +⇐
4);
pdc->MoveTo(rcBounds.right - m_BorderWidth - 4 , rcBounds.bottom - m_BorderWidth⇐
- 4);
pdc->LineTo(rcBounds.left + m_BorderWidth + 4, rcBounds.bottom - m_BorderWidth -⇐
4);
if (m_forepen.m_hObject == NULL)
m_forepen.CreatePen( PS_SOLID , 2 , TranslateColor( GetForeColor() ));
if (m_backbrush.m_hObject == NULL)
m_backbrush.CreateSolidBrush( TranslateColor( GetBackColor() ));
pdc->SelectObject( &m_forepen );
CBrush* pBrushSaved = pdc->SelectObject( &m_backbrush );
RECT rcHolder = rcBounds;
rcHolder.top += ( m_BorderWidth + 8 );
rcHolder.left += ( m_BorderWidth + 8 );
rcHolder.right -= ( m_BorderWidth + 8 );
rcHolder.bottom -= ( m_BorderWidth + 8 );
pdc->Rectangle( &rcHolder );
if (!IsOptimizedDraw())
{
// The container does not support optimized drawing.

// TODO: if you selected any GDI objects into the device context *pdc,
//restore the previously-selected objects here.
//For more information, please see MFC technical note #nnn,
//"Optimizing an ActiveX Control".
pdc->SelectObject( pOldPen );
pdc->SelectObject( pBrushSaved );
}
}
```

7. Move down to the `Persistence` method and enter the boldfaced code in Listing 3-23 to serialize the custom properties. Then move on down to the `Get/Set` methods for the custom properties and enter the boldfaced code in Listing 3-23 to handle these chores. Save the workspace.

Listing 3-23 ASPHT0304aCTL.CPP Get/Set methods source code

```
//////////////////////////////////////////////////////////////////////////////
// CAspht0304aCtrl::DoPropExchange - Persistence support

void CAspht0304aCtrl::DoPropExchange(CPropExchange* pPX)
{
ExchangeVersion(pPX, MAKELONG(_wVerMinor, _wVerMajor));
COleControl::DoPropExchange(pPX);

// TODO: Call PX_ functions for each persistent custom property.

PX_Color( pPX , _T("PanelColor"), m_PanelColor );
PX_Color( pPX , _T("HighlightColor"), m_HighlightColor );
PX_Color( pPX , _T("ShadowColor"), m_ShadowColor );
PX_Short( pPX , _T("BorderWidth"), m_BorderWidth );
}

//////////////////////////////////////////////////////////////////////////////
// CAspht0304aCtrl message handlers

short CAspht0304aCtrl::GetBorderWidth()
{
// TODO: Add your property handler here

return m_BorderWidth;
}

void CAspht0304aCtrl::SetBorderWidth(short nNewValue)
{
// TODO: Add your property handler here

SetModifiedFlag();
m_BorderWidth = nNewValue;
}

OLE_COLOR CAspht0304aCtrl::GetPanelColor()
{
// TODO: Add your property handler here

return m_PanelColor;
}

void CAspht0304aCtrl::SetPanelColor(OLE_COLOR nNewValue)
{
// TODO: Add your property handler here

SetModifiedFlag();
m_PanelColor = nNewValue;
}
```

continued on next page

continued from previous page

```
OLE_COLOR CAspht0304aCtrl::GetHighlightColor()
{
// TODO: Add your property handler here

return m_HighlightColor;
}

void CAspht0304aCtrl::SetHighlightColor(OLE_COLOR nNewValue)
{
// TODO: Add your property handler here

SetModifiedFlag();
m_HighlightColor = nNewValue;
m_highlightpen.DeleteObject();
}

OLE_COLOR CAspht0304aCtrl::GetShadowColor()
{
// TODO: Add your property handler here

return m_ShadowColor;
}

void CAspht0304aCtrl::SetShadowColor(OLE_COLOR nNewValue)
{
// TODO: Add your property handler here

SetModifiedFlag();
m_ShadowColor = nNewValue;
m_shadowpen.DeleteObject();
}
```

8. Activate the Class Wizard and move to the Message Maps tab. In the list of available messages, select `OnBackColorChanged` and `OnForeColorChanged` and press Add Function for each of them. When you are finished, your display should look very similar to Figure 3-17. Press OK to write the skeleton code and then save the workspace.

9. Back in the `ASPHT0304aCTL.CPP` file in the text editor, move to the new function skeletons the Class Wizard added and enter the boldfaced code in Listing 3-24 to respond to changes in the stock color properties. Save the workspace.

Listing 3-24 ASPHT0304aCTL.CPP stock color change notification message handlers source code

```
void CAspht0304aCtrl::OnBackColorChanged()
{
// TODO: Add your specialized code here and/or call the base class
```

```
COleControl::OnBackColorChanged();
m_backbrush.DeleteObject();
}

void CAspht0304aCtrl::OnForeColorChanged()
{
// TODO: Add your specialized code here and/or call the base class

COleControl::OnForeColorChanged();
m_forepen.DeleteObject();
}
```

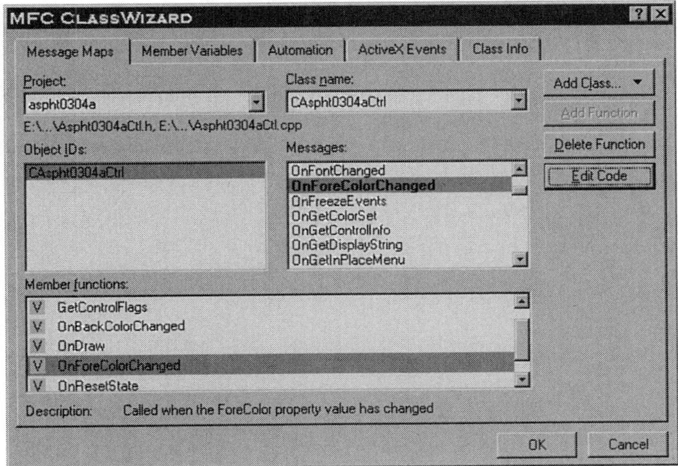

Figure 3-17 Add message map override functions to the Class Wizard for `OnBackColorChanged` and `OnForeColorChanged`

10. Build `ASPHT0304a.OCX`. Save the workspace, then create a new workspace named `ASPHT0304b`. In the MFC ActiveX Class Wizard, set the second page options the same as in the first project. Then in the Advanced Options, check the Windowless activation and Optimized drawing code check boxes as shown in Figure 3-18. Press OK, Finish, and OK to create the skeleton project.

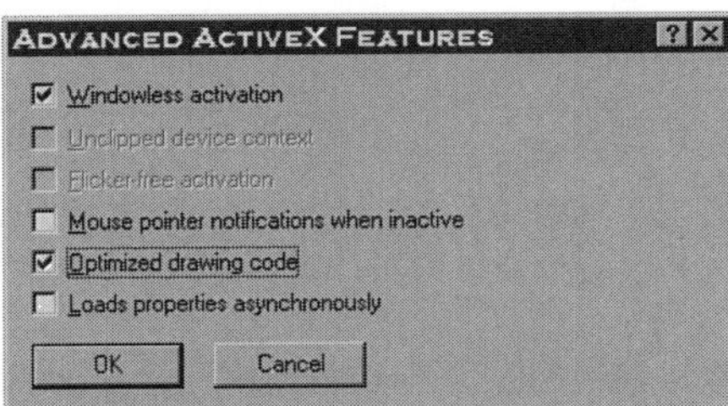

Figure 3-18 ASPHT0304b advanced options dialog

11. Re-create the project exactly as you did for **ASPHT0304a** in the previous steps, except enter the drawing code for the **OnDraw** function in Listing 3-25. Save the workspace and build **ASPHT0304b.OCX**.

Listing 3-25 ASPHT0304bCTL.CPP OnDraw source code

```
/////////////////////////////////////////////////////////////////////////////
// CAspht0304bCtrl::OnDraw - Drawing function

void CAspht0304bCtrl::OnDraw(
CDC* pdc, const CRect& rcBounds, const CRect& rcInvalid)
{
CBrush cbPanelBrush( TranslateColor( GetPanelColor() ));
RECT rcHolder = rcBounds;
rcHolder.bottom = rcHolder.top + m_BorderWidth + 4;
pdc->FillRect( rcHolder, &cbPanelBrush );
rcHolder.right = rcHolder.left + m_BorderWidth + 4;
rcHolder.bottom = rcBounds.bottom;
pdc->FillRect( rcHolder, &cbPanelBrush );
rcHolder.left = rcBounds.right - m_BorderWidth - 4;
rcHolder.right = rcBounds.right;
rcHolder.top = rcBounds.top;
rcHolder.bottom = rcBounds.bottom;
pdc->FillRect( rcHolder , &cbPanelBrush );
rcHolder.left = rcBounds.left;
rcHolder.top = rcBounds.bottom - m_BorderWidth - 4;
rcHolder.right = rcBounds.right;
rcHolder.bottom = rcBounds.bottom;
pdc->FillRect( rcHolder, &cbPanelBrush );
if (m_highlightpen.m_hObject == NULL)
m_highlightpen.CreatePen( PS_SOLID , 2 , TranslateColor( GetHighlightColor() ));
if (m_shadowpen.m_hObject == NULL)
m_shadowpen.CreatePen( PS_SOLID , 2 , TranslateColor( GetShadowColor() ));
CPen *pOldPen = pdc->SelectObject( &m_highlightpen );
pdc->MoveTo(rcBounds.left + 2 , rcBounds.top + 2);
pdc->LineTo(rcBounds.right - 2 , rcBounds.top + 2 );
pdc->MoveTo(rcBounds.left + 2 , rcBounds.top + 2 );
pdc->LineTo(rcBounds.left + 2 , rcBounds.bottom - 2);
pdc->SelectObject( &m_shadowpen );
pdc->MoveTo(rcBounds.right - 2 , rcBounds.bottom - 2 );
```

```
pdc->LineTo(rcBounds.right - 2 , rcBounds.top + 2);
pdc->MoveTo(rcBounds.right - 2 , rcBounds.bottom - 2);
pdc->LineTo(rcBounds.left + 2  , rcBounds.bottom - 2);
pdc->MoveTo(rcBounds.left + m_BorderWidth + 4 , rcBounds.top + m_BorderWidth + 4);
pdc->LineTo(rcBounds.right - m_BorderWidth - 4 , rcBounds.top + m_BorderWidth +⇐
4);
pdc->MoveTo(rcBounds.left + m_BorderWidth + 4 , rcBounds.top + m_BorderWidth + 4);
pdc->LineTo(rcBounds.left + m_BorderWidth + 4 , rcBounds.bottom - m_BorderWidth⇐
- 4);
pdc->SelectObject( &m_highlightpen );
pdc->MoveTo(rcBounds.right - m_BorderWidth - 4 , rcBounds.bottom - m_BorderWidth⇐
- 4);
pdc->LineTo(rcBounds.right - m_BorderWidth - 4 , rcBounds.top + m_BorderWidth +⇐
4);
pdc->MoveTo(rcBounds.right - m_BorderWidth - 4 , rcBounds.bottom - m_BorderWidth⇐
- 4);
pdc->LineTo(rcBounds.left + m_BorderWidth + 4, rcBounds.bottom - m_BorderWidth -⇐
4);
if (m_forepen.m_hObject == NULL)
m_forepen.CreatePen( PS_SOLID , 2 , TranslateColor( GetForeColor() ));
if (m_backbrush.m_hObject == NULL)
m_backbrush.CreateSolidBrush( TranslateColor( GetBackColor() ));
pdc->SelectObject( &m_forepen );
CBrush* pBrushSaved = pdc->SelectObject( &m_backbrush );
RECT rcHolder = rcBounds;
rcHolder.top += ( m_BorderWidth + 20 );
rcHolder.left += ( m_BorderWidth + 20 );
rcHolder.right -= ( m_BorderWidth + 20 );
rcHolder.bottom -= ( m_BorderWidth + 20 );
pdc->Ellipse( &rcHolder );
if (!IsOptimizedDraw())
{
// The container does not support optimized drawing.

// TODO: if you selected any GDI objects into the device context *pdc,
//restore the previously-selected objects here.
//For more information, please see MFC technical note #nnn,
//"Optimizing an ActiveX Control".
pdc->SelectObject( pOldPen );
pdc->SelectObject( pBrushSaved );
}
}
```

12. Start the ActiveX Control Test Container tool. Place a copy of `ASPHT0203a.OCX` and `ASPHT0304b.OCX` on the surface. Set `ForeColor` and `BackColor` of each to a new value, and set `PanelColor`, `HighlightColor`, and `ShadowColor` for `ASPHT0304a.OCX` to new values. Then drag the `ASPHT0304b.OCX` control over the edge of the `ASPHT0304a.OCX` and you will see a display similar to Figure 3-19. Your mastery of ActiveX controls is reaching completeness now with advanced features, including optimization and transparency.

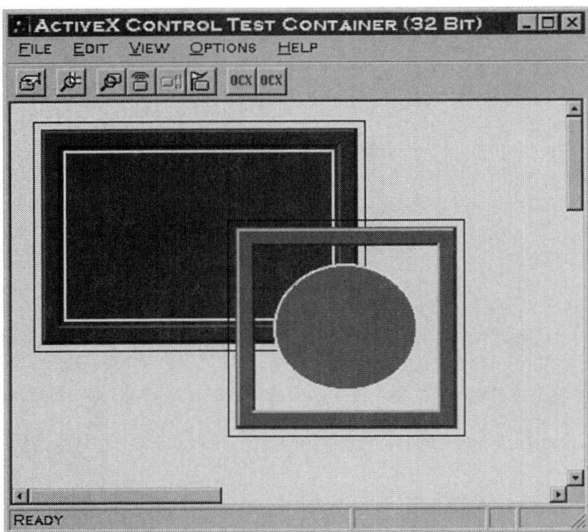

Figure 3-19 ASPHT0304a and ASPHT0304b showing advanced optimization features and transparency in the ActiveX Control Test Container tool

How It Works

Four major optimizations are available to an MFC ActiveX control: latent activation, minor graphics optimization, major graphics optimization, and windowless activation. Each is explained below.

Latent activation is the setting controlled by the Activates when visible setting in the Control Wizard. When this setting is `True`, the control's window is created immediately, even though it is not currently processing mouse messages (that is, active). Turning this setting off delays creation of the control's windows until the user interacts with it in some way, thereby saving a noticeable amount of time in the early creation and display of the control. It is a good idea to add the advanced setting Receive mouse pointer notifications when inactive whenever this option is chosen in case your control needs at some point to process `WM_SETCURSOR` and/or `WM_MOUSEMOVE` messages.

Minor graphics optimizations are the Unclipped device context and Flicker-free activation settings on the Advanced ActiveX options dialog from page 2 of the Control Wizard. Although they have no overt code created for them, in practice they speed drawing of ActiveX controls by a small degree, which can add up in complex displays and large controls. Unclipped device contexts require a promise by the control not to draw outside its bounding rectangle; this avoids a second or two overhead per control in creating a clipped PDC pointer. Flicker-free activation is more subtle; it should be used only when the inactive visual display of the control is the same as its active one (as is the case for these two controls). It eliminates the extra invalidation call whenever the control loses focus or otherwise goes inactive, which can result in "flicker" due to fast redraws of the same display.

The major graphics optimization (Optimized drawing code in the advanced options dialog) is to avoid calling **SelectObject** on previously saved GDI (Graphics Device Interface) objects such as pens and brushes. Notice this code fragment, part of which is automatically inserted by the Class Wizard when this optimization is selected:

```
if (!IsOptimizedDraw())
{
// The container does not support optimized drawing.

// TODO: if you selected any GDI objects into the device context *pdc,
//restore the previously-selected objects here.
//For more information, please see MFC technical note #nnn,
//"Optimizing an ActiveX Control".
pdc->SelectObject( pOldPen );
pdc->SelectObject( pBrushSaved );
}
}
```

The check against the member function **IsOptimizedDraw** allows the code to determine if the container will automatically reselect the old pens and brushes; if not, explicit **SelectObject** calls are made. In a small control like this, the gains from this are minor, but in a large and complex control, they are definitely noticeable! (Also notice the technique of stored pens and brushes in member variables and clearing them when their underlying data changes. This ties in neatly with the automatic cleanup system.)

The last optimization is by far the most powerful. It is controlled by the simple Windowless activation check box in the advanced ActiveX options dialog. Due to the sophistication of the MFC ActiveX system, this seems to have little effect; the **OnDraw** function remains the same, as do the other major functions of the control. However, there are two major effects of this change: First, the control becomes transparent (because it no longer owns its own **HWND** and thus does not automatically clear its background with a stock brush). Second, the control draws far more quickly because all the overhead of system window management is removed! For most Internet-oriented ActiveX controls, this is a major benefit and it should be used whenever possible. The only requirement this imposes on controls is to never automatically assume their window handle is valid; instead check it for a null value and, if necessary, force the system to produce a valid handle.

Comments

The transparency effect of **ASPHT0304b** could very easily be made a property by adding a custom property of type **BOOL** and checking it prior to drawing the four outer rectangles, and instead drawing a single full rectangle, as in the **ASPHT0304a** control.

3.5 How do I... Create a nonvisual ActiveX control in Visual C++ 5.0?

Problem

I need to create an ActiveX control that doesn't display anything on the screen. Do I have to code the control from scratch to do this?

Technique

Fortunately, MFC ActiveX controls support invisibility at runtime. We will demonstrate using this capability by creating a Timer control. The CD contains an already created workspace with the finished control under `CH03\HT05\ASPHT0305\`.

Steps

1. Activate Visual C++ 5.0 and create a new MFC ActiveX control using the Control Wizard. On the second dialog page, uncheck the Activates when visible check box and check the Invisible at runtime check box, as shown in Figure 3-20. Press Finish and OK to create the skeleton project.

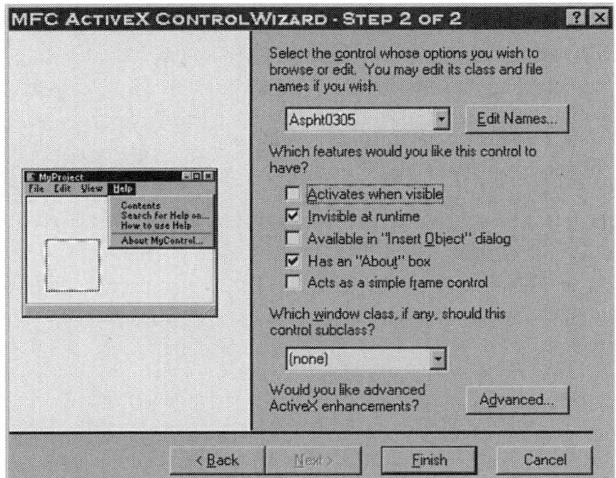

Figure 3-20 Using the MFC Control Wizard to create an ActiveX control that is invisible at runtime

2. Open the ASPHT0305CTL.H header file in the text editor. Enter the boldfaced code in Listing 3-26. Save the workspace.

Listing 3-26 ASPHT0305CTL.H header file source code

```
#if !defined(AFX_ASPHT0305CTL_H__4F2D1EF4_C13C_11D0_B7D8_444553540000__INCLUDED_)
#define AFX_ASPHT0305CTL_H__4F2D1EF4_C13C_11D0_B7D8_444553540000__INCLUDED_

#if _MSC_VER >= 1000
#pragma once
#endif // _MSC_VER >= 1000

/////////////////////////////////////////////////////////////////////////////
// Numeric constants

const DEFAULT_TIMER_INTERVAL  = 1000;


// Aspht0305Ctl.h : Declaration of the CAspht0305Ctrl ActiveX Control class.

/////////////////////////////////////////////////////////////////////////////
// CAspht0305Ctrl : See Aspht0305Ctl.cpp for implementation.

class CAspht0305Ctrl : public COleControl
{
DECLARE_DYNCREATE(CAspht0305Ctrl)

// Constructor
public:
CAspht0305Ctrl();

// Overrides
// ClassWizard generated virtual function overrides
//{{AFX_VIRTUAL(CAspht0305Ctrl)
public:
virtual void OnDraw(CDC* pdc, const CRect& rcBounds, const CRect& rcInvalid);
virtual void DoPropExchange(CPropExchange* pPX);
virtual void OnResetState();
//}}AFX_VIRTUAL

// Implementation
protected:
~CAspht0305Ctrl();

DECLARE_OLECREATE_EX(CAspht0305Ctrl)    // Class factory and guid
DECLARE_OLETYPELIB(CAspht0305Ctrl)      // GetTypeInfo
DECLARE_PROPPAGEIDS(CAspht0305Ctrl)     // Property page IDs
DECLARE_OLECTLTYPE(CAspht0305Ctrl)      // Type name and misc status

// Message maps
//{{AFX_MSG(CAspht0305Ctrl)
// NOTE - ClassWizard will add and remove member functions here.
//    DO NOT EDIT what you see in these blocks of generated code !
//}}AFX_MSG
DECLARE_MESSAGE_MAP()
```

continued on next page

continued from previous page

```
// Dispatch maps
//{{AFX_DISPATCH(CAspht0305Ctrl)
// NOTE - ClassWizard will add and remove member functions here.
//    DO NOT EDIT what you see in these blocks of generated code !
//}}AFX_DISPATCH
DECLARE_DISPATCH_MAP()

afx_msg void AboutBox();

// Event maps
//{{AFX_EVENT(CAspht0305Ctrl)
// NOTE - ClassWizard will add and remove member functions here.
//    DO NOT EDIT what you see in these blocks of generated code !
//}}AFX_EVENT
DECLARE_EVENT_MAP()

// Dispatch and event IDs
public:
enum {
//{{AFX_DISP_ID(CAspht0305Ctrl)
// NOTE: ClassWizard will add and remove enumeration elements here.
//    DO NOT EDIT what you see in these blocks of generated code !
//}}AFX_DISP_ID
};
protected:

void StartTimer();
void StopTimer();
};

//{{AFX_INSERT_LOCATION}}
// Microsoft Developer Studio will insert additional declarations immediately
before the previous line.

#endif //
!defined(AFX_ASPHT0305CTL_H__4F2D1EF4_C13C_11D0_B7D8_444553540000__INCLUDED)
```

3. Activate the Class Wizard dialog and select the Message Maps tab. Add override functions for the `OnAmbientPropertyChange`, `OnEnabledChanged`, `OnSetClientSite`, `WM_CREATE`, `WM_DESTROY`, `WM_ERASEBKGRND`, and `WM_TIMER` messages. When you are finished, the dialog should look very similar to Figure 3-21. Press OK and save the workspace.

4. Bring up the Class Wizard again, this time on the Automation tab. Enter an `Enabled` stock property, then a custom property named `Interval`, using a member variable of type `short`. When you are finished, the dialog box should look very similar to Figure 3-22. Press OK twice to add the changes to the project. Save the workspace.

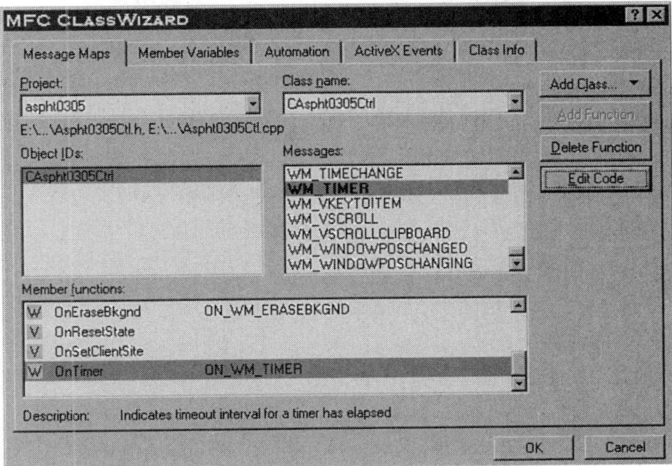

Figure 3-21 Adding message maps for overriding functions in `ASPHT0305CTL` with the Class Wizard

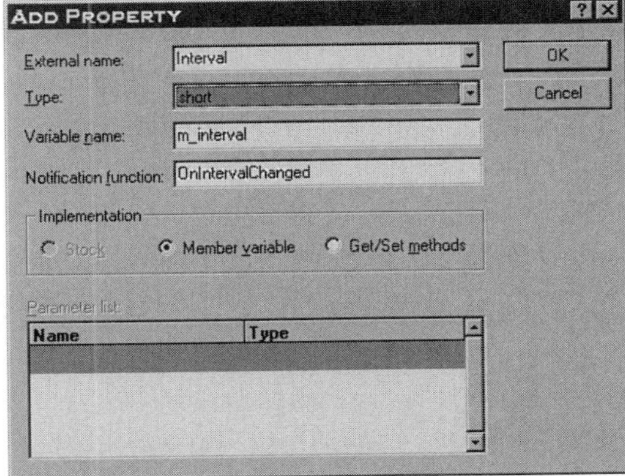

Figure 3-22 Using the Class Wizard to add a member variable–based notification property for the timer's interval

5. Open the Class Wizard one more time and select the ActiveX Events tab. Enter a custom event named `Timer`. When you are done, the display should look very similar to Figure 3-23. Press OK twice to add this change to the project. Save the workspace.

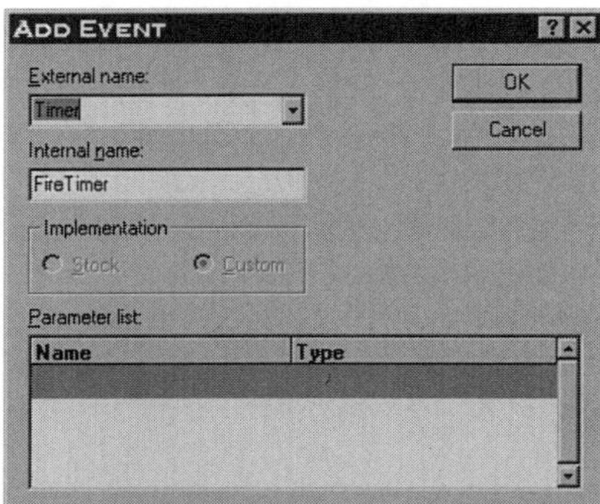

Figure 3-23 Adding the custom `Timer` event via the Class Wizard

6. Open the `IDB_ASPHT0305` bitmap in the Resource tab and edit it into something similar to that shown in Figure 3-24 to identify the component uniquely as relating to time. Save the workspace.

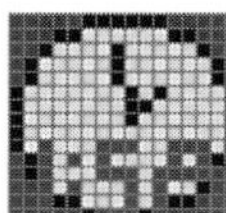

Figure 3-24 A custom bitmap for the project

7. Open the `IDD_PROPPAGE_ASPHT0305` dialog in the Resource tab and add controls in a pattern similar to that shown in Figure 3-25, with the Static control having a caption of `Firing Interval in Milliseconds`, the check box having a caption of `ASPHT0305 Timer Enabled`, and an Edit control to the right of the Static control. Save the workspace.

8. Press CTRL and double-click on the check box control. In the Class Wizard Add Member Variable dialog, set its name to `m_Enabled`, its category to `Value`, its type to `BOOL`, and its optional property to `Enabled`. Press OK. Then do the same to the Edit control and set its name to `m_Interval`, its category to `Value`, its type to `int`, and its optional property to `BorderStyle` (don't worry that this is wrong; you will fix it in a moment). The dialog should look similar to Figure 3-26 when you are done. Press OK and save the workspace.

9. Bring up `ASPHT0305PPG.CPP` in the text editor. Move to the `DoDataExchange` function and change the boldfaced code in Listing 3-27 to connect the Edit control to the correct `control` property. Save the workspace.

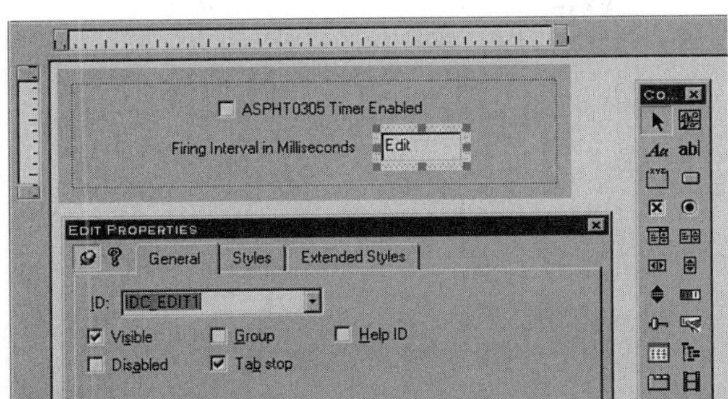

Figure 3-25 Adding controls to the property page dialog

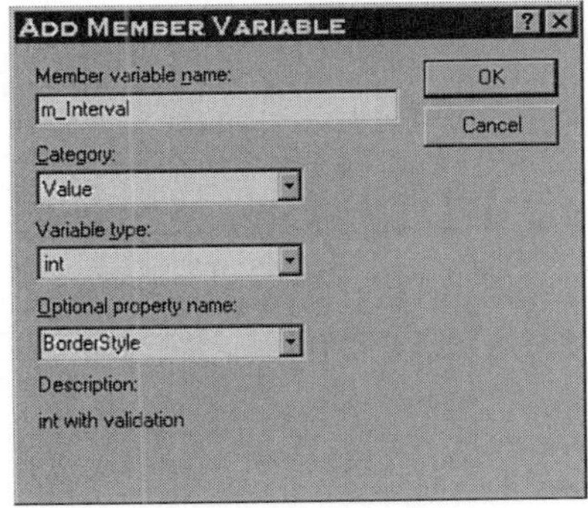

Figure 3-26 Connecting the dialog controls to member variables and properties

Listing 3-27 ASPHT0305PPG.CPP DoDataExchange source code

```
//////////////////////////////////////////////////////////////////////////////
// CAspht0305PropPage::DoDataExchange - Moves data between page and properties

void CAspht0305PropPage::DoDataExchange(CDataExchange* pDX)
{
//{{AFX_DATA_MAP(CAspht0305PropPage)
DDP_Check(pDX, IDC_CHECK1, m_Enabled, _T("Enabled") );
DDX_Check(pDX, IDC_CHECK1, m_Enabled);
DDP_Text(pDX, IDC_EDIT1, m_Interval, _T("Interval") );
DDX_Text(pDX, IDC_EDIT1, m_Interval);
//}}AFX_DATA_MAP
DDP_PostProcessing(pDX);
}
```

10. Bring up ASPHT0305CTL.CPP in the text editor. Move to the constructor function and add the boldfaced code in Listing 3-28 to initialize the control. Save the workspace.

Listing 3-28 ASPHT0305CTL.CPP constructor source code

```
/////////////////////////////////////////////////////////////////////////////
// CAspht0305Ctrl::CAspht0305Ctrl - Constructor

CAspht0305Ctrl::CAspht0305Ctrl()
{
InitializeIIDs(&IID_DAspht0305, &IID_DAspht0305Events);

// TODO: Initialize your control's instance data here.
SetInitialSize( 24, 22 ); //Keep size small since non-visible
m_Interval = (short) DEFAULT_TIMER_INTERVAL; //Initialize to 1 second
}
```

11. Move down to the OnDraw function. Enter the boldfaced code in Listing 3-29 to draw the design mode representation of the control. Save the workspace.

Listing 3-29 ASPHT0305CTL.CPP OnDraw source code

```
/////////////////////////////////////////////////////////////////////////////
// CAspht0305Ctrl::OnDraw - Drawing function

void CAspht0305Ctrl::OnDraw(
CDC* pdc, const CRect& rcBounds, const CRect& rcInvalid)
{
CBrush cbPanelBrush( RGB( 128 , 128 , 128 ));
pdc->FillRect( rcBounds, &cbPanelBrush );
CPen pHiLitePen(PS_SOLID, 2, RGB( 200 , 200 , 200 ));
CPen pShadowPen(PS_SOLID, 2, RGB( 32 , 32 , 32 ));
CPen *pOldPen = pdc->SelectObject( &pHiLitePen );
pdc->MoveTo(rcBounds.left + 2 , rcBounds.top + 2);
pdc->LineTo(rcBounds.right - 2 , rcBounds.top + 2 );
pdc->MoveTo(rcBounds.left + 2 , rcBounds.top + 2 );
pdc->LineTo(rcBounds.left + 2 , rcBounds.bottom - 2);
pdc->SelectObject( &pShadowPen );
pdc->MoveTo(rcBounds.right - 2 , rcBounds.bottom - 2 );
pdc->LineTo(rcBounds.right - 2 , rcBounds.top + 2);
pdc->MoveTo(rcBounds.right - 2 , rcBounds.bottom - 2);
pdc->LineTo(rcBounds.left + 2  , rcBounds.bottom - 2);
pdc->MoveTo(rcBounds.left + m_BorderWidth + 4 , rcBounds.top + m_BorderWidth + 4);
pdc->LineTo(rcBounds.right - m_BorderWidth - 4 , rcBounds.top + m_BorderWidth +⇐
4);
pdc->MoveTo(rcBounds.left + m_BorderWidth + 4 , rcBounds.top + m_BorderWidth + 4);
pdc->LineTo(rcBounds.left + m_BorderWidth + 4 , rcBounds.bottom - m_BorderWidth⇐
- 4);
pdc->SelectObject( &pHiLitePen );
pdc->MoveTo(rcBounds.right - m_BorderWidth - 4 , rcBounds.bottom - m_BorderWidth⇐
- 4);
pdc->LineTo(rcBounds.right - m_BorderWidth - 4 , rcBounds.top + m_BorderWidth +⇐
4);
```

```
pdc->MoveTo(rcBounds.right - m_BorderWidth - 4 , rcBounds.bottom - m_BorderWidth⇐
- 4);
pdc->LineTo(rcBounds.left + m_BorderWidth + 4, rcBounds.bottom - m_BorderWidth -⇐
4);
pdc->SelectObject(pOldPen);
HBITMAP hBmp = LoadBitmap( AfxGetInstanceHandle() , MAKEINTRESOURCE⇐
( IDB_ASPHT0305 ) );
CDC dcMem;
dcMem.CreateCompatibleDC( pdc );
CBitmap* pOldBMP = (CBitmap*) dcMem.SelectObject( hBmp );
pdc->BitBlt( rcBounds.left + 4 , rcBounds.bottom - 4 ,
16, 16 , &dcMem , 0 , 0 , SRCCOPY );
}
```

12. Move down to the `DoPropExchange` function. Enter the boldfaced code in Listing 3-30 to save the `Interval` property and make sure the value is updated. Save the workspace.

Listing 3-30 ASPHT0305CTL.CPP DoPropExchange source code

```
/////////////////////////////////////////////////////////////////////////////
// CAspht0305Ctrl::DoPropExchange - Persistence support

void CAspht0305Ctrl::DoPropExchange(CPropExchange* pPX)
{
ExchangeVersion(pPX, MAKELONG(_wVerMinor, _wVerMajor));
COleControl::DoPropExchange(pPX);

// TODO: Call PX_ functions for each persistent custom property.

short tInterval = m_interval;
PX_Short(pPX, _T("Interval"), (short) m_interval, (short) DEFAULT_TIMER_INTERVAL);

if (pPX->IsLoading())
{
if (tInterval != m_interval)
OnIntervalChanged(); // Update via notification function since don't use get/set
}
}
```

13. Move down to the `OnEnabledChanged` function. Enter the boldfaced code in Listing 3-31 to deal with turning the timer on and off as its `Enabled` property changes. Save the workspace.

Listing 3-31 ASPHT0305CTL.CPP OnEnabledChanged source code

```
void CAspht0305Ctrl::OnEnabledChanged()
{
// TODO: Add your specialized code here and/or call the base class

if (AmbientUserMode()) //Don't do this in design mode
{
if (GetEnabled())  //If Enabled is true
{
if (GetHwnd() != NULL) //And we have a handle for the function call
```

continued on next page

continued from previous page

```
StartTimer();       //Start the Timer
}
else
StopTimer(); //Stop the Timer
}
}
```

14. Move down to the `OnSetClientSite` function. Enter the boldfaced code in Listing 3-32 to force re-creation of the window when the control is connected. Save the workspace.

Listing 3-32 ASPHT0305CTL.CPP OnSetClientSite source code

```
void CAspht0305Ctrl::OnSetClientSite()
{
// TODO: Add your specialized code here and/or call the base class

RecreateControlWindow(); //Force recreation of the window
}
```

15. Move down to the `OnCreate` function. Enter the boldfaced code in Listing 3-33 to start the timer at once if it is enabled when the control is created. Save the workspace.

Listing 3-33 ASPHT0305CTL.CPP OnCreate source code

```
int CAspht0305Ctrl::OnCreate(LPCREATESTRUCT lpCreateStruct)
{
if (COleControl::OnCreate(lpCreateStruct) == -1)
return -1;

// TODO: Add your specialized creation code here

if (AmbientUserMode() && GetEnabled())
StartTimer(); //If not in design mode and enabled is true start the timer at once!

return 0;
}
```

16. Move down to the `OnDestroy` function. Enter the boldfaced code in Listing 3-34 to kill the timer if it is still running before the control is destroyed. Save the workspace.

Listing 3-34 ASPHT0305CTL.CPP OnDestroy source code

```
void CAspht0305Ctrl::OnDestroy()
{

// TODO: Add your message handler code here
StopTimer(); //Stop the timer if it is still running before we die!

COleControl::OnDestroy();

}
```

17. Move down to the `onEraseBkgrnd` function. Enter the boldfaced code in Listing 3-35 to prevent background repainting because this is a nonvisible control. Save the workspace.

Listing 3-35 ASPHT0305CTL.CPP OnEraseBkgrnd source code

```
BOOL CAspht0305Ctrl::OnEraseBkgnd(CDC* pDC)
{
// TODO: Add your message handler code here and/or call default

return TRUE; //Do this to prevent background erasing!
}
```

18. Move down to the `OnTimer` function. Enter the boldfaced code in Listing 3-36 to allow users to attach their code to the `Timer` events. Save the workspace.

Listing 3-36 ASPHT0305CTL.CPP OnTimer source code

```
void CAspht0305Ctrl::OnTimer(UINT nIDEvent)
{
// TODO: Add your message handler code here and/or call default

FireTimer(); //call our custom event so users can attach their code!
}
```

19. Move down to the `OnIntervalChanged` function. Enter the boldfaced code in Listing 3-37 to reset the timer if its `Interval` property changes when it is enabled at runtime. Save the workspace.

Listing 3-37 ASPHT0305CTL.CPP OnIntervalChanged source code

```
void CAspht0305Ctrl::OnIntervalChanged()
{
// TODO: Add notification handler code

if (GetEnabled() && AmbientUserMode()) //If not in design mode and enabled is true
{
StopTimer(); //Stop and start the Timer to take new value!
StartTimer();
}

SetModifiedFlag();
}
```

20. Move down to the `OnAmbientPropertyChange` function. Enter the boldfaced code in Listing 3-38 to reset the control when the user mode changes. Save the workspace.

Listing 3-38 ASPHT0305CTL.CPP OnAmbientPropertyChange source code

```
void CAspht0305Ctrl::OnAmbientPropertyChange(DISPID dispid)
{
// TODO: Add your specialized code here and/or call the base class

if (dispid == DISPID_AMBIENT_USERMODE) //If interface is for Ambient UserMode
change
{
if (GetEnabled()) //If Enabled is true
{
if (AmbientUserMode()) //If not in design mode then start timer
StartTimer();
else
StopTimer(); //else now in design mode, stop timer!
}

InvalidateControl();
}
}
```

21. Move down to the end of the file. Enter the boldfaced code in Listing 3-39 to supply the two custom methods you entered earlier in the header file. Save the workspace.

Listing 3-39 ASPHT0305CTL.CPP custom methods source code

```
/////////////////////////////////////////////////////////////////////////////
// CAspht0305Ctrl::StartTimer - Custom method to start the timer.

void CAspht0305Ctrl::StartTimer()
{
SetTimer(ID_TIMER, m_interval, NULL);
}


/////////////////////////////////////////////////////////////////////////////
// CAspht0305Ctrl::StopTimer - Custom method to stop the timer.

void CAspht0305Ctrl::StopTimer()
{
KillTimer(ID_TIMER);
}
```

22. Build `ASPHT0305.OCX`. Once the control has finished building and registering, start ActiveX Control Pad. Insert a copy of `ASPHT0305` into the page; you can bring up its property page if you would like to observe the controls you placed earlier; this display should look like Figure 3-27. Close the editor window to place the control on the HTML page. Then enter the HTML code in Listing 3-40 to script the control; you can also use the Script Wizard as shown in Figure 3-28. Save the file as

ASPHT0305.HTM. Bring it up in Internet Explorer and you will see a display similar to Figure 3-29 every 10 seconds as the timer fires. Press the button to turn it off. You have taken the big step of creating a complete custom nonvisible ActiveX control.

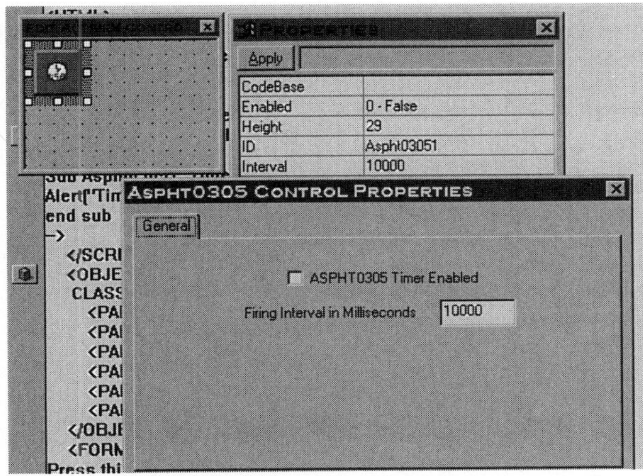

Figure 3-27 The functioning ASPHT0305 Timer control in ActiveX Control Pad

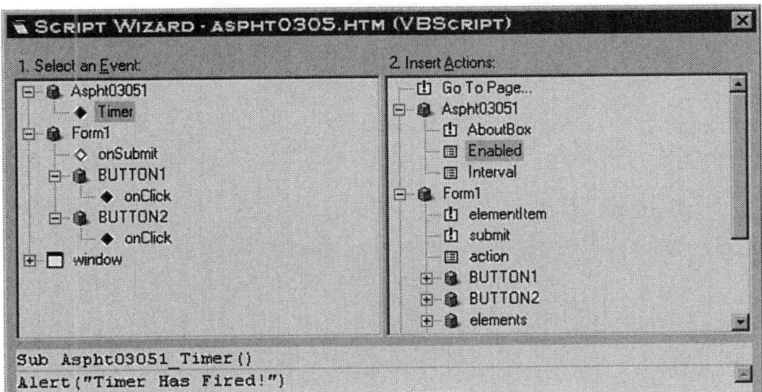

Figure 3-28 Scripting the ASPHT0305 Timer control in ActiveX Control Pad

Listing 3-40 ASPHT0305.HTM HTML source code

```
<HTML>
<HEAD>
    <SCRIPT LANGUAGE="VBScript">
<!--
Sub window_onLoad()
```

continued on next page

continued from previous page

```
Aspht03051.Enabled = True
Aspht03051.Interval = 10000
end sub
-->
    </SCRIPT>
<TITLE>Chapter Three How To Five Demo Page</TITLE>
</HEAD>
<BODY>
<H1>ASPHT0305 Timer Demo Page</H1>
    <SCRIPT LANGUAGE="VBScript">
<!--
Sub Aspht03051_Timer()
Alert("Timer Has Fired!")
end sub
-->
    </SCRIPT>
    <OBJECT ID="Aspht03051" WIDTH=39 HEIGHT=39
     CLASSID="CLSID:4F2D1EE6-C13C-11D0-B7D8-444553540000">
        <PARAM NAME="_Version" VALUE="65536">
        <PARAM NAME="_ExtentX" VALUE="1023">
        <PARAM NAME="_ExtentY" VALUE="1023">
        <PARAM NAME="_StockProps" VALUE="64">
       <PARAM NAME="Interval" VALUE="10000">
    </OBJECT>
    <FORM NAME="Form1">
You will see a timer message every ten seconds.<P>
<HR>
Press this button to turn off the timer.<P>
<HR>
        <INPUT LANGUAGE="VBScript" TYPE=BUTTON VALUE="Press To Stop Timer"
         ONCLICK="Aspht03051.Enabled = False" NAME="BUTTON2">
    </FORM>
<HR>
</BODY>
</HTML>
```

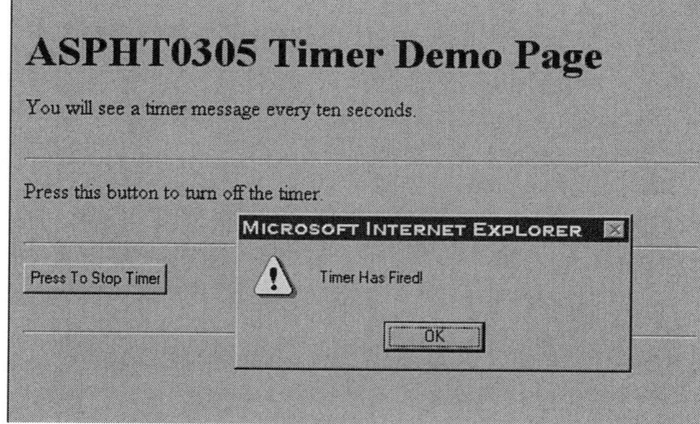

Figure 3-29 The ASPHT0305 Timer control in Internet Explorer

How It Works

Well, you may need your ActiveX coveralls, because you got a lot more than your hands dirty this time! This How-To illustrates a number of the down-and-dirty aspects of ActiveX coding, including adding custom methods, intercepting COM messages, and dealing with design versus runtime user modes.

Notice this code fragment from the `ASPHT0305CTL.H` file:

```
};
protected:

void StartTimer();
void StopTimer();
};
```

Those two methods are entirely hand-written; the MFC wizard system knows nothing about them. Therefore, you had to add the corresponding two method implementations in the `ASPHT0305CTL.CPP` file. This is the point in MFC ActiveX development where your C++ skills come into play; to add any custom methods that are not part of the ActiveX OLE system, you'll need to enter the code yourself.

Now note this method code from the same file:

```
void CAspht0305Ctrl::OnAmbientPropertyChange(DISPID dispid)
{
// TODO: Add your specialized code here and/or call the base class

if (dispid == DISPID_AMBIENT_USERMODE) //If interface is for Ambient UserMode
change
{
if (GetEnabled()) //If Enabled is true
{
if (AmbientUserMode()) //If not in design mode then start timer
StartTimer();
else
StopTimer(); //else now in design mode, stop timer!
}

InvalidateControl();
}
}
```

At this point, the `DISPID` passed in from the OLE system becomes important; prior to this, MFC has shielded you from this level of detail by processing all the messages itself and routing them as needed. Here, you need to find out whether the message involves a change in the user mode of the system, so you explicitly test for `DISPID_AMBIENT_USERMODE` in the parameter passed in. If you find it, make the appropriate tests and reset the system. Any interaction with the OLE system not automatically handled by MFC will use a variation of this technique.

Finally, study this often-repeated bit of code:

```
if (AmbientUserMode() && GetEnabled())
StartTimer(); //If not in design mode and enabled is true start the timer at once!
```

The AmbientUserMode function returns true if the control is not in design mode (such as in the ActiveX editor window) and false if it is. This prevents performing behaviors that would be superfluous (or even dangerous) when designing only when the control is actually running.

Comments

Note that no check of AmbientUserMode was needed for the OnDraw function; the reason is that no WM_PAINT messages reach the control at runtime because of this bit of boldfaced code:

```
static const DWORD BASED_CODE _dwAspht0305OleMisc =
OLEMISC_INVISIBLEATRUNTIME |
OLEMISC_SETCLIENTSITEFIRST |
OLEMISC_INSIDEOUT |
OLEMISC_CANTLINKINSIDE |
OLEMISC_RECOMPOSEONRESIZE;
```

When this flag is included in the flags for the control, the OLE system automatically screens out WM_PAINT messages for the control at runtime. However, remember that you had to kill WM_ERASEBKGRND messages explicitly. All nonvisible controls need to do this to cut down on overhead because this message *isn't* screened out.

3.6 How do I... Create an application that can use ActiveX controls at runtime with Visual C++ 5.0?

Problem

I'd like to use my custom ActiveX control in a regular application written with MFC. How do I handle this?

Technique

There is a particular option you need to set when creating your executable project, and some new steps to use in the IDE. This How-To illustrates using a custom ActiveX control in an MFC executable by reusing the control from How-To 3.3. Although these directions create the project from scratch, the CD contains a completed workspace under CH03\HT06\ASPHT0306\.

Steps

1. Activate Visual C++ 5.0. Choose File|New... and start a new MFC AppWizard executable with the name of `ASPHT0306` as a dialog-based project. On page 2 of the wizard dialog, make sure that the ActiveX Controls check box is enabled and enter a title of `ActiveX Control Container Demo`. The wizard page should look very similar to Figure 3-30 when you are finished. Press Finish and OK to create the skeleton project.

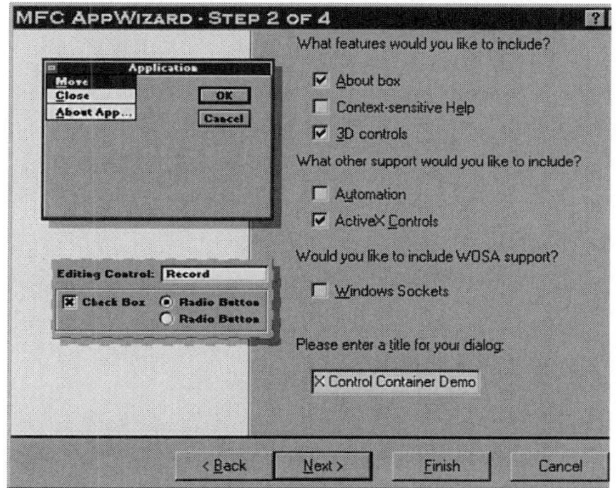

Figure 3-30 Preparing an MFC AppWizard executable project to use ActiveX controls

2. Open the main dialog for the project in the resource editor. Expand it considerably in both height and width. Then right-click on it to bring up its shortcut menu. Select the Insert ActiveX Control option, as shown in Figure 3-31.

3. In the dialog box that appears, select the `ASPHT0302` control, which contains the last version of the progressive control developed in How-To 3.3. Place it on the lower part of the dialog, leaving room above it for several controls. Right-click on it to bring up its property pages and select some interesting settings, as shown in Figure 3-32. Close the property pages and save the workspace.

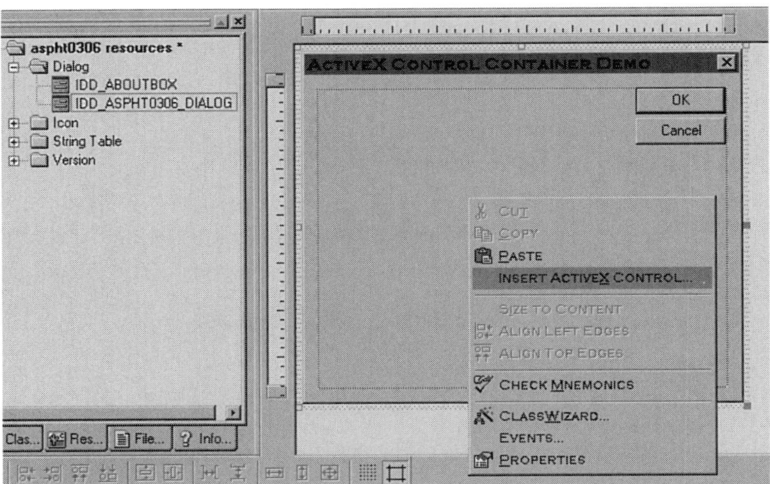

Figure 3-31 Shortcut menu for main dialog in ASPHT0306 project ready to insert ActiveX control

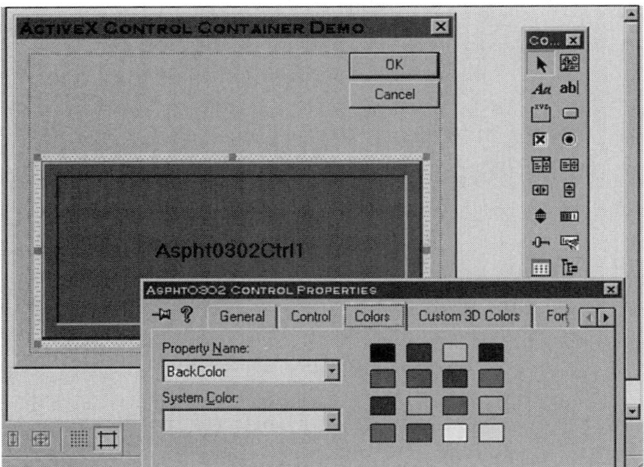

Figure 3-32 Setting interesting values for the ActiveX control with its property pages

4. Place a Static Text control with a caption of `New Control Caption:`, an Edit control, and two Push Button controls with captions of `Set Caption Property` and `Call FlipCOlors Control Method` as shown in Figure 3-33. Hold down CTRL and double-click on the Edit control and add a member variable named `m_Caption`, with a category of `Value` and type of `CString`, to allow interacting with its information. Save the workspace.

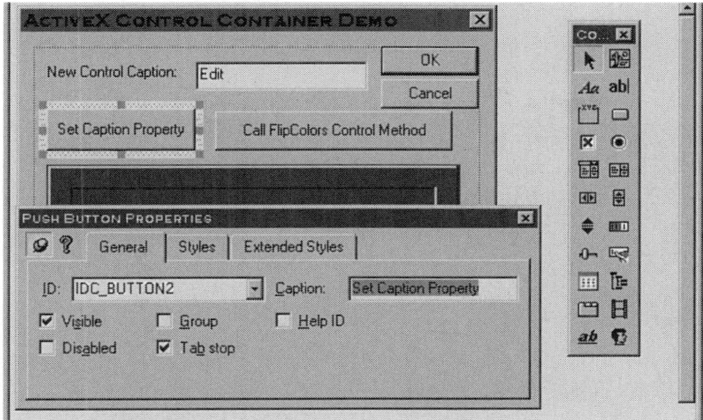

Figure 3-33 Placing controls on the project main dialog

5. Right-click again on one of the Push Button controls and select Events from the shortcut menu. Select its `BN_CLICKED` message, press the Add Handler button, and enter a name for the event handler method as shown in Figure 3-34. Add additional event handlers for a `BN_CLICKED` message for the other push button and for the `Click` and `InvertColors` events of the ActiveX control. Save the workspace.

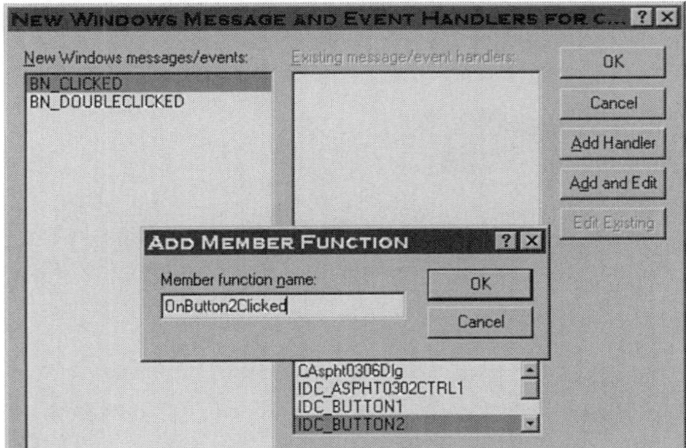

Figure 3-34 Adding an event handler method for a push button mouse click

6. Bring up the Class Wizard, select the Member Variables tab, and select the ActiveX control's ID. Press the Add Variable button, and a dialog box will appear as shown in Figure 3-35 as the Class Wizard realizes it needs to include a linked variable to the control in the project. Press OK and the system will create the needed information to allow using a member variable to access the ActiveX control.

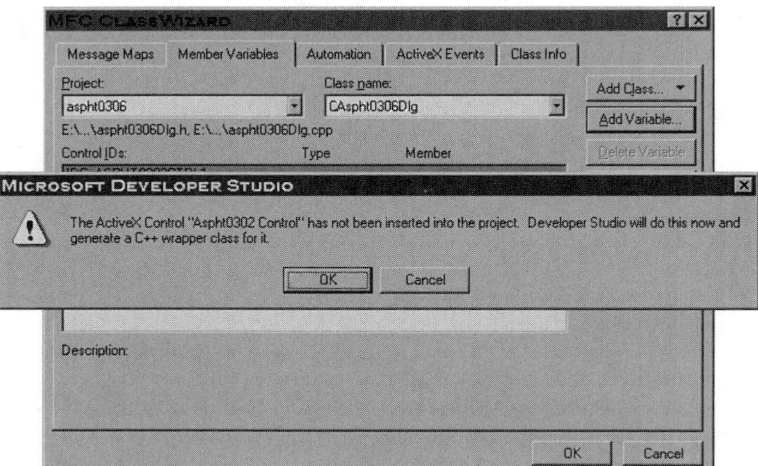

Figure 3-35 Creating wrapper classes for the ActiveX control in the `ASPHT0306` project

7. Shortly you will see a dialog box similar to that shown in Figure 3-36 listing the new classes derived from the control. Press OK to continue adding the control to your project.

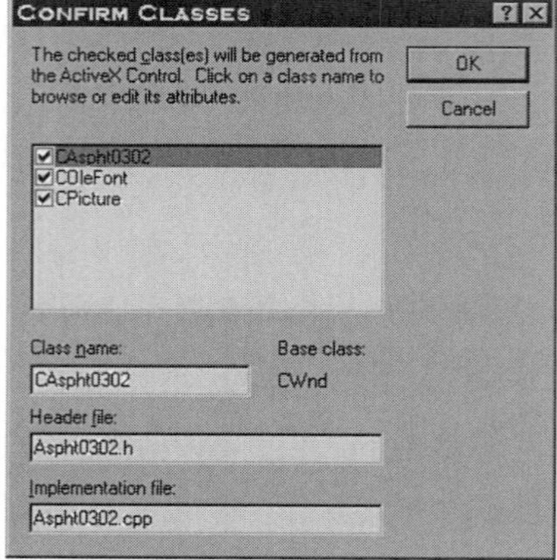

Figure 3-36 Added classes for the ActiveX control in the `ASPHT0306` project

8. Finally, you will reach the dialog shown in Figure 3-37. Enter `m_Aspht0302` as the variable name and press OK.

9. The Class Wizard should now strongly resemble the display shown in Figure 3-38. Note that now the control's ID value is mapped to the member variable, which can thus be used to interact with it in the project's CPP code. Press OK to complete adding the control's member variable to the project.

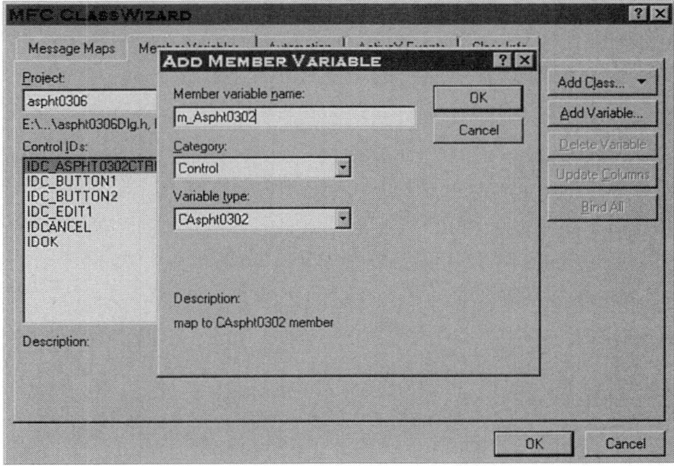

Figure 3-37 Adding the ActiveX control member variable in the ASPHT0306 project

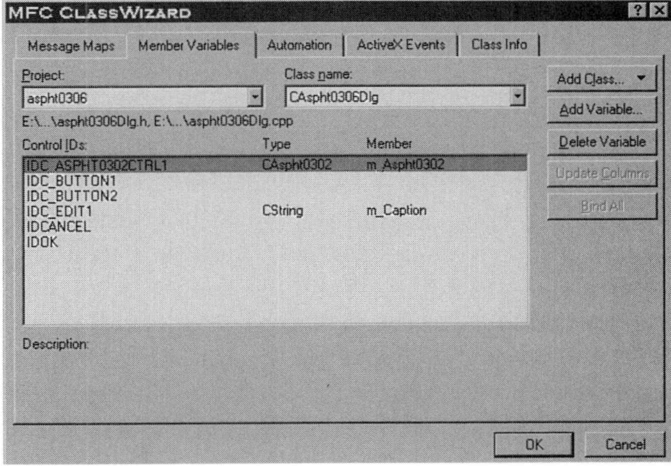

Figure 3-38 Shortcut menu for main dialog in ASPHT0306 project

10. Bring up the `ASPHT0306DLG.CPP` file in the text editor. Locate the four stubs written into the project by the Class Wizard, and enter the boldfaced code in Listing 3-41 to add functionality to the events and controls on the display. Save the workspace and build `ASPHT0306.EXE`.

Listing 3-41 ASPHT0306DLG.CPP event handlers source code

```
<
void CAspht0306Dlg::OnButton2Clicked()
{
// TODO: Add your control notification handler code here
SetWindowText(_T("ActiveX Control Container Demo"));
UpdateData( true );
m_Aspht0302.SetCaption( (LPCSTR) m_Caption );
}

void CAspht0306Dlg::OnClickAspht0302ctrl1Click()
{
// TODO: Add your control notification handler code here
SetWindowText(_T("ASPHT0302 Clicked!"));
m_Aspht0302.FlipColors( true );
}

void CAspht0306Dlg::OnInvertColorsAspht0302ctrl1(short ColorsToInvert)
{
// TODO: Add your control notification handler code here
SetWindowText(_T("ASPHT0302 InvertColors"));
m_Aspht0302.FlipColors( true );
}

void CAspht0306Dlg::OnButton1Click()
{
// TODO: Add your control notification handler code here
SetWindowText(_T("ActiveX Control Container Demo"));
m_Aspht0302.FlipColors( true );
}
```

11. Run the executable, enter a new caption in the Edit control, and press the Set Caption Property button; the new text should appear instantly in the control's caption. Then press the Call FlipColors Control Method button and the colors should invert themselves as shown in Figure 3-39. Now click on the control itself; the colors will return to normal and a message will appear in the caption title to notify you that an event handler for the control fired, as shown in Figure 3-40. You have learned how to use custom ActiveX controls properties, methods, and events in your MFC executable projects!

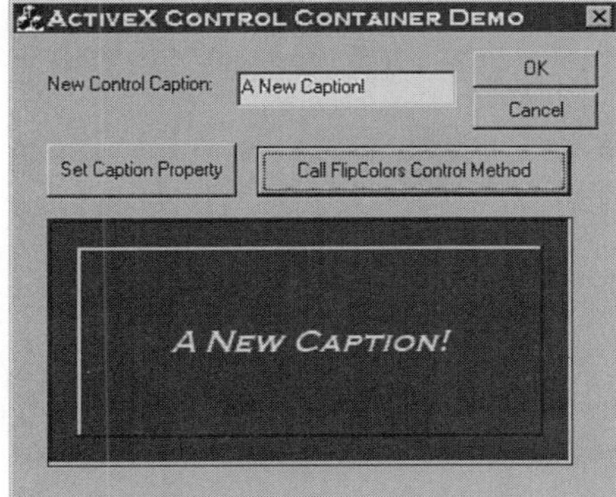

Figure 3-39 The ASPHT0306 executable showing the buttons' functionality

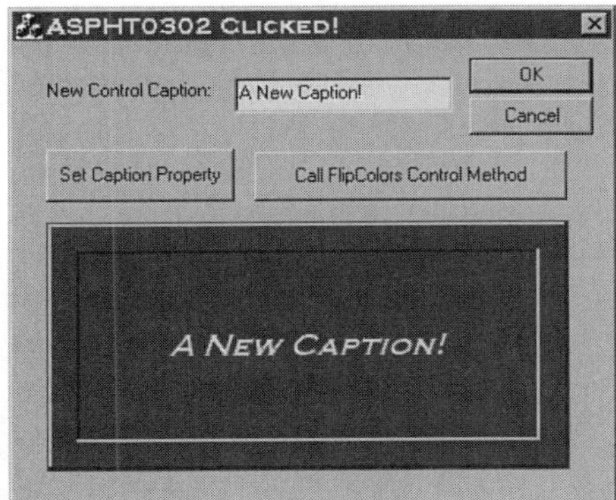

Figure 3-40 The ASPHT0306 executable showing the event handler method intercepting events for the ActiveX control

How It Works

MFC does all the work here, along with the Class Wizard. By checking the ActiveX Controls option when you created the project, all the background MFC code to handle OLE/ActiveX messaging and creation was automatically put in place. This allowed you to click on a menu option in the resource editor and place any ActiveX control you liked on your dialog box.

The other half of the work was done when you attempted to link the control's ID value on the dialog box with a member variable. The Class Wizard immediately knew that it needed to import the interfaces for the control into the current project and proceeded to do so; only after this was done were you allowed to create the variable and then use it.

Note that the events for the control were not handled directly by your code; instead they went into a special macro section of the `ASPHT0306DLG.CPP` file:

```
BEGIN_EVENTSINK_MAP(CAspht0306Dlg, CDialog)
//{{AFX_EVENTSINK_MAP(CAspht0306Dlg)
ON_EVENT(CAspht0306Dlg, IDC_ASPHT0302CTRL1, -600 /* Click */,
OnClickAspht0302ctrl1Click, VTS_NONE)
ON_EVENT(CAspht0306Dlg, IDC_ASPHT0302CTRL1, 1 /* InvertColors */,
OnInvertColorsAspht0302ctrl1, VTS_I2)
//}}AFX_EVENTSINK_MAP
END_EVENTSINK_MAP()
```

This has a drawback: The control's events cannot be fired from outside unless they are exposed via a method. Thus, although you wrote an event handler for the `InvertColors` event, it is never called by the control without scripting and so does not occur. To get around this, a new custom method could be exported from the `ASPHT0302` control just to call its internal `FireInvertColors` method. Other programs that want to use the event could then call this method to trigger it.

More interestingly, notice that the ActiveX control's `Caption` property is not accessed directly, but rather through its `SetCaption` method. This is because C++ is exposing the raw COM interfaces of the ActiveX object rather than using its `DispInterfaces` the way Visual Basic does. Although this is more powerful, it can also be frustrating, so be warned!

Comments

Note the call to `UpdateData( true )`. This little method is required to make sure that a member variable linked to a control has the latest value from the control's data. Attempting to use the member variable without calling `UpdateData` may result in older information being used. The `true` parameter means to load the member variable from the control; a value of `false` would load the control from the member variable. (You didn't need to bother with this on the property pages before because they do this automatically.)

COMPLEXITY
INTERMEDIATE

3.7 How do I… Create an ActiveX document server using Visual C++ 5.0?

Problem

I have an OLE server for a custom data type that I'd like to export onto the Web. Does MFC have support for this in VC 5?

Technique

Visual C++ 5.0 includes the capability to convert an older OLE server into an ActiveX document server. Unfortunately, the process is not currently automated, but this How-To takes you through the steps of converting the demonstration OLE server `SCRIBBLE` into an ActiveX document server. (This code is not shipped on the book CD because it is copyrighted by Microsoft, and because it is already available on all copies of VC 5!)

Steps

1. Activate Visual C++ 5.0 and locate the `SCRIBBLE` demonstration project that ships with the system (use the online help to find the hypertext link to copy the files if needed; the lesson you need is called `STEP 7`). Load and build the `SCRIBBLE.EXE` project and run it once to register it with the OLE system (because it's an older server, it does not self-register the way ActiveX controls do).

2. Open the `STDAFX.H` file associated with the project in the text editor and add the code in Listing 3-42 to include the `DocObject` classes. Save the workspace.

Listing 3-42 `STDAFX.H` header file source code

```
// stdafx.h : include file for standard system include files,
//  or project specific include files that are used frequently, but
//      are changed infrequently
//
// This is a part of the Microsoft Foundation Classes C++ library.
// Copyright (C) 1992-1997 Microsoft Corporation
// All rights reserved.
//
// This source code is only intended as a supplement to the
// Microsoft Foundation Classes Reference and related
// electronic documentation provided with the library.
// See these sources for detailed information regarding the
// Microsoft Foundation Classes product.

#include <afxwin.h>         // MFC core and standard components
#include <afxext.h>         // MFC extensions
#include <afxtempl.h>       // MFC templates

#ifndef _AFX_NO_AFXCMN_SUPPORT
#include <afxcmn.h>        // MFC support for Windows 95 Common Controls
#endif // _AFX_NO_AFXCMN_SUPPORT

#include <afxole.h>          // MFC OLE classes
#include <afxdocob.h>       //ActiveX Document Object classes
```

3. Open the `SCRIBBLE.CPP` file associated with the project in the text editor and add the boldfaced code in Listing 3-43 to register the server as an ActiveX document server. Save the workspace.

Listing 3-43 `SCRIBBLE.CPP UpdateRegistry` source code

```
// When a server application is launched stand-alone, it is a good idea
//  to update the system registry in case it has been damaged.
// Replace OAT_INPLACE_SERVER with OAT_DOC_OBJECT_SERVER for ActiveX Documents
m_server.UpdateRegistry(OAT_DOC_OBJECT_SERVER);

// Dispatch commands specified on the command line
```

4. Now, select Edit|Find In Files from the menu bar. In the dialog, enter `COleIPFrameWnd` as the search text for all files in the project, as shown in Figure 3-41. Make sure the Look in subfolders option is checked. Press Find and the system will locate all references to the text in the files of the project, as shown in Figure 3-42. Go to each reference and manually change the text to `COleDocIPFrameWnd`; an example is shown in Listing 3-44. DO NOT USE SEARCH AND REPLACE GLOBALLY! Save the workspace. (Note: You can simply double-click on each line in the output window and the IDE will automatically take you to the line of source code it represents. This is illustrated in Figure 3-43.)

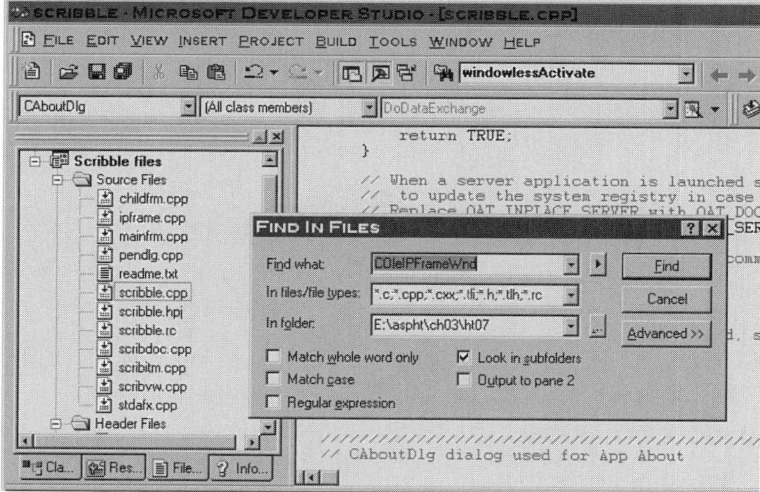

Figure 3-41 The Find In Files dialog preparing to search for `COleIPFrameWnd` in all files of the `SCRIBBLE` project

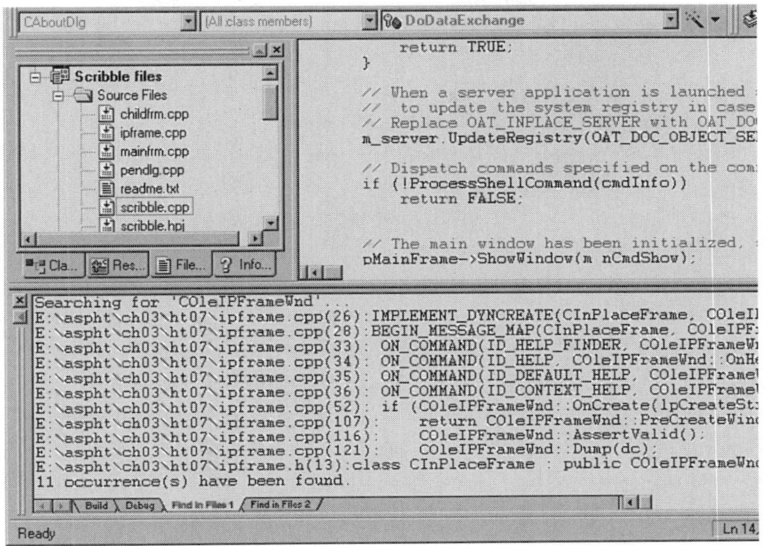

Figure 3-42 All occurrences of `COleIPFrameWnd` in `SCRIBBLE` project files found

Listing 3-44 `IPFRAME.CPP` `COleIPFrameWnd` replacement source code

```
/////////////////////////////////////////////////////////////////////////////
// CInPlaceFrame (Change to COleDocIPFrameWnd for ActiveX Document Server)

IMPLEMENT_DYNCREATE(CInPlaceFrame, COleDocIPFrameWnd)

BEGIN_MESSAGE_MAP(CInPlaceFrame, COleDocIPFrameWnd)
//{{AFX_MSG_MAP(CInPlaceFrame)
ON_WM_CREATE()
//}}AFX_MSG_MAP
// Global help commands
ON_COMMAND(ID_HELP_FINDER, COleDocIPFrameWnd::OnHelpFinder)
ON_COMMAND(ID_HELP, COleDocIPFrameWnd::OnHelp)
ON_COMMAND(ID_DEFAULT_HELP, COleDocIPFrameWnd::OnHelpFinder)
ON_COMMAND(ID_CONTEXT_HELP, COleDocIPFrameWnd::OnContextHelp)
END_MESSAGE_MAP()
```

5. Repeat the Find in Files procedure from step 4 for the text `COleServerItem`. Replace it by hand in all files with `CDocObjectServerItem`, as shown in Listing 3-45. Save the workspace.

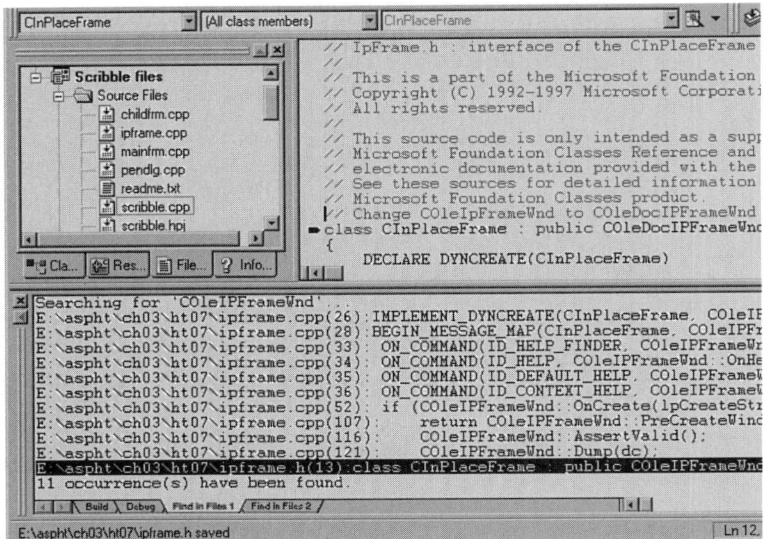

Figure 3-43 Double-clicking in the output pane to jump to exact source code lines for editing

Listing 3-45 SCRIBITM.H header file source code

```
// Change COleServerItem to CDocObjectServerItem for ActiveX Documents
class CScribbleItem : public CDocObjectServerItem
{
DECLARE_DYNAMIC(CScribbleItem)

// Constructors
```

6. Open the `SCRIBDOC.H` file associated with the project in the text editor and add the code in Listing 3-46 to include an OLE command message map for the document class. Save the workspace.

Listing 3-46 SCRIBDOC.H header file source code

```
// Generated message map functions
protected:
//{{AFX_MSG(CScribbleDoc)
afx_msg void OnEditClearAll();
afx_msg void OnPenThickOrThin();
afx_msg void OnUpdateEditClearAll(CCmdUI* pCmdUI);
afx_msg void OnUpdatePenThickOrThin(CCmdUI* pCmdUI);
afx_msg void OnPenWidths();
afx_msg void OnEditCopy();
//}}AFX_MSG
```

```
DECLARE_MESSAGE_MAP()
DECLARE_OLECMD_MAP()
};
```

7. Open the SCRIBDOC.CPP file associated with the project in the text editor and add the boldfaced code in Listing 3-47 to map the print handler to its OLE equivalent. Save the workspace.

Listing 3-47 SCRIBDOC.CPP OLECMD message maps source code

```
/////////////////////////////////////////////////////////////////////////////
// CScribbleDoc

IMPLEMENT_DYNCREATE(CScribbleDoc, COleServerDoc)

BEGIN_MESSAGE_MAP(CScribbleDoc, COleServerDoc)
//{{AFX_MSG_MAP(CScribbleDoc)
ON_COMMAND(ID_EDIT_CLEAR_ALL, OnEditClearAll)
ON_COMMAND(ID_PEN_THICK_OR_THIN, OnPenThickOrThin)
ON_UPDATE_COMMAND_UI(ID_EDIT_CLEAR_ALL, OnUpdateEditClearAll)
ON_UPDATE_COMMAND_UI(ID_PEN_THICK_OR_THIN, OnUpdatePenThickOrThin)
ON_COMMAND(ID_PEN_WIDTHS, OnPenWidths)
ON_COMMAND(ID_EDIT_COPY, OnEditCopy)
//}}AFX_MSG_MAP
END_MESSAGE_MAP()

BEGIN_OLECMD_MAP(CScribbleDoc, COleServerDoc)
  ON_OLECMD_PRINT()
END_OLECMD_MAP()
/////////////////////////////////////////////////////////////////////////////
// CScribbleDoc construction/destruction
```

8. Open the SCRIBDOC.H file associated with the project in the text editor again and add the boldfaced code in the upper part of Listing 3-48 to include the DocObjectServer method for the class; then add the boldfaced code in the lower part of the listing to SCRIBDOC.CPP. Save the workspace.

Listing 3-48 SCRIBDOC.H and CPP source code

```
// Attributes
protected:
// The document keeps track of the current pen width on
//PUT THIS IN SCRIBDOC.H
// behalf of all views. We'd like the user interface of
// Scribble to be such that if the user chooses the Draw
// Thick Line command, it will apply to all views, not just
// the view that currently has the focus.

UINT            m_nPenWidth;        // current user-selected pen width
BOOL            m_bThickPen;        // TRUE if current pen is thick
```

continued on next page

continued from previous page

```
UINT            m_nThinWidth;
UINT            m_nThickWidth;
CPen            m_penCur;           // pen created according to
// user-selected pen style (width)
public:
CTypedPtrList<CObList,CStroke*>     m_strokeList;
CPen*           GetCurrentPen() { return &m_penCur; }

protected:
CSize           m_sizeDoc;
public:
CSize GetDocSize() { return m_sizeDoc; }
CScribbleItem* GetEmbeddedItem()
{ return (CScribbleItem*)COleServerDoc::GetEmbeddedItem(); }
//Add this to create the DocObjectServer
CDocObjectServer* GetDocObjectServer(LPOLEDOCUMENTSITE pSite);
// Operations
//PUT THIS IN SCRIBDOC.CPP
CDocObjectServer* CScribDoc::GetDocObjectServer(LPOLEDOCUMENTSITE pSite)
{
return new CDocObjectServer(this, pSite);
}
```

9. Build `SCRIBBLE`. Run the application once to register it and create a simple scribble document ("hello world" drawn freehand is the one this example used). Save the scribble file as **`ASPHT0307.OSC`** in the local directory for the project. Then open ActiveX Control Pad and enter the HTML code in Listing 3-49. Save the file as **`ASPHT0307.HTM`** in the same directory as the SCB file you created earlier. Bring **`ASPHT0307.HTM`** up in Internet Explorer and you will see a display similar to Figure 3-44. You have reached ActiveX guru-dom now, creating an ActiveX document server for a custom data type.

Listing 3-49 `ASPHT0307.HTM` HTML source code

```
<HTML>
<HEAD>
<TITLE>Chapter Three How To Seven Demo</TITLE>
</HEAD>

<BODY>
<H1>This is a demo of an ActiveX Document!</H1>
<HR>
<IFRAME NAME="IFrame1" SRC="aspht0307.osc" WIDTH=300
HEIGHT=300 MARGINHEIGHT=0 MARGINWIDTH=0 FRAMEBORDER=1
SCROLLING="Yes"></IFRAME>
<HR>
</BODY>
</HTML>
```

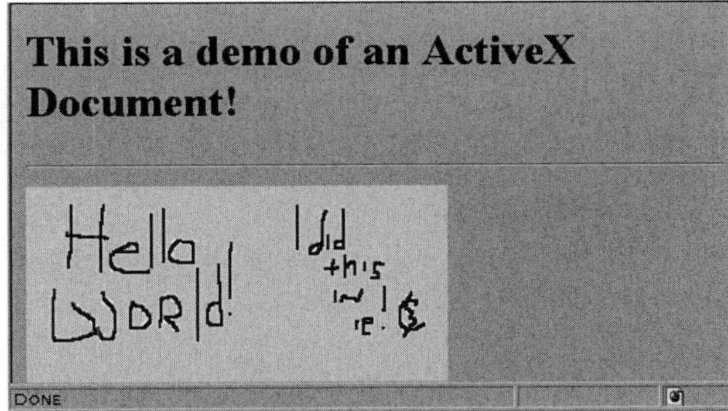

Figure 3-44 A scribble document in an HTML file in Internet Explorer

How It Works

The functionality of this How-To depends on replacing all the class members of standard OLE document management with the new `DocObject` classes. Believe it or not, this is all that is required to upgrade a older OLE server to the new power of ActiveX!

Comments

There is a peculiar problem with the step 7 code that sometimes causes it to fail to compile after these changes are made; if you encounter this problem, copy the `BINDSCRB` files to the directory instead of the step 7 code and compile them without making changes; they appear identical in every respect to the code above, but do not have the strange compilation error.

3.8 How do I… Create an ActiveX document container using Visual C++ 5.0?

Problem

Our company wants to distribute its own viewer application for our ActiveX document type and several others. Does MFC have support for this?

Technique

MFC does indeed have support for ActiveX document viewing through its Container option. This How-To develops a simple but complete ActiveX document container application using MFC. These steps create the application from scratch, but for your convenience the complete project is on the CD under `CH03\HT08\FINAL\ASPHT0308\`.

Steps

1. Activate Visual C++ 5.0. Begin a new MFC AppWizard EXE application as a single document application with no database support. As shown in Figure 3-45, choose the Container radio button, with support for compound files, automation, and ActiveX.

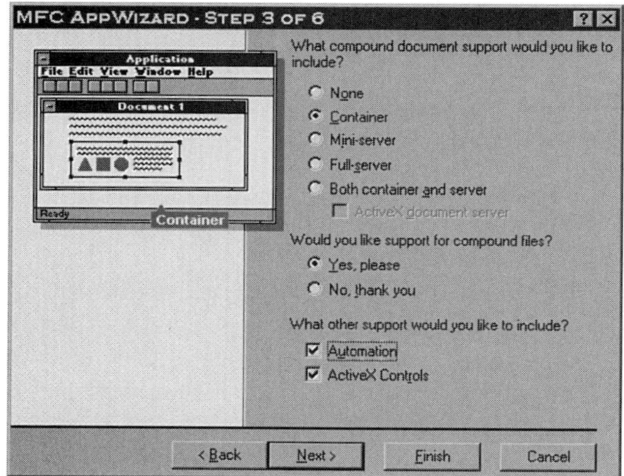

Figure 3-45 Creating an MFC AppWizard EXE with ActiveX document container support

2. Build `ASPHT0308.EXE`. When it is finished, run the application and choose Edit|Insert New Object, and place a new Microsoft Word object on the document. It will activate and work just as it does in the application itself, as shown in Figure 3-46. You have created an application with basic ActiveX document container support.

Figure 3-46 Using a Microsoft Word object in the ASPHT0308 document via ActiveX document containment

How It Works

MFC provides all the code to run ActiveX documents behind the scenes! Just by checking those three options during the AppWizard creation process, you don't have to do any hard work!

Comments

Unfortunately, the Container option currently supports only old-style OLE containers, not ActiveX document containers, due to last-minute problems at Microsoft. Microsoft says it will be releasing a patch for this shortly; please check the `README.TXT` file on the CD under "ActiveX Document Container Patch" for information on this upgrade.

3.9 How do I… Create ActiveX documents on an HTML page entirely at runtime with VBScript 2.0?

Problem

I'd like to be able to write the HTML code that creates my ActiveX documents directly rather than via ActiveX Control Pad. I understand VBScript 2.0 has some capability in this direction; how do I use it?

Technique

VBScript 2.0 allows runtime object creation, and the object can be an ActiveX document server! This How-To creates a copy of Microsoft Word dynamically with scripted HTML and loads a test file into it. The directions here create the project from scratch, but for your convenience a copy of the HTML file is on the CD under `\CH03\HT09\`.

Steps

1. Activate Notepad or some other simple text editor (Notepad is reported to be known at Microsoft these days as Visual Notepad++). Enter the HTML code in Listing 3-50 and save it as `ASPHT0309.HTM`.

Listing 3-50 `ASPHT0309.HTM` HTML source code

```
<HTML>
<HEAD>
<TITLE>Chapter Three How To Nine Demo Page</TITLE>
</HEAD>
<SCRIPT LANGUAGE=VBSCRIPT>
Dim WordDocument
Set WordDocument = CreateObject("Word.Document")
WordDocument.Application.Visible = True
WordDocument.Open "test1.doc"
</SCRIPT>
<BODY>
</BODY>
</HTML>
```

2. Bring up `ASPHT0309.HTM` in Internet Explorer and you will see a display similar to Figure 3-47 as the IE system creates the copy of Word entirely from scripting. You have learned to use VBScript 2.0's dynamic object system to create custom ActiveX documents at runtime with ActiveX Scripting.

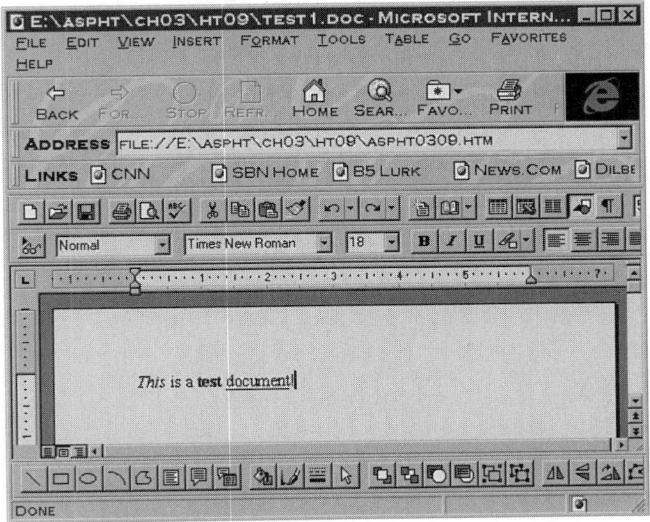

Figure 3-47 `ASPHT0309.HTM` in Internet Explorer showing the Microsoft Word ActiveX document dynamically created

How It Works

The key to this How-To is the inclusion of ActiveX document support in the VBScript object system. As long as the ActiveX document server is registered on the local system, Internet Explorer will automatically load it into memory and expose its automation interfaces to the script, just like an ActiveX control!

Comments

You need Word 97 for this How-To to function or you will receive a script error `Object not safe for scripting` because previous versions of Word were not written as script-safe ActiveX document servers.

AX--ASP

COMPLEXITY
ADVANCED

3.10 How do I... Use Active Server Pages with the VBScript 2.0 `TextStream` object to produce cookies that last between sessions?

Problem

I really need to keep track of user settings for my custom ActiveX control between sessions. Because cookies can't do this unless I give them expiration dates (and my users don't like that), does ASP offer any alternative?

Technique

Yes, with VBScript 2.0's **TextStream** object! This How-To takes the source code from How-To 2.10 and enhances it to use text streams and create "permanent cookies." Although the directions here create the project from scratch, the completed ASP files are on the book CD under **\CH03\HT10**. (If you have not created the **ASPEXEC** directory as requested in the Introduction, please refer to the "Creating an Executable Virtual Directory for ASP Scripting" section of the Introduction and create the directory now. You need it to do this How-To!)

Steps

1. Activate your copy of ActiveX Control Pad. Start a new HTML file and add the code in Listing 3-51. Then save the file as **ACTIVEXASP3.ASP** (choose All Files in the type combo box to prevent adding **.HTM** to the filename.) Make sure you save it into the **ASPEXEC** directory alias location!

Listing 3-51 ACTIVEXASP3.ASP ASP script file

```
<%@ LANGUAGE = VBScript %>
<%
      dim fs
      dim tf
      Set fs = CreateObject("Scripting.FileSystemObject")
      Set tf = fs.OpenTextFile("c:\storesets.txt",1,true)
      if IsEmpty( Request("Text1")) then
        if tf.AtEndOfStream = true then
          Response.Cookies("ASPHT0208")("BorderWidth") = "10"
        else
```

```
          Response.Cookies("ASPHT0208")("BorderWidth")=tf.ReadLine
        end if
      else
        Response.Cookies("ASPHT0208")("BorderWidth") = Request("Text1")
      end if
      if IsEmpty( Request("Text2")) then
        if tf.AtEndOfStream = true then
          Response.Cookies("ASPHT0208")("Caption") = "ActiveX is Cool!"
        else
          Response.Cookies("ASPHT0208")("Caption") = tf.ReadLine
      end if
      else
        Response.Cookies("ASPHT0208")("Caption") = Request("Text2")
      end if
      if IsEmpty( Request("Text3")) then
        if tf.AtEndOfStream = true then
          Response.Cookies("ASPHT0208")("PanelColor") = "&H0000AF00"
        else
          Response.Cookies("ASPHT0208")("PanelColor") = tf.ReadLine
        end if
      else
        Response.Cookies("ASPHT0208")("PanelColor") = Request("Text3")
      end if
      if IsEmpty( Request("Text4")) then
        if tf.AtEndOfStream = true then
          Response.Cookies("ASPHT0208")("HighlightColor") = "&H0000FF00"
        else
          Response.Cookies("ASPHT0208")("HighlightColor") = tf.ReadLine
        end if
      else
        Response.Cookies("ASPHT0208")("HighlightColor") = Request("Text4")
      end if
      if IsEmpty( Request("Text5")) then
        if tf.AtEndOfStream = true then
          Response.Cookies("ASPHT0208")("ShadowColor") = "&H00000A00"
        else
          Response.Cookies("ASPHT0208")("ShadowCOlor") = tf.ReadLine
        end if
      else
        Response.Cookies("ASPHT0208")("ShadowColor") = Request("Text5")
      end if
      tf.Close
      Set tf = fs.CreateTextFile("c:\storesets.txt", TRUE,FALSE)
      tf.WriteLine( Request.Cookies("ASPHT0208")("BorderWidth") )
      tf.WriteLine( Request.Cookies("ASPHT0208")("Caption"))
      tf.WriteLine( Request.Cookies("ASPHT0208")("PanelColor") )
      tf.WriteLine( Request.Cookies("Aspht0208")("HighlightColor") )
      tf.WriteLine( Request.Cookies("Aspht0208")("ShadowColor") )
      tf.Close
%>
<HTML>
<HEAD>
 <TITLE>ActiveX and ASP Cookies Demo Page</TITLE>
</HEAD>
<BODY>
<HTML>
```

continued on next page

continued from previous page

```
<HEAD>
<TITLE>Chapter Three Demo Page 10</TITLE>
</HEAD>
<BODY>
<H1>ASPHT0310 Demo Page</H1>
<HR>
    <SCRIPT LANGUAGE="VBScript">
<!--
Sub Aspht02081_Click()
call Aspht02081.FlipColors(1)
end sub
-->
    </SCRIPT>
    <OBJECT ID="Aspht02081" WIDTH=209 HEIGHT=165
     CLASSID="CLSID:EB303AA2-B4B9-11D0-B7D8-444553540000">
        <PARAM NAME="_Version" VALUE="65536">
        <PARAM NAME="_ExtentX" VALUE="5530">
        <PARAM NAME="_ExtentY" VALUE="4366">
        <PARAM NAME="_StockProps" VALUE="15">
        <PARAM NAME="Caption" VALUE="Script Me!">
        <PARAM NAME="ForeColor" VALUE="65535">
        <PARAM NAME="PanelColor" VALUE="255">
        <PARAM NAME="HighlightColor" VALUE="8421631">
        <PARAM NAME="ShadowColor" VALUE="4194432">
        <PARAM NAME="BorderWidth" VALUE="10">
    </OBJECT>
<HR>
    <FORM ACTION="http://default/ASPExec/activexasp3.asp" METHOD="POST"
     ONSUBMIT="Document.Form1.Text1.value = Aspht02081.BorderWidth
Document.Form1.Text2.value = Aspht02081.Caption
Document.Form1.Text3.value = Aspht02081.PanelColor
Document.Form1.Text4.value = Aspht02081.HighlightColor
Document.Form1.Text5.value = Aspht02081.ShadowColor"
     NAME="Form1">
        <INPUT TYPE=TEXT NAME="Text1">
        <INPUT LANGUAGE="VBScript" TYPE=BUTTON VALUE="Set BorderWidth"
ONCLICK="Aspht02081.BorderWidth = Document.Form1.Text1.value
call Aspht02081.Refresh()"
         NAME="Button1">
<P>
        <INPUT TYPE=TEXT NAME="Text2">
        <INPUT LANGUAGE="VBScript" TYPE=BUTTON VALUE="Set Caption"
ONCLICK="Aspht02081.Caption = Document.Form1.Text2.value
call Aspht02081.Refresh()"
         NAME="Button2">
<P>
        <INPUT TYPE=TEXT NAME="Text3">
        <INPUT LANGUAGE="VBScript" TYPE=BUTTON VALUE="Set Panel Color in Hex"
         ONCLICK="Aspht02081.PanelColor = Document.Form1.Text3.value
call Aspht02081.Refresh()"
         NAME="Button3">
<P>
        <INPUT TYPE=TEXT NAME="Text4">
        <INPUT LANGUAGE="VBScript" TYPE=BUTTON VALUE="Set HiLite Color in Hex"
         ONCLICK="Aspht02081.HighlightColor = Document.Form1.Text4.value
call Aspht02081.Refresh()"
         NAME="Button4">
```

```
<P>
        <INPUT TYPE=TEXT NAME="Text5">
        <INPUT LANGUAGE="VBScript" TYPE=BUTTON VALUE="Set Shadow Color in Hex"
         ONCLICK="Aspht02081.ShadowColor = Document.Form1.Text5.value
call Aspht02081.Refresh()"
         NAME="Button5">
<P>
<HR>
        <INPUT TYPE=SUBMIT VALUE="Press to Store Custom Settings!" NAME="Submit1">
    </FORM>
<HR>
<SCRIPT LANGUAGE="VBSCRIPT">
dim HoldBW
dim HoldCap
dim HoldPC
dim HoldHC
dim HoldSC
<%

   if IsEmpty( Request.Cookies("ASPHT0208")("BorderWidth") ) then
     Response.Write "HoldBW = 10"
   else
     Response.Write "HoldBW = " & CInt(
Request.Cookies("ASPHT0208")("BorderWidth"))
   end if
%>
   Aspht02081.BorderWidth = HoldBW
   Document.Form1.Text1.Value = holdBW
<%
   AString = "10"
   QuoteString = chr( 34 )
   if IsEmpty( Request.Cookies("ASPHT0208")("Caption") ) then
     Response.Write "HoldCap = " & QuoteString & "A Default Value" & QuoteString
   else
     Response.Write "HoldCap = " & QuoteString &
Request.Cookies("ASPHT0208")("Caption") & QuoteString
   end if
%>
   Aspht02081.Caption = HoldCap
   Document.Form1.Text2.Value = HoldCap
<%
   if IsEmpty( Request.Cookies("ASPHT0208")("PanelColor") ) then
     Response.Write "HoldPC = &H0000AF00"
   else
     Response.Write "HoldPC = " & CLng(Request.Cookies("ASPHT0208")("PanelColor"))
   end if
%>
   Aspht02081.PanelColor = HoldPC
  Document.Form1.Text3.Value = HoldPC
<%
   if IsEmpty( Request.Cookies("ASPHT0208")("HighlightColor") ) then
     Response.Write "HoldHC = &H0000FF00"
   else
     Response.Write "HoldHC = " &
CLng(Request.Cookies("ASPHT0208")("HighlightColor"))
   end if
```

continued on next page

continued from previous page

```
%>
   Aspht02081.HighlightColor = HoldHC
   Document.Form1.Text4.Value = HoldHC
<%
   if IsEmpty( Request.Cookies("ASPHT0208")("ShadowColor") ) then
     Response.Write "HoldSC = &H00000A00"
   else
     Response.Write "HoldSC = " &
CLng(Request.Cookies("ASPHT0208")("ShadowColor"))
   end if
%>
   Aspht02081.ShadowColor = HoldSC
   Document.Form1.Text5.Value = HoldSC
</SCRIPT>
</BODY>
</HTML>
```

2. Activate Internet Explorer. In the address field, type in `HTTP://DEFAULT/ASPEXEC/ACTIVEXASP3.ASP` and press Return. The page will initially display using the settings you gave it in ActiveX Control Pad. Use the Text and Button controls to change all the settings to new values, then press the Press to Store Custom Settings! button. The page will refresh and you will see that your settings are not lost, as shown in Figure 3-48. Shut down IE, then restart it and reload `ACTIVEXASP3.ASP`. Instead of coming up with the default settings from ActiveX Control Pad again (as it did in Chapter 2, "Intermediate ActiveX: Creating Customized ActiveX Controls"), it displays the custom settings you entered last time, as shown in Figure 3-49. Congratulations! You have learned to use ASP to store custom ActiveX control properties settings.

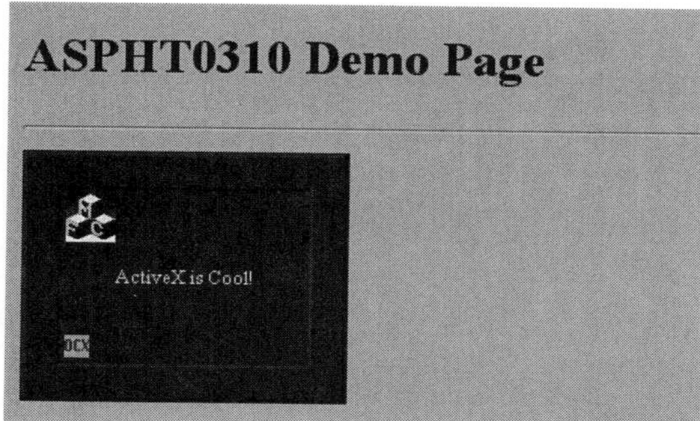

Figure 3-48 `ACTIVEXASP3.ASP` in Internet Explorer showing initial custom settings for the `ASPHT0302` control

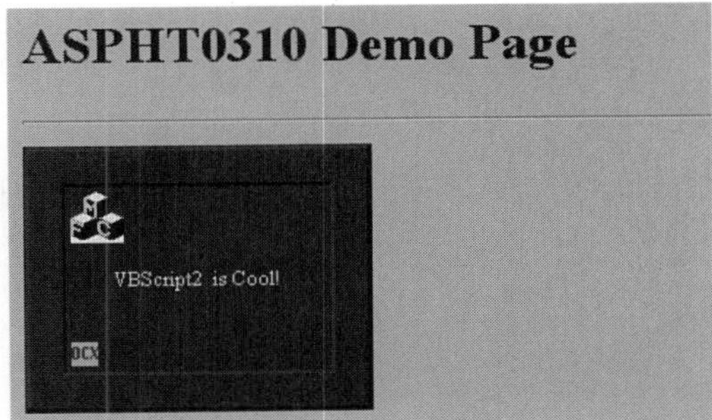

Figure 3-49 ACTIVEXASP3.ASP in Internet Explorer showing custom settings for the ASPHT0302 control preserved between sessions with VBScript's TextStream object

How It Works

VBScript 2.0 has added the powerful **FileSystem** object, which in turn can create **TextStream** objects that read and write text files on the server computer (*not* the client computer). This How-To illustrates a simple use for this capability; later How-To's will expand its use considerably!

There are two crucial parts of this How-To: the testing for an empty initial file and the guaranteed writing of data once the page has been loaded once. Notice this code block:

```
<%@ LANGUAGE = VBScript %>
<%
      dim fs
      dim tf
      Set fs = CreateObject("Scripting.FileSystemObject")
      Set tf = fs.OpenTextFile("c:\storesets.txt",1,true)
      if IsEmpty( Request("Text1")) then
        if tf.AtEndOfStream = true then
          Response.Cookies("ASPHT0208")("BorderWidth") = "10"
        else
          Response.Cookies("ASPHT0208")("BorderWidth")=tf.ReadLine
        end if
      else
        Response.Cookies("ASPHT0208")("BorderWidth") = Request("Text1")
      end if
```

After the initial opening of the file (which opens as a read-only file and creates a new file if one is not found due to the **1** and **true** parameters), a cascaded series of checks is made against each value. First, a test is made to see if there is any data in the **Form** objects (such as **Text1**); if so, this data is stored in the cookie for later use to reset the system to the new value. If not, one of two conditions is true. Possibly the page is being viewed for the first time ever (in which case the `TextStream` object's `AtEndOfStream` value is automatically `true` because the file is newly created and empty); in this case a default value is placed in the cookie. If the file is not empty, the page is being reopened after previously being used, so the stored text file data is read into the cookie.

Now consider the second part of the process, as shown in this code fragment:

```
        tf.Close
        Set tf = fs.CreateTextFile("c:\storesets.txt", TRUE,FALSE)
        tf.WriteLine( Request.Cookies("ASPHT0208")("BorderWidth") )
        tf.WriteLine( Request.Cookies("ASPHT0208")("Caption"))
        tf.WriteLine( Request.Cookies("ASPHT0208")("PanelColor") )
        tf.WriteLine( Request.Cookies("Aspht0208")("HighlightColor") )
        tf.WriteLine( Request.Cookies("Aspht0208")("ShadowColor") )
        tf.Close
%>
```

After the last data item is read in from the file or a `<FORM>` tag or its internal default, the `TextStream` object is re-created via `CreateTextFile`, with the same name, a `true` to indicate overwriting is allowed, and a `false` to prevent Unicode from being used. Then each of the cookie values is written to the file, because they are guaranteed to be the latest settings from the form, or the previous file settings, or the defaults. This way, the text file always has the latest values from the page stored.

(Note: The text file is created on the server computer, not on the local machine!)

Comments

One vital aspect of this How-To is that the file system object is not available outside the ASP `<%%>` blocks; any attempt to use it will result in an `Object not safe for scripting` error. (If you don't believe it, try running `Page2.HTM` in the `CH03\HT10\` directory.)

CHAPTER 4

BASIC ASP: SERVER- AND CLIENT-SIDE SCRIPTING

4

BASIC ASP: SERVER- AND CLIENT-SIDE SCRIPTING

How do I...

This chapter is a step off into another world of the active platform, namely that of HTML and Active Server Pages (ASP) scripting. If you are a hard-core ActiveX programmer, you may feel this chapter isn't for you. But consider this: Probably 90% of your ActiveX controls will end up being used on WWW pages, and Common Gateway Interface (CGI) scripting has long been the mechanism used by all nontrivial Web pages to give themselves sophisticated features. ASP is the odds-on favorite to replace CGI, and knowing how it works and how your ActiveX controls can take advantage of it may just boost your sales! This chapter starts from scratch with ASP, demonstrating every key feature in simple but clear How-To's that cover conditional HTML output, ASP variable output, form processing, CGI server variable handling, and simple and complex full-text output capabilities. More advanced topics are also covered, such as client- and server-side scripting and using ActiveX controls and ActiveX data objects (ADOs). After finishing this chapter, you'll be fully up and running in ASP.

4.1 Create an ASP Page

You've heard about it, now write one! This How-To shows you just what goes into creating the hottest thing on the Web since frames.

4.2 Send Output From My ASP Script to the HTML Page

The next major step up in ASP power is the capability to send values of ASP script variables directly into the HTML, and this How-To gives the secret away. (Hint: It's three characters!).

4.3 Use My ASP Page Like a CGI Script

CGI has long been king of the hill on the WWW because of its capability to process form input; a whole technology called Win-CGI was developed to let Windows programs do this, and not very well! Now ASP puts CGI out to well-deserved pasture with full, simple support for processing all types of HTML form input, and this How-To demonstrates it easily and effectively.

4.4 Get User Information for My ASP Page

The other side of CGI is the complex world of HTTP response variables, not seemingly a subject for a beginning chapter! But with ASP, it's almost child's play to obtain and manipulate these important aspects of WWW interaction; this How-To gives you the code to list every name and value an HTTP transaction has, and it's only six lines at that!

4.5 Control ASP Script Output

The really good stuff for ASP begins with being able to write text out to the HTML directly rather than as conditional HTML output. The key is the `Response.Write` method, and this How-To puts it through its paces.

4.6 Send Advanced ASP Output with the Response Object

Just like CGI, ASP can do funky things with your browser! This How-To demonstrates killing HTML processing, reverting to plain text, and sending the browser wherever you like (but not where the user thought he or she was going.).

4.7 Create a Script on a Client Computer with ASP

Scripts are not just the province of HTML; ASP has them too. This How-To illustrates using ASP to create user-requested scripts on demand that run on the client's computer rather than on the server.

4.8 Create a Server-Side ASP Script

Tired of all those nitpicky little `<%%>`s? Well, this How-To gets you into the big leagues with `<SCRIPT>` tags that work only on the server side, but with nary a `<%>` in sight! (The key is `RUNAT=SERVER` syntax.)

4.9 Create an HTML Page with an ActiveX Control Using ASP

You want ActiveX? You want ASP? You want them together? No problemo! This How-To uses ASP to create an ActiveX control, complete with custom parameters, entirely out of ASP Scripting statements. Now *that's* power!

4.10 Interact with ActiveX Data Objects Using ASP

Databases are what most of us professionals do, and ASP hasn't forgotten that. It uses a built-in `ADODB` object on the ASP server to activate ODBC-compliant databases and create SQL queries that can then be read using ActiveX data object (ADO) syntax and have their values placed directly into an HTML table with an ASP script. (And now if you'll excuse me, I'm going to go hide from the acronym police, since I just went over my daily limit in one sentence…)

4.1 How do I… Create an ASP page?

Problem

All right, I've heard a lot about this hot new ASP technology. How do I create an ASP page?

Technique

All you need is a simple text editor! This How-To creates an ASP page that displays different HTML depending on the time of day. Although these directions create the project from scratch, the CD contains a completed file under `CH04\HT01\`.

Steps

1. Activate Notepad or some other simple text editor. Enter the HTML code in Listing 4-1 and save it as `ASPHT0401.ASP`. Make sure you move it to the directory you aliased as `ASPEXEC` for use in executing ASP scripts.

Listing 4-1 `ASPHT0401.ASP` source code

```
<HTML>
<HEAD>
<TITLE>Active Server Pages How To Chapter Four How To One</TITLE>
</HEAD>
<BODY>
<% If Time >=#12:00:00 AM# And Time < #12:00:00 PM#  Then %>
 <H1>What a lovely morning!</H1>
<%Else %>
 <H1>Hey, it's almost quitting time!</H1>
<%End If%>

</BODY>
</HTML>
```

2. Activate Internet Explorer. In the address field, type in `HTTP://DEFAULT/ASPEXEC/ASPHT0401.ASP` and press Return. As shown in Figure 4-1, the resulting page will display either `What a lovely morning` or `Hey, it's almost quitting time!`, depending on whether it is currently before or after noon. Congratulations! You have learned to create an ASP page.

How It Works

ASP is a system that supports scripting languages that run on the HTTP server rather than on the client browser's computer; ASP provides many of the capabilities once relegated to CGI scripts. Microsoft's Internet Information Server (IIS) and Peer Web Services/Personal Web Server (PWS) support this capability (see the Introduction

Figure 4-1 `ASPHT0401.ASP` in Internet Explorer showing a variable HTML output depending on the time of day

section "Acquiring and Installing Active Server Pages" for more information on acquiring and installing ASP). This and the following How-To's explain how ASP scripts function and how to use them effectively.

Two important pieces of functionality come together to make ASP work: `<%%>` scripting and conditional HTML output. Notice this first portion of the HTML in the ASP page:

```
<% If Time >=#12:00:00 AM# And Time < #12:00:00 PM#  Then %>
 <H1>What a lovely morning!</H1>
```

The `<% If ... Then%>`s are called *ASP script statements*, and the `<%%>`s are called *ASP delimiters*. They are stripped out by the ASP engine when it creates the actual HTML pages that will be sent to the browser to display. Any line of text *not* bracketed by `<%%>` is assumed to be HTML and is automatically sent to the browser for display; this is why the `<H1>...</H1>` line will appear on the browser, because it has no bracketing script delimiters.

However, notice the remainder of the page:

```
<%Else %>
 <H1>Hey, it's almost quitting time!</H1>
<%End If%>
```

Due to the way ASP works, the first line about a lovely morning will *never be executed* if the time is after noon, so the standard HTML there will never be output to the browser! Instead, the second line of HTML about quitting time goes out. This feature is called *conditional HTML output*, and this is what gives ASP much of its power. You can write many different pages in the same HTML file, and output the appropriate one depending on whatever conditions your ASP scripts can test. Think about what this does for you, and you've already begun the process of being hooked on ASP, just like the rest of us serious Web developers.

Comments

If you don't feel impressed yet, stick around, or better yet, run the demo at the end of the chapter. This stuff only gets better!

COMPLEXITY
BEGINNING

4.2 How do I... Send output from my ASP script to the HTML page?

Problem

Okay, I know how to manipulate what HTML is displayed with an ASP script. But is there any way to send the value of an ASP script variable *directly* to the HTML rather than using nested conditional HTML output?

Technique

ASP has a special syntax for this, `<%=`. This How-To demonstrates using it to output the current date and time. Although these directions create the project from scratch, the CD contains a completed file under `CH04\HT02\`.

Steps

1. Activate Notepad or some other simple text editor. Enter the HTML code in Listing 4-2 and save it as `ASPHT0402.ASP`. Make sure you move it to the directory you aliased as `ASPEXEC` for use in executing ASP scripts.

Listing 4-2 `ASPHT0402.ASP` source code

```
<HTML>
<HEAD>
<TITLE>Active Server Pages How To Chapter Four How To Two</TITLE>
</HEAD>
<BODY>
<H1>The Current Time Is <%= now %></H1>
</BODY>
</HTML>
```

2. Activate Internet Explorer. In the address field, type in `HTTP://DEFAULT/ASPEXEC/ASPHT0402.ASP` and press Return. As shown in Figure 4-2, the resulting page will display the current time; if you like, keep hitting the Refresh button and the time will continually update itself. Congratulations! You have learned to use ASP to send ASP script variable values directly to HTML page output.

How It Works

Check out the critical difference in this HTML line from the last script:

```
<H1>The Current Time Is <%= now %></H1>
```

By using the `<%=` syntax, you sent the value of the VBScript function `Now` as text directly into the HTML output. This technique works not only with built-in variables but with any user-defined variable or function as well!

The Current Time Is 5/12/97 10:02:33 PM

Figure 4-2 `ASPHT0402.ASP` in Internet Explorer showing a direct ASP variable output in the HTML

Comments

The tricky part about using `<%=` is that there must be a terminating `%>` on the other side of the variable. This can make using a lot of these rather time consuming, particularly if you get one slightly out of place. Fortunately, as shown in How-To 4.4, there is a better way to send complicated output into the HTML.

4.3 How do I... Use my ASP page like a CGI script?

A lot of my work involves getting information from forms and sending back responses. I've been using CGI scripts written in Perl for this; can ASP take over this function for me?

Technique

Yes, it can! ASP files can be the targets of form submissions and can fully acquire and process their inputs. This How-To creates a simple form with two controls to demonstrate the technique. Although these directions create the project from scratch, the CD contains a completed file under `CH04\HT03\`.

Steps

1. Activate Notepad or some other simple text editor. Enter the HTML code in Listing 4-3 and save it as `ASPHT0403.ASP`. Make sure you move it to the directory you aliased as `ASPEXEC` for use in executing ASP scripts.

Listing 4-3 ASPHT0403.ASP source code

```
<HTML>
<HEAD>
<TITLE>Active Server Pages How To Chapter Four How To Three</TITLE>
</HEAD>
<BODY>
<H1>Welcome to Active Server Pages, <%= Request.Form("fullname") %></H1><P>
<I>Your current browser is </I><U><%= Request.Form("browsername") %></U>
</BODY>
</HTML>
```

2. Create a new text document after having saved the previous one, and enter the HTML code in Listing 4-4. Save it as `ASPHT0403.HTM`.

Listing 4-4 ASPHT0403.HTM source code

```
<HTML>
<HEAD>
<TITLE>Active Server Pages How To Chapter Four How To Three</TITLE>
</HEAD>
<BODY>
<H1>Enter the information below and press SUBMIT to see ASP form processing!</H1>
<form name="Form1" action="http://default/aspexec/aspht0403.asp" method="post">
<p>Enter Your Name: <input name="fullname" size=48>
<p>What is your current browser: <select name="browsername">
<option>Internet Explorer<option>Netscape Navigator<option>NCSA⇐
Mosaic<option>Online or Proprietary Browser
</select>
<p><input type=submit>
</form>
</BODY>
</HTML>
```

3. Activate Internet Explorer and bring up ASPHT0403.HTM. You will see a display similar to Figure 4-3; enter your name, select a browser, and press Submit. In a moment, your name and browser selection will be displayed in HTML formatting, as shown in Figure 4-4. Congratulations! You have learned to use ASP to process forms just like CGI scripts.

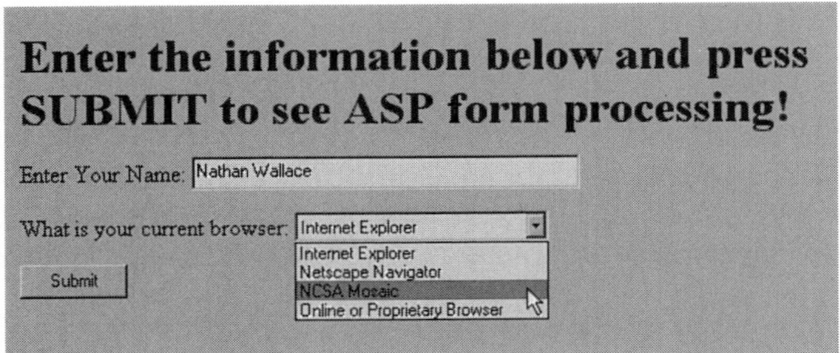

Figure 4-3 ASPHT0403.HTM in Internet Explorer showing the form the ASP file will process

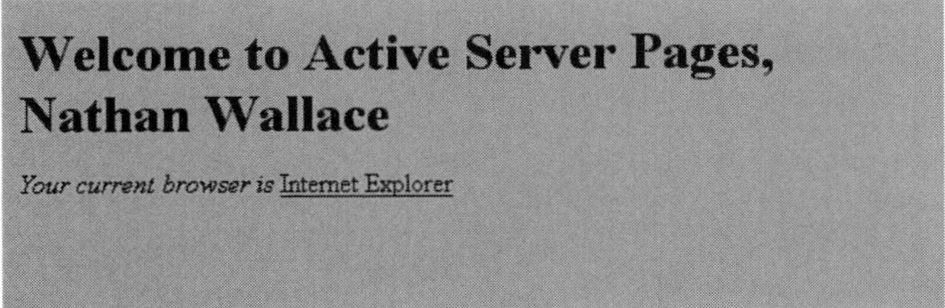

Figure 4-4 ASPHT0403.ASP in Internet Explorer showing the results of processing the previous form's output

How It Works

The key to processing form input to ASP files lies in the `Request.Form` collection. Study this code fragment:

```
<H1>Welcome to Active Server Pages, <%= Request.Form("fullname") %></H1><P>
<I>Your current browser is </I><U><%= Request.Form("browsername") %></U>
```

The `Request.Form("fullname")` call asks the collection of form variables sent to the ASP page if it has one by that name. If it does, it will be returned as a string; otherwise, an empty string will be returned (as will be the case if an empty value is sent for that form element). The type of underlying form element is not important; notice that both the Input Text control and the Select control return a string value!

Comments

The other vital fact to notice here is that you get all the overhead of CGI processing *for free* with ASP! That is (take it from someone who's been suffering through Perl and CGI since they began) no trivial matter!

4.4 How do I... Get user information for my ASP page?

Problem

There are times when I need to check on some of the HTTP headers the client's browser sent with its form data. I can easily do this in CGI scripts; does ASP have similar capabilities?

Technique

Yes, via the `Request` object's `ServerVariables` collection. This How-To demonstrates using the collection by creating an HTML table of all the HTTP headers sent with a simple `Form` request. Although these directions create the project from scratch, the CD contains a completed file under `CH04\HT04\`.

Steps

1. Activate Notepad or some other simple text editor. Enter the HTML code in Listing 4-5 and save it as `ASPHT0404.ASP`. Make sure you move it to the directory you aliased as `ASPEXEC` for use in executing ASP scripts.

Listing 4-5 ASPHT0404.ASP source code

```
<HTML>
<HEAD>
<TITLE>Active Server Pages How To Chapter Four How To Four</TITLE>
</HEAD>
<BODY>
<H1>Welcome to Active Server Pages, <%= Request.Form("fullname") %></H1><P>
<I>Your current browser is </I><U><%= Request.Form("browsername") %></U>
<HR>
Here is a table of all the Server Variables in the last HTTP Request:<P>
<HR>
<TABLE CELLSPACING=5 CELLPADDING=5 BORDER=5 ALIGN="Center"
VALIGN="Middle" BGCOLOR="Teal" BORDERCOLORLIGHT="AQUA" BORDERCOLORDARK="NAVY">
<TR><TD><B>Server Variable</B></TD><TD><B>Value</B></TD></TR>
<% For Each name In Request.ServerVariables %>
<TR><TD> <%= name %> </TD><TD>  <%= Request.ServerVariables(name) %> </TD></TR>
<% Next %>
</TABLE>
<HR>
</BODY>
</HTML>
```

2. Create a new text document after having saved the previous one, and enter the HTML code in Listing 4-6. Save it as `ASPHT0404.HTM`.

Listing 4-6 ASPHT0404.HTM source code

```
<HTML>
<HEAD>
<TITLE>Active Server Pages How To Chapter Four How To Four</TITLE>
</HEAD>

<BODY>
<H1>Enter the information below and press SUBMIT to see ASP server variable⇐
processing!</H1>
<form name="Form1" action="http://default/aspexec/aspht0404.asp" method="post">
<p>Enter Your Name: <input name="fullname" size=48>
<p>What is your current browser: <select name="browsername">
<option>Internet Explorer<option>Netscape Navigator<option>NCSA⇐
Mosaic<option>Online or Proprietary Browser
</select>
<p><input type=submit>
</form>


</BODY>
</HTML>
```

3. Activate Internet Explorer and bring up `ASPHT0404.HTM`. Enter your name and select a browser, and press Submit. In a moment, a large table will be displayed with all the HTTP headers sent in the `Form` request, as shown in Figure 4-5. Congratulations! You have learned to use the ASP `Request.ServerVariables` collection to obtain HTTP header information.

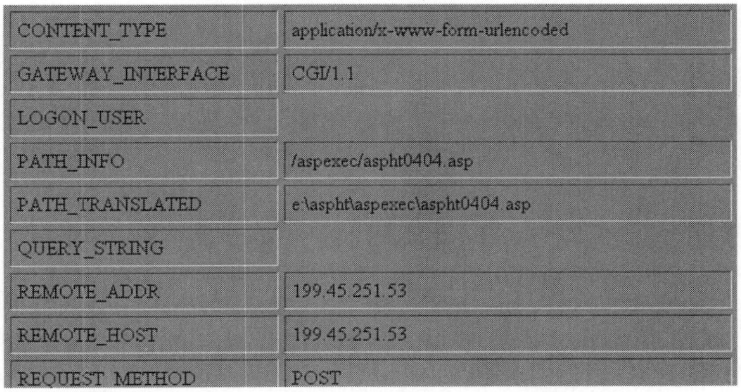

CONTENT_TYPE	application/x-www-form-urlencoded
GATEWAY_INTERFACE	CGI/1.1
LOGON_USER	
PATH_INFO	/aspexec/aspht0404.asp
PATH_TRANSLATED	e:\aspht\aspexec\aspht0404.asp
QUERY_STRING	
REMOTE_ADDR	199.45.251.53
REMOTE_HOST	199.45.251.53
REQUEST_METHOD	POST

Figure 4-5 ASPHT0404.ASP **in Internet Explorer showing the HTTP headers sent for the previous** Form **request**

How It Works

Two separate pieces of important and powerful functionality come together in this How-To: the `For Each` syntax and the `Request.ServerVariables` collection. Notice how the code that uses them is structured.

```
<% For Each name In Request.ServerVariables %>
<TR><TD> <%= name %> </TD><TD>  <%= Request.ServerVariables(name) %> </TD></TR>
<% Next %>
```

The `For Each` syntax uses a named field of the collection or other object after the `In` keyword; it then iterates (loops through) all the objects in the collection and sets the value of the named field to that of the current item. This permits both outputting the name value itself, as is done on the left-hand `<%=` statement, and getting its value as displayed by the right-hand `<%=` statement.

The `Request.ServerVariables` collection contains all the HTTP headers sent to the ASP system by the server when it received the current HTTP request the ASP file is processing. Although the values cannot be changed, new ones can be added to affect processing of the returned HTML, just as was done using the older CGI system.

Comments

You can use `For Each` with any collection object support by VBScript, not just the `ServerVariables` collection.

4.5 How do I... Control ASP script output?

Problem

Using the <%= technique is fine for returning variable values, but I need to send complex, formatted strings back in my ASP output. How do I do this?

Technique

You use the Response.Write method. This How-To demonstrates generating complex output values with this method, which would not be easily returned using <%. Although these directions create the project from scratch, the CD contains a completed file under CH04\HT05\.

Steps

1. Activate Notepad or some other simple text editor. Enter the HTML code in Listing 4-7 and save it as ASPHT0405.ASP. Make sure you move it to the directory you aliased as ASPEXEC for use in executing ASP scripts.

Listing 4-7 ASPHT0405.ASP source code

```
<HTML>
<HEAD>
<TITLE>Active Server Pages How To Chapter Four How To Five</TITLE>
</HEAD>
<BODY>
<H1>Welcome to Active Server Pages, <%= Request.Form("fullname") %></H1><P>
You are using <%= Request.Form("browsername")%> as a browser.<P>
<% if Request.Form("browsername") = "Internet Explorer" then
Response.Write("You have a full featured browser; congratulations!")
elseif Request.Form("browsername") = "Netscape Navigator" then
Response.Write("You are behind the curve; get Internet Explorer 3.2!")
elseif Request.Form("browsername") = "NCSA Mosaic" then
Response.Write("Did you know Internet Explorer has a UNIX version?")
else
Response.Write("You have our sympathy!")
end if %>
<HR>
</BODY>
</HTML>
```

2. Create a new text document after having saved the previous one, and enter the HTML code in Listing 4-8. Save it as ASPHT0405.HTM.

Listing 4-8 ASPHT0405.HTM source code

```
<HTML>
<HEAD>
<TITLE>Active Server Pages How To Chapter Four How To Five</TITLE>
</HEAD>
<BODY>
<H1>Enter the information below and press SUBMIT to see ASP Response.Write!</H1>
<form name="Form1" action="http://default/aspexec/aspht0405.asp" method="post">
<p>Enter Your Name: <input name="fullname" size=48>
<p>What is your current browser: <select name="browsername">
<option>Internet Explorer<option>Netscape Navigator<option>NCSA⇐
Mosaic<option>Online or Proprietary Browser
</select>
<p><input type=submit>
</form>

</BODY>
</HTML>
```

3. Activate Internet Explorer, bring up `ASPHT0406.HTM`, and press Return. As shown in Figure 4-6, a form will appear asking for your name and a selection of browser type. Select NCSA Mosaic, and you will see the interesting suggestion shown in Figure 4-7. Congratulations! You have learned to use the ASP `Response.Write` method to output sophisticated HTML strings.

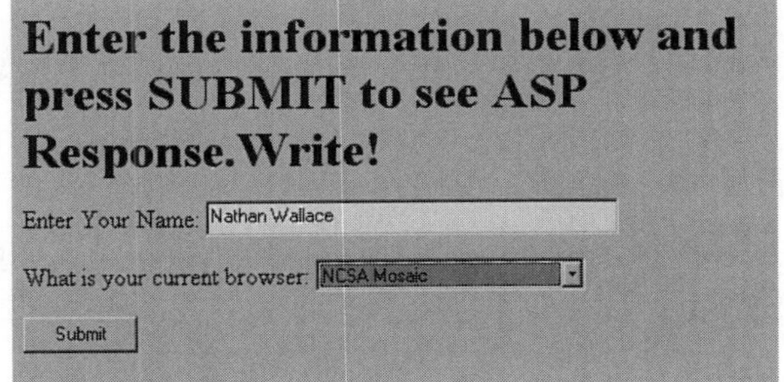

Figure 4-6 ASPHT0405.HTM in Internet Explorer showing the form ready to create a new page via ASP

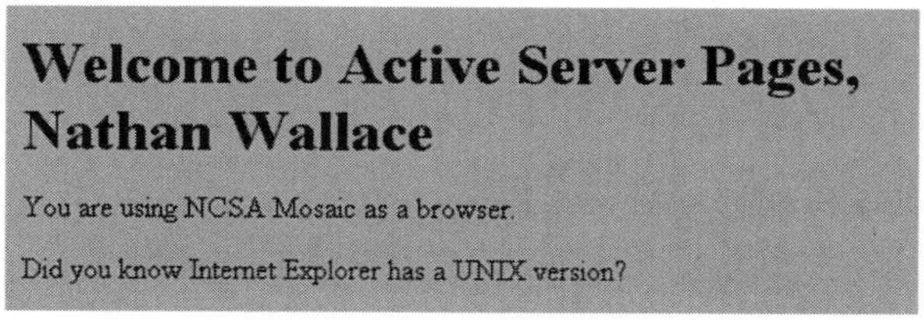

Welcome to Active Server Pages, Nathan Wallace

You are using NCSA Mosaic as a browser.

Did you know Internet Explorer has a UNIX version?

Figure 4-7 `ASPHT0405.ASP` in Internet Explorer showing the resulting suggestion from selecting NCSA Mosaic

How It Works

`Response.Write` sends anything in its parameter list (which must resolve to a string, but can use the `&` operator as shown in successive How-To's) as HTML to the finished page. This permits constructing more sophisticated outputs like this:

```
<% if Request.Form("browsername") = "Internet Explorer" then
Response.Write("You have a full featured browser; congratulations!")
elseif Request.Form("browsername") = "Netscape Navigator" then
Response.Write("You are behind the curve; get Internet Explorer 3.2!")
elseif Request.Form("browsername") = "NCSA Mosaic" then
Response.Write("Did you know Internet Explorer has a UNIX version?")
else
Response.Write("You have our sympathy!")
end if %>
```

Notice that there aren't the usual problems with correct placing of the `<%%>` delimiters; all the output takes place inside a single `<%%>` set.

Comments

This How-To was deliberately kept simple to acquaint you with how this method works. In the following How-To's you'll put together far more complex and powerful strings for the HTML output, all with `Response.Write`!

COMPLEXITY
BEGINNING

4.6 How do I... Send advanced ASP output with the `Response` object?

Problem

There are times when I need to control the HTML that goes back to the user from my ASP script completely, just as I was able to do with the older CGI system. Does ASP have similar advanced output manipulation features?

Technique

Yes, it does, via the `Response` object. This How-To demonstrates three key features of this powerful object in the context of the previous How-To's form response. Although these directions create the project from scratch, the CD contains a completed file under `CH03\HT06\`.

Steps

1. Activate Notepad or some other simple text editor. Enter the HTML code in Listing 4-9 and save it as `ASPHT0406.ASP`. Make sure you move it to the directory you aliased as `ASPEXEC` for use in executing ASP scripts.

Listing 4-9 ASPHT0406.ASP source code

```
<%
if Request.Form("browsername") = "Netscape Navigator" then
Response.Redirect( "http://www.microsoft.com/ie/default.asp")
elseif Request.Form("browsername") = "NCSA Mosaic" then
Response.ContentType = "text/plain"
elseif Request.Form("browsername")="Online or Proprietary Browser" then
Response.Buffer = true
end if %>
<%
if Request.Form("browsername") = "Internet Explorer" then%>
<HTML>
<HEAD>
<TITLE>Active Server Pages How To Chapter Four How To Six</TITLE>
</HEAD>
<BODY>
<H1>Welcome to Active Server Pages, <%= Request.Form("fullname") %></H1><P>
You are using <%= Request.Form("browsername")%> as a browser.<P>
<HR>
<%Response.Write("Bonus, Dude!")%>
<HR>
</BODY>
</HTML>
<%elseif Request.Form("browsername") = "NCSA Mosaic" then%>
<HTML>
<HEAD>
<TITLE>Active Server Pages How To Chapter Four How To Six</TITLE>
</HEAD>
<BODY>
<%Response.Write("You have failed the HTML entry level and will see plain text⇐
forevermore!")%>
</BODY>
</HTML>
<%else
Response.Clear
Response.Flush
end if %>
```

2. Create a new text document after having saved the previous one, and enter the HTML code in Listing 4-10. Save it as `ASPHT0406.HTM`.

Listing 4-10 ASPHT0406.HTM source code

```
<HTML>
<HEAD>
<TITLE>Active Server Pages How To Chapter Four How To Six</TITLE>
</HEAD>

<BODY>
<H1>Enter the information below and press SUBMIT to see ASP Response object⇐
methods!</H1>
<form name="Form1" action="http://default/aspexec/aspht0406.asp" method="post">
<p>Enter Your Name: <input name="fullname" size=48>
<p>What is your current browser: <select name="browsername">
<option>Internet Explorer<option>Netscape Navigator<option>NCSA⇐
Mosaic<option>Online or Proprietary Browser
</select>
<p><input type=submit>
</form>
</BODY>
</HTML>
```

3. Activate Internet Explorer, bring up **ASPHT0406.HTM**, and press Return. As shown in Figure 4-8, a form will appear asking for your name and a selection of browser types. Select each of the three choices other than Internet Explorer, and you will see the interesting behaviors shown in Figures 4-9, 4-10, and 4-11. Congratulations! You have learned to use the ASP **Response** object to control advanced output behavior.

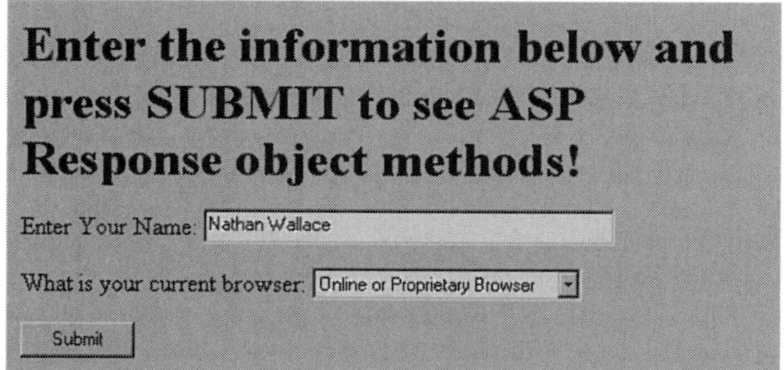

Figure 4-8 ASPHT0406.HTM in Internet Explorer showing the form ready to create a new page via ASP

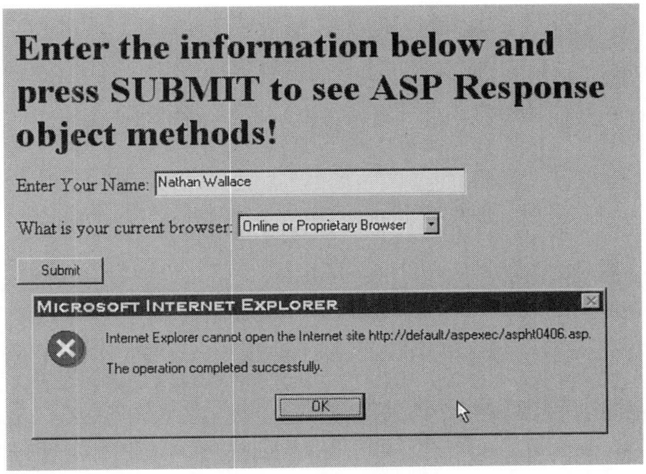

Figure 4-9 ASPHT0406.ASP in Internet Explorer showing the complete clearing of the HTTP output when Online Browser is selected

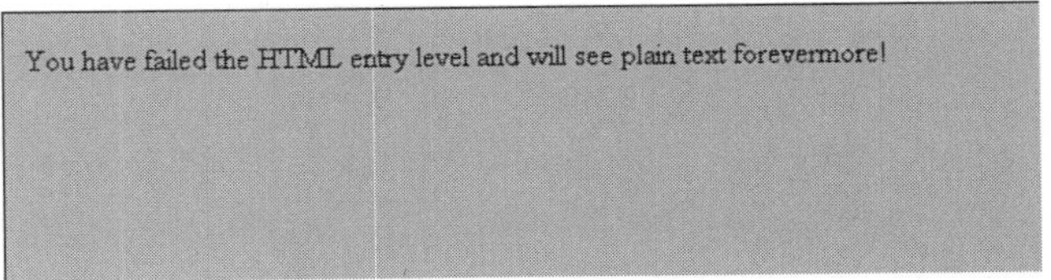

Figure 4-10 ASPHT0406.ASP in Internet Explorer showing the output of plain text when the NCSA Mosaic browser is selected

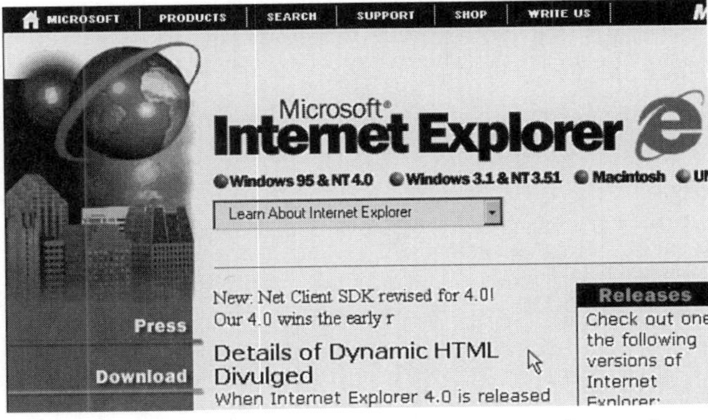

Figure 4-11 ASPHT0406.ASP in Internet Explorer showing the redirection to the IE home page when Netscape Navigator is selected

How It Works

Three separate things are going on in this How-To, all important for advanced browser control. First, notice these lines of ASP script code:

```
<%
if Request.Form("browsername") = "Netscape Navigator" then
Response.Redirect( "http://www.microsoft.com/ie/default.asp")
elseif Request.Form("browsername") = "NCSA Mosaic" then
Response.ContentType = "text/plain"
elseif Request.Form("browsername")="Online or Proprietary Browser" then
Response.Buffer = true
end if %>
```

Note that they are placed prior to the output of any HTML to the page. If they were placed after any text had been sent to the browser, an error would be generated because these lines modify the HTTP response headers sent by ASP's hosting server to the browsers. It is crucial to remember that any `Response` object method involving `ContentType` or `Redirection` must take place prior to emitting a single line that will go back to the browser!

The setting of `Response.ContentType` to `"text/plain"` is a way to tell a browser that the returning data is not HTML, but just text of some sort. IE will balk at this, but some browsers won't. There are other `ContentType` values; see any reference on HTML and CGI scripting for the entire list.

The setting of `Response.Buffer` to `true` is important because if it is `false`, every line of output text, HTML or otherwise, instantly vanishes down the network and cannot be stopped or recalled. If `Response.Buffer` is `true`, however, you can abort sending data back because it has not been sent until a `Response.End` or `Response.Flush` command is issued.

The `Response.Redirect` line is where the sending of a new page takes place; it is the easiest way to do such a midcourse correction, and will not result in extra load time on the client's browser because it takes place in the stream of HTTP information rather than onboard the HTML in the browser itself.

Now take a peek at the remaining ASP code:

```
<%
if Request.Form("browsername") = "Internet Explorer" then%>
<HTML>
<HEAD>
<TITLE>Active Server Pages How To Chapter Four How To Six</TITLE>
</HEAD>
<BODY>
<H1>Welcome to Active Server Pages, <%= Request.Form("fullname") %></H1><P>
You are using <%= Request.Form("browsername")%> as a browser.<P>
<HR>
<%Response.Write("Bonus, Dude!")%>
<HR>
</BODY>
</HTML>
<%elseif Request.Form("browsername") = "NCSA Mosaic" then%>
<HTML>
<HEAD>
```

```
<TITLE>Active Server Pages How To Chapter Four How To Six</TITLE>
</HEAD>
<BODY>
<%Response.Write("You have failed the HTML entry level and will see plain text⇐
forevermore!")%>
</BODY>
</HTML>
<%else
Response.Clear
Response.Flush
end if %>
```

Here is where the other end of the `Response.Buffer` comes in. Whereas the first two options write some sort of output to the user, the last one kills the entire transaction via `Response.Clear` and then prevents further modifications by calling `Response.Flush`. This results in an empty HTTP response, which generates the error message you saw in Figure 4-9.

Comments

There are more sophisticated methods and features than the ones covered here for the `Response` object; they have some additional demonstrations in Chapters 5, "Intermediate ASP: Active Server Components," and 6, "Advanced ASP: Creating ASP Components with Visual C++ 5.0."

4.7 How do I… Create a script on a client computer with ASP?

Problem

I need to include script statements in the output from my ASP. Because I don't want them running on the server, how do I do this?

Technique

The key to creating client-side scripts with ASP lies in mixing regular HTML with ASP scripts. This How-To demonstrates this technique to allow a user form to request the type of simple script the user would like. These steps create the application from scratch, but for your convenience the complete project is on the CD under `CH04\HT07\`.

Steps

1. Activate Notepad or some other simple text editor. Enter the HTML code in Listing 4-11 and save it as **ASPHT0407.ASP**. Make sure you move it to the directory you aliased as **ASPEXEC** for use in executing ASP scripts.

Listing 4-11 ASPHT0407.ASP source code

```
<HTML>
<HEAD>
<TITLE>Active Server Pages How To Chapter Four How To Seven</TITLE>
</HEAD>
<BODY>
<H1>Welcome to Active Server Pages, <%= Request.Form("fullname") %></H1><P>
    <FORM NAME="Form1">
<% if Request.Form("scripttype")="Enter URL" then%>
        <INPUT LANGUAGE="VBScript" TYPE=Button VALUE="Press Me!"⇐
ONCLICK="Window.location.href = GetURL()"
         NAME="Button1">
<P>
    </FORM>
</BODY>
<SCRIPT LANGUAGE="VBScript">
function GetURL
TheURL = prompt("Enter URL","http://www.microsoft.com/ie/default.asp")
GetURL = TheURL
end function
</SCRIPT>
<%else%>
<INPUT LANGUAGE="VBScript" TYPE=Button VALUE="Press Me!" ONCLICK="call⇐
ChangeColor()"
 NAME="Button2">
<P>
</FORM>
</BODY>
<SCRIPT LANGUAGE="VBScript">
sub ChangeColor
window.document.bgColor = "#FF0000"
end sub
</SCRIPT>
<%end if%>
</HTML>
```

2. Create a new text document after having saved the previous one, and enter the HTML code in Listing 4-12. Save it as **ASPHT0407.HTM**.

Listing 4-12 ASPHT0407.HTM source code

```
<HTML>
<HEAD>
<TITLE>Active Server Pages How To Chapter Four How To Six</TITLE>
</HEAD>
<BODY>
<H1>Enter the information below and press SUBMIT to see ASP-created Client-Side⇐
Scripting!</H1>
```

```
<form name="Form1" action="http://default/aspexec/aspht0407.asp" method="post">
<p>Enter Your Name: <input name="fullname" size=48>
<p>What type of script would you like: <select name="scripttype">
<option>Enter URL<option>Reset Background Color
</select>
<p><input type=submit>
</form>
</BODY>
</HTML>
```

3. Activate Internet Explorer, bring up `ASPHT0407.HTM`, and press Return. As shown in Figure 4-12, the previous How-To's form will appear. Select the `Background` color script and press Submit. After a moment, the new HTML page created by the ASP that processed the form request will appear; press the button, and the background will turn red as shown in Figure 4-13, due to an ASP-written client script! Congratulations! You have learned to use ASP client-side scripting.

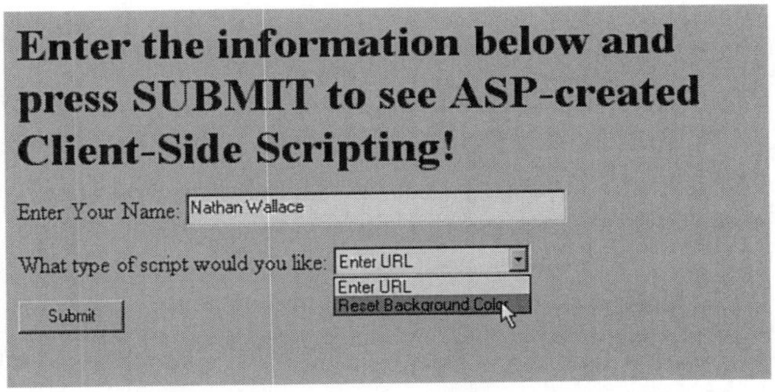

Figure 4-12 `ASPHT0407.HTM` in Internet Explorer showing the previous How-To's form ready to create a new page via ASP

Figure 4-13 `ASPHT0407.ASP` in Internet Explorer showing the client-side script created entirely via ASP output

How It Works

The key to this How-To is that statements outside <%%> are ignored on the server side and treated as standard HTML. Thus, this line of HTML code:

```
<%else%>
<INPUT LANGUAGE="VBScript" TYPE=Button VALUE="Press Me!" ONCLICK="call⇐
ChangeColor()"
 NAME="Button2">
<P>
</FORM>
</BODY>
<SCRIPT LANGUAGE="VBScript">
sub ChangeColor
window.document.bgColor = "#FF0000"
end sub
</SCRIPT>
<%end if%>
```

has no effect on the server, but does run very nicely on the client when the button is pressed. The <%else%> script statement does run on the server, however, thus allowing the ASP script to determine which HTML is output to the page.

Comments

It can take a while before you get used to just which statements will run on a server and which will run on the client browser. As shown in How-To 2.10, combining the two features can lead to some spectacularly powerful results.

4.8 How do I… Create a server-side ASP script?

Problem

I'm having problems keeping those blasted little <%%>s in the right place, and I can't use ActiveX Control Pad with them at all. Is there a way to write regular <SCRIPT> tags that will work with ASP?

Technique

Yes, via the server-side <SCRIPT> tag. This How-To illustrates redoing the ASP page from the previous How-To to run entirely inside a <SCRIPT> tag, rather than inside <%%>. These steps create the application from scratch, but for your convenience the complete project is on the CD under CH04\HT08\.

Steps

1. Activate Notepad or some other simple text editor. Enter the HTML code in Listing 4-13 and save it as `ASPHT0408.ASP`. Make sure you move it to the directory you aliased as `ASPEXEC` for use in executing ASP scripts.

Listing 4-13 `ASPHT0408.ASP` source code

```
<HTML>
<HEAD>
<TITLE>Active Server Pages How To Chapter Four How To Eight</TITLE>
</HEAD>

<BODY>
<% call SendTheOutput %>
</BODY>
<SCRIPT RUNAT="Server" LANGUAGE="VBScript">
Sub SendTheOutput
QuoteString = """"
QuoteVal = asc(QuoteString)
Response.Write("<H1>Welcome to Active Server Pages, ")
Response.Write(Request.Form("fullname"))
Response.Write( "</H1><P>")
Response.Write("<FORM NAME=Form1>")
if Request.Form("scripttype")="Enter URL" then
    Response.Write("<INPUT LANGUAGE=VBScript TYPE=Button VALUE=" & Chr(QuoteVal)⇐
&"Press Me!"  & Chr(QuoteVal) & "ONCLICK=" & Chr(42) & "Window.location.href =⇐
GetURL()" & Chr(QuoteVal) & "NAME=Button1>")
    Response.Write("<P></FORM><S")
    Response.Write("CRIPT LANGUAGE=VBScript>")
    Response.Write("function GetURL")
    Response.Write("TheURL = prompt(" & Chr(QuoteVal) & "Enter URL" &
Chr(QuoteVal) & "," & Chr(QuoteVal) & "http://www.microsoft.com/ie/default.asp" &
Chr(QuoteVal) & ")" )
    Response.Write("GetURL = TheURL")
    Response.Write("end function")
    Response.Write("</S")
    Response.Write("CRIPT>")
else
    Response.Write("<INPUT LANGUAGE=VBScript TYPE=Button VALUE=" & Chr(QuoteVal)⇐
& "Press Me!"  & Chr(QuoteVal) & "ONCLICK=" & Chr(QuoteVal) & "call⇐
ChangeColor()" & Chr(QuoteVal) & "NAME=Button2>" )
    Response.Write("<P></FORM><S")
    Response.Write("CRIPT LANGUAGE=VBScript>")
    Response.Write("sub ChangeColor " & Chr(10) & Chr(13))
    Response.Write("window.document.bgColor = " & Chr(QuoteVal) & "#FF0000" &⇐
Chr(QuoteVal) )
    Response.Write("end sub")
    Response.Write("</S")
    Response.Write("CRIPT>")
end if
End Sub
 </SCRIPT>
</HTML>
```

2. Create a new text document after having saved the previous one, and enter the HTML code in Listing 4-14. Save it as `ASPHT0408.HTM`.

Listing 4-14 `ASPHT0408.HTM` source code

```
<HTML>
<HEAD>
<TITLE>Active Server Pages How To Chapter Four How To Eight</TITLE>
</HEAD>

<BODY>
<H1>Enter the information below and press SUBMIT to see ASP Server-Side⇐
Scripting!</H1>
<form name="Form1" action="http://default/aspexec/aspht0408.asp" method="post">
<p>Enter Your Name: <input name="fullname" size=48>
<p>What type of script would you like: <select name="scripttype">
<option>Enter URL<option>Reset Background Color
</select>
<p><input type=submit>
</form>


</BODY>
</HTML>
```

3. Activate Internet Explorer, bring up `ASPHT0408.HTM`, and press Return. As shown in Figure 4-14, the previous How-To's form will appear. Select the `Background` color script and press Submit. After a moment, the new HTML page created by the ASP that processed the form request will appear; press the button, and the background will turn red just as it did in the previous How-To, as shown in Figure 4-15, but solely via the commands in a `<SCRIPT>` tag! Congratulations! You have learned to use ASP server-side scripting.

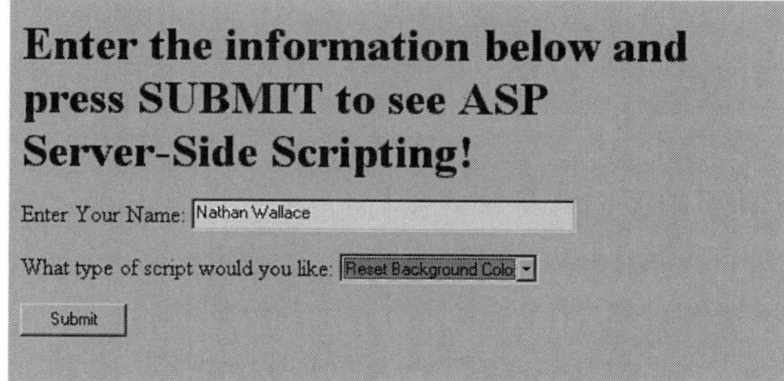

Figure 4-14 `ASPHT0408.HTM` in Internet Explorer showing the previous How-To's form ready to create a new page via ASP

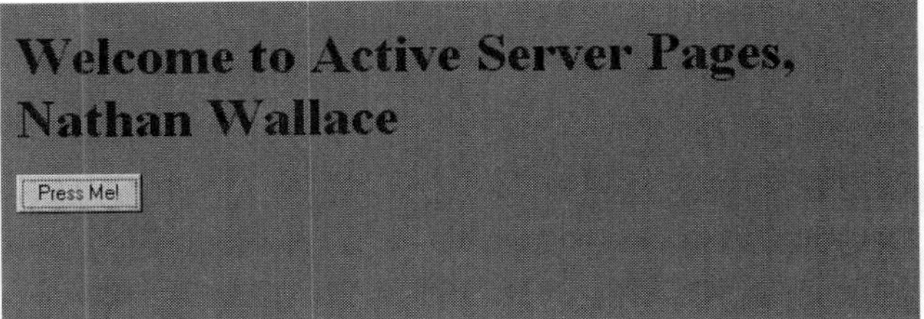

Figure 4-15 ASPHT0408.ASP in Internet Explorer showing the client-side script created entirely via server-side scripting

How It Works

Below is the actual HTML generated by the ASP file. Notice that none of the SCRIPT commands are present, but somehow they were processed:

```
<HTML>
<HEAD>
<TITLE>Active Server Pages How To Chapter Four How To Eight</TITLE>
</HEAD>

<BODY>
<H1>Welcome to Active Server Pages, Nathan Wallace</H1><P><FORM NAME=Form1>
<INPUT LANGUAGE=VBScript TYPE=Button VALUE="Press Me!"ONCLICK="call
ChangeColor()"NAME=Button2><P></FORM><SCRIPT LANGUAGE=VBScript>sub ChangeColor
window.document.bgColor = "#FF0000"end sub</SCRIPT>
</BODY>

</HTML>
```

The key is the parameter at the beginning of the script RUNAT=SERVER. By setting this parameter to any script statement, all its statements are *treated* as if they were enclosed in <%%> tags and thus handled only on the server side of things. That's all there is to it!

Comments

It is important to realize that if you try to include a <SCRIPT> tag in the output of an HTML page including RUNAT=SERVER, the browser will try to treat it like a normal <SCRIPT> tag, with spectacularly unsuccessful results. Make sure all the RUNAT=SERVER <SCRIPT> tags appear only in ASP files.

AXC-ASPS

4.9 How do I... Create an HTML page with an ActiveX control using ASP?

Problem

I need to be able to create complete ActiveX control tags for my HTML page in a CGI environment (that is, without using a special interface such as ActiveX Control Pad). Does ASP have any features that would help me?

Technique

The key to creating arbitrary ActiveX tags is to know the control's `CLSID` value and parameters. Once you have that information (which doesn't change over time), you can easily create your own ActiveX control tags in an HTML page with ASP scripts, as this How-To will demonstrate. The directions here create the project from scratch, but for your convenience, a copy of the HTML file is on the book CD under `\CH04\HT09\`.

Steps

1. Activate Notepad or some other simple text editor. (Notepad is reported to be known at Microsoft these days as "Visual Notepad++.") Enter the HTML code in Listing 4-15 and save it as `ASPHT0409.ASP`. Make sure you move it to the directory you aliased as `ASPEXEC` for use in executing ASP scripts.

Listing 4-15 ASPHT0409.ASP source code

```
<HTML>
<HEAD>
<TITLE>Active Server Pages How To Chapter Four How To Nine</TITLE>
</HEAD>
<BODY>
<H1> This is an ActiveX Control Created Entirely By an ASP Server-Side⇐
Script!</H1>
<HR>
<% Call MakeActiveXControl %>
<HR>
</BODY>
<SCRIPT RUNAT=SERVER LANGUAGE=VBSCRIPT>
sub MakeActiveXControl
    QuoteString = """"
    Response.Write("<OBJECT ID=" & QuoteString & "Aspht03021" & QuoteString &⇐
"WIDTH=324 HEIGHT=215"& Chr(10) & Chr(13))
    Response.Write(" CLASSID=" & QuoteString & "CLSID:503D9A9E-BF39-11D0-B7D8-⇐
444553540000" & QuoteString & ">"& Chr(10) & Chr(13))
```

```
    Response.Write("<PARAM NAME=" & QuoteString & "_Version" & QuoteString &⇐
"VALUE=" & QuoteString & "65536" & QuoteString & ">" & Chr(10) & Chr(13))
    Response.Write("<PARAM NAME=" & QuoteString & "_ExtentX" & QuoteString &⇐
"VALUE=" & QuoteString & "8567" & QuoteString & ">"& Chr(10) & Chr(13))
    Response.Write("<PARAM NAME=" & QuoteString & "_ExtentY" & QuoteString &⇐
"VALUE=" & QuoteString & "5657" & QuoteString & ">"& Chr(10) & Chr(13))
    Response.Write("<PARAM NAME=" & QuoteString & "_StockProps" & QuoteString⇐
& "VALUE=" & QuoteString & "15" & QuoteString & ">"& Chr(10) & Chr(13))
    Response.Write("<PARAM NAME=" & QuoteString & "Caption" & QuoteString &⇐
"VALUE=" & QuoteString & "An ActiveX Control from ASP!" & QuoteString & ">"&⇐
Chr(10) & Chr(13))
    Response.Write("<PARAM NAME=" & QuoteString & "ForeColor" & QuoteString &⇐
"VALUE=" & QuoteString & "65535" & QuoteString & ">"& Chr(10) & Chr(13))
    Response.Write(" <PARAM NAME=" & QuoteString & "PanelColor" & QuoteString⇐
& "VALUE=" & QuoteString & "16711680" & QuoteString & ">"& Chr(10) & Chr(13))
    Response.Write("<PARAM NAME=" & QuoteString & "HighlightColor" & QuoteString⇐
& "VALUE=" & QuoteString & "16776960" & QuoteString & ">"& Chr(10) & Chr(13))
    Response.Write("<PARAM NAME=" & QuoteString & "ShadowColor" & QuoteString⇐
& "VALUE=" & QuoteString & "10485760" & QuoteString & ">"& Chr(10) & Chr(13))
    Response.Write("<PARAM NAME=" & QuoteString & "BorderWidth" & QuoteString⇐
& "VALUE=" & QuoteString & "10" & QuoteString & ">"& Chr(10) & Chr(13))
    Response.Write("</OBJECT>"& Chr(10) & Chr(13))
End Sub
</SCRIPT>
</HTML>
```

2. Activate Internet Explorer. In the address field, type in `HTTP://DEFAULT/ASPEXEC/ASPHT0409.ASP` and press Return. As shown in Figure 4-16, a copy of the **ASPHT0302** custom ActiveX control will appear with specialized settings. Congratulations! You have learned to use ASP scripting to create custom ActiveX control HTML tags.

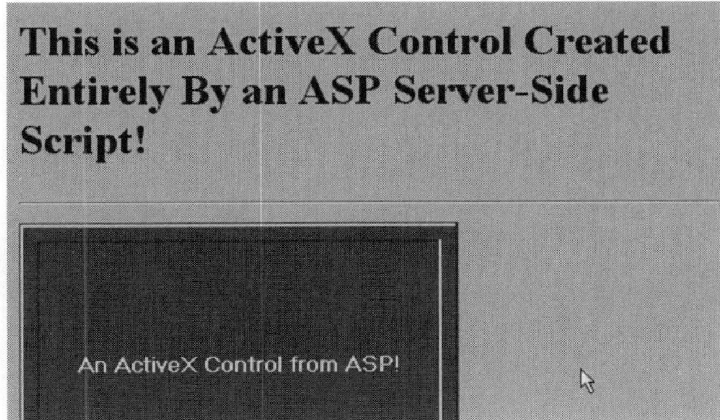

Figure 4-16 ASPHT0409.ASP in Internet Explorer showing the custom ActiveX control created with ASP scripting

How It Works

Although it might seem a trivial task to output the text strings needed to handle this task, it isn't. Observe these two lines of code:

```
Response.Write(" CLASSID=" & QuoteString & "CLSID:503D9A9E-BF39-11D0-B7D8-⇐
444553540000" & QuoteString & ">"& Chr(10) & Chr(13))
    Response.Write("<PARAM NAME="  & QuoteString & "_Version"  & QuoteString &⇐
"VALUE="  & QuoteString & "65536"  & QuoteString & ">" & Chr(10) & Chr(13))
```

Without the `Chr(10)Chr(13)` linefeed and carriage return characters, the line will not break and Internet Explorer will not be able to identify the `CLASSID` of the control to create it successfully. Also, because many of the parameters are sent as quoted strings, the `QuoteString` character is needed to send a double quote that won't be interpreted by the ASP system as a delimiter; it is created by using a double quote inside two double quotes to indicate it should be taken as a literal. (ASP doesn't always recognize this syntax in long strings to the `Write` method, so it is safer to use the workaround.)

Comments

Notice that all the parameters are created in the ASP script. They could have been easily read from a text file or cookies information, thus allowing even more customized ActiveX control creation.

ADO-ASPS

4.10 How do I… Interact with ActiveX data objects using ASP?

Problem

My company needs to use information in a Microsoft Access database in response to customer requests on our Web site. Can ASP help us out with this?

Technique

The key to connecting HTML, ASP, and Access database files is ActiveX data objects (ADO). This How-To demonstrates using an ODBC database to put information into an HTML table via an ASP script. Although the directions here create the project from scratch, the completed ASP files are on the book CD under `\CH04\HT10\`.

Steps

1. For this How-To, you'll use one of the tutorial databases supplied with ASP. (If you have removed them, you need to reinstall the `ADVWORKS.MDB` file to use this How-To.) First, you need to connect the ODBC drivers for Microsoft Access to the database, along with its alias. Open the control panel, then double-click on the 32-bit ODBC drivers icon. In the property pages dialog that appears, select the System DSN tab and click the Add button after selecting the MS Access Driver option. In the add dialog, enter `AWTutorial` for the datasource name, and in the database grouping, click the Select button and browse to the `AdventureWorks Tutorial` directory on your hard drive. Select the `ADVWORKS.MDB` file. Figure 4-17 shows how your configuration should look when you are done. Click OK twice to accept your new settings. (In case this seems mystifying, remember this is done on your *server* computer, where ASP is installed!)

2. Open ActiveX Control Pad and enter the program code in Listing 4-16. Save the file as `ASPHT0410.ASP`; then make sure to copy it to the directory on your hard drive that has ASP execute permissions.

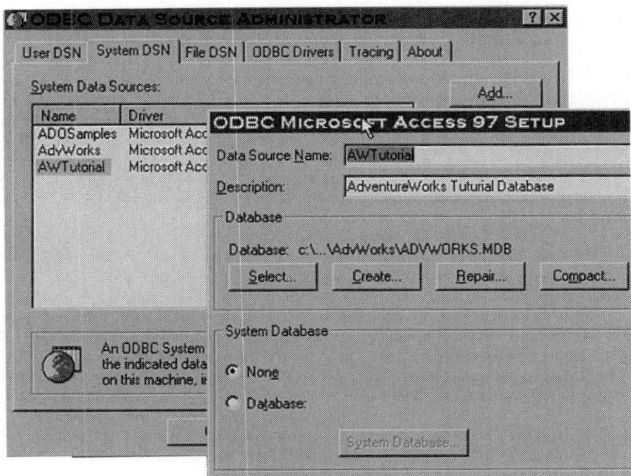

Figure 4-17 Setting the 32-bit ODBC drivers and alias for the Adventure Works demo database

Listing 4-16 ASPHT0410.ASP ASP script file

```
<%@ LANGUAGE = VBScript %>
<HTML>

1<HEAD>
<TITLE>Active Server Pages Chapter Four How To Ten</TITLE>
</HEAD>
<BODY>
<TABLE WIDTH=600 BORDER=0>
<TR>
<TD COLSPAN=3>
<FONT SIZE=4 FACE="ARIAL NARROW" COLOR="#800000">Customer Listing</FONT>
</TD>
</TR>
<TD VALIGN=TOP ALIGN=LEFT COLSPAN=3><FONT SIZE=2>
<% Set OBJdbConnection = Server.CreateObject("ADODB.Connection")
OBJdbConnection.Open "AWTutorial"
SQLQuery = "SELECT * FROM Customers"
Set RSCustomerList = OBJdbConnection.Execute(SQLQuery) %>
<TABLE COLSPAN=8 CELLPADDING=5 BORDER=0>
<TR>
<TD ALIGN=CENTER BGCOLOR="#800000">
<FONT STYLE="ARIAL NARROW" COLOR="#ffffff" SIZE=1>Company Name</FONT>
</TD>
<TD ALIGN=CENTER BGCOLOR="#800000">
<FONT STYLE="ARIAL NARROW" COLOR="#ffffff" SIZE=1>Contact Name</FONT>
</TD>
<TD ALIGN=CENTER WIDTH=150 BGCOLOR="#800000">
<FONT STYLE="ARIAL NARROW" COLOR="#ffffff" SIZE=1>E-mail address</FONT>
</TD>
<TD ALIGN=CENTER BGCOLOR="#800000">
<FONT STYLE="ARIAL NARROW" COLOR="#ffffff" SIZE=1>City</FONT>
</TD>
<TD ALIGN=CENTER BGCOLOR="#800000">
<FONT STYLE="ARIAL NARROW" COLOR="#ffffff" SIZE=1>State/Province</FONT>
</TD>
</TR>
<% Do While Not RScustomerList.EOF %>
  <TR>
  <TD BGCOLOR="f7efde" ALIGN=CENTER>
    <FONT STYLE="ARIAL NARROW" SIZE=1>
      <%= RSCustomerList("CompanyName")%>
    </FONT></TD>
  <TD BGCOLOR="f7efde" ALIGN=CENTER>
    <FONT STYLE="ARIAL NARROW" SIZE=1>
      <%= RScustomerList("ContactLastName") & ", " %>
      <%= RScustomerList("ContactFirstName") %>
    </FONT></TD>
  <TD BGCOLOR="f7efde" ALIGN=CENTER>
    <FONT STYLE="ARIAL NARROW" SIZE=1>
    <A HREF="mailto:">
      <%= RScustomerList("ContactLastName")%>
    </A></FONT></TD>
  <TD BGCOLOR="f7efde" ALIGN=CENTER>
    <FONT STYLE="ARIAL NARROW" SIZE=1>
      <%= RScustomerList("City")%>
```

```
        </FONT></TD>
    <TD BGCOLOR="f7efde" ALIGN=CENTER>
        <FONT STYLE="ARIAL NARROW" SIZE=1>
            <%= RScustomerList("StateOrProvince")%>
        </FONT></TD>
    </TR>
<% RScustomerList.MoveNext
Loop %>
</TABLE>
</TD>
</TR>
</TABLE>
</BODY>
</HTML>
```

3. Activate Internet Explorer. In the address field, type in `HTTP://DEFAULT/ASPEXEC/ASPHT0410.ASP` and press Return. As shown in Figure 4-18, a table will be created using the information from the ODBC database. Congratulations! You have learned to use ASP to interact with ODBC databases using ADO.

How It Works

Aside from the usual mechanics of interspersing ASP scripts with HTML text, this How-To shows a key part of ASP functionality, the `ADODB` object:

```
<% Set OBJdbConnection = Server.CreateObject("ADODB.Connection")
OBJdbConnection.Open "AWTutorial"
SQLQuery = "SELECT * FROM Customers"
Set RSCustomerList = OBJdbConnection.Execute(SQLQuery) %>
```

The `Server` object is used here, as it is where the connection to the `ADODB` object is stored (via the `GLOBAL.ASA` file, which is discussed in much more detail in Chapter 5, "Intermediate ASP: Active Server Components"). Once the object is successfully created, it is told to open the database with the alias `AWTutorial`, which you entered into your system in step 1. Finally, the last two statements create an SQL query and send it to the database, returning a `Collection` object that holds the results of that query.

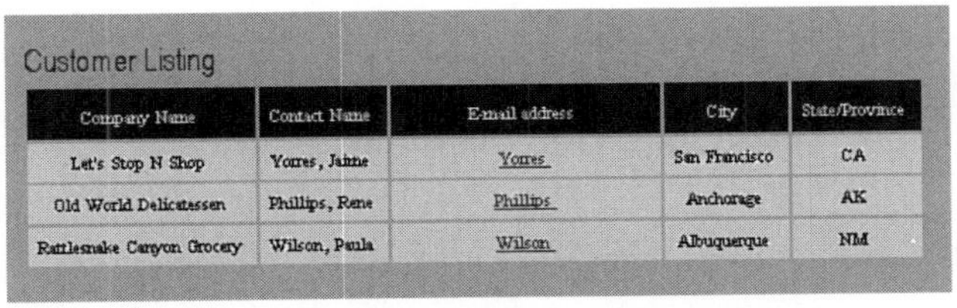

Customer Listing

Company Name	Contact Name	E-mail address	City	State/Province
Let's Stop N Shop	Yorres, Jaime	Yorres	San Francisco	CA
Old World Delicatessen	Phillips, Rene	Phillips	Anchorage	AK
Rattlesnake Canyon Grocery	Wilson, Paula	Wilson	Albuquerque	NM

Figure 4-18 ASPHT0410.ASP in Internet Explorer showing the successful creation of the HTML table from the ADO database via ASP

After having obtained the desired recordset, you must now use it to create the data for the HTML table.

```
<% Do While Not RScustomerList.EOF %>
  <TR>
  <TD BGCOLOR="f7efde" ALIGN=CENTER>
    <FONT STYLE="ARIAL NARROW" SIZE=1>
      <%= RSCustomerList("CompanyName")%>
    </FONT></TD>
  <TD BGCOLOR="f7efde" ALIGN=CENTER>
    <FONT STYLE="ARIAL NARROW" SIZE=1>
      <%= RScustomerList("ContactLastName") & ", " %>
      <%= RScustomerList("ContactFirstName") %>
    </FONT></TD>
  <TD BGCOLOR="f7efde" ALIGN=CENTER>
    <FONT STYLE="ARIAL NARROW" SIZE=1>
    <A HREF="mailto:">
      <%= RScustomerList("ContactLastName")%>
    </A></FONT></TD>
  <TD BGCOLOR="f7efde" ALIGN=CENTER>
    <FONT STYLE="ARIAL NARROW" SIZE=1>
      <%= RScustomerList("City")%>
    </FONT></TD>
  <TD BGCOLOR="f7efde" ALIGN=CENTER>
    <FONT STYLE="ARIAL NARROW" SIZE=1>
      <%= RScustomerList("StateOrProvince")%>
    </FONT></TD>
  </TR>
<% RScustomerList.MoveNext
Loop %>
```

The technique here is very simple: Output the values of fields of the `Collection` object returned by the SQL query by sending them into it as parameters. (More on using collections with ASP in Chapter 5.) By using a loop that runs until the end of the collection (`RScustomerList.EOF`), you can write all the data into the HTML table for clear display.

Comments

Despite the simplicity of this application, any type and complexity of database information can be displayed in this way, although more complex techniques are needed involving `BinaryWrite` for binary data (BLOB fields).

CHAPTER 5

INTERMEDIATE ASP: ACTIVE SERVER COMPONENTS

5

INTERMEDIATE ASP: ACTIVE SERVER COMPONENTS

How do I...

5.1 Create an ASP application?

5.2 Use the `GLOBAL.ASA` file to control my ASP application?

5.3 Handle multiple users with my ASP application?

5.4 Use the ASP Server component with my ASP application?

5.5 Use the ASP Session component with my ASP application?

5.6 Place random advertisement images on my ASP application's HTML pages?

5.7 Determine the capabilities of my users' browsers automatically in my ASP application?

5.8 Create HTML pages that automatically guide users along a "trail" of Web pages?

5.9 Create and use text files on my ASP server with my ASP application?

5.10 Use connection pooling with my ActiveX data objects in my ASP application?

Now that you know the basics of writing ASP scripts and using the very capable Request and Response components, it is time to move up to the really powerful components of ASP. This chapter covers all the remaining components supplied with ASP itself; Chapter 6, "Advanced ASP: Creating ASP Components with Visual C++ 5.0," guides you through creating your own! Here you will learn about ASP applications, the `GLOBAL.ASA` file and the potent `<OBJECT RUNAT=SERVER>` tag, and managing multiple users at the same time. Then you will delve into the powerful Server and Session components, learning how to control individual users as well as make sure your HTML is output correctly. Next is coverage of the `AdRotator`, `BrowserType`, and `ContentLinking` components that make up the starter set of ASP supplied by Microsoft, and more than enough to create killer Web sites! Finally, the last How-To's cover using text files on the ASP server and balancing ActiveX data object (ADO) demands on the database server with connection pooling.

5.1 Create an ASP Application

Because you might have always thought of applications as compiled binary code, the idea of a group of HTML pages as an "application" might seem a bit strange. This How-To will demonstrate how to use Personal Web Server (PWS, the little brother of Internet Information Server, IIS) to create an ASP application and how to take advantage of the amazing power of the Application component of ASP.

5.2 Use the `GLOBAL.ASA` File to Control My ASP Application

`GLOBAL.ASA` is a special ASP file used by the ASP system whenever an application is first started and finally stopped, and whenever a specific browser first connects and last leaves it. This How-To shows you the capabilities of `GLOBAL.ASA` scripts in keeping track of users and overall application usage.

5.3 Handle Multiple Users with My ASP Application

One of the goals of a professional Web site designer is to have heavy traffic, with many users at the site at the same time. This produces some unique challenges for the ASP Application component, and this How-To illustrates use of the `Lock` and `Unlock` methods that cope with the problem.

5.4 Use the ASP Server Component with My ASP Application

ASP supports a special Server component that represents the running instance of the ASP system. This How-To illustrates using its `MapPath`, `ScriptTimeOut`, and `HTML/URLEncode` methods and properties.

5.5 Use the ASP Session Component with My ASP Application

Another powerful ASP component is the Session component, which is created whenever a specific browser accesses a specific application. This How-To shows you the use of the powerful `SessionID` property, as well as the `Timeout` and `Abandon` methods, and the `session variables` collection that parallels the application variables used, starting in How-To 5.1.

5.6 Place Random Advertisement Images on My ASP Application's HTML Pages

Over a billion dollars in Web advertising revenue is projected for the next fiscal year, and the `AdRotator` ASP component is available to see that you get your share! This How-To demonstrates using the component's `schedule` and `redirection` files with the demo ads in the ASP documentation.

5.7 Determine the Capabilities of My Users' Browsers Automatically in My ASP Application

This has been a perennial CGI script favorite since multiple browsers became available, but now ASP levels the playing field with the potent `BrowserType` component and its companion `BROWSCAP.INI` file. This How-To covers this sophisticated component fully, along with breaking news about the new Microsoft `BROWSCAP` dedicated Web page.

5.8 Create HTML Pages that Automatically Guide Users Along a "Trail" of Web Pages

The "trail" was the initial concept behind hypertext, which in turn led to the WWW. Microsoft has returned to the Web's roots with the `ContentLinking` component, and this How-To shows you its information files and multiple methods in a simple but very powerful user-driven tour of the Microsoft ASP Web site.

5.9 Create and Use Text Files on My ASP Server with My ASP Application

Reading and writing text files in an HTML environment in the past required CGI scripts or ActiveX controls. Now `FileSystemObject` and `TextStreamObject` are available to do these important chores, and this How-To adds their capabilities to the developing ASP application in this chapter, giving you a fully functional guest book and demonstrating use of an ActiveX control with ASP components.

5.10 Use Connection Pooling with My ActiveX Data Objects in My ASP Application

Although connection pooling is the subject of Chapter 7," ActiveX Data Objects: OLE DB Made Easy," this How-To delves briefly but powerfully into the fairly deep subject of connection pooling, an option available with ADO and ASP to balance the load on a database server under heavy use. The `<OBJECT>` tags from How-To 5.2 are the key to this technology.

5.1 How do I… Create an ASP application?

Problem

I need to keep all my Web site's HTML pages working together, particularly in keeping track of who visits them. Does ASP have a way to help me with this?

Technique

Yes, it does! The concept is that of the ASP application, a specially marked directory containing all the HTML pages for the site. This How-To will show you how to use PWS to create an application, and then give you the ASP code to demonstrate a minimal guest book functionality. Although these directions create the project from scratch, the CD contains a completed file under `CH05\HT01\`.

Steps

1. First, create a new folder on an appropriate place of your system named `GuestBook`. If you have IIS installed instead of PWS, it to configure ASP. Otherwise, bring up the PWS Administration page in Internet Explorer. Click on the `WWW Administration` link, then click on the Directories tab, and scroll down if you need to, until the `Add` link is visible, as shown in Figure 5-1. Click on it to bring up the Directory Add page.

C:\Program Files\WebSvr\Htmla	/Htmla	Edit...	Delete
C:\Program Files\WebSvr\Htmlascr	/HtmlaScripts	Edit...	Delete
C:\Program Files\WebSvr\Docs	/IASDocs	Edit...	Delete
C:\WebShare\scripts	/Scripts	Edit...	Delete
			Add...

☑ Enable Default Document
Default Document : Default.htm

☑ Directory Browsing Allowed

OK Cancel Reset

Figure 5-1 The `Add` link for adding a new directory to the PWS administration system

2. On the Directory Add administration page, enter the root directory and drive letter where your `GuestBook` directory lives and press the Browse button, as shown in Figure 5-2. Then navigate via the links until you find the `GuestBook` directory, as shown in Figure 5-3. Press the OK button to accept the path for the new directory.

3. Back at the Directory Add page, scroll down and make sure the Virtual option is chosen, and enter `GuestBook` in the Alias text box. Then make sure the Execute check box is checked, as shown in Figure 5-4. Press OK to add the directory to the available ASP executable directories, as shown in Figure 5-5.

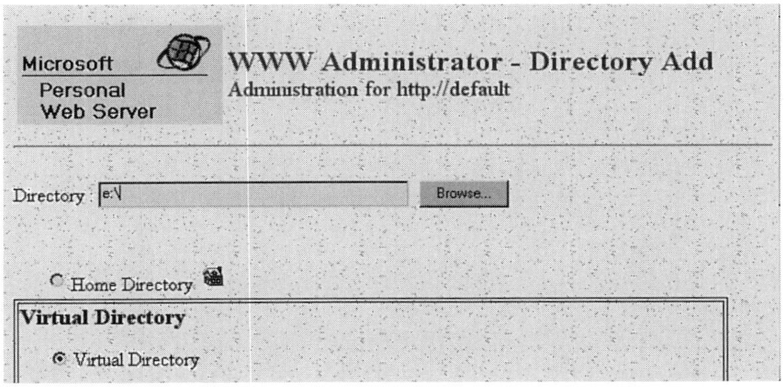

Figure 5-2 Starting to browse to find the `GuestBook` directory

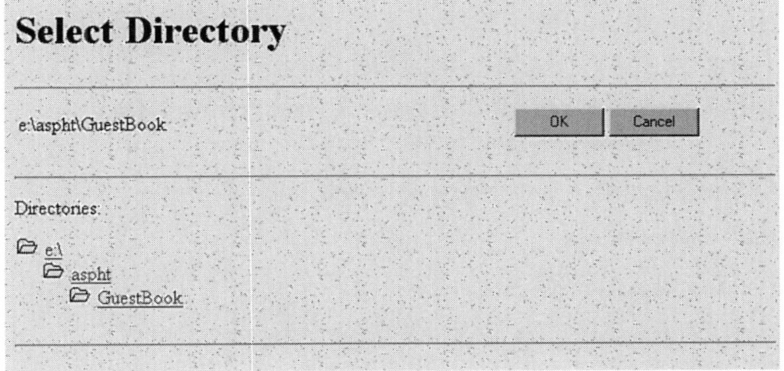

Figure 5-3 The complete path to the `GuestBook` directory

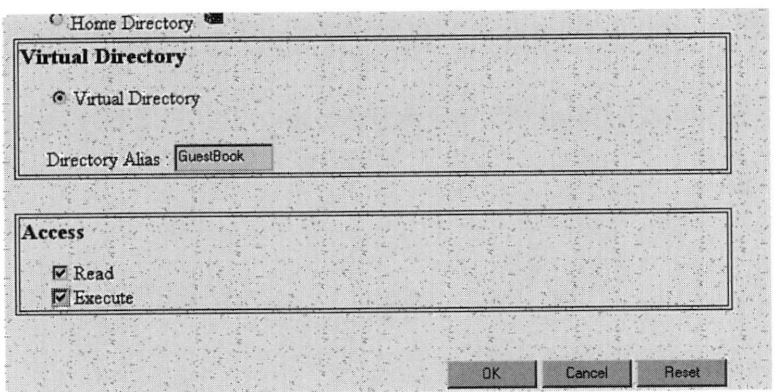

Figure 5-4 Setting the `Alias` and `Execute` properties

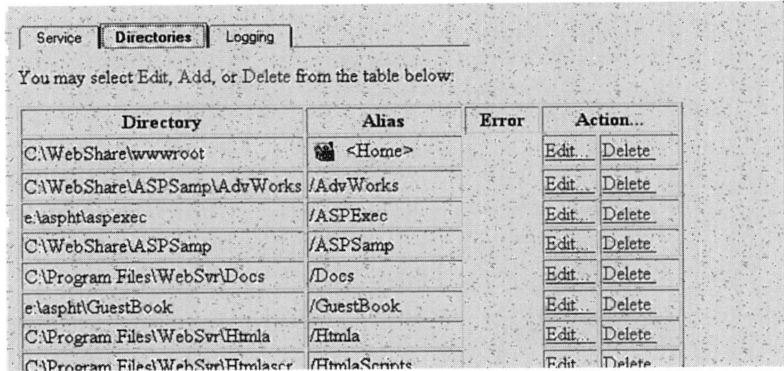

Figure 5-5 The newly added `GuestBook` ASP directory

4. Now you are ready to write your ASP application's first Web page. Activate ActiveX Control Pad. Enter the code in Listing 5-1 and save the file as `ASPHT0501.ASP` in the `GuestBook` directory.

Listing 5-1 `ASPHT0501.ASP` source code

```
<%@ LANGUAGE = VBScript %>
<%
UsersCount = Application("UsersCount")
dim UsersArray( 100 )
for counter1 = 1 to UsersCount
 UsersArray( counter1 ) = Application( "UserName" & CStr( counter1 ))
next
UserName = Request.Form("Text1")
if UserName <> "" then
  UserBrowser = Request.Form("Text2")
```

```
  WorkingString = UserName & " using " & UserBrowser
  UsersCount = UsersCount + 1
  UsersArray( UsersCount ) = WorkingString
  Application("UserName" & CStr( UsersCount) ) = WorkingString
  Application("UsersCount") = UsersCount
else
  UserName = "Ima User"
  UserBrowser = "Internet Explorer"
  Application("UsersCount") = UsersCount
  set Application("UsersArray") = UsersArray
end if
%>
<HTML>
<HEAD>
<TITLE>Active Server Pages How To Chapter Five How To One</TITLE>
</HEAD>
<BODY>
<FORM NAME="Form1" ACTION="aspht0501.asp" METHOD="POST" TARGET="_top">
<TABLE CELLPADDING=5 CELLSPACING=5 WIDTH=600 BORDER=5 ALIGN="CENTER"
VALIGN="MIDDLE" BGCOLOR="#008080">
<CAPTION>Welcome To The ASP How To GuestBook!</CAPTION>

<TR>
<TD ALIGN="CENTER" VALIGN="MIDDLE" BGCOLOR="#008080">Your Name
</TD>
<TD ALIGN="CENTER" VALIGN="MIDDLE" BGCOLOR="#008080">Your Browser
</TD>
<TD ALIGN="CENTER" VALIGN="MIDDLE" BGCOLOR="#008080">Other Guests
</TD>
</TR>
<TR>
<TD ALIGN="CENTER" VALIGN="MIDDLE" BGCOLOR="#008080">
<INPUT TYPE=Text NAME="Text1" VALUE="<%= UserName %>">
</TD>
<TD ALIGN="CENTER" VALIGN="MIDDLE" BGCOLOR="#008080">
<INPUT TYPE=Text NAME="Text2" VALUE="<%= UserBrowser %>">
</TD>
<TD ALIGN="CENTER" VALIGN="MIDDLE" BGCOLOR="#008080">
<%= "Total Visitors: " & UsersCount %><BR>
<% for Counter1 = 1 to UsersCount %>
<%= UsersArray( Counter1 ) %><BR>
<%next%>
</TD>
</TR>
<TR>
<TD COLSPAN=3 ALIGN="CENTER" VALIGN="MIDDLE" BGCOLOR="#008080">
<INPUT TYPE=Submit NAME="Submit1" VALUE="Sign GuestBook">
</TD>
</TR>
</TABLE>
</FORM>
</BODY>
</HTML>
```

5. Create a new blank file and enter the code in Listing 5-2. Save it in the `GuestBook` directory as `GLOBAL.ASA`.

Listing 5-2 GLOBAL.ASA source code

```
<SCRIPT LANGUAGE=VBScript RUNAT=Server>
SUB Application_OnStart
  Application("UsersCount") = 0
END SUB
</SCRIPT>
```

6. Activate Internet Explorer. In the address field, type in **HTTP://DEFAULT/GUESTBOOK/ASPHT0501.ASP** and press Return. Enter several usernames and browser types, and press Sign GuestBook after each one. As shown in Figure 5-6, the resulting page each time displays the current total and all the previous names you have entered. Now close and restart IE and go back to that directory; you will see that the names and count have been maintained! Congratulations! You have learned to create an ASP application and use the Application component to maintain state information about your users.

How It Works

The application concept is based on IIS/PWS executable directories. When an ASP file is loaded from any registered virtual IIS directory that has execute permissions, the ASP system checks several things. First, it checks to see if the directory is a "root" directory, that is, there are no execute-permitted directories above it. If not, it then checks to see if any file has been loaded from that directory since a certain interval (normally 30 minutes); if so, it connects itself to the `Application` object already created for that directory. If not, it creates a new `Application` object and maintains it until no page has been viewed from its directory or any subdirectory for the above-mentioned interval. This object then can be referenced from any ASP script in any HTML page in that root directory and any of its subdirectories. This grouping of HTML/ASP pages that all use the same `Application` object is known as an ASP application (for obvious reasons).

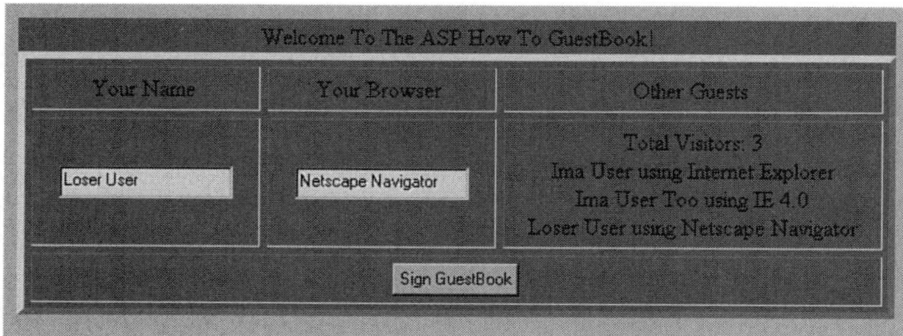

Figure 5-6 ASPHT0501.ASP in Internet Explorer, showing the Application component at work

In addition to creating the Application object the first time a HTML page is accessed since the PWS/IIS system was started or the last Application object was timed out, the ASP system automatically processes the Application_OnStart event handler in the GLOBAL.ASA file in the root directory of the application, if one is present. Objects and variables created in the GLOBAL.ASA file then remain available until the Application object is removed by timing out or by the IIS/PWS system shutting down. The GLOBAL.ASA file is covered in much more detail in How-To 5.2.

It is important to keep in mind the difference between an application and a session. An application starts whenever *any* browser or other HTTP process acquires any ASP file in the root directory or its subdirectories. A session starts whenever a *specific* browser program (not just a browser type, but an actual running program instance) acquires any ASP file in the same area. Thus, a single application can have as many sessions as there have been browser programs accessing its files. Like the Application object, Session objects also live on after their last access unless they are explicitly killed. Session objects are covered in much more detail in How-To 5.5.

When the system shuts down or a timeout interval has expired, the Application object is killed by the ASP system. At this time, the Application_OnEnd event handler in the GLOBAL.ASA file is processed, if one is present. All existing sessions are killed also, although in all likelihood they are long since gone because their timeout period is much shorter.

Once the Application object is created by the ASP system, it becomes available to ASP scripts. It has only two specific methods, covered in How-To 5.3, for use with multiple simultaneous users. Its main power lies in the ability of any ASP script to attach a variable of any name and type, except arrays, to the Application object and have that data persist until it is explicitly set to NOTHING or the Application object is killed. Note this line of code in the GLOBAL.ASA file:

```
Application("UsersCount") = 0
```

The collection object of the Application component is accessed by simply placing the name literal (it can be a constructed string also, as you'll see in a moment) inside parentheses attached to the application's name. You place a new value in the collection simply by assigning to it, as is done above. Now examine the reciprocal lines of code here to see how the data is taken out:

```
UsersCount = Application("UsersCount")
dim UsersArray( 100 )
for counter1 = 1 to UsersCount
 UsersArray( counter1 ) = Application( "UserName" & CStr( counter1 ))
next
```

If no such data variable has existed in the Application object's collection object, there would have been a return of Empty or "", and thus an error. But because you know that you've created the data item in the GLOBAL.ASA file, no such error handling is needed and the variable can be assumed to be safely initialized. Now notice that because of this, if no stored Application variables holding users are present, the loop will run from 1 to 0 and drop immediately through. If variables have been created, they can be accessed here via constructing a string with "UserName" and their numbers, and read into the local array for later display.

Similarly, the count can be increased and the new data added.

```
UserName = Request.Form("Text1")
if UserName <> "" then
  UserBrowser = Request.Form("Text2")
  WorkingString = UserName & " using " & UserBrowser
  UsersCount = UsersCount + 1
  UsersArray( UsersCount ) = WorkingString
  Application("UserName" & CStr( UsersCount) ) = WorkingString
  Application("UsersCount") = UsersCount
else
  UserName = "Ima User"
  UserBrowser = "Internet Explorer"
  Application("UsersCount") = UsersCount
  set Application("UsersArray") = UsersArray
end if
```

Again, only one data item needs to be added, so the unique name is constructed as before and then the incremented count variable is stored again. This lack of checking for a duplicate user is a potential bug, but we'll work on that in How-To 5.9!

Comments

If you are wondering why an array wasn't used, the answer lies in the next How-To.

5.2 How do I... Use the GLOBAL.ASA file to control my ASP application?

Problem

I need to be able to take actions when my ASP application starts and ends. I don't see any events on the Application component; how can I do this?

Technique

The GLOBAL.ASA file is where the On_Start and On_End events live. This How-To will demonstrate writing ASP code for them and using the powerful <OBJECT RUNAT-SERVER> tag. Although these directions create the project from scratch, the CD contains a completed file under CH05\HT02\.

Steps

1. Activate ActiveX Control Pad and reload the **ASPHT0501.ASP** file. Modify the code so it is identical to the code in Listing 5-3. Save it as ASPHT0502.ASP.

Listing 5-3 ASPHT0502.ASP source code

```
<%@ LANGUAGE = VBScript %>
<%
UsersCount = Application("UsersCount")
dim UsersArray( 100 )
UsersArray = Application("TheArray")
UserName = Request.Form("Text1")
if UserName <> "" then
  UserBrowser = Request.Form("Text2")
  WorkingString = UserName & " using " & UserBrowser
  UsersCount = UsersCount + 1
  UsersArray( UsersCount ) = WorkingString
  Application("UsersCount") = UsersCount
  Set Application("TheArray") = UsersArray
else
  UserName = "Ima User"
  UserBrowser = "Internet Explorer"
  Application("UsersCount") = UsersCount
  set Application("UsersArray") = UsersArray
end if
MyAdd.Border(0)
%>
<HTML>
<HEAD>
<TITLE>Active Server Pages How To Chapter Five How To Two</TITLE>
</HEAD>
<BODY>
<FORM NAME="Form1" ACTION="aspht0502.asp" METHOD="POST" TARGET="_top">
<TABLE CELLPADDING=5 CELLSPACING=5 WIDTH=600 BORDER=5 ALIGN="CENTER"
VALIGN="MIDDLE" BGCOLOR="#008080">
<CAPTION>Welcome To The ASP How To GuestBook!</CAPTION>

<TR>
<TD ALIGN="CENTER" VALIGN="MIDDLE" BGCOLOR="#008080">Your Name
</TD>
<TD ALIGN="CENTER" VALIGN="MIDDLE" BGCOLOR="#008080">Your Browser
</TD>
<TD ALIGN="CENTER" VALIGN="MIDDLE" BGCOLOR="#008080">Other Guests
</TD>
</TR>
<TR>
<TD ALIGN="CENTER" VALIGN="MIDDLE" BGCOLOR="#008080">
<INPUT TYPE=Text NAME="Text1" VALUE="<%= UserName %>">
</TD>
<TD ALIGN="CENTER" VALIGN="MIDDLE" BGCOLOR="#008080">
<INPUT TYPE=Text NAME="Text2" VALUE="<%= UserBrowser %>">
</TD>
<TD ALIGN="CENTER" VALIGN="MIDDLE" BGCOLOR="#008080">
```

continued on next page

continued from previous page

```
<%= "Total Visitors: " & UsersCount %><BR>
<% for Counter1 = 1 to UsersCount %>
<%= UsersArray( Counter1 ) %><BR>
<%next%>
</TD>
</TR>
<TR>
<TD COLSPAN=3 ALIGN="CENTER" VALIGN="MIDDLE" BGCOLOR="#008080">
<INPUT TYPE=Submit NAME="Submit1" VALUE="Sign GuestBook">
</TD>
</TR>
</TABLE>
</FORM>
</BODY>
</HTML>
```

2. Reload the `GLOBAL.ASA` file and modify it to match the code in Listing 5-4. Save it in the `GuestBook` directory as `GLOBAL.ASA`, overwriting the previous one.

Listing 5-4 `GLOBAL.ASA` source code

```
<SCRIPT LANGUAGE=VBScript RUNAT=Server>
SUB Application_OnStart
  Application("UsersCount") = 0
  dim HolderArray( 100 )
  Set Application("TheArray") = HolderArray
END SUB
</SCRIPT>

<SCRIPT LANGUAGE=VBScript RUNAT=Server>
SUB Application_OnEnd
  Set Application("TheArray") = Nothing
END SUB
</SCRIPT>

<OBJECT RUNAT=SERVER SCOPE=Application ID=MyAd PROGID= "MSWC.AdRotator">
</OBJECT>
```

3. Shut down and restart PWS or IIS to reset the `Application` object if you have run How-To 5.1 within the last hour. Activate Internet Explorer. In the address field, type in `HTTP://DEFAULT/GUESTBOOK /ASPHT0502.ASP` and press Return. Enter several usernames and browser types, and press Sign GuestBook after each one. As shown in Figure 5-7, the application behaves identically to its previous version, meaning that the `OnStart` code has run properly. You have learned to use `GLOBAL.ASA` to create persistent objects for your ASP application.

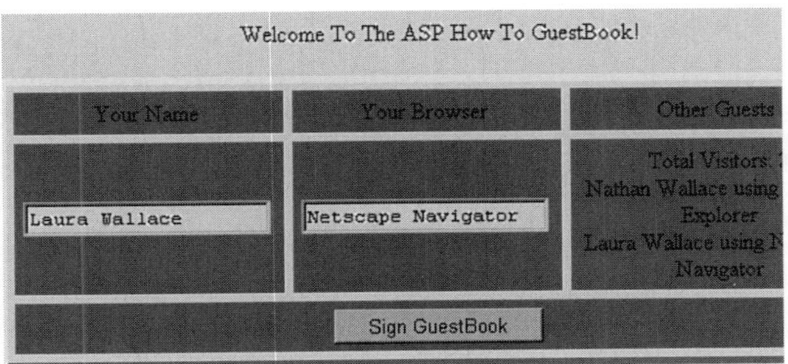

Figure 5-7 ASPHT0502.ASP **in Internet Explorer, showing the Application component at work using a** GLOBAL.ASA **array**

How It Works

There are three things going on in the GLOBAL.ASA file. First, notice these lines of code in the Application_OnStart event:

```
dim HolderArray( 100 )
Set Application("TheArray") = HolderArray
```

First an array is constructed in the GLOBAL.ASA file. Then it is added as a global object to the application's collection. Notice the Set syntax; this makes sure the contents of the array are preserved.

Now notice the corresponding line in the Application_OnEnd event:

```
Set Application("TheArray") = Nothing
```

Here, the array is set to Nothing to make sure the memory is cleaned up by the ASP system and a resource leak is avoided.

Finally, study this important code in the GLOBAL.ASA file:

```
<OBJECT RUNAT=SERVER SCOPE=Application ID=MyAd PROGID= "MSWC.AdRotator">
</OBJECT>
```

This special <OBJECT> tag creates an application-scope object containing an instance of the AdRotator component. The RUNAT=SERVER parameter is required to make sure ASP understands the object is to be kept around; the SCOPE= parameter can be Application or Session; more on this in How-To 5.5. Its ID= parameter gives it the unique name that can be referenced in later ASP files of the application. The last parameter is either a PROGID= or a CLSID=; PROGID is for the text representation of the object, whereas CLSID is for the GUID string assigned by the ActiveX system.

Note that there is no corresponding removal code for the object in the Application_OnEnd event handler; the ASP system takes care of this automatically.

Now look at how the objects are used in the ASP file.

```
dim UsersArray( 100 )
UsersArray = Application("TheArray")
UserName = Request.Form("Text1")
if UserName <> "" then
  UserBrowser = Request.Form("Text2")
  WorkingString = UserName & " using " & UserBrowser
  UsersCount = UsersCount + 1
  UsersArray( UsersCount ) = WorkingString
  Application("UsersCount") = UsersCount
  Set Application("TheArray") = UsersArray
else
  UserName = "Ima User"
  UserBrowser = "Internet Explorer"
  Application("UsersCount") = UsersCount
  set Application("UsersArray") = UsersArray
end if
MyAdd.Border(0)
```

The array is loaded using the normal application variable syntax and returned using the `Set` statement. The `MyAd` variable is not explicitly created in the ASP file, because it is automatically available via the `<OBJECT>` tag.

Comments

The `AdRotator` component isn't used more here to avoid adding complexity; the component is covered fully in How-To 5.6.

COMPLEXITY
INTERMEDIATE

5.3 How do I... Handle multiple users with my ASP application?

We've run into a problem when a large number of users are accessing our Web site at the same time, with inconsistent data being stored in the application variables. Does ASP have a way to prevent this?

Technique

The multiple user problem is one that the designers anticipated, and there is an easy fix, demonstrated in the code below. Although these directions create the project from scratch, the CD contains a completed file under `CH05\HT03\`.

Steps

1. Activate ActiveX Control Pad and reload the `ASPHT0502.ASP` file. Modify the code so it is identical to the code in Listing 5-5. Save it as `ASPHT0503.ASP`.

Listing 5-5 ASPHT0503.ASP source code

```
<%@ LANGUAGE = VBScript %>
<%
Application.Lock
UsersCount = Application("UsersCount")
dim UsersArray( 100 )
UsersArray = Application("TheArray")
UserName = Request.Form("Text1")
if UserName <> "" then
  UserBrowser = Request.Form("Text2")
  WorkingString = UserName & " using " & UserBrowser
  UsersCount = UsersCount + 1
  UsersArray( UsersCount ) = WorkingString
  Application("UsersCount") = UsersCount
  Set Application("TheArray") = UsersArray
else
  UserName = "Ima User"
  UserBrowser = "Internet Explorer"
  Application("UsersCount") = UsersCount
  set Application("UsersArray") = UsersArray
end if
Application.Unlock
MyAdd.Border(0)
%>
<HTML>
<HEAD>
<TITLE>Active Server Pages How To Chapter Five How To Three</TITLE>
</HEAD>
<BODY>
<FORM NAME="Form1" ACTION="aspht0503.asp" METHOD="POST" TARGET="_top">
<TABLE CELLPADDING=5 CELLSPACING=5 WIDTH=600 BORDER=5 ALIGN="CENTER"
VALIGN="MIDDLE" BGCOLOR="#008080">
<CAPTION>Welcome To The ASP How To GuestBook!</CAPTION>

<TR>
<TD ALIGN="CENTER" VALIGN="MIDDLE" BGCOLOR="#008080">Your Name
</TD>
<TD ALIGN="CENTER" VALIGN="MIDDLE" BGCOLOR="#008080">Your Browser
</TD>
<TD ALIGN="CENTER" VALIGN="MIDDLE" BGCOLOR="#008080">Other Guests
</TD>
</TR>
<TR>
<TD ALIGN="CENTER" VALIGN="MIDDLE" BGCOLOR="#008080">
<INPUT TYPE=Text NAME="Text1" VALUE="<%= UserName %>">
</TD>
<TD ALIGN="CENTER" VALIGN="MIDDLE" BGCOLOR="#008080">
<INPUT TYPE=Text NAME="Text2" VALUE="<%= UserBrowser %>">
</TD>
<TD ALIGN="CENTER" VALIGN="MIDDLE" BGCOLOR="#008080">
<%= "Total Visitors: " & UsersCount %><BR>
<% for Counter1 = 1 to UsersCount %>
<%= UsersArray( Counter1 ) %><BR>
<%next%>
```

continued on next page

continued from previous page

```
</TD>
</TR>
<TR>
<TD COLSPAN=3 ALIGN="CENTER" VALIGN="MIDDLE" BGCOLOR="#008080">
<INPUT TYPE=Submit NAME="Submit1" VALUE="Sign GuestBook">
</TD>
</TR>
</TABLE>
</FORM>
</BODY>
</HTML>
```

2. Shut down and restart PWS or IIS to reset the `Application` object if you have run How-To 5.1 within the last hour. Activate two copies of Internet Explorer. In the address field, type in `HTTP://DEFAULT/GUESTBOOK/ASPHT0503.ASP` and press Return. Enter several usernames and browser types from each copy, and press Sign GuestBook after each one. As shown in Figure 5-8, the application never gets confused and reports an incorrect value to the updating copy of the ASP page. Your ASP arsenal now includes locking and unlocking to prevent multiple user data corruption in an ASP application.

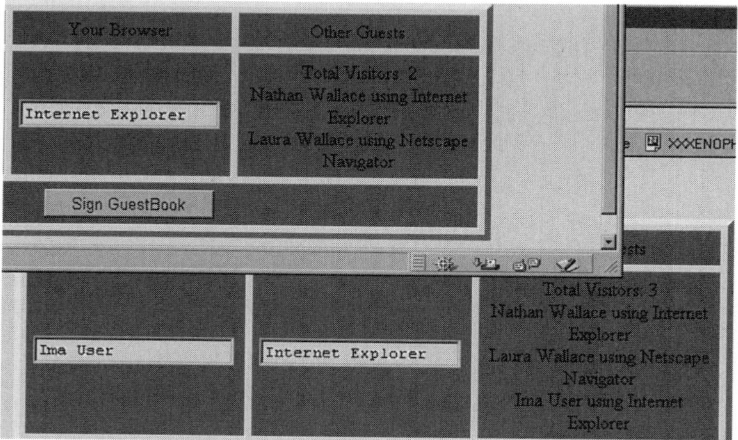

Figure 5-8 ASPHT0503.ASP in Internet Explorer, showing the Application component at work with multiple users

How It Works

This whole How-To hangs on two separate lines of code, boldfaced below to make them stand out:

```
Application.Lock
UsersCount = Application("UsersCount")
dim UsersArray( 100 )
UsersArray = Application("TheArray")
UserName = Request.Form("Text1")
if UserName <> "" then
  UserBrowser = Request.Form("Text2")
  WorkingString = UserName & " using " & UserBrowser
  UsersCount = UsersCount + 1
  UsersArray( UsersCount ) = WorkingString
  Application("UsersCount") = UsersCount
  Set Application("TheArray") = UsersArray
else
  UserName = "Ima User"
  UserBrowser = "Internet Explorer"
  Application("UsersCount") = UsersCount
  set Application("UsersArray") = UsersArray
end if
Application.Unlock
```

Notice that they completely wrap the application variable calls inside them. This is sometimes called a *mutex*, or mutual exclusion flag, and the code enclosed between mutexes is called a *critical section*. What this means in practical terms is that whenever the ASP system tries to access the `Application` object for a given application and finds it has been locked, ASP stops processing until the application is "unlocked." This way, the underlying application variables are always consistent, because only one ASP page can access them at a time.

Comments

Make *very* sure you always unlock the application before the page ends, especially in error situations, or you'll have to reset the PWS/IIS server to reinitialize the locked `Application` object!

COMPLEXITY
INTERMEDIATE

5.4 How do I... Use the ASP Server component with my ASP application?

Problem

We are having several problems with our ASP site. First, the scripts seem to hang and the users get frustrated. Second, we need to output HTML code sometimes but are having trouble with it choking the ASP parser. Does ASP have a component that can help us here?

Technique

The Server component has just what you need! This How-To will demonstrate setting the `ScriptTimeOut` property and using the `HTMLEncode` method to output the page's HTML to a table cell without choking the ASP parser. Although these directions create the project from scratch, the CD contains a completed file under `CH05\HT04\`.

Steps

1. Activate ActiveX Control Pad and reload the `ASPHT0503.ASP` file. Modify the code so it is identical to the code in Listing 5-6. Save it as `ASPHT0504.ASP`.

Listing 5-6 `ASPHT0504.ASP` source code

```
<%@ LANGUAGE = VBScript %>
<%
Application.Lock
UsersCount = Application("UsersCount")
dim UsersArray( 100 )
UsersArray = Application("TheArray")
UserName = Request.Form("Text1")
if UserName <> "" then
  UserBrowser = Request.Form("Text2")
  WorkingString = UserName & " using " & UserBrowser
  UsersCount = UsersCount + 1
  UsersArray( UsersCount ) = WorkingString
  Application("UsersCount") = UsersCount
  Set Application("TheArray") = UsersArray
else
  UserName = "Ima User"
  UserBrowser = "Internet Explorer"
  Application("UsersCount") = UsersCount
  set Application("UsersArray") = UsersArray
end if
Application.Unlock
MyAdd.Border(0)
'Keep the script from hanging
Server.ServerTimeout = 15
%>
<HTML>
<HEAD>
<TITLE>Active Server Pages How To Chapter Five How To Four</TITLE>
</HEAD>
<BODY>
<FORM NAME="Form1" ACTION="aspht0504.asp" METHOD="POST" TARGET="_top">
<TABLE CELLPADDING=5 CELLSPACING=5 WIDTH=600 BORDER=5 ALIGN="CENTER"
VALIGN="MIDDLE" BGCOLOR="#008080">
<CAPTION>Welcome To The ASP How To GuestBook!</CAPTION>

<TR>
<TD ALIGN="CENTER" VALIGN="MIDDLE" BGCOLOR="#008080">Your Name
</TD>
<TD ALIGN="CENTER" VALIGN="MIDDLE" BGCOLOR="#008080">Your Browser
```

```
</TD>
<TD ALIGN="CENTER" VALIGN="MIDDLE" BGCOLOR="#008080">Other Guests
</TD>
</TR>
<TR>
<TD ALIGN="CENTER" VALIGN="MIDDLE" BGCOLOR="#008080">
<INPUT TYPE=Text NAME="Text1" VALUE="<%= UserName %>">
</TD>
<TD ALIGN="CENTER" VALIGN="MIDDLE" BGCOLOR="#008080">
<INPUT TYPE=Text NAME="Text2" VALUE="<%= UserBrowser %>">
</TD>
<TD ALIGN="CENTER" VALIGN="MIDDLE" BGCOLOR="#008080">
<%= "Total Visitors: " & UsersCount %><BR>
<% for Counter1 = 1 to UsersCount %>
<%= UsersArray( Counter1 ) %><BR>
<%next%>
</TD>
</TR>
<TR>
<TD COLSPAN=3 ALIGN="CENTER" VALIGN="MIDDLE" BGCOLOR="#008080">
<INPUT TYPE=Submit NAME="Submit1" VALUE="Sign GuestBook">
</TD>
</TR>
<TR>
<TD COLSPAN=3>
Some Sample HTML Code
<%= Server.HTMLEncode("<TD COLSPAN=3 ALIGN=""CENTER"" VALIGN=""MIDDLE""⇐
BGCOLOR=""#008080"">")%>
</TD>
</TR>
</TABLE>
</FORM>
</BODY>
</HTML>
```

2. Activate Internet Explorer. In the address field, type in **HTTP://DEFAULT/GUESTBOOK/ASPHT0504.ASP** and press Return. As shown in Figure 5-9, the HTML has been successfully output without confusing ASP. Now reload the page and do something to block ASP from processing, such as starting up Word. After 15 seconds (give or take), an error dialog will appear, giving you the opportunity to kill the page because the script is taking too long. Your ASP repertoire now includes the Server component in an ASP application.

How It Works

There are two separate elements in this How-To, both using the Server component. First, note this line of code:

```
'Keep the script from hanging
Server.ServerTimeout = 15
```

The default timeout value is 60 seconds, which can seem pretty long to busy users, particularly if the multitasking system stretches that out due to delayed timer

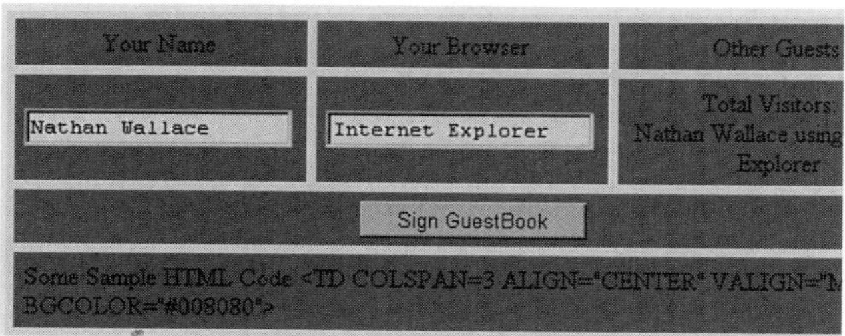

Figure 5-9 `ASPHT0504.ASP` in Internet Explorer showing `HTMLEncoding` from the Server component

messages. This value allows much faster response time. Note also that the `Server component` object is available automatically; it doesn't have to be created or stored.

Now look at how the `HTMLEncode` method is invoked:

```
<TD COLSPAN=3>
Some Sample HTML Code
<%= Server.HTMLEncode("<TD COLSPAN=3 ALIGN=""CENTER"" VALIGN=""MIDDLE""⇐
BGCOLOR=""#008080"">")%>
</TD>
```

It may seem silly to spit out HTML in the middle of a page, but consider how Microsoft displays HTML source code in its developer pages without using the <PLAIN-TEXT> tag! The double quotes allow quotation marks to be embedded safely in the stream sent to the encoder.

Comments

The `CreateObject` method of the `Server` object has been used already and will be shown again in later How-To's. The `URLEncode` method is mainly used to create complex parameterized URLs for links; the `MapPath` method is demonstrated in How-To 5.9.

COMPLEXITY
INTERMEDIATE

5.5 How do I... Use the ASP Session component with my ASP application?

Problem

We have some additional ASP problems: We need to keep track of individual users while they're logged on, and we also need to keep from tying up resources if users leave their browsers logged into our pages while they go to lunch. The `Server` object doesn't deal with this sort of thing; is there another ASP component that does?

Technique

The Session component is just what you need! This How-To will demonstrate using the `GLOBAL.ASA` file in combination with `Session` variables to keep track of a user's individual ID and kill his or her session if there are no page accesses in a short time or if the user deliberately shuts down the application. Although these directions create the project from scratch, the CD contains a completed file under `CH05\HT05\`.

Steps

1. Activate ActiveX Control Pad and reload the `ASPHT0504.ASP` file. Modify the code so it is identical to the code in Listing 5-7. Save it as `ASPHT0505.ASP`.

Listing 5-7 ASPHT0505.ASP source code

```
<%@ LANGUAGE = VBScript %>
<%
Application.Lock
Session("PageHits") = Session("PageHits") + 1
PageHits = Session("PageHits")
dim PageHitsArray( 100 )
PageHitsArray = Session("PageHitsArray")
PageHitsArray( PageHits ) = "ASPHT0505.ASP"
Set Session("PageHitsArray") = PageHitsArray
UsersCount = Application("UsersCount")
dim UsersArray( 100 )
UsersArray = Application("TheArray")
UserName = Request.Form("Text1")
if UserName <> "" then
  UserBrowser = Request.Form("Text2")
  WorkingString = UserName & " using " & UserBrowser
  UsersCount = UsersCount + 1
  UsersArray( UsersCount ) = WorkingString
  Application("UsersCount") = UsersCount
  Set Application("TheArray") = UsersArray
else
  UserName = "Ima User"
  UserBrowser = "Internet Explorer"
  Application("UsersCount") = UsersCount
  set Application("UsersArray") = UsersArray
end if
Application.Unlock
MyAdd.Border(0)
'Keep the script from hanging
Server.ServerTimeout = 15
%>
<HTML>
<HEAD>
<TITLE>Active Server Pages How To Chapter Five How To Five</TITLE>
</HEAD>
<BODY>
<FORM NAME="Form1" ACTION="aspht0505.asp" METHOD="POST" TARGET="_top">
```

continued on next page

continued from previous page

```
<TABLE CELLPADDING=5 CELLSPACING=5 WIDTH=600 BORDER=5 ALIGN="CENTER"
VALIGN="MIDDLE" BGCOLOR="#008080">
<CAPTION>Welcome To The ASP How To GuestBook!</CAPTION>
<TR>
<TD COLSPAN=2 ALIGN="CENTER" VALIGN="MIDDLE" BGCOLOR="#008080">
You are UserID <%= Session.SessionID%>. You have accessed <%=⇐
Session("PageHits")%> Pages in the GuestBook Application this session.
</TD>
<TD ALIGN="CENTER" VALIGN="MIDDLE" BGCOLOR="#008080">
Pages you have accessed this session:
<%for counter1 = 1 to PageHits%>
<%= PageHitsArray( counter1 ) %><BR>
<%next%>
</TD>
</TR>
<TR>
<TD ALIGN="CENTER" VALIGN="MIDDLE" BGCOLOR="#008080">Your Name
</TD>
<TD ALIGN="CENTER" VALIGN="MIDDLE" BGCOLOR="#008080">Your Browser
</TD>
<TD ALIGN="CENTER" VALIGN="MIDDLE" BGCOLOR="#008080">Other Guests
</TD>
</TR>
<TR>
<TD ALIGN="CENTER" VALIGN="MIDDLE" BGCOLOR="#008080">
<INPUT TYPE=Text NAME="Text1" VALUE="<%= UserName %>">
</TD>
<TD ALIGN="CENTER" VALIGN="MIDDLE" BGCOLOR="#008080">
<INPUT TYPE=Text NAME="Text2" VALUE="<%= UserBrowser %>">
</TD>
<TD ALIGN="CENTER" VALIGN="MIDDLE" BGCOLOR="#008080">
<%= "Total Visitors: " & UsersCount %><BR>
<% for Counter1 = 1 to UsersCount %>
<%= UsersArray( Counter1 ) %><BR>
<%next%>
</TD>
</TR>
<TD COLSPAN=3>
Some Sample HTML Code
<%= Server.HTMLEncode("<TD COLSPAN=3 ALIGN=""CENTER"" VALIGN=""MIDDLE""⇐
BGCOLOR=""#008080"">")%>
</TD>
</TR>
<TR>
<TD COLSPAN=3 ALIGN="CENTER" VALIGN="MIDDLE" BGCOLOR="#008080">
<A HREF="ASPHT0505AB.ASP">Click Here To Abandon Current Session</A>
</TD>
</TR>
<TR>
<TD COLSPAN=3 ALIGN="CENTER" VALIGN="MIDDLE" BGCOLOR="#008080">
<INPUT TYPE=Submit NAME="Submit1" VALUE="Sign GuestBook">
</TD>
</TR>
</TABLE>
</FORM>
</BODY>
</HTML>
```

2. Create a new blank ASP file and enter the code in Listing 5-8. Save it in the `GuestBook` directory as `ASPHT0505AB.ASP`.

Listing 5-8 ASPHT0505AB.ASP source code

```
<%@ LANGUAGE = VBScript %>
<%
Session.Abandon
Response.Redirect "ASPHT0505.ASP"
%>
<HTML>
<HEAD>
<TITLE>Active Server Pages How To Chapter Five How To Five Session Abandon⇐
Page</TITLE>
</HEAD>
<BODY>
</BODY>
</HTML>
```

3. Reload the `GLOBAL.ASA` file and modify it to match the code in Listing 5-9. Save it in the `GuestBook` directory as `GLOBAL.ASA`, overwriting the previous one.

Listing 5-9 GLOBAL.ASA source code

```
<SCRIPT LANGUAGE=VBScript RUNAT=Server>
SUB Application_OnStart
  Application("UsersCount") = 0
  dim HolderArray( 100 )
  Set Application("TheArray") = HolderArray
END SUB
</SCRIPT>

<SCRIPT LANGUAGE=VBScript RUNAT=Server>
SUB Application_OnEnd
  Set Application("TheArray") = Nothing
END SUB
</SCRIPT>

<OBJECT RUNAT=SERVER SCOPE=Application ID=MyAd PROGID= "MSWC.AdRotator">
</OBJECT>

<SCRIPT LANGUAGE=VBScript RUNAT=Server>
SUB Session_OnStart
  Session("PageHits") = 0
  dim PageHitsArray( 100 )
  Set Session("PageHitsArray") = PageHitsArray
END SUB
</SCRIPT>

<SCRIPT LANGUAGE=VBScript RUNAT=Server>
SUB Session_OnEnd
  Set Session("PageHitsArray") = Nothing
END SUB
</SCRIPT>
```

4. Reload the first four ASP pages from this chapter and add the lines to put their names into the `PageHitsArray Session` variable and increment the `PageHits Session` variable counter. (Modified versions are on the CD in the `\CH05\HT05\` directory.)

5. Shut down and restart PWS or IIS to reset the `Application` object if you have run How-To 5.1 within the last hour. Activate Internet Explorer. In the address field, type in `HTTP://DEFAULT/GUESTBOOK/ASPHT0505.ASP` and press Return. As shown in Figure 5-10, initially only the current page shows as having been accessed, along with the unique session ID. Now change to several of the other modified `GuestBook` pages and then back to `ASPHT0505.ASP`. As seen in Figure 5-11, the display now has the correct number of `GuestBook` pages hit, as well as their names. Now click on the `Abandon` link. As shown in Figure 5-12, after a moment the `ASPHT0505.ASP` page comes up with a new `SessionID` and only one page accessed. You have learned to use `GLOBAL.ASA` and the Session component to keep track of individual users of your ASP application.

How It Works

In many ways, the Session component is the most powerful one in ASP, simply because it allows developers to track individual users very precisely! The `Session` object is created when an individual browser first accesses any page in an application. A unique ID value is created, called the `SessionID`, as shown in this code:

```
You are UserID <%= Session.SessionID%>. You have accessed <%=⇐
Session("PageHits")%> Pages in the GuestBook Application this session.
```

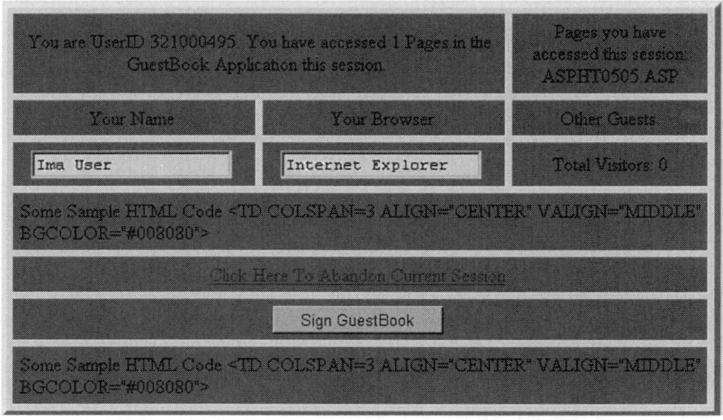

Figure 5-10 `ASPHT0505.ASP` in Internet Explorer, showing the initial session information

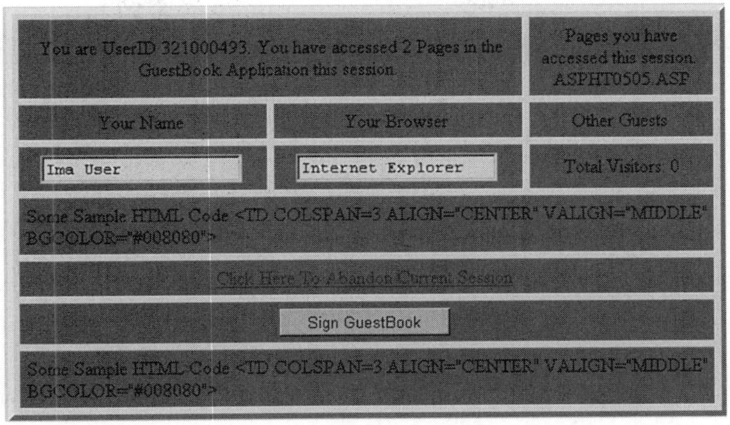

Figure 5-11 ASPHT0505.ASP in Internet Explorer, showing the Session object keeping track of multiple pages accessed by the same user

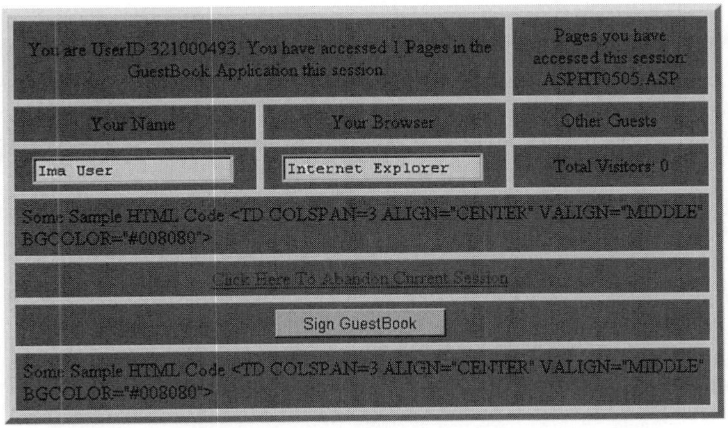

Figure 5-12 ASPHT0505.ASP in Internet Explorer, showing the Abandon method's effects

The actual value is a `LONG` integer number, synthesized with a combination of the date, time, machine, and browser. Although you can store it if you like, it has no real value beyond its internal system usage.

Like the application, the session triggers `OnStart` and `OnEnd` events in `GLOBAL.ASA`. Notice this code in the file:

```
<SCRIPT LANGUAGE=VBScript RUNAT=Server>
SUB Session_OnStart
  Session("PageHits") = 0
  dim PageHitsArray( 100 )
```

continued on next page

continued from previous page

```
  Set Session("PageHitsArray") = PageHitsArray
END SUB
</SCRIPT>

<SCRIPT LANGUAGE=VBScript RUNAT=Server>
SUB Session_OnEnd
  Set Session("PageHitsArray") = Nothing
END SUB
</SCRIPT>
```

The `PageHits` `Session` variable is created by simply assigning a value to it. Likewise, the array is stored by placing it in memory using the `Set` command. To prevent a memory leak, the array is set to `Nothing` at the session's end.

In the ASP file itself, notice how these variables are used:

```
Session("PageHits") = Session("PageHits") + 1
PageHits = Session("PageHits")
dim PageHitsArray( 100 )
PageHitsArray = Session("PageHitsArray")
PageHitsArray( PageHits ) = "ASPHT0505.ASP"
Set Session("PageHitsArray") = PageHitsArray
. . .
Pages you have accessed this session:
<%for counter1 = 1 to PageHits%>
<%= PageHitsArray( counter1 ) %>
<%next%>
```

The `PageHits` value is incremented without creating a local copy, which is perfectly workable syntax. A local copy is then created to allow indexing into the array of page names. The explicit filename is added to the `Names` array and it is resaved just like an `Application` variable. Then, in the appropriate location, the contents are printed out for the user.

Finally, examine this simple code in the `ASPHT0505AB.ASP` file:

```
<%
Session.Abandon
Response.Redirect "ASPHT0505.ASP"
%>
```

Here, the `Session.Abandon` method is called. It kills the existing session, triggers the `OnEnd` `GLOBAL.ASA` event, and closes out all the memory used by `Session` variables. A new access to an application page (via the `Response.Redirect` call) causes a new session to be started.

Comments

The one limitation on sessions is that they depend on the target browser accepting a "cookie," which is `SessionID`. If a user rejects this, the `SessionID` is not available and the `Session` object calls always start fresh, regardless of how many user accesses have occurred.

5.6 How do I... Place random advertisement images on my ASP application's HTML pages?

Problem

My boss recently got a contract to display several advertisers' ad images on our Web page. She wants them displayed randomly in a frequency based on the amount of money each advertiser is paying. Do I have to buy an ActiveX control to do this?

Technique

The `AdRotator` ASP component is supplied for free from Microsoft automatically with ASP! This How-To will show you how to use it to add an advertisement image based on a weighted random value to each instance of your Web page automatically. Although these directions create the project from scratch, the CD contains a completed file under `CH05\HT06\`.

Steps

1. Activate ActiveX Control Pad and reload the `ASPHT0505.ASP` file. Modify the code so it is identical to the code in Listing 5-10. Save it as `ASPHT0506.ASP`.

Listing 5-10 ASPHT0506.ASP source code

```
<%@ LANGUAGE = VBScript %>
<%
Application.Lock
Session("PageHits") = Session("PageHits") + 1
PageHits = Session("PageHits")
dim PageHitsArray( 100 )
PageHitsArray = Session("PageHitsArray")
PageHitsArray( PageHits ) = "ASPHT0506.ASP"
Set Session("PageHitsArray") = PageHitsArray
UsersCount = Application("UsersCount")
dim UsersArray( 100 )
UsersArray = Application("TheArray")
UserName = Request.Form("Text1")
if UserName <> "" then
  UserBrowser = Request.Form("Text2")
  WorkingString = UserName & " using " & UserBrowser
  UsersCount = UsersCount + 1
  UsersArray( UsersCount ) = WorkingString
```

continued on next page

continued from previous page

```
  Application("UsersCount") = UsersCount
  Set Application("TheArray") = UsersArray
else
  UserName = "Ima User"
  UserBrowser = "Internet Explorer"
  Application("UsersCount") = UsersCount
  set Application("UsersArray") = UsersArray
end if
Application.Unlock
 'Keep the script from hanging
Server.ServerTimeout = 15
%>
<HTML>
<HEAD>
<TITLE>Active Server Pages How To Chapter Five How To Six</TITLE>
</HEAD>
<BODY>
<% MyAdd.Border(0)
   MyAd.Clickable = true
   MyAd.TargetFrame = "_blank"%>
<%= MyAd.GetAdvertisement("aspht05ads.txt")%>
<FORM NAME="Form1" ACTION="aspht0506.asp" METHOD="POST" TARGET="_top">
<TABLE CELLPADDING=5 CELLSPACING=5 WIDTH=600 BORDER=5 ALIGN="CENTER"
VALIGN="MIDDLE" BGCOLOR="#008080">
<CAPTION>Welcome To The ASP How To GuestBook!</CAPTION>
<TR>
<TD COLSPAN=2 ALIGN="CENTER" VALIGN="MIDDLE" BGCOLOR="#008080">
You are UserID <%= Session.SessionID%>. You have accessed <%=⇐
Session("PageHits")%> Pages in the GuestBook Application this session.
</TD>
<TD ALIGN="CENTER" VALIGN="MIDDLE" BGCOLOR="#008080">
Pages you have accessed this session:
<%for counter1 = 1 to PageHits%>
<%= PageHitsArray( counter1 ) %><BR>
<%next%>
</TD>
</TR>
<TR>
<TD ALIGN="CENTER" VALIGN="MIDDLE" BGCOLOR="#008080">Your Name
</TD>
<TD ALIGN="CENTER" VALIGN="MIDDLE" BGCOLOR="#008080">Your Browser
</TD>
<TD ALIGN="CENTER" VALIGN="MIDDLE" BGCOLOR="#008080">Other Guests
</TD>
</TR>
<TR>
<TD ALIGN="CENTER" VALIGN="MIDDLE" BGCOLOR="#008080">
<INPUT TYPE=Text NAME="Text1" VALUE="<%= UserName %>">
</TD>
<TD ALIGN="CENTER" VALIGN="MIDDLE" BGCOLOR="#008080">
<INPUT TYPE=Text NAME="Text2" VALUE="<%= UserBrowser %>">
</TD>
<TD ALIGN="CENTER" VALIGN="MIDDLE" BGCOLOR="#008080">
<%= "Total Visitors: " & UsersCount %><BR>
<% for Counter1 = 1 to UsersCount %>
<%= UsersArray( Counter1 ) %><BR>
<%next%>
```

```
</TD>
</TR>
<TD COLSPAN=3>
Some Sample HTML Code
<%= Server.HTMLEncode("<TD COLSPAN=3 ALIGN=""CENTER"" VALIGN=""MIDDLE""⇐
BGCOLOR=""#008080"">")%>
</TD>
</TR>
<TR>
<TD COLSPAN=3 ALIGN="CENTER" VALIGN="MIDDLE" BGCOLOR="#008080">
<A HREF="ASPHT0505AB.ASP">Click Here To Abandon Current Session</A>
</TD>
</TR>
<TR>
<TD COLSPAN=3 ALIGN="CENTER" VALIGN="MIDDLE" BGCOLOR="#008080">
<INPUT TYPE=Submit NAME="Submit1" VALUE="Sign GuestBook">
</TD>
</TR>
</TABLE>
</FORM>
</BODY>
</HTML>
```

2. Create a new blank text file and enter the data in Listing 5-11. Save it in the `GuestBook` directory as `ASPHT0505ADS.TXT`.

Listing 5-11 `ASPHT0506ADS.TXT` source code

```
redirect aspht0506adredir.asp
width 460
height 60
border 1
*
ad_1.gif
http://www.microsoft.com
Astro Mt. Bike Company
20

ad_2.gif
http://www.microsoft.com
Arbor Shoes
20

ad_3.gif
http://www.microsoft.com
Clocktower Sporting Goods
30

ad_4.gif
http://www.microsoft.com
GG&G
30
```

3. Create another blank text file and enter the data in Listing 5-12. Save it in the `GuestBook` directory as `ASPHT0506ADREDIR.ASP`.

Listing 5-12 ASPHT0506ADREDIR.ASP source code

```
<% response.redirect (request.QueryString("url")) %>
```

4. Copy the sample images ad_1.gif, ad_2.gif, ad_3.gif, and ad_4.gif to the GuestBook directory from the ASP AdventureWorks samples directory. (These are copyright Microsoft and so cannot be placed on our CD.)

5. Activate Internet Explorer. In the address field, type in HTTP://DEFAULT/GUESTBOOK/ASPHT0506.ASP and press Return. As shown in Figure 5-13, a random advertiser's image now appears above the GuestBook table. Reload the page a number of times. As seen in Figure 5-14, a different image will appear in proportion to the percentages entered in the ASPHT0505ADS.TXT file. Now click on one of the advertisements. As shown in Figure 5-15, a new copy of IE is launched, linked to the Microsoft Web site, because this was the URL entered for each advertisement. The AdRotator ASP component has become one of your tools for revenue enhancement, through its capability to place random advertising images on your ASP application's pages.

How It Works

There are three properties of the AdRotator component, each of which is set in the ASP code:

```
<% MyAdd.Border(0)
   MyAd.Clickable = true
   MyAd.TargetFrame = "_blank"%>
```

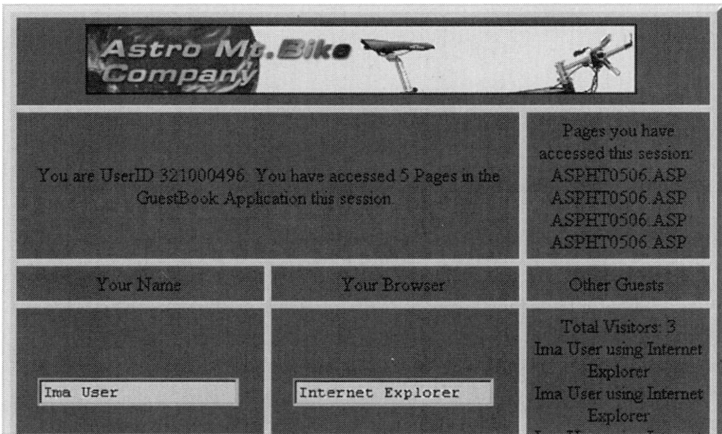

Figure 5-13 ASPHT0506.ASP in Internet Explorer, showing an initial random advertisement image

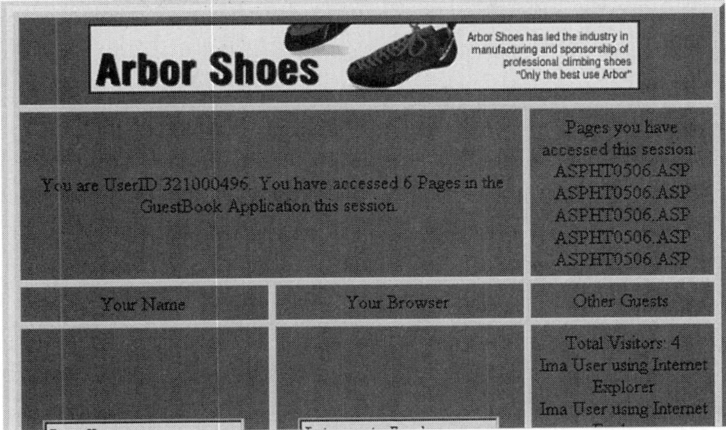

Figure 5-14 ASPHT0506.ASP in Internet Explorer, showing a different random advertisement image

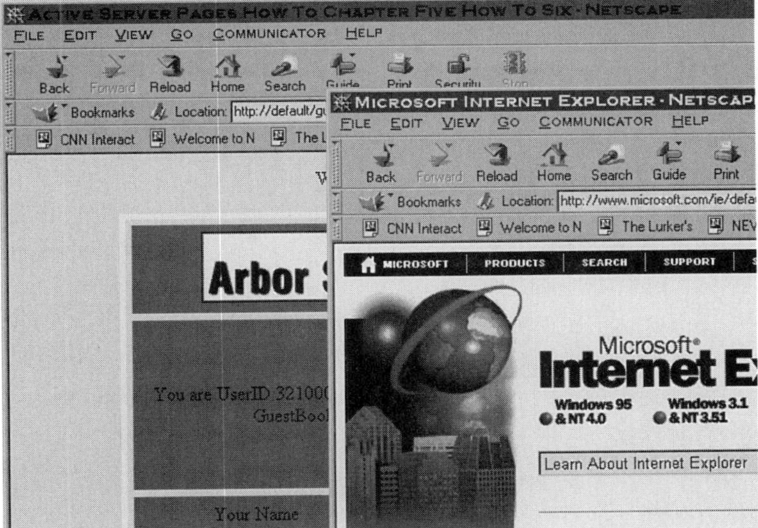

Figure 5-15 The advertisement redirect to the Microsoft Web site

The `Border` parameter determines whether a colored border is placed around the ad, and if so how many pixels wide it is. Setting the property to `0` cancels the border. By setting the `Clickable` property to `true`, the ad's URL is invoked by clicking on it; setting the property to `false` makes the ad merely an image. Finally, `TargetFrame` allows redirecting the URL from a click into a frame on the page, or into a new browser window, as was done here.

To get the HTML for the ad, you need this code:

```
<%= MyAd.GetAdvertisement("aspht05ads.txt")%>
```

The output is simply an <IMG> tag with an optional HREF wrapper to allow clicking. Notice that the string parameter to the call could have been constructed by the ASP script, thus creating more complex ad schemes.

The control information is kept in the two data files. Notice the information layout in the ASPHT0505ADS.TXT file.

```
redirect aspht0505adredir.asp
width 460
height 60
border 1
*
ad_1.gif
http://www.microsoft.com
Astro Mt. Bike Company
20
```

Here, the first line gives the ASP file to handle redirection if a click is allowed. Then the width and height of the image are set (based on the values of the images themselves, of course). A default border value is included, but it is overridden by the Border method call. After the separator, the list of ads is given. It starts with the name of the file (which can include an optional relative path), then the URL to be used if clicking is allowed, and an optional text caption for the ad. Finally, a number is given that is the percentage of the time this ad should be displayed. All the percentages for a given file must add up to 100.

In the redirection file, this simple line of code is used:

```
<% response.redirect (request.QueryString("url")) %>
```

It sends the browser to the URL parameter of the invoked string, created by the <IMG> link. Additional code could be used to keep statistics on how many people have used that particular ad and, if personal statistics are available in the Session object, who they are.

Comments

AdRotator can be used for other things besides advertisements. One project on the Web uses it for a clever trivia game!

5.7 How do I...
Determine the capabilities of my users' browsers automatically in my ASP application?

Problem

I need to know whether my users can display ActiveX controls on their browsers before I show them our Web page. I've heard that ASP has the capability to do this automatically; how can I take advantage of this feature?

Technique

The `BrowserType` component is your answer! This How-To shows you how to use it to determine whether your clients can use ActiveX controls and outputs either an ActiveX control or a standard HTML control as needed. These steps create the application from scratch, but for your convenience, the complete project is on the CD under `CH05\HT07\`.

Steps

1. Activate ActiveX Control Pad and reload the `ASPHT0506.ASP` file. Modify the code so it is identical to the code in Listing 5-13. Save it as `ASPHT0507.ASP`.

Listing 5-13 ASPHT0507.ASP source code

```
<%@ LANGUAGE = VBScript %>
<%
Application.Lock
Session("PageHits") = Session("PageHits") + 1
PageHits = Session("PageHits")
dim PageHitsArray( 100 )
PageHitsArray = Session("PageHitsArray")
PageHitsArray( PageHits ) = "ASPHT0507.ASP"
Set Session("PageHitsArray") = PageHitsArray
UsersCount = Application("UsersCount")
dim UsersArray( 100 )
UsersArray = Application("TheArray")
UserName = Request.Form("Text1")
if UserName <> "" then
  UserBrowser = Request.Form("Text2")
  WorkingString = UserName & " using " & UserBrowser
  UsersCount = UsersCount + 1
```

continued on next page

continued from previous page

```
  UsersArray( UsersCount ) = WorkingString
  Application("UsersCount") = UsersCount
  Set Application("TheArray") = UsersArray
else
  UserName = "Ima User"
  UserBrowser = "Internet Explorer"
  Application("UsersCount") = UsersCount
  set Application("UsersArray") = UsersArray
end if
Application.Unlock
 'Keep the script from hanging
Server.ServerTimeout = 15
%>
<HTML>
<HEAD>
<TITLE>Active Server Pages How To Chapter Five How To Seven</TITLE>
</HEAD>
<BODY>
<% MyAdd.Border(0)
   MyAd.Clickable = true
   MyAd.TargetFrame = "_blank"%>
<%= MyAd.GetAdvertisement("aspht05ads.txt")%>
<FORM NAME="Form1" ACTION="aspht0507.asp" METHOD="POST" TARGET="_top">
<TABLE CELLPADDING=5 CELLSPACING=5 WIDTH=600 BORDER=5 ALIGN="CENTER"
VALIGN="MIDDLE" BGCOLOR="#008080">
<CAPTION>Welcome To The ASP How To GuestBook!</CAPTION>
<TR>
<TD COLSPAN=2 ALIGN="CENTER" VALIGN="MIDDLE" BGCOLOR="#008080">
<% Set objBrowserCaps = Server.CreateObject("MSWC.BrowserType")
   if objBrowserCaps.ActiveXControls then%>
<% WorkingString = "You are UserID" & Session.SessionID & ".You have accessed "⇐
& Session("PageHits") & "Pages in the GuestBook Application this session."%>
<OBJECT ID="IeLabel1" WIDTH=831 HEIGHT=39
 CLASSID="CLSID:99B42120-6EC7-11CF-A6C7-00AA00A47DD2">
    <PARAM NAME="_ExtentX" VALUE="21960">
    <PARAM NAME="_ExtentY" VALUE="1005">
    <PARAM NAME="Caption" VALUE="<%= WorkingString %>">
    <PARAM NAME="Angle" VALUE="0">
    <PARAM NAME="Alignment" VALUE="4">
    <PARAM NAME="Mode" VALUE="1">
    <PARAM NAME="FillStyle" VALUE="0">
    <PARAM NAME="FillStyle" VALUE="0">
    <PARAM NAME="ForeColor" VALUE="#000000">
    <PARAM NAME="BackColor" VALUE="#D8C0A0">
    <PARAM NAME="FontName" VALUE="Arial">
    <PARAM NAME="FontSize" VALUE="12">
    <PARAM NAME="FontItalic" VALUE="0">
    <PARAM NAME="FontBold" VALUE="1">
    <PARAM NAME="FontUnderline" VALUE="0">
    <PARAM NAME="FontStrikeout" VALUE="0">
    <PARAM NAME="TopPoints" VALUE="0">
    <PARAM NAME="BotPoints" VALUE="0">
</OBJECT>
<% else %>
You are UserID <%= Session.SessionID%>. You have accessed <%=⇐
Session("PageHits")%> Pages in the GuestBook Application this session.
<% end if %>
```

```
</TD>
<TD ALIGN="CENTER" VALIGN="MIDDLE" BGCOLOR="#008080">
Pages you have accessed this session:
<%for counter1 = 1 to PageHits%>
<%= PageHitsArray( counter1 ) %><BR>
<%next%>
</TD>
</TR>
<TR>
<TD ALIGN="CENTER" VALIGN="MIDDLE" BGCOLOR="#008080">Your Name
</TD>
<TD ALIGN="CENTER" VALIGN="MIDDLE" BGCOLOR="#008080">Your Browser
</TD>
<TD ALIGN="CENTER" VALIGN="MIDDLE" BGCOLOR="#008080">Other Guests
</TD>
</TR>
<TR>
<TD ALIGN="CENTER" VALIGN="MIDDLE" BGCOLOR="#008080">
<INPUT TYPE=Text NAME="Text1" VALUE="<%= UserName %>">
</TD>
<TD ALIGN="CENTER" VALIGN="MIDDLE" BGCOLOR="#008080">
<INPUT TYPE=Text NAME="Text2" VALUE="<%= UserBrowser %>">
</TD>
<TD ALIGN="CENTER" VALIGN="MIDDLE" BGCOLOR="#008080">
<%= "Total Visitors: " & UsersCount %><BR>
<% for Counter1 = 1 to UsersCount %>
<%= UsersArray( Counter1 ) %><BR>
<%next%>
</TD>
</TR>
<TD COLSPAN=3>
Some Sample HTML Code
<%= Server.HTMLEncode("<TD COLSPAN=3 ALIGN=""CENTER"" VALIGN=""MIDDLE""⇐
BGCOLOR=""#008080"">")%>
</TD>
</TR>
<TR>
<TD COLSPAN=3 ALIGN="CENTER" VALIGN="MIDDLE" BGCOLOR="#008080">
<A HREF="ASPHT0505AB.ASP">Click Here To Abandon Current Session</A>
</TD>
</TR>
<TR>
<TD COLSPAN=3 ALIGN="CENTER" VALIGN="MIDDLE" BGCOLOR="#008080">
<INPUT TYPE=Submit NAME="Submit1" VALUE="Sign GuestBook">
</TD>
</TR>
</TABLE>
</FORM>
</BODY>
</HTML>
```

2. Activate Internet Explorer. In the address field, type in **HTTP://DEFAULT/GUESTBOOK/ASPHT0507.ASP** and press Return. As shown in Figure 5-16, the ActiveX control appears instead of the HTML text. If you have a copy of some non-ActiveX browser such as Netscape Navigator, use it to view

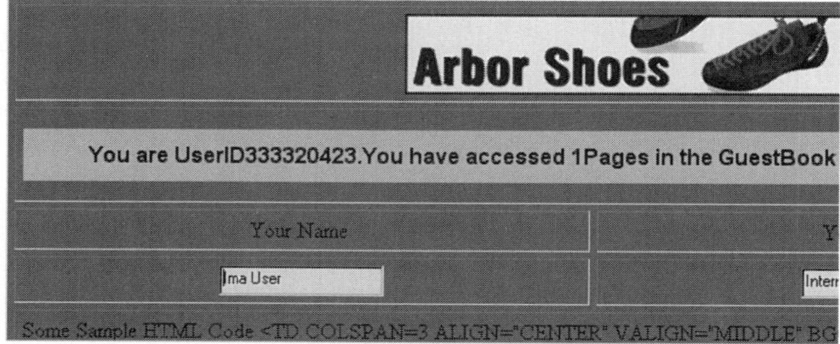

Figure 5-16 ASPHT0507.ASP in Internet Explorer, showing an ActiveX control

the same page (yes, NN can view ASP pages!). It will show the HTML text automatically instead of the ActiveX component. You have learned to use the `BrowserType` component to detect capabilities of your client's Web browsers for your ASP application automatically.

How It Works

The `BrowserType` component is created like the other non-system ASP components:

```
<% Set objBrowserCaps = Server.CreateObject("MSWC.BrowserType")
```

You might notice that the name used is `BrowserCaps` rather than `BrowserType`. The reason is explained in the comments. To use the `BrowserCaps` component, you simply check for the existence of a variable:

```
if objBrowserCaps.ActiveXControls then%>
<% WorkingString = "You are UserID" & Session.SessionID & ".You have accessed "⇐
& Session("PageHits") & "Pages in the GuestBook Application this session."%>
<OBJECT ID="IeLabel1" WIDTH=831 HEIGHT=39
 CLASSID="CLSID:99B42120-6EC7-11CF-A6C7-00AA00A47DD2">
    <PARAM NAME="_ExtentX" VALUE="21960">
    <PARAM NAME="_ExtentY" VALUE="1005">
    <PARAM NAME="Caption" VALUE="<%= WorkingString %>">
    <PARAM NAME="Angle" VALUE="0">
    <PARAM NAME="Alignment" VALUE="4">
    <PARAM NAME="Mode" VALUE="1">
    <PARAM NAME="FillStyle" VALUE="0">
    <PARAM NAME="FillStyle" VALUE="0">
    <PARAM NAME="ForeColor" VALUE="#000000">
    <PARAM NAME="BackColor" VALUE="#D8C0A0">
    <PARAM NAME="FontName" VALUE="Arial">
    <PARAM NAME="FontSize" VALUE="12">
    <PARAM NAME="FontItalic" VALUE="0">
    <PARAM NAME="FontBold" VALUE="1">
    <PARAM NAME="FontUnderline" VALUE="0">
    <PARAM NAME="FontStrikeout" VALUE="0">
```

```
    <PARAM NAME="TopPoints" VALUE="0">
    <PARAM NAME="BotPoints" VALUE="0">
</OBJECT>
<% else %>
You are UserID <%= Session.SessionID%>. You have accessed <%=⇐
Session("PageHits")%> Pages in the GuestBook Application this session.
<% end if %>
```

If the variable exists, either a `true` or a `false` value is returned; if it does not exist, a `false` is automatically returned without triggering an error. This can be paired with an `if then else` test to output appropriate HTML code, in this case either an ActiveX `<OBJECT>` tag or simple HTML text.

Here is a list of the most commonly found `BrowserType` variables (from the ASP documentation, copyright 1996 Microsoft):

- ✔ `ActiveXControls`: Specifies whether the browser supports ActiveX controls
- ✔ `backgroundsounds`: Specifies whether the browser supports background sounds
- ✔ `beta`: Specifies whether the browser is beta software
- ✔ `browser`: Specifies the name of the browser
- ✔ `cookies`: Specifies whether the browser supports cookies
- ✔ `frames`: Specifies whether the browser supports frames
- ✔ `javascript`: Specifies whether the browser supports JScript
- ✔ `platform`: Specifies the platform that the browser runs on
- ✔ `tables:` Specifies whether the browser supports tables
- ✔ `vbscript`: Specifies whether the browser supports VBScript
- ✔ `version`: Specifies the version number of the browser

Comments

The reason the component is named `BrowserCaps` is that to use the `BrowserType` component, you must have a `BROWSCAP.INI` file in your `Windows` directory. One is automatically put there whenever you install ASP, but because browsers change themselves like underwear these days, keeping it updated is a serious pain!

Fortunately, an IIS Web provider has anticipated this problem and created the new `BROWSCAP` Web site! Its URL is

```
http://www.cyscape.com/asp/browscap
```

This site allows you to download the latest `BROWSCAP.INI` file on a regular basis; if you are using IE 4, you can even arrange to download it automatically!

5.8 How do I… Create HTML pages that automatically guide users along a "trail" of Web pages?

Problem

We have a complex Web site that gets redesigned on an almost daily basis, and, because we use a graphical interface, maintaining all the `<IMG>` tag links has become a major problem. Can an ASP component help us out here?

Technique

The ASP `ContentLinking` component is part of the standard ASP installation, and it was created by Microsoft for exactly this problem! This How-To creates a simple tour of four Microsoft ASP sites inside an ASP page. The tour can be modified by changing a single simple text file. These steps create the application from scratch, but for your convenience the complete project is on the CD under `CH05\HT08\`.

Steps

1. Activate ActiveX Control Pad and reload the `ASPHT0507.ASP` file. Modify the code so it is identical to the code in Listing 5-14. Save it as `ASPHT0508.ASP`.

Listing 5-14 ASPHT0508.ASP source code

```
<%@ LANGUAGE = VBScript %>
<%
Application.Lock
Session("PageHits") = Session("PageHits") + 1
PageHits = Session("PageHits")
dim PageHitsArray( 100 )
PageHitsArray = Session("PageHitsArray")
PageHitsArray( PageHits ) = "ASPHT0508.ASP"
Set Session("PageHitsArray") = PageHitsArray
UsersCount = Application("UsersCount")
dim UsersArray( 100 )
UsersArray = Application("TheArray")
UserName = Request.Form("Text1")
if UserName <> "" then
  UserBrowser = Request.Form("Text2")
  WorkingString = UserName & " using " & UserBrowser
  UsersCount = UsersCount + 1
  UsersArray( UsersCount ) = WorkingString
```

```
  Application("UsersCount") = UsersCount
  Set Application("TheArray") = UsersArray
else
  UserName = "Ima User"
  UserBrowser = "Internet Explorer"
  Application("UsersCount") = UsersCount
  set Application("UsersArray") = UsersArray
end if
Application.Unlock
 'Keep the script from hanging
Server.ServerTimeout = 15
%>
<HTML>
<HEAD>
<TITLE>Active Server Pages How To Chapter Five How To Eight</TITLE>
</HEAD>
<BODY>
<% MyAdd.Border(0)
   MyAd.Clickable = true
   MyAd.TargetFrame = "_blank"%>
<%= MyAd.GetAdvertisement("aspht05ads.txt")%>
<FORM NAME="Form1" ACTION="aspht0508.asp" METHOD="POST" TARGET="_top">
<TABLE CELLPADDING=5 CELLSPACING=5 WIDTH=600 BORDER=5 ALIGN="CENTER"
VALIGN="MIDDLE" BGCOLOR="#008080">
<CAPTION>Welcome To The ASP How To GuestBook!</CAPTION>
<TR>
<TD COLSPAN=2 ALIGN="CENTER" VALIGN="MIDDLE" BGCOLOR="#008080">
<% Set objBrowserCaps = Server.CreateObject("MSWC.BrowserType")
   if objBrowserCaps.ActiveXControls then%>
<% WorkingString = "You are UserID" & Session.SessionID & ".You have accessed "⇐
& Session("PageHits") & "Pages in the GuestBook Application this session."%>
<OBJECT ID="IeLabel1" WIDTH=831 HEIGHT=39
 CLASSID="CLSID:99B42120-6EC7-11CF-A6C7-00AA00A47DD2">
    <PARAM NAME="_ExtentX" VALUE="21960">
    <PARAM NAME="_ExtentY" VALUE="1005">
    <PARAM NAME="Caption" VALUE="<%= WorkingString %>">
    <PARAM NAME="Angle" VALUE="0">
    <PARAM NAME="Alignment" VALUE="4">
    <PARAM NAME="Mode" VALUE="1">
    <PARAM NAME="FillStyle" VALUE="0">
    <PARAM NAME="FillStyle" VALUE="0">
    <PARAM NAME="ForeColor" VALUE="#000000">
    <PARAM NAME="BackColor" VALUE="#D8C0A0">
    <PARAM NAME="FontName" VALUE="Arial">
    <PARAM NAME="FontSize" VALUE="12">
    <PARAM NAME="FontItalic" VALUE="0">
    <PARAM NAME="FontBold" VALUE="1">
    <PARAM NAME="FontUnderline" VALUE="0">
    <PARAM NAME="FontStrikeout" VALUE="0">
    <PARAM NAME="TopPoints" VALUE="0">
    <PARAM NAME="BotPoints" VALUE="0">
</OBJECT>
<% else %>
You are UserID <%= Session.SessionID%>. You have accessed <%=⇐
Session("PageHits")%> Pages in the GuestBook Application this session.
<% end if %>
```

continued on next page

continued from previous page

```
</TD>
<TD ALIGN="CENTER" VALIGN="MIDDLE" BGCOLOR="#008080">
Pages you have accessed this session:
<%for counter1 = 1 to PageHits%>
<%= PageHitsArray( counter1 ) %><BR>
<%next%>
</TD>
</TR>
<TR>
<TD ALIGN="CENTER" VALIGN="MIDDLE" BGCOLOR="#008080">Your Name
</TD>
<TD ALIGN="CENTER" VALIGN="MIDDLE" BGCOLOR="#008080">Your Browser
</TD>
<TD ALIGN="CENTER" VALIGN="MIDDLE" BGCOLOR="#008080">Other Guests
</TD>
</TR>
<TR>
<TD ALIGN="CENTER" VALIGN="MIDDLE" BGCOLOR="#008080">
<INPUT TYPE=Text NAME="Text1" VALUE="<%= UserName %>">
</TD>
<TD ALIGN="CENTER" VALIGN="MIDDLE" BGCOLOR="#008080">
<INPUT TYPE=Text NAME="Text2" VALUE="<%= UserBrowser %>">
</TD>
<TD ALIGN="CENTER" VALIGN="MIDDLE" BGCOLOR="#008080">
<%= "Total Visitors: " & UsersCount %><BR>
<% for Counter1 = 1 to UsersCount %>
<%= UsersArray( Counter1 ) %><BR>
<%next%>
</TD>
</TR>
<TD COLSPAN=3>
Some Sample HTML Code
<%= Server.HTMLEncode("<TD COLSPAN=3 ALIGN=""CENTER"" VALIGN=""MIDDLE""⇐
BGCOLOR=""#008080"">")%>
</TD>
</TR>
<TR>
<TD COLSPAN=3 ALIGN="CENTER" VALIGN="MIDDLE" BGCOLOR="#008080">
<A HREF="ASPHT0505AB.ASP">Click Here To Abandon Current Session</A>
</TD>
</TR>
<TR>
<TD COLSPAN=3 ALIGN="CENTER" VALIGN="MIDDLE" BGCOLOR="#008080">
<INPUT TYPE=Submit NAME="Submit1" VALUE="Sign GuestBook">
</TD>
</TR>
<TR>
<TD COLSPAN=3 ALIGN="CENTER" VALIGN="MIDDLE" BGCOLOR="#008080">
The ASP Tour!<BR>
<IFRAME WIDTH=600 HEIGHT=300 NAME="IFrame1" SRC="ASPHT0508IF.ASP">
</TD>
</TR>
</TABLE>
</FORM>
</BODY>
</HTML>
```

2. Create a new ASP file and enter the code in Listing 5-15. Save it in the GuestBook directory as ASPHT0508IF.ASP.

Listing 5-15 ASPHT0508IF.ASP source code

```
<%@ LANGUAGE = VBScript %>
<%
%>
<HTML>
<HEAD>
<TITLE>Active Server Pages Tour</TITLE>
</HEAD>
<BODY>
<%  Set ContentsLinker = Server.CreateObject ("MSWC.NextLink") %>
<ol>
<%  Linkscount = ContentsLinker.GetListCount ("aspht0508links.txt") %>
<%  Counter1 = 1 %>

<ul>
<%  Do While (Counter1 <= Linkscount)  %>
<li><a href=" <%= ContentsLinker.GetNthURL ("aspht0508links.txt ", Counter1)⇐
%>  " Target="_blank">
<%= ContentsLinker.GetNthDescription ("aspht0508links.txt ", Counter1) %>  </a>
<%  Counter1 = (Counter1 + 1)  %>
<%  Loop  %>

</ul>
</ol>
</BODY>
</HTML>
```

3. Create a new blank text file and enter the data in Listing 5-16. Save it in the GuestBook directory as ASPHT0508LINKS.TXT.

Listing 5-16 ASPHT0508LINKS.TXT source code

```
---ASPHT0508LINKS.TXT---
link1.asp SiteBuilder Network Home Page
link2.asp ASP Home Page
link3.asp IIS Home Page
link4.asp ISAPI Home Page
```

4. Create four new ASP files and enter the code for each one in Listing 5-17. Save them in the GuestBook directory as LINK1.ASP, LINK2.ASP, LINK3.ASP, and LINK4.ASP.

Listing 5-17 The LINKn.ASP source code

LINK1.ASP:

```
<%@ LANGUAGE = VBScript %>
<%
%>
<HTML>
```

continued on next page

continued from previous page

```
<HEAD>
<TITLE>Active Server Pages Tour 1</TITLE>
</HEAD>
<BODY>
<%  Set ContentsLinker = Server.CreateObject ("MSWC.NextLink") %>
<%  If (ContentsLinker.GetListIndex ("aspht0508links.txt") > 1) Then %>

<a href="  <%= ContentsLinker.GetPreviousURL ("aspht0508links.txt")  %>  ">

Previous Page</a><BR>
<%  End If  %>
<a href="  <%= ContentsLinker.GetNextURL ("aspht0508links.txt")  %>  ">Next⇐
Page</a><P>
<IFRAME WIDTH= 600 HEIGHT=300 SRC="http://www.microsoft.com/sitebuilder⇐
/default.asp">
</BODY>
</HTML>
```

LINK2.ASP:

```
<%@ LANGUAGE = VBScript %>
<%
%>
<HTML>
<HEAD>
<TITLE>Active Server Pages Tour 2</TITLE>
</HEAD>
<BODY>
<%  Set ContentsLinker = Server.CreateObject ("MSWC.NextLink") %>
<%  If (ContentsLinker.GetListIndex ("aspht0508links.txt") > 1) Then %>

<a href="  <%= ContentsLinker.GetPreviousURL ("aspht0508links.txt")  %>  ">

Previous Page</a><BR>
<%  End If  %>
<a href="  <%= ContentsLinker.GetNextURL ("aspht0508links.txt")  %>  ">Next⇐
Page</a><P>
<IFRAME WIDTH= 600 HEIGHT=300 SRC="http://www.microsoft.com/asp/default.asp">
</BODY>
</HTML>
```

LINK3.ASP:

```
<%@ LANGUAGE = VBScript %>
<%
%>
<HTML>
<HEAD>
<TITLE>Active Server Pages Tour 3</TITLE>
</HEAD>
<BODY>
<%  Set ContentsLinker = Server.CreateObject ("MSWC.NextLink") %>
<%  If (ContentsLinker.GetListIndex ("aspht0508links.txt") > 1) Then %>

<a href="  <%= ContentsLinker.GetPreviousURL ("aspht0508links.txt")  %>  ">

Previous Page</a><BR>
<%  End If  %>
```

```
<a href="  <%= ContentsLinker.GetNextURL ("aspht0508links.txt")  %>  ">Next⇐
Page</a><P>
<IFRAME WIDTH= 600 HEIGHT=300 SRC="http://www.microsoft.com/iis/default.asp">
</BODY>
</HTML>
```

LINK4.ASP:

```
<%@ LANGUAGE = VBScript %>
<%
%>
<HTML>
<HEAD>
<TITLE>Active Server Pages Tour 4</TITLE>
</HEAD>
<BODY>
<%  Set ContentsLinker = Server.CreateObject ("MSWC.NextLink") %>
<%  If (ContentsLinker.GetListIndex ("aspht0508links.txt") > 1) Then %>

<a href="  <%= ContentsLinker.GetPreviousURL ("aspht0508links.txt")  %>  ">

Previous Page</a><BR>
<%  End If  %>
<a href="  <%= ContentsLinker.GetNextURL ("aspht0508links.txt")  %>  ">Next⇐
Page</a><P>
<IFRAME WIDTH= 600 HEIGHT=300 SRC="http://www.microsoft.com/isapi/default.asp">
</BODY>
</HTML>
```

5. Activate Internet Explorer. In the address field, type in `HTTP://DEFAULT/GUESTBOOK/ASPHT0508.ASP` and press Return. As shown in Figure 5-17, the list of available pages in the tour is shown in the IFrame. Click on one and it will appear in a separate browser window, complete with its own forward and backward buttons, as shown in Figure 5-18. Now the `ContentLinking` ASP component is available for you to create and display easily maintained lists of linked Web pages.

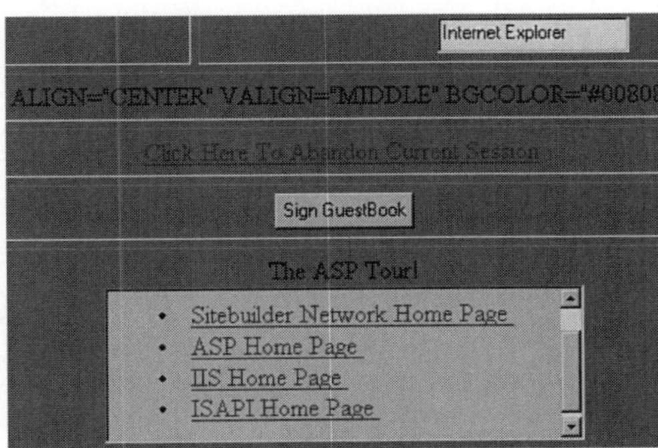

Figure 5-17 ASPHT0508.ASP in Internet Explorer, showing the list of tour Web pages

Figure 5-18 ASPHT0508.ASP in Internet Explorer, showing one of the tour pages with its forward and backward links

How It Works

At this point, things are getting somewhat complex! First, notice the way in which the output of the link's file is used:

```
<%  Linkscount = ContentsLinker.GetListCount ("aspht0508links.txt") %>
<%  Counter1 = 1 %>

<ul>
<%  Do While (Counter1 <= Linkscount)  %>
<li><a href=" <%= ContentsLinker.GetNthURL ("aspht0508links.txt ", Counter1)⇐
%>   " Target="_blank">
<%= ContentsLinker.GetNthDescription ("aspht0508links.txt ", Counter1) %>  </a>
<%  Counter1 = (Counter1 + 1)  %>
<%  Loop  %>
```

The GetNthURL method returns the URL portion of the link's file, whereas the GetNthDescription method returns the description portion of the link's text display. The GetListCount method returns the total links in the file. All these methods take the name of the link's file to read from, which can include an optional relative path. These methods are clearly designed to build display lists like this one.

By contrast, notice how the backward and forward links are created:

```
<%  Set ContentsLinker = Server.CreateObject ("MSWC.NextLink") %>
<%  If (ContentsLinker.GetListIndex ("aspht0508links.txt") > 1) Then %>

<a href="  <%= ContentsLinker.GetPreviousURL ("aspht0508links.txt")  %>  ">

Previous Page</a><BR>
<a href="  <%= ContentsLinker.GetNextURL ("aspht0508links.txt")  %>  ">Next⇐
Page</a><P>
```

Here, the GetListIndex method returns the position of the current URL in the file parameter (note that if the current URL is not in the file, a 0 is returned!). This can be used with the GetPreviousURL and GetNextURL methods to set up the backward and forward buttons.

The structure of the links file is very straightforward:

```
---ASPHT0508LINKS.TXT---
link1.asp SiteBuilder Network Home Page
link2.asp ASP Home Page
link3.asp IIS Home Page
link4.asp ISAPI Home Page
```

The first line is the name of the file, to make sure a valid link's file has been found. Then on each line, the URL is given (it must be relative; absolute URLs are not allowed!), followed by a required Tab character and the description portion (which can be blank). After a second Tab can come an optional comment portion.

Comments

Two additional methods, `GetNextDescription` and `GetPreviousDescription`, return the description portion of the URL for use in the text portion of backward and forward links.

5.9 How do I... Create and use text files on my ASP server with my ASP application?

Problem

We need to maintain a guest list even after the `Application` object is reset. Can we find some way to write it to a text file with ASP?

Technique

Yes, using the `FileSystemObject` and `TextStreamObject` components! This How-To demonstrates keeping `GuestBook` in a simple text file and loading and saving it in the `GLOBAL.ASA` file. The directions here create the project from scratch, but for your convenience, a copy of the HTML file is on the CD under `\CH05\HT09\`.

Steps

1. Activate ActiveX Control Pad and reload the `GLOBAL.ASA` file. Modify the code so it is identical to the code in Listing 5-18. Save it as `GLOBAL.ASA` in the `GuestBook` directory, replacing the existing file.

Listing 5-18 GLOBAL.ASA source code

```
<SCRIPT LANGUAGE=VBScript RUNAT=Server>
SUB Application_OnStart
  on error resume next
  WorkingPath = Server.MapPath("/GuestBook") + "\gb.txt"
  Set objFileSystem = CreateObject("Scripting.FileSystemObject")
  Set objTextFile = objFileSystem.OpenTextFile( WorkingPath, ForReading, FALSE)
  if err.Number = 0 then
    UsersCount = CInt( objTextFile.ReadLine )
    Application("UsersCount") = UsersCount
    dim HolderArray( 100 )
    counter1 = 1
    while not objTextFile.EOF
       HolderArray( counter1 ) = objTextFile.ReadLine
       counter1 = counter1 + 1
    wend
    objTextFile.Close
    Set Application("TheArray") = HolderArray
  else
    Err.Clear
    Application("UsersCount") = 0
    dim HolderArray( 100 )
    Set Application("TheArray") = HolderArray
end if
END SUB
</SCRIPT>

<SCRIPT LANGUAGE=VBScript RUNAT=Server>
SUB Application_OnEnd
on error resume next
  WorkingPath = Server.MapPath("/GuestBook") + "\gb.txt"
  Set objFileSystem = CreateObject("Scripting.FileSystemObject")
  Set objTextFile = objFileSystem.CreateTextFile( WorkingPath, TRUE)
  if err.Number = 0 then
    objTextFile.WriteLine( Application("UsersCount") )
    dim HolderArray( 100 )
    Set HolderArray = Application("TheArray")
    for counter1 = 1 to Application("UsersCount")
      objTextFile.WriteLine(HolderArray( counter1 ))
    next
    objTextFile.Close
end if
Set Application("TheArray") = Nothing
END SUB
</SCRIPT>

<OBJECT RUNAT=SERVER SCOPE=Application ID=MyAd PROGID= "MSWC.AdRotator">
</OBJECT>
```

```
<SCRIPT LANGUAGE=VBScript RUNAT=Server>
SUB Session_OnStart
  Session("PageHits") = 0
  dim PageHitsArray( 100 )
  Set Session("PageHitsArray") = PageHitsArray
END SUB
</SCRIPT>

<SCRIPT LANGUAGE=VBScript RUNAT=Server>
SUB Session_OnEnd
  Set Session("PageHitsArray") = Nothing
END SUB
</SCRIPT>
```

2. Close down IIS or PWS and reboot it. Activate Internet Explorer. In the address field, type in `HTTP://DEFAULT/ASPEXEC/ASPHT0508.ASP` and press Return. Enter some users in the file. Then close IE and reboot IIS or PWS and restart it. Again bring up `ASPHT0508`, and, as shown in Figure 5-19, `GuestBook` has been preserved! You can now maintain ASP information over multiple application sessions with text file objects.

How It Works

The `FileSystem` and `TextStream` objects are fairly powerful, and this How-To can show you only the basics. You open the existing text file with this code:

```
Set objFileSystem = CreateObject("Scripting.FileSystemObject")
  Set objTextFile = objFileSystem.OpenTextFile( WorkingPath, ForReading, FALSE)
```

First a `FileSystem` object must be created; this is always required. Then the text file is created via the `OpenTextFile` method, which outputs a `TextStream` object. It takes a path (more on that in a minute) to the file, a constant that is either `ForReading`

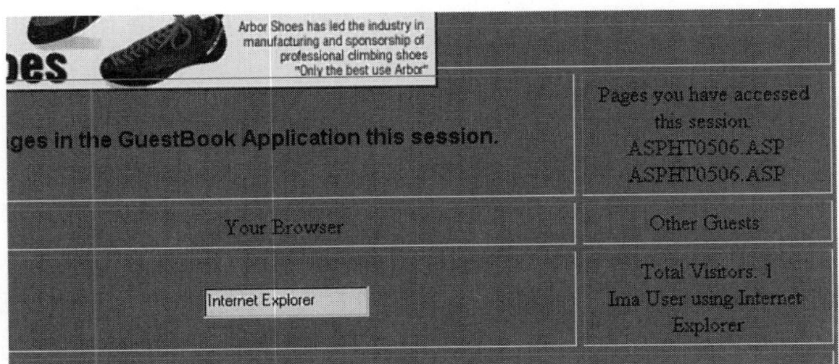

Figure 5-19 `ASPHT0507.ASP` in Internet Explorer, showing persistent `GuestBook` entries after resetting IIS/PWS

or `ForAppending`, depending on whether the file is to be just read or added to, and a parameter as to whether to use `UNICODE`. Now study the whole routine:

```
on error resume next
  WorkingPath = Server.MapPath("/GuestBook") + "\gb.txt"
  Set objFileSystem = CreateObject("Scripting.FileSystemObject")
  Set objTextFile = objFileSystem.OpenTextFile( WorkingPath, ForReading, FALSE)
  if err.Number = 0 then
    UsersCount = CInt( objTextFile.ReadLine )
    Application("UsersCount") = UsersCount
    dim HolderArray( 100 )
    counter1 = 1
    while not objTextFile.EOF
       HolderArray( counter1 ) = objTextFile.ReadLine
       counter1 = counter1 + 1
    wend
    objTextFile.Close
    Set Application("TheArray") = HolderArray
  else
    Err.Clear
    Application("UsersCount") = 0
    dim HolderArray( 100 )
    Set Application("TheArray") = HolderArray
end if
```

First, note that the local directory is obtained with the `Server.MapPath` method call. This is essential, because the `FileSystem` object is *not*, repeat *not*, hooked into the virtual directory system of ASP. The `MapPath` function keeps the two in sync; use it early and often!

Next, note the error trapping code. If the file has not yet been created, the attempt to open the file will generate an error, which can be caught with the `Err.Number` value check. In this case, a default initialization routine is performed. Otherwise, the first line of the file is read in with `ReadLine`; this is the `count` value. To demonstrate an additional way to process input, the `EOF` property is used to then read in the actual entries in the guestbook.

Now look at the code to write out `GuestBook`:

```
on error resume next
  WorkingPath = Server.MapPath("/GuestBook") + "\gb.txt"
  Set objFileSystem = CreateObject("Scripting.FileSystemObject")
  Set objTextFile = objFileSystem.CreateTextFile( WorkingPath, TRUE)
  if err.Number = 0 then
    objTextFile.WriteLine( Application("UsersCount") )
    dim HolderArray( 100 )
    Set HolderArray = Application("TheArray")
    for counter1 = 1 to Application("UsersCount")
      objTextFile.WriteLine(HolderArray( counter1 ))
    next
    objTextFile.Close
end if
```

Here is more error trapping code, in case the file can't be created for some reason. Then, after the obligatory `MapPath` call and `FileSystemObject` creation call, the `CreateTextFile` method is invoked, again with a path and the `true` value that indicates overwriting is allowed. Then the `WriteLine` method is used to output the data to the file.

Notice the `Close` methods in both these routines. This is to make sure the data is actually written to the file; if you leave it out and something happens to IIS, the data may never see the disk!

Comments

The documentation on the `FileSystem` and `TextStream` objects in the `ROADMAP.ASP` is very good, and you should memorize it!

COMPLEXITY
INTERMEDIATE

5.10 How do I… Use connection pooling with my ActiveX data objects in my ASP application?

Problem

We are having a problem with overloading the database server used by our ASP pages. Is there some way to reduce its load while keeping the same functionality and simple code structure?

Technique

ASP offers a special capability with ActiveX data objects (ADO) called *connection pooling* that handles just this problem. It is a system capability that maintains a connection even after it is closed explicitly in an ASP file, up to a specified limit of open connections (thus the "pooling" aspect). This How-To will show you how to access it easily and without major code rewrites. Although the directions here create the project from scratch, the completed ASP files are on the CD under `\CH05\HT10\`.

Steps

1. Activate ActiveX Control Pad again and reload the `ASPHT0508.ASP` file. Modify the code so it is identical to the code in Listing 5-19. Save it as `ASPHT05010.ASP`.

Listing 5-19 ASPHT0510.ASP source code

```
<%@ LANGUAGE = VBScript %>
<%
Application.Lock
Session("PageHits") = Session("PageHits") + 1
PageHits = Session("PageHits")
dim PageHitsArray( 100 )
PageHitsArray = Session("PageHitsArray")
PageHitsArray( PageHits ) = "ASPHT0510.ASP"
Set Session("PageHitsArray") = PageHitsArray
UsersCount = Application("UsersCount")
dim UsersArray( 100 )
UsersArray = Application("TheArray")
UserName = Request.Form("Text1")
if UserName <> "" then
  UserBrowser = Request.Form("Text2")
  WorkingString = UserName & " using " & UserBrowser
  UsersCount = UsersCount + 1
  UsersArray( UsersCount ) = WorkingString
  Application("UsersCount") = UsersCount
  Set Application("TheArray") = UsersArray
else
  UserName = "Ima User"
  UserBrowser = "Internet Explorer"
  Application("UsersCount") = UsersCount
  set Application("UsersArray") = UsersArray
end if
Application.Unlock
 'Keep the script from hanging
Server.ServerTimeout = 15
%>
<HTML>
<HEAD>
<TITLE>Active Server Pages How To Chapter Five How To Ten</TITLE>
</HEAD>
<BODY>
<% MyAdd.Border(0)
   MyAd.Clickable = true
   MyAd.TargetFrame = "_blank"%>
<%= MyAd.GetAdvertisement("aspht05ads.txt")%>
<FORM NAME="Form1" ACTION="aspht0510.asp" METHOD="POST" TARGET="_top">
<TABLE CELLPADDING=5 CELLSPACING=5 WIDTH=600 BORDER=5 ALIGN="CENTER"
VALIGN="MIDDLE" BGCOLOR="#008080">
<CAPTION>Welcome To The ASP How To GuestBook!</CAPTION>
<TR>
<TD COLSPAN=2 ALIGN="CENTER" VALIGN="MIDDLE" BGCOLOR="#008080">
<% Set objBrowserCaps = Server.CreateObject("MSWC.BrowserType")
   if objBrowserCaps.ActiveXControls then%>
<% WorkingString = "You are UserID" & Session.SessionID & ".You have accessed "⇐
& Session("PageHits") & "Pages in the GuestBook Application this session."%>
<OBJECT ID="IeLabel1" WIDTH=831 HEIGHT=39
 CLASSID="CLSID:99B42120-6EC7-11CF-A6C7-00AA00A47DD2">
    <PARAM NAME="_ExtentX" VALUE="21960">
    <PARAM NAME="_ExtentY" VALUE="1005">
    <PARAM NAME="Caption" VALUE="<%= WorkingString %>">
    <PARAM NAME="Angle" VALUE="0">
```

```
    <PARAM NAME="Alignment" VALUE="4">
    <PARAM NAME="Mode" VALUE="1">
    <PARAM NAME="FillStyle" VALUE="0">
    <PARAM NAME="FillStyle" VALUE="0">
    <PARAM NAME="ForeColor" VALUE="#000000">
    <PARAM NAME="BackColor" VALUE="#D8C0A0">
    <PARAM NAME="FontName" VALUE="Arial">
    <PARAM NAME="FontSize" VALUE="12">
    <PARAM NAME="FontItalic" VALUE="0">
    <PARAM NAME="FontBold" VALUE="1">
    <PARAM NAME="FontUnderline" VALUE="0">
    <PARAM NAME="FontStrikeout" VALUE="0">
    <PARAM NAME="TopPoints" VALUE="0">
    <PARAM NAME="BotPoints" VALUE="0">
</OBJECT>
<% else %>
You are UserID <%= Session.SessionID%>. You have accessed <%=⇐
Session("PageHits")%> Pages in the GuestBook Application this session.
<% end if %>
</TD>
<TD ALIGN="CENTER" VALIGN="MIDDLE" BGCOLOR="#008080">
Pages you have accessed this session:
<%for counter1 = 1 to PageHits%>
<%= PageHitsArray( counter1 ) %><BR>
<%next%>
</TD>
</TR>
<TR>
<TD ALIGN="CENTER" VALIGN="MIDDLE" BGCOLOR="#008080">Your Name
</TD>
<TD ALIGN="CENTER" VALIGN="MIDDLE" BGCOLOR="#008080">Your Browser
</TD>
<TD ALIGN="CENTER" VALIGN="MIDDLE" BGCOLOR="#008080">Other Guests
</TD>
</TR>
<TR>
<TD ALIGN="CENTER" VALIGN="MIDDLE" BGCOLOR="#008080">
<INPUT TYPE=Text NAME="Text1" VALUE="<%= UserName %>">
</TD>
<TD ALIGN="CENTER" VALIGN="MIDDLE" BGCOLOR="#008080">
<INPUT TYPE=Text NAME="Text2" VALUE="<%= UserBrowser %>">
</TD>
<TD ALIGN="CENTER" VALIGN="MIDDLE" BGCOLOR="#008080">
<%= "Total Visitors: " & UsersCount %><BR>
<% for Counter1 = 1 to UsersCount %>
<%= UsersArray( Counter1 ) %><BR>
<%next%>
</TD>
</TR>
<TD COLSPAN=3>
Some Sample HTML Code
<%= Server.HTMLEncode("<TD COLSPAN=3 ALIGN=""CENTER"" VALIGN=""MIDDLE""⇐
BGCOLOR=""#008080"">")%>
</TD>
</TR>
```

continued on next page

continued from previous page

```
<TR>
<TD COLSPAN=3 ALIGN="CENTER" VALIGN="MIDDLE" BGCOLOR="#008080">
<A HREF="ASPHT0505AB.ASP">Click Here To Abandon Current Session</A>
</TD>
</TR>
<TR>
<TD COLSPAN=3 ALIGN="CENTER" VALIGN="MIDDLE" BGCOLOR="#008080">
<INPUT TYPE=Submit NAME="Submit1" VALUE="Sign GuestBook">
</TD>
</TR>
<TR>
<TD COLSPAN=3 ALIGN="CENTER" VALIGN="MIDDLE" BGCOLOR="#008080">
The ASP Tour!<BR>
<IFRAME WIDTH=600 HEIGHT=300 NAME="IFrame1" SRC="ASPHT0508IF.ASP">
</TD>
</TR>
<TR>
<TD COLSPAN=3 ALIGN="CENTER" VALIGN="MIDDLE" BGCOLOR="#008080">
ADVENTURE WORKS!<BR>⇐
<IFRAME WIDTH=600 HEIGHT=300 NAME="IFrame2"
SRC="http://default/AdvWorks/default.asp">
</TD>
</TR>
</TABLE>
</FORM>
</BODY>
</HTML>
```

2. Reload the GLOBAL.ASA file. Modify the code so it is identical to the code in Listing 5-20. Save it as GLOBAL.ASA in the GuestBook directory, overwriting the old copy.

Listing 5-20 GLOBAL.ASA source code

```
<SCRIPT LANGUAGE=VBScript RUNAT=Server>
SUB Application_OnStart
  on error resume next
  WorkingPath = Server.MapPath("/GuestBook") + "\gb.txt"
  Set objFileSystem = CreateObject("Scripting.FileSystemObject")
  Set objTextFile = objFileSystem.OpenTextFile( WorkingPath, ForReading, FALSE)
  if err.Number = 0 then
    UsersCount = CInt( objTextFile.ReadLine )
    Application("UsersCount") = UsersCount
    dim HolderArray( 100 )
    counter1 = 1
    while not objTextFile.EOF
       HolderArray( counter1 ) = objTextFile.ReadLine
       counter1 = counter1 + 1
    wend
    objTextFile.Close
    Set Application("TheArray") = HolderArray
  else
    Err.Clear
    Application("UsersCount") = 0
    dim HolderArray( 100 )
    Set Application("TheArray") = HolderArray
```

```
end if
END SUB
</SCRIPT>

<SCRIPT LANGUAGE=VBScript RUNAT=Server>
SUB Application_OnEnd
on error resume next
  WorkingPath = Server.MapPath("/GuestBook") + "\gb.txt"
  Set objFileSystem = CreateObject("Scripting.FileSystemObject")
  Set objTextFile = objFileSystem.CreateTextFile( WorkingPath, TRUE)
  if err.Number = 0 then
    objTextFile.WriteLine( Application("UsersCount") )
    dim HolderArray( 100 )
    Set HolderArray = Application("TheArray")
    for counter1 = 1 to Application("UsersCount")
      objTextFile.WriteLine(HolderArray( counter1 ))
    next
    objTextFile.Close
end if
Set Application("TheArray") = Nothing
END SUB
</SCRIPT>

<OBJECT RUNAT=SERVER SCOPE=Application ID=MyAd PROGID= "MSWC.AdRotator">
</OBJECT>

<SCRIPT LANGUAGE=VBScript RUNAT=Server>
SUB Session_OnStart
  Session("ConnectionString") = "dsn=AdvWorks:uid=advworks:pwd=advworks"
  Session("PageHits") = 0
  dim PageHitsArray( 100 )
  Set Session("PageHitsArray") = PageHitsArray
END SUB
</SCRIPT>

<SCRIPT LANGUAGE=VBScript RUNAT=Server>
SUB Session_OnEnd
  Set Session("PageHitsArray") = Nothing
END SUB
</SCRIPT>
```

3. Activate Internet Explorer. In the address field, type in `HTTP://DEFAULT/ASPEXEC/ASPHT0510.ASP` and press Return. The `AdventureWorks` site will come up in the lowest IFrame. As shown in Figure 5-20, you can wander around in it easily even with a heavy server load. Congratulations! You have learned to use connection pooling to minimize database server load using ADO.

How It Works

The key line is in the `Session_OnStart` `GLOBAL.ASA` script:

```
Session("ConnectionString") = "dsn=AdvWorks:uid=advworks:pwd=advworks"
```

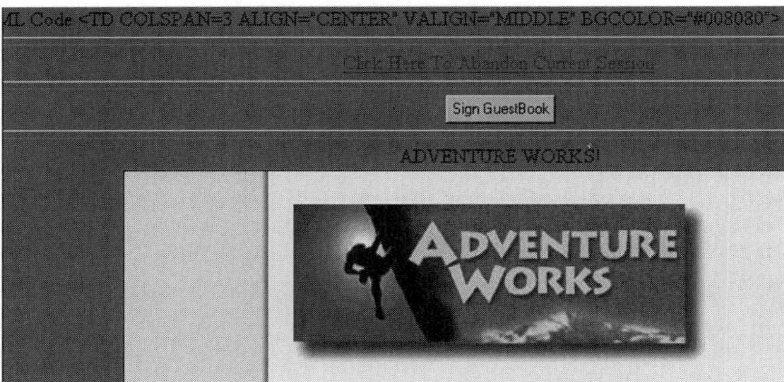

Figure 5-20 `ASPHT0510.ASP` in Internet Explorer, showing the `AdventureWorks` demo site

By storing the connection properties in the `Session` object, you can easily close and restart the connection on each ASP page that uses it, which is what the `AdventureWorks` sample does. The connection-pooling feature depends on this; if a connection is maintained (by keeping a copy of the recordset around in the `session` object, as is demonstrated in Chapter 7), the pooling feature won't work. But if the connection is closed when each page's ASP script terminates, the ADO manager can keep a "pool" of connections alive and reuse them quickly, thus minimizing server load.

Comments

The `AdventureWorks` sample is another excellent place to spend a lot of time if you really want to get into the guts of ADO and ASP!

CHAPTER 6

ADVANCED ASP: CREATING ASP COMPONENTS WITH VISUAL C++ 5.0

6

ADVANCED ASP: CREATING ASP COMPONENTS WITH VISUAL C++ 5.0

How do I...

- **6.1 Create an ASP component?**
- **6.2 Use page-level event methods with an ASP component?**
- **6.3 Use the scripting context interface with an ASP component?**
- **6.4 Write HTML output directly to an ASP page with an ASP component?**
- **6.5 Get HTML forms input directly with an ASP component?**
- **6.6 Interact with the ASP `Server` object in an ASP component?**
- **6.7 Interact with the ASP `Session` object in an ASP component?**

6.8 Interact with cookies in an ASP component?

6.9 Use a custom ASP component with an ActiveX control?

6.10 Use a custom ASP component with ActiveX data objects?

By now you are in the running to be an active platform guru! You've mastered creating and using ActiveX controls and writing Active Server Pages (ASP) scripts and interacting with the powerful system components of ASP. But there is another ASP level to master: creating your own custom ASP components with Visual C++ 5.0. This chapter takes you through the whole process, starting with a simple component that takes two strings and encrypts and decrypts one of them, allowing placement of encoded data in an HTML page. Further How-To's lead you through connecting with the ASP system via its `OnStartPage` and `OnEndPage` event methods and the potent Scripting Context Interface (SCI). Using the SCI, you will learn how to write and read HTML output and input, how to interact with ASP system objects such as `Session` and `Server`, and how to interact with cookies. Finally, two example How-To's use the custom ASP component with an ActiveX control and ActiveX data objects. This chapter will complete your control over Active Server Pages.

6.1 Create an ASP Component

Yes, you can do this! This How-To takes you through the steps of creating your own simple ASP component, `aspencrypt.Encryptor`.

6.2 Use Page-Level Event Methods with an ASP Component

The ASP system permits setup and termination code to be attached to two methods, `OnStartPage` and `OnEndPage`. These methods become de facto event handlers under ASP, and this How-To demonstrates adding them to the Encryptor component to permit storing the encoding key in a local file.

6.3 Use the Scripting Context Interface with an ASP Component

ASP exposes its full functionality to custom ASP components via the `IScriptingContext` interface. This How-To demonstrates fully how to add this interface to the Encryptor ASP component and interact with the `Application` object to store the encoding key as an `Application` variable.

6.4 Write HTML Output Directly to an ASP Page with an ASP Component

It is possible to override the script that calls an ASP component and write output directly to the `Response` object rather than exporting a string. This How-To gives you a complete working Encryptor example that permits bypassing scripts and reading and writing encoded and decoded information directly into the output HTML stream.

6.5 Get HTML Forms Input Directly with an ASP Component

The `Request` object is also available via `IScriptingContext`; this How-To illustrates using it to obtain specifically named text input and output fields and incorporate them into automatic encryption behavior of the Encryptor.

6.6 Interact with the ASP `Server` Object in an ASP Component

The `Server` object can also be used internally via `IScriptingContext`. This How-To uses this fact to obtain the `MapPath` function and store and retrieve the Encryptor's encoding key in the local directory rather than a fixed one.

6.7 Interact with the ASP `Session` Object in an ASP Component

The `Session` object is available to an ASP component internally as well. This How-To takes advantage of this knowledge to obtain and store a user's username and password in encrypted format in the `Session` object for that browser.

6.8 Interact with Cookies in an ASP Component

Cookies are available to ASP components internally both to read and to write; this How-To demonstrates using them to store the encrypted username and password with Encryptor over multiple sessions.

6.9 Use a Custom ASP Component with an ActiveX Control

Tying ActiveX controls to ASP components was illustrated in Chapter 5, "Intermediate ASP: Active Server Components," but there are some additional complexities if you are using a custom ASP component, and this How-To goes into all the details by showing how to create an ActiveX-based login page that uses Encryptor.

6.10 Use a Custom ASP Component with ActiveX Data Objects

Likewise, the ActiveX data objects (ADO) system can be interfaced with custom ASP components; this How-To shows you the complete details of adding an ODBC database connection to the Encryptor component so that encoded data can be stored and retrieved from an ADO database.

COMPLEXITY
ADVANCED

6.1 How do I... Create an ASP component?

Problem

My company needs to encrypt and decrypt some data on our Web site. Do I have to learn the massive Microsoft CryptoAPI to do this?

Technique

No, you need a custom ASP component. This How-To shows you all the steps to do this in Visual C++ 5.0, leaving you with a working simple Encryption and Decryption component that will become the basis for the remaining How-To's in this chapter. Although these directions create the project from scratch, the CD contains a completed file under `CH06\HT01\`.

Steps

1. Start Visual C++ 5.0 and bring up the New Workspace dialog. As shown in Figure 6-1, select MFC AppWizard[dll] from the list of icons to create a new ASP component dynamic link library (DLL). Choose an appropriate directory for the project and name it `ASPENCRYPT`.

2. When the wizard dialog appears, select a DLL with MFC as a shared DLL, and make sure that the Automation check box is checked and that source

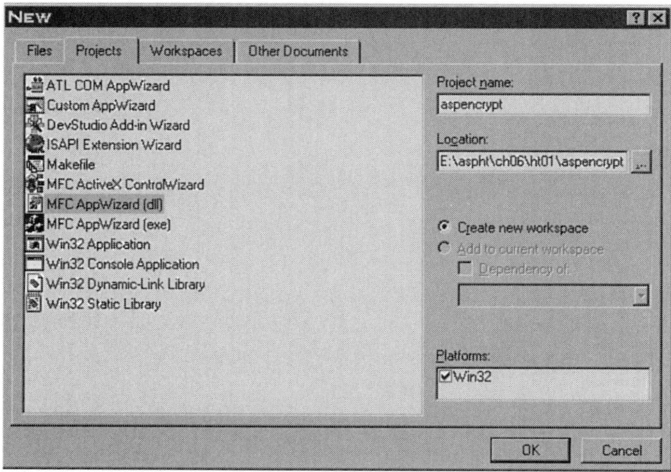

Figure 6-1 Selecting a new DLL project in VC 5

file comments are generated. The finished wizard dialog should look very similar to the one shown in Figure 6-2. Press Finish to create the new project skeleton.

3. After the project is created, use the menu to activate the Class Wizard. On the Automation page, press the Add Class button and select New… as shown in Figure 6-3. (Although automation was enabled for the project, the base class for the DLL never supports automation; this is the job of additional classes.)

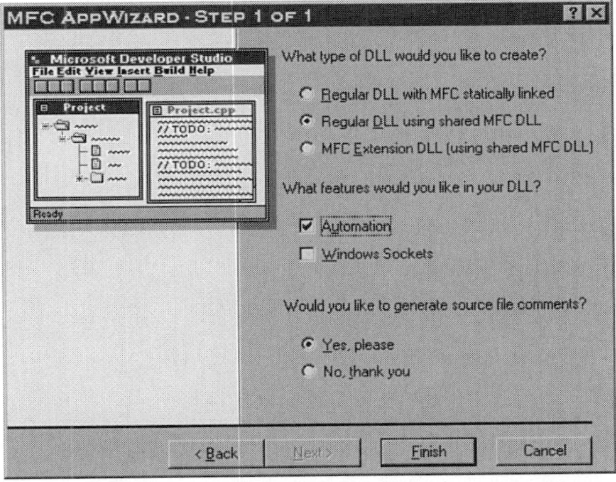

Figure 6-2 The MFC DLL Wizard in Visual C++ 5.0 set for automation

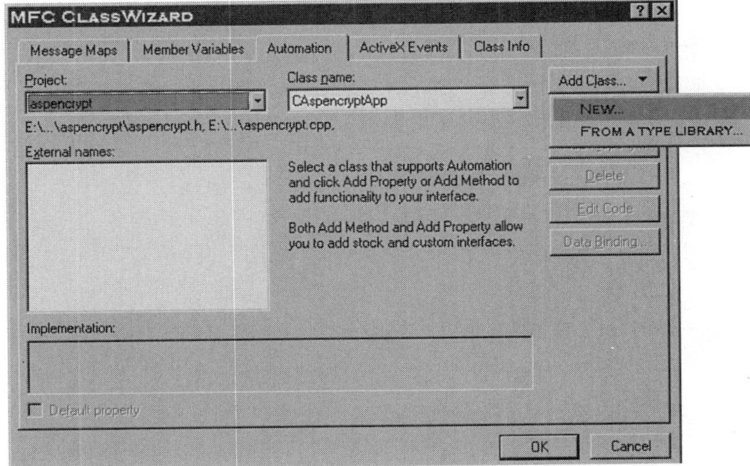

Figure 6-3 Adding a new automation-supporting class to the DLL

4. In the Add dialog, name the new class `Encryptor`. Set its base class to `CCmdTarget`, and select the Creatable by type ID radio button, leaving the default type name. Figure 6-4 shows how the dialog should look when you are finished. Press OK to add the class to the DLL.

5. Now that you have a class that supports automation, you can add methods and properties to it. (At this time, automation does not support events.) Press the Add Property button. In the Add dialog, enter the name of `EncryptionKey` and select a type of CString. Leave the implementation as Member Variable. Figure 6-5 shows how the completed dialog should look. Press OK to add the property to the `Automation` class.

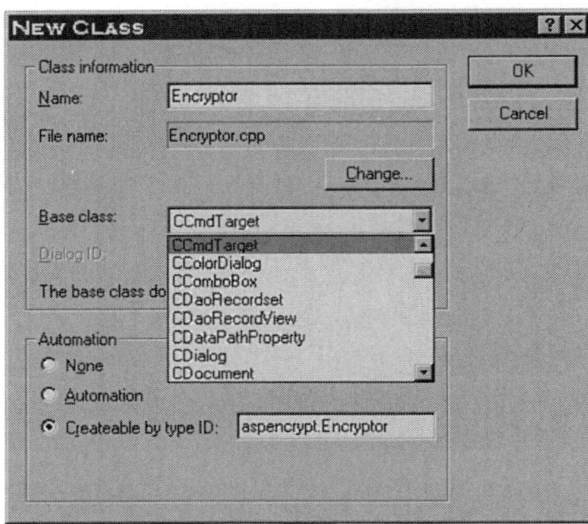

Figure 6-4 Adding a new automation-supporting class to the DLL

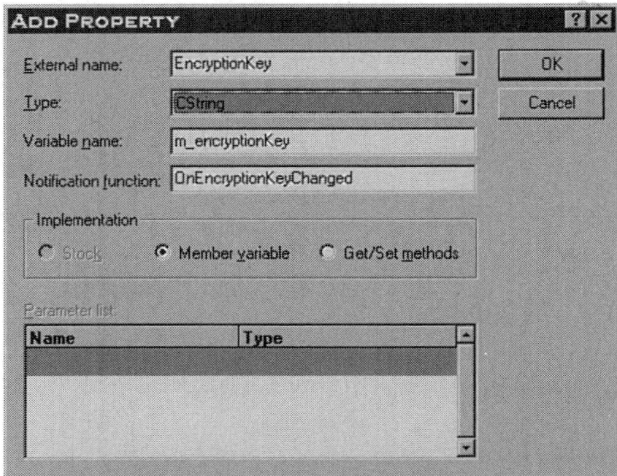

Figure 6-5 Adding a new property to the automation-supporting class

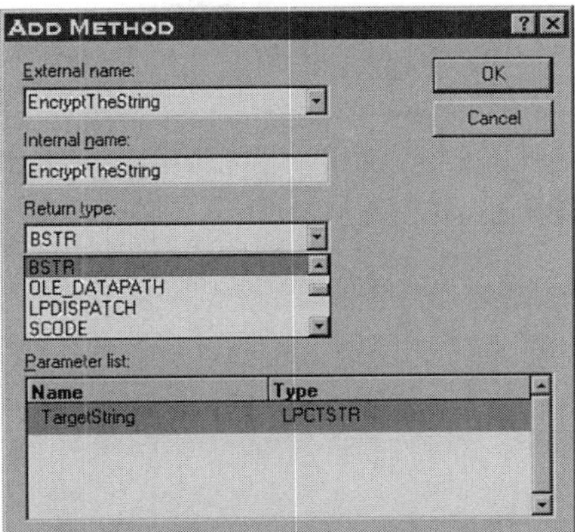

Figure 6-6 Adding a new method to the automation-supporting class

6. Next, press the Add Method button. In the Add dialog, enter a name of `EncryptTheString`, a type of `BSTR`, and a parameter named `TargetString` of type `LPCSTR`. Figure 6-6 shows how the completed dialog should appear. Press OK to add it to the class. Similarly, add a new method named `DecryptTheString`, of type `BSTR`, with a parameter named `SourceString` of type `LPCSTR`. Press OK to add it to the class and OK in the Class Wizard to add all the new information to the project.

7. Bring up the `ENCRYPTOR.CPP` source file in the text editor. Enter all the boldfaced code in Listing 6-1 to add functionality to the DLL. Save the project. Then select Build DLL from the menu. The project should create correctly with no errors or warnings.

Listing 6-1 ENCRYPTOR.CPP source code

```
CString HexStringFromByte( unsigned char TheByte )
{
    CString HexOutString1;
    CString HexOutString2;
    CString HexOutString;
    unsigned char HoldDivValue;
    unsigned char HoldModValue;
    unsigned char HoldInterimValue;

    HoldModValue = TheByte % 16;
    HoldInterimValue = TheByte - HoldModValue;
    HoldDivValue = HoldInterimValue / 16;
    switch( HoldDivValue )
    {
        case 0:
            HexOutString1 = "0";
            break;
```

continued on next page

continued from previous page

```
        case 1:
            HexOutString1 = "1";
            break;
        case 2:
            HexOutString1 = "2";
            break;
        case 3:
            HexOutString1 = "3";
            break;
        case 4:
            HexOutString1 = "4";
            break;
        case 5:
            HexOutString1 = "5";
            break;
        case 6:
            HexOutString1 = "6";
            break;
        case 7:
            HexOutString1 = "7";
            break;
        case 8:
            HexOutString1 = "8";
            break;
        case 9:
            HexOutString1 = "9";
            break;
        case 10:
            HexOutString1 = "A";
            break;
        case 11:
            HexOutString1 = "B";
            break;
        case 12:
            HexOutString1 = "C";
            break;
        case 13:
            HexOutString1 = "D";
            break;
        case 14:
            HexOutString1 = "E";
            break;
        case 15:
            HexOutString1 = "F";
            break;
    }
    switch( HoldModValue )
    {
        case 0:
            HexOutString2 = "0";
            break;
        case 1:
            HexOutString2 = "1";
            break;
        case 2:
            HexOutString2 = "2";
            break;
```

```
        case 3:
            HexOutString2 = "3";
            break;
        case 4:
            HexOutString2 = "4";
            break;
        case 5:
            HexOutString2 = "5";
            break;
        case 6:
            HexOutString2 = "6";
            break;
        case 7:
            HexOutString2 = "7";
            break;
        case 8:
            HexOutString2 = "8";
            break;
        case 9:
            HexOutString2 = "9";
            break;
        case 10:
            HexOutString2 = "A";
            break;
        case 11:
            HexOutString2 = "B";
            break;
        case 12:
            HexOutString2 = "C";
            break;
        case 13:
            HexOutString2 = "D";
            break;
        case 14:
            HexOutString2 = "E";
            break;
        case 15:
            HexOutString2 = "F";
            break;
    }
    HexOutString = HexOutString1 + HexOutString2;
    return HexOutString.AllocSysString();
}


unsigned char ByteFromHexString( CString TheHex )
{
    char HexSwitch;
    char HexSwitch2;
    int HoldValue;
    int HoldValue2;
    HexSwitch = TheHex[0];
    switch ( HexSwitch )
    {
        case '0':
```

continued on next page

continued from previous page

```
            HoldValue = 0;
            break;
        case '1':
            HoldValue = 1;
            break;
        case '2':
            HoldValue = 2;
            break;
        case '3':
            HoldValue = 3;
            break;
        case '4':
            HoldValue = 4;
            break;
        case '5':
            HoldValue = 5;
            break;
        case '6':
            HoldValue = 6;
            break;
        case '7':
            HoldValue = 7;
            break;
        case '8':
            HoldValue = 8;
            break;
        case '9':
            HoldValue = 9;
            break;
        case 'A':
            HoldValue = 10;
            break;
        case 'B':
            HoldValue = 11;
            break;
        case 'C':
            HoldValue = 12;
            break;
        case 'D':
            HoldValue = 13;
            break;
        case 'E':
            HoldValue = 14;
            break;
        case 'F':
            HoldValue = 15;
            break;
    }
    HexSwitch2 = TheHex[1];
    switch ( HexSwitch2 )
    {
        case '0':
            HoldValue2 = 0;
            break;
        case '1':
            HoldValue2 = 1;
            break;
```

```
            case '2':
                HoldValue2 = 2;
                break;
            case '3':
                HoldValue2 = 3;
                break;
            case '4':
                HoldValue2 = 4;
                break;
            case '5':
                HoldValue2 = 5;
                break;
            case '6':
                HoldValue2 = 6;
                break;
            case '7':
                HoldValue2 = 7;
                break;
            case '8':
                HoldValue2 = 8;
                break;
            case '9':
                HoldValue2 = 9;
                break;
            case 'A':
                HoldValue2 = 10;
                break;
            case 'B':
                HoldValue2 = 11;
                break;
            case 'C':
                HoldValue2 = 12;
                break;
            case 'D':
                HoldValue2 = 13;
                break;
            case 'E':
                HoldValue2 = 14;
                break;
            case 'F':
                HoldValue2 = 15;
                break;
        }
        return unsigned char ((( HoldValue * 16 ) + HoldValue2 ));
}


CString XORAByteToHex( unsigned char Byte1 ,
                       unsigned char Byte2   )
{
    unsigned char HoldXORValue;

    HoldXORValue = Byte1 ^ Byte2;
    return HexStringFromByte( HoldXORValue );
}
```

continued on next page

continued from previous page

```
unsigned char XORAByteToAByte( unsigned char Byte1 ,
                               unsigned char Byte2   )
{
    unsigned char ResultByte;

    ResultByte = Byte1 ^ Byte2;
    return ResultByte;
}

//////////////////////////////////////////////////////////////////////////////
// Encryptor message handlers

BSTR Encryptor::EncryptTheString(LPCTSTR TargetString)
{
    CString strResult;
    CString strWorkingString;
    int Counter1;
    int KeyCounter = 0;
    unsigned char HoldByte1;
    unsigned char HoldByte2;
    CString strHoldHex;
    CString strHoldKey;
    strWorkingString = CString( TargetString , strlen( TargetString ));
    strHoldKey = m_encryptionKey;
    for ( Counter1 = 0; Counter1 < strWorkingString.GetLength(); Counter1++ )
    {
        HoldByte1 = unsigned char( strWorkingString[ Counter1 ] );
        HoldByte2 = unsigned char( strHoldKey[ KeyCounter ]);
        KeyCounter++;
        if ( KeyCounter == strHoldKey.GetLength() )
        {
             KeyCounter = 0;
        }
        strHoldHex = XORAByteToHex( HoldByte1 , HoldByte2 );
        strResult = strResult +  strHoldHex;
    }
    return strResult.AllocSysString();
}

BSTR Encryptor::DecryptTheString(LPCTSTR SourceString)
{
    CString strResult;
    CString strWorkingString;
    int Counter1;
    int KeyCounter = 0;
    unsigned char HoldByte1;
    unsigned char HoldByte2;
    unsigned char HoldByte3;
    CString strHoldHex;
    CString strHoldKey;
    strWorkingString = CString( SourceString , strlen( SourceString ));
    strHoldKey = m_encryptionKey;
    for ( Counter1 = 0; Counter1 < strWorkingString.GetLength(); Counter1 = ⇐
Counter1 + 2 )
    {
        strHoldHex = SourceString[ 0 ];
```

```
        SourceString ++;
        strHoldHex = strHoldHex + SourceString[ 0 ];
        SourceString ++;
        HoldByte2 = unsigned char( strHoldKey[ KeyCounter ]);
        KeyCounter++;
        if ( KeyCounter == strHoldKey.GetLength() )
        {
            KeyCounter = 0;
        }
        HoldByte1 = ByteFromHexString( strHoldHex );
        HoldByte3 = XORAByteToAByte( HoldByte1 , HoldByte2 );
        strResult = strResult + char( HoldByte3 );
    }
    return strResult.AllocSysString();
}
```

8. Now bring up the Run dialog from the Start menu. As shown in Figure 6-7, enter `REGSVR32.EXE` with the path to your `ASPENCRYPT.DLL` file. Press OK to run `REGSVR32` to register the DLL for automation. As shown in Figure 6-8, the OLE system will give you a success dialog when it is finished.

9. Activate ActiveX Control Pad. Enter the ASP code in Listing 6-2 and save the file as `ASPHT0601.ASP`. Copy it into the `ASPEXEC` directory so it can be executed by the ASP system.

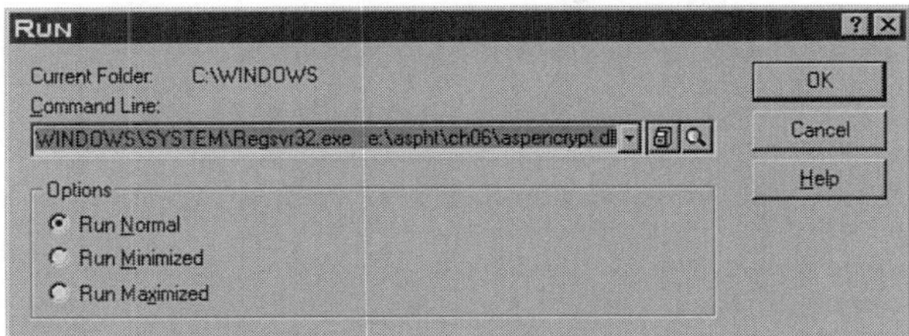

Figure 6-7 Registering the `Automation` class with `REGSVR32.EXE`

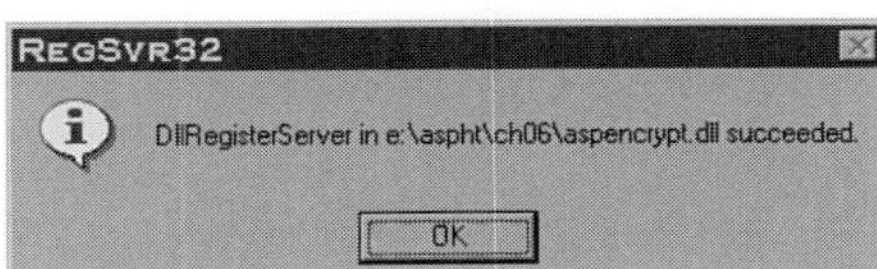

Figure 6-8 Success dialog from the OLE system

Listing 6-2 ASPHT0601.ASP source code

```
return strResult.AllocSysString();
<%@ LANGUAGE = VBScript %>
<%
EncryptionString = Request.Form("Text1")
if EncryptionString <> "" then
  StringToMessWith = Request.Form("Text2")
  Set objCrypto = Server.CreateObject("aspencrypt.Encryptor")
  objCrypto.EncryptionKey = EncryptionString
  EncryptedString = objCrypto.EncryptTheString( StringToMessWith )
  DecryptedString = objCrypto.DecryptTheString( EncryptedString )
else
  EncryptedString = ""
  DecryptedString = ""
end if
%>
<HTML>
<HEAD>
<TITLE>Active Server Pages How To Chapter Six How To One</TITLE>
</HEAD>
<BODY>
<FORM NAME="Form1" ACTION="aspht0601.asp" METHOD="POST" TARGET="_top">
<TABLE CELLPADDING=5 CELLSPACING=5 WIDTH=600 BORDER=5 ALIGN="CENTER"
VALIGN="MIDDLE" BGCOLOR="#008080">9<CAPTION>Welcome To The ASP How To Encryption⇐
Demo!</CAPTION>

<TR>
<TD ALIGN="CENTER" VALIGN="MIDDLE" BGCOLOR="#008080">Encryption Key
</TD>
<TD ALIGN="CENTER" VALIGN="MIDDLE" BGCOLOR="#008080">String To Encrypt
</TD>
<TD ALIGN="CENTER" VALIGN="MIDDLE" BGCOLOR="#008080">Encrypted String
</TD>
<TD ALIGN="CENTER" VALIGN="MIDDLE" BGCOLOR="#008080">Decrypted String
</TD>
</TR>
<TR>
<TD ALIGN="CENTER" VALIGN="MIDDLE" BGCOLOR="#008080">
<INPUT TYPE=Text NAME="Text1" VALUE="<%= EncryptionString %>">
</TD>
<TD ALIGN="CENTER" VALIGN="MIDDLE" BGCOLOR="#008080">
<INPUT TYPE=Text NAME="Text2" VALUE="<%= StringToMessWith %>">
</TD>
<TD ALIGN="CENTER" VALIGN="MIDDLE" BGCOLOR="#008080">
<INPUT TYPE=Text NAME="Text3" VALUE="<%= EncryptedString %>">
</TD>
<TD ALIGN="CENTER" VALIGN="MIDDLE" BGCOLOR="#008080">
<INPUT TYPE=Text NAME="Text4" VALUE="<%= DecryptedString %>">
</TD>
</TR>
<TR>
<TD COLSPAN=4 ALIGN="CENTER" VALIGN="MIDDLE" BGCOLOR="#008080">
<INPUT TYPE=Submit NAME="Submit1" VALUE="Encryption Demo!">
</TD>
</TR>
</TABLE>
```

```
</FORM>
</BODY>
</HTML>}
```

10. Activate Internet Explorer. In the address field, type in `HTTP://DEFAULT/ASPEXEC/ASPHT0601.ASP` and press Return. Enter a simple encryption key string and short string to encrypt and press the Encryption Demo! submit button. As shown in Figure 6-9, the resulting page will return with your two entered values, a string of hexadecimal code, and the original string decrypted from the hexadecimal string. Congratulations! You have learned to create an ASP component.

How It Works

An ASP component is simply an automation server DLL. Therefore, to create one, you just need to create an automation-enabled DLL and class, as shown above. Notice this code from the `ENCRYPTOR.CPP` file:

```
BEGIN_DISPATCH_MAP(Encryptor, CCmdTarget)
//{{AFX_DISPATCH_MAP(Encryptor)
DISP_PROPERTY_NOTIFY(Encryptor, "EncryptionKey", m_encryptionKey, ⇐
OnEncryptionKeyChanged, VT_BSTR)
DISP_FUNCTION(Encryptor, "EncryptTheString", EncryptTheString, VT_BSTR, VTS_BSTR)
DISP_FUNCTION(Encryptor, "DecryptTheString", DecryptTheString, VT_BSTR, VTS_BSTR)
//}}AFX_DISPATCH_MAP
END_DISPATCH_MAP()

// Note: we add support for IID_IEncryptor to support typesafe binding
//  from VBA.  This IID must match the GUID that is attached to the
//  dispinterface in the .ODL file.

// {B83A6244-D858-11D0-B7DF-444553540000}
static const IID IID_IEncryptor =
{ 0xb83a6244, 0xd858, 0x11d0, { 0xb7, 0xdf, 0x44, 0x45, 0x53, 0x54, 0x0, 0x0 } };

BEGIN_INTERFACE_MAP(Encryptor, CCmdTarget)
INTERFACE_PART(Encryptor, IID_IEncryptor, Dispatch)
END_INTERFACE_MAP()

// {B83A6245-D858-11D0-B7DF-444553540000}
IMPLEMENT_OLECREATE(Encryptor, "aspencrypt.Encryptor", 0xb83a6245, 0xd858, ⇐
0x11d0, 0xb7, 0xdf, 0x44, 0x45, 0x53, 0x54, 0x0, 0x0)
```

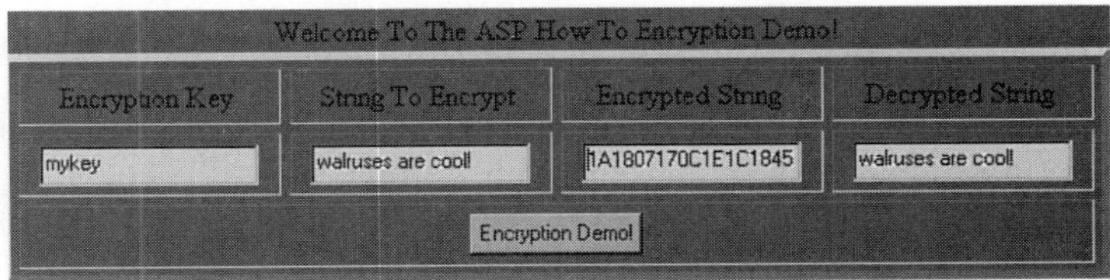

Figure 6-9 IE showing the Encryptor ASP component at work

The first section exports the property and two method functions for Encryptor. Then the IID (Interface ID) for the `IEncryptor` interface is exported so that other applications can use it, followed by the actual interface map that links the IID to the `Encryptor` class. Finally, the `TypeID` name for the interface is exported so that this creation method can be used rather than a GUID-based (Globally Unique ID) one.

Because this DLL needs to toss strings around and communicate with VBScript (not a trivial task!), some comments on how automation and MFC handle strings are in order. Note this code from the `Decryption` method:

```
BSTR Encryptor::DecryptTheString(LPCTSTR SourceString)
{
    CString strResult;
    CString strWorkingString;
...
    strWorkingString = CString( SourceString , strlen( SourceString ));
...
    for ( Counter1 = 0; Counter1 < strWorkingString.GetLength(); Counter1 =
Counter1 + 2 )
    {
        strHoldHex = SourceString[ 0 ];
        SourceString ++;
        strHoldHex = strHoldHex + SourceString[ 0 ];
...
        strResult = strResult + char( HoldByte3 );
    }
    return strResult.AllocSysString();
}
```

The method itself returns the OLE string type `BSTR`. Its parameter comes in as `LPCSTR`. Internally, MFC `CString` objects are used, with the conversion function to map the `LPCSTR` into one. (Make sure you use the CString conversion with a length value, or you'll get only the first character.) For diversity, older `char*` pointer-incrementing methods are used to obtain double-character groups from the imported string. The CString does its own memory management, so no `malloc` or `new` is required. Finally, the newly created character is added with a typecast and the `+` operator to the building output string. At the end, the internal string is allocated on the global heap with `AllocSysString` and returned. (I once lost a $3,000 consulting contract because I could not solve this little problem…)

Comments

You might wonder why an EXE server isn't used, because EXE servers are self-registering and somewhat easier to create. The answer in a nutshell is that ASP won't create an EXE-based (out-of-process) component without modifying the `Registry` value for the system (it defaults to in-process components only). This is not recommended because it greatly reduces the multithreading behavior of ASP and slows processing considerably. See the documentation in `ROADMAP.ASP` for more details.

6.2 How do I… Use page-level event methods with an ASP component?

Problem

We need to do some startup processing when each call is made to our component *before* the ASP script sees it; we don't want the methods used to be publicly exposed. Is there some way to do initialization processing for individual pages with ASP components?

Technique

Yes, use the `OnStartPage` and `OnEndPage` event methods. This How-To adds them to the Encryptor demo to illustrate saving and loading the encryption key from a file transparently each time a page is loaded and processed. Although these directions create the project from scratch, the CD contains a completed file under `CH06\HT02\`.

Steps

1. Copy the files from How-To 6.1 into a new directory and restart Visual C++ 5.0. Bring up the Class Wizard, and press Add Method. In the Add dialog, enter the name `OnStartPage`, of type `void`, with one parameter named `pUnk` of type `LPUNKNOWN`. Figure 6-10 shows how the dialog should look when you are done. Press OK to add the method. Add another method in the same manner named `OnEndPage` with identical settings. Save the project.

2. Bring up `ENCRYPTOR.CPP` in the text editor and enter the boldfaced code in Listing 6-3 to add the event handlers for the methods. Save the project.

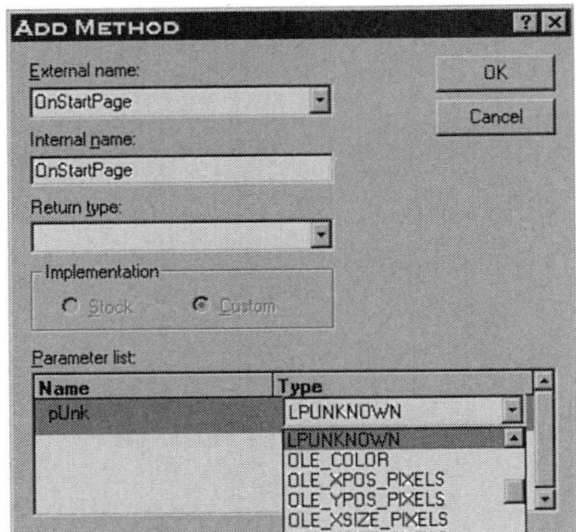

Figure 6-10 Adding page-level event methods to Encryptor

Listing 6-3 ENCRYPTOR.CPP event handler source code

```
void Encryptor::OnStartPage(LPUNKNOWN pUnk)
{
    char* pFileName = "c:\\windows\\encryptor.key";
    char strBuff[100];
    CStdioFile f1;
    if( !f1.Open( pFileName, CFile::modeRead ¦ CFile::typeText ) ) {
    #ifdef _DEBUG
      afxDump << "Unable to open file" << "\n";
    #endif
    exit( 1 );
    }
    f1.ReadString( strBuff , 100 );
    f1.Close();
    m_encryptionKey = strBuff;
}

void Encryptor::OnEndPage(LPUNKNOWN pUnk)
{
    char* pFileName = "c:\\windows\\encryptor.key";
    char strBuff[100];
    CStdioFile f1;
    if( !f1.Open( pFileName, CFile::modeCreate ¦ CFile::modeWrite ¦ ⇐
CFile::typeText ) ) {
    #ifdef _DEBUG
        afxDump << "Unable to open file" << "\n";
    #endif
    exit( 1 );
    }
    strcpy( strBuff , m_encryptionKey );
    f1.WriteString( strBuff );
    f1.Close();
}
```

3. Build the ASPENCRYPT.DLL again. Rerun REGSVR32.EXE on the new directory target for the new DLL. Then open ActiveX Control Pad and enter the ASP code in Listing 6-4. Save it as ASPHT0602.ASP and copy it into the ASPEXEC directory. Then create a text file in the C:\WINDOWS\ directory containing a single word of your choosing; save it as ENCRYPTOR.KEY.

Listing 6-4 ASPHT0602.ASP source code

```
<%@ LANGUAGE = VBScript %>
<%
EncryptionString = Request.Form("Text1")
if EncryptionString <> "" then
  StringToMessWith = Request.Form("Text2")
  Set objCrypto = Server.CreateObject("aspencrypt.Encryptor")
  objCrypto.EncryptionKey = EncryptionString
  EncryptedString = objCrypto.EncryptTheString( StringToMessWith )
  DecryptedString = objCrypto.DecryptTheString( EncryptedString )
else
  Set objCrypto = Server.CreateObject("aspencrypt.Encryptor")
  EncryptionString = objCrypto.EncryptionKey
  EncryptedString = ""
  DecryptedString = ""
end if
Set objCrypto = Nothing
%>
<HTML>
<HEAD>
<TITLE>Active Server Pages How To Chapter Six How To Two</TITLE>
</HEAD>
<BODY>
<FORM NAME="Form1" ACTION="aspht0602.asp" METHOD="POST" TARGET="_top">
<TABLE CELLPADDING=5 CELLSPACING=5 WIDTH=600 BORDER=5 ALIGN="CENTER"
VALIGN="MIDDLE" BGCOLOR="#008080">
<CAPTION>Welcome To The ASP How To Encryption Demo!</CAPTION>

<TR>
<TD ALIGN="CENTER" VALIGN="MIDDLE" BGCOLOR="#008080">Encryption Key
</TD>
<TD ALIGN="CENTER" VALIGN="MIDDLE" BGCOLOR="#008080">String To Encrypt
</TD>
<TD ALIGN="CENTER" VALIGN="MIDDLE" BGCOLOR="#008080">Encrypted String
</TD>
<TD ALIGN="CENTER" VALIGN="MIDDLE" BGCOLOR="#008080">Decrypted String
</TD>
</TR>
<TR>
<TD ALIGN="CENTER" VALIGN="MIDDLE" BGCOLOR="#008080">
<INPUT TYPE=Text NAME="Text1" VALUE="<%= EncryptionString %>">
</TD>
<TD ALIGN="CENTER" VALIGN="MIDDLE" BGCOLOR="#008080">
<INPUT TYPE=Text NAME="Text2" VALUE="<%= StringToMessWith %>">
</TD>
<TD ALIGN="CENTER" VALIGN="MIDDLE" BGCOLOR="#008080">
<INPUT TYPE=Text NAME="Text3" VALUE="<%= EncryptedString %>">
```

continued on next page

continued from previous page

```
</TD>
<TD ALIGN="CENTER" VALIGN="MIDDLE" BGCOLOR="#008080">
<INPUT TYPE=Text NAME="Text4" VALUE="<%= DecryptedString %>">
</TD>
</TR>
<TR>
<TD COLSPAN=4 ALIGN="CENTER" VALIGN="MIDDLE" BGCOLOR="#008080">
<INPUT TYPE=Submit NAME="Submit1" VALUE="Encryption Demo!">
</TD>
</TR>
</TABLE>
</FORM>
</BODY>
</HTML>
```

4. Activate Internet Explorer. In the address field, type in `HTTP://DEFAULT/ASPEXEC/ASPHT0602.ASP` and press Return. As shown in Figure 6-11, the page now comes up with the word you saved as the key in the first text control, read from the `ENCRYPTOR.KEY` file. Enter a new key encrypted, decrypt a string, and close IE. Reopen it after a moment and bring up `ASPHT0602.ASP` again. You will see, as shown in Figure 6-12, that the new key you entered has been saved for reuse. You can now employ the `OnStartPage` and `OnEndPage` event methods of ASP components.

How It Works

The two "event methods" are not true events. Instead, ASP checks all components referenced in an ASP page prior to processing its script, loads them,

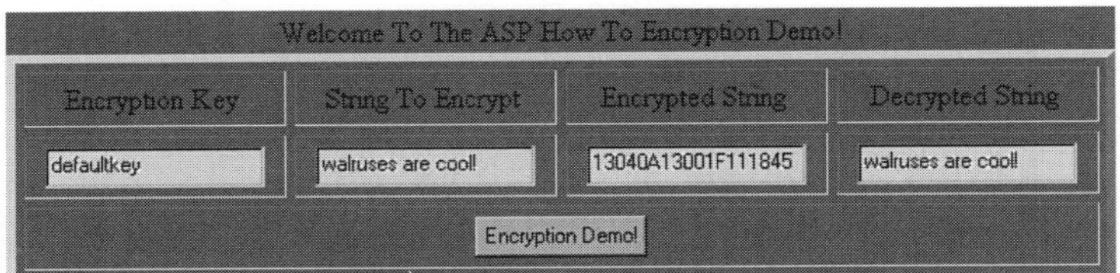

Figure 6-11 `ASPHT0602.ASP` in IE showing a default encryption key read during the `OnStartPage` event method

Figure 6-12 `ASPHT0602.ASP` in IE showing a custom encryption key saved during the `OnEndPage` event method and reloaded in the `OnStartPage` method

and checks whether they have the two methods defined as above. If not, execution of the component's interfaces proceeds normally. If either one is found, however, it is called first, before any actual script processing for **OnStartPage** and after all HTML has been output for **OnEndPage**. Note the crucial difference in the ASP code:

```
if EncryptionString <> "" then
  StringToMessWith = Request.Form("Text2")
  Set objCrypto = Server.CreateObject("aspencrypt.Encryptor")
  objCrypto.EncryptionKey = EncryptionString
  EncryptedString = objCrypto.EncryptTheString( StringToMessWith )
  DecryptedString = objCrypto.DecryptTheString( EncryptedString )
else
  Set objCrypto = Server.CreateObject("aspencrypt.Encryptor")
  EncryptionString = objCrypto.EncryptionKey
  EncryptedString = ""
  DecryptedString = ""
end if
Set objCrypto = Nothing
```

If this is the first time the ASP file has been processed, **objCrypto** still has information because of its **OnStartPage** event method. Thus, an object is created and its value is used as the default for the encryption key.

Also notice the setting of **objCrypto** to **nothing**; this can help defeat a bug that causes some **OnEndPage** event methods to fail without reason. Microsoft is working on this bug.

Comments

The code on the CD is actually somewhat different from the code above because the **OnEndPage** bug prevented me from using the correct code. If you encounter similar problems, consult the code on the CD; it contains a workaround. Also check the **README.TXT** file under "OnEndPage Bug" for last-minute information on this annoying bug.

6.3 How do I... Use the scripting context interface with an ASP component?

I have information I'd like to make available in the **Application** object that is created at initialization of my ASP component. Is there a way to store data in the ASP system objects directly from C++?

Technique

Microsoft thoughtfully provided an interface to the ASP system objects. It is called `IScriptingContext`, and this How-To illustrates using it to store the encryption key in the `Application` object as well as its own internal property. Although these directions create the project from scratch, the CD contains a completed file under `CH06\HT03\`.

Steps

1. Copy the files from the previous How-To into a new directory. Activate Visual C++ 5. As shown in Figure 6-13, select the Project|Add To Project... menu options. Move to the directory where ASP is installed and locate the file `ASPTLB.H`, as shown in Figure 6-14. Press OK to add it to the project. Then copy the file into the current working directory for the project. In the same way, locate the `INITGUID.H` file in the `\DEVSTUDIO\VC\INCLUDE\` directory and add it, as shown in Figure 6-15. Copy this file into the current working directory as well.

2. Bring up the text editor for `ENCRYPTOR.CPP` and enter the boldfaced code in Listing 6-5 in the initialization section and the `OnStartPage` event method. Save the project and build the DLL. Run `REGSVR32` on the new DLL as before. (It is especially important that the `INITGUID.H #INCLUDE` directive be *before* the `ASPTLB.H #INCLUDE` directive; otherwise linker errors will result!)

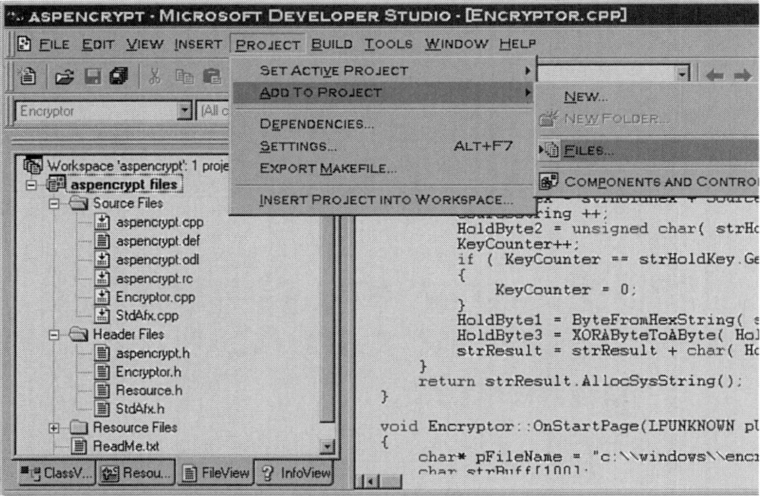

Figure 6-13 Adding a file to the project

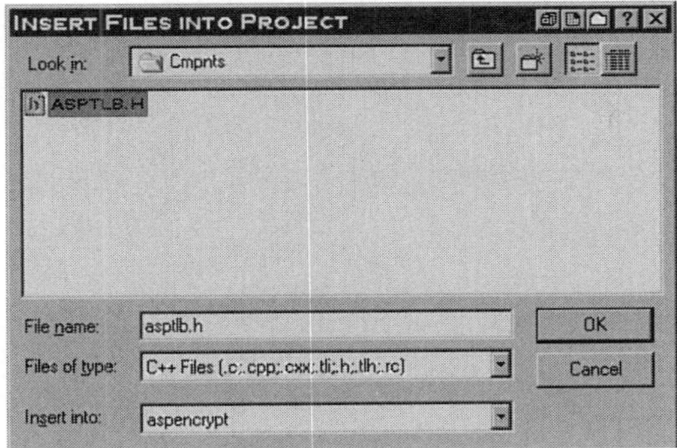

Figure 6-14 Getting the `ASPTLB.H` file in the project

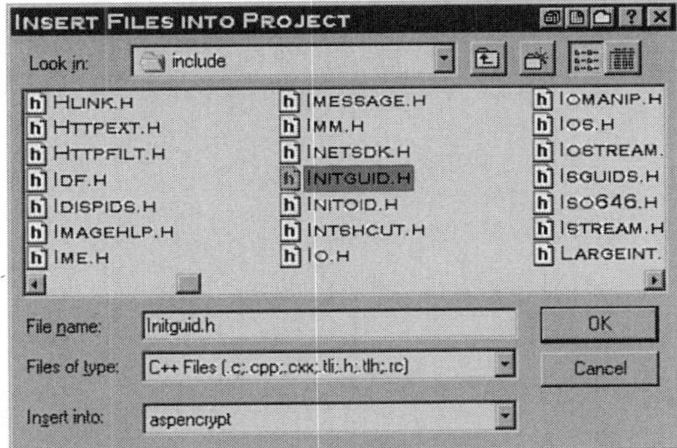

Figure 6-15 Getting the `INITGUID.H` file in the project

Listing 6-5 `ENCRYPTOR.CPP OnStartPage` source code

```
// Encryptor.cpp : implementation file
//

#include "stdafx.h"
#include "aspencrypt.h"
#include "Encryptor.h"
#include "initguid.h"
#include "asptlb.h"

#ifdef _DEBUG
#define new DEBUG_NEW
#undef THIS_FILE
static char THIS_FILE[] = __FILE__;
#endif
...
```

continued on next page

continued from previous page

```
void Encryptor::OnStartPage(LPUNKNOWN pUnk)
{
    char* pFileName = "c:\\windows\\encryptor.key";
    char strBuff[100];
    CStdioFile f1;
    if( !f1.Open( pFileName, CFile::modeRead ¦ CFile::typeText ) ) {
    #ifdef _DEBUG
      afxDump << "Unable to open file" << "\n";
      #endif
      exit( 1 );
    }
    f1.ReadString( strBuff , 100 );
    f1.Close();
    m_encryptionKey = strBuff;
    /////////////////////////////////////////////
    ///  IScriptingContext Section

    HRESULT hr;
    IScriptingContext *piContext;
    hr = pUnk->QueryInterface(IID_IScriptingContext , (void**)&piContext);
    IApplicationObject* piApplication = NULL;
    hr = piContext->get_Application( &piApplication );
    VARIANT vtOut;
    VariantInit(&vtOut);
    V_VT(&vtOut) = VT_BSTR;
    V_BSTR(&vtOut) = m_encryptionKey.AllocSysString();
    hr = piApplication->put_Value( OLESTR("EncryptKey"), vtOut );
    piApplication->Release();
    piContext->Release();
}
```

3. Activate ActiveX Control Pad and create a new ASP file with the contents of Listing 6-6. Save the file as ASPHT0603.ASP and move it into the ASPEXEC directory.

Listing 6-6 ASPHT0603.ASP source code

```
</BODY>
<%@ LANGUAGE = VBScript %>
<%
EncryptionString = Request.Form("Text1")
if EncryptionString <> "" then
  StringToMessWith = Request.Form("Text2")
  Set objCrypto = Server.CreateObject("aspencrypt.Encryptor")
  Application("EncryptKey") = EncryptionString
  objCrypto.EncryptionKey = EncryptionString
  EncryptedString = objCrypto.EncryptTheString( StringToMessWith )
  DecryptedString = objCrypto.DecryptTheString( EncryptedString )
else
  EncryptionString = Application("EncryptKey")
  EncryptedString = ""
  DecryptedString = ""
end if
Set objCrypto = Nothing
%>
<HTML>
<HEAD>
```

```
<TITLE>Active Server Pages How To Chapter Six How To Three</TITLE>
</HEAD>
<BODY>
<FORM NAME="Form1" ACTION="aspht0603.asp" METHOD="POST" TARGET="_top">
<TABLE CELLPADDING=5 CELLSPACING=5 WIDTH=600 BORDER=5 ALIGN="CENTER"
VALIGN="MIDDLE" BGCOLOR="#008080">
<CAPTION>Welcome To The ASP How To Encryption Demo!</CAPTION>

<TR>
<TD ALIGN="CENTER" VALIGN="MIDDLE" BGCOLOR="#008080">Encryption Key
</TD>
<TD ALIGN="CENTER" VALIGN="MIDDLE" BGCOLOR="#008080">String To Encrypt
</TD>
<TD ALIGN="CENTER" VALIGN="MIDDLE" BGCOLOR="#008080">Encrypted String
</TD>
<TD ALIGN="CENTER" VALIGN="MIDDLE" BGCOLOR="#008080">Decrypted String
</TD>
</TR>
<TR>
<TD ALIGN="CENTER" VALIGN="MIDDLE" BGCOLOR="#008080">
<INPUT TYPE=Text NAME="Text1" VALUE="<%= EncryptionString %>">
</TD>
<TD ALIGN="CENTER" VALIGN="MIDDLE" BGCOLOR="#008080">
<INPUT TYPE=Text NAME="Text2" VALUE="<%= StringToMessWith %>">
</TD>
<TD ALIGN="CENTER" VALIGN="MIDDLE" BGCOLOR="#008080">
<INPUT TYPE=Text NAME="Text3" VALUE="<%= EncryptedString %>">
</TD>
<TD ALIGN="CENTER" VALIGN="MIDDLE" BGCOLOR="#008080">
<INPUT TYPE=Text NAME="Text4" VALUE="<%= DecryptedString %>">
</TD>
</TR>
<TR>
<TD COLSPAN=4 ALIGN="CENTER" VALIGN="MIDDLE" BGCOLOR="#008080">
<INPUT TYPE=Submit NAME="Submit1" VALUE="Encryption Demo!">
</TD>
</TR>
</TABLE>
</FORM>
</BODY>
</HTML></HTML>
```

4. Activate Internet Explorer. In the address field, type in `HTTP://DEFAULT/ASPEXEC/ASPHT0603.ASP` and press Return. The display behaves identically to before, but uses the `Application` variable rather than the `Object` one. You have learned to use the `IScriptingContext` interface with ASP components, unlocking all the power of ASP in your C++ components.

How It Works

This is raw COM programming! The code you added is about as nasty as ActiveX programming in C++ can get until you reach ATL (ActiveX Template Library). Study these first three lines of code:

```
HRESULT hr;
IScriptingContext *piContext;
hr = pUnk->QueryInterface(IID_IScriptingContext , (void**)&piContext);
```

hr is of type HRESULT, the standard return type for OLE functions. This simple example does not check for error codes; a more complete one would use various macros that parse the HRESULT structure for things such as success or failure and error conditions. (See the online help on HRESULT.) Next, a pointer to the IScriptingContext interface is declared (this is where you start using ASPTLB.H), followed by a call to QueryInterface on the pUnk pointer. QueryInterface takes the IID of IScriptingContext along with the pointer to the interface itself and returns a valid interface structure in the pointer if one can be obtained.

Here is the next critical code section:

```
IApplicationObject* piApplication = NULL;
hr = piContext->get_Application( &piApplication );
```

In the first line, an IApplicationObject interface pointer is declared and set to NULL. Then, the previously obtained IScriptingContext pointer is called with its get_Application method to return a pointer to the underlying IApplicationObject. It also returns an HRESULT, which we blithely ignore.

Once you have the two interfaces, this code uses them to send in the value you want into the application's objects collection:

```
VARIANT vtOut;
VariantInit(&vtOut);
V_VT(&vtOut) = VT_BSTR;
V_BSTR(&vtOut) = m_encryptionKey.AllocSysString();
hr = piApplication->put_Value( OLESTR("EncryptKey"), vtOut );
```

Here, a variant is declared and initialized. Then it is cast into the type of a BSTR and given the contents of the m_encryptionKey CString via its AllocSysString method that sends out an exportable value. Finally, the critical method is called to put the actual information into the application's collection via put_Value and its two parameters, the name of the object and its value.

Finally, it's time for clean-up:

```
piApplication->Release();
piContext->Release();
```

Here the two interface pointers have their Release methods called to make sure their internal reference count is decreased properly so their resources can be reclaimed by the operating system when you are done.

In the ASP code itself, notice the simple but important changes:

```
else
  EncryptionString = Application("EncryptKey")
  EncryptedString = ""
  DecryptedString = ""
end if
```

Instead of creating a copy of the object and then reading its internal property, the default code for a first time display can use the now-created EncryptKey variable in the application's collection. This is very useful, as you will see later on, if you want to keep the way data appears in the **Application** object a secret!

Comments

The **#include** directive requirements for **INITGUID.H** are explained *only* in the ASP samples from Microsoft, not in any other documentation. If you have had problems compiling ASP components and getting **unresolved external symbol** errors, this is why!

6.4 How do I... Write HTML output directly to an ASP page with an ASP component?

Problem

We're using some internal data that we want to use for sending ASP output directly to the HTML stream to maintain confidentiality. Can ASP let our custom component do this?

Technique

If you ask it very nicely, yes! The **Response** object is available via the **IResponse** interface, and this How-To shows you the way to get at it, adding two new methods that send encrypted and decrypted text directly to the HTML stream. Although these directions create the project from scratch, the CD contains a completed file under **CH06\HT04**.

Steps

1. Copy the files from the previous How-To into a new directory. Activate Visual C++ 5.0. Bring up the text editor and enter the boldfaced code in Listing 6-7 to the **OnStartPage** event method.

Listing 6-7 ENCRYPTOR.CPP OnStartPage source code

```
void Encryptor::OnStartPage(LPUNKNOWN pUnk)
{
    char* pFileName = "c:\\windows\\encryptor.key";
    char strBuff[100];
    CStdioFile f1;
    if( !f1.Open( pFileName, CFile::modeRead ¦ CFile::typeText ) ) {
```

continued on next page

continued from previous page

```
    #ifdef _DEBUG
      afxDump << "Unable to open file" << "\n";
      #endif
      exit( 1 );
    }
    f1.ReadString( strBuff , 100 );
    f1.Close();
    m_encryptionKey = strBuff;
    ///////////////////////////////////////////////
    ///  IScriptingContext Section

    HRESULT hr;
    IScriptingContext *piContext;
    hr = pUnk->QueryInterface(IID_IScriptingContext , (void**)&piContext);
    IApplicationObject* piApplication = NULL;
    hr = piContext->get_Application( &piApplication );
    VARIANT vtOut;
    VariantInit(&vtOut);
    V_VT(&vtOut) = VT_BSTR;
    V_BSTR(&vtOut) = m_encryptionKey.AllocSysString();
    hr = piApplication->put_Value( OLESTR("EncryptKey"), vtOut );
    piApplication->Release();
    m_ContextHolder = piContext;
}
```

2. In the `ENCRYPTOR.H` file, add the boldfaced code in Listing 6-8 to place the member variable in the object itself to hold the scripting context. Make sure to enter the `#include` directives in the *exact* order listed!

Listing 6-8 ENCRYPTOR.H source code

```
#if !defined(AFX_ENCRYPTOR_H__B83A6246_D858_11D0_B7DF_444553540000__INCLUDED_)
#define AFX_ENCRYPTOR_H__B83A6246_D858_11D0_B7DF_444553540000__INCLUDED_

#if _MSC_VER >= 1000
#pragma once
#endif // _MSC_VER >= 1000
// Encryptor.h : header file
//
#include "initguid.h"
#include "asptlb.h"


/////////////////////////////////////////////////////////////////////////////
// Encryptor command target

class Encryptor : public CCmdTarget
{
DECLARE_DYNCREATE(Encryptor)

Encryptor();           // protected constructor used by dynamic creation

// Attributes
public:
```

```
// Operations
public:

// Overrides
// ClassWizard generated virtual function overrides
//{{AFX_VIRTUAL(Encryptor)
public:
virtual void OnFinalRelease();
//}}AFX_VIRTUAL

// Implementation
protected:
virtual ~Encryptor();

// Generated message map functions
//{{AFX_MSG(Encryptor)
// NOTE - the ClassWizard will add and remove member functions here.
//}}AFX_MSG

DECLARE_MESSAGE_MAP()
DECLARE_OLECREATE(Encryptor)

// Generated OLE dispatch map functions
//{{AFX_DISPATCH(Encryptor)
CString m_encryptionKey;
afx_msg void OnEncryptionKeyChanged();
afx_msg BSTR EncryptTheString(LPCTSTR TargetString);
afx_msg BSTR DecryptTheString(LPCTSTR SourceString);
afx_msg void OnStartPage(LPUNKNOWN pUnk);
afx_msg void SaveKey();
afx_msg void EncryptToHTML(LPCTSTR TargetString);
afx_msg void DecryptToHTML(LPCTSTR SourceString);
//}}AFX_DISPATCH
DECLARE_DISPATCH_MAP()
DECLARE_INTERFACE_MAP()
private:
IScriptingContext *m_ContextHolder;

};

/////////////////////////////////////////////////////////////////////////////

//{{AFX_INSERT_LOCATION}}
// Microsoft Developer Studio will insert additional declarations immediately ⇐
before the previous line.

#endif // !defined(AFX_ENCRYPTOR_H--B83A6246_D858_11D0_B7DF_444553540000--
INCLUDED_)
```

3. Bring up the Class Wizard and add three new methods. The first one should have a name of `EncryptToHTML`, a return type of `void`, and a parameter `TargetString` of type `LPCSTR`, as shown in Figure 6-16. The second one should have a name of `DecryptToHTML`, a return type of `void`, and a parameter `SourceString` of type `LPCSTR`. The third one should have an external name of `ReleaseContext`, a return type of `void`, and no parameters. Press OK to add them to the project. Then enter the source code in Listing 6-9 to ENCRYPTOR.CPP for each of the new methods (see Figure 6-16). Save the project.

Listing 6-9 ENCRYPTOR.CPP new methods source code

```
void Encryptor::EncryptToHTML(LPCTSTR TargetString)
{
    HRESULT hr;
    IResponse* piResponse = NULL;
    hr = m_ContextHolder->get_Response( &piResponse );
    VARIANT vtHTMLOut;
    VariantInit(&vtHTMLOut);
    V_VT(&vtHTMLOut) = VT_BSTR;
    V_BSTR(&vtHTMLOut) = EncryptTheString( TargetString );
    hr = piResponse->Write( vtHTMLOut );
}

void Encryptor::DecryptToHTML(LPCTSTR SourceString)
{
    HRESULT hr;
    IResponse* piResponse = NULL;
    hr = m_ContextHolder->get_Response( &piResponse );
    VARIANT vtHTMLOut;
    VariantInit(&vtHTMLOut);
    V_VT(&vtHTMLOut) = VT_BSTR;
    V_BSTR(&vtHTMLOut) = DecryptTheString( SourceString );
    hr = piResponse->Write( vtHTMLOut );
}

void Encryptor::ReleaseContext()
{
    m_ContextHolder->Release();
}
```

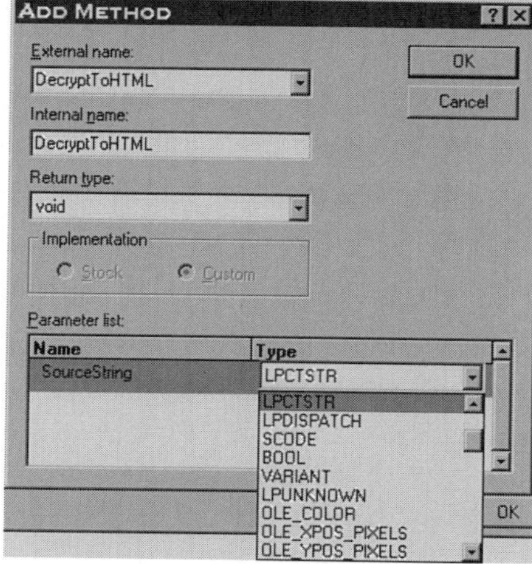

Figure 6-16 Adding two new methods

4. Build the DLL. Run **REGSVR32** to register the latest version. Then activate ActiveX Control Pad and enter the ASP source code in Listing 6-10. Save the file as **ASPHT0604.ASP** and move it to the **ASPEXEC** directory.

Listing 6-10 ASPHT0604.ASP source code

```
<%@ LANGUAGE = VBScript %>
<%
EncryptionString = Request.Form("Text1")
Set objCrypto = Server.CreateObject("aspencrypt.Encryptor")
if EncryptionString <> "" then
  StringToMessWith = Request.Form("Text2")
  objCrypto.EncryptionKey = EncryptionString
  Application("EncryptKey") = EncryptionString
else
  EncryptionString = Application("EncryptKey")
  EncryptedString = ""
  DecryptedString = ""
end if
%>
<HTML>
<HEAD>
<TITLE>Active Server Pages How To Chapter Six How To Four</TITLE>
</HEAD>
<BODY>
<FORM NAME="Form1" ACTION="aspht0604.asp" METHOD="POST" TARGET="_top">
<TABLE CELLPADDING=5 CELLSPACING=5 WIDTH=600 BORDER=5 ALIGN="CENTER"
VALIGN="MIDDLE" BGCOLOR="#008080">
<CAPTION>Welcome To The ASP How To Encryption Demo!</CAPTION>

<TR>
<TD ALIGN="CENTER" VALIGN="MIDDLE" BGCOLOR="#008080">Encryption Key
</TD>
<TD ALIGN="CENTER" VALIGN="MIDDLE" BGCOLOR="#008080">String To Encrypt
</TD>
<TD ALIGN="CENTER" VALIGN="MIDDLE" BGCOLOR="#008080">Encrypted String
</TD>
<TD ALIGN="CENTER" VALIGN="MIDDLE" BGCOLOR="#008080">Decrypted String
</TD>
</TR>
<TR>
<TD ALIGN="CENTER" VALIGN="MIDDLE" BGCOLOR="#008080">
<INPUT TYPE=Text NAME="Text1" VALUE="<%= EncryptionString %>">
</TD>
<TD ALIGN="CENTER" VALIGN="MIDDLE" BGCOLOR="#008080">
<INPUT TYPE=Text NAME="Text2" VALUE="<%= StringToMessWith %>">
</TD>
<TD ALIGN="CENTER" VALIGN="MIDDLE" BGCOLOR="#008080">
<INPUT TYPE=Text NAME="Text3" VALUE="
<%if StringToMessWith = "" then%>
<%= "" %>
<%else%>
<% objCrypto.EncryptToHTML( StringToMessWith ) %>
<% EncryptedString = objCrypto.EncryptTheString( StringToMessWith ) %>
<%end if%>
```

continued on next page

continued from previous page

```
">
</TD>
<TD ALIGN="CENTER" VALIGN="MIDDLE" BGCOLOR="#008080">
<INPUT TYPE=Text NAME="Text4" VALUE="
<%if StringToMessWith = "" then%>
<%= "" %>
<%else%>
<% objCrypto.DecryptToHTML( EncryptedString ) %>
<%end if%>
<% objCrypto.ReleaseContext%>
">
</TD>
</TR>
<TR>
<TD COLSPAN=4 ALIGN="CENTER" VALIGN="MIDDLE" BGCOLOR="#008080">
<INPUT TYPE=Submit NAME="Submit1" VALUE="Encryption Demo!">
</TD>
</TR>
</TABLE>
</FORM>
</BODY>
</HTML>
```

5. Activate Internet Explorer. In the address field, type in **HTTP://DEFAULT/ASPEXEC/ASPHT0604.ASP** and press Return. The display behaves identically to before, but uses the direct HTML output rather than explicit internal variables. You are now up to speed on using the **IResponse** interface with ASP components to write directly to the HTML output stream.

How It Works

The first problem faced by this How-To is to keep the **IScriptingContext** pointer around after the **OnStartPage** call. The answer lies in this modification to **ENCRYPTOR.H**:

```
private:
  IScriptingContext *m_ContextHolder;
```

Once the two **#include** directives give the header file access to the **ASPTLB.H** and **INITGUID.H** information, the compiler can easily add a member variable of the needed type. (Notice that the **#includes** are removed from the **ENCRYPTOR.CPP** file now to avoid duplication.) This member variable is then paired with this code:

```
piApplication->Release();
m_ContextHolder = piContext;
```

This is where the context pointer is stored so that later methods can use it. Notice also that the **Release** call is not made, for obvious reasons.

Once the **IScriptingContext** pointer stays around, other methods can freely call it. In the **EncryptToHTML** method, the following code uses it to obtain the **Response** object **Interface** pointer:

```
HRESULT hr;
IResponse* piResponse = NULL;
hr = m_ContextHolder->get_Response( &piResponse );
```

The `get_Response` method is designed to allow easy access to the interface for the `Response` object, without fiddling with `IDispatch` and `QueryInterface`. Once this is obtained, the following code shows how it is used to send the HTML to the output stream:

```
VARIANT vtHTMLOut;
VariantInit(&vtHTMLOut);
V_VT(&vtHTMLOut) = VT_BSTR;
V_BSTR(&vtHTMLOut) = EncryptTheString( TargetString );
hr = piResponse->Write( vtHTMLOut );
```

The variant conversions are similar to those in How-To 6.3. Notice that the output of `EncryptTheString` can be sent directly to the output variable, because it is a valid system string. The `Write` method sends the actual data just as it would in an ASP script.

But one problem remains: what to do with the `IScriptingContext` pointer when the script is done? The pointer is not valid beyond the immediate page where it is supplied by `ISAPI`, so storing it in the `Application` object isn't worth doing. On the other hand, the current code does not call `Release` on it, which would eat up memory very fast! The answer lies in this method:

```
void Encryptor::ReleaseContext()
{
    m_ContextHolder->Release();
}
```

Here, the `Release` method is called explicitly when needed. This allows the script writer to decide when the interface is finished and can be destroyed rather than forcing the component itself to decide this.

In the ASP file, notice how the HTML output methods are used:

```
<TD ALIGN="CENTER" VALIGN="MIDDLE" BGCOLOR="#008080">
<INPUT TYPE=Text NAME="Text3" VALUE="
<%if StringToMessWith = "" then%>
<%= "" %>
<%else%>
<% objCrypto.EncryptToHTML( StringToMessWith ) %>
<% EncryptedString = objCrypto.EncryptTheString( StringToMessWith ) %>
<%end if%>
">
</TD>
<TD ALIGN="CENTER" VALIGN="MIDDLE" BGCOLOR="#008080">
<INPUT TYPE=Text NAME="Text4" VALUE="
<%if StringToMessWith = "" then%>
<%= "" %>
<%else%>
<% objCrypto.DecryptToHTML( EncryptedString ) %>
<%end if%>
<% objCrypto.ReleaseContext%>
">
</TD>
```

Because they are going to write directly to the HTML, no `<%= %>` wrappers are needed around the calls. For simplicity, the encrypted output is stored in an internal variable and sent to the `DecodeToHTML` method, but other techniques could have been employed. Also notice that the `ReleaseContext` method is called only when both outputs are finished.

Comments

This How-To does have one hidden vulnerability. If `OnStartPage` is never called, a call to any method that relies on the `IScriptingContext` pointer will fail. This can happen if the object is created with application scope (that is, in `GLOBAL.ASA` as a server-level object), or if `Server.CreateObject` is not called to create the object (such as with passing a pointer through the `Application` object between different pages). If you rely on having the `IScriptingContext` pointer, make sure in your documentation that you warn against the two above possibilities!

6.5 How do I... Get HTML forms input directly with an ASP component?

Problem

I'd like to intercept HTML forms input directly with my ASP component. Does the `IScriptingContext` interface offer me a way to do this?

Technique

The various collections are available for the objects obtained via `IScriptingContext`, including the `Response.Forms` one. This How-To demonstrates obtaining the encryption key and string to encrypt directly from forms input in the component rather than with explicit ASP scripting calls. Although these directions create the project from scratch, the CD contains a completed file under `CH06\HT05\`.

Steps

1. Copy the files from the previous How-To into a new directory. Activate Visual C++ 5.0. Activate the Class Wizard and add two new methods to the `Automation` interface. The first one should have an external name of `EncryptFromForm`, a return type of `BSTR`, and no parameters. The second one should have an external name of `DecryptFromForm`, a return type of `BSTR`, and no parameters, as shown in Figure 6-17. Press OK to add the methods to the project.

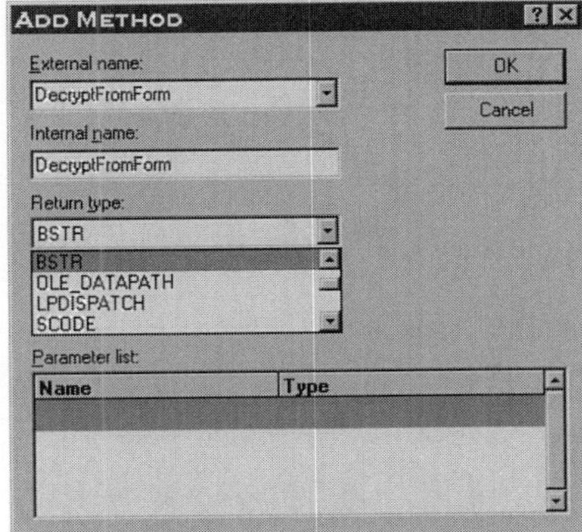

Figure 6-17 Entering the form's automation methods

2. Bring up ENCRYPTOR.CPP in the text editor and enter the boldfaced code in Listing 6-11. Save the project. Then build the DLL and run REGSVR32 to register it.

Listing 6-11 ENCRYPTOR.CPP form's methods source code

```
BSTR Encryptor::EncryptFromForm()
{
    CString strResult;
    HRESULT hr;
    IRequest* piRequest = NULL;
    hr = m_ContextHolder->get_Request( &piRequest );
    IRequestDictionary* piRequestDictionary = NULL;
    hr = piRequest->get_Form( &piRequestDictionary );

    VARIANT vtFormOut;
    VARIANT vtFormIn;
    VariantInit(&vtFormOut);
    VariantInit(&vtFormIn);

    V_VT(&vtFormIn) = VT_BSTR;
    V_BSTR(&vtFormIn) = SysAllocString(L"Text2");

    hr = piRequestDictionary->get_Item( vtFormIn, &vtFormOut );

    if (V_VT(&vtFormOut) !=VT_BSTR) VariantChangeType( &vtFormOut, &vtFormOut ⇐
, 0 , VT_BSTR );

    strResult = EncryptTheString( LPCSTR( &vtFormOut ));

    VariantClear( &vtFormIn);
    VariantClear( &vtFormOut );
```

continued on next page

continued from previous page

```
    piRequestDictionary->Release();
    piRequest->Release();

    return strResult.AllocSysString();
}

BSTR Encryptor::DecryptFromForm()
{
    CString strResult;
    HRESULT hr;
    IRequest* piRequest = NULL;
    hr = m_ContextHolder->get_Request( &piRequest );
    IRequestDictionary* piRequestDictionary = NULL;
    hr = piRequest->get_Form( &piRequestDictionary );

    VARIANT vtFormOut;
    VARIANT vtFormIn;
    VariantInit(&vtFormOut);
    VariantInit(&vtFormIn);

    V_VT(&vtFormIn) = VT_BSTR;
    V_BSTR(&vtFormIn) = SysAllocString(L"Text3");

    hr = piRequestDictionary->get_Item( vtFormIn, &vtFormOut );

    if (V_VT(&vtFormOut) !=VT_BSTR) VariantChangeType( &vtFormOut, &vtFormOut ⇐
, 0 , VT_BSTR );

    strResult = DecryptTheString( LPCSTR( &vtFormOut ));

    VariantClear( &vtFormIn);
    VariantClear( &vtFormOut );

    piRequestDictionary->Release();
    piRequest->Release();

    return strResult.AllocSysString();
}
```

3. Activate ActiveX Control Pad and enter the ASP source code in Listing 6-12. Save the file as `ASPHT0605.ASP` and move it to the `ASPEXEC` directory.

Listing 6-12 ASPHT0605.ASP source code

```
</BODY>
<%@ LANGUAGE = VBScript %>
<%
EncryptionString = Request.Form("Text1")
if EncryptionString <> "" then
  StringToMessWith = Request.Form("Text2")
  Set objCrypto = Server.CreateObject("aspencrypt.Encryptor")
  objCrypto.EncryptionKey = EncryptionString
  Application("EncryptKey") = EncryptionString
  EncryptedString = objCrypto.EncryptFromForm
  if Request.Form("Text3") <> "" then
    DecryptedString = objCrypto.DecryptFromForm
```

```
  else
    DecryptedString = objCrypto.DecryptTheString( EncryptedString )
  end if
else
  EncryptionString = Application("EncryptKey")
  EncryptedString = ""
  DecryptedString = ""
end if
objCrypto.ReleaseContext
Set objCrypto = Nothing
%>
<HTML>
<HEAD>
<TITLE>Active Server Pages How To Chapter Six How To Five</TITLE>
</HEAD>
<BODY>
<FORM NAME="Form1" ACTION="aspht0605.asp" METHOD="POST" TARGET="_top">
<TABLE CELLPADDING=5 CELLSPACING=5 WIDTH=600 BORDER=5 ALIGN="CENTER"
VALIGN="MIDDLE" BGCOLOR="#008080">
<CAPTION>Welcome To The ASP How To Encryption Demo!</CAPTION>

<TR>
<TD ALIGN="CENTER" VALIGN="MIDDLE" BGCOLOR="#008080">Encryption Key
</TD>
<TD ALIGN="CENTER" VALIGN="MIDDLE" BGCOLOR="#008080">String To Encrypt
</TD>
<TD ALIGN="CENTER" VALIGN="MIDDLE" BGCOLOR="#008080">Encrypted String
</TD>
<TD ALIGN="CENTER" VALIGN="MIDDLE" BGCOLOR="#008080">Decrypted String
</TD>
</TR>
<TR>
<TD ALIGN="CENTER" VALIGN="MIDDLE" BGCOLOR="#008080">
<INPUT TYPE=Text NAME="Text1" VALUE="<%= EncryptionString %>">
</TD>
<TD ALIGN="CENTER" VALIGN="MIDDLE" BGCOLOR="#008080">
<INPUT TYPE=Text NAME="Text2" VALUE="<%= StringToMessWith %>">
</TD>
<TD ALIGN="CENTER" VALIGN="MIDDLE" BGCOLOR="#008080">
<INPUT TYPE=Text NAME="Text3" VALUE="<%= EncryptedString %>">
</TD>
<TD ALIGN="CENTER" VALIGN="MIDDLE" BGCOLOR="#008080">
<INPUT TYPE=Text NAME="Text4" VALUE="<%= DecryptedString %>">
</TD>
</TR>
<TR>
<TD COLSPAN=4 ALIGN="CENTER" VALIGN="MIDDLE" BGCOLOR="#008080">
<INPUT TYPE=Submit NAME="Submit1" VALUE="Encryption Demo!">
</TD>
</TR>
</TABLE>
</FORM>
</BODY>
</HTML>
```

4. Activate Internet Explorer. In the address field, type in `HTTP://DEFAULT/ASPEXEC/ASPHT0605.ASP` and press Return. The display behaves identically to before, but uses the forms input via the component rather than explicit internal scripting. You have learned to use the `IRequestDictionary` interface with ASP components to obtain form information directly from the ASP system.

How It Works

The key to interaction with collections in the `IScriptingContext` ASP component system is the `IRequestDictionary` interface. Notice this code in the `EncodeFromForm` method:

```
HRESULT hr;
IRequest* piRequest = NULL;
hr = m_ContextHolder->get_Request( &piRequest );
IRequestDictionary* piRequestDictionary = NULL;
hr = piRequest->get_Form( &piRequestDictionary );
```

First, an `IRequest` interface must be obtained via the `get_Request` call. This in turn exposes the `get_Form` method. It returns a collection interface that is the `IRequestDictionary` pointer. Once this interface has been obtained, special variants must be constructed to interact with it, shown in this code fragment:

```
VARIANT vtFormOut;
VARIANT vtFormIn;
VariantInit(&vtFormOut);
VariantInit(&vtFormIn);

V_VT(&vtFormIn) = VT_BSTR;
V_BSTR(&vtFormIn) = SysAllocString(L"Text2");

hr = piRequestDictionary->get_Item( vtFormIn, &vtFormOut );

if (V_VT(&vtFormOut) !=VT_BSTR) VariantChangeType( &vtFormOut, &vtFormOut ⇐
, 0 , VT_BSTR );
```

The `vtFormIn` variant is used to send the text representation of the collection item whose value is desired. It is then sent along with the other variant to the `get_Item` method. This method returns either a `VT_EMPTY` type or one of some other valid variant types to represent the underlying data. In this case, you want a string type, and so if the variant is in the wrong form, you coerce into the right one with the `VariantChangeType` method call. The coerced variant is then typecast into an `LPCSTR` and sent directly into the normal `EncryptTheString` method.

In the ASP script file, notice this code section:

```
EncryptionString = Request.Form("Text1")
if EncryptionString <> "" then
  StringToMessWith = Request.Form("Text2")
  Set objCrypto = Server.CreateObject("aspencrypt.Encryptor")
  objCrypto.EncryptionKey = EncryptionString
```

```
  Application("EncryptKey") = EncryptionString
  EncryptedString = objCrypto.EncryptFromForm
  if Request.Form("Text3") <> "" then
    DecryptedString = objCrypto.DecryptFromForm
  else
    DecryptedString = objCrypto.DecryptTheString( EncryptedString )
  end if
else
  EncryptionString = Application("EncryptKey")
  EncryptedString = ""
  DecryptedString = ""
end if
objCrypto.ReleaseContext
Set objCrypto = Nothing
%>
```

Because the names of the desired form elements are hard-coded into the ASP component, all that is needed is to determine that there is indeed data in them and invoke the methods. Because they output strings rather than writing to the HTML directly, their results go into intermediate variables.

Comments

It would be more elegant to store the names of the form variables in the **Session** object under preset keys and obtain them when the form methods are invoked, rather than hard-wiring the form variable names into the methods directly.

COMPLEXITY
ADVANCED

6.6 How do I... Interact with the ASP Server object in an ASP component?

Problem

We are having trouble losing text files written by our ASP components. The **Server.MapPath** function would solve this, but can we access it directly in our C++ ASP component?

Technique

The **Server** object is also exposed via the **IScriptingContext** interface! This How-To demonstrates using the **IServer** interface and its **MapPath** method. Although these directions create the project from scratch, the CD contains a completed file under **CH06\HT06**.

Steps

1. Copy the files from the previous How-To into a new directory. Activate Visual C++ 5.0. Bring up `ENCRYPTOR.CPP` in the text editor and enter the boldfaced code in Listing 6-13 in the `OnStartPage` and `OnEndPage` methods. Save the project. Then build the DLL and run `REGSVR32` to register it.

Listing 6-13 ENCRYPTOR.CPP server interface source code

```
void Encryptor::OnStartPage(LPUNKNOWN pUnk)
{
    ///////////////////////////////////////////////
    ///  IScriptingContext Section

    HRESULT hr;
    IScriptingContext *piContext;
     hr = pUnk->QueryInterface(IID_IScriptingContext , (void**)&piContext);

    ///////////////////////////////////////////////
    /// IServer MapPath modified encryption key save

    IServer* piServer = NULL;
    hr = piContext->get_Server( &piServer );

    char FileName[255];
    char strBuff[100];
    CStdioFile f1;
    BSTR* strPath;

    hr = piServer->MapPath( SysAllocString(L"/ASPEXEC") , strPath );

    strcpy( FileName , LPCSTR( &strPath ));
    strcat( FileName , "\\encryptor.key" );
    if( !f1.Open( FileName, CFile::modeRead | CFile::typeText ) )
    {
    #ifdef _DEBUG
      afxDump << "Unable to open file" << "\n";
    #endif
    exit( 1 );
    }
    f1.ReadString( strBuff , 100 );
    f1.Close();
    m_encryptionKey = strBuff;

    piServer->Release();

    IApplicationObject* piApplication = NULL;
    hr = piContext->get_Application( &piApplication );
    VARIANT vtOut;
    VariantInit(&vtOut);
    V_VT(&vtOut) = VT_BSTR;
    V_BSTR(&vtOut) = m_encryptionKey.AllocSysString();
    hr = piApplication->put_Value( OLESTR("EncryptKey"), vtOut );
    piApplication->Release();
    m_ContextHolder = piContext;
```

```
}

void Encryptor::OnEndPage(LPUNKNOWN pUnk)
{
    HRESULT hr;
    char FileName[255];
    char strBuff[100];
    CStdioFile f1;
    BSTR* strPath;

    IServer* piServer = NULL;
    hr = m_ContextHolder->get_Server( &piServer );

    hr = piServer->MapPath( SysAllocString(L"/ASPEXEC") , strPath  );

    strcpy( FileName , LPCSTR( &strPath ));
    strcat( FileName , "\\encryptor.key" );
    if( !f1.Open( FileName, CFile::modeCreate ¦ CFile::modeWrite ¦ ⇐
CFile::typeText ) )
    {
    #ifdef _DEBUG
      afxDump << "Unable to open file" << "\n";
    #endif
    exit( 1 );
    }
    strcpy( strBuff , m_encryptionKey );
    f1.WriteString( strBuff );
    f1.Close();

    piServer->Release();

}
```

2. Activate ActiveX Control Pad and enter the ASP source code in Listing 6-14. Save the file as `ASPHT0606.ASP` and move it to the `ASPEXEC` directory.

Listing 6-14 ASPHT0606.ASP source code

```
<%@ LANGUAGE = VBScript %>
<%
EncryptionString = Request.Form("Text1")
if EncryptionString <> "" then
  StringToMessWith = Request.Form("Text2")
  Set objCrypto = Server.CreateObject("aspencrypt.Encryptor")
  objCrypto.EncryptionKey = EncryptionString
  Application("EncryptKey") = EncryptionString
  EncryptedString = objCrypto.EncryptFromForm
  if Request.Form("Text3") <> "" then
    DecryptedString = objCrypto.DecryptFromForm
  else
    DecryptedString = objCrypto.DecryptTheString( EncryptedString )
  end if
else
  EncryptionString = Application("EncryptKey")
  EncryptedString = ""
```

continued on next page

continued from previous page

```
  DecryptedString = ""
end if
objCrypto.ReleaseContext
Set objCrypto = Nothing
%>
<HTML>
<HEAD>
<TITLE>Active Server Pages How To Chapter Six How To Six</TITLE>
</HEAD>
<BODY>
<FORM NAME="Form1" ACTION="aspht0606.asp" METHOD="POST" TARGET="_top">
<TABLE CELLPADDING=5 CELLSPACING=5 WIDTH=600 BORDER=5 ALIGN="CENTER"
VALIGN="MIDDLE" BGCOLOR="#008080">
<CAPTION>Welcome To The ASP How To Encryption Demo!</CAPTION>

<TR>
<TD ALIGN="CENTER" VALIGN="MIDDLE" BGCOLOR="#008080">Encryption Key
</TD>
<TD ALIGN="CENTER" VALIGN="MIDDLE" BGCOLOR="#008080">String To Encrypt
</TD>
<TD ALIGN="CENTER" VALIGN="MIDDLE" BGCOLOR="#008080">Encrypted String
</TD>
<TD ALIGN="CENTER" VALIGN="MIDDLE" BGCOLOR="#008080">Decrypted String
</TD>
</TR>
<TR>
<TD ALIGN="CENTER" VALIGN="MIDDLE" BGCOLOR="#008080">
<INPUT TYPE=Text NAME="Text1" VALUE="<%= EncryptionString %>">
</TD>
<TD ALIGN="CENTER" VALIGN="MIDDLE" BGCOLOR="#008080">
<INPUT TYPE=Text NAME="Text2" VALUE="<%= StringToMessWith %>">
</TD>
<TD ALIGN="CENTER" VALIGN="MIDDLE" BGCOLOR="#008080">
<INPUT TYPE=Text NAME="Text3" VALUE="<%= EncryptedString %>">
</TD>
<TD ALIGN="CENTER" VALIGN="MIDDLE" BGCOLOR="#008080">
<INPUT TYPE=Text NAME="Text4" VALUE="<%= DecryptedString %>">
</TD>
</TR>
<TR>
<TD COLSPAN=4 ALIGN="CENTER" VALIGN="MIDDLE" BGCOLOR="#008080">
<INPUT TYPE=Submit NAME="Submit1" VALUE="Encryption Demo!">
</TD>
</TR>
</TABLE>
</FORM>
</BODY>
</HTML>
```

3. Activate Internet Explorer. In the address field, type in `HTTP://DEFAULT/ASPEXEC/ASPHT0606.ASP` and press Return. The display behaves identically to before. Close IE and bring up the regular explorer and examine your `ASPEXEC` directory. As shown in Figure 6-18, the `ENCRYPTOR.KEY` file now resides there rather than in the `C:\WINDOWS\` directory. The `IServer` interface is now part of your ASP arsenal; you can use it with ASP components to obtain the `MapPath` local directory.

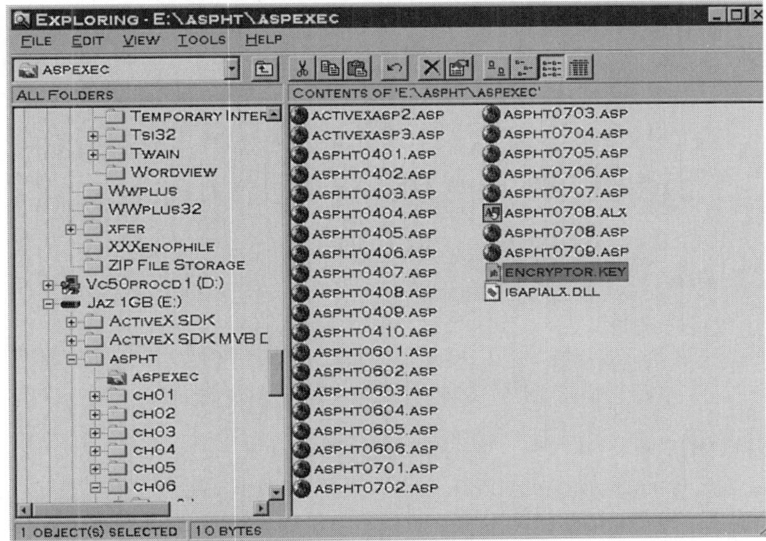

Figure 6-18 Locally saved copy of ENCRYPTOR.KEY due to server map path

How It Works

The `IServer` interface is obtained in the same way as the other `IScriptingContext` interfaces:

```
IServer* piServer = NULL;
hr = piContext->get_Server( &piServer );
```

Once the `IServer` interface has been obtained, its `MapPath` method can then be called. Unlike other methods, `MapPath` takes `BSTR` string pointers rather than variants;

```
BSTR* strPath;

hr = piServer->MapPath( SysAllocString(L"/ASPEXEC") , strPath );

strcpy( FileName , LPCSTR( &strPath ));
```

The `ASPEXEC` parameter is the default value for this How-To; in a real component it might have to be read from an application system variable.

Comments

The code on the CD is slightly different than the code here due to the `OnEndPage` bug.

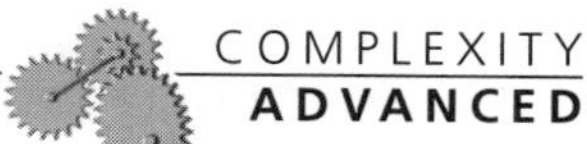

6.7 How do I... Interact with the ASP Session object in an ASP component?

Problem

We need to keep hidden information about individual users during their sessions. Can the IScriptingContext interface provide my ASP component access to the Session object?

Technique

The ISessionObject interface is what you need! This How-To illustrates keeping the encryption key in a Session variable rather than an Application one, stored entirely via the ASP component. These steps create the application from scratch, but for your convenience the complete project is on the CD under CH06\HT07\.

Steps

1. Copy the files from the previous How-To into a new directory. Activate Visual C++ 5.0. Bring up ENCRYPTOR.CPP in the text editor and enter the boldfaced code in Listing 6-15 in the OnStartPage method. Save the project. Then build the DLL and run REGSVR32 to register it.

Listing 6-15 ENCRYPTOR.CPP SessionObject **interface source code**

```
void Encryptor::OnStartPage(LPUNKNOWN pUnk)
{
    ///////////////////////////////////////////////
    ///  IScriptingContext Section

    HRESULT hr;
    IScriptingContext *piContext;
    hr = pUnk->QueryInterface(IID_IScriptingContext , (void**)&piContext);

    ///////////////////////////////////////////////
    /// IServer MapPath modified encryption key save

    IServer* piServer = NULL;
    hr = piContext->get_Server( &piServer );

    char FileName[255];
    char strBuff[100];
    CStdioFile f1;
    BSTR* strPath;
```

```
    hr = piServer->MapPath( SysAllocString(L"/ASPEXEC") , strPath );

    strcpy( FileName , LPCSTR( &strPath ));
    strcat( FileName , "\\encryptor.key" );
    if( !f1.Open( FileName, CFile::modeRead | CFile::typeText ) )
    {
    #ifdef _DEBUG
      afxDump << "Unable to open file" << "\n";
    #endif
    exit( 1 );
    }
    f1.ReadString( strBuff , 100 );
    f1.Close();
    m_encryptionKey = strBuff;

    piServer->Release();

    ISessionObject* piSession = NULL;
    hr = piContext->get_Session( &piSession );
    VARIANT vtOut;
    VariantInit(&vtOut);
    V_VT(&vtOut) = VT_BSTR;
    V_BSTR(&vtOut) = m_encryptionKey.AllocSysString();
    hr = piSession->put_Value( OLESTR("EncryptKey"), vtOut );
    piSession->Release();
    m_ContextHolder = piContext;

}
```

2. Activate ActiveX Control Pad and enter the ASP source code in Listing 6-16. Save the file as `ASPHT0607.ASP` and move it to the `ASPEXEC` directory.

Listing 6-16 ASPHT0607.ASP source code

```
<%@ LANGUAGE = VBScript %>
<%
EncryptionString = Request.Form("Text1")
if EncryptionString <> "" then
  StringToMessWith = Request.Form("Text2")
  Set objCrypto = Server.CreateObject("aspencrypt.Encryptor")
  objCrypto.EncryptionKey = EncryptionString
  Session("EncryptKey") = EncryptionString
  EncryptedString = objCrypto.EncryptFromForm
  if Request.Form("Text3") <> "" then
    DecryptedString = objCrypto.DecryptFromForm
  else
    DecryptedString = objCrypto.DecryptTheString( EncryptedString )
  end if
else
  EncryptionString = Session("EncryptKey")
  EncryptedString = ""
  DecryptedString = ""
end if
objCrypto.ReleaseContext
Set objCrypto = Nothing
```

continued on next page

continued from previous page

```
%>
<HTML>
<HEAD>
<TITLE>Active Server Pages How To Chapter Six How To Seven</TITLE>
</HEAD>
<BODY>
<FORM NAME="Form1" ACTION="aspht0607.asp" METHOD="POST" TARGET="_top">
<TABLE CELLPADDING=5 CELLSPACING=5 WIDTH=600 BORDER=5 ALIGN="CENTER"
VALIGN="MIDDLE" BGCOLOR="#008080">
<CAPTION>Welcome To The ASP How To Encryption Demo!</CAPTION>

<TR>
<TD ALIGN="CENTER" VALIGN="MIDDLE" BGCOLOR="#008080">Encryption Key
</TD>
<TD ALIGN="CENTER" VALIGN="MIDDLE" BGCOLOR="#008080">String To Encrypt
</TD>
<TD ALIGN="CENTER" VALIGN="MIDDLE" BGCOLOR="#008080">Encrypted String
</TD>
<TD ALIGN="CENTER" VALIGN="MIDDLE" BGCOLOR="#008080">Decrypted String
</TD>
</TR>
<TR>
<TD ALIGN="CENTER" VALIGN="MIDDLE" BGCOLOR="#008080">
<INPUT TYPE=Text NAME="Text1" VALUE="<%= EncryptionString %>">
</TD>
<TD ALIGN="CENTER" VALIGN="MIDDLE" BGCOLOR="#008080">
<INPUT TYPE=Text NAME="Text2" VALUE="<%= StringToMessWith %>">
</TD>
<TD ALIGN="CENTER" VALIGN="MIDDLE" BGCOLOR="#008080">
<INPUT TYPE=Text NAME="Text3" VALUE="<%= EncryptedString %>">
</TD>
<TD ALIGN="CENTER" VALIGN="MIDDLE" BGCOLOR="#008080">
<INPUT TYPE=Text NAME="Text4" VALUE="<%= DecryptedString %>">
</TD>
</TR>
<TR>
<TD COLSPAN=4 ALIGN="CENTER" VALIGN="MIDDLE" BGCOLOR="#008080">
<INPUT TYPE=Submit NAME="Submit1" VALUE="Encryption Demo!">
</TD>
</TR>
</TABLE>
</FORM>
</BODY>
</HTML>
```

3. Activate Internet Explorer. In the address field, type in `HTTP://DEFAULT/ASPEXEC/ASPHT0607.ASP` and press Return. The display behaves identically to before, but now the encryption key value is stored in a `Session` object. You can now use the `ISessionObject` interface with ASP components to store information local to a session.

How It Works

The code changes are extremely straightforward, and are simple only because you've already done this with the **Application** object:

```
ISessionObject* piSession = NULL;
hr = piContext->get_Session( &piSession );
VARIANT vtOut;
VariantInit(&vtOut);
V_VT(&vtOut) = VT_BSTR;
V_BSTR(&vtOut) = m_encryptionKey.AllocSysString();
hr = piSession->put_Value( OLESTR("EncryptKey"), vtOut );
piSession->Release();
```

Each place **Application** appeared is now replaced by **Session**, and the behavior moves from the **Application** object to the **Session** object. *Voila*!

Comments

At this point, you should be feeling like this is old hat, and you're right! Once you've mastered the techniques of ASP **IScriptingContext** programming, using a new interface is just a matter of changing a few names; the behaviors are almost identical across the entire system.

COMPLEXITY
ADVANCED

6.8 How do I... Interact with cookies in an ASP component?

Problem

I need to use my ASP component to read and write cookie data internally in C++. Does the **IScriptingContext** interface support this?

Technique

The **IResponse** and **IRequest** interfaces both support a **get_Cookies** method. These methods return another pointer that is actually an **IRequestDictionary** interface, as used in How-To 6.5. In this case, however, **get_Item** returns cookies information. This How-To demonstrates writing the encryption key to a cookie rather than the **Session** object. These steps create the application from scratch, but for your convenience the complete project is on the CD under CH06\HT08\.

Steps

1. Copy the files from the previous How-To into a new directory. Activate Visual C++ 5.0. Bring up `ENCRYPTOR.CPP` in the text editor and enter the boldfaced code in Listing 6-17 in the `OnStartPage` method. Save the project. Then build the DLL and run `REGSVR32` to register it.

Listing 6-17 `ENCRYPTOR.CPP` `SessionObject` interface source code

```
void Encryptor::OnStartPage(LPUNKNOWN pUnk)
{
    ///////////////////////////////////////////////
    ///  IScriptingContext Section

    HRESULT hr;
    IScriptingContext *piContext;
    hr = pUnk->QueryInterface(IID_IScriptingContext , (void**)&piContext);
    m_ContextHolder = piContext;

    ///////////////////////////////////////////////
    /// IServer MapPath modified encryption key save

    IServer* piServer = NULL;
    hr = piContext->get_Server( &piServer );
    char FileName[255];
    char strBuff[100];
    CStdioFile f1;
    BSTR* strPath;
    hr = piServer->MapPath( SysAllocString(L"/ASPEXEC") , strPath );
    strcpy( FileName , LPCSTR( &strPath ));
    strcat( FileName , "\\encryptor.key" );
    if( !f1.Open( FileName, CFile::modeRead ¦ CFile::typeText ) )
    {
    #ifdef _DEBUG
      afxDump << "Unable to open file" << "\n";
    #endif
    exit( 1 );
    }
    f1.ReadString( strBuff , 100 );
    f1.Close();
    m_encryptionKey = strBuff;
    piServer->Release();

    IResponse* piResponse = NULL;
    hr = m_ContextHolder->get_Response( &piResponse );
    IRequestDictionary* piRequestDictionary = NULL;
    hr = piResponse->get_Cookies( &piRequestDictionary );

    VARIANT vtFormIn2;
    VARIANT vtFormIn;
    VariantInit(&vtFormIn2);
    VariantInit(&vtFormIn);

    V_VT(&vtFormIn) = VT_BSTR;
    V_VT(&vtFormIn2) = VT_BSTR;
```

```
    V_BSTR(&vtFormIn) = SysAllocString(L"EncryptKey");
    V_BSTR(&vtFormIn2) = m_encryptionKey.AllocSysString();

    hr = piRequestDictionary->get_Item( vtFormIn, &vtFormIn2 );
    piRequestDictionary->Release();
    piResponse->Release();
}
```

2. Activate ActiveX Control Pad and enter the ASP source code in Listing 6-18. Save the file as ASPHT0608.ASP and move it to the ASPEXEC directory.

Listing 6-18 ASPHT0608.ASP source code

```
<%@ LANGUAGE = VBScript %>
<%
EncryptionString = Request.Form("Text1")
if EncryptionString <> "" then
  StringToMessWith = Request.Form("Text2")
  Set objCrypto = Server.CreateObject("aspencrypt.Encryptor")
  objCrypto.EncryptionKey = EncryptionString
  EncryptedString = objCrypto.EncryptFromForm
  if Request.Form("Text3") <> "" then
    DecryptedString = objCrypto.DecryptFromForm
  else
    DecryptedString = objCrypto.DecryptTheString( EncryptedString )
  end if
else
  if Request.Cookies("EncryptKey") = "" then
    EncryptionString = "defaultkey"
  else
   EncryptionString = Request.Cookies("EncryptKey")
  end if
  EncryptedString = ""
  DecryptedString = ""
end if
objCrypto.ReleaseContext
Set objCrypto = Nothing
%>
<HTML>
<HEAD>
<TITLE>Active Server Pages How To Chapter Six How To Eight</TITLE>
</HEAD>
<BODY>
<FORM NAME="Form1" ACTION="aspht0608.asp" METHOD="POST" TARGET="_top">
<TABLE CELLPADDING=5 CELLSPACING=5 WIDTH=600 BORDER=5 ALIGN="CENTER"
VALIGN="MIDDLE" BGCOLOR="#008080">
<CAPTION>Welcome To The ASP How To Encryption Demo!</CAPTION>

<TR>
<TD ALIGN="CENTER" VALIGN="MIDDLE" BGCOLOR="#008080">Encryption Key
</TD>
<TD ALIGN="CENTER" VALIGN="MIDDLE" BGCOLOR="#008080">String To Encrypt
</TD>
<TD ALIGN="CENTER" VALIGN="MIDDLE" BGCOLOR="#008080">Encrypted String
</TD>
<TD ALIGN="CENTER" VALIGN="MIDDLE" BGCOLOR="#008080">Decrypted String
```

continued on next page

continued from previous page

```
</TD>
</TR>
<TR>
<TD ALIGN="CENTER" VALIGN="MIDDLE" BGCOLOR="#008080">
<INPUT TYPE=Text NAME="Text1" VALUE="<%= EncryptionString %>">
</TD>
<TD ALIGN="CENTER" VALIGN="MIDDLE" BGCOLOR="#008080">
<INPUT TYPE=Text NAME="Text2" VALUE="<%= StringToMessWith %>">
</TD>
<TD ALIGN="CENTER" VALIGN="MIDDLE" BGCOLOR="#008080">
<INPUT TYPE=Text NAME="Text3" VALUE="<%= EncryptedString %>">
</TD>
<TD ALIGN="CENTER" VALIGN="MIDDLE" BGCOLOR="#008080">
<INPUT TYPE=Text NAME="Text4" VALUE="<%= DecryptedString %>">
</TD>
</TR>
<TR>
<TD COLSPAN=4 ALIGN="CENTER" VALIGN="MIDDLE" BGCOLOR="#008080">
<INPUT TYPE=Submit NAME="Submit1" VALUE="Encryption Demo!">
</TD>
</TR>
</TABLE>
</FORM>
</BODY>
</HTML>
```

3. Activate Internet Explorer. In the address field, type in `HTTP://DEFAULT/ASPEXEC/ASPHT0608.ASP` and press Return. The display behaves identically to before, but now the encryption key value is stored in a cookie. You have now mastered using the **IResponse** and **IRequestDictionary** interfaces with ASP components to store information in cookies.

How It Works

The code is almost boilerplate by now:

```
IResponse* piResponse = NULL;
hr = m_ContextHolder->get_Response( &piResponse );
IRequestDictionary* piRequestDictionary = NULL;
hr = piResponse->get_Cookies( &piRequestDictionary );

VARIANT vtFormIn2;
VARIANT vtFormIn;
VariantInit(&vtFormIn2);
VariantInit(&vtFormIn);

V_VT(&vtFormIn) = VT_BSTR;
V_VT(&vtFormIn2) = VT_BSTR;
V_BSTR(&vtFormIn) = SysAllocString(L"EncryptKey");
V_BSTR(&vtFormIn2) = m_encryptionKey.AllocSysString();

hr = piRequestDictionary->get_Item( vtFormIn, &vtFormIn2 );
piRequestDictionary->Release();
piResponse->Release();
```

The critical differences here are the use of the `get_Cookies` method to return an `IRequestDictionary` object linked to the cookies collection and the need to send in two strings rather than send one and get one back. Other than that, this is standard ASP `IScriptingContext` code.

Comments

You can also use `QueryInterface` on the `IRequestDictionary` interface to obtain the `IReadCookies` and `IWriteCookies` interfaces. See the ASP documentation for more information on these very useful interfaces.

AXC-ASPS

6.9 How do I... Use a custom ASP component with an ActiveX control?

Problem

We'd like to send the output from our ASP component directly to an ActiveX control. Can an ASP component do this?

Technique

Yes, it can! The key is remembering that the output from an ASP component is still text, and that's what ActiveX needs! This How-To illustrates adding an ActiveX control to display the encrypted and decrypted strings along with the normal table interface. The directions here create the project from scratch, but for your convenience a copy of the HTML file is on the CD under `\CH06\HT09\`.

Steps

1. Activate Notepad or some other simple text editor (Notepad is reported to be known at Microsoft these days as Visual Notepad++). Enter the HTML code in Listing 6-19 and save it as `ASPHT0609.ASP`. Make sure you move it to the directory you aliased as `ASPEXEC` for use in executing ASP scripts.

Listing 6-19 ASPHT0609.ASP source code

```
</SCRIPT>
<%@ LANGUAGE = VBScript %>
<%
EncryptionString = Request.Form("Text1")
if EncryptionString <> "" then
```

continued on next page

continued from previous page

```
  StringToMessWith = Request.Form("Text2")
  Set objCrypto = Server.CreateObject("aspencrypt.Encryptor")
  objCrypto.EncryptionKey = EncryptionString
  EncryptedString = objCrypto.EncryptFromForm
  if Request.Form("Text3") <> "" then
    DecryptedString = objCrypto.DecryptFromForm
  else
    DecryptedString = objCrypto.DecryptTheString( EncryptedString )
  end if
else
  if Request.Cookies("EncryptKey") = "" then
    EncryptionString = "defaultkey"
  else
   EncryptionString = Request.Cookies("EncryptKey")
  end if
  EncryptedString = ""
  DecryptedString = ""
end if
objCrypto.ReleaseContext
Set objCrypto = Nothing
%>
<HTML>
<HEAD>
<TITLE>Active Server Pages How To Chapter Six How To Nine</TITLE>
</HEAD>
<BODY>
<FORM NAME="Form1" ACTION="aspht0609.asp" METHOD="POST" TARGET="_top">
<TABLE CELLPADDING=5 CELLSPACING=5 WIDTH=600 BORDER=5 ALIGN="CENTER"
VALIGN="MIDDLE" BGCOLOR="#008080">
<CAPTION>Welcome To The ASP How To Encryption Demo!</CAPTION>

<TR>
<TD ALIGN="CENTER" VALIGN="MIDDLE" BGCOLOR="#008080">Encryption Key
</TD>
<TD ALIGN="CENTER" VALIGN="MIDDLE" BGCOLOR="#008080">String To Encrypt
</TD>
<TD ALIGN="CENTER" VALIGN="MIDDLE" BGCOLOR="#008080">Encrypted String
</TD>
<TD ALIGN="CENTER" VALIGN="MIDDLE" BGCOLOR="#008080">Decrypted String
</TD>
</TR>
<TR>
<TD ALIGN="CENTER" VALIGN="MIDDLE" BGCOLOR="#008080">
<INPUT TYPE=Text NAME="Text1" VALUE="<%= EncryptionString %>">
</TD>
<TD ALIGN="CENTER" VALIGN="MIDDLE" BGCOLOR="#008080">
<INPUT TYPE=Text NAME="Text2" VALUE="<%= StringToMessWith %>">
</TD>
<TD ALIGN="CENTER" VALIGN="MIDDLE" BGCOLOR="#008080">
<INPUT TYPE=Text NAME="Text3" VALUE="<%= EncryptedString %>">
</TD>
<TD ALIGN="CENTER" VALIGN="MIDDLE" BGCOLOR="#008080">
<INPUT TYPE=Text NAME="Text4" VALUE="<%= DecryptedString %>">
</TD>
</TR>
<TR>
<TD COLSPAN = 2 ALIGN="CENTER" VALIGN="MIDDLE" BGCOLOR="#008080">
```

```
<OBJECT ID="IeLabel1" WIDTH=489 HEIGHT=39
 CLASSID="CLSID:99B42120-6EC7-11CF-A6C7-00AA00A47DD2">
    <PARAM NAME="_ExtentX" VALUE="12938">
    <PARAM NAME="_ExtentY" VALUE="1005">
    <PARAM NAME="Caption" VALUE="<%= EncryptedString %>">
    <PARAM NAME="Angle" VALUE="0">
    <PARAM NAME="Alignment" VALUE="4">
    <PARAM NAME="Mode" VALUE="1">
    <PARAM NAME="FillStyle" VALUE="0">
    <PARAM NAME="FillStyle" VALUE="0">
    <PARAM NAME="ForeColor" VALUE="#000000">
    <PARAM NAME="BackColor" VALUE="#D8C0A0">
    <PARAM NAME="FontName" VALUE="Arial">
    <PARAM NAME="FontSize" VALUE="12">
    <PARAM NAME="FontItalic" VALUE="0">
    <PARAM NAME="FontBold" VALUE="1">
    <PARAM NAME="FontUnderline" VALUE="0">
    <PARAM NAME="FontStrikeout" VALUE="0">
    <PARAM NAME="TopPoints" VALUE="0">
    <PARAM NAME="BotPoints" VALUE="0">
</OBJECT>

</TD>
<TD COLSPAN = 2 ALIGN="CENTER" VALIGN="MIDDLE" BGCOLOR="#008080">

<OBJECT ID="IeLabel2" WIDTH=489 HEIGHT=39
 CLASSID="CLSID:99B42120-6EC7-11CF-A6C7-00AA00A47DD2">
    <PARAM NAME="_ExtentX" VALUE="12938">
    <PARAM NAME="_ExtentY" VALUE="1005">
    <PARAM NAME="Caption" VALUE="<%= DecryptedString %>">
    <PARAM NAME="Angle" VALUE="0">
    <PARAM NAME="Alignment" VALUE="4">
    <PARAM NAME="Mode" VALUE="1">
    <PARAM NAME="FillStyle" VALUE="0">
    <PARAM NAME="FillStyle" VALUE="0">
    <PARAM NAME="ForeColor" VALUE="#000000">
    <PARAM NAME="BackColor" VALUE="#D8C0A0">
    <PARAM NAME="FontName" VALUE="Arial">
    <PARAM NAME="FontSize" VALUE="12">
    <PARAM NAME="FontItalic" VALUE="0">
    <PARAM NAME="FontBold" VALUE="1">
    <PARAM NAME="FontUnderline" VALUE="0">
    <PARAM NAME="FontStrikeout" VALUE="0">
    <PARAM NAME="TopPoints" VALUE="0">
    <PARAM NAME="BotPoints" VALUE="0">
</OBJECT>

</TD>
</TR>
<TR>
<TD COLSPAN=4 ALIGN="CENTER" VALIGN="MIDDLE" BGCOLOR="#008080">
<INPUT TYPE=Submit NAME="Submit1" VALUE="Encryption Demo!">
</TD>
</TR>
</TABLE>
</FORM>
</BODY>
</HTML>
```

2. Activate Internet Explorer. In the address field, type in HTTP://DEFAULT/ASPEXEC/ASPHT0609.ASP and press Return. As shown in Figure 6-19, the ActiveX controls appear with the encrypted and decrypted data. You have now learned to use an ASP custom component with ActiveX controls.

How It Works

Notice the critical bit of code, highlighted below in boldface:

```
<OBJECT ID="IeLabel1" WIDTH=489 HEIGHT=39
 CLASSID="CLSID:99B42120-6EC7-11CF-A6C7-00AA00A47DD2">
    <PARAM NAME="_ExtentX" VALUE="12938">
    <PARAM NAME="_ExtentY" VALUE="1005">
    <PARAM NAME="Caption" VALUE="<%= EncryptedString %>">
    <PARAM NAME="Angle" VALUE="0">
    <PARAM NAME="Alignment" VALUE="4">
    <PARAM NAME="Mode" VALUE="1">
    <PARAM NAME="FillStyle" VALUE="0">
    <PARAM NAME="FillStyle" VALUE="0">
    <PARAM NAME="ForeColor" VALUE="#000000">
    <PARAM NAME="BackColor" VALUE="#D8C0A0">
    <PARAM NAME="FontName" VALUE="Arial">
    <PARAM NAME="FontSize" VALUE="12">
    <PARAM NAME="FontItalic" VALUE="0">
    <PARAM NAME="FontBold" VALUE="1">
    <PARAM NAME="FontUnderline" VALUE="0">
    <PARAM NAME="FontStrikeout" VALUE="0">
    <PARAM NAME="TopPoints" VALUE="0">
    <PARAM NAME="BotPoints" VALUE="0">
</OBJECT>

</TD>
```

The key to linking ASP components with ActiveX is to use their text-oriented output methods, either with `<%=` or directly in the case of `Response.Write` supporting methods (such as `EncodeToHTML`). The text they output can be directly sent to the browser and picked up by the created ActiveX controls, as is the case here.

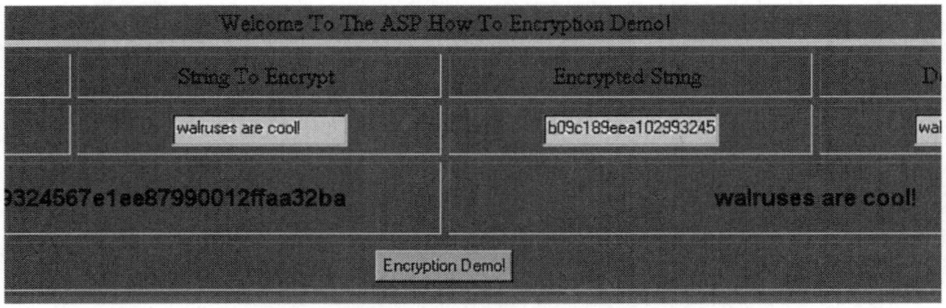

Figure 6-19 ASPHT0609.ASP in IE showing the ActiveX controls interacting with the ASP custom component

Comments

This may seem like a trivial How-To, but many people actually are stumped by how to do this sort of thing, because the two technologies are so radically different. A vital rule of thumb in the ActiveX world is: If you can't figure out how it works, send a string!

ADO-ASPS

COMPLEXITY
ADVANCED

6.10 How do I... Use a custom ASP component with ActiveX data objects?

Problem

My company needs to use information in a Microsoft Access database in response to customer requests on our Web site. Can ASP help us out with this?

Technique

The key to connecting HTML, ASP, and Access databases file is ActiveX data objects (ADO). This How-To demonstrates using an ODBC database to put information into an HTML table via an ASP script. Although the directions here create the project from scratch, the completed ASP files are on the CD under `\CH06\HT10\`.

Steps

1. For this How-To, you'll use one of the tutorial databases supplied with ASP. (If you have removed them, you need to reinstall the `ADVWORKS.MDB` file to use this How-To.) If you have already configured this database from How-To 4.10, you can skip this step. First, you need to connect the ODBC drivers for Microsoft Access to the database along with its alias. Open the control panel, then double-click on the 32-bit ODBC drivers icon. In the property pages dialog that appears, select the System DSN tab and click the Add button. In the Add dialog, enter `AWTutorial` for the datasource name, and in the database grouping, click the Select button; browse to the `AdventureWorks Tutorial` directory on your hard drive and select the `ADVWORKS.MDB` file. Figure 6-20 shows how your configuration should look when you are done. Click OK twice to accept your new settings.

2. Open ActiveX Control Pad and enter the program code in Listing 6-20. Save the file as `ASPHT0610.ASP`; then make sure to copy it to the directory on your hard drive that has ASP execute permissions.

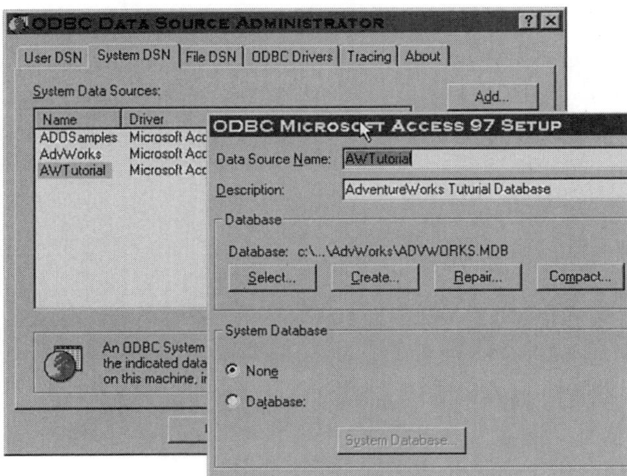

Figure 6-20 Setting the 32-bit ODBC drivers and alias for the Adventure Works demo database

Listing 6-20 `ASPHT0610.ASP` ASP script file

```
<%@ LANGUAGE = VBScript %>
<HTML>

<HEAD>
<TITLE>Active Server Pages Chapter Six How To Ten</TITLE>
</HEAD>
<BODY>
<TABLE WIDTH=600 BORDER=0>
<TR>
<TD COLSPAN=3>
<FONT SIZE=4 FACE="ARIAL NARROW" COLOR="#800000">Customer Listing</FONT>
</TD>
</TR>
<TD VALIGN=TOP ALIGN=LEFT COLSPAN=3><FONT SIZE=2>
<% Set OBJdbConnection = Server.CreateObject("ADODB.Connection")
OBJdbConnection.Open "AWTutorial"
SQLQuery = "SELECT * FROM Customers"
Set RSCustomerList = OBJdbConnection.Execute(SQLQuery) %>
<TABLE COLSPAN=8 CELLPADDING=5 BORDER=0>
<TR>
<TD ALIGN=CENTER BGCOLOR="#800000">
<FONT STYLE="ARIAL NARROW" COLOR="#ffffff" SIZE=1>Company Name</FONT>
</TD>
<TD ALIGN=CENTER BGCOLOR="#800000">
<FONT STYLE="ARIAL NARROW" COLOR="#ffffff" SIZE=1>Contact Name</FONT>
</TD>
<TD ALIGN=CENTER WIDTH=150 BGCOLOR="#800000">
<FONT STYLE="ARIAL NARROW" COLOR="#ffffff" SIZE=1>E-mail address</FONT>
</TD>
<TD ALIGN=CENTER BGCOLOR="#800000">
<FONT STYLE="ARIAL NARROW" COLOR="#ffffff" SIZE=1>City</FONT>
```

```
</TD>
<TD ALIGN=CENTER BGCOLOR="#800000">
<FONT STYLE="ARIAL NARROW" COLOR="#ffffff" SIZE=1>State/Province</FONT>
</TD>
</TR>
<% Do While Not RScustomerList.EOF %>
  <TR>
  <TD BGCOLOR="f7efde" ALIGN=CENTER>
    <FONT STYLE="ARIAL NARROW" SIZE=1>
      <%= RSCustomerList("CompanyName")%>
    </FONT></TD>
  <TD BGCOLOR="f7efde" ALIGN=CENTER>
    <FONT STYLE="ARIAL NARROW" SIZE=1>
      <%= RScustomerList("ContactLastName") & ", " %>
      <%= RScustomerList("ContactFirstName") %>
    </FONT></TD>
  <TD BGCOLOR="f7efde" ALIGN=CENTER>
    <FONT STYLE="ARIAL NARROW" SIZE=1>
    <A HREF="mailto:">
      <%= RScustomerList("ContactLastName")%>
    </A></FONT></TD>
  <TD BGCOLOR="f7efde" ALIGN=CENTER>
    <FONT STYLE="ARIAL NARROW" SIZE=1>
      <%= RScustomerList("City")%>
    </FONT></TD>
  <TD BGCOLOR="f7efde" ALIGN=CENTER>
    <FONT STYLE="ARIAL NARROW" SIZE=1>
      <%= RScustomerList("StateOrProvince")%>
    </FONT></TD>
  </TR>
<% RScustomerList.MoveNext
Loop %>
</TABLE>
</TD>
</TR>
</TABLE>
</BODY>
</HTML>
```

3. Activate Internet Explorer. In the address field, type in `HTTP://DEFAULT/ASPEXEC/ASPHT0610.ASP` and press Return. As shown in Figure 6-21, a table will be created using the information from the ODBC database. Congratulations! You have learned to use ASP to interact with ODBC databases using ADO.

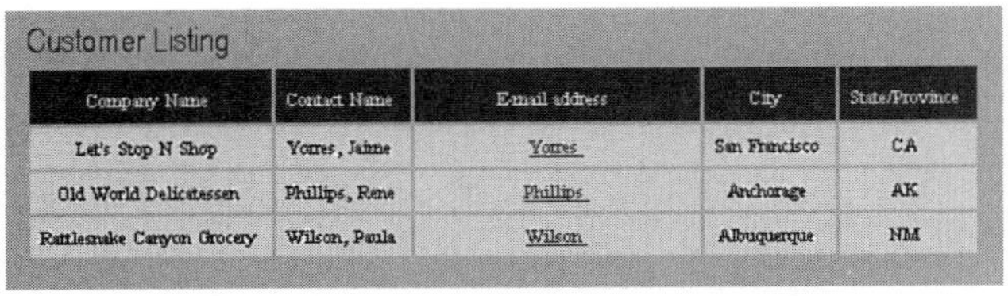

Customer Listing

Company Name	Contact Name	E-mail address	City	State/Province
Let's Stop N Shop	Yorres, Jaime	Yorres	San Francisco	CA
Old World Delicatessen	Phillips, Rene	Phillips	Anchorage	AK
Rattlesnake Canyon Grocery	Wilson, Paula	Wilson	Albuquerque	NM

Figure 6-21 ASPHT0610.ASP in IE showing the successful creation of the HTML table from the ADO database via ASP

How It Works

Aside from the usual mechanics of interspersing ASP scripts with HTML text, this How-To shows a key part of ASP functionality, the **ADODB** object:

```
<% Set OBJdbConnection = Server.CreateObject("ADODB.Connection")
OBJdbConnection.Open "AWTutorial"
SQLQuery = "SELECT * FROM Customers"
Set RSCustomerList = OBJdbConnection.Execute(SQLQuery) %>
```

The `Server` object is used here, as it is where the connection to the **ADODB** object is stored (via the **GLOBAL.ASA** file, which is discussed in much more detail in Chapter 5, "Intermediate ASP: Active Server Components"). Once the object is successfully created, it is told to open the database with the alias `AWTutorial` that you entered into your system in step 1. Finally, the last two statements create an SQL query and send it to the database, returning a `collection` object that holds the results of that query.

After having obtained the desired recordset, you use it to create the data for the HTML table:

```
<% Do While Not RScustomerList.EOF %>
  <TR>
  <TD BGCOLOR="f7efde" ALIGN=CENTER>
    <FONT STYLE="ARIAL NARROW" SIZE=1>
      <%= RSCustomerList("CompanyName")%>
    </FONT></TD>
  <TD BGCOLOR="f7efde" ALIGN=CENTER>
    <FONT STYLE="ARIAL NARROW" SIZE=1>
      <%= RScustomerList("ContactLastName") & ", " %>
      <%= RScustomerList("ContactFirstName") %>
    </FONT></TD>
  <TD BGCOLOR="f7efde" ALIGN=CENTER>
    <FONT STYLE="ARIAL NARROW" SIZE=1>
    <A HREF="mailto:">
      <%= RScustomerList("ContactLastName")%>
    </A></FONT></TD>
  <TD BGCOLOR="f7efde" ALIGN=CENTER>
    <FONT STYLE="ARIAL NARROW" SIZE=1>
      <%= RScustomerList("City")%>
    </FONT></TD>
  <TD BGCOLOR="f7efde" ALIGN=CENTER>
```

```
    <FONT STYLE="ARIAL NARROW" SIZE=1>
      <%= RScustomerList("StateOrProvince")%>
    </FONT></TD>
  </TR>
<% RScustomerList.MoveNext
Loop %>
```

The technique here is very simple: Output the values of fields of the `collection` object returned by the SQL query by sending them into it as parameters. (More on using collections with ASP in Chapter 5.) By using a loop that runs until the end of the collection (`RScustomerList.EOF`), you write all the data into the HTML table for clear display.

Comments

Despite the simplicity of the format, any type and complexity of database information can be displayed in this way, although more complex techniques are needed involving `BinaryWrite` (`BLOB` fields) for binary data.

CHAPTER 7

ACTIVEX DATA OBJECTS: OLE DB MADE EASY

7

ACTIVEX DATA OBJECTS: OLE DB MADE EASY

How do I...

- 7.1 Use ActiveX data objects on my Web page?
- 7.2 Make my ASP ADO Web page interactive?
- 7.3 Use an ASP component with my interactive ASP ADO page?
- 7.4 Allow user navigation in my ASP ADO Web page?
- 7.5 Allow user updates in my ASP ADO Web page?
- 7.6 Use an ActiveX control with my ASP ADO information?
- 7.7 Add client-side scripting to the ActiveX control on my ASP ADO page?
- 7.8 Use an HTML Layout control with client-side scripting on my ASP ADO page?

7.9 Invoke an ISAPI extension DLL on my ASP ADO page?

7.10 Use an ISAPI filter with my ASP ADO page?

One of the major weaknesses of the World Wide Web has been the lack of an easy-to-use database system that can generate HTML directly rather than going through complex Common Gateway Interface (CGI) processes. Active Server Pages (ASP) provides half the required capabilities to get around this problem (namely, a simple but powerful replacement for CGI), and ActiveX data objects (ADO) provide the other half. Microsoft's previous database encapsulations, data access objects (DAO) from the Jet system, and the distributed database system remote data objects (RDO) of the Visual Basic 4.0 Enterprise Edition, both contributed to the new ADO system, but ADO also draws heavily on the OLEDB Applications Programming Interface (API) (OLE for databases). It is possible to program the OLEDB API directly in Visual C++ 5.0 (full support is included), but most developers will be interested in using ADO instead, because it provides a complete, simple, and easy-to-use wrapper around the OLEDB API calls. Although many aspects of the system are not covered here due to lack of space, this chapter will provide detailed coverage of the following points.

7.1 Use ActiveX Data Objects on My Web Page

Want your data on the World Wide Web? This How-To shows you the way to create an ASP-driven HTML page that displays a table with the entire contents of an ODBC database.

7.2 Make My ASP ADO Web Page Interactive

Now that your users can see your data, what's next? Answer: Give them control! This How-To shows a simple but effective mechanism to allow users to specify which database record they want and have it returned via the self-referencing power of an ASP page.

7.3 Use an ASP Component with My Interactive ASP ADO Page

ASP components are incredibly powerful, and this is certainly true in the world of ADO! This How-To shows you precisely how to create a state-maintaining copy of the ADO recordset your users are displaying, making navigation much easier and more intuitive!

7.4 Allow User Navigation in My ASP ADO Web Page

Really powerful databases often require complex user interactions. ADO supports the concept of cursors, sophisticated display mechanisms for interacting with database recordsets. This How-To implements a dynamic cursor that permits forward and backward navigation through a database using the interactive ASP system developed in previous How-To's in this chapter.

7.5 Allow User Updates in My ASP ADO Web Page

The pinnacle of database utilization is to permit users to change data online! This How-To develops an updatable system using HTML forms and the `Update` method of the ADO recordset.

7.6 Use an ActiveX Control with My ASP ADO Information

At this point in the chapter, ADO has pretty much been maxed out; a number of sophisticated internal capabilities are still left to discuss, but they are advanced DBMS topics and beyond the scope of this book. But fear not! What is left is equally important: tying ADO and ASP into the ActiveX system! This How-To demonstrates adding a simple but effective ActiveX control to the database display from previous How-To's, and setting its properties using ASP and ADO.

7.7 Add Client-Side Scripting to the ActiveX Control on My ASP ADO Page

ASP is server-side scripting, but many times client-side scripting (CSS) is needed also. This How-To shows you the way to add CSS to the ADO, ASP, and ActiveX project from the previous How-To, allowing a sophisticated drop-down menu for user interaction.

7.8 Use an HTML Layout Control with Client-Side Scripting on My ASP ADO Page

Now for the good stuff. HTML Layout controls offer complete design control over the placement of ActiveX controls on a Web page. This How-To shows you exactly how to tie an HTML layout into the ASP/ADO system (which is not a trivial task, as you will see).

7.9 Invoke an ISAPI Extension DLL on My ASP ADO Page

ISAPI? What's ISAPI? Well, it stands for Internet Server API, and it is the big brother of ASP. Through ISAPI, you can perform the same tasks as in CGI and ASP but in a full C++ (or VB or Delphi) environment. This How-To shows all the steps to create an ISAPI extension Dynamic Link Library (DLL) that exports the HTML Layout control's ALX file used in the previous How-To, but does so as the result of an HTML `<SRC>` tag rather than ASP!

7.10 Use an ISAPI Filter with My ASP ADO Page

ISAPI filters are even more powerful than ISAPI extensions! This How-To shows you how to use one that checks all incoming ASP pages for ADO references and writes the queried database to a log file. It can easily be scaled up to become a powerful statistical data collector for Internet interactions.

7.1 How do I... Use ActiveX data objects on my Web page?

Problem

I need to make some of my company's database information available on our Web page. Do I have to go and spend thousands of dollars for a Web database product?

Technique

Nope! With either Internet Information Server (IIS) or Personal Web Server (PWS), you automatically get ODBC-compliant database technology, namely ActiveX data objects. This How-To shows you the way to access this amazing power from simple HTML. Although these directions create the project from scratch, the CD contains a completed file under `CH07\HT01\`.

> **NOTE**
>
> This and all the subsequent How-To's in this chapter assume you have already installed the ODBC database AWTutorial. If you have not, bring up the `ROADMAP.ASP` sample and follow its directions to make the sample database available on your system.

Steps

1. Activate ActiveX Control Pad. (If you have not done this before, bring up the URL `http://www.microsoft.com/workshop/author/cpad/` and download it, then run the self-extracting executable to install it.) Enter the code in Listing 7-1 and save the file as `ASPHT0701.ASP`.

Listing 7-1 ASPHT0701.ASP source code

```
<%@ LANGUAGE = VBScript %>
<HTML>

<HEAD>
<TITLE>Active Server Pages Chapter Seven How To One</TITLE>
</HEAD>
<BODY>
<% Set OBJdbConnection = Server.CreateObject("ADODB.Connection")
OBJdbConnection.Open "AWTutorial"
SQLQuery = "SELECT * FROM Customers"
Set RSCustomerList = OBJdbConnection.Execute(SQLQuery) %>
```

```
<TABLE WIDTH=600 COLSPAN=8 BORDER=5 CELLSPACING=5
CELLPADDING=5 ALIGN="CENTER" VALIGN="MIDDLE" BGCOLOR="Teal">
<TR>
<TD COLSPAN=5 ALIGN="CENTER">
Customer Listing
</TD>
</TR>
<TR>
<TD>
Company Name
</TD>
<TD>
Contact Name
</TD>
<TD>
E-mail address
</TD>
<TD>
City
</TD>
<TD>
State/Province
</TD>
</TR>
<% Do While Not RScustomerList.EOF %>
  <TR>
  <TD>
      <%= RSCustomerList("CompanyName")%>
  </TD>
  <TD>
      <%= RScustomerList("ContactLastName") & ", " %>
      <%= RScustomerList("ContactFirstName") %>
  </TD>
  <TD>
    <A HREF="mailto:">
      <%= RScustomerList("ContactLastName")%>
    </A></TD>
  <TD>
      <%= RScustomerList("City")%>
  </TD>
  <TD>
      <%= RScustomerList("StateOrProvince")%>
  </TD>
  </TR>
<% RScustomerList.MoveNext
Loop %>
</TD>
</TR>
</TABLE>
</BODY>
</HTML>
```

2. Activate Internet Explorer. In the address field, type in `HTTP://DEFAULT/ASPEXEC/ASPHT0701.ASP` and press Return. As shown in Figure 7-1, the resulting page will display the contents of the sample

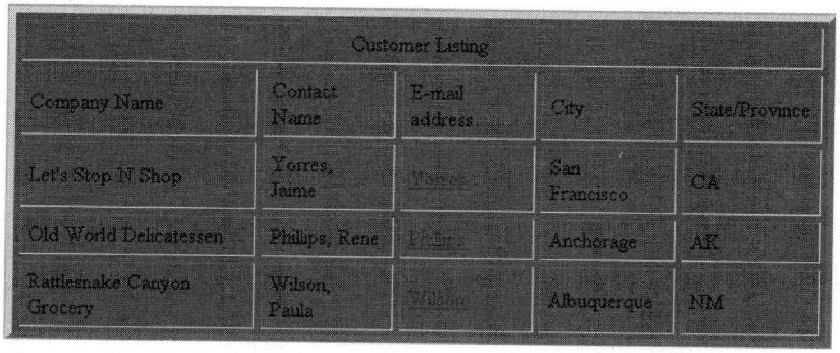

Customer Listing				
Company Name	Contact Name	E-mail address	City	State/Province
Let's Stop N Shop	Yorres, Jaime	Yorres	San Francisco	CA
Old World Delicatessen	Phillips, Rene	Phillips	Anchorage	AK
Rattlesnake Canyon Grocery	Wilson, Paula	Wilson	Albuquerque	NM

Figure 7-1 ASPHT0701.ASP in IE showing an ODBC database displayed in HTML

AWTutorial database in the HTML. Congratulations! You have learned to use ADO on the World Wide Web.

How It Works

First, the entire system is based on this simple line of code:

```
<% Set OBJdbConnection = Server.CreateObject("ADODB.Connection")
```

The ADODB object encapsulates the entire ADO functionality for ASP. There are complete details on it in the ASP documentation, as well as in the Visual C++ 5.0 help system. This and subsequent How-To's won't attempt to cover all the functionality of this object, but will instead aim for giving you a practical feel for using it.

After you create an ADO, you need to link it to a database. That's done with this statement:

```
OBJdbConnection.Open "AWTutorial"
```

The `Open` method of the `Connection` object is the central way to connect into a database with ADO, but there are others. The parameter of the method is the alias you give the database to the ODBC system, as explained in the note above.

Next, a recordset has to be created to allow you to get at the underlying data. These statements do that:

```
SQLQuery = "SELECT * FROM Customers"
Set RSCustomerList = OBJdbConnection.Execute(SQLQuery) %>
```

The `SQLQuery` variable holds a text string that contains, appropriately enough, an SQL syntax query statement. It becomes the parameter to the `Execute` method, which returns a pointer to a `RecordSet` object. This recordset will then be used to get the database information in the following loop:

```
<% Do While Not RScustomerList.EOF %>
  <TR>
```

```
  <TD>
      <%= RSCustomerList("CompanyName")%>
  </TD>
  <TD>
      <%= RScustomerList("ContactLastName") & ", " %>
      <%= RScustomerList("ContactFirstName") %>
  </TD>
  <TD>
    <A HREF="mailto:">
      <%= RScustomerList("ContactLastName")%>
    </A></TD>
  <TD>
      <%= RScustomerList("City")%>
  </TD>
  <TD>
      <%= RScustomerList("StateOrProvince")%>
  </TD>
  </TR>
<% RScustomerList.MoveNext
Loop %>
```

Notice the standard database logic of testing for `EOF` and incrementing with a `MoveNext` statement. There are more sophisticated ways to move around in a database, of course, but this is the easiest, and it works quite nicely. Note that the actual fields are acquired using the collection syntax from Chapter 5, "Intermediate ASP: Active Server Components." Also notice that the data is made part of the HTML with the `<%= %>` constructs; always remember this or the whole exercise will fly right past your viewers into the WWW ether!

Comments

To recap, you access the ODBC database by creating an ADO, opening a database alias, executing an SQL query or similar method, and then obtaining actual data via direct references to the field names using collection syntax. Simple and effective, but it's only the beginning!

7.2 How do I... Make my ASP ADO Web page interactive?

Problem

All right, my users can see my data now and I haven't mortgaged my eyeteeth to do it—great! Now they want to be able to decide which record to display directly from the HTML page. Am I sunk without a trace here?

Technique

You're riding high, thanks to the self-referencing capabilities of ASP! This How-To will add simple but effective interactivity to the demo from How-To 7.1, and in the process exploit another major ASP advantage. Although these directions create the project from scratch, the CD contains a completed file under **CH07\HT02**.

Steps

1. Activate ActiveX Control Pad and reload the **ASPHT0701.ASP** file. Modify the code so it is identical to the code in Listing 7-2. Save it as ASPHT0702.ASP.

Listing 7-2 ASPHT0702.ASP source code

```
<%@ LANGUAGE = VBScript %>
<HTML>
<HEAD>
<TITLE>Active Server Pages Chapter Seven How To Two</TITLE>
</HEAD>
<BODY>
<% Set OBJdbConnection = Server.CreateObject("ADODB.Connection")
OBJdbConnection.Open "AWTutorial"
SQLQuery = "SELECT * FROM Customers"
Set RSCustomerList = OBJdbConnection.Execute(SQLQuery)
dim HoldNumber
if Request.Form("Text1")="" then
  HoldNumber = 0
else
  HoldNumber = Cint(Request.Form("Text1"))
  if HoldNumber < 0 then HoldNumber = 0
end if
dim counter1
for counter1 = 0 to HoldNumber
  on error resume next
  RSCustomerList.MoveNext
next
%>
    <FORM NAME="Form1" ACTION="http://default/aspexec/aspht0702.asp⇐
    "METHOD="POST" TARGET="_top">
<TABLE WIDTH=600 COLSPAN=8 BORDER=5 CELLSPACING=5
CELLPADDING=5 ALIGN="CENTER" VALIGN="MIDDLE" BGCOLOR="Teal">
<TR>
<TD COLSPAN=3 ALIGN="CENTER">
Customer Listing
</TD>
<TD>
<INPUT Type="Text" NAME="Text1" VALUE="<%=HoldNumber%>">
</TD>
<INPUT Type="Submit" NAME="Submit1" Value ="Get Record Number">
</TR>
```

```
<TR>
<TD>
Company Name
</TD>
<TD>
Contact Name
</TD>
<TD>
E-mail address
</TD>
<TD>
City
</TD>
<TD>
State/Province
</TD>
</TR>
  <TR>
  <TD>
      <%= RSCustomerList("CompanyName")%>
  </TD>
  <TD>
      <%= RScustomerList("ContactLastName") & ", " %>
      <%= RScustomerList("ContactFirstName") %>
  </TD>
  <TD>
    <A HREF="mailto:">
      <%= RScustomerList("ContactLastName")%>
    </A></TD>
  <TD>
      <%= RScustomerList("City")%>
  </TD>
  <TD>
      <%= RScustomerList("StateOrProvince")%>
  </TD>
  </TR>
</TD>
</TR>
</TABLE>
    </FORM>
</BODY>
</HTML>
```

2. Activate Internet Explorer. In the address field, type in **HTTP://DEFAULT/ASPEXEC/ASPHT0702.ASP** and press Return. When a database display appears, enter **2** in the Text control and press the Submit button. The page will refresh, and, as shown in Figure 7-2, the return page will show the new record. You have learned to use ADO interactively with the self-referencing capabilities of ASP.

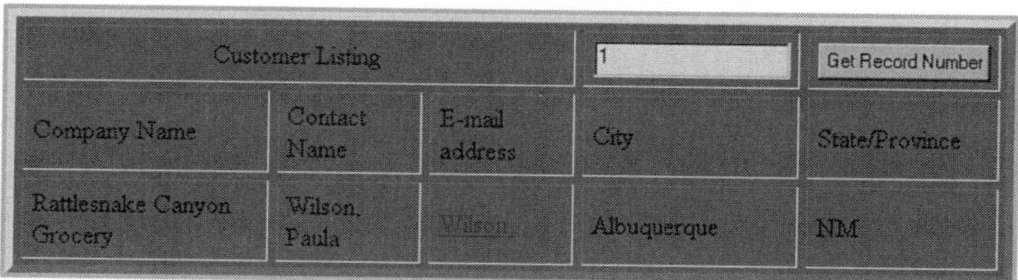

Figure 7-2 ASPHT0702.ASP in IE showing a new database record called up via self-referencing ASP scripting

How It Works

Notice these new lines of ASP code:

```
dim HoldNumber
if Request.Form("Text1")="" then
  HoldNumber = 0
else
  HoldNumber = Cint(Request.Form("Text1"))
  if HoldNumber < 0 then HoldNumber = 0
end if
```

The `Request.Form` call allows determining whether this is the first time the page is hit or if it is referencing itself in a form submission call. In the former case, the form variable will be empty and the `HoldNumber` variable will be set to `0`, the starting record. Otherwise, the form variable will return a value and be set to either that value or `0` (if the user accidentally entered a negative number).

Now notice how the value is put to use:

```
dim counter1
for counter1 = 0 to HoldNumber
  on error resume next
  RSCustomerList.MoveNext
next
```

This is brute force, and more sophisticated databases would use ADO properties such as `AbsolutePage` and `RecordCount` for this task and its error trapping; unfortunately, the simple test database doesn't support these features, so you have to get your fingernails dirty. Isn't that so like the real world?

Now take a look at this <FORM> tag:

```
<FORM NAME="Form1" ACTION="http://default/aspexec/aspht0702.asp" METHOD="POST"⇐
TARGET="_top">
```

It is calling itself! As shown in How-To 7.1, ASP can take advantage of the "stateless" nature of HTTP interactions to perform smooth and powerful self-referencing tasks that would tie other systems in knots. (This is known in the computer science jargon as *recursion*; it is the main reason older programmers have little or no hair, having pulled it out trying to debug recursive programs...)

Of course, we could have written a separate ASP file to handle this chore, but this way is more elegant.

Comments

There should be an error trapping statement around the code to convert the `Text1` string into an integer, in case the user tries to access record `Fred`.

7.3 How do I... Use an ASP component with my interactive ASP ADO page?

Problem

My database is a little too sophisticated for this "enter a record number" technique. Is there some way I can keep track of where my users are in the database using ADO itself?

Technique

Thanks to the power of ASP components, you can! This How-To uses the potent `Session` object to make a copy of the working recordset that remains available from page to page. Although these directions create the project from scratch, the CD contains a completed file under `CH07\HT03\`.

Steps

1. Activate ActiveX Control Pad and reload the `ASPHT0702.ASP` file. Modify the code so it is identical to the code in Listing 7-3. Save it as `ASPHT0703.ASP`.

Listing 7-3 ASPHT0703.ASP source code

```
<%@ LANGUAGE = VBScript %>
<HTML>
<HEAD>
<TITLE>Active Server Pages Chapter Seven How To Three</TITLE>
</HEAD>
<BODY>
<% if IsObject(Session("objRecordSet")) then
     set objRecordSet = Session("objRecordSet")
   else
     Set objConnection = Server.CreateObject("ADODB.Connection")
     objConnection.Open "AWTutorial"
```

continued on next page

continued from previous page

```
      SQLQuery = "SELECT * FROM Customers"
      Set objRecordSet = objConnection.Execute( SQLQuery )
      Set Session("objRecordSet") = objRecordSet
    end if
    on error resume next
    if not objRecordSet.EOF then
      objRecordSet.MoveNext
    else
       objRecordSet.MoveFirst
    end if
%>
     <FORM NAME="Form1" ACTION="http://default/aspexec/aspht0703.asp"⇐
      METHOD="POST" TARGET="_top">
<TABLE WIDTH=600 COLSPAN=8 BORDER=5 CELLSPACING=5
CELLPADDING=5 ALIGN="CENTER" VALIGN="MIDDLE" BGCOLOR="Teal">
<TR>
<TD COLSPAN=4 ALIGN="CENTER">
Customer Listing
</TD>
<INPUT Type="Submit" NAME="Submit1" Value ="Get Next Record">
</TR>
<TR>
<TD>
Company Name
</TD>
<TD>
Contact Name
</TD>
<TD>
E-mail address
</TD>
<TD>
City
</TD>
<TD>
State/Province
</TD>
</TR>
  <TR>
  <TD>
      <%= objRecordSet("CompanyName")%>
  </TD>
  <TD>
      <%= objRecordSet("ContactLastName") & ", " %>
      <%= objRecordSet("ContactFirstName") %>
  </TD>
  <TD>
    <A HREF="mailto:">
      <%= objRecordSet("ContactLastName")%>
    </A></TD>
  <TD>
      <%= objRecordSet("City")%>
  </TD>
  <TD>
      <%= objRecordSet("StateOrProvince")%>
```

```
  </TD>
  </TR>
</TD>
</TR>
</TABLE>
    </FORM>
</BODY>
</HTML>
```

2. Activate Internet Explorer and bring up **ASPHT0703.ASP**. Press the Get Next Record button several times, and each time the correct display will appear until the end of the data is reached, as shown in Figure 7-3. You have learned to use ASP components to keep ADO databases alive between user pages.

How It Works

The most important lines of code in the whole shebang are these:

```
<% if IsObject(Session("objRecordSet")) then
     set objRecordSet = Session("objRecordSet")
   else
```

The key test is whether the Session component has an object in its collection named `objRecordSet`. If so, the object is retrieved and put into the new copy of `objRecordSet`. If not, these lines of code take over:

```
else
     Set objConnection = Server.CreateObject("ADODB.Connection")
     objConnection.Open "AWTutorial"
     SQLQuery = "SELECT * FROM Customers"
     Set objRecordSet = objConnection.Execute( SQLQuery )
     Set Session("objRecordSet") = objRecordSet
   end if
```

They, of course, are the standard recordset creation code from before, but now they make the call to store a copy of the recordset into the Session component's collection. This simple bit of functionality then allows removal of all the clumsy form code, replacing it with this much more sophisticated solution:

Customer Listing				Get Next Record
Company Name	Contact Name	E-mail address	City	State/Province
Rattlesnake Canyon Grocery	Wilson, Paula	Wilson	Albuquerque	NM

Figure 7-3 ASPHT0703.ASP in IE showing the new ASP-component-driven interactive database

```
on error resume next
   if not objRecordSet.EOF then
     objRecordSet.MoveNext
   else
      objRecordSet.MoveFirst
   end if
```

Now the user can simply press one button and move to the end of the database or back to the beginning once the end is reached.

Comments

If you are concerned about the capability to move in either direction, stay tuned!

COMPLEXITY
INTERMEDIATE

7.4 How do I… Allow user navigation in my ASP ADO Web page?

Problem

Okay, I'm scrolling forward just fine here in my ASP ADO database system. But when I try to go backward, nothing happens. What am I missing here?

Technique

The problem is that full-blown backward and forward navigation in a database, particularly a complicated one, is not a trivial task. To conserve system resources, therefore, the concept of a cursor was invented. This How-To shows you how to modify the ongoing project to add a dynamic cursor that will allow navigation in the user database both forward and backward. Although these directions create the project from scratch, the CD contains a completed file under `CH04\HT04\`.

Steps

1. Activate ActiveX Control Pad and reload the `ASPHT0703.ASP` file. Modify the code so it is identical to the code in Listing 7-4. Save it as `ASPHT0704.ASP`.

Listing 7-4 ASPHT0704.ASP source code

```
<%@ LANGUAGE = VBScript %>
<HTML>
<HEAD>
<TITLE>Active Server Pages Chapter Seven How To Four</TITLE>
</HEAD>
```

```
<BODY>
<% if IsObject(Session("objRecordSet")) then
     set objRecordSet = Session("objRecordSet")
   else
     Set objConnection = Server.CreateObject("ADODB.Connection")
     objConnection.Open "AWTutorial"
     SQLQuery = "SELECT * FROM Customers"
     Set objRecordSet = objConnection.Execute( SQLQuery )
     objRecordSet.Close
     objRecordSet.Open , , 3
     Set Session("objRecordSet") = objRecordSet
   end if
   dim HoldAction
   HoldAction = Request.Form("Text1")
   HoldAction = UCase( HoldAction )
   if HoldAction = "" then HoldAction = "FORWARD"
   if HoldAction = "FORWARD" then
     on error resume next
     if not objRecordSet.EOF then
        objRecordSet.MoveNext
     else
        objRecordSet.MoveFirst
     end if
   else
     on error resume next
     if not objRecordSet.BOF then
        objRecordSet.MovePrevious
     else
        objRecordSet.MoveLast
     end if
   end if
%>
    <FORM NAME="Form1" ACTION="http://default/aspexec/aspht0704.asp"⇐
    METHOD="POST" TARGET="_top">
<TABLE WIDTH=600 COLSPAN=8 BORDER=5 CELLSPACING=5
CELLPADDING=5 ALIGN="CENTER" VALIGN="MIDDLE" BGCOLOR="Teal">
<TR>
<TD COLSPAN=3 ALIGN="CENTER">
Customer Listing
</TD>
<TD>
<INPUT Type="Text" Name="Text1" Value = "<%= HoldAction %>">
</TD>
<INPUT Type="Submit" NAME="Submit1" Value ="Get Record">
</TR>
<TR>
<TD>
Company Name
</TD>
<TD>
Contact Name
</TD>
<TD>
E-mail address
</TD>
```

continued on next page

continued from previous page

```
<TD>
City
</TD>
<TD>
State/Province
</TD>
</TR>
  <TR>
  <TD>
      <%= objRecordSet("CompanyName")%>
  </TD>
  <TD>
      <%= objRecordSet("ContactLastName") & ", " %>
      <%= objRecordSet("ContactFirstName") %>
  </TD>
  <TD>
    <A HREF="mailto:">
      <%= objRecordSet("ContactLastName")%>
    </A></TD>
  <TD>
      <%= objRecordSet("City")%>
  </TD>
  <TD>
      <%= objRecordSet("StateOrProvince")%>
  </TD>
  </TR>
</TD>
</TR>
</TABLE>
    </FORM>
</BODY>
</HTML>
```

2. Activate Internet Explorer and bring up `ASPHT0704.ASP`. Enter **`Backwards`** in the Text control and press the Submit button. As shown in Figure 7-4, you can now move backward as well as forward in the ADO ASP database system. You have learned to use cursors with the ADO system in ASP.

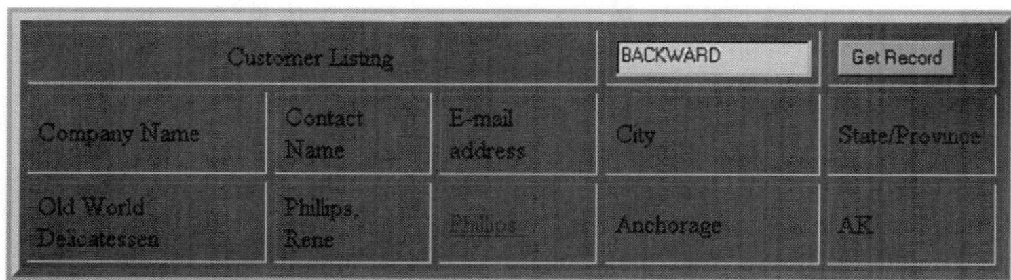

Figure 7-4 `ASPHT0704.ASP` in IE showing the backward navigation capability using an active cursor

How It Works

The whole process depends on two lines of ASP code:

```
objRecordSet.Close
objRecordSet.Open , , 3
```

Like the 10-cent washer, the trick is knowing where to put the code. Once a recordset is opened, its cursor cannot be changed. Instead, the recordset must be closed and reopened using a new cursor type. Once this is done, any new operations supported by the cursor are immediately available.

Okay, now what in the world is a cursor, really? Well, it is a term in database jargon for the way the system allows the user to look at the data in his recordset. This optimizes system resources, but imposes constraints on what can be done without some specific requests of the system. By asking explicitly for a more powerful cursor type, you can easily give your users more flexibility while keeping the more casual database environments resource-friendly.

Comments

Look under `Recordset.CursorType` for the online documentation of all the various cursor types available in ADO.

COMPLEXITY
INTERMEDIATE

7.5 How do I... Allow user updates in my ASP ADO Web page?

Problem

Well, my boss has had an attack of the clevers, and has promised our customers immediate online modifications of the ASP ADO database I've developed. Is it time for me to start job hunting in Redmond?

Technique

Microsoft won't get you over this one. Instead, you simply need to add one extra parameter to the recordset manipulation code and use the `Update` method, along with some powerful form code, of course. This How-To gives you all the details. Although these directions create the project from scratch, the CD contains a completed file under `CH07\HT05\`.

Steps

1. Activate ActiveX Control Pad and reload the **ASPHT0704.ASP** file. Modify the code so it is identical to the code in Listing 7-5. Save it as ASPHT0705.ASP.

Listing 7-5 ASPHT0705.ASP source code

```
<%@ LANGUAGE = VBScript %>
<HTML>
<HEAD>
<TITLE>Active Server Pages Chapter Seven How To Five</TITLE>
</HEAD>
<BODY>
<% if IsObject(Session("objRecordSet")) then
     set objRecordSet = Session("objRecordSet")
   else
     Set objConnection = Server.CreateObject("ADODB.Connection")
     objConnection.Open "AWTutorial"
     SQLQuery = "SELECT * FROM Customers"
     Set objRecordSet = objConnection.Execute( SQLQuery )
     objRecordSet.Close
     objRecordSet.Open , , 3 , 4
     Set Session("objRecordSet") = objRecordSet
   end if
   dim HoldAction
   HoldAction = Request.Form("Text1")
   HoldAction = UCase( HoldAction )
   if HoldAction = "" then HoldAction = "FORWARD"
   if HoldAction = "FORWARD" then
     on error resume next
     if not objRecordSet.EOF then
       objRecordSet.MoveNext
     else
       objRecordSet.MoveFirst
     end if
   elseif HoldAction = "BACKWARD" then
     on error resume next
     if not objRecordSet.BOF then
        objRecordSet.MovePrevious
     else
        objRecordSet.MoveLast
     end if
   elseif HoldAction = "UPDATE" then
     objRecordSet("CompanyName") = Request.Form("Text2")
     objRecordSet("ContactLastName") = Request.Form("Text3")
     objRecordSet("ContactFirstName") = Request.Form("Text4")
     objRecordSet("City") = Request.Form("Text5")
     objRecordSet("StateOrProvince") = Request.Form("Text6")
     ObjRecordSet.Update
    end if
%>
    <FORM NAME="Form1" ACTION="http://default/aspexec/aspht0705.asp"⇐
    METHOD="POST" TARGET="_top">
<TABLE WIDTH=600 COLSPAN=8 BORDER=5 CELLSPACING=5
```

```
CELLPADDING=5 ALIGN="CENTER" VALIGN="MIDDLE" BGCOLOR="Teal">
<TR>
<TD COLSPAN=3 ALIGN="CENTER">
Customer Listing
</TD>
<TD>
<INPUT Type="Text" Name="Text1" Value = "<%= HoldAction %>">
</TD>
<INPUT Type="Submit" NAME="Submit1" Value ="Next Action">
</TR>
<TR>
<TD>
Company Name
</TD>
<TD>
Contact Name
</TD>
<TD>
E-mail address
</TD>
<TD>
City
</TD>
<TD>
State/Province
</TD>
</TR>
  <TR>
  <TD>
  <INPUT Type = "Text" Name="Text2" Value = "<%= objRecordSet("CompanyName")%>">
  </TD>
  <TD>
  <INPUT Type = "Text" Name="Text3" Value = "<%= objRecordSet("ContactLastName")⇐
  %>">
  <INPUT Type = "Text" Name="Text4" Value = "<%= objRecordSet("ContactFirstName")⇐
  %>">
  </TD>
  <TD>
    <A HREF="mailto:">
      <%= objRecordSet("ContactLastName")%>
    </A></TD>
  <TD>
  <INPUT Type = "Text" Name="Text5" Value = "<%= objRecordSet("City")%>">
  </TD>
  <TD>
  <INPUT Type = "Text" Name="Text6" Value = "<%= objRecordSet("StateOrProvince")⇐
  %>">
  </TD>
  </TR>
</TD>
</TR>
</TABLE>
    </FORM>
</BODY>
</HTML>
```

2. Activate Internet Explorer and bring up `ASPHT0405.ASP`. Change some data, enter `UPDATE` in the text box, and press the Submit button. As shown in Figure 7-5, the new data will reflect the change. You have learned to use the `Update` method to allow users to change database information over the WWW with ADO.

How It Works

Aside from the HTML form code, two important pieces need to be in place to permit user updates. The first one is shown in this ASP code:

```
objRecordSet.Close
objRecordSet.Open , , 3 , 4
```

Notice the extra parameter after the cursor type. It is called a `LockType`, and it reflects whether or not the database can be updated by users. The default setting is `0`, which is read only, and thus no updates are allowed. The `4` setting is the easiest and allows multiple users to change the information at will.

The other critical bit of code is this:

```
elseif HoldAction = "UPDATE" then
     objRecordSet("CompanyName") = Request.Form("Text2")
     objRecordSet("ContactLastName") = Request.Form("Text3")
     objRecordSet("ContactFirstName") = Request.Form("Text4")
     objRecordSet("City") = Request.Form("Text5")
     objRecordSet("StateOrProvince") = Request.Form("Text6")
     ObjRecordSet.Update
    end if
```

In this code segment, if an `Update` command is received, the data from the form text elements is used to change the values of the fields. Note that no edit method is needed; ADO's property handlers do the edit method implicitly rather than explicitly, in keeping with object-oriented programming (OOP) practices. The `Update` method simply tells the database system to change the underlying recordset to the new values, and the system does so automatically.

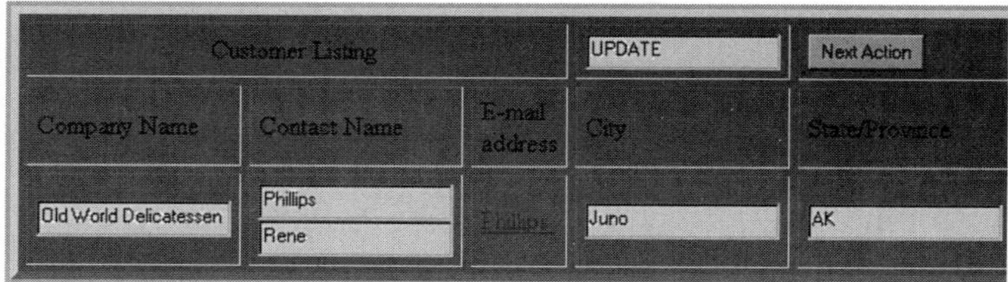

Figure 7-5 `ASPHT0705.ASP` in IE showing an updated database element via the WWW

Comments

Look under `RecordSet.LockType` for the various database locks and their documentation. Also check out the Transactions systems for more advanced methods of updating data from users.

7.6 How do I... Use an ActiveX control with my ASP ADO information?

Problem

I don't mean to complain, but my users are saying that the HTML interface is really outdated. Can I find some way to spiff up my display of the ADO ASP database data?

Technique

Okay, you just jumped into the deep end of the pool! Let's climb back out and walk in from the shallow end, starting with a simple ActiveX control—the Label control. Although these directions create the project from scratch, the CD contains a completed file under `CH07\HT06\`.

Steps

1. Activate ActiveX Control Pad and reload the `ASPHT0705.ASP` file. Modify the code so it is identical to the code in Listing 7-6. Save it as `ASPHT0706.ASP`.

Listing 7-6 ASPHT0706.ASP source code

```
<%@ LANGUAGE = VBScript %>
<HTML>
<HEAD>
<TITLE>Active Server Pages Chapter Seven How To Six</TITLE>
</HEAD>
<BODY>
<% if IsObject(Session("objRecordSet")) then
     set objRecordSet = Session("objRecordSet")
   else
     Set objConnection = Server.CreateObject("ADODB.Connection")
     objConnection.Open "AWTutorial"
     SQLQuery = "SELECT * FROM Customers"
     Set objRecordSet = objConnection.Execute( SQLQuery )
```

continued on next page

continued from previous page

```
     objRecordSet.Close
     objRecordSet.Open , , 2 , 4
     Set Session("objRecordSet") = objRecordSet
   end if
   dim HoldAction
   HoldAction = Request.Form("Text1")
   HoldAction = UCase( HoldAction )
   if HoldAction = "" then HoldAction = "FORWARD"
   if HoldAction = "FORWARD" then
     on error resume next
     if not objRecordSet.EOF then
       objRecordSet.MoveNext
     else
       objRecordSet.MoveFirst
     end if
   elseif HoldAction = "BACKWARD" then
     on error resume next
     if not objRecordSet.BOF then
       objRecordSet.MovePrevious
     else
       objRecordSet.MoveLast
     end if
   elseif HoldAction = "UPDATE" then
     objRecordSet("CompanyName") = Request.Form("Text2")
     objRecordSet("ContactLastName") = Request.Form("Text3")
     objRecordSet("ContactFirstName") = Request.Form("Text4")
     objRecordSet("City") = Request.Form("Text5")
     objRecordSet("StateOrProvince") = Request.Form("Text6")
     ObjRecordSet.Update
    end if
%>
    <FORM NAME="Form1" ACTION="http://default/aspexec/aspht0706.asp"⇐
    METHOD="POST" TARGET="_top">
<TABLE WIDTH=600 COLSPAN=8 BORDER=5 CELLSPACING=5
CELLPADDING=5 ALIGN="CENTER" VALIGN="MIDDLE" BGCOLOR="Teal">
<TR>
<TD COLSPAN=3 ALIGN="CENTER">
Customer Listing
</TD>
<TD>
<INPUT Type="Text" Name="Text1" Value = "<%= HoldAction %>">
</TD>
<INPUT Type="Submit" NAME="Submit1" Value ="Next Action">
</TR>
<TR>
<TD>
Company Name
</TD>
<TD>
Contact Name
</TD>
<TD>
E-mail address
</TD>
<TD>
```

```
City
</TD>
<TD>
State/Province
</TD>
</TR>
  <TR>
  <TD>
  <INPUT Type = "Text" Name="Text2" Value = "<%= objRecordSet("CompanyName")%>">
  </TD>
  <TD>
  <INPUT Type = "Text" Name="Text3" Value = "<%= objRecordSet("ContactLastName")⇐
  %>">
  <INPUT Type = "Text" Name="Text4" Value = "<%=⇐
  objRecordSet("ContactFirstName") %>">
  </TD>
  <TD>

<OBJECT ID="IeLabel1" WIDTH=225 HEIGHT=27
 CLASSID="CLSID:99B42120-6EC7-11CF-A6C7-00AA00A47DD2">
    <PARAM NAME="_ExtentX" VALUE="5953">
    <PARAM NAME="_ExtentY" VALUE="714">
    <PARAM NAME="Caption" VALUE="Mailto: <%= objRecordSet("ContactLastName")%>">
    <PARAM NAME="Angle" VALUE="0">
    <PARAM NAME="Alignment" VALUE="4">
    <PARAM NAME="Mode" VALUE="1">
    <PARAM NAME="FillStyle" VALUE="0">
    <PARAM NAME="FillStyle" VALUE="1">
    <PARAM NAME="ForeColor" VALUE="#000000">
    <PARAM NAME="BackColor" VALUE="#D8C0A0">
    <PARAM NAME="FontName" VALUE="Arial">
    <PARAM NAME="FontSize" VALUE="12">
    <PARAM NAME="FontItalic" VALUE="0">
    <PARAM NAME="FontBold" VALUE="1">
    <PARAM NAME="FontUnderline" VALUE="0">
    <PARAM NAME="FontStrikeout" VALUE="0">
    <PARAM NAME="TopPoints" VALUE="0">
    <PARAM NAME="BotPoints" VALUE="0">
</OBJECT>

   </TD>
  <TD>
  <INPUT Type = "Text" Name="Text5" Value = "<%= objRecordSet("City")%>">
  </TD>
  <TD>
  <INPUT Type = "Text" Name="Text6" Value = "<%= objRecordSet("StateOrProvince")⇐
  %>">
  </TD>
  </TR>
</TD>
</TR>
</TABLE>
    </FORM>
</BODY>
</HTML>
```

2. Activate Internet Explorer and bring up **ASPHT0706.ASP**. Move forward or backward in the database and the Label control, which replaced the **MAILTO** link, will change each time to reflect the new last name, shown in Figure 7-6. You have learned to use ActiveX, ADO, and ASP all at the same time.

How It Works

They key to this entire scenario is this little fragment of code:

```
<OBJECT ID="IeLabel1" WIDTH=225 HEIGHT=27
 CLASSID="CLSID:99B42120-6EC7-11CF-A6C7-00AA00A47DD2">
    <PARAM NAME="_ExtentX" VALUE="5953">
    <PARAM NAME="_ExtentY" VALUE="714">
    <PARAM NAME="Caption" VALUE="Mailto: <%= objRecordSet("ContactLastName")%>">
```

Notice that the value portion of the **<PARAM>** tag is filled in with the **<%= %>** syntax. That is the key to controlling ActiveX with ASP and ADO! By simply determining via server-side variables from ADO recordsets what information goes into the **<PARAM>** tags of the ActiveX controls, you can use them to display as much information as you like from your ADO databases.

Comments

This may seem a bit trivial, but it gets your feet wet for the big stuff to come. And make no mistake, far bigger fish are about to land in the frying pan!

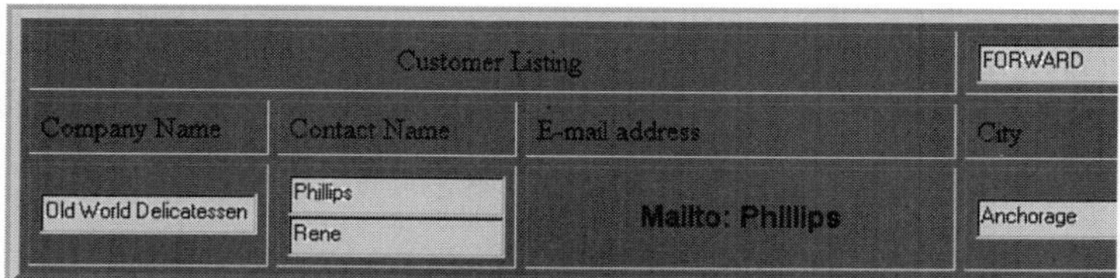

Figure 7-6 ASPHT0706.ASP in IE showing an ActiveX Label control updated by the ASP and ADO functionality

7.7 How do I…
Add client-side scripting to the ActiveX control on my ASP ADO page?

Problem

Okay, my boss is adamant: The dorky user interface has to go! I have to have Windows-style pull-down menus implemented by Wednesday or I'm knocking on Bill Gates' door. Time for the golden parachute?

Technique

Don't pull the ripcord just yet. The Menu ActiveX control from Microsoft's Internet Explorer 3.0 control set is just what you need, and this How-To shows you all the steps needed to implement it. These steps create the application from scratch, but for your convenience the complete project is on the CD under `CH07\HT07\`.

Steps

1. Activate ActiveX Control Pad and reload the `ASPHT0706.ASP` file. Modify the code so it is identical to the code in Listing 7-7. Save it as `ASPHT0707.ASP`.

Listing 7-7 `ASPHT0707.ASP` source code

```
<%@ LANGUAGE = VBScript %>
<HTML>
<HEAD>
<TITLE>Active Server Pages Chapter Seven How To Seven</TITLE>
</HEAD>
<BODY>
<% if IsObject(Session("objRecordSet")) then
     set objRecordSet = Session("objRecordSet")
   else
```

continued on next page

continued from previous page

```
      Set objConnection = Server.CreateObject("ADODB.Connection")
      objConnection.Open "AWTutorial"
      SQLQuery = "SELECT * FROM Customers"
      Set objRecordSet = objConnection.Execute( SQLQuery )
      objRecordSet.Close
      objRecordSet.Open , , 3 , 4
      Set Session("objRecordSet") = objRecordSet
    end if
    dim HoldAction
    HoldAction = Request.Form("Text1")
    HoldAction = UCase( HoldAction )
    if HoldAction = "" then HoldAction = "FORWARD"
    if HoldAction = "FORWARD" then
      on error resume next
      if not objRecordSet.EOF then
        objRecordSet.MoveNext
      else
        objRecordSet.MoveFirst
      end if
    elseif HoldAction = "BACKWARD" then
      on error resume next
      if not objRecordSet.BOF then
        objRecordSet.MovePrevious
      else
        objRecordSet.MoveLast
      end if
    elseif HoldAction = "UPDATE" then
      objRecordSet("CompanyName") = Request.Form("Text2")
      objRecordSet("ContactLastName") = Request.Form("Text3")
      objRecordSet("ContactFirstName") = Request.Form("Text4")
      objRecordSet("City") = Request.Form("Text5")
      objRecordSet("StateOrProvince") = Request.Form("Text6")
      ObjRecordSet.Update
     end if
%>
    <FORM ACTION="http://default/aspexec/aspht0707.asp" METHOD="POST" NAME="Form1"
     TARGET="_top">
<TABLE WIDTH=600 COLSPAN=8 BORDER=5 CELLSPACING=5
CELLPADDING=5 ALIGN="CENTER" VALIGN="MIDDLE" BGCOLOR="Teal">
<TR>
<TD COLSPAN=2 ALIGN="CENTER">
Customer Listing
</TD>
<TD>
        <SCRIPT LANGUAGE="VBScript">
<!--
Sub menu2_Select(item)
select case item
  case 1
    Document.Form1.Text1.value = "FORWARD"
    call Document.Form1.Submit1.click()
  case 2
    Document.Form1.Text1.value = "BACKWARD"
    call Document.Form1.Submit1.click()
  case 3
```

```
    Document.Form1.Text1.value = "UPDATE"
    call Document.Form1.Submit1.click()
end select
end sub
-->
</SCRIPT>
        <OBJECT ID="menu2" WIDTH=80 HEIGHT=25 align=middle
         CLASSID="CLSID:52DFAE60-CEBF-11CF-A3A9-00A0C9034920">
            <PARAM NAME="Menuitem[0]" VALUE="Forward">
            <PARAM NAME="Menuitem[1]" VALUE="Backward">
            <PARAM NAME="Menuitem[2]" VALUE="Update">
            <PARAM NAME="Caption" VALUE="Actions">
        </OBJECT>
</TD>
<TD>
        <INPUT TYPE=Text VALUE="<%= HoldAction %>" NAME="Text1">
</TD>
        <INPUT TYPE=Submit VALUE="Next Action" NAME="Submit1">
</TR>
<TR>
<TD>
Company Name
</TD>
<TD>
Contact Name
</TD>
<TD>
E-mail address
</TD>
<TD>
City
</TD>
<TD>
State/Province
</TD>
</TR>
  <TR>
  <TD>
        <INPUT TYPE=Text NAME="Text2" VALUE="<%= objRecordSet("CompanyName")%>">
</TD>
  <TD>
        <INPUT TYPE=Text NAME="Text3" VALUE="<%=⇐
        objRecordSet("ContactLastName") %>">
        <INPUT TYPE=Text NAME="Text4" VALUE="<%=⇐
        objRecordSet("ContactFirstName") %>">
</TD>
  <TD>
        <OBJECT ID="IeLabel1" WIDTH=225 HEIGHT=27
         CLASSID="CLSID:99B42120-6EC7-11CF-A6C7-00AA00A47DD2">
            <PARAM NAME="_ExtentX" VALUE="5953">
            <PARAM NAME="_ExtentY" VALUE="714">
            <PARAM NAME="Caption" VALUE="Mailto: <%=⇐
            objRecordSet("ContactLastName")%>">
    <PARAM NAME="Angle" VALUE="0">
```

continued on next page

continued from previous page

```
    <PARAM NAME="Alignment" VALUE="4">
    <PARAM NAME="Mode" VALUE="1">
    <PARAM NAME="FillStyle" VALUE="0">
    <PARAM NAME="FillStyle" VALUE="1">
    <PARAM NAME="ForeColor" VALUE="#000000">
    <PARAM NAME="BackColor" VALUE="#D8C0A0">
    <PARAM NAME="FontName" VALUE="Arial">
    <PARAM NAME="FontSize" VALUE="12">
    <PARAM NAME="FontItalic" VALUE="0">
    <PARAM NAME="FontBold" VALUE="1">
    <PARAM NAME="FontUnderline" VALUE="0">
    <PARAM NAME="FontStrikeout" VALUE="0">
    <PARAM NAME="TopPoints" VALUE="0">
    <PARAM NAME="BotPoints" VALUE="0">
</OBJECT>

    </TD>
   <TD>
   <INPUT Type = "Text" Name="Text5" Value = "<%= objRecordSet("City")%>">
   </TD>
   <TD>
   <INPUT Type = "Text" Name="Text6" Value = "<%=⇐
   objRecordSet("StateOrProvince")%>">
   </TD>
   </TR>
</TD>
</TR>
</TABLE>
    </FORM>
</BODY>
</HTML>
        </OBJECT>
    </FORM>
</BODY>
```

2. Activate Internet Explorer, bring up `ASPHT0707.ASP`, and select the Backward option from the pull-down ActiveX menu. As shown in Figure 7-7, the command is relayed to the ASP file and the proper record is displayed. You have learned to use a full-featured ActiveX control with your ASP/ADO database system.

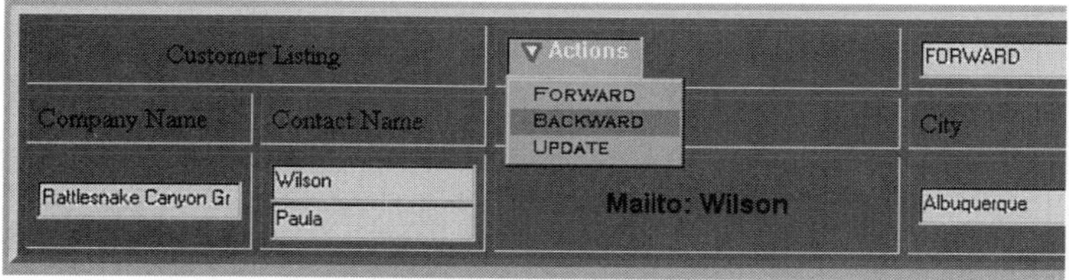

Figure 7-7 `ASPHT0707.ASP` in IE showing the pull-down menu ActiveX control working with the ASP ADO system

How It Works

The key to this How-To is client-side scripting, as shown in these lines of code:

```
<SCRIPT LANGUAGE="VBScript">
<!--
Sub menu2_Select(item)
select case item
  case 1
    Document.Form1.Text1.value = "FORWARD"
    call Document.Form1.Submit1.click()
  case 2
    Document.Form1.Text1.value = "BACKWARD"
    call Document.Form1.Submit1.click()
  case 3
    Document.Form1.Text1.value = "UPDATE"
    call Document.Form1.Submit1.click()
end select
end sub
-->
</SCRIPT>
```

Notice that the `Select` subroutine isn't explicitly tied to the ActiveX control; this is because it is a native event exposed by the control, and so is automatically available. By making calls to the appropriate form elements from its scripting code, you can make the menu work just like the real ones in Windows!

Comments

Notice that although the menu items start at index `0`, the item parameter into the `Select` event starts at `1`!

COMPLEXITY
INTERMEDIATE

7.8 How do I... Use an HTML Layout control with client-side scripting on my ASP ADO page?

Problem

I need a really lovely user interface now, because the boss has seen the pretty pull-down menus. I can't get the ActiveX controls to position themselves right, even in a table. Is there some other ActiveX technology that can help me here?

Technique

The HTML Layout control is your salvation! This How-To shows you exactly how to create one from an ASP script. These steps create the application from scratch, but for your convenience the complete project is on the CD under CH07\HT08\.

Steps

1. Activate ActiveX Control Pad and reload the ASPHT0707.ASP file. Modify the code so it is identical to the code in Listing 7-8. Save it as ASPHT0708.ASP.

Listing 7-8 ASPHT0708.ASP source code

```
<%@ LANGUAGE = VBScript %>
<HTML>
<HEAD>
<TITLE>Active Server Pages Chapter Seven How To Eight</TITLE>
</HEAD>
<BODY>
<% if IsObject(Session("objRecordSet")) then
     set objRecordSet = Session("objRecordSet")
   else
     Set objConnection = Server.CreateObject("ADODB.Connection")
        objConnection.Open "AWTutorial"
        SQLQuery = "SELECT * FROM Customers"
        Set objRecordSet = objConnection.Execute( SQLQuery )
        objRecordSet.Close
        objRecordSet.Open , , 3 , 4
        Set Session("objRecordSet") = objRecordSet
   end if
   dim HoldAction
   HoldAction = Request.Form("Text1")
   HoldAction = UCase( HoldAction )
   if HoldAction = "" then HoldAction = "FORWARD"
   if HoldAction = "FORWARD" then
     on error resume next
     if not objRecordSet.EOF then
          objRecordSet.MoveNext
     else
          objRecordSet.MoveFirst
     end if
   elseif HoldAction = "BACKWARD" then
     on error resume next
     if not objRecordSet.BOF then
          objRecordSet.MovePrevious
     else
          objRecordSet.MoveLast
     end if
   elseif HoldAction = "UPDATE" then
     objRecordSet("CompanyName") = Request.Form("Text2")
     objRecordSet("ContactLastName") = Request.Form("Text3")
        objRecordSet("ContactFirstName") = Request.Form("Text4")
```

```
        objRecordSet("City") = Request.Form("Text5")
        objRecordSet("StateOrProvince") = Request.Form("Text6")
        ObjRecordSet.Update
    end if
%>
    <FORM ACTION="http://default/aspexec/aspht0708.asp" METHOD="POST" NAME="Form1"
     TARGET="_top">
<TABLE WIDTH=600 COLSPAN=8 BORDER=5 CELLSPACING=5
CELLPADDING=5 ALIGN="CENTER" VALIGN="MIDDLE" BGCOLOR="Teal">
<TR>
<TD COLSPAN=2 ALIGN="CENTER">
Customer Listing
</TD>
<TD>
        <SCRIPT LANGUAGE="VBScript">
<!--
Sub menu2_Select(item)
select case item
  case 1
    Document.Form1.Text1.value = "FORWARD"
    call Document.Form1.Submit1.click()
  case 2
    Document.Form1.Text1.value = "BACKWARD"
    call Document.Form1.Submit1.click()
  case 3
    Document.Form1.Text1.value = "UPDATE"
    call Document.Form1.Submit1.click()
end select
end sub
-->
        </SCRIPT>
        <OBJECT ID="menu2" WIDTH=80 HEIGHT=25 align=middle
         CLASSID="CLSID:52DFAE60-CEBF-11CF-A3A9-00A0C9034920">
            <PARAM NAME="Menuitem[0]" VALUE="Forward">
            <PARAM NAME="Menuitem[1]" VALUE="Backward">
            <PARAM NAME="Menuitem[2]" VALUE="Update">
            <PARAM NAME="Caption" VALUE="Actions">
        </OBJECT>
</TD>
<TD>
        <INPUT TYPE=Text VALUE="<%= HoldAction %>" NAME="Text1">
</TD>
        <INPUT TYPE=Submit VALUE="Next Action" NAME="Submit1">
</TR>
<TR>
<TD>
Company Name
</TD>
<TD>
Contact Name
</TD>
<TD>
E-mail address
</TD>
```

continued on next page

continued from previous page

```
<TD>
City
</TD>
<TD>
State/Province
</TD>
</TR>
  <TR>
  <TD>
        <INPUT TYPE=Text NAME="Text2" VALUE="<%= objRecordSet("CompanyName")%>">
</TD>
  <TD>
        <INPUT TYPE=Text NAME="Text3" VALUE="<%=⇐
        objRecordSet("ContactLastName")%>">
        <INPUT TYPE=Text NAME="Text4" VALUE="<%=⇐
        objRecordSet("ContactFirstName")%>">
</TD>
  <TD>
        <OBJECT ID="IeLabel1" WIDTH=225 HEIGHT=27
         CLASSID="CLSID:99B42120-6EC7-11CF-A6C7-00AA00A47DD2">
            <PARAM NAME="_ExtentX" VALUE="5953">
            <PARAM NAME="_ExtentY" VALUE="714">
            <PARAM NAME="Caption" VALUE="Mailto: <%=⇐
            objRecordSet("ContactLastName")%>">
    <PARAM NAME="Angle" VALUE="0">
    <PARAM NAME="Alignment" VALUE="4">
    <PARAM NAME="Mode" VALUE="1">
    <PARAM NAME="FillStyle" VALUE="0">
    <PARAM NAME="FillStyle" VALUE="1">
    <PARAM NAME="ForeColor" VALUE="#000000">
    <PARAM NAME="BackColor" VALUE="#D8C0A0">
    <PARAM NAME="FontName" VALUE="Arial">
    <PARAM NAME="FontSize" VALUE="12">
    <PARAM NAME="FontItalic" VALUE="0">
    <PARAM NAME="FontBold" VALUE="1">
    <PARAM NAME="FontUnderline" VALUE="0">
    <PARAM NAME="FontStrikeout" VALUE="0">
    <PARAM NAME="TopPoints" VALUE="0">
    <PARAM NAME="BotPoints" VALUE="0">
</OBJECT>

   </TD>
  <TD>
  <INPUT Type = "Text" Name="Text5" Value = "<%= objRecordSet("City")%>">
  </TD>
  <TD>
  <INPUT Type = "Text" Name="Text6" Value = "<%=⇐
  objRecordSet("StateOrProvince")%>">
  </TD>
  </TR>
</TD>
</TR>
<TR >
<TD COLSPAN = 5>
```

```
<OBJECT CLASSID="CLSID:812AE312-8B8E-11CF-93C8-00AA00C08FDF"
ID="aspht0708_alx" STYLE="LEFT:0;TOP:0">
<PARAM NAME="ALXPATH" REF VALUE="aspht0708.alx">
 </OBJECT>


</TD>
</TD>
</TABLE>
    </FORM>
<%
Set objFileSys = Server.CreateObject("Scripting.FileSystemObject")
Dim strALXPath
strALXPath = Server.MapPath("/ASPExec") & "/aspht0708.alx"
Set objALXOut = objFileSys.CreateTextFile( strALXPath ,True)
strOut = "<SCRIPT LANGUAGE=""VBScript"">"
objALXOut.WriteLine( strOut )
strOut = "<!--"
objALXOut.WriteLine( strOut )
strOut = "Sub CommandButton3_Click()"
objALXOut.WriteLine( strOut )
strOut = "parent.Document.Form1.text1.value = ""UPDATE"""
objALXOut.WriteLine( strOut )
strOut = "call parent.Document.Form1.Submit1.click()"
objALXOut.WriteLine( strOut )
strOut = "end sub"
objALXOut.WriteLine( strOut )
strOut = "-->"
objALXOut.WriteLine( strOut )
strOut = "</SCRIPT>"
objALXOut.WriteLine( strOut )
strOut = "<SCRIPT LANGUAGE=""VBScript"">"
objALXOut.WriteLine( strOut )
strOut = "<!--"
objALXOut.WriteLine( strOut )
strOut = "Sub CommandButton2_Click()"
objALXOut.WriteLine( strOut )
strOut = "parent.Document.Form1.text1.value = ""FORWARD"""
objALXOut.WriteLine( strOut )
strOut = "call parent.Document.Form1.Submit1.click()"
objALXOut.WriteLine( strOut )
strOut = "end sub"
objALXOut.WriteLine( strOut )
strOut = "-->"
objALXOut.WriteLine( strOut )
strOut = "</SCRIPT>"
objALXOut.WriteLine( strOut )
strOut = "<SCRIPT LANGUAGE=""VBScript"">"
objALXOut.WriteLine( strOut )
strOut = "<!--"
objALXOut.WriteLine( strOut )
strOut = "Sub CommandButton1_Click()"
objALXOut.WriteLine( strOut )
strOut = "parent.Document.Form1.text1.value = ""BACKWARD"""
```

continued on next page

continued from previous page

```
objALXOut.WriteLine( strOut )
strOut = "call parent.Document.Form1.Submit1.click()"
objALXOut.WriteLine( strOut )
strOut = "end sub"
objALXOut.WriteLine( strOut )
strOut = "-->"
objALXOut.WriteLine( strOut )
strOut = "</SCRIPT>"
objALXOut.WriteLine( strOut )
strOut = "<SCRIPT LANGUAGE=""VBScript"">"
objALXOut.WriteLine( strOut )
strOut = "<!--"
objALXOut.WriteLine( strOut )
strOut = "Sub TextBox2_Change()"
objALXOut.WriteLine( strOut )
strOut = "parent.Document.Form1.Text5.Value = TextBox2.Text"
objALXOut.WriteLine( strOut )
strOut = "end sub"
objALXOut.WriteLine( strOut )
strOut = "-->"
objALXOut.WriteLine( strOut )
strOut = "</SCRIPT>"
objALXOut.WriteLine( strOut )
strOut = "<SCRIPT LANGUAGE=""VBScript"">"
objALXOut.WriteLine( strOut )
strOut = "<!--"
objALXOut.WriteLine( strOut )
strOut = "Sub TextBox1_Change()"
objALXOut.WriteLine( strOut )
strOut = "parent.Document.Form1.Text2.Value = TextBox1.Text"
objALXOut.WriteLine( strOut )
strOut = "end sub"
objALXOut.WriteLine( strOut )
strOut = "-->"
objALXOut.WriteLine( strOut )
strOut = "</SCRIPT>"
objALXOut.WriteLine( strOut )
strOut = "<DIV ID=""Layout1"" STYLE=""LAYOUT:FIXED;WIDTH:530pt;HEIGHT:92pt;"">"
objALXOut.WriteLine( strOut )
strOut = "<OBJECT ID=""Label1"""
objALXOut.WriteLine( strOut )
strOut = "CLASSID=""CLSID:978C9E23-D4B0-11CE-BF2D-00AA003F40D0""
STYLE=""TOP:25pt;LEFT:8pt;WIDTH:107pt;HEIGHT:17pt;ZINDEX:0;"">"
objALXOut.WriteLine( strOut )
strOut = "<PARAM NAME=""Caption"" VALUE=""Business Name"">"
objALXOut.WriteLine( strOut )
strOut = "<PARAM NAME=""Size"" VALUE=""3793;600"">"
objALXOut.WriteLine( strOut )
strOut = "<PARAM NAME=""FontCharSet"" VALUE=""0"">"
objALXOut.WriteLine( strOut )
strOut = "<PARAM NAME=""FontPitchAndFamily"" VALUE=""2"">"
objALXOut.WriteLine( strOut )
strOut = "<PARAM NAME=""FontWeight"" VALUE=""0"">"
objALXOut.WriteLine( strOut )
strOut = "</OBJECT>"
```

```
objALXOut.WriteLine( strOut )
strOut = "<OBJECT ID=""Label2"""
objALXOut.WriteLine( strOut )
strOut = "CLASSID=""CLSID:978C9E23-D4B0-11CE-BF2D-00AA003F40D0""
STYLE=""TOP:50pt;LEFT:8pt;WIDTH:107pt;HEIGHT:25pt;ZINDEX:1;"">"
objALXOut.WriteLine( strOut )
strOut = "<PARAM NAME=""Caption"" VALUE=""City"">"
objALXOut.WriteLine( strOut )
strOut = "<PARAM NAME=""Size"" VALUE=""3793;882"">"
objALXOut.WriteLine( strOut )
strOut = "<PARAM NAME=""FontCharSet"" VALUE=""0"">"
objALXOut.WriteLine( strOut )
strOut = "<PARAM NAME=""FontPitchAndFamily"" VALUE=""2"">"
objALXOut.WriteLine( strOut )
strOut = "<PARAM NAME=""FontWeight"" VALUE=""0"">"
objALXOut.WriteLine( strOut )
strOut = "</OBJECT>"
objALXOut.WriteLine( strOut )
strOut = "<OBJECT ID=""TextBox1"""
objALXOut.WriteLine( strOut )
strOut = "CLASSID=""CLSID:8BD21D10-EC42-11CE-9E0D-00AA006002F3""
STYLE=""TOP:17pt;LEFT:124pt;WIDTH:215pt;HEIGHT:25pt;TABINDEX:2;ZINDEX:2;"">"
objALXOut.WriteLine( strOut )
strOut = "<PARAM NAME=""VariousPropertyBits"" VALUE=""746604571"">"
objALXOut.WriteLine( strOut )
strOut = "<PARAM NAME=""Size"" VALUE=""7585;882"">"
objALXOut.WriteLine( strOut )
strOut = "<PARAM NAME=""Value"" VALUE=""" & objRecordSet("CompanyName") & """>"
objALXOut.WriteLine( strOut )
strOut = "<PARAM NAME=""FontCharSet"" VALUE=""0"">"
objALXOut.WriteLine( strOut )
strOut = "<PARAM NAME=""FontPitchAndFamily"" VALUE=""2"">"
objALXOut.WriteLine( strOut )
strOut = "<PARAM NAME=""FontWeight"" VALUE=""0"">"
objALXOut.WriteLine( strOut )
strOut = "</OBJECT>"
objALXOut.WriteLine( strOut )
strOut = "<OBJECT ID=""TextBox2"""
objALXOut.WriteLine( strOut )
strOut = "CLASSID=""CLSID:8BD21D10-EC42-11CE-9E0D-00AA006002F3""
STYLE=""TOP:50pt;LEFT:124pt;WIDTH:215pt;HEIGHT:26pt;TABINDEX:3;ZINDEX:3;"">"
objALXOut.WriteLine( strOut )
strOut = "<PARAM NAME=""VariousPropertyBits"" VALUE=""746604571"">"
objALXOut.WriteLine( strOut )
strOut = "<PARAM NAME=""Size"" VALUE=""7585;917"">"
objALXOut.WriteLine( strOut )
strOut = "<PARAM NAME=""Value"" VALUE=""" & objRecordSet("City") &""">"
objALXOut.WriteLine( strOut )
strOut = "<PARAM NAME=""FontCharSet"" VALUE=""0"">"
objALXOut.WriteLine( strOut )
strOut = "<PARAM NAME=""FontPitchAndFamily"" VALUE=""2"">"
objALXOut.WriteLine( strOut )
strOut = "<PARAM NAME=""FontWeight"" VALUE=""0"">"
objALXOut.WriteLine( strOut )
strOut = "</OBJECT>"
```

continued on next page

continued from previous page

```
objALXOut.WriteLine( strOut )
strOut = "<OBJECT ID=""CommandButton1"""
objALXOut.WriteLine( strOut )
strOut = "CLASSID=""CLSID:D7053240-CE69-11CD-A777-00DD01143C57""
STYLE=""TOP:17pt;LEFT:347pt;WIDTH:74pt;HEIGHT:25pt;TABINDEX:4;ZINDEX:4;"">"
objALXOut.WriteLine( strOut )
strOut = "<PARAM NAME=""Caption"" VALUE=""Backward"">"
objALXOut.WriteLine( strOut )
strOut = "<PARAM NAME=""Size"" VALUE=""2619;873"">"
objALXOut.WriteLine( strOut )
strOut = "<PARAM NAME=""FontCharSet"" VALUE=""0"">"
objALXOut.WriteLine( strOut )
strOut = "<PARAM NAME=""FontPitchAndFamily"" VALUE=""2"">"
objALXOut.WriteLine( strOut )
strOut = "<PARAM NAME=""ParagraphAlign"" VALUE=""3"">"
objALXOut.WriteLine( strOut )
strOut = "<PARAM NAME=""FontWeight"" VALUE=""0"">"
objALXOut.WriteLine( strOut )
strOut = "</OBJECT>"
objALXOut.WriteLine( strOut )
strOut = "<OBJECT ID=""CommandButton2"""
objALXOut.WriteLine( strOut )
strOut = "CLASSID=""CLSID:D7053240-CE69-11CD-A777-00DD01143C57""
STYLE=""TOP:17pt;LEFT:429pt;WIDTH:83pt;HEIGHT:25pt;TABINDEX:5;ZINDEX:5;"">"
objALXOut.WriteLine( strOut )
strOut = "<PARAM NAME=""Caption"" VALUE=""Forward"">"
objALXOut.WriteLine( strOut )
strOut = "<PARAM NAME=""Size"" VALUE=""2911;873"">"
objALXOut.WriteLine( strOut )
strOut = "<PARAM NAME=""FontCharSet"" VALUE=""0"">"
objALXOut.WriteLine( strOut )
strOut = "<PARAM NAME=""FontPitchAndFamily"" VALUE=""2"">"
objALXOut.WriteLine( strOut )
strOut = "<PARAM NAME=""ParagraphAlign"" VALUE=""3"">"
objALXOut.WriteLine( strOut )
strOut = "<PARAM NAME=""FontWeight"" VALUE=""0"">"
objALXOut.WriteLine( strOut )
strOut = "</OBJECT>"
objALXOut.WriteLine( strOut )
strOut = "<OBJECT ID=""CommandButton3"""
objALXOut.WriteLine( strOut )
strOut = "CLASSID=""CLSID:D7053240-CE69-11CD-A777-00DD01143C57"" "
strOut = strOut &⇐
"STYLE=""TOP:50pt;LEFT:388pt;WIDTH:91pt;HEIGHT:25pt;TABINDEX:6;ZINDEX:6;"">"
objALXOut.WriteLine( strOut )
strOut = "<PARAM NAME=""Caption"" VALUE=""Update"">"
objALXOut.WriteLine( strOut )
strOut = "<PARAM NAME=""Size"" VALUE=""3210;873"">"
objALXOut.WriteLine( strOut )
strOut = "<PARAM NAME=""FontCharSet"" VALUE=""0"">"
objALXOut.WriteLine( strOut )
strOut = "<PARAM NAME=""FontPitchAndFamily"" VALUE=""2"">"
objALXOut.WriteLine( strOut )
strOut = "<PARAM NAME=""ParagraphAlign"" VALUE=""3"">"
objALXOut.WriteLine( strOut )
```

```
strOut = "<PARAM NAME=""FontWeight"" VALUE=""0"">"
objALXOut.WriteLine( strOut )
strOut = "</OBJECT>"
objALXOut.WriteLine( strOut )
strOut = "</DIV>"
objALXOut.WriteLine( strOut )
objALXOut.Close
%>
</BODY>
</HTML>
```

2. Activate Internet Explorer and bring up `ASPHT0708.ASP`. As shown in Figure 7-8, when you change data in the HTML Layout control, the data in the form controls changes; when you move to a new record, the data in the HTML layout changes; and when you press the HTML layout command buttons, the ASP ADO code is triggered. You have learned to use HTML Layout controls with ASP and ADO.

How It Works

Rather than relist all the complex output code, I'd prefer that you simply look over Listing 7-8. The key features of this How-To are clearly seen in the `textfile` object `WriteLine` calls. This system allows creation of the ALX file needed by the ASP component on-the-fly, thus mating the two technologies smoothly.

Comments

This is one of the "kludgy" places warned about in the introduction. But this technique works, works reliably, and users need never know…

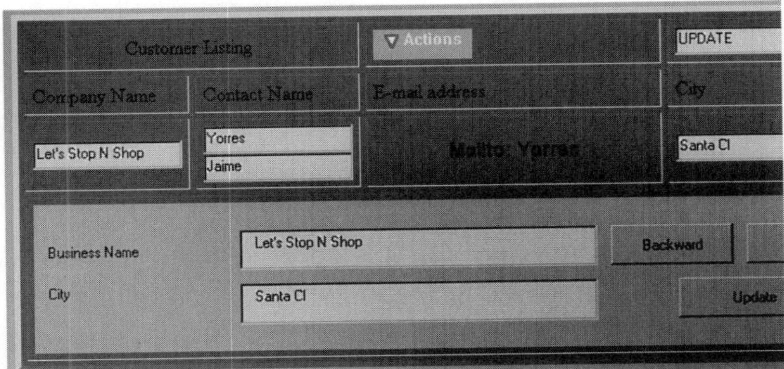

Figure 7-8 `ASPHT0708.ASP` in IE showing an HTML Layout control working with an ASP and ADO database page

7.9 How do I... Invoke an ISAPI extension DLL on my ASP ADO page?

Problem

We need to output complex HTML code from a C++ DLL. I've tried calling it from the CGI system, but the results are poor to say the least. Does the active platform have more to offer here?

Technique

The technology of the future for the Web is ISAPI (Internet Server API). This How-To demonstrates using an ISAPI DLL with the ADO application to create the HTML Layout control in a frame via an extension DLL call rather than explicit code. The directions here create the project from scratch, but for your convenience a copy of the HTML file is on the CD under `\CH07\HT09\`.

Steps

1. Activate ActiveX Control Pad and reload the `ASPHT0708.ASP` file. Modify the code so it is identical to the code in Listing 7-9. Save it as `ASPHT0709.ASP`.

Listing 7-9 ASPHT0709.ASP source code

```
<%@ LANGUAGE = VBScript %>
<HTML>
<HEAD>
<TITLE>Active Server Pages Chapter Seven How To Nine</TITLE>
</HEAD>
<BODY>
<% if IsObject(Session("objRecordSet")) then
     set objRecordSet = Session("objRecordSet")
  else
    Set objConnection = Server.CreateObject("ADODB.Connection")
       objConnection.Open "AWTutorial"
       SQLQuery = "SELECT * FROM Customers"
       Set objRecordSet = objConnection.Execute( SQLQuery )
       objRecordSet.Close
       objRecordSet.Open , , 3 , 4
       Set Session("objRecordSet") = objRecordSet
  end if
  dim HoldAction
  HoldAction = Request.Form("Text1")
  HoldAction = UCase( HoldAction )
```

```
  if HoldAction = "" then HoldAction = "FORWARD"
  if HoldAction = "FORWARD" then
    on error resume next
    if not objRecordSet.EOF then
         objRecordSet.MoveNext
    else
         objRecordSet.MoveFirst
    end if
  elseif HoldAction = "BACKWARD" then
    on error resume next
    if not objRecordSet.BOF then
         objRecordSet.MovePrevious
    else
         objRecordSet.MoveLast
    end if
  elseif HoldAction = "UPDATE" then
    objRecordSet("CompanyName") = Request.Form("Text2")
    objRecordSet("ContactLastName") = Request.Form("Text3")
       objRecordSet("ContactFirstName") = Request.Form("Text4")
       objRecordSet("City") = Request.Form("Text5")
       objRecordSet("StateOrProvince") = Request.Form("Text6")
       ObjRecordSet.Update
  end if
%>
    <FORM ACTION="http://default/aspexec/aspht0709.asp" METHOD="POST" NAME="Form1"
     TARGET="_top">
<TABLE WIDTH=600 COLSPAN=8 BORDER=5 CELLSPACING=5
CELLPADDING=5 ALIGN="CENTER" VALIGN="MIDDLE" BGCOLOR="Teal">
<TR>
<TD COLSPAN=2 ALIGN="CENTER">
Customer Listing
</TD>
<TD>
        <SCRIPT LANGUAGE="VBScript">
<!--
Sub menu2_Select(item)
select case item
  case 1
    Document.Form1.Text1.value = "FORWARD"
    call Document.Form1.Submit1.click()
  case 2
    Document.Form1.Text1.value = "BACKWARD"
    call Document.Form1.Submit1.click()
  case 3
    Document.Form1.Text1.value = "UPDATE"
    call Document.Form1.Submit1.click()
end select
end sub
-->
        </SCRIPT>
        <OBJECT ID="menu2" WIDTH=80 HEIGHT=25 align=middle
         CLASSID="CLSID:52DFAE60-CEBF-11CF-A3A9-00A0C9034920">
            <PARAM NAME="Menuitem[0]" VALUE="Forward">
            <PARAM NAME="Menuitem[1]" VALUE="Backward">
            <PARAM NAME="Menuitem[2]" VALUE="Update">
```

continued on next page

continued from previous page

```
            <PARAM NAME="Caption" VALUE="Actions">
        </OBJECT>
</TD>
<TD>
        <INPUT TYPE=Text VALUE="<%= HoldAction %>" NAME="Text1">
</TD>
        <INPUT TYPE=Submit VALUE="Next Action" NAME="Submit1">
</TR>
<TR>
<TD>
Company Name
</TD>
<TD>
Contact Name
</TD>
<TD>
E-mail address
</TD>
<TD>
City
</TD>
<TD>
State/Province
</TD>
</TR>
  <TR>
  <TD>
        <INPUT TYPE=Text NAME="Text2" VALUE="<%= objRecordSet("CompanyName")%>">
</TD>
  <TD>
        <INPUT TYPE=Text NAME="Text3" VALUE="<%=⇐
        objRecordSet("ContactLastName")%>">
        <INPUT TYPE=Text NAME="Text4" VALUE="<%=⇐
        objRecordSet("ContactFirstName")%>">
</TD>
  <TD>
        <OBJECT ID="IeLabel1" WIDTH=225 HEIGHT=27
         CLASSID="CLSID:99B42120-6EC7-11CF-A6C7-00AA00A47DD2">
            <PARAM NAME="_ExtentX" VALUE="5953">
            <PARAM NAME="_ExtentY" VALUE="714">
            <PARAM NAME="Caption" VALUE="Mailto: <%=⇐
            objRecordSet("ContactLastName")%>">
    <PARAM NAME="Angle" VALUE="0">
    <PARAM NAME="Alignment" VALUE="4">
    <PARAM NAME="Mode" VALUE="1">
    <PARAM NAME="FillStyle" VALUE="0">
    <PARAM NAME="FillStyle" VALUE="1">
    <PARAM NAME="ForeColor" VALUE="#000000">
    <PARAM NAME="BackColor" VALUE="#D8C0A0">
    <PARAM NAME="FontName" VALUE="Arial">
    <PARAM NAME="FontSize" VALUE="12">
    <PARAM NAME="FontItalic" VALUE="0">
    <PARAM NAME="FontBold" VALUE="1">
    <PARAM NAME="FontUnderline" VALUE="0">
    <PARAM NAME="FontStrikeout" VALUE="0">
```

```
    <PARAM NAME="TopPoints" VALUE="0">
    <PARAM NAME="BotPoints" VALUE="0">
</OBJECT>

   </TD>
  <TD>
  <INPUT Type = "Text" Name="Text5" Value = "<%= objRecordSet("City")%>">
  </TD>
  <TD>
  <INPUT Type = "Text" Name="Text6" Value = "<%=⇐
  objRecordSet("StateOrProvince")%>">
  </TD>
  </TR>
</TD>
</TR>
<TR >
<TD COLSPAN = 5>
<IFRAME NAME="IFrame1" SRC="isapialx.dll" WIDTH=750 HEIGHT=200 MARGINHEIGHT=0⇐|
MARGINWIDTH=0
ALIGN=MIDDLE FRAMEBORDER=1 SCROLLING="YES"></IFRAME>
</TD>
</TR>
</TABLE>
    </FORM>
<%
Set objFileSys = Server.CreateObject("Scripting.FileSystemObject")
Dim strALXPath
strALXPath = Server.MapPath("/ASPExec") & "/aspht0708.alx"
Set objALXOut = objFileSys.CreateTextFile( strALXPath ,True)
strOut = "<SCRIPT LANGUAGE=""VBScript"">"
objALXOut.WriteLine( strOut )
strOut = "<!--"
objALXOut.WriteLine( strOut )
strOut = "Sub CommandButton3_Click()"
objALXOut.WriteLine( strOut )
strOut = "parent.Document.Form1.text1.value = ""UPDATE"""
objALXOut.WriteLine( strOut )
strOut = "call parent.Document.Form1.Submit1.click()"
objALXOut.WriteLine( strOut )
strOut = "end sub"
objALXOut.WriteLine( strOut )
strOut = "-->"
objALXOut.WriteLine( strOut )
strOut = "</SCRIPT>"
objALXOut.WriteLine( strOut )
strOut = "<SCRIPT LANGUAGE=""VBScript"">"
objALXOut.WriteLine( strOut )
strOut = "<!--"
objALXOut.WriteLine( strOut )
strOut = "Sub CommandButton2_Click()"
objALXOut.WriteLine( strOut )
strOut = "parent.Document.Form1.text1.value = ""FORWARD"""
objALXOut.WriteLine( strOut )
strOut = "call parent.Document.Form1.Submit1.click()"
```

continued on next page

continued from previous page

```
objALXOut.WriteLine( strOut )
strOut = "end sub"
objALXOut.WriteLine( strOut )
strOut = "-->"
objALXOut.WriteLine( strOut )
strOut = "</SCRIPT>"
objALXOut.WriteLine( strOut )
strOut = "<SCRIPT LANGUAGE=""VBScript"">"
objALXOut.WriteLine( strOut )
strOut = "<!--"
objALXOut.WriteLine( strOut )
strOut = "Sub CommandButton1_Click()"
objALXOut.WriteLine( strOut )
strOut = "parent.Document.Form1.text1.value = ""BACKWARD"""
objALXOut.WriteLine( strOut )
strOut = "call parent.Document.Form1.Submit1.click()"
objALXOut.WriteLine( strOut )
strOut = "end sub"
objALXOut.WriteLine( strOut )
strOut = "-->"
objALXOut.WriteLine( strOut )
strOut = "</SCRIPT>"
objALXOut.WriteLine( strOut )
strOut = "<SCRIPT LANGUAGE=""VBScript"">"
objALXOut.WriteLine( strOut )
strOut = "<!--"
objALXOut.WriteLine( strOut )
strOut = "Sub TextBox2_Change()"
objALXOut.WriteLine( strOut )
strOut = "parent.Document.Form1.Text5.Value = TextBox2.Text"
objALXOut.WriteLine( strOut )
strOut = "end sub"
objALXOut.WriteLine( strOut )
strOut = "-->"
objALXOut.WriteLine( strOut )
strOut = "</SCRIPT>"
objALXOut.WriteLine( strOut )
strOut = "<SCRIPT LANGUAGE=""VBScript"">"
objALXOut.WriteLine( strOut )
strOut = "<!--"
objALXOut.WriteLine( strOut )
strOut = "Sub TextBox1_Change()"
objALXOut.WriteLine( strOut )
strOut = "parent.Document.Form1.Text2.Value = TextBox1.Text"
objALXOut.WriteLine( strOut )
strOut = "end sub"
objALXOut.WriteLine( strOut )
strOut = "-->"
objALXOut.WriteLine( strOut )
strOut = "</SCRIPT>"
objALXOut.WriteLine( strOut )
strOut = "<DIV ID=""Layout1"" STYLE=""LAYOUT:FIXED;WIDTH:530pt;HEIGHT:92pt;"">"
objALXOut.WriteLine( strOut )
strOut = "<OBJECT ID=""Label1"""
objALXOut.WriteLine( strOut )
```

```
strOut = "CLASSID=""CLSID:978C9E23-D4B0-11CE-BF2D-00AA003F40D0""
STYLE=""TOP:25pt;LEFT:8pt;WIDTH:107pt;HEIGHT:17pt;ZINDEX:0;"">"
objALXOut.WriteLine( strOut )
strOut = "<PARAM NAME=""Caption"" VALUE=""Business Name"">"
objALXOut.WriteLine( strOut )
strOut = "<PARAM NAME=""Size"" VALUE=""3793;600"">"
objALXOut.WriteLine( strOut )
strOut = "<PARAM NAME=""FontCharSet"" VALUE=""0"">"
objALXOut.WriteLine( strOut )
strOut = "<PARAM NAME=""FontPitchAndFamily"" VALUE=""2"">"
objALXOut.WriteLine( strOut )
strOut = "<PARAM NAME=""FontWeight"" VALUE=""0"">"
objALXOut.WriteLine( strOut )
strOut = "</OBJECT>"
objALXOut.WriteLine( strOut )
strOut = "<OBJECT ID=""Label2"""
objALXOut.WriteLine( strOut )
strOut = "CLASSID=""CLSID:978C9E23-D4B0-11CE-BF2D-00AA003F40D0""
STYLE=""TOP:50pt;LEFT:8pt;WIDTH:107pt;HEIGHT:25pt;ZINDEX:1;"">"
objALXOut.WriteLine( strOut )
strOut = "<PARAM NAME=""Caption"" VALUE=""City"">"
objALXOut.WriteLine( strOut )
strOut = "<PARAM NAME=""Size"" VALUE=""3793;882"">"
objALXOut.WriteLine( strOut )
strOut = "<PARAM NAME=""FontCharSet"" VALUE=""0"">"
objALXOut.WriteLine( strOut )
strOut = "<PARAM NAME=""FontPitchAndFamily"" VALUE=""2"">"
objALXOut.WriteLine( strOut )
strOut = "<PARAM NAME=""FontWeight"" VALUE=""0"">"
objALXOut.WriteLine( strOut )
strOut = "</OBJECT>"
objALXOut.WriteLine( strOut )
strOut = "<OBJECT ID=""TextBox1"""
objALXOut.WriteLine( strOut )
strOut = "CLASSID=""CLSID:8BD21D10-EC42-11CE-9E0D-00AA006002F3""
STYLE=""TOP:17pt;LEFT:124pt;WIDTH:215pt;HEIGHT:25pt;TABINDEX:2;ZINDEX:2;"">"
objALXOut.WriteLine( strOut )
strOut = "<PARAM NAME=""VariousPropertyBits"" VALUE=""746604571"">"
objALXOut.WriteLine( strOut )
strOut = "<PARAM NAME=""Size"" VALUE=""7585;882"">"
objALXOut.WriteLine( strOut )
strOut = "<PARAM NAME=""Value"" VALUE=""" & objRecordSet("CompanyName") & """>"
objALXOut.WriteLine( strOut )
strOut = "<PARAM NAME=""FontCharSet"" VALUE=""0"">"
objALXOut.WriteLine( strOut )
strOut = "<PARAM NAME=""FontPitchAndFamily"" VALUE=""2"">"
objALXOut.WriteLine( strOut )
strOut = "<PARAM NAME=""FontWeight"" VALUE=""0"">"
objALXOut.WriteLine( strOut )
strOut = "</OBJECT>"
objALXOut.WriteLine( strOut )
strOut = "<OBJECT ID=""TextBox2"""
objALXOut.WriteLine( strOut )
strOut = "CLASSID=""CLSID:8BD21D10-EC42-11CE-9E0D-00AA006002F3""
STYLE=""TOP:50pt;LEFT:124pt;WIDTH:215pt;HEIGHT:26pt;TABINDEX:3;ZINDEX:3;"">"
```

continued on next page

continued from previous page

```
objALXOut.WriteLine( strOut )
strOut = "<PARAM NAME=""VariousPropertyBits"" VALUE=""746604571"">"
objALXOut.WriteLine( strOut )
strOut = "<PARAM NAME=""Size"" VALUE=""7585;917"">"
objALXOut.WriteLine( strOut )
strOut = "<PARAM NAME=""Value"" VALUE=""" & objRecordSet("City") &""">"
objALXOut.WriteLine( strOut )
strOut = "<PARAM NAME=""FontCharSet"" VALUE=""0"">"
objALXOut.WriteLine( strOut )
strOut = "<PARAM NAME=""FontPitchAndFamily"" VALUE=""2"">"
objALXOut.WriteLine( strOut )
strOut = "<PARAM NAME=""FontWeight"" VALUE=""0"">"
objALXOut.WriteLine( strOut )
strOut = "</OBJECT>"
objALXOut.WriteLine( strOut )
strOut = "<OBJECT ID=""CommandButton1"""
objALXOut.WriteLine( strOut )
strOut = "CLASSID=""CLSID:D7053240-CE69-11CD-A777-00DD01143C57""
STYLE=""TOP:17pt;LEFT:347pt;WIDTH:74pt;HEIGHT:25pt;TABINDEX:4;ZINDEX:4;"">"
objALXOut.WriteLine( strOut )
strOut = "<PARAM NAME=""Caption"" VALUE=""Backward"">"
objALXOut.WriteLine( strOut )
strOut = "<PARAM NAME=""Size"" VALUE=""2619;873"">"
objALXOut.WriteLine( strOut )
strOut = "<PARAM NAME=""FontCharSet"" VALUE=""0"">"
objALXOut.WriteLine( strOut )
strOut = "<PARAM NAME=""FontPitchAndFamily"" VALUE=""2"">"
objALXOut.WriteLine( strOut )
strOut = "<PARAM NAME=""ParagraphAlign"" VALUE=""3"">"
objALXOut.WriteLine( strOut )
strOut = "<PARAM NAME=""FontWeight"" VALUE=""0"">"
objALXOut.WriteLine( strOut )
strOut = "</OBJECT>"
objALXOut.WriteLine( strOut )
strOut = "<OBJECT ID=""CommandButton2"""
objALXOut.WriteLine( strOut )
strOut = "CLASSID=""CLSID:D7053240-CE69-11CD-A777-00DD01143C57""
STYLE=""TOP:17pt;LEFT:429pt;WIDTH:83pt;HEIGHT:25pt;TABINDEX:5;ZINDEX:5;"">"
objALXOut.WriteLine( strOut )
strOut = "<PARAM NAME=""Caption"" VALUE=""Forward"">"
objALXOut.WriteLine( strOut )
strOut = "<PARAM NAME=""Size"" VALUE=""2911;873"">"
objALXOut.WriteLine( strOut )
strOut = "<PARAM NAME=""FontCharSet"" VALUE=""0"">"
objALXOut.WriteLine( strOut )
strOut = "<PARAM NAME=""FontPitchAndFamily"" VALUE=""2"">"
objALXOut.WriteLine( strOut )
strOut = "<PARAM NAME=""ParagraphAlign"" VALUE=""3"">"
objALXOut.WriteLine( strOut )
strOut = "<PARAM NAME=""FontWeight"" VALUE=""0"">"
objALXOut.WriteLine( strOut )
strOut = "</OBJECT>"
objALXOut.WriteLine( strOut )
strOut = "<OBJECT ID=""CommandButton3"""
objALXOut.WriteLine( strOut )
```

```
strOut = "CLASSID=""CLSID:D7053240-CE69-11CD-A777-00DD01143C57"" "
strOut = strOut &⇐
"STYLE=""TOP:50pt;LEFT:388pt;WIDTH:91pt;HEIGHT:25pt;TABINDEX:6;ZINDEX:6;"">"
objALXOut.WriteLine( strOut )
strOut = "<PARAM NAME=""Caption"" VALUE=""Update"">"
objALXOut.WriteLine( strOut )
strOut = "<PARAM NAME=""Size"" VALUE=""3210;873"">"
objALXOut.WriteLine( strOut )
strOut = "<PARAM NAME=""FontCharSet"" VALUE=""0"">"
objALXOut.WriteLine( strOut )
strOut = "<PARAM NAME=""FontPitchAndFamily"" VALUE=""2"">"
objALXOut.WriteLine( strOut )
strOut = "<PARAM NAME=""ParagraphAlign"" VALUE=""3"">"
objALXOut.WriteLine( strOut )
strOut = "<PARAM NAME=""FontWeight"" VALUE=""0"">"
objALXOut.WriteLine( strOut )
strOut = "</OBJECT>"
objALXOut.WriteLine( strOut )
strOut = "</DIV>"
objALXOut.WriteLine( strOut )
objALXOut.Close
%>
</BODY>
</HTML>
```

2. Activate Internet Explorer. In the address field, type in `HTTP://DEFAULT/ASPEXEC/ASPHT0709.ASP` and press Return. As shown in Figure 7-9, the HTML Layout control will now appear correctly in its IFrame window. You have learned to use an ISAPI extension DLL with ASP and ADO.

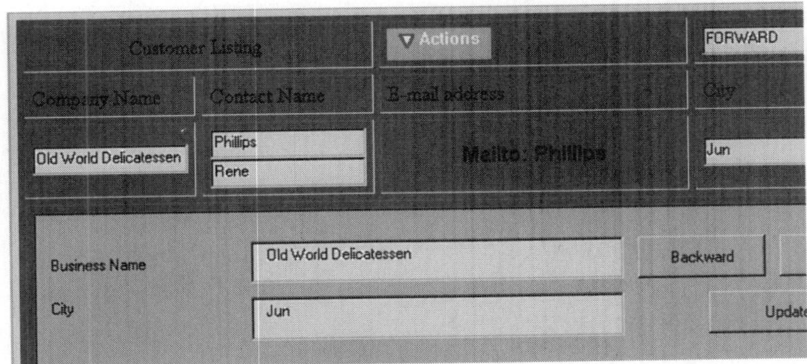

Figure 7.9 ASPHT0709.ASP in IE showing ISAPI extension DLL's output as an HTML Layout control

How It Works

These two lines of code are all it takes to use an ISAPI extension DLL:

```
<IFRAME NAME="IFrame1" SRC="isapialx.dll" WIDTH=750 HEIGHT=200 MARGINHEIGHT=0⇐
MARGINWIDTH=0
ALIGN=MIDDLE FRAMEBORDER=1 SCROLLING="YES"></IFRAME>
```

The DLL is treated as the source of an HTML document, thus inputting its HTML output stream into the browser. Internally, as is shown in Chapter 9, "ISAPI Filters: Customizing Internet Information Server," the DLL obtains information about the request and then sends back needed HTML code.

Comments

The best way to think about an ISAPI extension DLL is as a compiled CGI program. Use it that way and you'll never go wrong!

COMPLEXITY
ADVANCED

7.10 How do I... Use an ISAPI filter with my ASP ADO page?

Problem

We need to start keeping some statistics about when our Web pages are hit, particularly the database ones. Is there a way ISAPI can help us out here?

Technique

ISAPI filters are your solution. By using an ISAPI filter written to look for ADO references in the triggered ASP page and entering the page name and URL into a log file, you can start the process of gathering potent WWW statistics! Although the directions create the project from scratch, the completed ASP files are on the book CD under `\CH07\HT10\`. (Before using this How-To, make sure you have completed How-To 9.1 in Chapter 9 and entered its Filter into the IIS/PWS system.)

Steps

1. This How-To does not show you how to create the ISAPI filter, because that's the province of Chapter 9. Instead, it shows you how to use its output in an HTML page with the ADO system already developed. Activate ActiveX Control Pad and reload the `ASPHT0709.ASP` file. Modify

the code so it is identical to the code in Listing 7-10. Save it as ASPHT0710.ASP.

Listing 7-10 ASPHT0710.ASP ASP script file

```
<%@ LANGUAGE = VBScript %>
<HTML>
<HEAD>
<TITLE>Active Server Pages Chapter Seven How To Ten</TITLE>
</HEAD>
<BODY>
<% if IsObject(Session("objRecordSet")) then
     set objRecordSet = Session("objRecordSet")
   else
     Set objConnection = Server.CreateObject("ADODB.Connection")
        objConnection.Open "AWTutorial"
        SQLQuery = "SELECT * FROM Customers"
        Set objRecordSet = objConnection.Execute( SQLQuery )
        objRecordSet.Close
        objRecordSet.Open , , 3 , 4
        Set Session("objRecordSet") = objRecordSet
   end if
   dim HoldAction
   HoldAction = Request.Form("Text1")
   HoldAction = UCase( HoldAction )
   if HoldAction = "" then HoldAction = "FORWARD"
   if HoldAction = "FORWARD" then
     on error resume next
     if not objRecordSet.EOF then
          objRecordSet.MoveNext
     else
          objRecordSet.MoveFirst
     end if
   elseif HoldAction = "BACKWARD" then
     on error resume next
     if not objRecordSet.BOF then
          objRecordSet.MovePrevious
     else
          objRecordSet.MoveLast
     end if
   elseif HoldAction = "UPDATE" then
     objRecordSet("CompanyName") = Request.Form("Text2")
     objRecordSet("ContactLastName") = Request.Form("Text3")
        objRecordSet("ContactFirstName") = Request.Form("Text4")
        objRecordSet("City") = Request.Form("Text5")
        objRecordSet("StateOrProvince") = Request.Form("Text6")
        ObjRecordSet.Update
    end if
%>
    <FORM ACTION="http://default/aspexec/aspht0709.asp" METHOD="POST" NAME="Form1"
     TARGET="_top">
<TABLE WIDTH=600 COLSPAN=8 BORDER=5 CELLSPACING=5
CELLPADDING=5 ALIGN="CENTER" VALIGN="MIDDLE" BGCOLOR="Teal">
<TR>
```

continued on next page

continued from previous page

```
<TD COLSPAN=2 ALIGN="CENTER">
Customer Listing
</TD>
<TD>
        <SCRIPT LANGUAGE="VBScript">
<!--
Sub menu2_Select(item)
select case item
  case 1
    Document.Form1.Text1.value = "FORWARD"
    call Document.Form1.Submit1.click()
  case 2
    Document.Form1.Text1.value = "BACKWARD"
    call Document.Form1.Submit1.click()
  case 3
    Document.Form1.Text1.value = "UPDATE"
    call Document.Form1.Submit1.click()
end select
end sub
-->
        </SCRIPT>
        <OBJECT ID="menu2" WIDTH=80 HEIGHT=25 align=middle
         CLASSID="CLSID:52DFAE60-CEBF-11CF-A3A9-00A0C9034920">
            <PARAM NAME="Menuitem[0]" VALUE="Forward">
            <PARAM NAME="Menuitem[1]" VALUE="Backward">
            <PARAM NAME="Menuitem[2]" VALUE="Update">
            <PARAM NAME="Caption" VALUE="Actions">
        </OBJECT>
</TD>
<TD>
        <INPUT TYPE=Text VALUE="<%= HoldAction %>" NAME="Text1">
</TD>
        <INPUT TYPE=Submit VALUE="Next Action" NAME="Submit1">
</TR>
<TR>
<TD>
Company Name
</TD>
<TD>
Contact Name
</TD>
<TD>
E-mail address
</TD>
<TD>
City
</TD>
<TD>
State/Province
</TD>
</TR>
  <TR>
  <TD>
        <INPUT TYPE=Text NAME="Text2" VALUE="<%= objRecordSet("CompanyName")%>">
</TD>
```

```
  <TD>
        <INPUT TYPE=Text NAME="Text3" VALUE="<%=⇐
        objRecordSet("ContactLastName")%>">
        <INPUT TYPE=Text NAME="Text4" VALUE="<%=⇐
        objRecordSet("ContactFirstName")%>">
</TD>
  <TD>
        <OBJECT ID="IeLabel1" WIDTH=225 HEIGHT=27
         CLASSID="CLSID:99B42120-6EC7-11CF-A6C7-00AA00A47DD2">
            <PARAM NAME="_ExtentX" VALUE="5953">
            <PARAM NAME="_ExtentY" VALUE="714">
            <PARAM NAME="Caption" VALUE="Mailto: <%=⇐
            objRecordSet("ContactLastName")%>">
    <PARAM NAME="Angle" VALUE="0">
    <PARAM NAME="Alignment" VALUE="4">
    <PARAM NAME="Mode" VALUE="1">
    <PARAM NAME="FillStyle" VALUE="0">
    <PARAM NAME="FillStyle" VALUE="1">
    <PARAM NAME="ForeColor" VALUE="#000000">
    <PARAM NAME="BackColor" VALUE="#D8C0A0">
    <PARAM NAME="FontName" VALUE="Arial">
    <PARAM NAME="FontSize" VALUE="12">
    <PARAM NAME="FontItalic" VALUE="0">
    <PARAM NAME="FontBold" VALUE="1">
    <PARAM NAME="FontUnderline" VALUE="0">
    <PARAM NAME="FontStrikeout" VALUE="0">
    <PARAM NAME="TopPoints" VALUE="0">
    <PARAM NAME="BotPoints" VALUE="0">
</OBJECT>

   </TD>
  <TD>
  <INPUT Type = "Text" Name="Text5" Value = "<%= objRecordSet("City")%>">
  </TD>
  <TD>
  <INPUT Type = "Text" Name="Text6" Value = "<%=⇐
  objRecordSet("StateOrProvince")%>">
  </TD>
  </TR>
</TD>
</TR>
<TR >
<TD COLSPAN = 5>
<IFRAME NAME="IFrame1" SRC="isapialx.dll" WIDTH=750 HEIGHT=200 MARGINHEIGHT=0
MARGINWIDTH=0
ALIGN=MIDDLE FRAMEBORDER=1 SCROLLING="YES"></IFRAME>
</TD>
</TR>
</TABLE>
    </FORM>
<%
Set objFileSys = Server.CreateObject("Scripting.FileSystemObject")
Dim strALXPath
strALXPath = Server.MapPath("/ASPExec") & "/aspht0708.alx"
Set objALXOut = objFileSys.CreateTextFile( strALXPath ,True)
```

continued on next page

continued from previous page

```
strOut = "<SCRIPT LANGUAGE=""VBScript"">"
objALXOut.WriteLine( strOut )
strOut = "<!--"
objALXOut.WriteLine( strOut )
strOut = "Sub CommandButton3_Click()"
objALXOut.WriteLine( strOut )
strOut = "parent.Document.Form1.text1.value = ""UPDATE"""
objALXOut.WriteLine( strOut )
strOut = "call parent.Document.Form1.Submit1.click()"
objALXOut.WriteLine( strOut )
strOut = "end sub"
objALXOut.WriteLine( strOut )
strOut = "-->"
objALXOut.WriteLine( strOut )
strOut = "</SCRIPT>"
objALXOut.WriteLine( strOut )
strOut = "<SCRIPT LANGUAGE=""VBScript"">"
objALXOut.WriteLine( strOut )
strOut = "<!--"
objALXOut.WriteLine( strOut )
strOut = "Sub CommandButton2_Click()"
objALXOut.WriteLine( strOut )
strOut = "parent.Document.Form1.text1.value = ""FORWARD"""
objALXOut.WriteLine( strOut )
strOut = "call parent.Document.Form1.Submit1.click()"
objALXOut.WriteLine( strOut )
strOut = "end sub"
objALXOut.WriteLine( strOut )
strOut = "-->"
objALXOut.WriteLine( strOut )
strOut = "</SCRIPT>"
objALXOut.WriteLine( strOut )
strOut = "<SCRIPT LANGUAGE=""VBScript"">"
objALXOut.WriteLine( strOut )
strOut = "<!--"
objALXOut.WriteLine( strOut )
strOut = "Sub CommandButton1_Click()"
objALXOut.WriteLine( strOut )
strOut = "parent.Document.Form1.text1.value = ""BACKWARD"""
objALXOut.WriteLine( strOut )
strOut = "call parent.Document.Form1.Submit1.click()"
objALXOut.WriteLine( strOut )
strOut = "end sub"
objALXOut.WriteLine( strOut )
strOut = "-->"
objALXOut.WriteLine( strOut )
strOut = "</SCRIPT>"
objALXOut.WriteLine( strOut )
strOut = "<SCRIPT LANGUAGE=""VBScript"">"
objALXOut.WriteLine( strOut )
strOut = "<!--"
objALXOut.WriteLine( strOut )
strOut = "Sub TextBox2_Change()"
objALXOut.WriteLine( strOut )
strOut = "parent.Document.Form1.Text5.Value = TextBox2.Text"
```

```
objALXOut.WriteLine( strOut )
strOut = "end sub"
objALXOut.WriteLine( strOut )
strOut = "-->"
objALXOut.WriteLine( strOut )
strOut = "</SCRIPT>"
objALXOut.WriteLine( strOut )
strOut = "<SCRIPT LANGUAGE=""VBScript"">"
objALXOut.WriteLine( strOut )
strOut = "<!--"
objALXOut.WriteLine( strOut )
strOut = "Sub TextBox1_Change()"
objALXOut.WriteLine( strOut )
strOut = "parent.Document.Form1.Text2.Value = TextBox1.Text"
objALXOut.WriteLine( strOut )
strOut = "end sub"
objALXOut.WriteLine( strOut )
strOut = "-->"
objALXOut.WriteLine( strOut )
strOut = "</SCRIPT>"
objALXOut.WriteLine( strOut )
strOut = "<DIV ID=""Layout1"" STYLE=""LAYOUT:FIXED;WIDTH:530pt;HEIGHT:92pt;"">"
objALXOut.WriteLine( strOut )
strOut = "<OBJECT ID=""Label1"""
objALXOut.WriteLine( strOut )
strOut = "CLASSID=""CLSID:978C9E23-D4B0-11CE-BF2D-00AA003F40D0""
STYLE=""TOP:25pt;LEFT:8pt;WIDTH:107pt;HEIGHT:17pt;ZINDEX:0;"">"
objALXOut.WriteLine( strOut )
strOut = "<PARAM NAME=""Caption"" VALUE=""Business Name"">"
objALXOut.WriteLine( strOut )
strOut = "<PARAM NAME=""Size"" VALUE=""3793;600"">"
objALXOut.WriteLine( strOut )
strOut = "<PARAM NAME=""FontCharSet"" VALUE=""0"">"
objALXOut.WriteLine( strOut )
strOut = "<PARAM NAME=""FontPitchAndFamily"" VALUE=""2"">"
objALXOut.WriteLine( strOut )
strOut = "<PARAM NAME=""FontWeight"" VALUE=""0"">"
objALXOut.WriteLine( strOut )
strOut = "</OBJECT>"
objALXOut.WriteLine( strOut )
strOut = "<OBJECT ID=""Label2"""
objALXOut.WriteLine( strOut )
strOut = "CLASSID=""CLSID:978C9E23-D4B0-11CE-BF2D-00AA003F40D0""
STYLE=""TOP:50pt;LEFT:8pt;WIDTH:107pt;HEIGHT:25pt;ZINDEX:1;"">"
objALXOut.WriteLine( strOut )
strOut = "<PARAM NAME=""Caption"" VALUE=""City"">"
objALXOut.WriteLine( strOut )
strOut = "<PARAM NAME=""Size"" VALUE=""3793;882"">"
objALXOut.WriteLine( strOut )
strOut = "<PARAM NAME=""FontCharSet"" VALUE=""0"">"
objALXOut.WriteLine( strOut )
strOut = "<PARAM NAME=""FontPitchAndFamily"" VALUE=""2"">"
objALXOut.WriteLine( strOut )
strOut = "<PARAM NAME=""FontWeight"" VALUE=""0"">"
objALXOut.WriteLine( strOut )
```

continued on next page

continued from previous page

```
strOut = "</OBJECT>"
objALXOut.WriteLine( strOut )
strOut = "<OBJECT ID=""TextBox1"""
objALXOut.WriteLine( strOut )
strOut = "CLASSID=""CLSID:8BD21D10-EC42-11CE-9E0D-00AA006002F3""
STYLE=""TOP:17pt;LEFT:124pt;WIDTH:215pt;HEIGHT:25pt;TABINDEX:2;ZINDEX:2;"">"
objALXOut.WriteLine( strOut )
strOut = "<PARAM NAME=""VariousPropertyBits"" VALUE=""746604571"">"
objALXOut.WriteLine( strOut )
strOut = "<PARAM NAME=""Size"" VALUE=""7585;882"">"
objALXOut.WriteLine( strOut )
strOut = "<PARAM NAME=""Value"" VALUE=""" & objRecordSet("CompanyName") & """>"
objALXOut.WriteLine( strOut )
strOut = "<PARAM NAME=""FontCharSet"" VALUE=""0"">"
objALXOut.WriteLine( strOut )
strOut = "<PARAM NAME=""FontPitchAndFamily"" VALUE=""2"">"
objALXOut.WriteLine( strOut )
strOut = "<PARAM NAME=""FontWeight"" VALUE=""0"">"
objALXOut.WriteLine( strOut )
strOut = "</OBJECT>"
objALXOut.WriteLine( strOut )
strOut = "<OBJECT ID=""TextBox2"""
objALXOut.WriteLine( strOut )
strOut = "CLASSID=""CLSID:8BD21D10-EC42-11CE-9E0D-00AA006002F3""
STYLE=""TOP:50pt;LEFT:124pt;WIDTH:215pt;HEIGHT:26pt;TABINDEX:3;ZINDEX:3;"">"
objALXOut.WriteLine( strOut )
strOut = "<PARAM NAME=""VariousPropertyBits"" VALUE=""746604571"">"
objALXOut.WriteLine( strOut )
strOut = "<PARAM NAME=""Size"" VALUE=""7585;917"">"
objALXOut.WriteLine( strOut )
strOut = "<PARAM NAME=""Value"" VALUE=""" & objRecordSet("City") &""">"
objALXOut.WriteLine( strOut )
strOut = "<PARAM NAME=""FontCharSet"" VALUE=""0"">"
objALXOut.WriteLine( strOut )
strOut = "<PARAM NAME=""FontPitchAndFamily"" VALUE=""2"">"
objALXOut.WriteLine( strOut )
strOut = "<PARAM NAME=""FontWeight"" VALUE=""0"">"
objALXOut.WriteLine( strOut )
strOut = "</OBJECT>"
objALXOut.WriteLine( strOut )
strOut = "<OBJECT ID=""CommandButton1"""
objALXOut.WriteLine( strOut )
strOut = "CLASSID=""CLSID:D7053240-CE69-11CD-A777-00DD01143C57""
STYLE=""TOP:17pt;LEFT:347pt;WIDTH:74pt;HEIGHT:25pt;TABINDEX:4;ZINDEX:4;"">"
objALXOut.WriteLine( strOut )
strOut = "<PARAM NAME=""Caption"" VALUE=""Backward"">"
objALXOut.WriteLine( strOut )
strOut = "<PARAM NAME=""Size"" VALUE=""2619;873"">"
objALXOut.WriteLine( strOut )
strOut = "<PARAM NAME=""FontCharSet"" VALUE=""0"">"
objALXOut.WriteLine( strOut )
strOut = "<PARAM NAME=""FontPitchAndFamily"" VALUE=""2"">"
objALXOut.WriteLine( strOut )
strOut = "<PARAM NAME=""ParagraphAlign"" VALUE=""3"">"
objALXOut.WriteLine( strOut )
```

```
strOut = "<PARAM NAME=""FontWeight"" VALUE=""0"">"
objALXOut.WriteLine( strOut )
strOut = "</OBJECT>"
objALXOut.WriteLine( strOut )
strOut = "<OBJECT ID=""CommandButton2"""
objALXOut.WriteLine( strOut )
strOut = "CLASSID=""CLSID:D7053240-CE69-11CD-A777-00DD01143C57""
STYLE=""TOP:17pt;LEFT:429pt;WIDTH:83pt;HEIGHT:25pt;TABINDEX:5;ZINDEX:5;"">"
objALXOut.WriteLine( strOut )
strOut = "<PARAM NAME=""Caption"" VALUE=""Forward"">"
objALXOut.WriteLine( strOut )
strOut = "<PARAM NAME=""Size"" VALUE=""2911;873"">"
objALXOut.WriteLine( strOut )
strOut = "<PARAM NAME=""FontCharSet"" VALUE=""0"">"
objALXOut.WriteLine( strOut )
strOut = "<PARAM NAME=""FontPitchAndFamily"" VALUE=""2"">"
objALXOut.WriteLine( strOut )
strOut = "<PARAM NAME=""ParagraphAlign"" VALUE=""3"">"
objALXOut.WriteLine( strOut )
strOut = "<PARAM NAME=""FontWeight"" VALUE=""0"">"
objALXOut.WriteLine( strOut )
strOut = "</OBJECT>"
objALXOut.WriteLine( strOut )
strOut = "<OBJECT ID=""CommandButton3"""
objALXOut.WriteLine( strOut )
strOut = "CLASSID=""CLSID:D7053240-CE69-11CD-A777-00DD01143C57"" "
strOut = strOut &⇐
"STYLE=""TOP:50pt;LEFT:388pt;WIDTH:91pt;HEIGHT:25pt;TABINDEX:6;ZINDEX:6;"">"
objALXOut.WriteLine( strOut )
strOut = "<PARAM NAME=""Caption"" VALUE=""Update"">"
objALXOut.WriteLine( strOut )
strOut = "<PARAM NAME=""Size"" VALUE=""3210;873"">"
objALXOut.WriteLine( strOut )
strOut = "<PARAM NAME=""FontCharSet"" VALUE=""0"">"
objALXOut.WriteLine( strOut )
strOut = "<PARAM NAME=""FontPitchAndFamily"" VALUE=""2"">"
objALXOut.WriteLine( strOut )
strOut = "<PARAM NAME=""ParagraphAlign"" VALUE=""3"">"
objALXOut.WriteLine( strOut )
strOut = "<PARAM NAME=""FontWeight"" VALUE=""0"">"
objALXOut.WriteLine( strOut )
strOut = "</OBJECT>"
objALXOut.WriteLine( strOut )
strOut = "</DIV>"
objALXOut.WriteLine( strOut )
objALXOut.Close
%>
</BODY>
</HTML>
```

2. Activate Internet Explorer. In the address field, type in **HTTP://DEFAULT/ASPEXEC/ASPHT0710.ASP** and press Return. A table will be created using the information from the ODBC database. Now check the **ASPHT0901.LOG** file in NotePad or a similar text editor; you will see that the call to the

ADODB object has been logged. Congratulations! You have learned to use ISAPI filters to interact with ODBC databases using ADO.

How It Works

Aside from the usual mechanics of interspersing ASP scripts with HTML text, this How-To shows a key part of ASP functionality, the ADODB object:

```
<% Set OBJdbConnection = Server.CreateObject("ADODB.Connection")
OBJdbConnection.Open "AWTutorial"
SQLQuery = "SELECT * FROM Customers"
Set RSCustomerList = OBJdbConnection.Execute(SQLQuery) %>
```

The Server object is used here, as it is where the connection to the ADODB object is stored (via the GLOBAL.ASA file, which is discussed in much more detail in Chapter 5, "Intermediate ASP: Active Server Components"). Once the object is successfully created, it is told to open the database with the alias AWTutorial, which you entered into your system in step 1. Finally, the last two statements create an SQL query and send it to the database, returning a collection object that holds the results of that query.

After having obtained the desired recordset, you must next use it to create the data for the HTML table:

```
<% Do While Not RScustomerList.EOF %>
  <TR>
  <TD BGCOLOR="f7efde" ALIGN=CENTER>
    <FONT STYLE="ARIAL NARROW" SIZE=1>
      <%= RSCustomerList("CompanyName")%>
    </FONT></TD>
  <TD BGCOLOR="f7efde" ALIGN=CENTER>
    <FONT STYLE="ARIAL NARROW" SIZE=1>
      <%= RScustomerList("ContactLastName") & ", " %>
      <%= RScustomerList("ContactFirstName") %>
    </FONT></TD>
  <TD BGCOLOR="f7efde" ALIGN=CENTER>
    <FONT STYLE="ARIAL NARROW" SIZE=1>
    <A HREF="mailto:">
      <%= RScustomerList("ContactLastName")%>
    </A></FONT></TD>
  <TD BGCOLOR="f7efde" ALIGN=CENTER>
    <FONT STYLE="ARIAL NARROW" SIZE=1>
      <%= RScustomerList("City")%>
    </FONT></TD>
  <TD BGCOLOR="f7efde" ALIGN=CENTER>
    <FONT STYLE="ARIAL NARROW" SIZE=1>
      <%= RScustomerList("StateOrProvince")%>
    </FONT></TD>
  </TR>
<% RScustomerList.MoveNext
Loop %>
```

The technique here is very simple: Output the values of fields of the collection object returned by the SQL query by sending them into it as parameters. (More on using collections with ASP in Chapter 5.) By using a loop that runs until the end of the collection (`RScustomerList.EOF`), you write all the data into the HTML table for clear display.

Comments

Despite the simplicity, any type and complexity of database information can be displayed in this way, although more complex techniques are needed involving `BinaryWrite` for binary data (`BLOB` fields).

CHAPTER 8

ISAPI EXTENSIONS: USING ACTIVEX DLLS TO REPLACE CGI

8

ISAPI EXTENSIONS: USING ACTIVEX DLLS TO REPLACE CGI

How do I...

8.9 Use an ASP script with an ISAPI extension DLL?

8.10 Interact with ActiveX data objects with an ISAPI extension DLL?

Active Server Pages (ASP) works very well in many situations as a replacement for Common Gateway Interface (CGI) scripting. But in some areas, its text-based design imposes limitations that even the additional powerful ASP components cannot fully remedy. Microsoft understood this during the design phase of ASP and added a powerful feature to the overall Internet Information Server/Personal Web Server (IIS/PWS) system: the ISAPI extension. ISAPI stands for Internet Server Applications Programming Interface (API), and an extension is a Dynamic Link Library (DLL) that behaves exactly like a CGI executable inside IIS/PWS. With extension DLLs, you can send back complex HTML text, obtain HTTP server variables, and obtain complete form data elements easily and quickly. The extension system also permits sending data to the server, both directly in the case of errors and via header fields, as well as redirection of the client browser to a new URL. This chapter provides complete code examples in Visual C++ 5.0 for creating ISAPI extension DLLs.

8.1 Create an ISAPI Extension DLL in Visual C++ 5.0

Visual C++ 5.0 has an ISAPI Wizard, and this How-To gives you complete instructions on using it to create a simple DLL that sends back an HTML Layout control for using it in an ADO page.

8.2 Get Server Information with an ISAPI Extension DLL

The ISAPI extension system is encapsulated inside the `CHttpServer` and `CHttpServerContext` objects in MFC. This How-To demonstrates using the `GetServerVariable` method of `CHttpServerContext` to determine which browser is being used to access an HTML page and send back the appropriate HTML content.

8.3 Interact With HTML Forms Using Parse Maps with an ISAPI Extension DLL

CGI's principal focus is to retrieve HTML form variables with preset names, process their input, and send back appropriate output. ISAPI extension DLLs provide the same functionality via their parse map macro system. This How-To details using parse maps to respond to users' input.

8.4 Send Server Information with an ISAPI Extension DLL

Another powerful feature of CGI is its capability to send information to the server that controls HTTP processing behavior directly, something not possible with ASP scripts or components. This How-To shows you the way to send a complete HTML file as output of the extension DLL via the `ServerSupportFunction` method of the extension `Control Block` object.

8.5 Handle Error Conditions with an ISAPI Extension DLL

Sometimes, despite the best efforts of developers, error conditions happen during an HTTP request. This How-To illustrates using the `WriteClient` method of the extension `Control Block` object to send a user-friendly error message when a problem happens.

8.6 Send Customized HTML Output with an ISAPI Extension DLL

CGI also shines at sending specialized response headers to the server, and extension DLLs have the same capability. This How-To details the steps needed to send a specialized response header and binary data output via the methods of the extension control block (ECB).

8.7 Redirect the Client Browser to a New URL with an ISAPI Extension DLL

One of the most common uses for CGI scripts has been URL redirection, either due to a server change or due to internal reorganization of a Web site. This How-To focuses on the `ServerSupportFunction` method of the ECB again, this time using it to perform remote URL redirection to another link when needed.

8.8 Link an ActiveX Control to an ISAPI Extension DLL

Now that you're up to speed on the major functionality of ISAPI extension DLLs, you need to start using them in an active platform environment! This How-To shows you exactly how to use extension features to control the behavior of an ActiveX control on an HTML page precisely.

8.9 Use an ASP Script with an ISAPI Extension DLL

At first glance, this might seem trivial, until you remember that the output of an extension DLL *bypasses* the ASP system and goes directly into HTML output! Getting around this is one of the little tricks that will put your capabilities into the "guru" class, and this How-To shows you the exact procedure required.

8.10 Interact With ActiveX Data Objects with an ISAPI Extension DLL

Because ADO lives only in ASP scripts for now, typing an ISAPI extension DLL with ADO is a serious challenge! This How-To gives you one technique that uses ASP `#include` syntax and custom text file output.

8.1 How do I...
Create an ISAPI extension DLL in Visual C++ 5.0?

Problem

Although ASP is great, my company has invested considerable time and money into Win-CGI executables (written in VB) for our Web site. Some of them require interaction with the Windows API that ASP cannot duplicate. Is there another active platform technology that can duplicate full CGI functionality?

Technique

The technology you need is called ISAPI extension DLLs. They are C++ DLLs that have full access to the Windows API as well as complete CGI functionality. This How-To shows you the basics of using Visual C++ 5.0 to create an ISAPI extension DLL that exports an HTML Layout control to an ASP file's output. Although these directions create the project from scratch, the CD contains a completed file under `CH08\HT01\`.

Steps

1. Start Visual C++ 5.0 and bring up the New Workspace dialog. As shown in Figure 8-1, select MFC ISAPI Extension Wizard from the list of icons to create a new ASP component DLL. Choose an appropriate directory for the project and name it `ISAPIALX`.

2. When the wizard dialog appears, select an extension DLL with MFC as a shared DLL. The finished wizard dialog should look very similar to the one shown in Figure 8-2. Press Finish to create the new project skeleton.

3. Bring up the `ISAPIALX.CPP` source file in the text editor. Enter all the boldfaced code in Listing 8-1 to add functionality to the extension DLL. Save the project. Then select Build DLL from the menu. The project should create correctly with no errors or warnings. Copy it into the `ASPEXEC` directory (if you have already completed Chapter 7, "ActiveX Data Objects: OLE DB Made Easy," you will overwrite the existing copy placed there earlier).

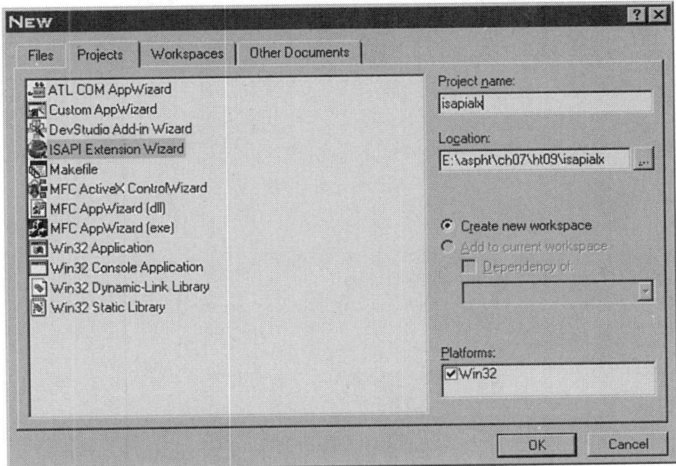

Figure 8-1 Selecting a new ISAPI extension DLL project in VC 5

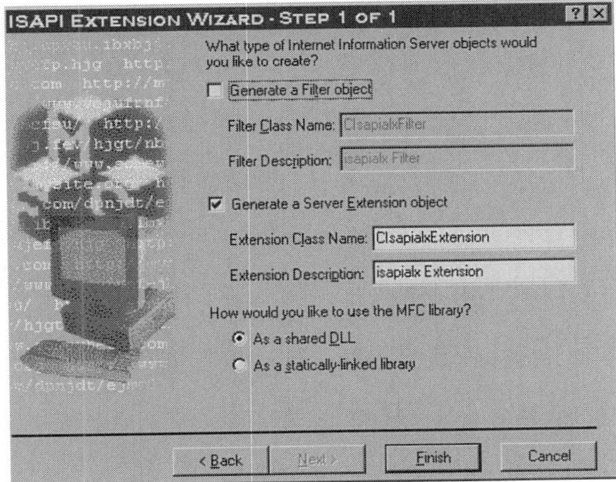

Figure 8-2 The MFC ISAPI Wizard in Visual C++ 5.0 set for an extension DLL

Listing 8-1 ISAPIALX.CPP source code

```
return strResult.AllocSysString();
// ISAPIALX.CPP - Implementation file for your Internet Server
//    isapialx Extension

#include "stdafx.h"
#include "isapialx.h"
```

continued on next page

continued from previous page

```
///////////////////////////////////////////////////////////////////////
// The one and only CWinApp object
// NOTE: You may remove this object if you alter your project to no
// longer use MFC in a DLL.

CWinApp theApp;

///////////////////////////////////////////////////////////////////////
// command-parsing map

BEGIN_PARSE_MAP(CIsapialxExtension, CHttpServer)
// TODO: insert your ON_PARSE_COMMAND() and
// ON_PARSE_COMMAND_PARAMS() here to hook up your commands.
// For example:

ON_PARSE_COMMAND(Default, CIsapialxExtension, ITS_EMPTY)
DEFAULT_PARSE_COMMAND(Default, CIsapialxExtension)
END_PARSE_MAP(CIsapialxExtension)


///////////////////////////////////////////////////////////////////////
// The one and only CIsapialxExtension object

CIsapialxExtension theExtension;


///////////////////////////////////////////////////////////////////////
// CIsapialxExtension implementation

CIsapialxExtension::CIsapialxExtension()
{
}

CIsapialxExtension::~CIsapialxExtension()
{
}

BOOL CIsapialxExtension::GetExtensionVersion(HSE_VERSION_INFO* pVer)
{
// Call default implementation for initialization
CHttpServer::GetExtensionVersion(pVer);

// Load description string
TCHAR sz[HSE_MAX_EXT_DLL_NAME_LEN+1];
ISAPIVERIFY(::LoadString(AfxGetResourceHandle(),
IDS_SERVER, sz, HSE_MAX_EXT_DLL_NAME_LEN));
_tcscpy(pVer->lpszExtensionDesc, sz);
return TRUE;
}

///////////////////////////////////////////////////////////////////////
// CIsapialxExtension command handlers

void CIsapialxExtension::Default(CHttpServerContext* pCtxt)
{
```

```
    StartContent(pCtxt);
    WriteTitle(pCtxt);

    *pCtxt << _T("<OBJECT CLASSID=""CLSID:812AE312-8B8E-11CF-93C8-
00AA00C08FDF""");
    *pCtxt << _T("ID=""aspht0708_alx"" STYLE=""LEFT:0;TOP:0"">");
    *pCtxt << _T("<PARAM NAME=""ALXPATH"" REF VALUE=""aspht0708.alx"">");
    *pCtxt << _T("</OBJECT>\r\n");

    EndContent(pCtxt);
}

// Do not edit the following lines, which are needed by ClassWizard.
#if 0
BEGIN_MESSAGE_MAP(CIsapialxExtension, CHttpServer)
//{{AFX_MSG_MAP(CIsapialxExtension)
//}}AFX_MSG_MAP
END_MESSAGE_MAP()
#endif// 0



///////////////////////////////////////////////////////////////////////
// If your extension will not use MFC, you'll need this code to make
// sure the extension objects can find the resource handle for the
// module.  If you convert your extension to not be dependent on MFC,
// remove the comments around the following AfxGetResourceHandle()
// and DllMain() functions, as well as the g_hInstance global.

/****

static HINSTANCE g_hInstance;

HINSTANCE AFXISAPI AfxGetResourceHandle()
{
return g_hInstance;
}

BOOL WINAPI DllMain(HINSTANCE hInst, ULONG ulReason,
LPVOID lpReserved)
{
if (ulReason == DLL_PROCESS_ATTACH)
{
g_hInstance = hInst;
}

return TRUE;
}

****/
```

4. Activate ActiveX Control Pad. Enter the ASP code in Listing 8-2 and save the file as ASPHT0801.ASP. Copy it into the ASPEXEC directory so it can be executed by the ASP system.

Listing 8-2 ASPHT0801.ASP source code

```
<%@ LANGUAGE = VBScript %>
<HTML>
<HEAD>
<TITLE>Active Server Pages Chapter Eight How To One</TITLE>
</HEAD>
<BODY>
<% if IsObject(Session("objRecordSet")) then
     set objRecordSet = Session("objRecordSet")
   else
     Set objConnection = Server.CreateObject("ADODB.Connection")
objConnection.Open "AWTutorial"
SQLQuery = "SELECT * FROM Customers"
Set objRecordSet = objConnection.Execute( SQLQuery )
objRecordSet.Close
objRecordSet.Open , , 3 , 4
Set Session("objRecordSet") = objRecordSet
   end if
   dim HoldAction
   HoldAction = Request.Form("Text1")
   HoldAction = UCase( HoldAction )
   if HoldAction = "" then HoldAction = "FORWARD"
   if HoldAction = "FORWARD" then
     on error resume next
     if not objRecordSet.EOF then
objRecordSet.MoveNext
     else
objRecordSet.MoveFirst
     end if
   elseif HoldAction = "BACKWARD" then
     on error resume next
     if not objRecordSet.BOF then
objRecordSet.MovePrevious
     else
objRecordSet.MoveLast
     end if
   elseif HoldAction = "UPDATE" then
     objRecordSet("CompanyName") = Request.Form("Text2")
     objRecordSet("ContactLastName") = Request.Form("Text3")
     objRecordSet("ContactFirstName") = Request.Form("Text4")
     objRecordSet("City") = Request.Form("Text5")
     objRecordSet("StateOrProvince") = Request.Form("Text6")
     ObjRecordSet.Update
    end if
%>
    <FORM ACTION="http://default/aspexec/aspht0801.asp" METHOD="POST" NAME="Form1"
     TARGET="_top">
<TABLE WIDTH=600 COLSPAN=8 BORDER=5 CELLSPACING=5
CELLPADDING=5 ALIGN="CENTER" VALIGN="MIDDLE" BGCOLOR="Teal">
<TR>
<TD COLSPAN=2 ALIGN="CENTER">
Customer Listing
</TD>
<TD>
        <SCRIPT LANGUAGE="VBScript">
<!--
Sub menu2_Select(item)
```

```
select case item
  case 1
    Document.Form1.Text1.value = "FORWARD"
    call Document.Form1.Submit1.click()
  case 2
    Document.Form1.Text1.value = "BACKWARD"
    call Document.Form1.Submit1.click()
  case 3
    Document.Form1.Text1.value = "UPDATE"
    call Document.Form1.Submit1.click()
end select
end sub
-->
        </SCRIPT>
        <OBJECT ID="menu2" WIDTH=80 HEIGHT=25 align=middle
         CLASSID="CLSID:52DFAE60-CEBF-11CF-A3A9-00A0C9034920">
            <PARAM NAME="Menuitem[0]" VALUE="Forward">
            <PARAM NAME="Menuitem[1]" VALUE="Backward">
            <PARAM NAME="Menuitem[2]" VALUE="Update">
            <PARAM NAME="Caption" VALUE="Actions">
        </OBJECT>
</TD>
<TD>
        <INPUT TYPE=Text VALUE="<%= HoldAction %>" NAME="Text1">
</TD>
        <INPUT TYPE=Submit VALUE="Next Action" NAME="Submit1">
</TR>
<TR>
<TD>
Company Name
</TD>
<TD>
Contact Name
</TD>
<TD>
E-mail address
</TD>
<TD>
City
</TD>
<TD>
State/Province
</TD>
</TR>
  <TR>
  <TD>
        <INPUT TYPE=Text NAME="Text2" VALUE="<%= objRecordSet("CompanyName")%>">
</TD>
  <TD>
        <INPUT TYPE=Text NAME="Text3" VALUE="<%=⇐
objRecordSet("ContactLastName")%>">
        <INPUT TYPE=Text NAME="Text4" VALUE="<%=⇐
objRecordSet("ContactFirstName")%>">
</TD>
  <TD>
```

continued on next page

continued from previous page

```
        <OBJECT ID="IeLabel1" WIDTH=225 HEIGHT=27
         CLASSID="CLSID:99B42120-6EC7-11CF-A6C7-00AA00A47DD2">
            <PARAM NAME="_ExtentX" VALUE="5953">
            <PARAM NAME="_ExtentY" VALUE="714">
            <PARAM NAME="Caption" VALUE="Mailto: <%=⇐
objRecordSet("ContactLastName")%>">
    <PARAM NAME="Angle" VALUE="0">
    <PARAM NAME="Alignment" VALUE="4">
    <PARAM NAME="Mode" VALUE="1">
    <PARAM NAME="FillStyle" VALUE="0">
    <PARAM NAME="FillStyle" VALUE="1">
    <PARAM NAME="ForeColor" VALUE="#000000">
    <PARAM NAME="BackColor" VALUE="#D8C0A0">
    <PARAM NAME="FontName" VALUE="Arial">
    <PARAM NAME="FontSize" VALUE="12">
    <PARAM NAME="FontItalic" VALUE="0">
    <PARAM NAME="FontBold" VALUE="1">
    <PARAM NAME="FontUnderline" VALUE="0">
    <PARAM NAME="FontStrikeout" VALUE="0">
    <PARAM NAME="TopPoints" VALUE="0">
    <PARAM NAME="BotPoints" VALUE="0">
</OBJECT>

   </TD>
  <TD>
  <INPUT Type = "Text" Name="Text5" Value = "<%= objRecordSet("City")%>">
  </TD>
  <TD>
  <INPUT Type = "Text" Name="Text6" Value = "<%=⇐
objRecordSet("StateOrProvince")%>">
  </TD>
  </TR>
</TD>
</TR>
<TR >
<TD COLSPAN = 5>
<IFRAME NAME="IFrame1" SRC="isapialx.dll" WIDTH=750 HEIGHT=200 MARGINHEIGHT=0⇐
MARGINWIDTH=0
ALIGN=MIDDLE FRAMEBORDER=1 SCROLLING="YES"></IFRAME>
</TD>
</TR>
</TABLE>
    </FORM>
<%
Set objFileSys = Server.CreateObject("Scripting.FileSystemObject")
Dim strALXPath
strALXPath = Server.MapPath("/ASPExec") & "/aspht0708.alx"
Set objALXOut = objFileSys.CreateTextFile( strALXPath ,True)
strOut = "<SCRIPT LANGUAGE=""VBScript"">"
objALXOut.WriteLine( strOut )
strOut = "<!--"
objALXOut.WriteLine( strOut )
strOut = "Sub CommandButton3_Click()"
objALXOut.WriteLine( strOut )
strOut = "parent.Document.Form1.text1.value = ""UPDATE"""
objALXOut.WriteLine( strOut )
strOut = "call parent.Document.Form1.Submit1.click()"
objALXOut.WriteLine( strOut )
```

```
strOut = "end sub"
objALXOut.WriteLine( strOut )
strOut = "-->"
objALXOut.WriteLine( strOut )
strOut = "</SCRIPT>"
objALXOut.WriteLine( strOut )
strOut = "<SCRIPT LANGUAGE=""VBScript"">"
objALXOut.WriteLine( strOut )
strOut = "<!--"
objALXOut.WriteLine( strOut )
strOut = "Sub CommandButton2_Click()"
objALXOut.WriteLine( strOut )
strOut = "parent.Document.Form1.text1.value = ""FORWARD"""
objALXOut.WriteLine( strOut )
strOut = "call parent.Document.Form1.Submit1.click()"
objALXOut.WriteLine( strOut )
strOut = "end sub"
objALXOut.WriteLine( strOut )
strOut = "-->"
objALXOut.WriteLine( strOut )
strOut = "</SCRIPT>"
objALXOut.WriteLine( strOut )
strOut = "<SCRIPT LANGUAGE=""VBScript"">"
objALXOut.WriteLine( strOut )
strOut = "<!--"
objALXOut.WriteLine( strOut )
strOut = "Sub CommandButton1_Click()"
objALXOut.WriteLine( strOut )
strOut = "parent.Document.Form1.text1.value = ""BACKWARD"""
objALXOut.WriteLine( strOut )
strOut = "call parent.Document.Form1.Submit1.click()"
objALXOut.WriteLine( strOut )
strOut = "end sub"
objALXOut.WriteLine( strOut )
strOut = "-->"
objALXOut.WriteLine( strOut )
strOut = "</SCRIPT>"
objALXOut.WriteLine( strOut )
strOut = "<SCRIPT LANGUAGE=""VBScript"">"
objALXOut.WriteLine( strOut )
strOut = "<!--"
objALXOut.WriteLine( strOut )
strOut = "Sub TextBox2_Change()"
objALXOut.WriteLine( strOut )
strOut = "parent.Document.Form1.Text5.Value = TextBox2.Text"
objALXOut.WriteLine( strOut )
strOut = "end sub"
objALXOut.WriteLine( strOut )
strOut = "-->"
objALXOut.WriteLine( strOut )
strOut = "</SCRIPT>"
objALXOut.WriteLine( strOut )
strOut = "<SCRIPT LANGUAGE=""VBScript"">"
objALXOut.WriteLine( strOut )
strOut = "<!--"
objALXOut.WriteLine( strOut )
strOut = "Sub TextBox1_Change()"
```

continued on next page

continued from previous page

```
objALXOut.WriteLine( strOut )
strOut = "parent.Document.Form1.Text2.Value = TextBox1.Text"
objALXOut.WriteLine( strOut )
strOut = "end sub"
objALXOut.WriteLine( strOut )
strOut = "-->"
objALXOut.WriteLine( strOut )
strOut = "</SCRIPT>"
objALXOut.WriteLine( strOut )
strOut = "<DIV ID=""Layout1"" STYLE=""LAYOUT:FIXED;WIDTH:530pt;HEIGHT:92pt;"">"
objALXOut.WriteLine( strOut )
strOut = "<OBJECT ID=""Label1"""
objALXOut.WriteLine( strOut )
strOut = "CLASSID=""CLSID:978C9E23-D4B0-11CE-BF2D-00AA003F40D0""
STYLE=""TOP:25pt;LEFT:8pt;WIDTH:107pt;HEIGHT:17pt;ZINDEX:0;"">"
objALXOut.WriteLine( strOut )
strOut = "<PARAM NAME=""Caption"" VALUE=""Business Name"">"
objALXOut.WriteLine( strOut )
strOut = "<PARAM NAME=""Size"" VALUE=""3793;600"">"
objALXOut.WriteLine( strOut )
strOut = "<PARAM NAME=""FontCharSet"" VALUE=""0"">"
objALXOut.WriteLine( strOut )
strOut = "<PARAM NAME=""FontPitchAndFamily"" VALUE=""2"">"
objALXOut.WriteLine( strOut )
strOut = "<PARAM NAME=""FontWeight"" VALUE=""0"">"
objALXOut.WriteLine( strOut )
strOut = "</OBJECT>"
objALXOut.WriteLine( strOut )
strOut = "<OBJECT ID=""Label2"""
objALXOut.WriteLine( strOut )
strOut = "CLASSID=""CLSID:978C9E23-D4B0-11CE-BF2D-00AA003F40D0""
STYLE=""TOP:50pt;LEFT:8pt;WIDTH:107pt;HEIGHT:25pt;ZINDEX:1;"">"
objALXOut.WriteLine( strOut )
strOut = "<PARAM NAME=""Caption"" VALUE=""City"">"
objALXOut.WriteLine( strOut )
strOut = "<PARAM NAME=""Size"" VALUE=""3793;882"">"
objALXOut.WriteLine( strOut )
strOut = "<PARAM NAME=""FontCharSet"" VALUE=""0"">"
objALXOut.WriteLine( strOut )
strOut = "<PARAM NAME=""FontPitchAndFamily"" VALUE=""2"">"
objALXOut.WriteLine( strOut )
strOut = "<PARAM NAME=""FontWeight"" VALUE=""0"">"
objALXOut.WriteLine( strOut )
strOut = "</OBJECT>"
objALXOut.WriteLine( strOut )
strOut = "<OBJECT ID=""TextBox1"""
objALXOut.WriteLine( strOut )
strOut = "CLASSID=""CLSID:8BD21D10-EC42-11CE-9E0D-00AA006002F3""
STYLE=""TOP:17pt;LEFT:124pt;WIDTH:215pt;HEIGHT:25pt;TABINDEX:2;ZINDEX:2;"">"
objALXOut.WriteLine( strOut )
strOut = "<PARAM NAME=""VariousPropertyBits"" VALUE=""746604571"">"
objALXOut.WriteLine( strOut )
strOut = "<PARAM NAME=""Size"" VALUE=""7585;882"">"
objALXOut.WriteLine( strOut )
strOut = "<PARAM NAME=""Value"" VALUE=""" & objRecordSet("CompanyName") & """>"
objALXOut.WriteLine( strOut )
strOut = "<PARAM NAME=""FontCharSet"" VALUE=""0"">"
objALXOut.WriteLine( strOut )
```

```
strOut = "<PARAM NAME=""FontPitchAndFamily"" VALUE=""2"">"
objALXOut.WriteLine( strOut )
strOut = "<PARAM NAME=""FontWeight"" VALUE=""0"">"
objALXOut.WriteLine( strOut )
strOut = "</OBJECT>"
objALXOut.WriteLine( strOut )
strOut = "<OBJECT ID=""TextBox2"""
objALXOut.WriteLine( strOut )
strOut = "CLASSID=""CLSID:8BD21D10-EC42-11CE-9E0D-00AA006002F3""
STYLE=""TOP:50pt;LEFT:124pt;WIDTH:215pt;HEIGHT:26pt;TABINDEX:3;ZINDEX:3;"">"
objALXOut.WriteLine( strOut )
strOut = "<PARAM NAME=""VariousPropertyBits"" VALUE=""746604571"">"
objALXOut.WriteLine( strOut )
strOut = "<PARAM NAME=""Size"" VALUE=""7585;917"">"
objALXOut.WriteLine( strOut )
strOut = "<PARAM NAME=""Value"" VALUE=""" & objRecordSet("City") &""">"
objALXOut.WriteLine( strOut )
strOut = "<PARAM NAME=""FontCharSet"" VALUE=""0"">"
objALXOut.WriteLine( strOut )
strOut = "<PARAM NAME=""FontPitchAndFamily"" VALUE=""2"">"
objALXOut.WriteLine( strOut )
strOut = "<PARAM NAME=""FontWeight"" VALUE=""0"">"
objALXOut.WriteLine( strOut )
strOut = "</OBJECT>"
objALXOut.WriteLine( strOut )
strOut = "<OBJECT ID=""CommandButton1"""
objALXOut.WriteLine( strOut )
strOut = "CLASSID=""CLSID:D7053240-CE69-11CD-A777-00DD01143C57""
STYLE=""TOP:17pt;LEFT:347pt;WIDTH:74pt;HEIGHT:25pt;TABINDEX:4;ZINDEX:4;"">"
objALXOut.WriteLine( strOut )
strOut = "<PARAM NAME=""Caption"" VALUE=""Backward"">"
objALXOut.WriteLine( strOut )
strOut = "<PARAM NAME=""Size"" VALUE=""2619;873"">"
objALXOut.WriteLine( strOut )
strOut = "<PARAM NAME=""FontCharSet"" VALUE=""0"">"
objALXOut.WriteLine( strOut )
strOut = "<PARAM NAME=""FontPitchAndFamily"" VALUE=""2"">"
objALXOut.WriteLine( strOut )
strOut = "<PARAM NAME=""ParagraphAlign"" VALUE=""3"">"
objALXOut.WriteLine( strOut )
strOut = "<PARAM NAME=""FontWeight"" VALUE=""0"">"
objALXOut.WriteLine( strOut )
strOut = "</OBJECT>"
objALXOut.WriteLine( strOut )
strOut = "<OBJECT ID=""CommandButton2"""
objALXOut.WriteLine( strOut )
strOut = "CLASSID=""CLSID:D7053240-CE69-11CD-A777-00DD01143C57""
STYLE=""TOP:17pt;LEFT:429pt;WIDTH:83pt;HEIGHT:25pt;TABINDEX:5;ZINDEX:5;"">"
objALXOut.WriteLine( strOut )
strOut = "<PARAM NAME=""Caption"" VALUE=""Forward"">"
objALXOut.WriteLine( strOut )
strOut = "<PARAM NAME=""Size"" VALUE=""2911;873"">"
objALXOut.WriteLine( strOut )
strOut = "<PARAM NAME=""FontCharSet"" VALUE=""0"">"
objALXOut.WriteLine( strOut )
strOut = "<PARAM NAME=""FontPitchAndFamily"" VALUE=""2"">"
objALXOut.WriteLine( strOut )
```

continued on next page

continued from previous page

```
strOut = "<PARAM NAME=""ParagraphAlign"" VALUE=""3"">"
objALXOut.WriteLine( strOut )
strOut = "<PARAM NAME=""FontWeight"" VALUE=""0"">"
objALXOut.WriteLine( strOut )
strOut = "</OBJECT>"
objALXOut.WriteLine( strOut )
strOut = "<OBJECT ID=""CommandButton3"""
objALXOut.WriteLine( strOut )
strOut = "CLASSID=""CLSID:D7053240-CE69-11CD-A777-00DD01143C57"" "
strOut = strOut &
"STYLE=""TOP:50pt;LEFT:388pt;WIDTH:91pt;HEIGHT:25pt;TABINDEX:6;ZINDEX:6;"">"
objALXOut.WriteLine( strOut )
strOut = "<PARAM NAME=""Caption"" VALUE=""Update"">"
objALXOut.WriteLine( strOut )
strOut = "<PARAM NAME=""Size"" VALUE=""3210;873"">"
objALXOut.WriteLine( strOut )
strOut = "<PARAM NAME=""FontCharSet"" VALUE=""0"">"
objALXOut.WriteLine( strOut )
strOut = "<PARAM NAME=""FontPitchAndFamily"" VALUE=""2"">"
objALXOut.WriteLine( strOut )
strOut = "<PARAM NAME=""ParagraphAlign"" VALUE=""3"">"
objALXOut.WriteLine( strOut )
strOut = "<PARAM NAME=""FontWeight"" VALUE=""0"">"
objALXOut.WriteLine( strOut )
strOut = "</OBJECT>"
objALXOut.WriteLine( strOut )
strOut = "</DIV>"
objALXOut.WriteLine( strOut )
objALXOut.Close
%>
</BODY>
</HTML>
```

5. Activate Internet Explorer. In the address field, type in `HTTP://DEFAULT/ASPEXEC/ASPHT0801.ASP` and press Return. The display shown in Figure 8-3 appears, as the HTML Layout control is created in the HTML output stream by the ISAPI extension DLL. Congratulations! You have learned to create a working ISAPI extension DLL.

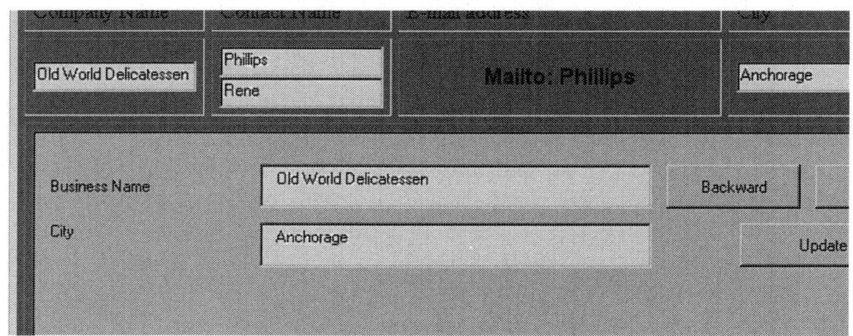

Figure 8-3 IE showing `ASPHT0801.ASP` with an ISAPI extension-created HTML Layout control

How It Works

As noted above, ISAPI stands, for Internet Server Application Programming Interface. ISAPI allows DLL and application projects created with MFC (Microsoft Foundation Classes) to access the underlying functionality of IIS/PWS directly, rather than via a scripting shell such as ASP or CGI. To see how the pieces fit together, let's examine some of the boilerplate code added to the project by the ISAPI Extension Wizard. First, notice the `GetExtensionVersion` method that is part of the extension-derived class created by the wizard:

```
BOOL CIsapialxExtension::GetExtensionVersion(HSE_VERSION_INFO* pVer)
{
// Call default implementation for initialization
CHttpServer::GetExtensionVersion(pVer);

// Load description string
TCHAR sz[HSE_MAX_EXT_DLL_NAME_LEN+1];
ISAPIVERIFY(::LoadString(AfxGetResourceHandle(),
IDS_SERVER, sz, HSE_MAX_EXT_DLL_NAME_LEN));
_tcscpy(pVer->lpszExtensionDesc, sz);
return TRUE;
}
```

This is one of the two points where the ISAPI system "hooks" into the extension DLL. Here, all that is done is to load a resource string that gives a user-friendly text description of the DLL. In the DLL on the CD, this string is `"isapialx Extension"`. Your version created from scratch may have a different string based on the name you gave the extension DLL. The `pVer` parameter points to a structure named `HSE_VERSION_INFO`. It consists of a doubleword and a string pointer; the string pointer is the `lpszExtensionDesc` string pointer used above; the other is `dwExtensionVersion`, a doubleword used to hold a version number. This is already set for you by the MFC system before the `GetExtensionVersion` method is called, so you should not change it. (ISAPI uses this to determine what functionality to expect from the DLL as additional ISAPI versions are released.)

If you wish to do additional initialization tasks for your DLL, this is the place to do them, because your DLL is called before any other DLL functions and only once when the DLL is first loaded into memory. Make sure to return a `TRUE` value when you are done to reassure ISAPI that your DLL initialized correctly. If you forget to return a value, or return `FALSE`, ISAPI will unload your DLL and return an error message to whoever called it, assuming you are signaling an internal error condition.

The other "hook" for ISAPI into your DLL is the default method of the `Extension` object. However, this method is not called automatically! Instead, examine the parse map macro code below:

```
///////////////////////////////////////////////////////////////////////
// command-parsing map

BEGIN_PARSE_MAP(CIsapialxExtension, CHttpServer)
```

```
// TODO: insert your ON_PARSE_COMMAND() and
// ON_PARSE_COMMAND_PARAMS() here to hook up your commands.
// For example:

ON_PARSE_COMMAND(Default, CIsapialxExtension, ITS_EMPTY)
DEFAULT_PARSE_COMMAND(Default, CIsapialxExtension)
END_PARSE_MAP(CIsapialxExtension)
```

Notice that only one command is registered with an `ON_PARSE_COMMAND` macro, which is named `Default`, has a type of `ITS_EMPTY`, and is linked to the `Extension` object in question. (The `ITS_EMPTY` type indicates that the method accepts no parameters.) Next, the `DEFAULT_PARSE_COMMAND` macro is used to indicate that when there are no recognized parameters in the URL containing the DLL reference, the `Default` method of the `Extension` object should be called. This set of code is needed to inform ISAPI of what to do when you aren't looking for specific information in the URL query string.

Once the parse map macros are in place, a matching method must be added to fit the name and parameters in the map. Here is its code:

```
///////////////////////////////////////////////////////////////////////
// CIsapialxExtension command handlers

void CIsapialxExtension::Default(CHttpServerContext* pCtxt)
{
    StartContent(pCtxt);
    WriteTitle(pCtxt);

    *pCtxt << _T("<OBJECT CLASSID=""CLSID:812AE312-8B8E-11CF-93C8-⇐
00AA00C08FDF""");
    *pCtxt << _T("ID=""aspht0708_alx"" STYLE=""LEFT:0;TOP:0"">");
    *pCtxt << _T("<PARAM NAME=""ALXPATH"" REF VALUE=""aspht0708.alx"">");
    *pCtxt << _T("</OBJECT>\r\n");

    EndContent(pCtxt);
}
```

Note the `CHttpServerContext` pointer passed into the method. This is critical to later use of the extension system, and will be the focus of the remaining How-To's in this chapter. For now, note that it has an overloaded `<<` operator that permits sending `tchar` typecast (with the `_T` macro) strings directly to the HTML stream. Here, a set of `<OBJECT>` tag HTML strings is exported to allow the display of an HTML Layout control. At this point, that is all this extension DLL can ever do. However, in the remaining How-To's, you'll greatly increase extension functionality!

Now, take a peek at how the extension is invoked:

```
<TD COLSPAN = 5>
<IFRAME NAME="IFrame1" SRC="isapialx.dll" WIDTH=750 HEIGHT=200 MARGINHEIGHT=0⇐
MARGINWIDTH=0
ALIGN=MIDDLE FRAMEBORDER=1 SCROLLING="YES"></IFRAME>
</TD>
```

Just like a CGI script, the extension DLL is made part of a URL in a link tag or `<SRC>` tag in a `Frame` or `IFrame` reference. The ISAPI system loads it and parses its query string (which in this case is nothing) and calls the extension, first hitting its `GetExtensionVersion` hook and then grabbing the default method handler because none is explicitly given in the URL. (Giving an explicit method handler is covered in How-To 8.3.)

Comments

It is important to note that the output from an ISAPI extension does not go through the ASP parser, even when invoked from an ASP file! This will have important consequences when you get ready to link ASP scripts with ISAPI extension DLLs.

8.2 How do I... Get server information with an ISAPI extension DLL?

Problem

Wow, ISAPI extensions are great! Our next problem is to get some specific server variables, just as we do with Win-CGI. How do you do this in an ISAPI extension?

Technique

The MFC system encapsulates the CGI system in two objects: `CHttpServer` and `CHttpServerContext`. One of the methods of `CHttpServerContext` is `GetServerVariable`. This How-To demonstrates creating a function that uses `GetServerVariable` to obtain any and all server variables desired and then use this information to determine whether a client browser is Internet Explorer so that the appropriate HTML can be exported. Although these directions create the project from scratch, the CD contains a completed file under `CH08\HT02\`.

Steps

1. Restart Visual C++ 5.0. Create an ISAPI extension DLL with the ISAPI Extension Wizard as shown in How-To 8.1, naming it `ISAPIALX2`. Then bring up the `ISAPIALX2.H` file in the text editor and enter the boldfaced code in Listing 8-3. Save the project.

Listing 8-3 ISAPIALX2.H source code

```
#if !defined(AFX_ISAPIALX2_H__49CFE6A5_E958_11D0_B7DF_444553540000__INCLUDED_)
#define AFX_ISAPIALX2_H__49CFE6A5_E958_11D0_B7DF_444553540000__INCLUDED_

// ISAPIALX2.H - Header file for your Internet Server
//    isapialx2 Extension

#include "resource.h"

class CIsapialx2Extension : public CHttpServer
{
public:
CIsapialx2Extension();
~CIsapialx2Extension();
// ServerVariable Method
CString GetServerVariable( CHttpServerContext* pCtxt, LPTSTR pstrSVar );

// Overrides
// ClassWizard generated virtual function overrides
// NOTE - the ClassWizard will add and remove member functions here.
//    DO NOT EDIT what you see in these blocks of generated code !
//{{AFX_VIRTUAL(CIsapialx2Extension)
public:
virtual BOOL GetExtensionVersion(HSE_VERSION_INFO* pVer);
//}}AFX_VIRTUAL

// TODO: Add handlers for your commands here.
// For example:

void Default(CHttpServerContext* pCtxt);

DECLARE_PARSE_MAP()

//{{AFX_MSG(CIsapialx2Extension)
//}}AFX_MSG
};


//{{AFX_INSERT_LOCATION}}
// Microsoft Developer Studio will insert additional declarations immediately
//before the previous line.

#endif //
!defined(AFX_ISAPIALX2_H__49CFE6A5_E958_11D0_B7DF_444553540000__INCLUDED)
```

2. Bring up ISAPIALX2.CPP in the text editor and enter the boldfaced code in Listing 8-4 to structure the output based on a server variable. Save the project.

Listing 8-4 ISAPIALX2.CPP source code

```
void CIsapialx2Extension::Default(CHttpServerContext* pCtxt)
{
    CString BrowserType;
    static const LPTSTR USER_AGENT = _T("HTTP_USER_AGENT");
    BrowserType = GetServerVariable( pCtxt , USER_AGENT );
```

```
    if ( BrowserType.Find( "MSIE 3" ) != -1 )
    {
        StartContent(pCtxt);
        WriteTitle(pCtxt);

        *pCtxt << _T("<OBJECT CLASSID=""CLSID:812AE312-8B8E-11CF-93C8-⇐
00AA00C08FDF""");
        *pCtxt << _T("ID=""aspht0708_alx"" STYLE=""LEFT:0;TOP:0"">");
        *pCtxt << _T("<PARAM NAME=""ALXPATH"" REF VALUE=""aspht0708.alx"">");
        *pCtxt << _T("</OBJECT>\r\n");

        EndContent(pCtxt);
    }
    else
    {
        StartContent(pCtxt);
        WriteTitle(pCtxt);

        *pCtxt << _T("Your browser cannot display this content!");
        *pCtxt << _T("To obtain a compatible browser, please jump to ");
        *pCtxt << _T("<A HREF= ""http://www.microsoft.com/ie/default.asp"">");
        *pCtxt << _T("The Internet Explorer Home Page.</A>\r\n");

        EndContent(pCtxt);
    }
}

CString CIsapialx2Extension::GetServerVariable( CHttpServerContext* pCtxt,
LPTSTR pstrSVar )
{
    LPTSTR pstrInputBuffer[ 256 ];
    CString strOutput;
    DWORD dwReturnSize;
    UINT nReturnCode;

    nReturnCode = pCtxt->GetServerVariable(pstrSVar , pstrInputBuffer ,
&dwReturnSize );
    switch (nReturnCode)
    {
        case ERROR_INVALID_PARAMETER:
            return "ISAPI ERROR: BAD CONNECTION HANDLE";
            break;
        case ERROR_INVALID_INDEX:
            return "ISAPI ERROR: BAD OR UNSUPPORTED VARIABLE IDENTIFIER";
            break;
        case ERROR_INSUFFICIENT_BUFFER:
            return "ISAPI ERROR: TOO MUCH DATA FOR SUPPLIED BUFFER";
            break;
        case ERROR_MORE_DATA:
            return "ISAPI ERROR: TOO MUCH DATA FOR SUPPLIED BUFFER; SIZE UNKNOWN";
            break;
        case ERROR_NO_DATA:
            return "ISAPI ERROR: REQUESTED DATA NOT AVAILABLE";
            break;
    }
    strOutput = (LPCTSTR)pstrInputBuffer;
    return strOutput;
}
```

3. Build the DLL and copy it to the `ASPEXEC` directory. Then activate ActiveX Control Pad and enter the ASP code in Listing 8-5. Save it as `ASPHT0802.ASP`. Move it to the `ASPEXEC` directory as well.

Listing 8-5 `ASPHT0802.ASP` source code

```
<%@ LANGUAGE = VBScript %>
<HTML>
<HEAD>
<TITLE>Active Server Pages Chapter Eight How To Two</TITLE>
</HEAD>
<BODY>
<% if IsObject(Session("objRecordSet")) then
     set objRecordSet = Session("objRecordSet")
   else
     Set objConnection = Server.CreateObject("ADODB.Connection")
        objConnection.Open "AWTutorial"
        SQLQuery = "SELECT * FROM Customers"
        Set objRecordSet = objConnection.Execute( SQLQuery )
        objRecordSet.Close
        objRecordSet.Open , , 3 , 4
        Set Session("objRecordSet") = objRecordSet
   end if
   dim HoldAction
   HoldAction = Request.Form("Text1")
   HoldAction = UCase( HoldAction )
   if HoldAction = "" then HoldAction = "FORWARD"
   if HoldAction = "FORWARD" then
     on error resume next
     if not objRecordSet.EOF then
          objRecordSet.MoveNext
     else
          objRecordSet.MoveFirst
     end if
   elseif HoldAction = "BACKWARD" then
     on error resume next
     if not objRecordSet.BOF then
          objRecordSet.MovePrevious
     else
          objRecordSet.MoveLast
     end if
   elseif HoldAction = "UPDATE" then
     objRecordSet("CompanyName") = Request.Form("Text2")
     objRecordSet("ContactLastName") = Request.Form("Text3")
        objRecordSet("ContactFirstName") = Request.Form("Text4")
        objRecordSet("City") = Request.Form("Text5")
        objRecordSet("StateOrProvince") = Request.Form("Text6")
        ObjRecordSet.Update
    end if
%>
    <FORM ACTION="http://default/aspexec/aspht0802.asp" METHOD="POST" NAME="Form1"
     TARGET="_top">
<TABLE WIDTH=600 COLSPAN=8 BORDER=5 CELLSPACING=5
CELLPADDING=5 ALIGN="CENTER" VALIGN="MIDDLE" BGCOLOR="Teal">
<TR>
<TD COLSPAN=2 ALIGN="CENTER">
Customer Listing
```

```
</TD>
<TD>
        <SCRIPT LANGUAGE="VBScript">
<!--
Sub menu2_Select(item)
select case item
  case 1
    Document.Form1.Text1.value = "FORWARD"
    call Document.Form1.Submit1.click()
  case 2
    Document.Form1.Text1.value = "BACKWARD"
    call Document.Form1.Submit1.click()
  case 3
    Document.Form1.Text1.value = "UPDATE"
    call Document.Form1.Submit1.click()
end select
end sub
-->
        </SCRIPT>
        <OBJECT ID="menu2" WIDTH=80 HEIGHT=25 align=middle
         CLASSID="CLSID:52DFAE60-CEBF-11CF-A3A9-00A0C9034920">
            <PARAM NAME="Menuitem[0]" VALUE="Forward">
            <PARAM NAME="Menuitem[1]" VALUE="Backward">
            <PARAM NAME="Menuitem[2]" VALUE="Update">
            <PARAM NAME="Caption" VALUE="Actions">
        </OBJECT>
</TD>
<TD>
        <INPUT TYPE=Text VALUE="<%= HoldAction %>" NAME="Text1">
</TD>
        <INPUT TYPE=Submit VALUE="Next Action" NAME="Submit1">
</TR>
<TR>
<TD>
Company Name
</TD>
<TD>
Contact Name
</TD>
<TD>
E-mail address
</TD>
<TD>
City
</TD>
<TD>
State/Province
</TD>
</TR>
  <TR>
  <TD>
        <INPUT TYPE=Text NAME="Text2" VALUE="<%= objRecordSet("CompanyName")%>">
</TD>
  <TD>
        <INPUT TYPE=Text NAME="Text3" VALUE="<%=⇐
objRecordSet("ContactLastName")%>">
```

continued on next page

continued from previous page

```
        <INPUT TYPE=Text NAME="Text4" VALUE="<%=⇐
objRecordSet("ContactFirstName")%>">
</TD>
  <TD>
        <OBJECT ID="IeLabel1" WIDTH=225 HEIGHT=27
         CLASSID="CLSID:99B42120-6EC7-11CF-A6C7-00AA00A47DD2">
            <PARAM NAME="_ExtentX" VALUE="5953">
            <PARAM NAME="_ExtentY" VALUE="714">
            <PARAM NAME="Caption" VALUE="Mailto: <%=⇐
objRecordSet("ContactLastName")%>">
    <PARAM NAME="Angle" VALUE="0">
    <PARAM NAME="Alignment" VALUE="4">
    <PARAM NAME="Mode" VALUE="1">
    <PARAM NAME="FillStyle" VALUE="0">
    <PARAM NAME="FillStyle" VALUE="1">
    <PARAM NAME="ForeColor" VALUE="#000000">
    <PARAM NAME="BackColor" VALUE="#D8C0A0">
    <PARAM NAME="FontName" VALUE="Arial">
    <PARAM NAME="FontSize" VALUE="12">
    <PARAM NAME="FontItalic" VALUE="0">
    <PARAM NAME="FontBold" VALUE="1">
    <PARAM NAME="FontUnderline" VALUE="0">
    <PARAM NAME="FontStrikeout" VALUE="0">
    <PARAM NAME="TopPoints" VALUE="0">
    <PARAM NAME="BotPoints" VALUE="0">
</OBJECT>

   </TD>
  <TD>
  <INPUT Type = "Text" Name="Text5" Value = "<%= objRecordSet("City")%>">
  </TD>
  <TD>
  <INPUT Type = "Text" Name="Text6" Value = "<%=⇐
objRecordSet("StateOrProvince")%>">
  </TD>
  </TR>
</TD>
</TR>
<TR >
<TD COLSPAN = 5>
<FRAMESET COLS="100%" ROWS="100%">
       <FRAME NAME="Frame 1" SRC="isapialx2.dll" SCROLLING="AUTO">
</FRAMESET>
</TD>
</TR>
</TABLE>
    </FORM>
<%
Set objFileSys = Server.CreateObject("Scripting.FileSystemObject")
Dim strALXPath
strALXPath = Server.MapPath("/ASPExec") & "/aspht0708.alx"
Set objALXOut = objFileSys.CreateTextFile( strALXPath ,True)
strOut = "<SCRIPT LANGUAGE=""VBScript"">"
objALXOut.WriteLine( strOut )
strOut = "<!--"
objALXOut.WriteLine( strOut )
strOut = "Sub CommandButton3_Click()"
objALXOut.WriteLine( strOut )
```

```
strOut = "parent.Document.Form1.text1.value = ""UPDATE"""
objALXOut.WriteLine( strOut )
strOut = "call parent.Document.Form1.Submit1.click()"
objALXOut.WriteLine( strOut )
strOut = "end sub"
objALXOut.WriteLine( strOut )
strOut = "-->"
objALXOut.WriteLine( strOut )
strOut = "</SCRIPT>"
objALXOut.WriteLine( strOut )
strOut = "<SCRIPT LANGUAGE=""VBScript"">"
objALXOut.WriteLine( strOut )
strOut = "<!--"
objALXOut.WriteLine( strOut )
strOut = "Sub CommandButton2_Click()"
objALXOut.WriteLine( strOut )
strOut = "parent.Document.Form1.text1.value = ""FORWARD"""
objALXOut.WriteLine( strOut )
strOut = "call parent.Document.Form1.Submit1.click()"
objALXOut.WriteLine( strOut )
strOut = "end sub"
objALXOut.WriteLine( strOut )
strOut = "-->"
objALXOut.WriteLine( strOut )
strOut = "</SCRIPT>"
objALXOut.WriteLine( strOut )
strOut = "<SCRIPT LANGUAGE=""VBScript"">"
objALXOut.WriteLine( strOut )
strOut = "<!--"
objALXOut.WriteLine( strOut )
strOut = "Sub CommandButton1_Click()"
objALXOut.WriteLine( strOut )
strOut = "parent.Document.Form1.text1.value = ""BACKWARD"""
objALXOut.WriteLine( strOut )
strOut = "call parent.Document.Form1.Submit1.click()"
objALXOut.WriteLine( strOut )
strOut = "end sub"
objALXOut.WriteLine( strOut )
strOut = "-->"
objALXOut.WriteLine( strOut )
strOut = "</SCRIPT>"
objALXOut.WriteLine( strOut )
strOut = "<SCRIPT LANGUAGE=""VBScript"">"
objALXOut.WriteLine( strOut )
strOut = "<!--"
objALXOut.WriteLine( strOut )
strOut = "Sub TextBox2_Change()"
objALXOut.WriteLine( strOut )
strOut = "parent.Document.Form1.Text5.Value = TextBox2.Text"
objALXOut.WriteLine( strOut )
strOut = "end sub"
objALXOut.WriteLine( strOut )
strOut = "-->"
objALXOut.WriteLine( strOut )
strOut = "</SCRIPT>"
objALXOut.WriteLine( strOut )
strOut = "<SCRIPT LANGUAGE=""VBScript"">"
```

continued on next page

continued from previous page

```
objALXOut.WriteLine( strOut )
strOut = "<!--"
objALXOut.WriteLine( strOut )
strOut = "Sub TextBox1_Change()"
objALXOut.WriteLine( strOut )
strOut = "parent.Document.Form1.Text2.Value = TextBox1.Text"
objALXOut.WriteLine( strOut )
strOut = "end sub"
objALXOut.WriteLine( strOut )
strOut = "-->"
objALXOut.WriteLine( strOut )
strOut = "</SCRIPT>"
objALXOut.WriteLine( strOut )
strOut = "<DIV ID=""Layout1"" STYLE=""LAYOUT:FIXED;WIDTH:530pt;HEIGHT:92pt;"">"
objALXOut.WriteLine( strOut )
strOut = "<OBJECT ID=""Label1"""
objALXOut.WriteLine( strOut )
strOut = "CLASSID=""CLSID:978C9E23-D4B0-11CE-BF2D-00AA003F40D0""
STYLE=""TOP:25pt;LEFT:8pt;WIDTH:107pt;HEIGHT:17pt;ZINDEX:0;"">"
objALXOut.WriteLine( strOut )
strOut = "<PARAM NAME=""Caption"" VALUE=""Business Name"">"
objALXOut.WriteLine( strOut )
strOut = "<PARAM NAME=""Size"" VALUE=""3793;600"">"
objALXOut.WriteLine( strOut )
strOut = "<PARAM NAME=""FontCharSet"" VALUE=""0"">"
objALXOut.WriteLine( strOut )
strOut = "<PARAM NAME=""FontPitchAndFamily"" VALUE=""2"">"
objALXOut.WriteLine( strOut )
strOut = "<PARAM NAME=""FontWeight"" VALUE=""0"">"
objALXOut.WriteLine( strOut )
strOut = "</OBJECT>"
objALXOut.WriteLine( strOut )
strOut = "<OBJECT ID=""Label2"""
objALXOut.WriteLine( strOut )
strOut = "CLASSID=""CLSID:978C9E23-D4B0-11CE-BF2D-00AA003F40D0""
STYLE=""TOP:50pt;LEFT:8pt;WIDTH:107pt;HEIGHT:25pt;ZINDEX:1;"">"
objALXOut.WriteLine( strOut )
strOut = "<PARAM NAME=""Caption"" VALUE=""City"">"
objALXOut.WriteLine( strOut )
strOut = "<PARAM NAME=""Size"" VALUE=""3793;882"">"
objALXOut.WriteLine( strOut )
strOut = "<PARAM NAME=""FontCharSet"" VALUE=""0"">"
objALXOut.WriteLine( strOut )
strOut = "<PARAM NAME=""FontPitchAndFamily"" VALUE=""2"">"
objALXOut.WriteLine( strOut )
strOut = "<PARAM NAME=""FontWeight"" VALUE=""0"">"
objALXOut.WriteLine( strOut )
strOut = "</OBJECT>"
objALXOut.WriteLine( strOut )
strOut = "<OBJECT ID=""TextBox1"""
objALXOut.WriteLine( strOut )
strOut = "CLASSID=""CLSID:8BD21D10-EC42-11CE-9E0D-00AA006002F3""
STYLE=""TOP:17pt;LEFT:124pt;WIDTH:215pt;HEIGHT:25pt;TABINDEX:2;ZINDEX:2;"">"
objALXOut.WriteLine( strOut )
strOut = "<PARAM NAME=""VariousPropertyBits"" VALUE=""746604571"">"
objALXOut.WriteLine( strOut )
strOut = "<PARAM NAME=""Size"" VALUE=""7585;882"">"
objALXOut.WriteLine( strOut )
```

```
strOut = "<PARAM NAME=""Value"" VALUE=""" & objRecordSet("CompanyName") & """>"
objALXOut.WriteLine( strOut )
strOut = "<PARAM NAME=""FontCharSet"" VALUE=""0"">"
objALXOut.WriteLine( strOut )
strOut = "<PARAM NAME=""FontPitchAndFamily"" VALUE=""2"">"
objALXOut.WriteLine( strOut )
strOut = "<PARAM NAME=""FontWeight"" VALUE=""0"">"
objALXOut.WriteLine( strOut )
strOut = "</OBJECT>"
objALXOut.WriteLine( strOut )
strOut = "<OBJECT ID=""TextBox2"""
objALXOut.WriteLine( strOut )
strOut = "CLASSID=""CLSID:8BD21D10-EC42-11CE-9E0D-00AA006002F3""
STYLE=""TOP:50pt;LEFT:124pt;WIDTH:215pt;HEIGHT:26pt;TABINDEX:3;ZINDEX:3;"">"
objALXOut.WriteLine( strOut )
strOut = "<PARAM NAME=""VariousPropertyBits"" VALUE=""746604571"">"
objALXOut.WriteLine( strOut )
strOut = "<PARAM NAME=""Size"" VALUE=""7585;917"">"
objALXOut.WriteLine( strOut )
strOut = "<PARAM NAME=""Value"" VALUE=""" & objRecordSet("City") &""">"
objALXOut.WriteLine( strOut )
strOut = "<PARAM NAME=""FontCharSet"" VALUE=""0"">"
objALXOut.WriteLine( strOut )
strOut = "<PARAM NAME=""FontPitchAndFamily"" VALUE=""2"">"
objALXOut.WriteLine( strOut )
strOut = "<PARAM NAME=""FontWeight"" VALUE=""0"">"
objALXOut.WriteLine( strOut )
strOut = "</OBJECT>"
objALXOut.WriteLine( strOut )
strOut = "<OBJECT ID=""CommandButton1"""
objALXOut.WriteLine( strOut )
strOut = "CLASSID=""CLSID:D7053240-CE69-11CD-A777-00DD01143C57""
STYLE=""TOP:17pt;LEFT:347pt;WIDTH:74pt;HEIGHT:25pt;TABINDEX:4;ZINDEX:4;"">"
objALXOut.WriteLine( strOut )
strOut = "<PARAM NAME=""Caption"" VALUE=""Backward"">"
objALXOut.WriteLine( strOut )
strOut = "<PARAM NAME=""Size"" VALUE=""2619;873"">"
objALXOut.WriteLine( strOut )
strOut = "<PARAM NAME=""FontCharSet"" VALUE=""0"">"
objALXOut.WriteLine( strOut )
strOut = "<PARAM NAME=""FontPitchAndFamily"" VALUE=""2"">"
objALXOut.WriteLine( strOut )
strOut = "<PARAM NAME=""ParagraphAlign"" VALUE=""3"">"
objALXOut.WriteLine( strOut )
strOut = "<PARAM NAME=""FontWeight"" VALUE=""0"">"
objALXOut.WriteLine( strOut )
strOut = "</OBJECT>"
objALXOut.WriteLine( strOut )
strOut = "<OBJECT ID=""CommandButton2"""
objALXOut.WriteLine( strOut )
strOut = "CLASSID=""CLSID:D7053240-CE69-11CD-A777-00DD01143C57""
STYLE=""TOP:17pt;LEFT:429pt;WIDTH:83pt;HEIGHT:25pt;TABINDEX:5;ZINDEX:5;"">"
objALXOut.WriteLine( strOut )
strOut = "<PARAM NAME=""Caption"" VALUE=""Forward"">"
objALXOut.WriteLine( strOut )
strOut = "<PARAM NAME=""Size"" VALUE=""2911;873"">"
objALXOut.WriteLine( strOut )
```

continued on next page

continued from previous page

```
strOut = "<PARAM NAME=""FontCharSet"" VALUE=""0"">"
objALXOut.WriteLine( strOut )
strOut = "<PARAM NAME=""FontPitchAndFamily"" VALUE=""2"">"
objALXOut.WriteLine( strOut )
strOut = "<PARAM NAME=""ParagraphAlign"" VALUE=""3"">"
objALXOut.WriteLine( strOut )
strOut = "<PARAM NAME=""FontWeight"" VALUE=""0"">"
objALXOut.WriteLine( strOut )
strOut = "</OBJECT>"
objALXOut.WriteLine( strOut )
strOut = "<OBJECT ID=""CommandButton3"""
objALXOut.WriteLine( strOut )
strOut = "CLASSID=""CLSID:D7053240-CE69-11CD-A777-00DD01143C57"" "
strOut = strOut &
"STYLE=""TOP:50pt;LEFT:388pt;WIDTH:91pt;HEIGHT:25pt;TABINDEX:6;ZINDEX:6;"">"
objALXOut.WriteLine( strOut )
strOut = "<PARAM NAME=""Caption"" VALUE=""Update"">"
objALXOut.WriteLine( strOut )
strOut = "<PARAM NAME=""Size"" VALUE=""3210;873"">"
objALXOut.WriteLine( strOut )
strOut = "<PARAM NAME=""FontCharSet"" VALUE=""0"">"
objALXOut.WriteLine( strOut )
strOut = "<PARAM NAME=""FontPitchAndFamily"" VALUE=""2"">"
objALXOut.WriteLine( strOut )
strOut = "<PARAM NAME=""ParagraphAlign"" VALUE=""3"">"
objALXOut.WriteLine( strOut )
strOut = "<PARAM NAME=""FontWeight"" VALUE=""0"">"
objALXOut.WriteLine( strOut )
strOut = "</OBJECT>"
objALXOut.WriteLine( strOut )
strOut = "</DIV>"
objALXOut.WriteLine( strOut )
objALXOut.Close
%>
</BODY>
</HTML>
```

4. Activate Internet Explorer. In the address field, type in **HTTP://DEFAULT/ASPEXEC/ASPHT0802.ASP** and press Return. As shown in Figure 8-4, the HTML Layout control is displayed, because the IFrame's call to **ISAPIALX2.DLL** detected that the browser was Internet Explorer and exported the proper **<OBJECT>** tag. Now close IE, and if you have one available, start a different browser, such as Netscape Communicator or Navigator. In its address field, type in **HTTP://DEFAULT/ASPEXEC/ISAPIALX2.DLL**. As shown in Figure 8-5, rather than getting the **<OBJECT>** tag that the non-IE browser cannot understand, you see the error message because **ISAPIALX2** detected the non-IE browser. You have learned to acquire server variables and use them in ISAPI extension DLLs.

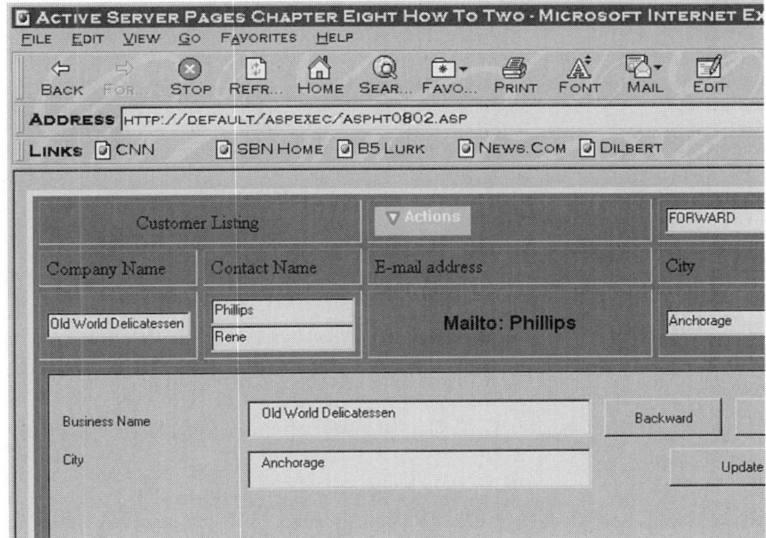

Figure 8-4 ASPHT0804.ASP in IE showing the HTML Layout control exported by ISAPIALX2.DLL

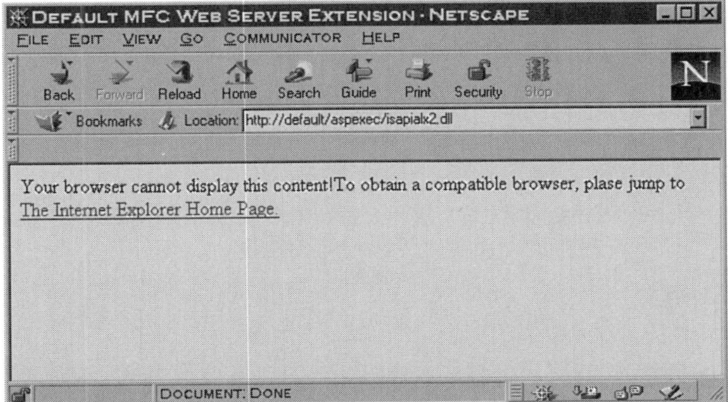

Figure 8-5 ISAPIALX2.DLL in Netscape Communicator showing the error message for a non-IE browser

How It Works

The key function call is found in this code of the helper method:

```
CString CIsapialx2Extension::GetServerVariable( CHttpServerContext* pCtxt,
LPTSTR pstrSVar )
{
    LPTSTR pstrInputBuffer[ 256 ];
    CString strOutput;
```

continued on next page

continued from previous page

```
    DWORD dwReturnSize;
    UINT nReturnCode;

    nReturnCode = pCtxt->GetServerVariable(pstrSVar , pstrInputBuffer ,
&dwReturnSize );
```

The CHttpServerContext pointer is sent in, allowing access to the GetServerVariable method. It takes a pointer to the variable name to attempt to obtain a pointer for the returned value and a pointer for a size variable that can be used if there is too much data for the supplied buffer. (In this function, ignore that value because you are interested only in simple server variables with small data footprints.)

The return code will either be 0 or an error, as the error handling switch statement shows. In case of an error, the return string will contain error information. Otherwise, the returned value is typecast into a CString and exported. Once back in the calling default handler, notice how the information is used:

```
void CIsapialx2Extension::Default(CHttpServerContext* pCtxt)
{
    CString BrowserType;
    static const LPTSTR USER_AGENT = _T("HTTP_USER_AGENT");
    BrowserType = GetServerVariable( pCtxt , USER_AGENT );

    if ( BrowserType.Find( "MSIE 3" ) != -1 )
    {
        StartContent(pCtxt);
        WriteTitle(pCtxt);

        *pCtxt << _T("<OBJECT CLASSID=""CLSID:812AE312-8B8E-11CF-93C8-⇐
00AA00C08FDF""");
```

The CString Find method returns the starting position of a match on the supplied substring, or -1 if no match is found. By testing for "MSIE 3", the code returns the <OBJECT> tag for the HTML Layout control only if the browser is a variation of Internet Explorer version 3.0; otherwise, the default HTML is sent back.

Comments

By defining different constants other than USER_AGENT, you can use the GetServerVariable method to obtain virtually any available server variable in a convenient CString format.

8.3 How do I... Interact with HTML forms using parse maps with an ISAPI extension DLL?

Problem

Now for a hard one: We need to retrieve a lot of complex HTML forms' data and process it. The information seems to be available in raw format in one of the server variables, but is there an easier way to get form data in ISAPI extensions?

Technique

Because forms processing is the core business of CGI, the MFC version of extensions provides powerful support for it using parse map macros. This How-To demonstrates getting each of the three major `<INPUT>` tags' data with a parse map and responding to it. Although these directions create the project from scratch, the CD contains a completed file under `CH08\HT03\`.

Steps

1. Activate Visual C++ 5.0. Create a new ISAPI extension DLL with the wizard, naming it `ISAPIXFORMS`. Bring up the `ISAPIXFORMS.CPP` file in the text editor and enter the boldfaced code in Listing 8-6 in the Parse Map Macros area. Save the project.

Listing 8-6 ISAPIXFORMS.CPP parse map macros source code

```
///////////////////////////////////////////////////////////////////////////
// command-parsing map

BEGIN_PARSE_MAP(CIsapixformsExtension, CHttpServer)
    // TODO: insert your ON_PARSE_COMMAND() and
    // ON_PARSE_COMMAND_PARAMS() here to hook up your commands.
    // For example:

    ON_PARSE_COMMAND(Default, CIsapixformsExtension, ITS_EMPTY)
    DEFAULT_PARSE_COMMAND(Default, CIsapixformsExtension)
    ON_PARSE_COMMAND(HandleFormData, CIsapixformsExtension, ITS_PSTR ITS_PSTR
ITS_PSTR)
    ON_PARSE_COMMAND_PARAMS("MyName MyBrowser=Internet_Explorer IUseASP=Yes")
END_PARSE_MAP(CIsapixformsExtension)
```

2. While still in the text editor for ISAPIXFORMS.CPP, move down below the code for the default command handler method and enter the boldfaced code in Listing 8-7 to process the form's data. Save the project.

Listing 8-7 ISAPIXFORMS.CPP HandleFormData method source code

```
void CIsapixformsExtension::HandleFormData(CHttpServerContext* pCtxt, LPCTSTR⇐
UserName, LPCTSTR UserBrowser, LPCTSTR UsesASP)
{
    StartContent(pCtxt);
    WriteTitle(pCtxt);

    CString TheMessage = "Hello ";
    TheMessage += UserName;
    TheMessage += "!<P>";
    TheMessage += "Your browser is ";
    TheMessage += UserBrowser;
    CString TestASP = UsesASP;
    if ( TestASP == "on" )
    {
        TheMessage += "<P>You use Active Server Pages!";
    }
    else
    {
        TheMessage += "<P>You do not use Active Server Pages!";
    }
    *pCtxt << _T(TheMessage);
    EndContent(pCtxt);
}
```

3. Now move in the text editor to the ISAPIXFORMS.H file and enter the boldfaced code in Listing 8-8. Save the project. Build the DLL and move it into the ASPEXEC directory.

Listing 8-8 ISAPIXFORMS.H header file source code

```
//
#if !defined(AFX_ISAPIXFORMS_H__BAAB6A85_EBD2_11D0_B7DF_444553540000__INCLUDED_)
#define AFX_ISAPIXFORMS_H__BAAB6A85_EBD2_11D0_B7DF_444553540000__INCLUDED_

// ISAPIXFORMS.H - Header file for your Internet Server
//    isapixforms Extension

#include "resource.h"

class CIsapixformsExtension : public CHttpServer
{
public:
CIsapixformsExtension();
~CIsapixformsExtension();
void HandleFormData(CHttpServerContext* pCtxt,
LPCTSTR UserName,
LPCTSTR UserBrowser,
LPCTSTR UsesASP );

// Overrides
```

```
// ClassWizard generated virtual function overrides
// NOTE - the ClassWizard will add and remove member functions here.
//    DO NOT EDIT what you see in these blocks of generated code !
//{{AFX_VIRTUAL(CIsapixformsExtension)
public:
virtual BOOL GetExtensionVersion(HSE_VERSION_INFO* pVer);
//}}AFX_VIRTUAL

// TODO: Add handlers for your commands here.
// For example:

void Default(CHttpServerContext* pCtxt);

DECLARE_PARSE_MAP()

//{{AFX_MSG(CIsapixformsExtension)
//}}AFX_MSG
};


//{{AFX_INSERT_LOCATION}}
// Microsoft Developer Studio will insert additional declarations immediately
//before the previous line.

#endif //
!defined(AFX_ISAPIXFORMS_H__BAAB6A85_EBD2_11D0_B7DF_444553540000__INCLUDED)
```

4. Activate ActiveX Control Pad and create a new HTML file with the contents of Listing 8-9. Save the file as `ASPHT0803.HTM` and move it into the `ASPEXEC` directory.

Listing 8-9 `ASPHT0803.HTM` source code

```
<HTML>
<HEAD>
<TITLE>Active Server Pages How To Chapter Eight How To Three</TITLE>
</HEAD>

<BODY>
This is a test of the forms processing capabilities of an ISAPI extension DLL.
Please enter the appropriate data and press the SUBMIT button for a response.<P>
<HR>
<FORM action="http://default/aspexec/isapixforms.dll?HandleFormData"⇐
method="post">

Your Name:<BR>
<INPUT TYPE=TEXT NAME="MyName"><P>
<HR>
Your Browser:
<br>
<INPUT type="radio" name="MyBrowser" value="Internet_Explorer">Internet
Explorer<BR>
<INPUT type="radio" name="MyBrowser" value="Netscape_Product">Netscape Product<BR>
<P>
<HR>
<INPUT NAME="IUseASP" type=checkbox checked>
```

continued on next page

continued from previous page

```
I Use Active Server Pages!
<P>
<HR><INPUT type=submit value="SUBMIT">
</BODY>
</HTML>
```

5. Activate Internet Explorer and bring up `ASPHT0803.HTM`. As shown in Figure 8-6, it consists of several input fields. Fill them out with some data and press the SUBMIT button. As shown in Figure 8-7, the DLL is called and responds correctly to the form data. Your expertise now includes using HTML forms with ISAPI extension DLL parse maps.

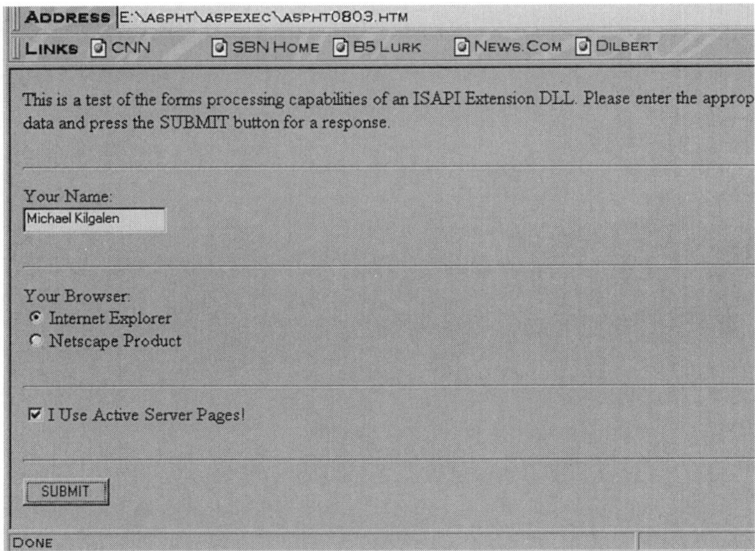

Figure 8-6 `ASPHT0803` in IE showing the input form elements

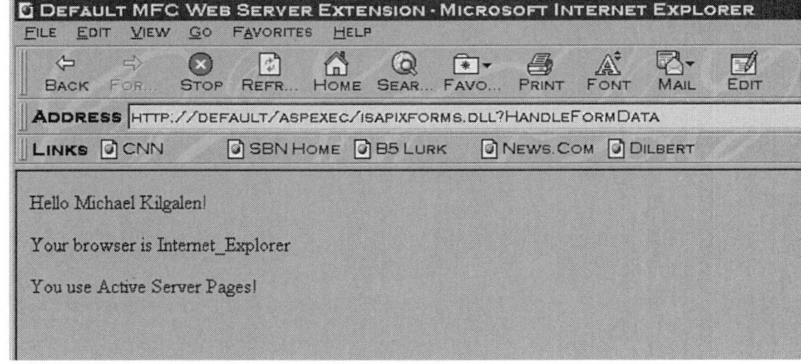

Figure 8-7 `ISAPIXFORMS` returned HTML after processing the form's input

How It Works

This is a particularly finicky level of programming for ISAPI, principally because it is the intersection of HTML and ISAPI, and thus errors are easy to make and hard to understand. To deal with the first level of problems, notice how the parse maps are laid out:

```
    ON_PARSE_COMMAND(HandleFormData, CIsapixformsExtension, ITS_PSTR ITS_PSTR⇐
ITS_PSTR)
    ON_PARSE_COMMAND_PARAMS("MyName MyBrowser=Internet_Explorer IUseASP=Yes")
```

First, the number and kind of parameter types in the `ON_PARSE_COMMAND` macro must exactly match those in the `ON_PARSE_COMMAND_PARAMS` macro and those in the HTML. In this case, three string parameters are expected, with names of `MyName`, `MyBrowser`, and `IUseASP`. If there are too many or too few parameters to either of these macros or the HTML output from the form, you will get either nothing on the return or a system error message saying it cannot find the DLL file. This is misleading, because what has happened is not that the DLL is not found, but rather that it failed to send any output due to an internal error condition at the assembly language level (which happens when the parameter numbers and types don't match up). Any of four things can cause this: too many parameters, too few parameters, incorrect names for the parameters (case is important), and wrong data types for the parameters. This is the principal weak point of the ISAPI extensions forms-processing system, so make sure you keep everything in synchronization here!

Once you have your parse map in place, you need to write the actual handler (and put it in the header file).

```
void CIsapixformsExtension::HandleFormData(CHttpServerContext* pCtxt, LPCTSTR⇐
UserName, LPCTSTR UserBrowser, LPCTSTR UsesASP)
{
    StartContent(pCtxt);
    WriteTitle(pCtxt);

    CString TheMessage = "Hello ";
    TheMessage += UserName;
    TheMessage += "!<P>";
    TheMessage += "Your browser is ";
    TheMessage += UserBrowser;
```

Notice that all the input strings are matched with the assigned parameters automatically. This means that you can be sure that `UserName` has the value from the `MyName` form element, without having to parse any browser input strings yourself. You then can structure appropriate output strings as shown above to respond to the information. You can also process it as shown in this section:

```
    CString TestASP = UsesASP;
    if ( TestASP == "on" )
    {
        TheMessage += "<P>You use Active Server Pages!";
    }
```

continued on next page

continued from previous page

```
    else
    {
        TheMessage += "<P>You do not use Active Server Pages!";
    }
    *pCtxt << _T(TheMessage);
    EndContent(pCtxt);
}
```

The imported values can be tested using normal string mechanics for desired values and the output can be sent based on matches or misses. The HTML from this method is quite minimal, but of course much more sophisticated output is easily arranged.

Now notice how the DLL is invoked in the HTML page:

```
<FORM action="http://default/aspexec/isapixforms.dll?HandleFormData"⇐
method="post">
```

Along with the exact executable path to the DLL, a `?` character followed by the exact name of the method desired is appended. This is critical, because without it no output will occur. The extensions system must have the method name to start with to check for parameter matches and call the right code. The only exception is the default method, which is invoked automatically even if it not called explicitly in the DLL invocation.

Comments

There is another finicky point about using this system: It is very browser-dependent! It is guaranteed to work only with IE; Netscape products send different URL strings that may cause it to fail. To remedy this, Microsoft included a special "fix" inside the extensions form processing system called `MfcISAPICommand`. If you make this the very first parameter on the form output, the extensions system will work around any ambiguities in the URL query and function correctly. See the online help in VC 5 on this topic for more details.

8.4 How do I… Send server information with an ISAPI extension DLL?

Problem

CGI lets us send control commands directly to the HTTP server. Do ISAPI extensions provide similar capabilities?

Technique

The MFC object `HttpServerContext` provides a powerful method named `ServerSupportFunction`. With it, all the control CGI provides over HTTP servers is made available. This How-To demonstrates using the method `ServerSupportFunction` to send a complete file as its response using a server output command. Although these directions create the project from scratch, the CD contains a completed file under `CH08\HT04\`.

Steps

1. Create a new ISAPI extension DLL using the wizard. Name it `ISAPIXURL`. Open the `ISAPIXURL.CPP` file in the text editor and enter the boldfaced code in Listing 8-10 to add an override method for `HttpExtensionProc`. Save the project.

Listing 8-10 `ISAPIXURL.CPP HttpExtensionProc` source code

```
DWORD CIsapixurlExtension::
HttpExtensionProc( EXTENSION_CONTROL_BLOCK *pECB )
{

    CHAR    szNewUrl[1024] = { 0 };
    CHAR    szBrowserType[ 1024 ] = { 0 };
    DWORD   dwLen = 1024;
    static const LPTSTR USER_AGENT = _T("HTTP_USER_AGENT");

    pECB->GetServerVariable( pECB->ConnID, USER_AGENT, szBrowserType, &dwLen);
    CString strGetBT = CString( szBrowserType , strlen( szBrowserType ));
    if ( strGetBT.Find( "MSIE 3" ) != - 1 )
    {

        lstrcpy(szNewUrl, "/aspexec/aspht0804a.htm" );
        dwLen = lstrlen( szNewUrl );
        pECB->ServerSupportFunction( pECB->ConnID,
        HSE_REQ_SEND_URL, szNewUrl, &dwLen, (LPDWORD)NULL );
    }
    else
    {
        lstrcpy(szNewUrl, "/aspexec/aspht0804b.htm" );
        dwLen = lstrlen( szNewUrl );
        pECB->ServerSupportFunction( pECB->ConnID,
        HSE_REQ_SEND_URL, szNewUrl, &dwLen, (LPDWORD)NULL );
    }

    return HSE_STATUS_SUCCESS;
}
```

2. In the `ISAPIXURL`.H file, add the boldfaced code in Listing 8-11 to enable the override of the `HttpExtensionProc` method. Save the project. Build the DLL and copy it into the `ASPEXEC` directory.

Listing 8-11 ISAPIXURL.H source code

```
// ISAPIXURL.H - Header file for your Internet Server
//    isapixurl Extension

#include "resource.h"

class CIsapixurlExtension : public CHttpServer
{
public:
CIsapixurlExtension();
~CIsapixurlExtension();

// Overrides
// ClassWizard generated virtual function overrides
// NOTE - the ClassWizard will add and remove member functions here.
//    DO NOT EDIT what you see in these blocks of generated code !
//{{AFX_VIRTUAL(CIsapixurlExtension)
public:
virtual BOOL GetExtensionVersion(HSE_VERSION_INFO* pVer);
//}}AFX_VIRTUAL

// TODO: Add handlers for your commands here.
// For example:

void Default(CHttpServerContext* pCtxt);
DWORD   HttpExtensionProc(EXTENSION_CONTROL_BLOCK *pECB);

DECLARE_PARSE_MAP()

//{{AFX_MSG(CIsapixurlExtension)
//}}AFX_MSG
};


//{{AFX_INSERT_LOCATION}}
// Microsoft Developer Studio will insert additional declarations immediately
//before the previous line.

#endif //
!defined(AFX_ISAPIXURL_H__3F4E20A5_EBE4_11D0_B7DF_444553540000__INCLUDED)
```

3. Activate ActiveX Control Pad and enter the HTML code in Listing 8-12. Save it as ASPHT0804.HTM and copy it into the ASPEXEC directory.

Listing 8-12 ASPHT0804.HTM source code

```
<HTML>
<HEAD>
<TITLE>Active Server Pages How To Chapter Eight How To Four</TITLE>
</HEAD>
<BODY>
Here is the link to
<A HREF="http://default/aspexec/isapixurl.dll" TARGET="_self">Test ISAPI Local⇐
Server Redirection</A>
</BODY>
</HTML>
```

4. Create a new HTML file in ActiveX Control Pad and enter the HTML code in Listing 8-13. Save it as **ASPHT0804A.HTM** and copy it into the **ASPEXEC** directory.

Listing 8-13 ASPHT0804A.HTM source code

```
<HTML>
<HEAD>
<TITLE>Active Server Pages How To Chapter Eight How To Four A</TITLE>
</HEAD>

<BODY>
You have received this page because your browser is Microsoft Internet Explorer⇐
3+!
Please click <A HREF="http://default/aspexec/aspht0404.asp">here</A> to display⇐
an ASP page!
</BODY>
</HTML>
```

5. Create another new HTML file in ActiveX Control Pad and enter the HTML code in Listing 8-14. Save it as **ASPHT0804B.HTM** and copy it into the **ASPEXEC** directory.

Listing 8-14 ASPHT0804B.HTM source code

```
<HTML>
<HEAD>
<TITLE>Active Server Pages How To Chapter Eight How To Four B</TITLE>
</HEAD>

<BODY>
You have received this page because your browser is not Internet Explorer 3+!
Please click <A HREF="http://www.microsoft.com/ie/default.asp">here</A> to obtain
a free copy!
</BODY>
</HTML>
```

6. Activate Internet Explorer and bring up **ASPHT0804.HTM**. Then activate another browser if you have one (such as Netscape Communicator). Figure 8-8 shows the file in both browsers at the same time. Click on each of the redirection links and the IE browser will bring up the file for Internet Explorer, whereas the non-IE browser will bring up the non-IE page, as shown in Figure 8-9. You can now do local server redirection in an ISAPI extension DLL.

How It Works

This How-To illustrates a major problem of the active platform: Sometimes things don't work well together! You have access to `ServerSupportFunction` inside the `CHttpServerContext` system encapsulated by the `CHttpServer` object, and you would expect that sending out an `HSE_REQ_SEND_URL` message would send the server off to the new URL.

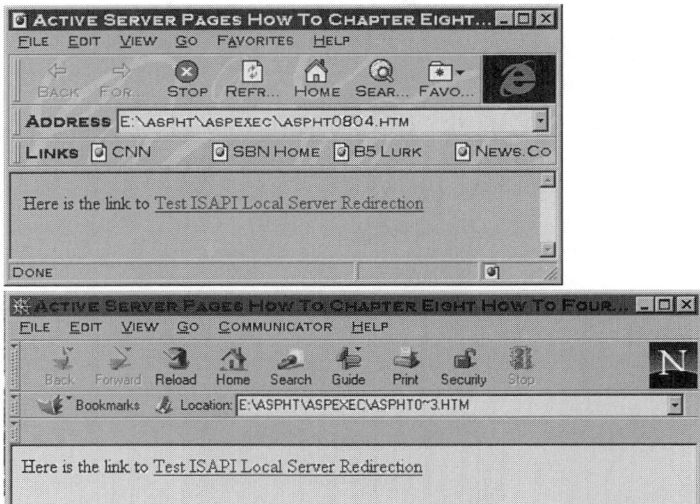

Figure 8-8 `ASPHT0804.HTM` in both Internet Explorer and Netscape Communicator

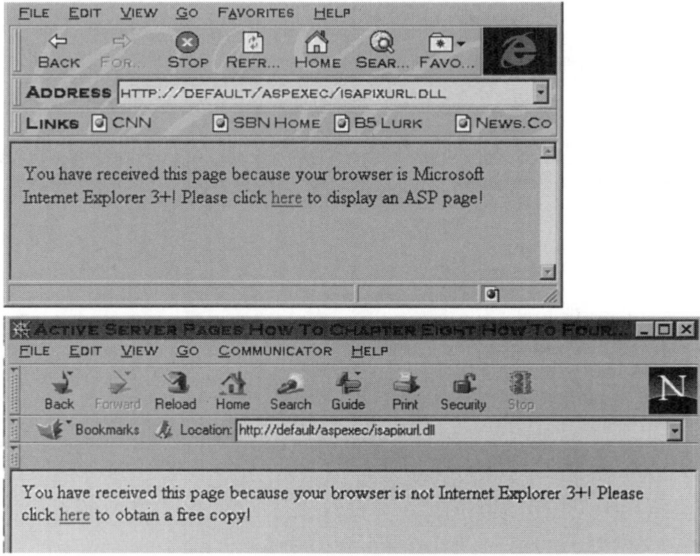

Figure 8-9 `ISAPIXURL` displaying different files in each browser via local URL redirection

Unfortunately, it doesn't!

Instead, it bypasses the normal HTML parsing mechanism and either fails in various ways or ends up being displayed as plain text rather than HTML. To avoid this problem, you must move one level up in the hierarchy and interact directly with the `CHttpServer` object's extension control block (ECB) data structure. ECB directly connects the `CHttpServer` object with the CGI processing stream from the server itself. `HttpExtensionProc` the supplied method, uses the ECB to initialize the response stream and create the `CHttpServerContext` object. The price of this is that by the time the `CHttpServerContext` is provided, response headers have already been sent, and so redirection is no longer functional. Thus, the problem!

To solve it, override the `HttpExtensionProc` method and provide your own:

```
DWORD CIsapixurlExtension::
HttpExtensionProc( EXTENSION_CONTROL_BLOCK *pECB )
{

    CHAR    szNewUrl[1024] = { 0 };
    CHAR    szBrowserType[ 1024 ] = { 0 };
    DWORD   dwLen = 1024;
    static const LPTSTR USER_AGENT = _T("HTTP_USER_AGENT");

    pECB->GetServerVariable( pECB->ConnID, USER_AGENT, szBrowserType, &dwLen);
    CString strGetBT = CString( szBrowserType , strlen( szBrowserType ));
    if ( strGetBT.Find( "MSIE 3" ) != - 1 )
    {

        lstrcpy(szNewUrl, "/aspexec/aspht0804a.htm" );
        dwLen = lstrlen( szNewUrl );
        pECB->ServerSupportFunction( pECB->ConnID,
        HSE_REQ_SEND_URL, szNewUrl, &dwLen, (LPDWORD)NULL );
    }
```

The method doesn't have access to the higher-level methods of the `CHttpServerContext`, but can call the lower-level ones of the ECB. First, it calls `GetServerVariable` using the `ConnID` field, which is the Internet handle of the server process, and two strings, one of which is the variable to obtain and the other the buffer to fill if it is found. The major difference between this method and the higher-level one is that the strings must be low-level `char` arrays rather than `CString` or `tchar` pointers. Once it obtains the variable value, the value is copied into a CString and the `Find` method is used to determine whether `MSIE 3` is present, indicating that Internet Explorer is the browser. Once this is determined, a string is created and sent into the `ServerSupportFunction` method of the ECB, again using the `ConnID` and low-level string pointers. Because this takes place before any response headers are sent (in fact, none are because they have been overridden) the redirection takes place correctly!

Note also the way the extension is invoked:

```
<A HREF="http://default/aspexec/isapixurl.dll" TARGET="_self">Test ISAPI Local⇐
Server Redirection</A>
```

It takes no parameters and does not even do default processing, because it cannot take advantage of the higher-level `CHttpServerContext` object's features. But due to its capability to intercept data at the ECB level, it still does the proper redirection.

Comments

One additional flaw is that you cannot do any form of ASP redirection with this method; the ASP filter is not invoked by the redirection request (a bug?) and so the attempt fails. Only HTM files can be redirected using this technique.

COMPLEXITY
INTERMEDIATE

8.5 How do I… Handle error conditions with an ISAPI extension DLL?

Problem

At times we need to output specialized error information to our clients. CGI lets us do this, but can ISAPI extensions write HTML error output directly?

Technique

Yes, this can be done using the `WriteClient` method of the ECB along with `ServerSupportFunction`. This How-To demonstrates sending a formatted error page rather than a simple error message when a problem occurs. Although these directions create the project from scratch, the CD contains a completed file under `CH08\HT05\`.

Steps

1. Activate Visual C++ 5.0 and create a new ISAPI extension DLL named `ISAPIXERR` using the wizard. Bring up the `ISAPIXERR.H` file in the text editor and enter the boldfaced code in Listing 8-15 to provide the override of the `HttpExtensionProc` method.

Listing 8-15 `ISAPIXERR.H` header file source code

```
#if !defined(AFX_ISAPIXERR_H__D70D30C5_EC02_11D0_B7DF_444553540000__INCLUDED_)
#define AFX_ISAPIXERR_H__D70D30C5_EC02_11D0_B7DF_444553540000__INCLUDED_

// ISAPIXERR.H - Header file for your Internet Server
//    isapixerr Extension

#include "resource.h"
```

```
class CIsapixerrExtension : public CHttpServer
{
public:
CIsapixerrExtension();
~CIsapixerrExtension();

// Overrides
// ClassWizard generated virtual function overrides
// NOTE - the ClassWizard will add and remove member functions here.
//    DO NOT EDIT what you see in these blocks of generated code !
//{{AFX_VIRTUAL(CIsapixerrExtension)
public:
virtual BOOL GetExtensionVersion(HSE_VERSION_INFO* pVer);
//}}AFX_VIRTUAL

// TODO: Add handlers for your commands here.
// For example:

    void Default(CHttpServerContext* pCtxt);
    DWORD   HttpExtensionProc(EXTENSION_CONTROL_BLOCK *pECB);

DECLARE_PARSE_MAP()

//{{AFX_MSG(CIsapixerrExtension)
/}}AFX_MSG
};


//{{AFX_INSERT_LOCATION}}
// Microsoft Developer Studio will insert additional declarations immediately
//before the previous line.
```

2. Bring up ISAPIXERR.CPP in the text editor and enter the boldfaced code in Listing 8-16. Save the project. Then build the DLL and copy it to the ASPEXEC directory.

Listing 8-16 ISAPIXERR.CPP CHttpExtensionProc source code

```
DWORD CIsapixerrExtension::
HttpExtensionProc( EXTENSION_CONTROL_BLOCK *pECB )
{

    CHAR    szBuff[4096] = { 0 };
    DWORD   dwLen = 0;
    BOOL    bSuccess = FALSE;

    wsprintf( szBuff,
             "<html>\n"
             "Content-Type: text/html\r\n"
             "\r\n"
             "<head>"
             "<title>Formatted Error Message Demo</title></head>\n");

    dwLen = lstrlen( szBuff );
    pECB->ServerSupportFunction( pECB->ConnID,
    HSE_REQ_SEND_RESPONSE_HEADER, "200 OK", &dwLen, ( LPDWORD )
```

continued on next page

continued from previous page

```
    szBuff );


    wsprintf(szBuff, "<body>");
    dwLen = lstrlen( szBuff );
    pECB->WriteClient( pECB->ConnID, szBuff, &dwLen, dwLen);

    wsprintf(szBuff, "<H1>158 Simulated Error Message</H1>This is a simulated⇐
error message.");
    dwLen = lstrlen( szBuff );
    pECB->WriteClient( pECB->ConnID, szBuff, &dwLen, dwLen);
    wsprintf(szBuff, "<P>Had this been a real error, you would be in deep⇐
trouble!</body>");
    dwLen = lstrlen( szBuff );
    pECB->WriteClient( pECB->ConnID, szBuff, &dwLen, dwLen);

    wsprintf(szBuff, "</html>");
    dwLen = lstrlen( szBuff );
    pECB->WriteClient( pECB->ConnID, szBuff, &dwLen, dwLen);


    pECB->ServerSupportFunction( pECB->ConnID,
    HSE_REQ_DONE_WITH_SESSION, "200 OK", NULL, NULL );

    return HSE_STATUS_SUCCESS;
}
```

3. Activate ActiveX Control Pad and enter the HTML source code in Listing 8-17. Save the file as `ASPHT0805.HTM` and move it to the `ASPEXEC` directory.

Listing 8-17 ASPHT0805.ASP source code

```
<HTML>
<HEAD>
<TITLE>Active Server Pages How To Chapter Eight How To Five</TITLE>
</HEAD>
<BODY>
Here is the link to
<A HREF="http://default/aspexec/isapixerr.dll" TARGET="_self">display a custom⇐
error message!</A>
</BODY>
</HTML>
```

4. Activate Internet Explorer and bring up `ASPHT0805.HTM`. As shown in Figure 8-10, the initial file is a simple hyperlink. But as shown in Figure 8-11, when the hyperlink is clicked on, it displays a simulated error message that could replace the one normally generated from a failed HTTP transaction. You have learned to output headers with `ServerSupportFunction` and direct HTML to the output stream with `WriteClient` in ISAPI extension DLLs.

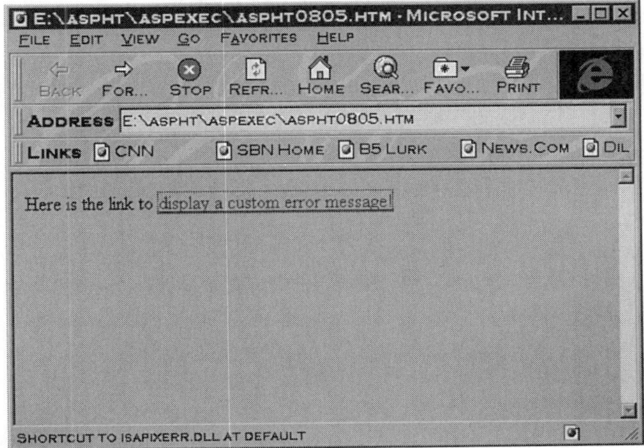

Figure 8-10 ASPHT0805.HTM in Internet Explorer prior to the custom error message

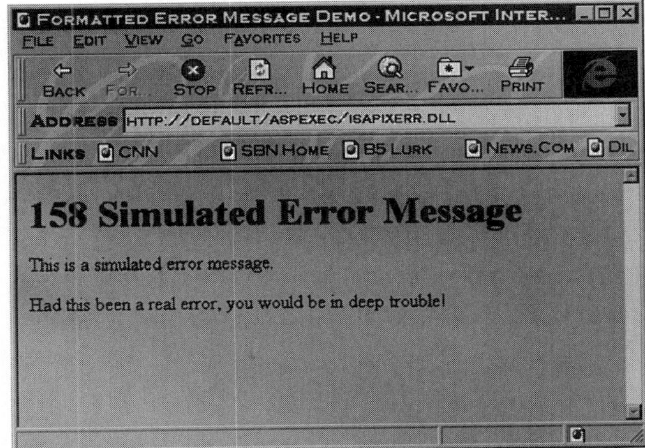

Figure 8-11 The custom error message from ISAPIXERR.DLL

How It Works

The key bit of code is right up front in this How-To:

```
CHAR    szBuff[4096] = { 0 };
DWORD   dwLen = 0;
BOOL    bSuccess = FALSE;

wsprintf( szBuff,
          "<html>\n"
```

continued on next page

continued from previous page

```
                "Content-Type: text/html\r\n"
                "\r\n"
                "<head>"
                "<title>Formatted Error Message Demo</title></head>\n");

    dwLen = lstrlen( szBuff );
    pECB->ServerSupportFunction( pECB->ConnID,
    HSE_REQ_SEND_RESPONSE_HEADER, "200 OK", &dwLen, ( LPDWORD )
    szBuff );
```

A character buffer is created and assigned a set of values with `wsprintf`. Note that it includes both `\r` and `\n` characters at the end of important lines. Once the string is built, its length is taken and it is then sent the `ServerSupportFunction` of the ECB, with a code of `HSE_REQ_SEND_ RESPONSE_HEADER`. Along with it goes a `200 OK` message to tell the system that everything is fine. (Of course, it isn't in an error situation, but the purpose of the How-To is to demonstrate successful error messages with HTML; the HTML message isn't having an error!) It is particularly important to note the `Content-Type` line; this is what tells the browser what to expect from the response stream. If a specialized header had been desired, it would have been added to the stream just before the `Content-Type` header.

Once the header is output (and note that it contains some HTML itself), the remaining body of the file is sent by simply placing the HTML text into the string buffers and flushing them out with the `WriteClient` method:

```
    wsprintf(szBuff, "<body>");
    dwLen = lstrlen( szBuff );
    pECB->WriteClient( pECB->ConnID, szBuff, &dwLen, dwLen);

    wsprintf(szBuff, "<H1>158 Simulated Error Message</H1>This is a simulated⇐
error message.");
    dwLen = lstrlen( szBuff );
    pECB->WriteClient( pECB->ConnID, szBuff, &dwLen, dwLen);
    wsprintf(szBuff, "<P>Had this been a real error, you would be in deep⇐
trouble!</body>");
    dwLen = lstrlen( szBuff );
    pECB->WriteClient( pECB->ConnID, szBuff, &dwLen, dwLen);
```

`WriteClient` is a method that sends its text directly back to the browser, bypassing the ISAPI initial filter system, and thus is not suitable for ASP or other complex formatting/parsing chores. But in terms of raw HTML, it is perfect! You can write HTML files of arbitrary complexity this way, subject to the elements in the Comments section. It takes parameters of the ECB Internet handle, the buffer to write, and a pointer and a value for the length of the string. (See the Comments section on this item.)

To finish up sending the HTML response, this code is needed:

```
    wsprintf(szBuff, "</html>");
    dwLen = lstrlen( szBuff );
    pECB->WriteClient( pECB->ConnID, szBuff, &dwLen, dwLen);
```

```
pECB->ServerSupportFunction( pECB->ConnID,
HSE_REQ_DONE_WITH_SESSION, "200 OK", NULL, NULL );

return HSE_STATUS_SUCCESS;
```

Notice first that the </HTML> tag is sent to close off the HTML portion of the stream. Next, ServerSupportFunction is called again to let it know that the DLL has finished processing (HSE_REQ_DONE_WITH_SESSION). Finally, the return value is HSE_STATUS_SUCCESS, which is the default success code. Failing to return it, however, will cause your DLL to always fail!

Comments

There are some deadly omissions and mistakes in the documentation for this material! First, the final parameter of the WriteClient method is supposed to be 0, but it has been changed to a value parameter for the length of the imported string. Second, the initial <HTML> and <HEAD> tags must be written with the ServerSupportFunction call to HSE_REQ_SEND_REPONSE_HEADER or the output will fail with a cryptic error message. Finally, a call needs to be made with the HSE_REQ_DONE_WITH_SESSION value to release the server from the DLL and close the output stream. All these issues are either undocumented or incorrect in the documentation.

COMPLEXITY
INTERMEDIATE

8.6 How do I... Send customized HTML output with an ISAPI extension DLL?

Problem

We need to return images from our CGI applications; can ISAPI extension DLLs return custom binary output to the client's browser?

Technique

ServerSupportFunction steps in again to fill this need. This How-To demonstrates using it to send a GIF file back to an <IMG> tag. Although these directions create the project from scratch, the CD contains a completed file under CH08\HT06\.

Steps

1. Activate Visual C++ 5.0 and create a new ISAPI extension DLL with the wizard named ISAPIXBIN. Open its ISAPIXBIN.H file in the text editor and add the boldfaced code in Listing 8-18. Save the project.

Listing 8-18 ISAPIXBIN.H header file source code

```
#if !defined(AFX_ISAPIXBIN_H__E58A88C8_EC73_11D0_B7DF_444553540000__INCLUDED_)
#define AFX_ISAPIXBIN_H__E58A88C8_EC73_11D0_B7DF_444553540000__INCLUDED_

// ISAPIXBIN.H - Header file for your Internet Server
//    isapixbin Extension

#include "resource.h"

class CIsapixbinExtension : public CHttpServer
{
public:
CIsapixbinExtension();
~CIsapixbinExtension();

// Overrides
// ClassWizard generated virtual function overrides
// NOTE - the ClassWizard will add and remove member functions here.
//    DO NOT EDIT what you see in these blocks of generated code !
//{{AFX_VIRTUAL(CIsapixbinExtension)
public:
virtual BOOL GetExtensionVersion(HSE_VERSION_INFO* pVer);
//}}AFX_VIRTUAL

// TODO: Add handlers for your commands here.
// For example:

void Default(CHttpServerContext* pCtxt);
    DWORD   HttpExtensionProc(EXTENSION_CONTROL_BLOCK *pECB);

DECLARE_PARSE_MAP()

//{{AFX_MSG(CIsapixbinExtension)
//}}AFX_MSG
};


//{{AFX_INSERT_LOCATION}}
// Microsoft Developer Studio will insert additional declarations immediately
//before the previous line.

#endif //
!defined(AFX_ISAPIXBIN_H__E58A88C8_EC73_11D0_B7DF_444553540000__INCLUDED)
```

2. Move to the ISAPIXBIN.CPP file in the text editor and enter the boldfaced code in Listing 8-19 to define the overriding HttpExtensionProc function. Save the project, build the DLL, and move it to the ASPEXEC directory.

Listing 8-19 ISAPIXBIN.CPP HttpExtensionProc source code

```
DWORD CIsapixbinExtension::
HttpExtensionProc( EXTENSION_CONTROL_BLOCK *pECB )
{

    CHAR    szBuff[4096] = { 0 };
```

```
    DWORD   dwLen = 0;
    try
    {
        CFile   file("test.gif", CFile::modeRead);
        DWORD   dwLength = file.GetLength();
        wsprintf( szBuff,
        "Content-Type: image/gif\r\n\r\n"
                  "Content-length: %d\r\n\r\n", dwLength);
        dwLen = lstrlen( szBuff );
        pECB->ServerSupportFunction( pECB->ConnID,
          HSE_REQ_SEND_RESPONSE_HEADER, "200 OK", &dwLen, ( LPDWORD )
          szBuff );
        try
        {
            char *  pData = new char[dwLength];
            try
            {
                file.Read(pData, dwLength);
            }
            catch(CFileException * e)
            {
                e->Delete();
            }
            pECB->WriteClient( pECB->ConnID, pData, &dwLength, dwLength);
            delete pData;
        }
        catch(CMemoryException * e)
        {
            e->Delete();
        }
    }
    catch(CFileException * e)
    {
        e->Delete();
    }
    pECB->ServerSupportFunction( pECB->ConnID,
      HSE_REQ_DONE_WITH_SESSION, "200 OK", NULL, NULL );

    return HSE_STATUS_SUCCESS;
}
```

3. Activate ActiveX Control Pad and enter the HTML source code in Listing 8-20. Save the file as `ASPHT0806.HTM` and move it to the `ASPEXEC` directory.

Listing 8-20 `ASPHT0806.HTM` source code

```
<HTML>
<HEAD>
<TITLE>Active Server Pages How To Chapter Eight How To Six</TITLE>
</HEAD>
<BODY>
<IMG SRC="http://default/aspexec/isapixbin.dll">
</BODY>
</HTML>
```

4. Activate Internet Explorer and display `ASPHT0806.HTM`. As shown in Figure 8-12, `ISAPIXBIN.DLL` sends back a GIF that the `<IMG>` tag displays. You have learned to use custom HTML binary output with an ISAPI extension DLL.

How It Works

The controlling difference between sending back HTML output and sending a GIF file is in this bit of code:

```
wsprintf( szBuff,
"Content-Type: image/gif\r\n\r\n"
         "Content-length: %d\r\n\r\n", dwLength);
dwLen = lstrlen( szBuff );
pECB->ServerSupportFunction( pECB->ConnID,
  HSE_REQ_SEND_RESPONSE_HEADER, "200 OK", &dwLen, ( LPDWORD )
  szBuff );
```

The `Content-Type: image/gif` header indicates that when the client browser receives the response stream, it should treat it as a GIF image rather than as HTML. The `Content-Length` parameter is optional but can be helpful to some browsers. Other content types will trigger download dialogs or helper applications, depending on the specific browser.

Once the header is sent, the next step is to send the file data. This requires opening the file, getting its data, and then writing the data to the output stream.

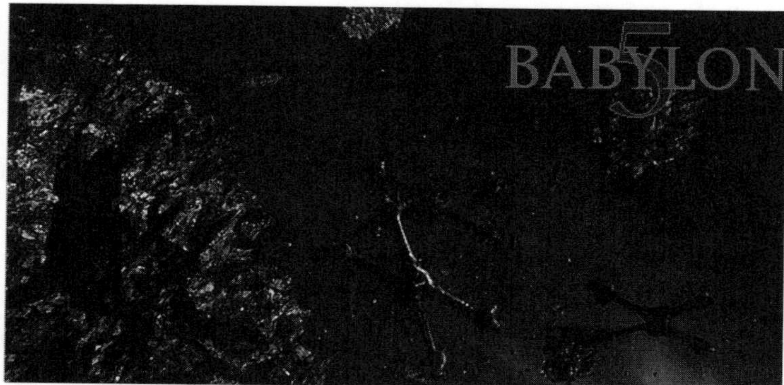

Figure 8-12 A GIF file displayed from an extension DLL's custom HTML output

```
char *  pData = new char[dwLength];
try
{
    file.Read(pData, dwLength);
}
catch(CFileException * e)
{
    e->Delete();
}
pECB->WriteClient( pECB->ConnID, pData, &dwLength, dwLength);
delete pData;
```

This is where `WriteClient` comes into its own! Unlike the redirection via << to the `pCTxt` pointer in the `CHttpServerContext` system, `WriteClient` can send pure binary output. (The << redirection will attempt to convert nonprinting characters to escape sequences.)

Comments

This is really a very powerful How-To because it can be used to send *any* kind of binary data to the browser: applications, zipped files, Java applets, even ActiveX controls! (An ISAPI extension DLL can be the target of an `FTP://` protocol, for example.)

COMPLEXITY
INTERMEDIATE

8.7 How do I... Redirect the client browser to a new URL with an ISAPI extension DLL?

Problem

Our Web site gets redesigned a lot, and we depend on using CGI to do redirection when a URL becomes invalid. Can ISAPI extensions generate server redirection requests?

Technique

Using `ServerSupportFunction`, an ISAPI extension DLL can send any of several server redirection requests when needed. This How-To shows you the steps required to send a client request to a new URL. These steps create the application from scratch, but for your convenience the complete project is on the CD under `CH08\HT07\`.

Steps

1. Activate Visual C++ 5.0 and create a new ISAPI extension DLL named `ISAPIXREMREDIR` with the wizard. Bring up the `ISAPIXREMREDIR.H` file in the text editor and add the boldfaced code in Listing 8-21. Save the project.

Listing 8-21 `ISAPIXREMREDIR.H` header file source code

```
#if
!defined(AFX_ISAPIXREMREDIR_H__374420E5_EC8D_11D0_B7DF_444553540000__INCLUDED_)
#define AFX_ISAPIXREMREDIR_H__374420E5_EC8D_11D0_B7DF_444553540000__INCLUDED_

// ISAPIXREMREDIR.H - Header file for your Internet Server
//    isapixremredir Extension

#include "resource.h"

class CIsapixremredirExtension : public CHttpServer
{
public:
CIsapixremredirExtension();
~CIsapixremredirExtension();

// Overrides
// ClassWizard generated virtual function overrides
// NOTE - the ClassWizard will add and remove member functions here.
//    DO NOT EDIT what you see in these blocks of generated code !
//{{AFX_VIRTUAL(CIsapixremredirExtension)
public:
virtual BOOL GetExtensionVersion(HSE_VERSION_INFO* pVer);
//}}AFX_VIRTUAL

// TODO: Add handlers for your commands here.
// For example:

    void Default(CHttpServerContext* pCtxt);
    DWORD   HttpExtensionProc(EXTENSION_CONTROL_BLOCK *pECB);

DECLARE_PARSE_MAP()

//{{AFX_MSG(CIsapixremredirExtension)
//}}AFX_MSG
};


//{{AFX_INSERT_LOCATION}}
// Microsoft Developer Studio will insert additional declarations immediately
//before the previous line.

#endif //
!defined(AFX_ISAPIXREMREDIR_H__374420E5_EC8D_11D0_B7DF_444553540000__INCLUDED)
```

2. Now bring up `ISAPIXREMREDIR.CPP` in the text editor and add the boldfaced code in Listing 8-22. Save the project, build the DLL, and move it to the `ASPEXEC` directory.

Listing 8-22 ISAPIXREMREDIR.CPP HttpExtensionProc source code

```
DWORD CIsapixremredirExtension::
HttpExtensionProc( EXTENSION_CONTROL_BLOCK *pECB )
{

    CHAR    szNewUrl[1024] = { 0 };
    CHAR    szBrowserType[ 1024 ] = { 0 };
    DWORD   dwLen = 1024;
    static const LPTSTR USER_AGENT = _T("HTTP_USER_AGENT");

    pECB->GetServerVariable( pECB->ConnID, USER_AGENT, szBrowserType, &dwLen);
    CString strGetBT = CString( szBrowserType , strlen( szBrowserType ));
    if ( strGetBT.Find( "MSIE 3" ) != - 1 )
    {
        lstrcpy(szNewUrl,⇐
"http://www.microsoft.com/sitebuilder/features/channelbuild.asp" );
        dwLen = lstrlen( szNewUrl );
        pECB->ServerSupportFunction( pECB->ConnID,
        HSE_REQ_SEND_URL_REDIRECT_RESP, szNewUrl, &dwLen, (LPDWORD)NULL );
    }
    else
    {

        lstrcpy(szNewUrl, "http://www.microsoft.com/ie/default.asp" );
        dwLen = lstrlen( szNewUrl );
        pECB->ServerSupportFunction( pECB->ConnID,
        HSE_REQ_SEND_URL_REDIRECT_RESP, szNewUrl, &dwLen, (LPDWORD)NULL );
    }

    return HSE_STATUS_SUCCESS;
}
```

3. Activate ActiveX Control Pad and enter the HTML code in Listing 8-23. Save the file as ASPHT0807.HTM and move it to the ASPEXEC directory.

Listing 8-23 ASPHT0807.HTM source code

```
<HTML>
<HEAD>
<TITLE>Active Server Pages How To Chapter Eight How To Seven</TITLE>
</HEAD>
<BODY>This is the link to
<A HREF="http://default/aspexec/isapixremredir.dll">Test Remote Server⇐
Redirection!</A>
</BODY>
</HTML>
```

4. Activate Internet Explorer and display ASPHT0807.HTM. Then activate another browser (such as Netscape Communicator); Figure 8-13 shows the two browsers displaying the same page. Now click on each link; the IE browser will go to the SiteBuilder Network page, whereas the non-IE browser will go to the default IE page as a hint (see Figure 8-14). You can now redirect to remote URLs with an ISAPI extension DLL.

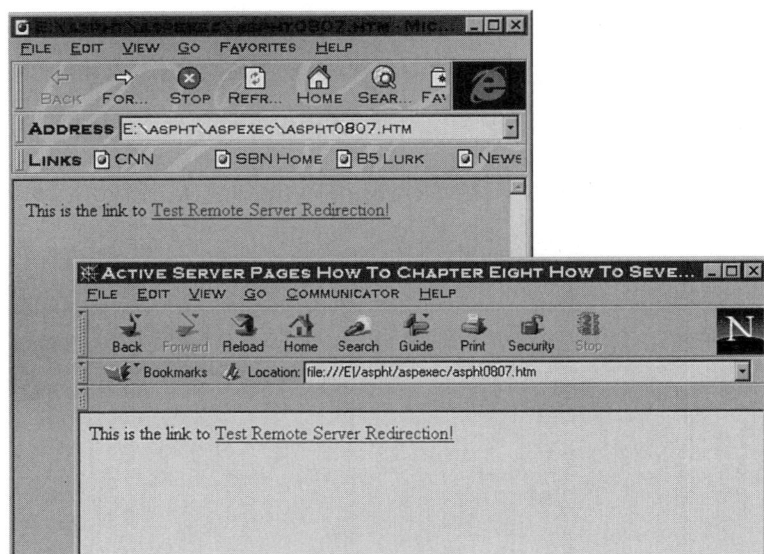

Figure 8-13 The redirection HTML file in both IE and NC

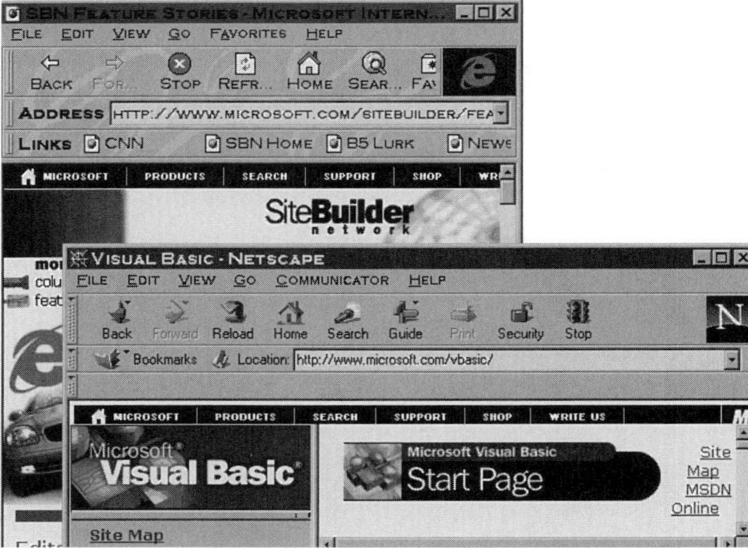

Figure 8-14 IE goes to the SiteBuilder Network page, whereas NC goes to the IE main page

How It Works

This How-To is virtually identical to How-To 8.4, except for this critical change to the code:

```
        lstrcpy(szNewUrl,⇐
"http://www.microsoft.com/sitebuilder/features/channelbuild.asp" );
        dwLen = lstrlen( szNewUrl );
        pECB->ServerSupportFunction( pECB->ConnID,
        HSE_REQ_SEND_URL_REDIRECT_RESP, szNewUrl, &dwLen, (LPDWORD)NULL );
```

Note first that the URL string is now a fully qualified one (with protocol and remote server name). Second, the constant sent to `ServerSupportFunction` is `HSE_REQ_SEND_URL_REDIRECT_RESP`, rather than `HSE_REQ_SEND_URL`. This constant tells the browser to redirect to a remote URL rather than one on the same server. That's all there is to it!

Comments

Believe it or not, this is all there is to URL redirection. At their core, all those fancy redirection components use this simple technique.

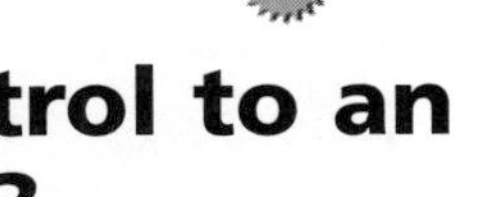

COMPLEXITY
ADVANCED

8.8 How do I... Link an ActiveX control to an ISAPI extension DLL?

Problem

We've completed our changeover from CGI to ISAPI extensions, but now we need to send extension information that can be displayed in an ActiveX control. How do you link ISAPI extensions with ActiveX controls?

Technique

ActiveX controls live entirely on the client machine via HTML `<OBJECT>` tags. To link them with an ISAPI extension requires the output of these tags mixed with data from the extension itself. This How-To illustrates using an ISAPI DLL to output a directory of files on the server computer in an ActiveX menu control. These steps create the application from scratch, but for your convenience the complete project is on the CD under `CH08\HT08\`.

Steps

1. Activate Visual C++ 5.0. Create a new ISAPI extension DLL named `ISAPIXAX` with the wizard. Bring up the `ISAPIXAX.CPP` file in the text editor and enter the boldfaced code in Listing 8-24. Save the project, build the DLL, and copy it into the `ASPEXEC` directory. (Note: Be sure to replace the directory string in the `_findfirst` call with the one on your local machine!)

Listing 8-24 ISAPIXAX.CPP default method source code

```
//////////////////////////////////////////////////////////////////////
// CIsapixaxExtension command handlers

void CIsapixaxExtension::Default(CHttpServerContext* pCtxt)
{
    StartContent(pCtxt);
    WriteTitle(pCtxt);

    *pCtxt << _T("<OBJECT ID=""menu2"" WIDTH=160 HEIGHT=25 align=middle\n");
    *pCtxt << _T("CLASSID=""CLSID:52DFAE60-CEBF-11CF-A3A9-00A0C9034920"">\n");
    int counter1 = 0;
    struct _finddata_t htm_file;
    long hFile;
    char strOutput[ 256 ];

    if( (hFile = _findfirst( "e:\\aspht\\aspexec\\*.htm", &htm_file )) == -1L )
    {
       wsprintf( strOutput , "<PARAM NAME=""Menuitem[%d]""
VALUE=""No_HTM_Files_In_Dir"">\n"
       , counter1);
       *pCtxt << _T( strOutput );
    }
    else
    {
          wsprintf( strOutput , "<PARAM NAME=""Menuitem[%d]"" VALUE=""%s"">\n" ,
counter1 , htm_file.name);
        *pCtxt << _T( strOutput );
        counter1++;
       while( _findnext( hFile, &htm_file ) == 0 )
       {
              wsprintf( strOutput , "<PARAM NAME=""Menuitem[%d]"" VALUE=""%s"">\n"
, counter1 , htm_file.name)
         *pCtxt << _T( strOutput );
         counter1++;
       }

       findclose( hFile );
    }
    *pCtxt << _T("<PARAM NAME=""Caption"" VALUE=""HTM_Files"">\n");
    *pCtxt << _T("</OBJECT>\n");
    *pCtxt << _T("\r\n");

    EndContent(pCtxt);
}
```

2. Activate ActiveX Control Pad and enter the HTML source code in Listing 8-25. Save the file as ASPHT0808.HTM and move it to the ASPEXEC directory.

Listing 8-25 ASPHT0808.HTM source code

```
<HTML>
<HEAD>
<TITLE>Active Server Pages How To Chapter Eight How To Eight</TITLE>
</HEAD>
<BODY>This is the link to
<A HREF="http://default/aspexec/isapixax3.dll">Test ISAPI/ActiveX Interaction!</A>
</BODY>
</HTML>
```

3. Activate Internet Explorer and bring up ASPHT0808.HTM. Click on the link, and, as shown in Figure 8-15, the Menu ActiveX control appears that, when clicked, gives a drop-down list of all the HTM files in the ASPEXEC directory. Now select View Source. As shown in Figure 8-16, the source code has been mechanically created with PARAM values for all the filenames. Your mastery of ISAPI now includes linking an ISAPI extension DLL with an ActiveX control.

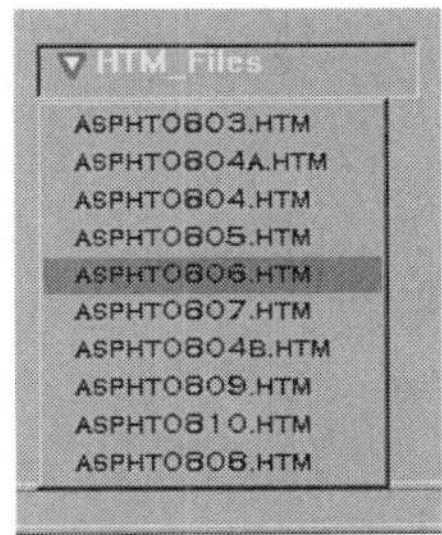

Figure 8-15 IE showing the mechanically created ActiveX menu control with a server files listing

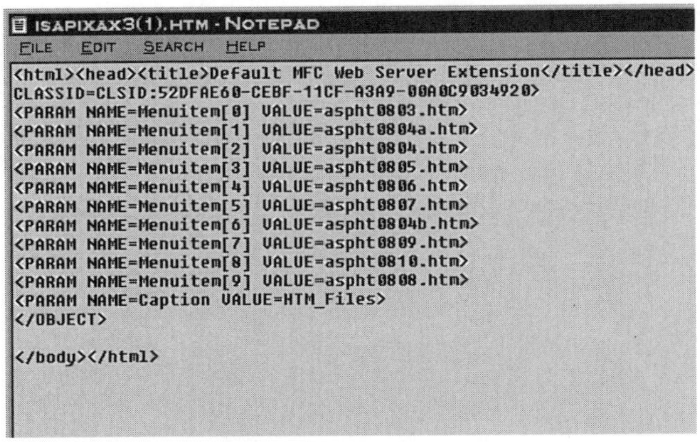

```
ISAPIXAX3(1).HTM - NOTEPAD
FILE  EDIT  SEARCH  HELP
<html><head><title>Default MFC Web Server Extension</title></head>
CLASSID=CLSID:52DFAE60-CEBF-11CF-A3A9-00A0C9034920>
<PARAM NAME=Menuitem[0] VALUE=aspht0803.htm>
<PARAM NAME=Menuitem[1] VALUE=aspht0804a.htm>
<PARAM NAME=Menuitem[2] VALUE=aspht0804.htm>
<PARAM NAME=Menuitem[3] VALUE=aspht0805.htm>
<PARAM NAME=Menuitem[4] VALUE=aspht0806.htm>
<PARAM NAME=Menuitem[5] VALUE=aspht0807.htm>
<PARAM NAME=Menuitem[6] VALUE=aspht0804b.htm>
<PARAM NAME=Menuitem[7] VALUE=aspht0809.htm>
<PARAM NAME=Menuitem[8] VALUE=aspht0810.htm>
<PARAM NAME=Menuitem[9] VALUE=aspht0808.htm>
<PARAM NAME=Caption VALUE=HTM_Files>
</OBJECT>

</body></html>
```

Figure 8-16 Viewing the mechanically created HTM source for the ActiveX Menu control's data

How It Works

Aside from the API calls to obtain the filenames, notice this vital piece of code:

```
while( _findnext( hFile, &htm_file ) == 0 )
{
   wsprintf( strOutput , "<PARAM NAME=""Menuitem[%d]"" VALUE=""%s"">\n" ,
   counter1 , htm_file.name)
  *pCtxt << _T( strOutput );
  counter1++;
}
```

Using `wsprintf`, you can merge the output text to the HTML file with C++ variables easily! This allows creating arbitrarily complex HTML outputs from within ISAPI extensions, just as is done with CGI scripts. The difference, of course, is that unlike with CGI, you have all the power of both C++ and the Windows API at your disposal!

Comments

A useful refinement of this How-To would be to add logic in client-side scripting, or a frameset system, to allow clicking on the menu items to display them.

IEXT-ASPS

8.9 How do I...
Use an ASP script with an ISAPI extension DLL?

Problem

We desperately need to output an ASP script with our ISAPI extension DLL, but the output never gets to the ASP parser; it always shows up as strange text on the client's browser. Can ISAPI extensions output ASP scripts?

Technique

Yes, they can, but only using a clever trick! This How-To demonstrates this trick, which involves internal server redirection. The directions here create the project from scratch, but for your convenience a copy of the HTML file is on the CD under `\CH08\HT09\`.

Steps

1. Activate Visual C++ 5.0 and create a new ISAPI extension named `ISAPIXASP` using the wizard. Bring up the `ISAPIXASP.H` file in the text editor and enter the boldfaced code in Listing 8-26. Save the project.

Listing 8-26 `ISAPIXASP.H` header file source code

```
#if !defined(AFX_ISAPIXASP_H__374420F0_EC8D_11D0_B7DF_444553540000__INCLUDED_)
#define AFX_ISAPIXASP_H__374420F0_EC8D_11D0_B7DF_444553540000__INCLUDED_

// ISAPIXASP.H - Header file for your Internet Server
//    isapixasp Extension

#include "resource.h"

class CIsapixaspExtension : public CHttpServer
{
public:
CIsapixaspExtension();
~CIsapixaspExtension();

// Overrides
// ClassWizard generated virtual function overrides
// NOTE - the ClassWizard will add and remove member functions here.
//    DO NOT EDIT what you see in these blocks of generated code !
//{{AFX_VIRTUAL(CIsapixaspExtension)
public:
virtual BOOL GetExtensionVersion(HSE_VERSION_INFO* pVer);
//}}AFX_VIRTUAL
```

continued on next page

continued from previous page

```
// TODO: Add handlers for your commands here.
// For example:

    void Default(CHttpServerContext* pCtxt);
    DWORD   HttpExtensionProc(EXTENSION_CONTROL_BLOCK *pECB);

DECLARE_PARSE_MAP()

//{{AFX_MSG(CIsapixaspExtension)
//}}AFX_MSG
};


//{{AFX_INSERT_LOCATION}}
// Microsoft Developer Studio will insert additional declarations immediately
//before the previous line.

#endif //
!defined(AFX_ISAPIXASP_H__374420F0_EC8D_11D0_B7DF_444553540000__INCLUDED)</HTML>
```

2. Move to the `ISAPIXASP.CPP` file in the text editor and enter the boldfaced code in Listing 8-27 for the `HttpExtensionProc` override method. Save the project, build the DLL, and move it into the `ASPEXEC` directory.

Listing 8-27 `ISAPIXASP.CPP HttpExtensionProc` source code

```
DWORD CIsapixaspExtension::
HttpExtensionProc( EXTENSION_CONTROL_BLOCK *pECB )
{

    CHAR     szNewUrl[1024] = { 0 };
    CHAR     szBrowserType[ 1024 ] = { 0 };
    DWORD    dwLen = 1024;
    static const LPTSTR USER_AGENT = _T("HTTP_USER_AGENT");

    pECB->GetServerVariable( pECB->ConnID, USER_AGENT, szBrowserType, &dwLen);
    CString strGetBT = CString( szBrowserType , strlen( szBrowserType ));
    if ( strGetBT.Find( "MSIE 3" ) != - 1 )
    {

        lstrcpy(szNewUrl, "http://default/aspexec/aspht0809a.asp" );
        dwLen = lstrlen( szNewUrl );
        pECB->ServerSupportFunction( pECB->ConnID,
      HSE_REQ_SEND_URL_REDIRECT_RESP, szNewUrl, &dwLen, (LPDWORD)NULL );
    }
    else
    {

        lstrcpy(szNewUrl, "http://default/aspexec/aspht0809b.asp" );
        dwLen = lstrlen( szNewUrl );
        pECB->ServerSupportFunction( pECB->ConnID,
        HSE_REQ_SEND_URL_REDIRECT_RESP, szNewUrl, &dwLen, (LPDWORD)NULL );
    }

    return HSE_STATUS_SUCCESS;
}
```

3. Activate ActiveX Control Pad and enter the HTML code in Listing 8-28. Save the file as ASPHT0809.HTM and move it into the ASPEXEC directory. To save time, copy the ASPHT0809A.ASP and ASPHT0809B.ASP files from the CD (they are just reworked versions of ASPHT0404.ASP and ASPHT0402.ASP).

Listing 8-28 ISAPIXASP.H header file source code

```
<HTML>
<HEAD>
<TITLE>Active Server Pages How To Chapter Eight How To Nine</TITLE>
</HEAD>
<BODY>This is the link to
<A HREF="http://default/aspexec/isapixasp.dll">test ASP redirection!</A>
</BODY>
</HTML>
```

4. Activate Internet Explorer and another non-IE browser and bring up ASPHT0809.HTM. Click on the link in each browser; the IE browser should display the list of HTTP headers, whereas the non-IE browser should show the current time, as shown in Figure 8-17, due to the redirection by the DLL to appropriate ASP files, which are correctly processed because they are using remote redirection. You have learned to use ASP files with ISAPI extension DLLs.

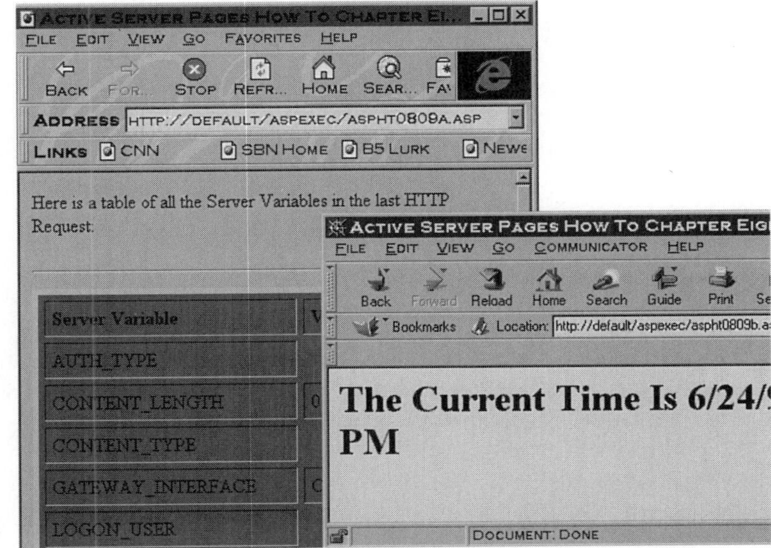

Figure 8-17 The redirected ASP files from ISAPIXASP.DLL properly processed

How It Works

If you are beginning to believe that `HttpExtensionProc` is the servant of all work in ISAPI extensions, you are right! Notice how this bit of magic was worked:

```
lstrcpy(szNewUrl, "http://default/aspexec/aspht0809a.asp" );
 dwLen = lstrlen( szNewUrl );
 pECB->ServerSupportFunction( pECB->ConnID,
HSE_REQ_SEND_URL_REDIRECT_RESP, szNewUrl, &dwLen, (LPDWORD)NULL );
```

The ASP files displayed were activated by remote redirection, thus bypassing the problem with local redirection or direct HTML output not triggering the ASP filter and processing correctly. This may seem trivial, but at present it is the *only* way to handle ASP output correctly from inside an ISAPI extension DLL!

Comments

There are other ways to merge ASP and ISAPI extensions, but they involve using ASP components in the C++ code directly and do not address the problem of failing to parse ASP script statements in the HTML output stream.

ISAPI-ADO-ASP

COMPLEXITY
ADVANCED

8.10 How do I... Interact with ActiveX data objects with an ISAPI extension DLL?

Problem

We need the ASP files redirected via our ISAPI extension DLL to do customized interaction with ADO using an ODBC database. Can ISAPI extensions modify the ASP code to which they redirect output?

Technique

Yes, via the powerful server-side include capability of ASP. This How-To demonstrates outputting a simple text file from the ISAPI extension DLL that is then included in the ASP file to control the ADO behavior under ASP. Although the directions here create the project from scratch, the completed ASP files are on the CD under `\CH08\HT10\`.

Steps

1. For this How-To, you'll use one of the tutorial databases supplied with ASP. (If you have removed them, you need to reinstall the `ADVWORKS.MDB` file to use this How-To.) If you have already done Chapter 7, "ActiveX

Data Objects: OLE DB Made Easy," or How-To 4.10, you can skip this step. First, you need to connect the ODBC drivers for Microsoft Access to the database along with its alias. Open the control panel, then double-click on the 32-bit ODBC drivers icon. In the property pages dialog that appears, select the System DSN tab and click the Add button. In the Add Dialog, enter `AWTutorial` for the datasource name; in the database grouping, click the Select button and browse to the `AdventureWorks Tutorial` directory on your hard drive; select the `ADVWORKS.MDB` file. Click OK twice to accept your new settings.

2. Activate Visual C++ 5.0. Create a new ISAPI extension DLL named `ISAPIXADOASP` with the wizard. Bring up its `ISAPIXADOASP.H` header file in the text editor and enter the boldfaced code in Listing 8-29. Save the project.

Listing 8-29 `ISAPIXADOASP.H` header file source code

```
#if !defined(AFX_ISAPIXADOASP_H__374420FB_EC8D_11D0_B7DF_444553540000__INCLUDED_)
#define AFX_ISAPIXADOASP_H__374420FB_EC8D_11D0_B7DF_444553540000__INCLUDED_

// ISAPIXADOASP.H - Header file for your Internet Server
//    isapixadoasp Extension

#include "resource.h"

class CIsapixadoaspExtension : public CHttpServer
{
public:
CIsapixadoaspExtension();
~CIsapixadoaspExtension();

// Overrides
// ClassWizard generated virtual function overrides
// NOTE - the ClassWizard will add and remove member functions here.
//    DO NOT EDIT what you see in these blocks of generated code !
//{{AFX_VIRTUAL(CIsapixadoaspExtension)
public:
virtual BOOL GetExtensionVersion(HSE_VERSION_INFO* pVer);
//}}AFX_VIRTUAL

// TODO: Add handlers for your commands here.
// For example:

    void Default(CHttpServerContext* pCtxt);
    DWORD   HttpExtensionProc(EXTENSION_CONTROL_BLOCK *pECB);

DECLARE_PARSE_MAP()

//{{AFX_MSG(CIsapixadoaspExtension)
//}}AFX_MSG
};


//{{AFX_INSERT_LOCATION}}
```

continued on next page

continued from previous page

```
// Microsoft Developer Studio will insert additional declarations immediately
//before the previous line.

#endif //!defined(AFX_ISAPIXADOASP_H__374420FB_EC8D_11D0_B7DF_444553540000__
INCLUDED)
```

3. Bring up the `ISAPIXADOASP.CPP` file in the text editor. Enter the boldfaced code in Listing 8-30 to supply the `HttpExtensionProc` override method. Save the project, build the DLL, and move it into the `ASPEXEC` directory.

Listing 8-30 `ISAPIXADOASP.CPP HttpExtensionProc` source code

```
DWORD CIsapixadoaspExtension::
HttpExtensionProc( EXTENSION_CONTROL_BLOCK *pECB )
{

    CHAR    szNewUrl[1024] = { 0 };
    CHAR    szBrowserType[ 1024 ] = { 0 };
    DWORD   dwLen = 1024;
    static const LPTSTR USER_AGENT = _T("HTTP_USER_AGENT");

    pECB->GetServerVariable( pECB->ConnID, USER_AGENT, szBrowserType, &dwLen);
    CString strGetBT = CString( szBrowserType , strlen( szBrowserType ));
    if ( strGetBT.Find( "MSIE 3" ) != - 1 )
    {
        char* pFileName = "e:\\aspht\\aspexec\\aspht0810inc.asp";
        CStdioFile   file;
        file.Open( pFileName, CFile::modeCreate ¦ CFile::modeWrite ¦⇐
CFile::typeText );
        try
        {
            CString pstrOutput;
            try
            {
                pstrOutput = "<% dim HoldAction %>\n";
                file.WriteString(pstrOutput);
                pstrOutput = "<% HoldAction = ""FORWARD"" %>\n";
                file.WriteString(pstrOutput);
            }
            catch(CFileException * e)
            {
                e->Delete();
            }
        }
        catch(CMemoryException * e)
        {
            e->Delete();
        }
        catch(CFileException * e)
        {
            e->Delete();
        }
        lstrcpy(szNewUrl, "http://default/aspexec/aspht0810.asp" );
        dwLen = lstrlen( szNewUrl );
        pECB->ServerSupportFunction( pECB->ConnID,
       HSE_REQ_SEND_URL_REDIRECT_RESP, szNewUrl, &dwLen, (LPDWORD)NULL );
```

```
    }
    else
    {
        char* pFileName = "e:\\aspht\\aspexec\\aspht0810inc.asp";
        CStdioFile   file;
        file.Open( pFileName, CFile::modeCreate ¦ CFile::modeWrite ¦⇐
CFile::typeText );
        try
        {
            CString pstrOutput;
            try
            {
                pstrOutput = "<% dim HoldAction %>\n";
                file.WriteString(pstrOutput);
                pstrOutput = "<% HoldAction = ""BACKWARD"" %\n>";
                file.WriteString(pstrOutput);
            }
            catch(CFileException * e)
            {
                e->Delete();
            }
        }
        catch(CMemoryException * e)
        {
            e->Delete();
        }
        catch(CFileException * e)
        {
            e->Delete();
        }
        lstrcpy(szNewUrl, "http://default/aspexec/aspht0810.asp" );
        dwLen = lstrlen( szNewUrl );
        pECB->ServerSupportFunction( pECB->ConnID,
        HSE_REQ_SEND_URL_REDIRECT_RESP, szNewUrl, &dwLen, (LPDWORD)NULL );
    }

    return HSE_STATUS_SUCCESS;
}
```

4. Activate ActiveX Control Pad. Enter the HTML code in Listing 8-31. Save it as ASPHT0810.HTM and move it into the ASPEXEC directory.

Listing 8-31 ASPHT0810.HTM source code

```
<HTML>
<HEAD>
<TITLE>Active Server Pages How To Chapter Eight How To Ten</TITLE>
</HEAD>
<BODY>This is the link to
<A HREF="http://default/aspexec/isapixadoasp.dll">test ISAPI/ADO/ASP⇐
interaction!</A>
</BODY>
</HTML>
```

5. Create a new file in ActiveX Control Pad. Enter the ASP code in Listing 8-32. Save it as ASPHT0810.ASP and move it into the ASPEXEC directory.

Listing 8-32 ASPHT0810.ASP source code

```
<%@ LANGUAGE = VBScript %>
<HTML>
<HEAD>
<TITLE>Active Server Pages Chapter Eight How To Ten</TITLE>
</HEAD>
<BODY>
<% if IsObject(Session("objRecordSet")) then
     set objRecordSet = Session("objRecordSet")
   else
     Set objConnection = Server.CreateObject("ADODB.Connection")
   objConnection.Open "AWTutorial"
   SQLQuery = "SELECT * FROM Customers"
   Set objRecordSet = objConnection.Execute( SQLQuery )
   objRecordSet.Close
   objRecordSet.Open , , 2 , 4
   Set Session("objRecordSet") = objRecordSet
   end if
%>
<!--#INCLUDE FILE = "aspht0810inc.asp"-->
<%
   HoldAction = UCase( HoldAction )
   if HoldAction = "" then HoldAction = "FORWARD"
   if HoldAction = "FORWARD" then
     on error resume next
     if not objRecordSet.EOF then
objRecordSet.MoveNext
     else
objRecordSet.MoveFirst
     end if
   elseif HoldAction = "BACKWARD" then
     on error resume next
     if not objRecordSet.BOF then
objRecordSet.MovePrevious
     else
objRecordSet.MoveLast
     end if
   elseif HoldAction = "UPDATE" then
     objRecordSet("CompanyName") = Request.Form("Text2")
     objRecordSet("ContactLastName") = Request.Form("Text3")
objRecordSet("ContactFirstName") = Request.Form("Text4")
objRecordSet("City") = Request.Form("Text5")
objRecordSet("StateOrProvince") = Request.Form("Text6")
ObjRecordSet.Update
    end if
%>
    <FORM NAME="Form1" >
<TABLE WIDTH=600 COLSPAN=8 BORDER=5 CELLSPACING=5
CELLPADDING=5 ALIGN="CENTER" VALIGN="MIDDLE" BGCOLOR="Teal">
<TR>
<TD COLSPAN=5 ALIGN="CENTER">
Customer Listing
</TD>
</TR>
<TR>
<TD>
```

```
Company Name
</TD>
<TD>
Contact Name
</TD>
<TD>
E-mail address
</TD>
<TD>
City
</TD>
<TD>
State/Province
</TD>
</TR>
  <TR>
  <TD>
  <INPUT Type = "Text" Name="Text2" Value = "<%= objRecordSet("CompanyName")%>">
  </TD>
  <TD>
  <INPUT Type = "Text" Name="Text3" Value = "<%=⇐
objRecordSet("ContactLastName")%>">
  <INPUT Type = "Text" Name="Text4" Value = "<%=⇐
objRecordSet("ContactFirstName")%>">
  </TD>
  <TD>
    <A HREF="mailto:">
      <%= objRecordSet("ContactLastName")%>
    </A></TD>
  <TD>
  <INPUT Type = "Text" Name="Text5" Value = "<%= objRecordSet("City")%>">
  </TD>
  <TD>
  <INPUT Type = "Text" Name="Text6" Value = "<%=⇐
objRecordSet("StateOrProvince")%>">
  </TD>
  </TR>
</TD>
</TR>
</TABLE>
    </FORM>
</BODY>
</HTML>
```

6. Bring up ASPHT0810.HTM in both Internet Explorer and another browser such as Netscape Communicator. Click on the link to the ISAPI DLL in each browser. In both cases, you will start at the initial record because the dataset had not been previously initialized. Move back to the ASPHT0810.HTM page in each browser and click on the link again. In the IE browser, you will move to the second record in the database. In the non-IE browser, you will move to the end record of the database, as shown in Figure 8-18. These different results are caused by the included ASP code created by the DLL and picked up by the ASP file. Congratulations! You have learned to use server-side include files with ASP scripts to control ODBC database data display using ADOs.

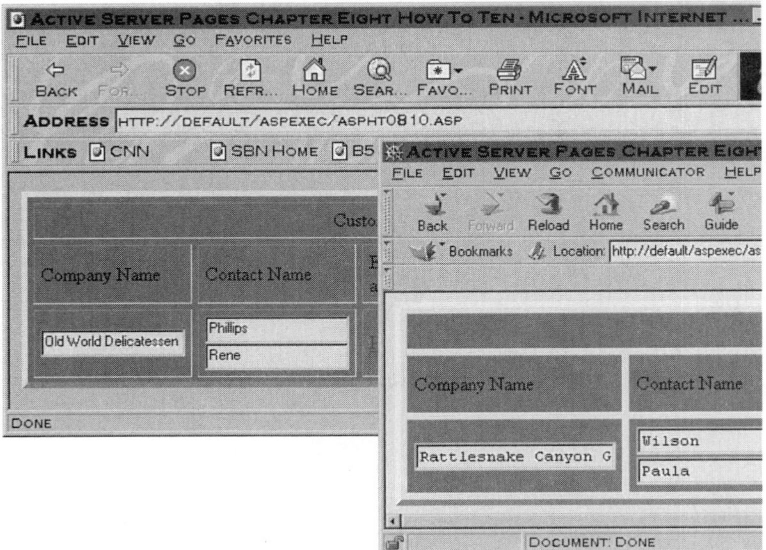

Figure 8-18 IE and NC showing the different navigation results in ASPHT0810.ASP via the server-side include file from the ISAPIADOASP ISAPI extension

How It Works

This How-To's C++ code is quite standard by now: It detects which browser is being used and redirects to an appropriate ASP file. However, notice what is written out to a text file before the redirection:

```
char* pFileName = "e:\\aspht\\aspexec\\aspht0810inc.asp";
CStdioFile   file;
file.Open( pFileName, CFile::modeCreate | CFile::modeWrite | CFile::typeText );
try
{
    CString pstrOutput;
    try
    {
        pstrOutput = "<% dim HoldAction %>\n";
        file.WriteString(pstrOutput);
        pstrOutput = "<% HoldAction = ""FORWARD"" %>\n";
        file.WriteString(pstrOutput);
    }
```

An ASP file is created and two lines of ASP code are written to it. One set of code sends the browser forward; the other sends it backward. (This is, of course, an extremely simple example; in practice, any amount of sophisticated ASP code could be written here!) The redirection then sends both browser types to the same ASP file for display.

This is where the critical piece of new functionality comes in:

```
<% if IsObject(Session("objRecordSet")) then
     set objRecordSet = Session("objRecordSet")
   else
     Set objConnection = Server.CreateObject("ADODB.Connection")
   objConnection.Open "AWTutorial"
   SQLQuery = "SELECT * FROM Customers"
   Set objRecordSet = objConnection.Execute( SQLQuery )
   objRecordSet.Close
   objRecordSet.Open , , 2 , 4
   Set Session("objRecordSet") = objRecordSet
   end if
%>
<!--#INCLUDE FILE = "aspht0810inc.asp"-->
<%
   HoldAction = UCase( HoldAction )
   if HoldAction = "" then HoldAction = "FORWARD"
   if HoldAction = "FORWARD" then
```

The line that looks like a comment is actually a powerful `#include` directive for ASP! It tells the ASP parser to locate the named file and insert its complete contents into the hosting ASP file at that point. All this is done prior to any script execution, allowing arbitrarily complex ASP scripts to be created this way dynamically! Once all `#include` directives have been processed, the ASP scripts are then evaluated and their HTML is generated normally.

There are extra subtleties to using `#include` directives with ASP, such as `VIRTUAL` versus `FILE` inclusions; please consult the ASP documentation for more details.

Comments

It may seem strange to use simple text files to control powerful technology such as ISAPI, ASP, and ADO. However, to a certain degree this is because the Windows world has relied much more heavily on compiled executable files for program behavior. In the workstation environment of UNIX, using program-created text files to manipulate other programs is routine, and some of the most powerful computer programs available (such as supercomputers) rely on precisely this technique. (I've written simulations of living neural networks on Intel supercomputers that did almost all their work swapping text files around!)

CHAPTER 9

ISAPI FILTERS: CUSTOMIZING INTERNET INFORMATION SERVER

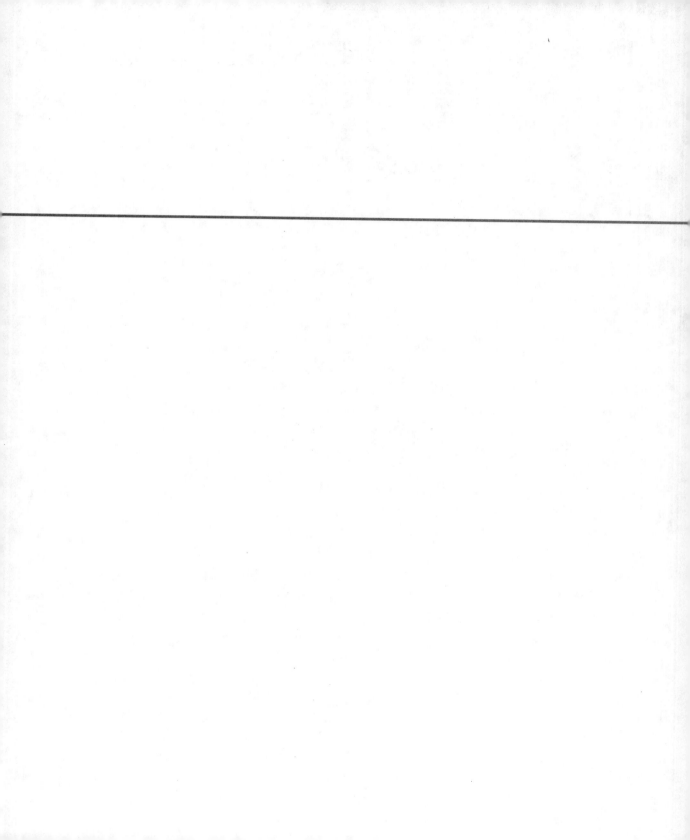

9

ISAPI FILTERS: CUSTOMIZING INTERNET INFORMATION SERVER

How do I...

9.7 Interact with an ISAPI extension DLL in an ISAPI filter?

9.8 Link an ActiveX control to an ISAPI filter?

9.9 Use ActiveX Scripting with an ISAPI filter?

9.10 Use Active Server Pages and ActiveX data objects with an ISAPI filter?

Although ISAPI extension DLLs have many powerful uses, they all suffer a common limitation: They must be explicitly invoked in a URL to function. Some tasks once handled by the Common Gateway Interface (CGI) via hooks into the Web server's system cannot be handled by ISAPI extensions for this reason. To fill this gap, Microsoft added a second layer of ISAPI functionality: the Internet Server Application Programming Interface (ISAPI) filter. ISAPI filters are also Dynamic Link Libraries (DLLs), and they hook directly into the server to intercept and process all instances of specific server interactions. They can detect secure or nonsecure ports, maintain Web site counters, and allow custom design of URLs not directly linked to physical file locations. ISAPI filters can also detect header information such as `USER_AGENT` values and append and modify the outgoing HTML stream. This chapter provides complete code examples in Visual C++ 5.0 for all these capabilities and more.

9.1 Create an ISAPI Filter DLL in Visual C++ 5.0

Visual C++ 5.0 has an ISAPI Filter Wizard, and this How-To shows you how to use it to create a simple filter that writes a log file with HTTP header information for each access to a Web site.

9.2 Create a Web Site Counter with an ISAPI Filter

Counters are still widely used on the Web; this How-To gives you exact instructions for creating your own counter via an ISAPI filter that detects which virtual directory is being accessed and increments a counter in a log file for each one.

9.3 Use Custom URLs with an ISAPI Filter

Most surfers assume that URLs are exact mappings of file structures on the server computer for that file. In fact, the server often translates URLs into physical mappings that are quite different from the URL itself. This How-To gives you complete information on creating an ISAPI filter that detects any URL with the UNIX ~ in it and redirects that URL to a real physical path on the local hard drive.

9.4 Control Browser Access to a Web Site with an ISAPI Filter

Another important aspect of ISAPI filter functionality is its capability to intercept the raw HTML headers prior to actual retrieval and processing of the URL. This How-To outlines an ISAPI filter that detects non-Internet Explorer browsers and redirects them to a special physical portion of the Web site using URL redirection.

9.5 Add Custom HTML to All Pages Requested from a Web Site with an ISAPI Filter

Some Web sites like to advertise themselves on all HTML pages retrieved from their servers; this How-To gives your Web site this capability with an ISAPI filter DLL that uses the `SEND_RAW_DATA` event handler.

9.6 Change Internal HTML from Pages Requested from a Web Site with an ISAPI Filter

Not only can ISAPI filters add HTML to the outgoing data stream, they can modify it as well! This How-To shows you the technique needed to expand all space-delimited instances of `ASP` in a returned HTML file into `Active Server Pages`.

9.7 Interact with an ISAPI Extension DLL in an ISAPI Filter

Because ISAPI extension DLLs must be explicitly invoked in a URL, this How-To gives you the code to write an ISAPI filter that watches for a particular extension DLL and prevents a bug by modifying its parameter stream.

9.8 Link an ActiveX Control to an ISAPI Filter

Because ISAPI filters can output HTML on their own, they can add ActiveX controls to Web pages as well! This How-To demonstrates adding a colorful ActiveX Label control with the counter information for a particular Web application to every page obtained from it.

9.9 Use ActiveX Scripting with an ISAPI Filter

Along with HTML, ISAPI filters can output ActiveX Scripting information. This How-To guides you through modifying the example from How-To 9.8 to permit changing display characteristics at runtime on the client machine.

9.10 Use Active Server Pages and ActiveX Data Objects with an ISAPI Filter

Although direct Active Server Pages (ASP) output isn't possible via an ISAPI filter any more than with an ISAPI extension DLL, the same include file technique also works around the problem for ISAPI filters. This How-To reproduces the browser detection behavior in an ActiveX data object (ADO) and ASP environment but at the filter level rather than the extension level.

NOTE

You should not keep all the filters created in these How-To's running at once; when you have examined the behavior of Internet Information Server (IIS) with a given filter or two running, remove the filter from the registry or filters list to free up system resources and reduce the complexity in case errors happen.

9.1 How do I... Create an ISAPI filter DLL in Visual C++ 5.0?

Problem

ISAPI extensions are great, but we have some Common Gateway Interface (CGI) applications that ISAPI extensions can't duplicate because they hook directly into the server itself. Does ISAPI have another technology that can help us get rid of CGI for good?

Technique

Yes, the ISAPI filter DLL! These DLLs are connected directly into Internet Information Server/Personal Web Server (IIS/PWS) and can handle parts of CGI that ISAPI extensions can't. This How-To demonstrates creating a simple ISAPI filter with Visual C++ 5.0's MFC (Microsoft Foundation Classes) ISAPI Wizard. Although these directions create the project from scratch, the CD contains a completed file under `CH09\HT01\`.

Steps

1. Start Visual C++ 5.0 and bring up the New Workspace dialog. As shown in Figure 9-1, select MFC ISAPI Extension Wizard from the list of icons to create a new ISAPI filter DLL. Choose an appropriate directory for the project and name it `ISAPIFLOG`.

2. When the wizard dialog appears, select a filter DLL with MFC as a shared DLL, unchecking the Extension option. The finished wizard dialog should look similar to the one shown in Figure 9-2. Press Next to create the new project skeleton.

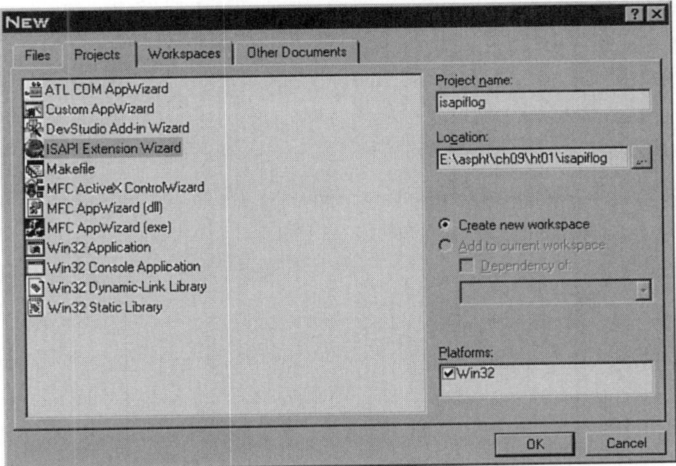

Figure 9-1 Selecting a new ISAPI filter DLL project in VC 5

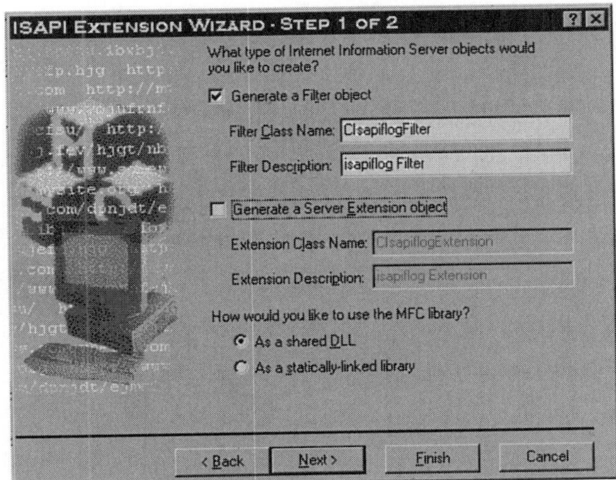

Figure 9-2 The MFC ISAPI Wizard in VC 5 set for a filter DLL

3. When the next wizard page appears, select only the Nonsecure port sessions and URL mapping requests notification check boxes; clear all the others for this demonstration. Leave the notification priority set to low. When you are done, the dialog should look very similar to Figure 9-3. Press Finish to create the new skeleton project.

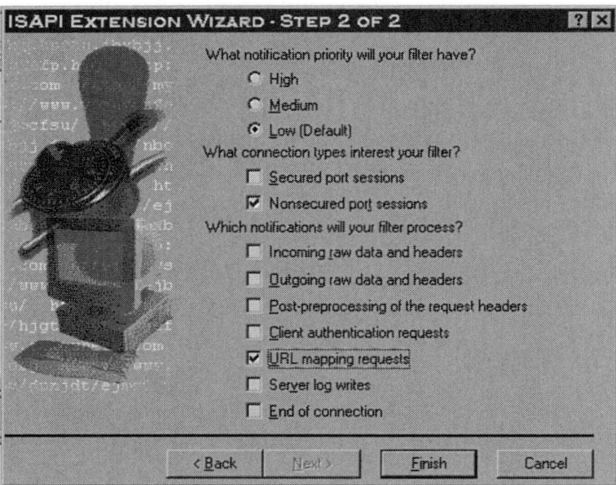

Figure 9-3 The MFC ISAPI Wizard in VC 5 set for a filter DLL and requesting notification of URL mapping requests

4. Bring up the `ISAPIFLOG.CPP` source file in the text editor. Move up to the constructor and destructor skeleton code and add the boldfaced code in Listing 9-1. Save the project. (Be sure to change the pathname for the log file to one appropriate for your system.)

Listing 9-1 `ISAPIFLOG.CPP` constructor and destructor source code

```
// ISAPIFLOG.CPP - Implementation file for your Internet Server
//  isapiflog Filter

#include "stdafx.h"
#include "isapiflog.h"

#define VARIABLE_SIZE 4182

///////////////////////////////////////////////////////////////////////
// The one and only CWinApp object
// NOTE: You may remove this object if you alter your project to no
// longer use MFC in a DLL.

CWinApp theApp;



///////////////////////////////////////////////////////////////////////
// The one and only CIsapiflogFilter object

CIsapiflogFilter theFilter;

// m_hLogFile
```

```
// global handle for the log file which will be used for
// writing out user-agent and URL mapping strings.
HANDLE m_hLogFile = INVALID_HANDLE_VALUE;

///////////////////////////////////////////////////////////////////////
// CIsapiflogFilter implementation

CIsapiflogFilter::CIsapiflogFilter()
{
  DWORD cb;
  CHAR rgchBuff[1024];

  if (m_hLogFile == INVALID_HANDLE_VALUE)
  {
    m_hLogFile = CreateFileW(L"c:\\aspht0901.log",
    GENERIC_WRITE,
    FILE_SHARE_READ ¦ FILE_SHARE_WRITE,
    NULL,
    OPEN_ALWAYS,
    0,
    NULL);

    if (m_hLogFile != INVALID_HANDLE_VALUE)
    {
      if (SetFilePointer(m_hLogFile, 0, NULL, FILE_END) == (DWORD) -1L)
      {
        CloseHandle(m_hLogFile);
        m_hLogFile = INVALID_HANDLE_VALUE;
      }
      else
      {
        CTime t = CTime::GetCurrentTime();
        cb = wsprintf(rgchBuff, "--> log started %s\n", t.Format("%m/%d/%y⇐
        %H:%M:%S"));
        DWORD cbWritten = 0;
        WriteFile(m_hLogFile,
              rgchBuff,
              cb,
              &cbWritten,
              NULL);
      }
    }
  }
}

CIsapiflogFilter::~CIsapiflogFilter()
{
  // close the file
  if (m_hLogFile != INVALID_HANDLE_VALUE)
  {
    CloseHandle(m_hLogFile);
    m_hLogFile = INVALID_HANDLE_VALUE;
  }
}
```

5. Move down to the event handler for the URL mapping notification and add the boldfaced code in Listing 9-2. Save the project. Build the DLL.

Listing 9-2 ISAPIFPORT.CPP OnURLMap event handler source code

```
BOOL CIsapiflogFilter::GetFilterVersion(PHTTP_FILTER_VERSION pVer)
{
// Call default implementation for initialization
CHttpFilter::GetFilterVersion(pVer);

// Clear the flags set by base class
pVer->dwFlags &= ~SF_NOTIFY_ORDER_MASK;

// Set the flags we are interested in
pVer->dwFlags |= SF_NOTIFY_ORDER_LOW | SF_NOTIFY_NONSECURE_PORT |
SF_NOTIFY_URL_MAP;

// Load description string
TCHAR sz[SF_MAX_FILTER_DESC_LEN+1];
ISAPIVERIFY(::LoadString(AfxGetResourceHandle(),
IDS_FILTER, sz, SF_MAX_FILTER_DESC_LEN));
tcscpy(pVer->lpszFilterDesc, sz);
return TRUE;
}

DWORD CIsapiflogFilter::OnUrlMap(CHttpFilterContext* pCtxt,
PHTTP_FILTER_URL_MAP pMapInfo)
{
  CHAR achReferer[VARIABLE_SIZE];
  DWORD cbReferer = VARIABLE_SIZE;
  DWORD cb;
  CHAR rgchBuff[1024];
  CString strPhysicalPath, strOriginalPath;
  int nPos = 0;

  // copy the original physical path string
  strOriginalPath = pMapInfo->pszPhysicalPath;
  strPhysicalPath = strOriginalPath;
  // Get referer from server
  if (!pCtxt->GetServerVariable("HTTP_REFERER", achReferer, &cbReferer))
  {
    // the Client did not supply the referer string
    achReferer[0] = '-';
    achReferer[1] = '\0';
    cbReferer = 2;
  }
  //
  // generate the log record and write it to log file
  //
  cb = wsprintf(rgchBuff, "[%s] -> [%s] refered by: %s\n",
  strOriginalPath, strPhysicalPath, achReferer);
  if (m_hLogFile != INVALID_HANDLE_VALUE)
  {
    DWORD cbWritten = 0;
    WriteFile(m_hLogFile, rgchBuff, cb, &cbWritten, NULL);
  }
```

```
    return SF_STATUS_REQ_NEXT_NOTIFICATION;
}

// Do not edit the following lines, which are needed by ClassWizard.
#if 0
BEGIN_MESSAGE_MAP(CIsapiflogFilter, CHttpFilter)
//{{AFX_MSG_MAP(CIsapiflogFilter)
//}}AFX_MSG_MAP
END_MESSAGE_MAP()
#endif// 0
```

6. Using Explorer or some other file manager, move to the `WINDOWS` directory and run `REGEDIT.EXE` (`REGEDT32.EXE` on Windows NT). Navigate down through the keys to `HKEY_LOCAL_MACHINE\System\CurrentControlSet\Services\W3SCVC\Parameters\Filter Dlls`. Double-click on it and the modification dialog will appear, as shown in Figure 9-4. Enter `,[path to your dll]isapiflog.dll` after the existing entry or entries and press OK. Figure 9-5 shows the registry with the new entry. Close the registry editor.

NOTE

These directions are for PWS 1.0 or IIS 3.0. If you have 4.0, please see the `README.TXT` file under "Installing and Configuring IIS/PWS" for details on setting up filters under other versions of IIS/PWS.

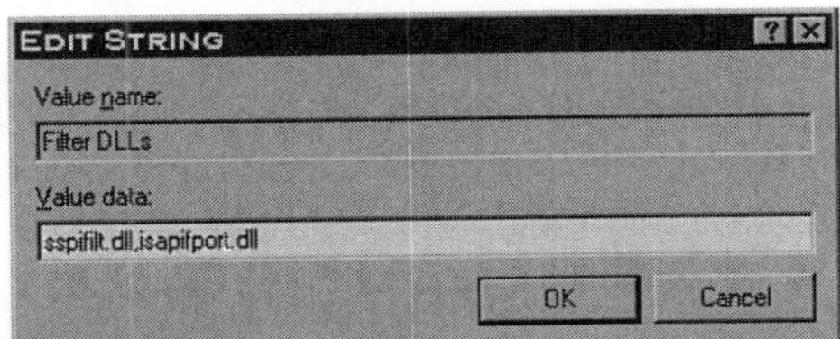

Figure 9-4 Use `REGEDIT32.EXE` to add the `ISAPIFLOG` filter to PWS's registry settings

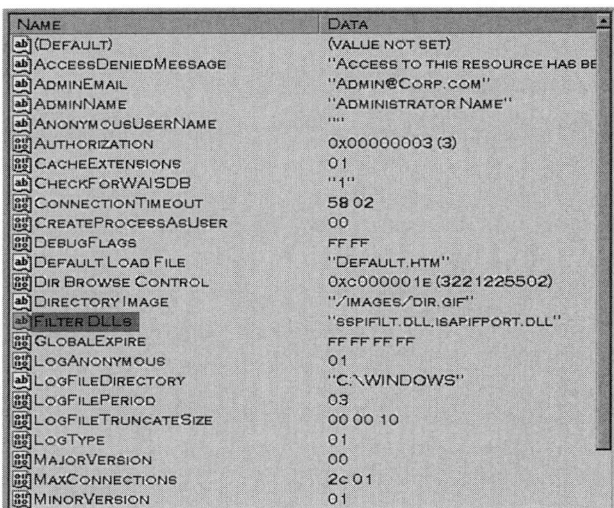

Name
Data
(Default)
(value not set)
AccessDeniedMessage
"Access to this resource has be
AdminEmail
"Admin@Corp.com"
AdminName
"Administrator Name"
AnonymousUserName
""
Authorization
0x00000003 (3)
CacheExtensions
01
CheckForWAISDB
"1"
ConnectionTimeout
58 02
CreateProcessAsUser
00
DebugFlags
FF FF
Default Load File
"Default.htm"
Dir Browse Control
0xc000001e (3221225502)
Directory Image
"/images/dir.gif"
Filter DLLs
"sspifilt.dll,isapifport.dll"
GlobalExpire
FF FF FF FF
LogAnonymous
01
LogFileDirectory
"C:\WINDOWS"
LogFilePeriod
03
LogFileTruncateSize
00 00 10
LogType
01
MajorVersion
00
MaxConnections
2c 01
MinorVersion
01

Figure 9-5 The new filter DLL entered in the registry

7. Restart IIS or PWS, depending on which one you are using. View several of the ASP and/or HTM files from previous How-To's that activate the PWS/IIS system on your machine. Then move to the directory you chose for the log file and open it. As shown in Figure 9-6, the file will contain entries for all the pages you activated. Congratulations! You have learned to create an ISAPI filter DLL and use it with the IIS/PWS system to create log information about the server.

Figure 9-6 The log file created by the `ISAPIFLOG` filter

How It Works

An ISAPI filter is a DLL that is loaded into memory when IIS/PWS first starts. It is then given the opportunity to examine and modify data from every HTTP request the server handles. By attaching itself to specific server events, the filter determines what data it sees for each request and what actions it can take in response to the requests.

Filters work considerably differently than extensions, so I have to plow some fairly deep ground here even though the code is easy. Like extensions, filters have required DLL entry points that the IIS/PWS system calls. Unlike extensions, which are loaded only when referenced by a URL, filters are loaded when IIS/PWS first runs. The `GetFilterVersion` entry point is always called first to obtain vital information about what the filter wants to do. Notice this section of code from the `GetFilterVersion` function:

```
// Set the flags we are interested in
pVer->dwFlags |= SF_NOTIFY_ORDER_LOW | SF_NOTIFY_NONSECURE_PORT |⇐
SF_NOTIFY_URL_MAP;
```

This entry is where ISAPI learns from the filter two vital pieces of information. The first piece of data is the `SF_NOTIFY_ORDER_XXX` constant. This is used when more than one filter is attempting to process the same notification (notifications are discussed in about two sentences). In cases of two or more filters competing for a notification, the `NOTIFY_ORDER` priority settings control which one gets the data stream first, second, and so on. This can make a difference depending on how vital it is that one filter do its work before others are invoked.

Notifications are the other critical bit of data in this line of code. This particular DLL uses two of them, `SF_NOTIFY_URL_MAP` and `SF_NOTIFY_NONSECURE_PORT`. By including these two constants and no others, the DLL indicates that it wishes to be called only when a URL mapping request is made (to transform the raw header URL into a physical path on the server machine). Of course, in effect this means all requests will be routed to this filter because all URLs must be remapped. A number of other notifications are available, with different effects; they are the focus of the remaining How-To's in this chapter.

It is critical to understand that *all* filter DLLs are called for *almost every request* made to the IIS/PWS system because they all use the various services covered in the notification codes. Therefore, it is important to select only the notifications the filter absolutely requires; otherwise, the system will soon bog down with useless processing chores!

The ISAPI filter MFC classes have built-in handler methods for the various notifications. Our code lives inside the `OnURLMap` event handler.

```
DWORD CIsapiflogFilter::OnUrlMap(CHttpFilterContext* pCtxt,
PHTTP_FILTER_URL_MAP pMapInfo)
{
  CHAR achReferer[VARIABLE_SIZE];
  DWORD cbReferer = VARIABLE_SIZE;
  DWORD cb;
  CHAR rgchBuff[1024];
  CString strPhysicalPath, strOriginalPath;
  int nPos = 0;

  // copy the original physical path string
  strOriginalPath = pMapInfo->pszPhysicalPath;
  strPhysicalPath = strOriginalPath;
  // Get referer from server
  if (!pCtxt->GetServerVariable("HTTP_REFERER", achReferer, &cbReferer))
  {
    // the Client did not supply the referer string
    achReferer[0] = '-';
    achReferer[1] = '\0';
    cbReferer = 2;
  }
  //
  // generate the log record and write it to log file
  //
  cb = wsprintf(rgchBuff, "[%s] -> [%s] refered by: %s\n",
  strOriginalPath, strPhysicalPath, achReferer);
  if (m_hLogFile != INVALID_HANDLE_VALUE)
  {
    DWORD cbWritten = 0;
    WriteFile(m_hLogFile, rgchBuff, cb, &cbWritten, NULL);
  }
  return SF_STATUS_REQ_NEXT_NOTIFICATION;
}
```

Each notification type passes a different data structure to its event handler with information relevant to that notification. In the case of the URL mapping notification, this data structure is `HTTP_FILTER_URL_MAP`. It contains two strings: one with the raw URL and one with the physical path the raw URL has been translated into, plus a doubleword holding the length of the translated path. In the code above, you simply set a second variable for the raw path equal to the physical because on a Windows machine they are identical (such translation is needed normally only to deal with the UNIX ~ alias character).

The `HttpFilterContext` variable also sent into the event handler has words virtually identical to the `HttpExtensionContext` sent into the `Extension` methods from Chapter 8, "ISAPI Extensions: Using ActiveX DLLs to Replace CGI." Here, you use it to get the server variable `HTTP_REFERER` (which, by the way, is misspelled, but if you use the correct spelling, the variable comes back empty). This information is then written to the log file along with the URLs referenced.

Simply creating the DLL is not enough, however. The IIS/PWS system must also be informed to use the DLL as a filter. This is where the registry entry comes in. By adding the name (and optionally the full path) of the DLL to the filter DLL's entry of the registry, IIS/PWS will automatically load the DLL when it starts, and from checking its desired notifications on loading in the `GetFilterVersion` hook, be ready to call it when needed for registered events.

As a final note, you can see that the file opening and closing chores are dealt with in the constructor and destructor code rather than in the actual event handler. For a logging filter, this is reasonable because these two methods are called only when IIS/PWS starts and stops, creating and destroying all its filter DLLs when it does so.

Comments

This is a simple filter example, but it illustrates many of the basic techniques all filters use. Once you've mastered this How-To, it is a good idea to go back and remove it from the registry because, otherwise, it will create a large and relatively useless log file on your server as well as eat processor cycles for no good purpose.

9.2 How do I... Create a Web site counter with an ISAPI filter?

Problem

We need to maintain a counter for our Web site. Previously we used Win-CGI, but now that we've converted to ISAPI, can it provide us with the same capability?

Technique

Yes, an ISAPI filter can easily be written to provide full-featured counters for Web sites. This How-To implements a simple filter that will log hits on the two applications created in this book, **ASPEXEC** and **GUESTBOOK**. Although these directions create the project from scratch, the CD contains a completed file under **CH09\HT02**.

Steps

1. Activate Visual C++ 5.0. Create a new ISAPI filter named **ISAPIFCTR** with the wizard. Set its notifications to Nonsecured port sessions and URL mapping requests only. Open its **ISAPIFCTR.CPP** file and enter the boldfaced code in Listing 9-3 for the **OnURLMap** event handler. Be sure to change the path for the log file to one appropriate for your system. Save the project and build the DLL.

Listing 9-3 ISAPIFCTR.CPP OnURLMap event handler source code

```
// ISAPIFCTR.CPP - Implementation file for your Internet Server
//  isapifctr filter

#include "stdafx.h"
#include "isapifctr.h"

///////////////////////////////////////////////////////////////////////
// The one and only CWinApp object
// NOTE: You may remove this object if you alter your project to no
// longer use MFC in a DLL.

CWinApp theApp;



///////////////////////////////////////////////////////////////////////
// The one and only CIsapifctrFilter object

CIsapifctrFilter theFilter;


///////////////////////////////////////////////////////////////////////
// CIsapifctrFilter implementation

CIsapifctrFilter::CIsapifctrFilter()
{
}

CIsapifctrFilter::~CIsapifctrFilter()
{
}

BOOL CIsapifctrFilter::GetFilterVersion(PHTTP_FILTER_VERSION pVer)
{
// Call default implementation for initialization
CHttpFilter::GetFilterVersion(pVer);

// Clear the flags set by base class
pVer->dwFlags &= ~SF_NOTIFY_ORDER_MASK;

// Set the flags we are interested in
pVer->dwFlags |= SF_NOTIFY_ORDER_LOW | SF_NOTIFY_NONSECURE_PORT |⇐
SF_NOTIFY_URL_MAP;

// Load description string
TCHAR sz[SF_MAX_FILTER_DESC_LEN+1];
ISAPIVERIFY(::LoadString(AfxGetResourceHandle(),
IDS_FILTER, sz, SF_MAX_FILTER_DESC_LEN));
tcscpy(pVer->lpszFilterDesc, sz);
return TRUE;
}
```

```
DWORD CIsapifctrFilter::OnUrlMap(CHttpFilterContext* pCtxt,
PHTTP_FILTER_URL_MAP pMapInfo)
{
  LPTSTR pstrPhysPath = pMapInfo->pszPhysicalPath;
  CString HoldPPath = CString( pstrPhysPath , strlen( pstrPhysPath ));
  CString pstrBuffer;
  CString pstrBuffer2;
  int aspexeccounter;
  int guestbookcounter;
  // Change this to a path appropriate to your system!!!
  char* pFileName = "e:\\aspht\\counter.log";
  CStdioFile  file;
  file.Open( pFileName, CFile::modeRead ¦ CFile::shareexclusive ¦⇐
CFile::typeText );
  try
  {
    try
    {
      file.ReadString(pstrBuffer);
      file.ReadString(pstrBuffer2);
    }
    catch(CFileException * e)
    {
      e->Delete();
    }
    file.Close();
  }
  catch(CMemoryException * e)
  {
    e->Delete();
  }
  catch(CFileException * e)
  {
    e->Delete();
  }
  aspexeccounter = atoi( pstrBuffer );
  guestbookcounter = atoi( pstrBuffer2 );
  if ( HoldPPath.Find("aspexec") !=-1) aspexeccounter++;
  if ( HoldPPath.Find("ASPEXEC") !=-1) aspexeccounter++;
  if ( HoldPPath.Find("guestbook") !=-1) guestbookcounter++;
  if ( HoldPPath.Find("GUESTBOOK") !=-1) guestbookcounter++;
  char buffer1[ 255 ];
  char buffer2[ 255 ];
  itoa( aspexeccounter , buffer1 , 10 );
  itoa( guestbookcounter , buffer2 , 10 );
  pstrBuffer = CString( buffer1 , strlen( buffer1 ));
  pstrBuffer2 = CString( buffer2 , strlen( buffer2 ));
  file.Open( pFileName, CFile::modeWrite ¦ CFile::typeText );
  try
  {
    try
    {
      file.WriteString(pstrBuffer);
      file.WriteString(pstrBuffer2);
    }
```

continued on next page

continued from previous page

```
    catch(CFileException * e)
    {
e->Delete();
    }
    file.Close();
  }
  catch(CMemoryException * e)
  {
    e->Delete();
  }
  catch(CFileException * e)
  {
    e->Delete();
  }
  return SF_STATUS_REQ_NEXT_NOTIFICATION;
}

// Do not edit the following lines, which are needed by ClassWizard.
#if 0
BEGIN_MESSAGE_MAP(CIsapifctrFilter, CHttpFilter)
//{{AFX_MSG_MAP(CIsapifctrFilter)
//}}AFX_MSG_MAP
END_MESSAGE_MAP()
#endif// 0
```

2. Activate `REGEDIT.EXE` or `REGEDT32.EXE` (for Windows 95 or Windows NT) and locate the `HKEY_LOCAL_MACHINE\System\CurrentControlSet\Services\W3SCVC\Parameters\Filter Dlls` key. Edit it and add a comma at the end, followed by the path for the new DLL. Close the registry editor and restart IIS/PWS to load the new filter.

3. Now load several pages in the `ASPEXEC` application, and do the same for the `GUESTBOOK` application. Then locate the log file you created and open it. As shown in Figure 9-7, the log file now contains two integers, reflecting the total hits on the two application directories. You have learned to create a Web site counter with an ISAPI filter DLL.

Figure 9-7 The ISAPI filter log file showing counters for the two applications

How It Works

If you have noticed that both of these filters use the **OnURLMap** event, you have picked up on the central issue of filter development: There are essentially three key notifications: **OnReadRawData**, **OnURLMap**, and **OnSendRawData**. The remaining notifications are available for specialized tasks, but these three are used by almost every filter. They are where the critical data for the HTTP request is made available by the IIS system. **OnReadRawData** is called before any processing is done; it is the place to intercept the headers prior to their being processed by the target file. **OnURLMap** is where the URL information is made available and where filters can do counters (such as this one), URL remapping, and other similar chores. **OnSendRawData** is the outgoing data stream, after processing the URL by its extension, CGI file, ASP handler, or HTML loader. This is the place where changes can be made in the HTML stream going back to the browser. All the How-To's in this chapter use one or more of these notifications.

This How-To focuses on the **OnURLMap** notification. Notice how the URL information is used.

```
LPTSTR pstrPhysPath = pMapInfo->pszPhysicalPath;
CString HoldPPath = CString( pstrPhysPath , strlen( pstrPhysPath ));
```

First, the string pointer from the **pMapInfo** structure is moved into a standard **LPTSTR** pointer. It is then loaded into a CString with the constructor call. This is important because the underlying data structure for **HTTP_FILTER_URL_MAP** uses a simple **CHAR *** pointer rather than a **LPTSTR**. Other data structures of the ISAPI filter system will supply their strings in different formats; by transforming all of them this way, you can handle specific idiosyncrasies of individual **HTTP_FILTER_XXX** data structures more easily.

Once the string has been placed into a CString, the next step is to determine what information it contains.

```
if ( HoldPPath.Find("guestbook") !=-1) guestbookcounter++;
if ( HoldPPath.Find("GUESTBOOK") !=-1) guestbookcounter++;
```

The CString **Find** method returns the starting position of a match on the supplied substring, or **-1** if no match is found. This allows checking the URL for a call into a specific directory (because either upper- or lowercase letters may be used, both are checked; a more robust implementation would uppercase or lowercase the whole string first before checking) and incrementing the counter appropriately. The counters are then rewritten to the log file (which is re-created each time for simplicity).

Notice the return code for the function.

```
return SF_STATUS_REQ_NEXT_NOTIFICATION;
```

This is important because it is required by IIS to make sure that the filter has neither encountered an error that should abort returning a response to the client browser nor completed processing on the request so that no other filter is allowed to process it. `SF_STATUS_REQ_NEXT_NOTIFICATION` is the default and indicates that no error happened and all additional filter processing can take place normally. Other return codes are `SF_STATUS_REQ_HANDLED_NOTIFICATION` (used to indicate that no further filters should process the notification for that request) and `SF_STATUS_REQ_ERROR` (which indicates an error has occurred and will send an error message to the client rather than the requested HTML). Some more sophisticated return codes are also possible in special situations; please see the online documentation on `SF_STATUS_REQ*` for more details.

Comments

Notice the `CFile::ShareExclusive` flag in the file creation logic. This is important due to the need to keep filters thread-safe. Rather than use a critical section, you simply lock the file when it is open to prevent another write while it is open. This will cause the second copy of the filter's attempt to fail and be safely handled by the exceptions. In a more robust application, though, critical sections should be used to make sure all the hits are recorded properly.

COMPLEXITY
INTERMEDIATE

9.3 How do I… Use custom URLs with an ISAPI filter?

My Web site uses artificial URLs to send information to our server; we've previously remapped those URLs to real files with CGI applications. Can ISAPI filters handle URL remapping for us?

Technique

The `OnURLMap` event handler for an ISAPI filter permits changing the physical path output to the system prior to actual page loading. This How-To will demonstrate a simple "tilde" filter that strips out UNIX ~ aliases from URLs. Although these directions create the project from scratch, the CD contains a completed file under `CH09\HT03\`.

NOTE

A tip of my virtual hat to Steven Genusa (`steveg@onramp.com`), the leading ASP/ISAPI developer, who provided the inspiration for this particular How-To. Thanks, Steve, and keep up the good work!

Steps

1. Activate Visual C++ 5.0. Create a new ISAPI filter named ISAPIFTILDE with the wizard. Set its notifications to Nonsecured port sessions and URL mapping requests only. Open its ISAPIFTILDE.CPP file and enter the boldfaced code in Listing 9-4 for the OnURLMap event handler. Save the project and build the DLL.

Listing 9-4 ISAPIFTILDE.CPP OnURLMap source code

```
DWORD CIsapiftildeFilter::OnUrlMap(CHttpFilterContext* pCtxt,
PHTTP_FILTER_URL_MAP pMapInfo)
{
  CString strOutputPath;
  int nPosition = 0;
  strOutputPath = pMapInfo->pszPhysicalPath;
  nPosition = strOutputPath.Find("\\~");
  if (nPosition != -1)
  {
    CString strHoldPath = strOutputPath.Left(nPosition + 1);
    strHoldPath += strOutputPath.Mid(nPosition + 2);
    strOutputPath = strHoldPath;
    strcpy (pMapInfo->pszPhysicalPath, (LPCTSTR)strOutputPath);
  }
  return SF_STATUS_REQ_NEXT_NOTIFICATION;
}
```

2. Activate REGEDIT.EXE or REGEDT32.EXE (for Windows 95 or Windows NT) and locate the HKEY_LOCAL_MACHINE\System\CurrentControlSet\Services\W3SCVC\Parameters\Filter Dlls key. Edit it and add a comma at the end, followed by the path for the new DLL. Close the registry editor and restart IIS/PWS to load the new filter.

3. Bring up Internet Explorer and enter the following address: HTTP://DEFAULT/ASPEXEC/~ASPHT0801.ASP. As shown in Figure 9-8, the ISAPIFTILDE filter will catch the ~ reference and remove it, allowing the correct URL to be loaded. You have learned to use ISAPI filter DLLs to modify URL physical paths.

How It Works

This How-To relies on the fact that when the OnURLMap event is fired, the actual physical path has not yet been loaded into the server for processing. First, the actual URL has to be obtained.

```
strOutputPath = pMapInfo->pszPhysicalPath;
nPosition = strOutputPath.Find("\\~");
```

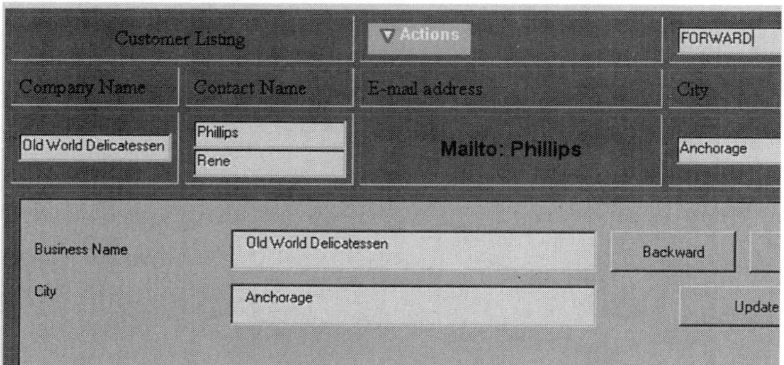

Figure 9-8 ASPHT0801 in IE after removal of the ~ from the physical path by the ISAPIFTILDE filter

This is done by placing the `pszPhysicalPath` member variable of the `HTTP_FILTER_URL_MAP` structure into a CString. Then the `Find` method works again, this time to determine whether a `\~` combination is found in the URL.

If it is, then the output path has to be rebuilt.

```
if (nPosition != -1)
{
  CString strHoldPath = strOutputPath.Left(nPosition + 1);
  strHoldPath += strOutputPath.Mid(nPosition + 2);
  strOutputPath = strHoldPath;
```

First, the left-hand portion up to the position of the `\~` is peeled off and stored (including the `\` character). Then, the right portion after the `\~` is tacked on to it, thereby neatly cutting out the ~ but leaving everything else in.

Finally, the modified path has to be returned to the IIS/PWS system.

```
  strcpy (pMapInfo->pszPhysicalPath, (LPCTSTR)strOutputPath);
}
return SF_STATUS_REQ_NEXT_NOTIFICATION;
```

This is done by recasting the CString back into its pointer and copying it into the buffer held in the `HTTP_FILTER_URL_MAP` structure. The nonerror status code allows the URL request to continue processing normally.

Comments

The crucial lesson from this How-To is that you can change the output URL from the `OnURLMap` event to *anything* you like. This will be demonstrated even more noticeably in the next How-To.

9.4 How do I... Control browser access to a Web site with an ISAPI filter?

Problem

We need to be able to detect the browser used for all requests to our server automatically so we can redirect it appropriately. Extensions handle this just fine, but only when they are the target of the URL; can filters do this sort of redirection?

Technique

Yes, via trapping raw input to search for the `HTTP_USER_AGENT` server variable. This How-To will demonstrate recasting all URLs viewed by IE into one directory, and all URLs viewed from other browsers into another. Although these directions create the project from scratch, the CD contains a completed file under `CH09\HT04\`.

Steps

1. Activate Visual C++ 5.0. Create a new ISAPI filter named `ISAPIFBROWSCTL` with the wizard. Set its notifications to Nonsecured port sessions and URL mapping requests only. Open its `ISAPIFBROWSCTL.CPP` file and enter the boldfaced code in Listing 9-5 for the `OnURLMap` event handler. Save the project and build the DLL.

Listing 9-5 `ISAPIFBROWSCTL.CPP OnURLMap` **source code**

```
DWORD CIsapifbrowsctlFilter::OnUrlMap(CHttpFilterContext* pCtxt,
PHTTP_FILTER_URL_MAP pMapInfo)
{
  CHAR achUserAgent[1026];
  DWORD cbUserAgent = 1026;
  CString strPhysicalPath, strOriginalPath, HoldUA;
  int nPos = 0;

  pCtxt->GetServerVariable("HTTP_USER_AGENT", achUserAgent, &cbUserAgent);
  HoldUA = CString( achUserAgent , strlen( achUserAgent ));
  if ( HoldUA.Find("MSIE" ) != -1 )
  {
    strOriginalPath = pMapInfo->pszPhysicalPath;
    strPhysicalPath = strOriginalPath;
    nPos = strPhysicalPath.Find("\\aspexec");
```

continued on next page

continued from previous page

```
    if (nPos != -1)
    {
      CString strPath = strPhysicalPath.Left(nPos + 1);
      strPath += "ieaspexec\\";
      strPath += strPhysicalPath.Mid(nPos + 9);
      strPhysicalPath = strPath;
      strcpy (pMapInfo->pszPhysicalPath, (LPCTSTR)strPhysicalPath);
    }
  }
  else
  {
    strOriginalPath = pMapInfo->pszPhysicalPath;
    strPhysicalPath = strOriginalPath;
    nPos = strPhysicalPath.Find("\\aspexec");
    if (nPos != -1)
    {
      CString strPath = strPhysicalPath.Left(nPos + 1);
      strPath += "ncaspexec\\";
      strPath += strPhysicalPath.Mid(nPos + 9);
      strPhysicalPath = strPath;
      strcpy (pMapInfo->pszPhysicalPath, (LPCTSTR)strPhysicalPath);
    }

  }
  return SF_STATUS_REQ_NEXT_NOTIFICATION;
}
```

2. Activate `REGEDIT.EXE` or `REGEDT32.EXE` (for Windows 95 or Windows NT) and locate the `HKEY_LOCAL_MACHINE\System\CurrentControlSet\Services\W3SCVC\Parameters\Filter Dlls` key. Edit it and add a comma at the end, followed by the path for the new DLL. Close the registry editor and restart IIS/PWS to load the new filter.

3. Create two new directories on your machine. Use the IIS/PWS administration facilities to make them executable for ASP scripts and extensions and name them `IEASPEXEC` and `NCASPEXEC`. Copy `ASPHT0801.ASP` into the `IEASPEXEC` directory and rename it `ASPHT0904.ASP`. Copy `ASPHT0802.ASP` into the `NCASPEXEC` directory and rename it `ASPHT0904.ASP` as well.

4. Bring up Internet Explorer and enter the following address: `HTTP://DEFAULT\ASPEXEC\ASPHT0904.ASP`. As shown in Figure 9-9, the `ISAPIFBROWSCTL` filter will detect that IE is being used along with `ASPEXEC` and redirect to the `IEASPEXEC` directory. Now try the URL with a non-IE browser such as Netscape Communicator. As shown in Figure 9-10, you are redirected to the file in the `NCASPEXEC` directory. You have learned to use ISAPI filter DLLs to modify URL physical paths based on browser type.

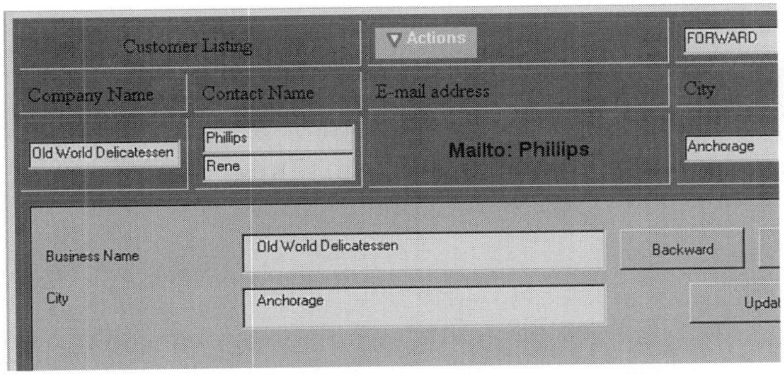

Figure 9-9 ASPHT0904 in IE after redirection to IEASPEXEC by the ISAPIFBROWSCTL filter

HTTP_CONNECTION	Keep-Alive
HTTP_HOST	default
HTTP_USER_AGENT	Mozilla/2.0 (compatible; MSIE 3.02; Update a; Windows 95)
HTTP_UA_PIXELS	1024x768
HTTP_UA_COLOR	color32
HTTP_UA_OS	Windows 95
HTTP_UA_CPU	x86

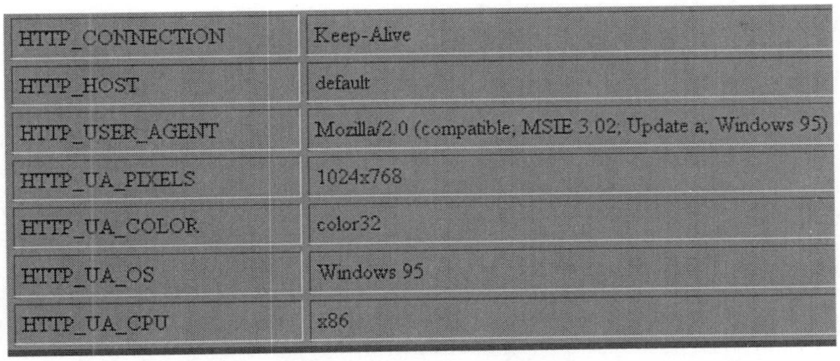

Figure 9-10 ASPHT0904 in Netscape Communicator after redirection to NCASPEXEC by the ISAPIFBROWSCTL filter

How It Works

The key to this How-To lies in the `CHttpFilterContext` object.

```
pCtxt->GetServerVariable("HTTP_USER_AGENT", achUserAgent, &cbUserAgent);
HoldUA = CString( achUserAgent , strlen( achUserAgent ));
if ( HoldUA.Find("MSIE" ) != -1 )
```

It supports a `GetServerVariable` method like the `CHttpExtensionContext` object did in Chapter 8, "ISAPI Extensions: Using ActiveX DLLs to Replace CGI." Here it is used to obtain the string holding the `USER_AGENT` server variable. If it contains `MSIE`, then the following occurs:

```
if ( HoldUA.Find("MSIE" ) != -1 )
{
  strOriginalPath = pMapInfo->pszPhysicalPath;
  strPhysicalPath = strOriginalPath;
  nPos = strPhysicalPath.Find("\\aspexec");
```

continued on next page

continued from previous page

```
    if (nPos != -1)
    {
      CString strPath = strPhysicalPath.Left(nPos + 1);
      strPath += "ieaspexec\\";
      strPath += strPhysicalPath.Mid(nPos + 9);
      strPhysicalPath = strPath;
      strcpy (pMapInfo->pszPhysicalPath, (LPCTSTR)strPhysicalPath);
    }
  }
```

This section illustrates an important concept, namely making sure a specific filter acts only when appropriate. Remember that filters see every HTTP request, regardless of what it may be. The preceding code checks to see whether the URL contains `\aspexec`; if it does, then the browser-based remapping takes place. Otherwise, nothing gets changed, regardless of what browser type is being used!

Comments

As noted prior to How-To 9.1, you should consider removing this filter and some of the others to reduce the load on your server and to follow the remaining How-To's more easily; if you haven't removed filters yet, this would be a good time.

COMPLEXITY
INTERMEDIATE

9.5 How do I... Add custom HTML to all pages requested from a Web site with an ISAPI filter?

Problem

We need to append some HTML to every page returned from our site for advertising reasons. At present, a very complex and fragile CGI script does this; can ISAPI filters take over this chore?

Technique

The `OnSendRawData` event notification in the ISAPI filter system is tailor-made for this task! This How-To will demonstrate using it to add a simple HTML tag line to all page requests. Although these directions create the project from scratch, the CD contains a completed file under `CH09\HT05\`.

Steps

1. Activate Visual C++ 5.0. Create a new ISAPI filter named **ISAPIFADDSIG** with the wizard. Set its notifications to Nonsecured port sessions and `SendRawData` requests only. Open its **ISAPIFADDSIG.CPP** file and enter the boldfaced code in Listing 9-6 for the **OnSendRawData** event handler. Save the project and build the DLL.

Listing 9-6 ISAPIFADDSIG.CPP OnSendRawData source code

```
DWORD CIsapifaddsigFilter::OnSendRawData(CHttpFilterContext* pCtxt,
PHTTP_FILTER_RAW_DATA pRawData)
{
  LPTSTR pstrIn;
  DWORD cbBuffer;
  DWORD cbTemp;
  pstrIn = (LPTSTR) pRawData->pvInData;
  CString strHoldIn = CString( pstrIn , strlen( pstrIn ));
  cbBuffer = 0;
  cbTemp = 0;
  if (pCtxt->m_pFC->pFilterContext == NULL)
  {
    while (cbBuffer < pRawData->cbInData)
    {
      if (pstrIn[cbBuffer] == '\n' &&
      pstrIn[cbBuffer+2] == '\n')
      {
        cbBuffer += 3;
        break;
      }
      cbBuffer++;
    }
    while (cbTemp < cbBuffer)
    {
      if (pstrIn[cbTemp] == '/' && pstrIn[cbTemp+1] == 'h' &&
      pstrIn[cbTemp+2] == 't' && pstrIn[cbTemp+3] == 'm')
      {
        pCtxt->m_pFC->pFilterContext = (VOID*) 2;
        break;
      }
      cbTemp++;
    }
    if (cbTemp == cbBuffer)
     pCtxt->m_pFC->pFilterContext = (VOID *) 1;
  }
  if (pCtxt->m_pFC->pFilterContext == (VOID *) 2)
  {
    DWORD nPos;
    nPos = strHoldIn.Find( "</body>" );
    if ( nPos = -1 ) nPos = strHoldIn.Find( "</BODY>" );
```

continued on next page

continued from previous page

```
    if ( nPos != -1 )
    {
      strOut += "<HR><H1>This Page Brought To You by CIUPKC WebSite!</H1><HR>";
      strOut += strHoldIn.Mid(nPos);
      strcpy ( (LPTSTR)pRawData->pvInData, (LPCTSTR)strOut);
      pRawData->cbInData = (DWORD) strlen( (LPTSTR) pRawData->pvInData );

    }
  }

  return SF_STATUS_REQ_NEXT_NOTIFICATION;
}
```

2. Activate REGEDIT.EXE or REGEDT32.EXE (for Windows 95 or Windows NT) and locate the HKEY_LOCAL_MACHINE\System\CurrentControlSet\Services\W3SCVC\Parameters\Filter Dlls key. Edit it and add a comma at the end, followed by the path for the new DLL. Close the registry editor and restart IIS/PWS to load the new filter.

3. Bring up Internet Explorer and enter the following address: HTTP://DEFAULT\ASPEXEC\ASPHT0801.ASP. As shown in Figure 9-11, the ISAPIFADDSIG filter will add the signature line to the HTML page generated by the ASP code. Try several similar URLs and you'll see the same result. You have learned to use ISAPI filter DLLs to add customized HTML to all pages requested from your IIS/PWS server.

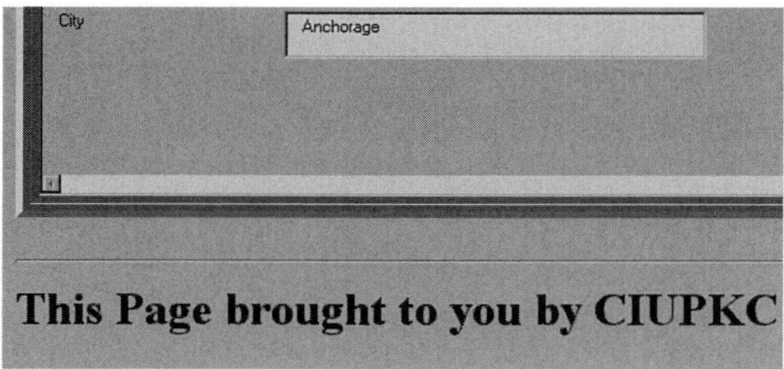

Figure 9-11 ASPHT0801 in IE showing the custom HTML code added by the ISAPIFADDSIG filter

How It Works

This How-To moves from the ubiquitous `OnURLMap` event notification to the more powerful `OnSendRawData`. URL mapping can determine only what file is loaded by the server in response to the client request. When the `OnSendRawData` event is called, the *complete HTML stream* that is going back to the browser is contained in the parameters of the `HTTP_FILTER_RAW_DATA` structure.

```
pstrIn = (LPTSTR) pRawData->pvInData;
CString strHoldIn = CString( pstrIn , strlen( pstrIn ));
```

The `pvInData` member variable of the `pRawData` structure contains the entire HTML to be returned to the client in one long string. The preceding code puts it in a CString for later use.

One very important consideration must be dealt with in this type of filter: Not all requests are for HTML! It would be catastrophic to add HTML text to the end of, say, a JPEG or GIF file or a downloaded ZIP file. To get around this problem, the following code searches for the end of the HTML header:

```
while (cbBuffer < pRawData->cbInData)
{
  if (pstrIn[cbBuffer] == '\n' &&
  pstrIn[cbBuffer+2] == '\n')
  {
    cbBuffer += 3;
    break;
  }
  cbBuffer++;
}
```

This code inches along the pointer looking for the end of the headers. The key to detecting the end of the header is the double `\n`; this separates the headers from the content type, which is what we are really interested in.

```
while (cbTemp < cbBuffer)
{
  if (pstrIn[cbTemp] == '/' && pstrIn[cbTemp+1] == 'h' &&
  pstrIn[cbTemp+2] == 't' && pstrIn[cbTemp+3] == 'm')
  {
    pCtxt->m_pFC->pFilterContext = (VOID*) 2;
    break;
  }
  cbTemp++;
}
if (cbTemp == cbBuffer)
 pCtxt->m_pFC->pFilterContext = (VOID*) 1;
}
```

The preceding code meets one of two criteria: If it finds /htm before it runs out of data, then it assumes the file is HTML text and sets the pFilterContext tag variable to 2. Otherwise, it sets the variable to 1. The reason for this involution is crucial: This event can be called more than once. It can be called once when the header is written and once or more when the main data stream is written. The content type will be in the first call, but the data will be in the second. The pFilterContext tag variable is available for just such flag passing as this, although, of course, another member variable can also be used.

If a second call is made with the actual data or after the first check, this code is used:

```
if (pCtxt->m_pFC->pFilterContext == (VOID *) 2)
{
  DWORD nPos;
```

Now a check is made to see whether, indeed, an HTML file is being sent. If so, the tag will be 2; otherwise, it will be 1. The following code then attempts to find the end of the HTML stream:

```
nPos = strHoldIn.Find( "</body>" );
if ( nPos = -1 ) nPos = strHoldIn.Find( "</BODY>" );
if ( nPos != -1 )
{
  CString strOut = strHoldIn.Left(nPos - 1);
  strOut += "<HR><H1>This Page Brought To You by CIUPKC WebSite!</H1><HR>";
  strOut += strHoldIn.Mid(nPos);
  strcpy ( (LPTSTR)pRawData->pvInData, (LPCTSTR)strOut);
  pRawData->cbInData = (DWORD) strlen( (LPTSTR) pRawData->pvInData );

}
```

On any call before the end of the data stream is sent, of course, both tests will fail. On the last time, though, the </body> or </BODY> tags should be present. If so, the standard string stitching code you're heartily sick of by now is employed to shove in the little blurb about the company.

Comments

Notice that after the chimera HTML is inserted, the CString has to be recast into the char pointer of the pRawData structure. Also, its length must be put in the cbInData doubleword member variable of the pRawData structure because not all clients use null-terminated strings and so have to have a numerical string length to work with. Forgetting this step will guarantee you a night in front of the debugger!

9.6 How do I... Change internal HTML from pages requested from a Web site with an ISAPI filter?

Problem

Certain clients want to do specialized processing on the HTML output by their Web pages. We've used CGI to do this, but it keeps breaking down on us. Can ISAPI *modify* HTML output on its way to the client (as opposed to just adding things to it)?

Technique

A string is a string, as far as the ISAPI filter system is concerned. This How-To will modify all the occurrences of `ASP` in a file into `Active Server Pages` as a demonstration of this concept. Although these directions create the project from scratch, the CD contains a completed file under `CH09\HT06\`.

Steps

1. Activate Visual C++ 5.0. Create a new ISAPI filter named `ISAPIFEXPASP` with the wizard. Set its notifications to Nonsecured port sessions and Send raw data requests only. Open its `ISAPIFEXPASP.CPP` file and enter the boldfaced code in Listing 9-7 for the `OnSendRawData` event handler. Save the project and build the DLL.

Listing 9-7 `ISAPIEXPASP.CPP` `OnSendRawData` source code

```
DWORD CIsapifexpaspFilter::OnSendRawData(CHttpFilterContext* pCtxt,
PHTTP_FILTER_RAW_DATA pRawData)
{
  LPTSTR pstrIn;
  DWORD cbBuffer;
  DWORD cbTemp;

  pstrIn = (LPTSTR) pRawData->pvInData;
  CString strHoldIn = CString( pstrIn , strlen( pstrIn ));
  cbBuffer = 0;
  cbTemp = 0;
```

continued on next page

continued from previous page

```
  if (pCtxt->m_pFC->pFilterContext == NULL )
  {
    while (cbBuffer < pRawData->cbInData)
    {
      if (pstrIn[cbBuffer] == '\n' &&
      pstrIn[cbBuffer+2] == '\n')
      {
        cbBuffer += 3;
        break;
      }
      cbBuffer++;
    }

    while (cbTemp < cbBuffer)
    {
      if (pstrIn[cbTemp] == '/' && pstrIn[cbTemp+1] == 'h' &&
      pstrIn[cbTemp+2] == 't' && pstrIn[cbTemp+3] == 'm')
      {
        pCtxt->m_pFC->pFilterContext = (VOID*) 2;
        break;
      }

      cbTemp++;
    }

    if (cbTemp == cbBuffer)
     pCtxt->m_pFC->pFilterContext = (VOID *) 1;
  }
  if (pCtxt->m_pFC->pFilterContext == (VOID *) 2)
  {
    DWORD nPos;
    int flag = 0;
    CString strWorker = strHoldIn;
    CString strOut;
    CString strXfer;
    do
    {
      nPos = strWorker.Find( "ASP " );
      if ( nPos != -1 )
      {
        strOut += strWorker.Left(nPos - 1);
        strOut += "Active Server Pages ";
        strXfer = strWorker.Mid(nPos + 5);
        strWorker = strXfer;
      }
      else
      {
        flag = 1;
        strcpy ( (LPTSTR)pRawData->pvInData, (LPCTSTR)strOut);
        pRawData->cbInData = (DWORD) strlen( (LPTSTR) pRawData->pvInData );
      }
    } while (flag != 1 );
  }

  return SF_STATUS_REQ_NEXT_NOTIFICATION;
}
```

2. Activate `REGEDIT.EXE` or `REGEDT32.EXE` (for Windows 95 or Windows NT) and locate the `HKEY_LOCAL_MACHINE\System\CurrentControlSet\Services\W3SCVC\Parameters\Filter Dlls` key. Edit it and add a comma at the end, followed by the path for the new DLL. Close the registry editor and restart IIS/PWS to load the new filter.

3. Activate ActiveX Control Pad. Create a new HTML file with the source code in Listing 9-8. Save the file as `ASPHT0906.HTM`. Move it into the `ASPEXEC` directory.

Listing 9-8 ASPHT0906.HTM source code

```
<HTML>
<HEAD>
<TITLE>Active Server Pages How To Chapter Nine How To Six</TITLE>
</HEAD>
<BODY>
This is a test of the ASP filtering system.<P>
Everywhere you see "ASP" you should see ASP .<P>
But where you see ASPwithout a trailing space, you don't see ASP .<P>
</BODY>
</HTML>
```

4. Bring up Internet Explorer and enter the following address: `HTTP://DEFAULT\ASPEXEC\ASPHT0906.HTM`. As shown in Figure 9-12, the `ISAPIFEXPASP` filter will expand all the `ASP` references in the returned text to `Active Server Pages`. You have learned to use ISAPI filter DLLs to customize the HTML output from IIS/PWS pages.

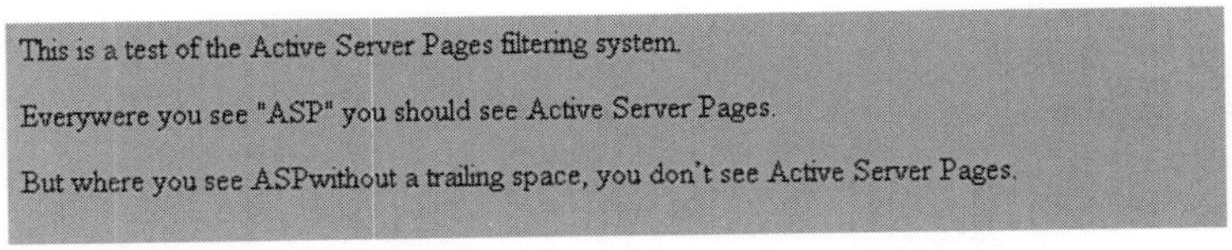

This is a test of the Active Server Pages filtering system.

Everywere you see "ASP" you should see Active Server Pages.

But where you see ASPwithout a trailing space, you don't see Active Server Pages.

Figure 9-12 ASPHT0906 in IE showing the ASP strings expanded to Active Server Pages

How It Works

This How-To is identical to How-To 9.5 until you get to this code:

```
DWORD nPos;
int flag = 0;
CString strWorker = strHoldIn;
CString strOut;
CString strXfer;
do
{
  nPos = strWorker.Find( "ASP " );
  if ( nPos != -1 )
  {
```

The critical difference in this How-To is that the outgoing HTML stream, contained in `strHoldIn`, must be broken up and modified without losing its arbitrarily complex HTML formatting. To do this, two additional strings are created, `strOut` and `strXfer`. A flag is set to `0`, and a loop is started.

The loop checks the `strWorker` string for the next occurrence of `ASP` , with the trailing space to allow for including ASP as part of larger words or by itself if it ends with a punctuation mark. Once an occurrence has been found, this code takes over:

```
if ( nPos != -1 )
{
  strOut += strWorker.Left(nPos - 1);
  strOut += "Active Server Pages ";
  strXfer = strWorker.Mid(nPos + 5);
  strWorker = strXfer;
}
```

The current worker string has its leftmost portion added to the output string, and `Active Server Pages` is then added to the output string. The remaining worker string has four characters chopped off it and is placed into the `Xfer` string. The `Xfer` string then is assigned to the `worker` string, and the loop continues.

Eventually the loop will run out of `ASP` tokens. Then this code takes over:

```
else
{
  flag = 1;
  strcpy ( (LPTSTR)pRawData->pvInData, (LPCTSTR)strOut);
  pRawData->cbInData = (DWORD) strlen( (LPTSTR) pRawData->pvInData );
 }
} while (flag != 1 );
```

Here, the flag is set to `1` and the output string is copied to the `pRawData`'s string pointer, followed by setting its length variable as well. Because the flag is now `1`, the loop ends and the method terminates.

Comments

The take-home message of this How-To is that *all* the characters in the HTML output stream are up for grabs in the `OnSendRawData` event handler. You can change it as much as you like, as long as the HTML formatting is kept in place and you make sure to do the string conversion and length calculation when you're done.

IFIL-IEXT

9.7 How do I... Interact with an ISAPI extension DLL in an ISAPI filter?

Problem

We have peculiar situations that arise at times where one CGI script needs to modify the input to another one. This doesn't seem possible with the ISAPI extensions system; do ISAPI filters have the ability to interact with ISAPI extensions?

Technique

The `OnURLMap` event comes to the rescue here. Remember that to the IIS/PWS system at the filter level, an ISAPI extension is just part of a URL. This How-To will change the mapping from one ISAPI extension to another to simulate altering extension parameters during HTTP processing. These steps create the application from scratch, but for your convenience the complete project is on the CD under `CH09\HT07\`.

Steps

1. Activate Visual C++ 5.0. Create a new ISAPI filter named `ISAPIFMODEX` with the wizard. Set its notifications to Nonsecured port sessions and URL mapping requests only. Open its `ISAPIFMODEX.CPP` file and enter the boldfaced code in Listing 9-9 for the `OnURLMap` event handler. Save the project and build the DLL.

Listing 9-9 ISAPIFMODEX.CPP OnURLMap source code

```
DWORD CIsapifmodexFilter::OnUrlMap(CHttpFilterContext* pCtxt,
PHTTP_FILTER_URL_MAP pMapInfo)
{
    LPTSTR pstrIn;
    pstrIn = (LPTSTR) pMapInfo->pszPhysicalPath;
    CString strHoldIn = CString( pstrIn , strlen( pstrIn ));
    CString strOut;
    DWORD nPos;
    nPos = strHoldIn.Find("\\isapixbin");
    if ( nPos != -1 )
    {
        strOut = strHoldIn.Left(nPos - 1);
        strOut += "\\isapixbin2";
        strOut = strHoldIn.Mid(nPos + 10);
        strcpy ( (LPTSTR)pMapInfo->pszPhysicalPath, (LPCTSTR)strOut);
        pMapInfo->cbPathBuff = (DWORD) strlen( (LPTSTR) pMapInfo->pszPhysicalPath
);
    }
    return SF_STATUS_REQ_NEXT_NOTIFICATION;
}
```

2. Activate REGEDIT.EXE or REGEDT32.EXE (for Windows 95 or Windows NT) and locate the HKEY_LOCAL_MACHINE\System\CurrentControlSet\Services\W3SCVC\Parameters\Filter Dlls key. Edit it and add a comma at the end, followed by the path for the new DLL. Close the registry editor and restart IIS/PWS to load the new filter.

3. Locate ISAPIXBIN.DLL, created in How-To 8.6, and copy it to ISAPIXBIN2.DLL; then remove ISAPIXBIN.DLL from the ASPEXEC directory to simulate the need for last-minute extension changes.

4. Bring up Internet Explorer and enter the following address: HTTP://DEFAULT\ASPEXEC\ASPHT0806.HTM. As shown in Figure 9-13, the ISAPIFMODEX filter will intercept the extension URL and change it to the new name, bringing up the picture normally even though the DLL named in the HTML file is no longer available. You have learned to use ISAPI filter DLLs to interact at the system level with ISAPI extension DLLs.

How It Works

As mentioned in the initial paragraph in this section, the key to interacting with ISAPI extensions at the filter level lies in the fact that they are always part of a URL.

```
nPos = strHoldIn.Find("\\isapixbin");
if ( nPos != -1 )
{
    strOut = strHoldIn.Left(nPos - 1);
    strOut += "\\isapixbin2";
```

```
    strOut = strHoldIn.Mid(nPos + 10);
    strcpy ( (LPTSTR)pMapInfo->pszPhysicalPath, (LPCTSTR)strOut);
    pMapInfo->cbPathBuff = (DWORD) strlen( (LPTSTR) pMapInfo->pszPhysicalPath);
}
```

Figure 9-13 ASPHT0806.HTM in IE showing its picture even though the DLL is no longer there

The name of the extension in question is part of the URL input string. If it is found, any modifications to the DLL name or its parameter string are allowed, as long as the final path is a valid physical path and the length variable is set correctly. That's all there is to it!

Comments

Although this example may seem simple with all the power of ISAPI behind it, doing this in CGI is hard. (Trust me, I've had to...)

IFIL-AXC

COMPLEXITY
INTERMEDIATE

9.8 How do I... Link an ActiveX control to an ISAPI filter?

Problem

We need to put our company's logo on each HTML page we display. The problem is, our logo is actually displayed by an ActiveX control. How do we get the ISAPI filter we wrote to add the ActiveX control to every page?

Technique

ActiveX controls live entirely on the client machine via HTML `<OBJECT>` tags. To link them with an ISAPI filter requires output of these tags mixed with data from the filter itself. This How-To illustrates using an ISAPI filter DLL to output a simple Label ActiveX control with the figures for site hits from a previous filter. These steps create the application from scratch, but for your convenience the complete project is on the CD under `CH09\HT08\`.

Steps

1. Activate Visual C++ 5.0. Create a new ISAPI filter named `ISAPIFAXSIG` with the wizard. Set its notifications to Nonsecured port sessions and `OnSendRawData` requests only. Open its `ISAPIFAXSIG.CPP` file and enter the boldfaced code in Listing 9-10 for the `OnSendRawData` event handler. Save the project and build the DLL. (Be sure to modify the path to the log file to the same one you used in How-To 9.2.)

Listing 9-10 ISAPIfAXSIG.CPP OnSendRawData source code

```
DWORD CIsapifaxsigFilter::OnSendRawData(CHttpFilterContext* pCtxt,
PHTTP_FILTER_RAW_DATA pRawData)
{
    CString pstrBuffer;
    CString pstrBuffer2;
    char* pFileName = "e:\\aspht\\counter.log";
    CStdioFile   file;
    file.Open( pFileName, CFile::modeRead ¦ CFile::typeText );
    try
    {
        try
        {
            file.ReadString(pstrBuffer);
            file.ReadString(pstrBuffer2);
        }
        catch(CFileException * e)
        {
            e->Delete();
        }
        file.Close();
    }
    catch(CMemoryException * e)
    {
        e->Delete();
    }
    catch(CFileException * e)
    {
        e->Delete();
    }
    CString strCaption;
    strCaption = "AspExec hits: ";
    strCaption += pstrBuffer;
    strCaption += " -- Guestbook hits: ";
```

```
strCaption += pstrBuffer2;
LPTSTRpstrIn;
DWORD cbBuffer;
DWORD cbTemp;
pstrIn = (LPTSTR) pRawData->pvInData;
CString strHoldIn = CString( pstrIn , strlen( pstrIn ));
cbBuffer = 0;
cbTemp = 0;
if (pCtxt->m_pFC->pFilterContext == NULL)
{
    while (cbBuffer < pRawData->cbInData)
    {
        if (pstrIn[cbBuffer] == '\n' &&
        pstrIn[cbBuffer+2] == '\n')
        {
            cbBuffer += 3;
            break;
        }
        cbBuffer++;
    }
    while (cbTemp < cbBuffer)
    {
        if (pstrIn[cbTemp] == '/' && pstrIn[cbTemp+1] == 'h' &&
        pstrIn[cbTemp+2] == 't' && pstrIn[cbTemp+3] == 'm')
        {
            pCtxt->m_pFC->pFilterContext = (VOID*) 2;
            break;
        }
        cbTemp++;
    }

    if (cbTemp == cbBuffer)
     pCtxt->m_pFC->pFilterContext = (VOID *) 1;
}
if (pCtxt->m_pFC->pFilterContext == (VOID *) 2)
{
    DWORD nPos;
    nPos = strHoldIn.Find( "</body>" );
    if ( nPos = -1 ) nPos = strHoldIn.Find( "</BODY>" );
    if ( nPos != -1 )
    {
        CString strOut = strHoldIn.Left(nPos - 1);
        strOut += "<HR><H1>This Page Brought To You by CIUPKC⇐
        WebSite!</H1><HR>";
        strOut += "<OBJECT ID=""IeLabel1"" WIDTH=611 HEIGHT=60\n";
        strOut += "CLASSID=""CLSID:99B42120-6EC7-11CF-A6C7-00AA00A47DD2"">\n";
        strOut += "<PARAM NAME=""_ExtentX"" VALUE=""16140"">\n";
        strOut += "<PARAM NAME=""_ExtentY"" VALUE=""1588"">\n";
        strOut += "<PARAM NAME=""Caption"" VALUE=""\n";
        strOut += strCaption;
        strOut += """>\n";
        strOut += "<PARAM NAME=""Angle"" VALUE=""0"">\n";
        strOut += "<PARAM NAME=""Alignment"" VALUE=""4"">\n";
        strOut += "<PARAM NAME=""Mode"" VALUE=""1"">\n";
        strOut += "<PARAM NAME=""FillStyle"" VALUE=""1"">\n";
        strOut += "<PARAM NAME=""ForeColor"" VALUE=""#70DA01"">\n";
```

continued on next page

continued from previous page

```
            strOut += "<PARAM NAME=""BackColor"" VALUE=""#000000"">\n";
            strOut += "<PARAM NAME=""FontName"" VALUE=""Arial""\n>";
            strOut += "<PARAM NAME=""FontSize"" VALUE=""20"">\n";
            strOut += "<PARAM NAME=""FontItalic"" VALUE=""0""\n>";
            strOut += "<PARAM NAME=""FontBold"" VALUE=""1"">\n";
            strOut += "<PARAM NAME=""FontUnderline"" VALUE=""0"">\n";
            strOut += "<PARAM NAME=""FontStrikeout"" VALUE=""0"">\n";
            strOut += "<PARAM NAME=""TopPoints"" VALUE=""0"">\n";
            strOut += "<PARAM NAME=""BotPoints"" VALUE=""0"">\n";
            strOut += strHoldIn.Mid(nPos);
            strcpy ( (LPTSTR)pRawData->pvInData, (LPCTSTR)strOut);
            pRawData->cbInData = (DWORD) strlen( (LPTSTR) pRawData->pvInData );

        }
    }

    return SF_STATUS_REQ_NEXT_NOTIFICATION;

}
```

2. Activate `REGEDIT.EXE` or `REGEDT32.EXE` (for Windows 95 or Windows NT) and locate the `HKEY_LOCAL_MACHINE\System\CurrentControlSet\Services\W3SCVC\Parameters\Filter Dlls` key. Edit it and add a comma at the end, followed by the path for the new DLL. Close the registry editor and restart IIS/PWS to load the new filter.

3. Make sure that the `Counter` filter from How-To 9.2 is installed while you bring up some pages in the `ASPEXEC` and `GUESTBOOK` directories, to build up the counter's log file.

4. Bring up Internet Explorer and enter the following address: `HTTP://DEFAULT\ASPEXEC\ASPHT801.ASP`. As shown in Figure 9-14, the `ISAPIFAXSIG` filter will add the ActiveX Label control to the page with the count for each application. You have learned to use ISAPI filter DLLs to add ActiveX controls to all the pages from your IIS/PWS server.

How It Works

The filter first has to obtain the counters from the log file.

```
CString pstrBuffer;
CString pstrBuffer2;
char* pFileName = "e:\\aspht\\counter.log";
CStdioFile   file;
file.Open( pFileName, CFile::modeRead | CFile::typeText );
try
{
    try
    {
        file.ReadString(pstrBuffer);
        file.ReadString(pstrBuffer2);
    }
```

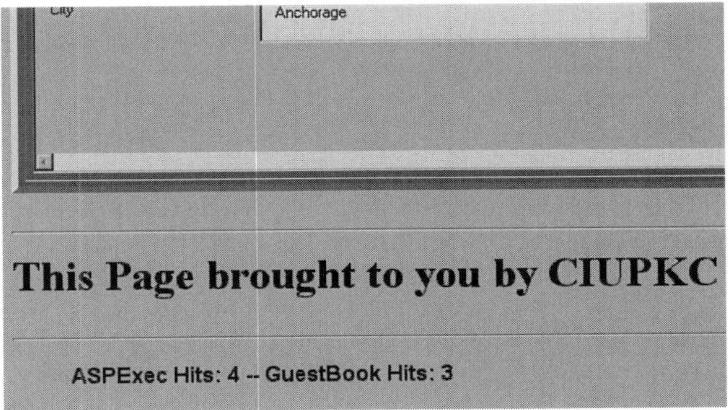

Figure 9-14 ASPHT0801.ASP in IE showing the ActiveX control added by the ISAPIFAXSIG filter

These counters are read in using normal file techniques. Once in memory, though, they are used a bit differently than before.

```
CString strCaption;
strCaption = "AspExec hits: ";
strCaption += pstrBuffer;
strCaption += " -- Guestbook hits: ";
strCaption += pstrBuffer2;
```

Here, they are kept as strings, added to some explanatory text, and kept in another string buffer. Once the boilerplate code finds the end of the HTML stream, this text gets sent out into the stream in a special way, mixing C++ CStrings and literal text.

```
CString strOut = strHoldIn.Left(nPos - 1);
strOut += "<HR><H1>This Page Brought To You by CIUPKC WebSite!</H1><HR>";
strOut += "<OBJECT ID=""IeLabel1"" WIDTH=611 HEIGHT=60\n";
strOut += "CLASSID=""CLSID:99B42120-6EC7-11CF-A6C7-00AA00A47DD2"">\n";
strOut += "<PARAM NAME=""_ExtentX"" VALUE=""16140"">\n";
strOut += "<PARAM NAME=""_ExtentY"" VALUE=""1588"">\n";
strOut += "<PARAM NAME=""Caption"" VALUE=""\n";
strOut += strCaption;
strOut += """>\n";
strOut += "<PARAM NAME=""Angle"" VALUE=""0"">\n";
strOut += "<PARAM NAME=""Alignment"" VALUE=""4"">\n";
strOut += "<PARAM NAME=""Mode"" VALUE=""1"">\n";
strOut += "<PARAM NAME=""FillStyle"" VALUE=""1"">\n";
strOut += "<PARAM NAME=""ForeColor"" VALUE=""#70DA01"">\n";
strOut += "<PARAM NAME=""BackColor"" VALUE=""#000000"">\n";
strOut += "<PARAM NAME=""FontName"" VALUE=""Arial""\n>";
strOut += "<PARAM NAME=""FontSize"" VALUE=""20"">\n";
strOut += "<PARAM NAME=""FontItalic"" VALUE=""0""\n>";
strOut += "<PARAM NAME=""FontBold"" VALUE=""1"">\n";
strOut += "<PARAM NAME=""FontUnderline"" VALUE=""0"">\n";
```

continued on next page

continued from previous page

```
strOut += "<PARAM NAME=""FontStrikeout"" VALUE=""0"">\n";
strOut += "<PARAM NAME=""TopPoints"" VALUE=""0"">\n";
strOut += "<PARAM NAME=""BotPoints"" VALUE=""0"">\n";
strOut += strHoldIn.Mid(nPos);
strcpy ( (LPTSTR)pRawData->pvInData, (LPCTSTR)strOut);
pRawData->cbInData = (DWORD) strlen( (LPTSTR) pRawData->pvInData );
```

The data has to be inserted as part of the `<PARAM>` tags or the ActiveX control won't display it properly. Notice also the double `""` characters to make sure quotes go out properly in the HTML data. Finally, note that the caption was built as a CString and not a literal; this is the special mixture you need to link these technologies.

Comments

The text here with all the arbitrary GUIDs (Globally Unique IDs) and formatting didn't come out of thin air; it was taken from ActiveX Control Pad, used to insert a control into a test HTML page. The text was then lifted into the C++ project and reformatted appropriately for C++.

IFIL-AXS

COMPLEXITY
ADVANCED

9.9 How do I... Use ActiveX Scripting with an ISAPI filter?

Problem

Now that we can put out an ActiveX control with our ISAPI filter, can we also add client-side ActiveX Scripting to the ActiveX control's behavior this way?

Technique

Yes, but you have to watch out for several "gotchas." This How-To adds a mouse click client-side script to the ActiveX control output from the previous How-To. The directions here create the project from scratch, but for your convenience a copy of the HTML file is on the book CD under `\CH09\HT09\`.

Steps

1. Activate Visual C++ 5.0. Reload the `ISAPIFAXSIG` project. Open its `ISAPIFAXSIG.CPP` file and enter the boldfaced code in Listing 9-11 for the `OnSendRawData` event handler. Save the project and build the DLL.

Listing 9-11 ISAPIFAXSIG.CPP OnSendRawData source code

```
DWORD CIsapifaxsigFilter::OnSendRawData(CHttpFilterContext* pCtxt,
PHTTP_FILTER_RAW_DATA pRawData)
{
    CString pstrBuffer;
    CString pstrBuffer2;
    char* pFileName = "e:\\aspht\\counter.log";
    CStdioFile   file;
    file.Open( pFileName, CFile::modeRead ¦ CFile::typeText );
    try
    {
        try
        {
            file.ReadString(pstrBuffer);
            file.ReadString(pstrBuffer2);
        }
        catch(CFileException * e)
        {
            e->Delete();
        }
        file.Close();
    }
    catch(CMemoryException * e)
    {
        e->Delete();
    }
    catch(CFileException * e)
    {
        e->Delete();
    }
    CString strCaption;
    strCaption = "AspExec hits: ";
    strCaption += pstrBuffer;
    strCaption += " -- Guestbook hits: ";
    strCaption += pstrBuffer2;
    LPTSTRpstrIn;
    DWORD cbBuffer;
    DWORD cbTemp;
    pstrIn = (LPTSTR) pRawData->pvInData;
    CString strHoldIn = CString( pstrIn , strlen( pstrIn ));
    cbBuffer = 0;
    cbTemp = 0;
    if (pCtxt->m_pFC->pFilterContext == NULL)
    {
        while (cbBuffer < pRawData->cbInData)
        {
            if (pstrIn[cbBuffer] == '\n' &&
            pstrIn[cbBuffer+2] == '\n')
            {
                cbBuffer += 3;
                break;
            }
            cbBuffer++;
        }
```

continued on next page

continued from previous page

```
        while (cbTemp < cbBuffer)
        {
            if (pstrIn[cbTemp] == '/' && pstrIn[cbTemp+1] == 'h' &&
            pstrIn[cbTemp+2] == 't' && pstrIn[cbTemp+3] == 'm')
            {
                pCtxt->m_pFC->pFilterContext = (VOID*) 2;
                break;
            }
            cbTemp++;
        }

        if (cbTemp == cbBuffer)
         pCtxt->m_pFC->pFilterContext = (VOID *) 1;
    }
    if (pCtxt->m_pFC->pFilterContext == (VOID *) 2)
    {
        DWORD nPos;
        nPos = strHoldIn.Find( "</body>" );
        if ( nPos = -1 ) nPos = strHoldIn.Find( "</BODY>" );
        if ( nPos != -1 )
        {
            CString strOut = strHoldIn.Left(nPos - 1);
            strOut += "<HR><H1>This Page Brought To You by CIUPKC⇐
            WebSite!</H1><HR>";
           strOut += "<SCRIPT LANGUAGE=""VBScript"">\n";
           strOut += "<!--\n";
           strOut += "Sub IeLabel1_Click()\n";
           strOut += "IeLabel1.ForeColor = Int((16000000 - 0 + 1) * Rnd )\n";
           strOut += "end sub\n";
           strOut += "-->\n";
           strOut += "</SCRIPT>\n";
            strOut += "<OBJECT ID=""IeLabel1"" WIDTH=611 HEIGHT=60\n";
            strOut += "CLASSID=""CLSID:99B42120-6EC7-11CF-A6C7-00AA00A47DD2"">\n";
            strOut += "<PARAM NAME=""_ExtentX"" VALUE=""16140"">\n";
            strOut += "<PARAM NAME=""_ExtentY"" VALUE=""1588"">\n";
            strOut += "<PARAM NAME=""Caption"" VALUE=""\n";
            strOut += strCaption;
            strOut += """>\n";
            strOut += "<PARAM NAME=""Angle"" VALUE=""0"">\n";
            strOut += "<PARAM NAME=""Alignment"" VALUE=""4"">\n";
            strOut += "<PARAM NAME=""Mode"" VALUE=""1"">\n";
            strOut += "<PARAM NAME=""FillStyle"" VALUE=""1"">\n";
            strOut += "<PARAM NAME=""ForeColor"" VALUE=""#70DA01"">\n";
            strOut += "<PARAM NAME=""BackColor"" VALUE=""#000000"">\n";
            strOut += "<PARAM NAME=""FontName"" VALUE=""Arial""\n>";
            strOut += "<PARAM NAME=""FontSize"" VALUE=""20"">\n";
            strOut += "<PARAM NAME=""FontItalic"" VALUE=""0""\n>";
            strOut += "<PARAM NAME=""FontBold"" VALUE=""1"">\n";
            strOut += "<PARAM NAME=""FontUnderline"" VALUE=""0"">\n";
            strOut += "<PARAM NAME=""FontStrikeout"" VALUE=""0"">\n";
            strOut += "<PARAM NAME=""TopPoints"" VALUE=""0"">\n";
            strOut += "<PARAM NAME=""BotPoints"" VALUE=""0"">\n";
            strOut += strHoldIn.Mid(nPos);
            strcpy ( (LPTSTR)pRawData->pvInData, (LPCTSTR)strOut);
```

```
            pRawData->cbInData = (DWORD) strlen( (LPTSTR) pRawData->pvInData );

        }
    }

    return SF_STATUS_REQ_NEXT_NOTIFICATION;

}
```

2. Activate `REGEDIT.EXE` or `REGEDT32.EXE` (for Windows 95 or Windows NT) and locate the `HKEY_LOCAL_MACHINE\System\CurrentControlSet\Services\W3SCVC\Parameters\Filter Dlls` key. Edit it and add a comma at the end, followed by the path for the new DLL. Close the registry editor and restart IIS/PWS to load the new filter.

3. Make sure that the `Counter` filter from How-To 9.2 is installed while you bring up some pages in the `ASPEXEC` and `GUESTBOOK` directories, to build up the counter's log file.

4. Bring up Internet Explorer and enter the following address: `HTTP://DEFAULT\ASPEXEC\ASPHT801.ASP`. The page comes up with the ActiveX Label control at the bottom. Now click on it several times; as shown in Figure 9-15, the `ISAPIFAXSIG` filter has added code that flips the color of the text randomly whenever the control is clicked with the mouse. You have learned to use ISAPI filter DLLs to add client-side scripting to ActiveX controls.

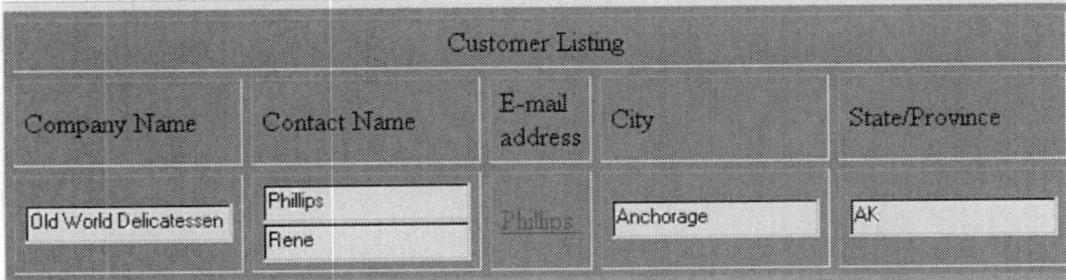

Figure 9-15 `ASPHT0801.ASP` in IE showing the ActiveX control added by the `ISAPIFAXSIG` filter responding to mouse clicks with client-side scripting

How It Works

The key lines are added before the inclusion of the ActiveX control.

```
CString strOut = strHoldIn.Left(nPos - 1);
strOut += "<HR><H1>This Page Brought To You by CIUPKC WebSite!</H1><HR>";
strOut += "<SCRIPT LANGUAGE=""VBScript"">\n";
strOut += "<!--\n";
strOut += "Sub IeLabel1_Click()\n";
strOut += "IeLabel1.ForeColor = Int((16000000 - 0 + 1) * Rnd )\n";
strOut += "end sub\n";
strOut += "-->\n";
strOut += "</SCRIPT>\n";
strOut += "<OBJECT ID=""IeLabel1"" WIDTH=611 HEIGHT=60\n";
strOut += "CLASSID=""CLSID:99B42120-6EC7-11CF-A6C7-00AA00A47DD2"">\n";
```

To get client-side scripting to work properly with output as program-written HTML, you must fulfill two major requirements. First, you must enclose the script in `<SCRIPT>` tags and then comment tags (`<!---->`) to keep older browsers from trying to interpret the script code. Second, you must terminate each line of the script with a `\n`, or the parser will likely become confused. These two gotchas will cause many an ISAPI developer to become addicted to caffeine and late night TV shows.

Comments

If it seems a bit strange that control over powerful technologies such as ActiveX Scripting and ISAPI depends in the final analysis on moving little bits of text around, just wait until you meet dynamic HTML in Windows 98. It uses ActiveX Scripting to do what is now considered the province of compiled C++ and Visual Basic applications: manipulate the Windows desktop.

IFIL-ADO-ASP

COMPLEXITY
ADVANCED

9.10 How do I... Use Active Server Pages and ActiveX data objects with an ISAPI filter?

Problem

We need to use the information from an ISAPI filter in the creation of ADO and ASP output to the client. Because ISAPI filters can't write ASP code, how do we do this?

Technique

Once again, server-side includes come to your aid. This How-To will reproduce the functionality of How-To 8.10, but using a filter rather than an extension. Although the directions here create the project from scratch, the completed ASP files are on the book CD under `\CH09\HT10\`.

Steps

1. For this How-To, you'll use one of the tutorial databases supplied with ASP. (If you have removed them, you need to reinstall the `ADVWORKS.MDB` file to use this How-To.) If you have already done Chapter 7, "ActiveX Data Objects: OLE DB Made Easy," or How-To 4.10, you can skip this step. First, you need to connect the ODBC drivers for Microsoft Access to the database along with its alias. Open the control panel; then double-click on the 32-bit ODBC drivers icon. In the property pages dialog that appears, select the System DSN tab and click the Add button. In the Add dialog, enter `AWTutorial` for the datasource name, and in the database grouping, click the Select button and browse to the `AdventureWorks Tutorial` directory on your hard drive. Select the `ADVWORKS.MDB` file. Click OK twice to accept your new settings.

2. Activate Visual C++ 5.0. Create a new ISAPI filter named `ISAPIFADOASP` with the wizard. Set its notifications to Nonsecured port sessions and URL mapping requests only. Open its `ISAPIFADOASP.CPP` file and enter the boldfaced code in Listing 9-12 for the `OnURLMap` event handler. Save the project and build the DLL. (Be sure to modify the path to the include file to the same one you used in How-To 8.10.)

Listing 9-12 `ISAPIFADOASP.CPP OnURLMap` source code

```
DWORD CIsapifadoaspFilter::OnUrlMap(CHttpFilterContext* pCtxt,
PHTTP_FILTER_URL_MAP pMapInfo)
{
    CHAR achUserAgent[1026];
    DWORD cbUserAgent = 1026;
    BOOL bChange = FALSE;
    CString strPhysicalPath, strOriginalPath, HoldUA;
    int nPos = 0;

    pCtxt->GetServerVariable("HTTP_USER_AGENT", achUserAgent, &cbUserAgent);
    HoldUA = CString( achUserAgent , strlen( achUserAgent ));
    if ( HoldUA.Find("MSIE" ) != -1 )
    {
        strOriginalPath = pMapInfo->pszPhysicalPath;
        strPhysicalPath = strOriginalPath;
        nPos = strPhysicalPath.Find("\\aspht0910.asp");
        if (nPos != -1)
        {
```

continued on next page

continued from previous page

```
            char* pFileName = "e:\\aspht\\aspexec\\aspht0910inc.asp";
            CStdioFile   file;
            file.Open( pFileName, CFile::modeCreate ¦ CFile::modeWrite ¦⇐
            CFile::typeText );
            try
            {
                CString pstrOutput;
                try
                {
                    pstrOutput = "<% dim HoldAction %>\n";
                    file.WriteString(pstrOutput);
                    pstrOutput = "<% HoldAction = ""FORWARD"" %>\n";
                    file.WriteString(pstrOutput);
                }
                catch(CFileException * e)
                {
                    e->Delete();
                }
            }
            catch(CMemoryException * e)
            {
                e->Delete();
            }
            catch(CFileException * e)
            {
                e->Delete();
            }
        }
    }
    else
    {
        strOriginalPath = pMapInfo->pszPhysicalPath;
        strPhysicalPath = strOriginalPath;
        nPos = strPhysicalPath.Find("\\aspht0910.asp");
        if (nPos != -1)
        {
            char* pFileName = "e:\\aspht\\aspexec\\aspht0910inc.asp";
            CStdioFile   file;
            file.Open( pFileName, CFile::modeCreate ¦ CFile::modeWrite ¦⇐
            zCFile::typeText );
            try
            {
                CString pstrOutput;
                try
                {
                    pstrOutput = "<% dim HoldAction %>\n";
                    file.WriteString(pstrOutput);
                    pstrOutput = "<% HoldAction = ""BACKWARD"" %>\n";
                    file.WriteString(pstrOutput);
                }
                catch(CFileException * e)
                {
                    e->Delete();
                }
            }
            catch(CMemoryException * e)
            {
```

```
                e->Delete();
            }
            catch(CFileException * e)
            {
                e->Delete();
            }
        }

    }
    return SF_STATUS_REQ_NEXT_NOTIFICATION;
}
```

3. Activate `REGEDIT.EXE` or `REGEDT32.EXE` (for Windows 95 or Windows NT) and locate the `HKEY_LOCAL_MACHINE\System\CurrentControlSet\Services\W3SCVC\Parameters\Filter Dlls` key. Edit it and add a comma at the end, followed by the path for the new DLL. Close the registry editor and restart IIS/PWS to load the new filter.

4. Bring up ActiveX Control Pad. Create a new ASP file and enter the ASP code in Listing 9-13. Save it as `ASPHT0910.ASP` and move it into the `ASPEXEC` directory.

Listing 9-13 ASPHT0910.ASP source code

```
<%@ LANGUAGE = VBScript %>
<HTML>
<HEAD>
<TITLE>Active Server Pages Chapter Nine How To Ten</TITLE>
</HEAD>
<BODY>
<% if IsObject(Session("objRecordSet")) then
     set objRecordSet = Session("objRecordSet")
   else
     Set objConnection = Server.CreateObject("ADODB.Connection")
objConnection.Open "AWTutorial"
SQLQuery = "SELECT * FROM Customers"
Set objRecordSet = objConnection.Execute( SQLQuery )
objRecordSet.Close
objRecordSet.Open , , 2 , 4
Set Session("objRecordSet") = objRecordSet
   end if
%>
<!--#INCLUDE FILE = "aspht0910inc.asp"-->
<%
   HoldAction = UCase( HoldAction )
   if HoldAction = "" then HoldAction = "FORWARD"
   if HoldAction = "FORWARD" then
     on error resume next
     if not objRecordSet.EOF then
objRecordSet.MoveNext
     else
objRecordSet.MoveFirst
     end if
```

continued on next page

continued from previous page

```
   elseif HoldAction = "BACKWARD" then
     on error resume next
     if not objRecordSet.BOF then
objRecordSet.MovePrevious
     else
objRecordSet.MoveLast
     end if
   elseif HoldAction = "UPDATE" then
     objRecordSet("CompanyName") = Request.Form("Text2")
     objRecordSet("ContactLastName") = Request.Form("Text3")
objRecordSet("ContactFirstName") = Request.Form("Text4")
objRecordSet("City") = Request.Form("Text5")
objRecordSet("StateOrProvince") = Request.Form("Text6")
ObjRecordSet.Update
    end if
%>
    <FORM NAME="Form1" >
<TABLE WIDTH=600 COLSPAN=8 BORDER=5 CELLSPACING=5
CELLPADDING=5 ALIGN="CENTER" VALIGN="MIDDLE" BGCOLOR="Teal">
<TR>
<TD COLSPAN=5 ALIGN="CENTER">
Customer Listing
</TD>
</TR>
<TR>
<TD>
Company Name
</TD>
<TD>
Contact Name
</TD>
<TD>
E-mail address
</TD>
<TD>
City
</TD>
<TD>
State/Province
</TD>
</TR>
  <TR>
  <TD>
  <INPUT Type = "Text" Name="Text2" Value = "<%= objRecordSet("CompanyName")%>">
  </TD>
  <TD>
  <INPUT Type = "Text" Name="Text3" Value = "<%= objRecordSet⇐
  ("ContactLastName")%>">
  <INPUT Type = "Text" Name="Text4" Value = "<%= objRecordSet⇐
  ("ContactFirstName")%>">
  </TD>
  <TD>
    <A HREF="mailto:">
      <%= objRecordSet("ContactLastName")%>
    </A></TD>
```

```
    <TD>
    <INPUT Type = "Text" Name="Text5" Value = "<%= objRecordSet("City")%>">
    </TD>
    <TD>
    <INPUT Type = "Text" Name="Text6" Value = "<%= objRecordSet⇐
    ("StateOrProvince")%>">
    </TD>
    </TR>
  </TD>
  </TR>
  </TABLE>
  </FORM>
  </BODY>
  </HTML>
```

5. Bring up Internet Explorer and enter the following address: `HTTP://DEFAULT\ASPEXEC\ASPHT0910.ASP`. When it comes up, navigate to another page in the `ASPEXEC` directory and then come back. As shown in Figure 9-16, the include file written by the `ISAPIFADOASP` filter has moved the browser forward automatically. Do the same with a non-IE browser such as Netscape Communicator, and you will see that the include file automatically moves the browser backward, as shown in Figure 9-17. Congratulations! You have learned to use ISAPI filter DLLs and server-side include files to manipulate ASP and ADOs.

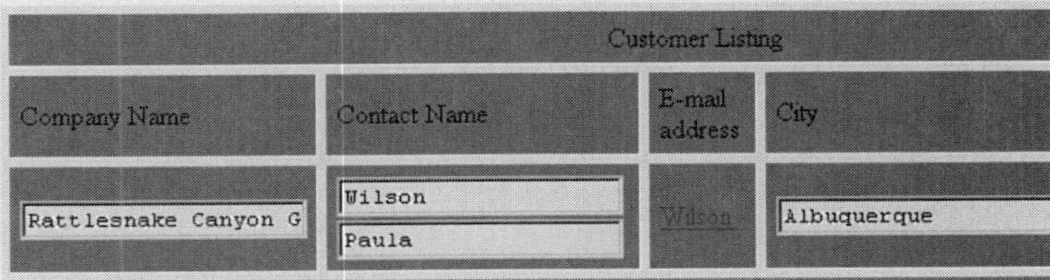

Figure 9-16 `ASPHT0910.ASP` in IE showing automatic ADO navigation using a filter-written server-side include file

How It Works

This How-To is really a combination of other How-To's in this chapter. The central problem it faces is that, unlike the extension version, this DLL will be called in cases where its output is not appropriate. The initial code is to obtain the `USER_AGENT` value.

```
pCtxt->GetServerVariable("HTTP_USER_AGENT", achUserAgent, &cbUserAgent);
HoldUA = CString( achUserAgent , strlen( achUserAgent ));
if ( HoldUA.Find("MSIE" ) != -1 )
{
    strOriginalPath = pMapInfo->pszPhysicalPath;
    strPhysicalPath = strOriginalPath;
    nPos = strPhysicalPath.Find("\\aspht0910.asp");
```

The `CHttpFilterContext` object is used to get the `HTTP_USER_AGENT` value. When it is obtained, then a check needs to be made to find out whether the URL being hit is `ASPHT0910.ASP`; if not, nothing else is done. Otherwise, the next bit of code is executed:

```
if (nPos != -1)
{
   char* pFileName = "e:\\aspht\\aspexec\\aspht0910inc.asp";
   CStdioFile   file;
   file.Open( pFileName, CFile::modeCreate ¦ CFile::modeWrite ¦ CFile::typeText );
   try
   {
            CString pstrOutput;
            try
            {
                pstrOutput = "<% dim HoldAction %>\n";
                file.WriteString(pstrOutput);
                pstrOutput = "<% HoldAction = ""FORWARD"" %>\n";
                file.WriteString(pstrOutput);
            }
```

Notice that the include file is written just as before, using a hard-wired pathname and the `CStdioFile` object. The contents of the file depend on whether the browser is Internet Explorer or any other one, as before. The include file is dealt with similarly.

```
Set Session("objRecordSet") = objRecordSet
   end if
%>
<!--#INCLUDE FILE = "aspht0910inc.asp"-->
<%
   HoldAction = UCase( HoldAction )
```

The include filename used in the ASP file is now the proper name to match that output by the filter.

Comments

As a final note, you might notice that the path delimiters used in all these C++ files are `\` rather than the `/` you see in the address bar. The reason is that the translation is already complete to a physical URL when the URL string is interpreted, and in Windows `/` becomes `\`.

CHAPTER 10

OLE DB: ACTIVEX DATA OBJECTS IN VISUAL C++ 5.0

10

OLE DB: ACTIVEX DATA OBJECTS IN VISUAL C++ 5.0

How do I...

10.9 Use ADO in a Visual C++ 5.0 ISAPI extension?

10.10 Use ADO in a Visual C++ 5.0 ISAPI filter?

Be warned: This chapter is not for the timid! You need to know Visual C++ fairly well and understand ISAPI extension and ISAPI filter creation. This chapter unleashes all the power of the OLE DB interfaces via the wonderful new wrapper, the ActiveX data objects (ADO) system! In this chapter, you will develop a C++ ActiveX control that fully implements interactions with an ODBC database, and learn to modify that control so that client-side scripts can interact with the database directly. Next, you'll create an Active Server Pages (ASP) component with identical functionality. Finally, you'll create an ISAPI extension and ISAPI filter that use ADO to implement a complete restricted URL system that requires users to supply unique personal information to gain access to a Web page.

10.1 Use ActiveX Data Objects in a Visual C++ 5.0 ActiveX Control

If you thought ADOs were available only to ASP scripts, think again! Thanks to the OLE DB Software Development Kit (SDK), you can now add all the power of OLE DB/ADO to a Visual C++ 5.0 ActiveX control! This How-To develops a simple control for an ODBC employee database supplied with the OLE DB SDK.

10.2 Allow User Navigation in ADO with My C++ ActiveX Control

Now that you have leapt the hurdle of using ADO in Visual C++, you can master the next level: user navigation. This How-To enhances the `EmployeeViewer` control from How-To 10.1 to permit users to move forward and backward inside the ODBC database.

10.3 Allow User Updates in ADO with My C++ ActiveX Control

Users also want to change things, and this includes information in the database. This How-To gives you complete directions for adding record updating to the ODBC database via ADO in the `EmployeeViewer` ActiveX control.

10.4 Find Records in the Database with ADO in My C++ ActiveX Control

One of the most vital tasks any database interface must handle is finding records. This How-To shows you exactly how to add this capability via the ADO system to the `EmployeeViewer` ActiveX control created in the previous How-To.

10.5 Add and Delete Records in the Database with ADO in My C++ ActiveX Control

Databases don't just materialize out of thin air; somebody has to create them! This How-To illustrates using ADO to add new records and delete old ones from the Employees database with the `EmployeeViewer` control.

10.6 Make ADO Functionality Available to ActiveX Scripting in My C++ ActiveX Control

ADO has been available since the start of ASP, but only on the server side of things. This How-To shows you the way to provide ADO capabilities to the client-side scripting environment with properties and methods of the EmployeeViewer ActiveX control.

10.7 Use ADO in a Visual C++ 5.0 ASP Component

There are times when you want to access ODBC or other data inside an ASP component, particularly when the database contains proprietary information you don't want available on the Internet. This How-To demonstrates creating a version of the EmployeeViewer control as an ASP component that returns an entire employee record as an HTML table.

10.8 Make ADO Functionality Available to ASP Scripting in My C++ ASP Component

Because an ASP component can provide "canned" database access that removes a lot of the complexity involved in script-based ADO programming, it's only fair to make its capabilities available to ASP scripts too. This How-To enhances the EmployeeViewer ASP component from the previous How-To, exposing its internal data as scriptable properties and methods.

10.9 Use ADO in a Visual C++ 5.0 ISAPI Extension

ISAPI extensions need databases too, and this How-To makes the power of the EmployeeViewer control and component part of an ISAPI extension that reads a form for an employee's last name and phone number and, if this information is verified, outputs an HTML page sending the user to a restricted URL.

10.10 Use ADO in a Visual C++ 5.0 ISAPI Filter

Because this is the last How-To in the book, it is only fitting that it be a capstone project, one that uses every bit of ASP know-how you've acquired in the last 99 How-To's. It develops an ISAPI filter that uses ADO to check each URL for a ~~ character string, followed by a user's first name. If this is detected, the application checks the first name against an ADO database; if a match is found, the user is sent to an HTML page that contains the target URL and is the same as that used in How-To 10.9. Together, these last two How-To's demonstrate a complete secure URL system that can be scaled for use on either a corporate intranet or the World Wide Web. Welcome to the 21st century!

ADO-AXC

10.1 How do I… Use ActiveX Data Objects in a Visual C++ 5.0 ActiveX Control?

Problem

We really, really need to use OLE DB in a C++ ActiveX control for our corporate intranet. We looked over the raw OLE DB COM interfaces and almost had heart failure! Is there any way to use OLE DB without all the headaches of COM?

Technique

Via the magic of the newly released OLE DB SDK, you can now use the powerful ADO wrapper for OLE DB in Visual C++. This How-To demonstrates creating a simple but effective ActiveX control that uses ADO to open and display a record from an employee database. Although these directions create the project from scratch, the CD contains a completed file under `CH010\HT01\EMPLOYEEVIEWER\`.

Steps

1. Bring up Internet Explorer, Netscape Communicator, or your Web browser of choice and navigate to `http://www.microsoft.com/oledb/`. As shown in Figure 10-1, this is the OLE DB home page at Microsoft, featuring a very useful collection of OLE DB resources.

2. Click on the `Download` link, and you will find a page of downloadable items, as shown in Figure 10-2. Move down to the `OLEDBSDK` download link, click on it, find a suitable directory to store the 12-megabyte file, and download the SDK, as shown in Figure 10-3.

3. Once the download is finished, make sure you have about 50 megabytes of free hard-disk space and double-click on the `OLEDBSDK.EXE` file you downloaded. It will open up a DOS window and decompress its files, then run a setup program. When the setup is finished, you will have the needed tools and samples to develop with OLE DB in C++ (as well as Java and Visual Basic…).

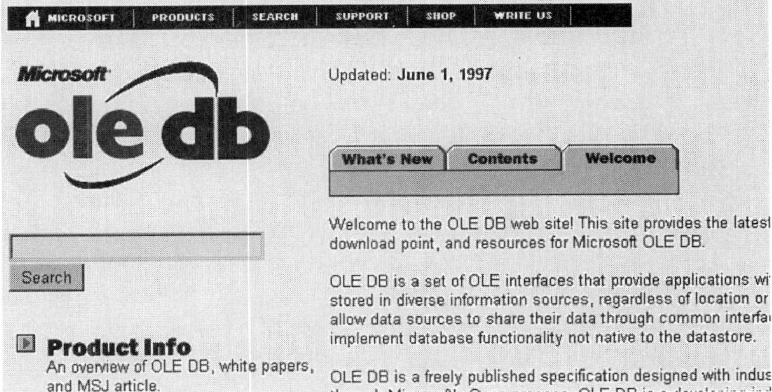

Figure 10-1 The OLE DB home page

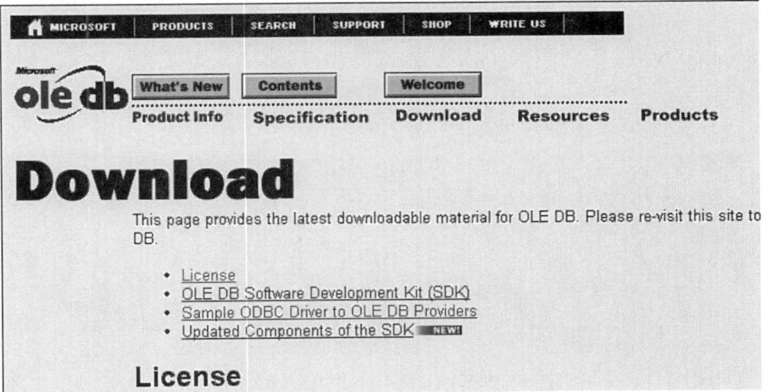

Figure 10-2 The OLE DB downloads page

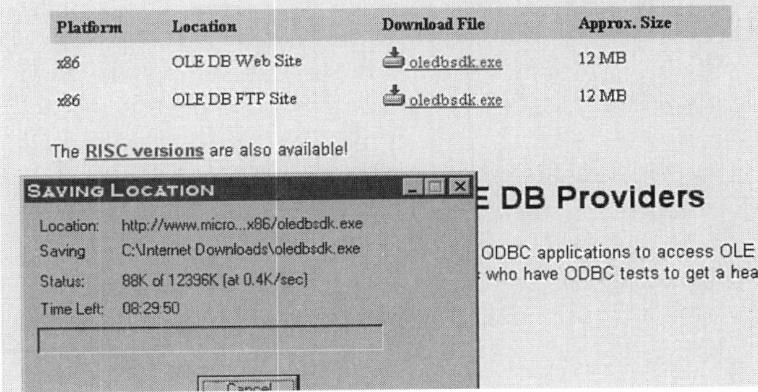

Figure 10-3 Downloading the OLE DB SDK

4. To prepare for this and the following How-To's, you need to make sure the ODBC database provided with the OLE DB SDK has been properly registered with the 32-bit ODBC manager. As shown in Figure 10-4, move to the control panel, double-click on the 32-bit ODBC icon, and check to see that the `OLE_DB_NWind_Jet` database is installed. If it is, click on it and make sure that the directory is the correct one; the installation program won't change this entry to a new directory if you change the installation to one other than the default. Change the directory entry to the one where the database is located if needed. If the database is not installed, you suffered a failure during the installation of the OLE DB SDK and should consult its Release Notes and `README` files to help you diagnose the error and install the database before continuing with this How-To.

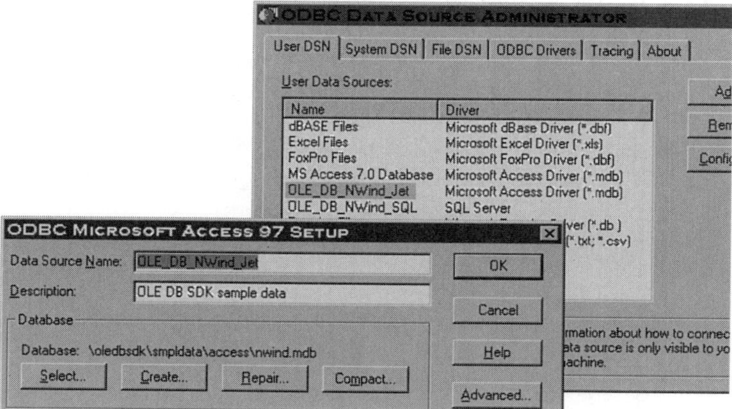

Figure 10-4 Verifying the installation of the `OLE_DB_NWind_Jet` database in the 32-bit ODBC manager

5. Start Visual C++ 5.0 and select the Tools|Options menu item. In the dialog box that appears, move to the Directories tab, select the Include Files combo box setting, scroll down the list to an empty line, and press the New button (the empty red square). As shown in Figure 10-5, enter the location of the OLE DB include files directory (default installation is in `\OLEDBSDK\INCLUDE\`). Press OK to add this directory to the system path. Then select the Library Files combo box setting, scroll down to an empty line, click on the New button, and, as shown in Figure 10-6, add the location of the OLE DB library files directory (default installation is in `\OLDEBSDK\LIB\`). Press OK to add your changes to the system.

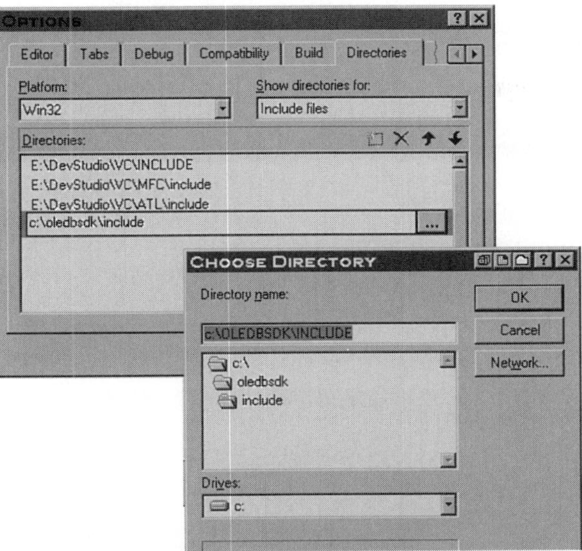

Figure 10-5 Adding the OLE DB SDK include files to the system path

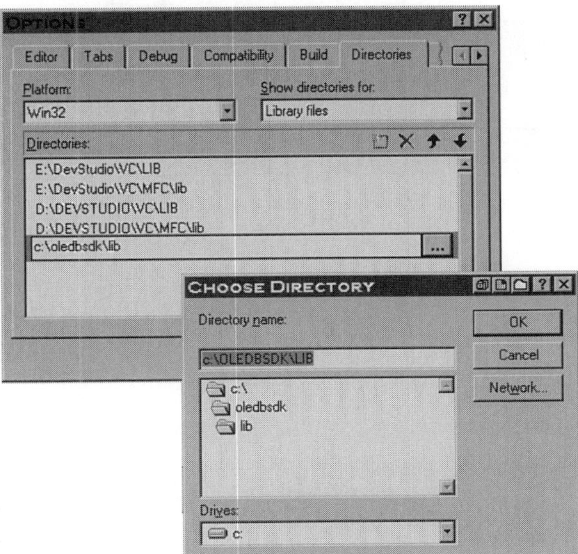

Figure 10-6 Adding the OLE DB SDK library files to the system path

6. Select File|New and choose an MFC ActiveX control project, with a name of `EMPLOYEEVIEWER`, as shown in Figure 10-7. Accept the default options and save the project.

NOTE

If you are creating your project on a drive other than `C:`, you must make sure the actual ActiveX control is output to drive `C:` (using the Project|Options dialog's `Output` directory entry), or you will get errors from the ADO system. This is a known bug and will be fixed in the next OLE DB SDK release.

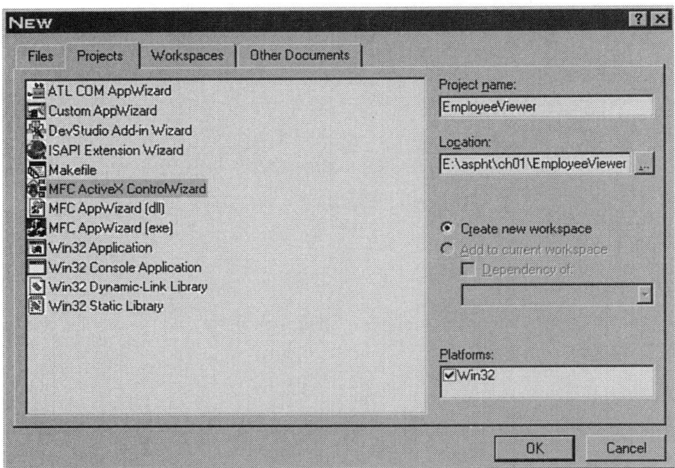

Figure 10-7 Creating the MFC ActiveX control project

7. Select File|New again and choose a new C++ header file, with a name of `ADOHEADERS.H`, as shown in Figure 10-8. Do the same procedure to add another new header file named `ADOWRAPPER.H` and a new C++ file named `ADOWRAPPER.CPP`. Save the project.

8. Bring up `ADOHEADERS.H` in the text editor. Add all the code in Listing 10-1 to the file to link the needed headers for the ADO system to the project and include support for a special `VARIANT` class used by ADO. Save the project.

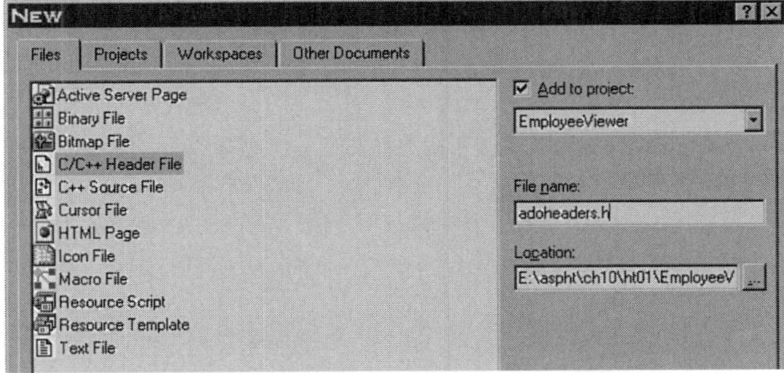

Figure 10-8 Adding new files to the project

Listing 10-1 ADOHEADERS.H header file source code

```
#include <objbase.h>
#include <afxdisp.h>
#include <tchar.h>                    // Unicode
#include "Initguid.h"
#include "Adoid.h"                    // ADO C++ header
#include "Adoint.h"                   // ADO C++ header

#ifndef __AFXWIN_H__
      #error include 'stdafx.h' before including this file for PCH
#endif

#include "resource.h"                 // main symbols


////////////////////////////////////////////////////////////////////////////


////////////////////////////////////////////////////////////////////////////
// Conversion macros/inline functions - Variant

inline CString VTOCSTR(VARIANT *v)
{
      if(v->vt==VT_BSTR)
      {
            CString str((LPCWSTR)v->bstrVal);
            return str;
      }
      else
      {
            return CString("");
      }
}

#define VTOLONG(v)        ((v).vt==VT_I4 ? (LONG)(v).lVal:0L)
#define VTODATE(v)        ((v).vt==VT_DATE ? (CTime)(v).iVal:0L)
```

continued on next page

continued from previous page

```
class CVar : public VARIANT
      {
public:
      CVar()
            {
            VariantInit(this);
            }
      CVar(VARTYPE vt, SCODE scode = 0)
            {
            VariantInit(this);
            this->vt = vt;
            this->scode = scode;
            }
      CVar(VARIANT var)
            {
            *this = var;
            }
      ~CVar()
            {
            VariantClear(this);
            }

      // ASSIGNMENT OPS.
      CVar & operator=(PCWSTR pcwstr)
            {
            VariantClear(this);
            if (NULL == (this->bstrVal = SysAllocStringLen(pcwstr, ⇐
                          wcslen(pcwstr))))
                  throw E_OUTOFMEMORY;
            this->vt = VT_BSTR;
            return *this;
            }
      CVar & operator=(VARIANT var)
            {
            HRESULT hr;

            VariantClear(this);
            if (FAILED(hr = VariantCopy(this, &var)))
                  throw hr;
            return *this;
            }

      // CAST OPS.
      // doesn't change type. only returns BSTR if variant is of type
      // bstr. asserts otherwise.
      operator BSTR() const
      {
            if(VT_BSTR == this->vt)
                  return this->bstrVal;
            else
                  return NULL;
      }
```

```
    HRESULT Clear()
    {
        return VariantClear(this);
    }
};
```

WARNING

The addition of the `INITGUID.H` file is critical. It is required at this *exact* point to allow the linker to understand the expanded macros that create the `CLSID` and `IID` GUIDs for the project; if you do not place the include file here, you will get unresolved symbol errors from the linker for all the GUIDs in the project. Believe me, this is one marginally documented feature of ActiveX development that can cause developers to buy cases of Maalox!

9. Likewise, bring up `ADOWRAPPER.H` in the text editor and add all the code in Listing 10-2 to define the `AdoWrapper` class for use in encapsulating ADO methods and properties. Save the project.

Listing 10-2 `ADOWRAPPER.H` header file source code

```
// adowrapper.h : header file
//
#include "Adoint.h"

/////////////////////////////////////////////////////////////////////////////
// CAdoWrapper dialog

class CAdoWrapper
{
// Construction
public:
    CAdoWrapper();      // standard constructor
    ~CAdoWrapper();

// Attributes
public:
    ADORecordset*      m_piEmployeeRecordSet;
    BOOL               m_fConnectedtoDB;
    BOOL               m_fRecordsetIsEmpty;

protected:
    ADOConnection*            m_piADOConnection;
    COleVariant            m_varTheLastGoodRecord;
// Operations
public:
    BOOL      ConnectToDB(); //Opens a database
    long      GetTheEmployeeId();
    CString GetTheFirstName();
```

continued on next page

continued from previous page

```
      CString GetTheLastName();
      CString GetThePhoneNumber() ;
      CString GetTheJobTitle() ;
};


#define THE_EMPLOYEE_ID         L"EmployeeID"
#define THE_LAST_NAME           L"LastName"
#define THE_FIRST_NAME          L"FirstName"
#define THE_TITLE               L"Title"
#define THE_PHONE_NUMBER        L"HomePhone"
```

10. Next, bring up `ADOWRAPPER.CPP` in the text editor and add all the code in Listing 10-3 to write the code for the `AdoWrapper` class for use in encapsulating ADO methods and properties. (You will add more functionality later.) Save the project.

Listing 10-3 ADOWRAPPER.CPP ADO interface source code

```
#include "stdafx.h"
#include "adoheaders.h"
#include "adowrapper.h"

#ifdef _DEBUG
#undef THIS_FILE
static char THIS_FILE[] = __FILE__;
#endif

#define THROW_ERR(exp)      if (FAILED(hr = (exp))) throw hr

const LPCWSTR g_lpcwszSource = L"OLE_DB_NWind_Jet;";
const LPCWSTR g_lpcwszUser = L"Admin";
const LPCWSTR g_lpcwszPwd = L"";
const LPCWSTR g_lpcwszSQL = L"select EmployeeId, LastName, FirstName, Title, ⇐
                            HomePhone from Employees";

CAdoWrapper::CAdoWrapper()
{
      m_piADOConnection = NULL;
      m_piEmployeeRecordSet = NULL;
      m_fConnectedtoDB = FALSE;
      m_fRecordsetIsEmpty = TRUE;
}

CAdoWrapper::~CAdoWrapper()
{
      if ( m_piADOConnection != NULL )
            m_piADOConnection->Release();
      if ( m_piEmployeeRecordSet != NULL )
            m_piEmployeeRecordSet->Release();
```

```
    m_varTheLastGoodRecord.Clear();
    m_piADOConnection = NULL;
    m_piEmployeeRecordSet = NULL;
}


long CAdoWrapper::GetTheEmployeeId()
{
    HRESULT                     hr;
    COleVariant                 vFldName, vID;

    if (!m_fConnectedtoDB)
        return 0;

    if(m_fRecordsetIsEmpty)
        return 0;

    vFldName.bstrVal = CString(THE_EMPLOYEE_ID).AllocSysString();
    vFldName.vt = VT_BSTR;
    THROW_ERR(      m_piEmployeeRecordSet->get_Collect(vFldName, vID)       );

    return VTOLONG(vID);
}


CString CAdoWrapper::GetTheFirstName()
{
    HRESULT                     hr;
    COleVariant                vFldName, vFirstName;

    if (!m_fConnectedtoDB)
        return "";

    if(m_fRecordsetIsEmpty)
        return "";

    vFldName.bstrVal = CString(THE_FIRST_NAME).AllocSysString();
    vFldName.vt = VT_BSTR;
    THROW_ERR(      m_piEmployeeRecordSet->get_Collect(vFldName, vFirstName) );

    return VTOCSTR(vFirstName);
}

CString CAdoWrapper::GetTheLastName()
{
    HRESULT                     hr;
    COleVariant                vFldName, vLastName;

    if (!m_fConnectedtoDB)
        return "";

    if(m_fRecordsetIsEmpty)
        return "";
```

continued on next page

continued from previous page

```
	vFldName.bstrVal = CString(THE_LAST_NAME).AllocSysString();
	vFldName.vt = VT_BSTR;
	THROW_ERR(	m_piEmployeeRecordSet->get_Collect(vFldName, vLastName) );

	return VTOCSTR(vLastName);
}

CString CAdoWrapper::GetThePhoneNumber()
{
	HRESULT			hr;
	COleVariant		vFldName, vHomePhone;

	 if (!m_fConnectedtoDB)
		return "";

	if(m_fRecordsetIsEmpty)
		return "";

	vFldName.bstrVal = CString(THE_PHONE_NUMBER).AllocSysString();
	vFldName.vt = VT_BSTR;
	THROW_ERR(	m_piEmployeeRecordSet->get_Collect(vFldName, vHomePhone) );

	return VTOCSTR(vHomePhone);
}

CString CAdoWrapper::GetTheJobTitle()
{
	HRESULT			hr;
	COleVariant		vFldName, vTitle;

	 if (!m_fConnectedtoDB)
		return "";

	if(m_fRecordsetIsEmpty)
		return "";

	vFldName.bstrVal = CString(THE_TITLE).AllocSysString();
	vFldName.vt = VT_BSTR;
	THROW_ERR(	m_piEmployeeRecordSet->get_Collect(vFldName, vTitle) );

	return VTOCSTR(vTitle);
}

BOOL CAdoWrapper::ConnectToDB()
{

	CVar		varDataSource, varUserId, varPwd, varSQL;
	HRESULT		  hr;
	CVar		vNull(VT_ERROR, DISP_E_PARAMNOTFOUND);
	VARIANT_BOOL	  vbEOF, vbBOF;
```

```
    varDataSource       = g_lpcwszSource;
    varUserId           = g_lpcwszUser;
    varPwd              = g_lpcwszPwd;
    varSQL              = g_lpcwszSQL;

    try
    {
        if ( m_piADOConnection == NULL || m_piEmployeeRecordSet == NULL)
        {
            THROW_ERR(        CoInitialize(NULL) );
            THROW_ERR(        CoCreateInstance(CLSID_CADOConnection, NULL,
CLSCTX_INPROC_SERVER, IID_IADOConnection, (LPVOID *)&m_piADOConnection) );
            THROW_ERR(        m_piADOConnection->Open( varDataSource, ⇐
                              varUserId, varPwd ) );

            THROW_ERR(        CoCreateInstance(CLSID_CADORecordset, NULL,
CLSCTX_INPROC_SERVER, IID_IADORecordset, (LPVOID *)&m_piEmployeeRecordSet) );
            THROW_ERR(        m_piEmployeeRecordSet-
>putref_ActiveConnection(m_piADOConnection) );
            THROW_ERR(        m_piEmployeeRecordSet->put_Source(varSQL) );

            vNull.vt = VT_ERROR;
            vNull.scode = DISP_E_PARAMNOTFOUND;
            THROW_ERR(        m_piEmployeeRecordSet->Open(vNull, vNull, ⇐
                              adOpenKeyset, adLockOptimistic, adCmdText) );

            THROW_ERR(       m_piEmployeeRecordSet->get_EOF(&vbEOF) );
            THROW_ERR(       m_piEmployeeRecordSet->get_BOF(&vbBOF) );
            if(vbEOF && vbBOF)
                m_fRecordsetIsEmpty  = TRUE;
            else
                m_fRecordsetIsEmpty  = FALSE;
        }

        return TRUE;
    }
    catch (HRESULT hr)
    {
        TCHAR szBuf[256];
        wsprintf(szBuf, _T("Error: %d \n"), hr);
        AfxMessageBox(szBuf);

        return (FALSE);
    }
}
```

11. Now activate the Class Wizard and select the `EmployeeViewerCtl` class's `WM_CREATE` message on the Message Maps tab. Press the Add Function button to override the existing method, as shown in Figure 10-9. Then click on the Edit Code button and enter the boldface code in Listing 10-4 to the event handler. Save the project.

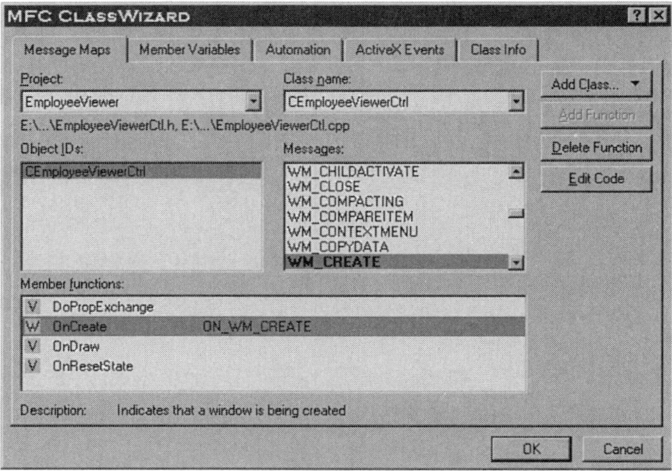

Figure 10-9 Overriding the `OnCreate` method via the Class Wizard

Listing 10.4 EMPLOYEEVIEWERCTL.CPP OnCreate event handler source code

```
int CEmployeeViewerCtrl::OnCreate(LPCREATESTRUCT lpCreateStruct)
{
      if (COleControl::OnCreate(lpCreateStruct) == -1)
            return -1;

      // TODO: Add your specialized creation code here
      m_FirstName.Create( WS_CHILD¦ WS_VISIBLE ¦ WS_BORDER ¦ ES_AUTOHSCROLL ,
            CRect( 20 , 50 , 220 , 75 ), this , IDC_FIRSTNAME );
      m_LastName.Create( WS_CHILD¦ WS_VISIBLE ¦ WS_BORDER ¦ ES_AUTOHSCROLL ,
            CRect( 250 , 50 , 450 , 75 ), this , IDC_LASTNAME );
      m_JobTitle.Create( WS_CHILD¦ WS_VISIBLE ¦ WS_BORDER ¦ ES_AUTOHSCROLL ,
            CRect( 20 , 150 , 220 , 175 ), this , IDC_JOBTITLE );
      m_EmployeeID.Create( WS_CHILD¦ WS_VISIBLE ¦ WS_BORDER ¦ ES_AUTOHSCROLL ,
            CRect( 250 , 150 , 450 , 175 ), this , IDC_EMPLOYEEID );
    m_Connect.Create("Connect to Database",WS_CHILD ¦ WS_VISIBLE ¦ WS_BORDER ⇐
                  ¦BS_PUSHBUTTON ,
            CRect( 20 , 200 , 300 , 240) , this , IDC_CONNECT );
      m_Disconnect.Create("Disconnect from Database",WS_CHILD ¦ WS_VISIBLE ¦ ⇐
                     WS_BORDER ¦BS_PUSHBUTTON ,
            CRect( 20 , 250 , 300 , 290) , this , IDC_DISCONNECT );
        return 0;
}
```

12. Next, select the View|Resource Symbols menu option. In the dialog box, press the New button and enter `IDC_FIRSTNAME` in the Name text control, leaving 101 in the Value control. Press OK to add this named resource to the project. Add `IDC_LASTNAME`, `IDC_JOBTITLE`, `IDC_EMPLOYEEID`, `IDC_CONNECT`, and `IDC_DISCONNECT` the same way. Figure 10-10 shows how the dialog box should look on the last entry. Press OK to add the symbols. Save the project.

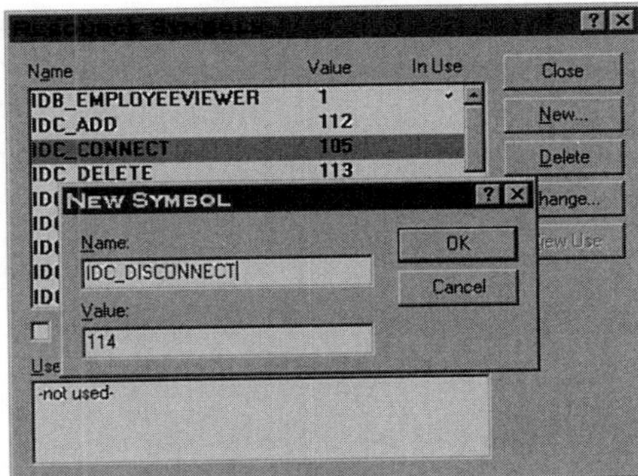

Figure 10-10 Adding named resource IDs to the project

13. Back in `EMPLOYEEVIEWERCTL.CPP`, find the `OnDraw` event handler and delete the boilerplate ellipse drawing statement (but not the `FillRect` one!) provided by the wizard. Replace it with the boldface code in Listing 10-5 to draw the four captions above the Edit controls. Save the project. (The MFC controls will automatically draw themselves and don't need any code in the `OnDraw` event handler.)

Listing 10-5 `EMPLOYEEVIEWERCTL.CPP OnDraw` event handler source code

```
void CEmployeeViewerCtrl::OnDraw(CDC* pdc, const ⇐
                              CRect& rcBounds, const CRect& rcInvalid)
{
        pdc->FillRect(rcBounds, CBrush::FromHandle((HBRUSH)GetStockObject⇐
                    (WHITE_BRUSH)));
      pdc->TextOut( 20 , 20 , "Employee First Name" );
     pdc->TextOut( 250 ,20 , "Employee Last Name" );
     pdc->TextOut( 20 , 120 , "Employee Job Title" );
     pdc->TextOut( 250 , 120 , "Employee ID Number" );
}
```

14. Return to `EMPLOYEEVIEWERCTL.H` in the text editor. Add the boldface lines in Listing 10-6 to the file to load the ADO header files, provide `Connection` and `RecordSet` objects to the ActiveX control's class, add the Edit controls and button objects to the main class, and connect the Button controls with their click event handlers. Save the project.

Listing 10-6 `EMPLOYEEVIEWERCTL.H` header file source code

```
#if
!defined(AFX_EMPLOYEEVIEWERCTL_H__A7BAC253_FDCA_11D0_B7DF_444553540000__INCLUDED_)
#define AFX_EMPLOYEEVIEWERCTL_H__A7BAC253_FDCA_11D0_B7DF_444553540000__INCLUDED_

#if _MSC_VER >= 1000
#pragma once
#endif // _MSC_VER >= 1000

#include "adowrapper.h"

// EmployeeViewerCtl.h : Declaration of the CEmployeeViewerCtrl ActiveX Control
// class.


/////////////////////////////////////////////////////////////////////////////
// CEmployeeViewerCtrl : See EmployeeViewerCtl.cpp for implementation.

class CEmployeeViewerCtrl : public COleControl
{
      DECLARE_DYNCREATE(CEmployeeViewerCtrl)

// Constructor
public:
      CEmployeeViewerCtrl();
      CEdit m_FirstName;
      CEdit m_LastName;
      CEdit m_JobTitle;
      CEdit m_EmployeeID;
      CButton m_Connect;
      CButton m_Disconnect;
      CAdoWrapper*      m_pAdoWrapper;

    // Overrides
      // ClassWizard generated virtual function overrides
      //{{AFX_VIRTUAL(CEmployeeViewerCtrl)
      public:
      virtual void OnDraw(CDC* pdc, const CRect& rcBounds, const CRect& ⇐
                    rcInvalid);
      virtual void DoPropExchange(CPropExchange* pPX);
      virtual void OnResetState();
      //}}AFX_VIRTUAL
```

```
// Implementation
protected:
      ~CEmployeeViewerCtrl();

      DECLARE_OLECREATE_EX(CEmployeeViewerCtrl)     // Class factory and guid
      DECLARE_OLETYPELIB(CEmployeeViewerCtrl)       // GetTypeInfo
      DECLARE_PROPPAGEIDS(CEmployeeViewerCtrl)      // Property page IDs
      DECLARE_OLECTLTYPE(CEmployeeViewerCtrl)       // Type name and misc status

// Message maps
      //{{AFX_MSG(CEmployeeViewerCtrl)
      afx_msg int OnCreate(LPCREATESTRUCT lpCreateStruct);
      afx_msg void OnConnectClicked();
      afx_msg void OnDisconnectClicked();
      //}}AFX_MSG
      DECLARE_MESSAGE_MAP()

// Dispatch maps
      //{{AFX_DISPATCH(CEmployeeViewerCtrl)
      //}}AFX_DISPATCH
      DECLARE_DISPATCH_MAP()

      afx_msg void AboutBox();

// Event maps
      //{{AFX_EVENT(CEmployeeViewerCtrl)
      //}}AFX_EVENT
      DECLARE_EVENT_MAP()

// Dispatch and event IDs
public:
      enum {
      //{{AFX_DISP_ID(CEmployeeViewerCtrl)
      //}}AFX_DISP_ID
      };
};

//{{AFX_INSERT_LOCATION}}
// Microsoft Developer Studio will insert additional declarations immediately
// before the previous line.

#endif //
!defined(AFX_EMPLOYEEVIEWERCTL_H__A7BAC253_FDCA_11D0_B7DF_444553540000__INCLUDED)
```

15. Back in the `EMPLOYEEVIEWERCTL.CPP` file, move down to the Message Map section and add the boldface lines of code in Listing 10-7 to the file to connect the buttons with their event handler methods. Save the project.

Listing 10-7 EMPLOYEEVIEWERCTL.CPP message map macros source code

```
/////////////////////////////////////////////////////////////////////////////
// Message map

BEGIN_MESSAGE_MAP(CEmployeeViewerCtrl, COleControl)
	//{{AFX_MSG_MAP(CEmployeeViewerCtrl)
	ON_WM_CREATE()
	//}}AFX_MSG_MAP
	ON_OLEVERB(AFX_IDS_VERB_PROPERTIES, OnProperties)
	 ON_BN_CLICKED(IDC_CONNECT, OnConnectClicked )
	 ON_BN_CLICKED(IDC_DISCONNECT, OnDisconnectClicked )
END_MESSAGE_MAP()
```

16. Move down to the constructor and destructor method stubs and add the boldface code in Listing 10-8 to shut down the database connection when the control is destroyed, in case the user forgets to press the Disconnect button. Save the project.

Listing 10-8 EMPLOYEEVIEWERCTL.CPP destructor source code

```
/////////////////////////////////////////////////////////////////////////////
// CEmployeeViewerCtrl::~CEmployeeViewerCtrl - Destructor

CEmployeeViewerCtrl::~CEmployeeViewerCtrl()
{
	// TODO: Cleanup your control's instance data here.
		if (m_pAdoWrapper != NULL)
		delete m_pAdoWrapper;
}
```

17. Move to the end of the file and add the code in Listing 10-9 for the button click event handlers. Save the project.

Listing 10-9 EMPLOYEEVIEWERCTL.CPP button click event handlers source code

```
void CEmployeeViewerCtrl::OnConnectClicked()
{
	if(!m_pAdoWrapper->ConnectToDB())
	{
		m_pAdoWrapper->m_fConnectedtoDB = FALSE;
		return;
	}

	m_pAdoWrapper->m_fConnectedtoDB = TRUE;
```

```
        m_FirstName.SetWindowText( m_pAdoWrapper->GetTheFirstName() );
        m_LastName.SetWindowText( m_pAdoWrapper->GetTheLastName() );
        m_JobTitle.SetWindowText( m_pAdoWrapper->GetTheJobTitle() );
        char idstring[5];
        wsprintf( idstring , "%d" , m_pAdoWrapper->GetTheEmployeeId() );
        m_EmployeeID.SetWindowText( idstring );
}

void CEmployeeViewerCtrl::OnDisconnectClicked()
{
            if (m_pAdoWrapper != NULL)
            delete m_pAdoWrapper;
}
```

18. Make sure you have copied the `Initguid.h` file from the CD to your project directory (it is done automatically when the CD installation program is run if you install the How-To code; otherwise, you will need to copy it manually and reset its `READONLY` flag). Select the Build|Build OCX menu option. If you get linker errors, you have most likely forgotten the `INITGUID.H` file. Aside from these problems, your control should build and register itself normally.

19. Start ActiveX Control Pad. Create a new HTML file and enter the HTML code in Listing 10-10 *except* for the `<OBJECT>` tag. Then use the Edit|Insert ActiveX control to place a copy of the EmployeeViewer control on the page between the `<HR>` tags, as shown in Figure 10-11. After you have inserted the control, change its `ExtentX` and `ExtentY` parameters to those in Listing 10-10. Save the file as `ASPHT1001.HTM`. (You need to insert it yourself because the control created on your machine will have a different `CLASSID`.)

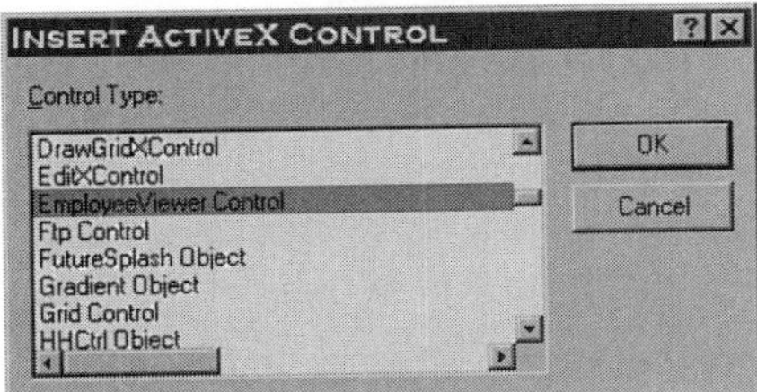

Figure 10-11 Placing the EmployeeViewer ActiveX control into the HTML file in ActiveX Control Pad

Listing 10-10 ASPHT1001.HTM HTML source code

```
<HTML>
<HEAD>
<TITLE>Active Server Pages How To Chapter Ten How To One</TITLE>
</HEAD>
<BODY>
This is a demo of an ActiveX Control using an ActiveX Data Objects Database!<P>
<HR>

<OBJECT ID="EmployeeViewer1" WIDTH=924 HEIGHT=407
 CLASSID="CLSID:A7BAC245-FDCA-11D0-B7DF-444553540000">
    <PARAM NAME="_Version" VALUE="65536">
    <PARAM NAME="_ExtentX" VALUE="24448">
    <PARAM NAME="_ExtentY" VALUE="10769">
    <PARAM NAME="_StockProps" VALUE="0">
</OBJECT>
<HR>
Press "Connect To Database" to see the first employee record.<P>
Press "Disconnect From Database" before navigating or closing IE!<P>
</BODY>
</HTML>
```

20. Bring up ASPHT1001.HTM in Internet Explorer. Press the Connect To Database button, and the first employee record should appear in the control's edit boxes, as shown in Figure 10-12. Congratulations! You now know how to use ADOs and OLE DB in Visual C++ with an ActiveX control.

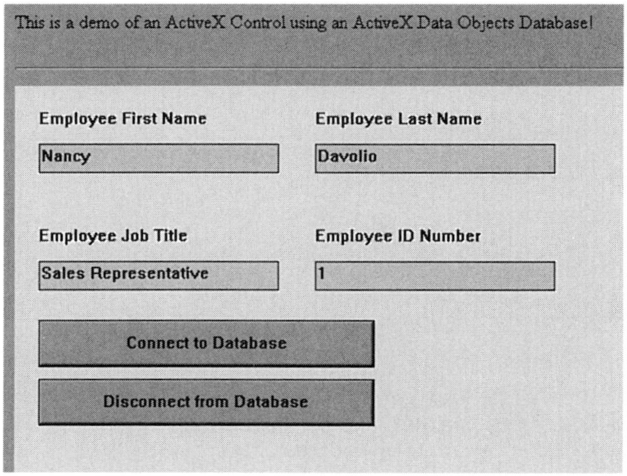

Figure 10-12 The EmployeeViewer control in IE showing the first record from the database

How It Works

Because this entire chapter is about ADO in C++, I'll defer some issues from this code to later How-To's for discussion. There are three points of major interest here: learning how to call ADO methods without documentation for C++, using MFC controls in an MFC ActiveX control (because it has no equivalent of the dialog editor for ActiveX controls), and the basics of raw COM programming.

In regard to using ADO without documentation, notice this section of code from the ADOINT.H file:

```
EXTERN_C const IID IID__Command;
#if defined(__cplusplus) && !defined(CINTERFACE)

    interface _ADOCommand : public _ADO
    {
    public:
        virtual /* [propget] */ HRESULT STDMETHODCALLTYPE get_ActiveConnection(
            /* [retval][out] */ _ADOConnection __RPC_FAR *__RPC_FAR *ppvObject) ⇐
            = 0;

        virtual /* [propputref] */ HRESULT STDMETHODCALLTYPE ⇐
            putref_ActiveConnection(
            /* [in] */ _ADOConnection __RPC_FAR *pCon) = 0;

        virtual /* [propput] */ HRESULT STDMETHODCALLTYPE put_ActiveConnection(
            /* [in] */ BSTR bstrConn) = 0;

        virtual /* [propget] */ HRESULT STDMETHODCALLTYPE get_CommandText(
            /* [retval][out] */ BSTR __RPC_FAR *pbstr) = 0;

        virtual /* [propput] */ HRESULT STDMETHODCALLTYPE put_CommandText(
            /* [in] */ BSTR bstr) = 0;

        virtual /* [propget] */ HRESULT STDMETHODCALLTYPE get_CommandTimeout(
            /* [retval][out] */ LONG __RPC_FAR *pl) = 0;

        virtual /* [propput] */ HRESULT STDMETHODCALLTYPE put_CommandTimeout(
            /* [in] */ LONG Timeout) = 0;

        virtual /* [propget] */ HRESULT STDMETHODCALLTYPE get_Prepared(
            /* [retval][out] */ VARIANT_BOOL __RPC_FAR *pfPrepared) = 0;

        virtual /* [propput] */ HRESULT STDMETHODCALLTYPE put_Prepared(
            /* [in] */ VARIANT_BOOL fPrepared) = 0;

        virtual /* [helpstring][helpcontext] */ HRESULT STDMETHODCALLTYPE Execute(
            /* [optional][out] */ VARIANT __RPC_FAR *RecordsAffected,
            /* [optional][in] */ VARIANT __RPC_FAR *Parameters,
            /* [defaultvalue][in] */ long Options,
            /* [retval][out] */ ADORecordset __RPC_FAR *__RPC_FAR *ppirs) = 0;

        virtual HRESULT STDMETHODCALLTYPE CreateParameter(
            /* [defaultvalue][in] */ BSTR Name,
```

continued on next page

continued from previous page

```
            /* [defaultvalue][in] */ DataTypeEnum Type,
            /* [defaultvalue][in] */ ParameterDirectionEnum Direction,
            /* [defaultvalue][in] */ long Size,
            /* [optional][in] */ VARIANT Value,
            /* [retval][out] */ _ADOParameter __RPC_FAR *__RPC_FAR *ppiprm) = 0;

        virtual /* [helpstring][helpcontext][id][propget] */ HRESULT ⇐
                STDMETHODCALLTYPE get_Parameters(
            /* [retval][out] */ ADOParameters __RPC_FAR *__RPC_FAR *ppvObject) ⇐
               = 0;

        virtual /* [propput] */ HRESULT STDMETHODCALLTYPE put_CommandType(
            /* [in] */ CommandTypeEnum lCmdType) = 0;

        virtual /* [propget] */ HRESULT STDMETHODCALLTYPE get_CommandType(
            /* [retval][out] */ CommandTypeEnum __RPC_FAR *plCmdType) = 0;

    };
```

This is where the C++ interfaces to the ADO system are documented. By carefully studying this and the **ADOID.H** header files, you can learn exactly how to match up the documented VBScript ADO functionality with C++ equivalents. As of this release of the OLE DB SDK, this is all the help you're going to get.

If you are a veteran MFC programmer, you may well be used to manipulating MFC controls outside the visual environment of the dialog editor. However, for many users new to MFC, the lack of a visual editor for ActiveX controls comes as a nasty surprise. The technique covered here is very useful for including MFC controls in situations where there is no visual editor or wizard to help out.

The technique breaks down into six steps. First, the objects that will create and display the controls must be added to the header file for the ActiveX control where they will live.

```
class CEmployeeViewerCtrl : public COleControl
{
      DECLARE_DYNCREATE(CEmployeeViewerCtrl)

// Constructor
public:
      CEmployeeViewerCtrl();
      CEdit m_FirstName;
      CEdit m_LastName;
      CEdit m_JobTitle;
      CEdit m_EmployeeID;
      CButton m_Connect;
      CButton m_Disconnect;
      CAdoWrapper*      m_pAdoWrapper;
```

Next, they must be added to the message map for the control so they can communicate with it using the standard message-handling macros. Notice that at this point the methods being referenced do not exist.

```
  // Message maps
//{{AFX_MSG(CEmployeeViewerCtrl)
afx_msg int OnCreate(LPCREATESTRUCT lpCreateStruct);
afx_msg void OnConnectClicked();
afx_msg void OnDisconnectClicked();
//}}AFX_MSG
DECLARE_MESSAGE_MAP()
```

Third, in the control's CPP file, the matching macros must be added to the Message Map section so that the appropriate messages are sent to the correct handler method. Although the `ON_BN_CLICKED` message macro is the only one used here, any other message could be handled as well, provided the base control generates it.

```
/////////////////////////////////////////////////////////////////////////////
// Message map

BEGIN_MESSAGE_MAP(CEmployeeViewerCtrl, COleControl)
      //{{AFX_MSG_MAP(CEmployeeViewerCtrl)
      ON_WM_CREATE()
      //}}AFX_MSG_MAP
      ON_OLEVERB(AFX_IDS_VERB_PROPERTIES, OnProperties)
      ON_BN_CLICKED(IDC_CONNECT, OnConnectClicked )
      ON_BN_CLICKED(IDC_DISCONNECT, OnDisconnectClicked )
END_MESSAGE_MAP()
```

Next, the control IDs must be created using the tool built into the VC++ Integrated Development Environment (the only automated part of this whole process). Remember to watch out for duplicate identifiers.

Fifth, the controls must be created by their `create` methods with the appropriate parameters. By doing this, you create their visual elements automatically, with no additional code needed in the `OnDraw` event handler. Also, any desired additional method or property interactions prior to display could take place here. Remember that you will have to override the `OnCreate` message handler supplied by MFC by attaching a message handler to `WM_CREATE`.

Each control type has a different constructor; for a CEdit control, the first parameter is a set of `OR`ed flags that control the appearance and behavior of the control. Then comes a `CRect` structure that is in pixels and defines the size of the control (don't forget that the third and fourth coordinates are absolute, not relative). Then comes a pointer to the object that will display the control (this serves quite handily here), followed by the integer constant used by the system to identify the control uniquely. Other constructors will have more data, such as a caption for the button controls, but most will have at least this much data.

```
int CEmployeeViewerCtrl::OnCreate(LPCREATESTRUCT lpCreateStruct)
{
      if (COleControl::OnCreate(lpCreateStruct) == -1)
            return -1;

      // TODO: Add your specialized creation code here
      m_FirstName.Create( WS_CHILD¦ WS_VISIBLE ¦ WS_BORDER ¦ ES_AUTOHSCROLL ,
            CRect( 20 , 50 , 220 , 75 ), this , IDC_FIRSTNAME );
      m_LastName.Create( WS_CHILD¦ WS_VISIBLE ¦ WS_BORDER ¦ ES_AUTOHSCROLL ,
            CRect( 250 , 50 , 450 , 75 ), this , IDC_LASTNAME );
      m_JobTitle.Create( WS_CHILD¦ WS_VISIBLE ¦ WS_BORDER ¦ ES_AUTOHSCROLL ,
            CRect( 20 , 150 , 220 , 175 ), this , IDC_JOBTITLE );
      m_EmployeeID.Create( WS_CHILD¦ WS_VISIBLE ¦ WS_BORDER ¦ ES_AUTOHSCROLL ,
            CRect( 250 , 150 , 450 , 175 ), this , IDC_EMPLOYEEID );
    m_Connect.Create("Connect to Database",WS_CHILD ¦ WS_VISIBLE ¦ WS_BORDER ⇐
            ¦BS_PUSHBUTTON ,
            CRect( 20 , 200 , 300 , 240) , this , IDC_CONNECT );
      m_Disconnect.Create("Disconnect from Database",WS_CHILD ¦ WS_VISIBLE ¦ ⇐
            WS_BORDER ¦BS_PUSHBUTTON ,
            CRect( 20 , 250 , 300 , 290) , this , IDC_DISCONNECT );
        return 0;
}
```

Finally, the actual message handlers must be defined and written so that everything will work. Unfortunately, all this must be done by hand, because at this time there isn't any support at all for this process.

```
void CEmployeeViewerCtrl::OnDisconnectClicked()
{
            if (m_pAdoWrapper != NULL)
            delete m_pAdoWrapper;
}
```

Let's look at how the actual `ADOConnection` and `ADORecordset` objects are created. Unfortunately, it isn't as simple as calling a `Create` constructor.

```
varDataSource           = g_lpcwszSource;
varUserId               = g_lpcwszUser;
varPwd                  = g_lpcwszPwd;
varSQL                  = g_lpcwszSQL;

try
{
      if ( m_piADOConnection == NULL ¦¦ m_piEmployeeRecordSet == NULL)
      {
            THROW_ERR(        CoInitialize(NULL) );
            THROW_ERR(        CoCreateInstance(CLSID_CADOConnection, NULL,
```

```
                    CLSCTX_INPROC_SERVER, IID_IADOConnection,
                    (LPVOID *)&m_piADOConnection) );
THROW_ERR(      m_piADOConnection->Open( varDataSource, varUserId,⇐
                varPwd ) );

THROW_ERR(      CoCreateInstance(CLSID_CADORecordset, NULL,
                    CLSCTX_INPROC_SERVER, IID_IADORecordset,
                    (LPVOID *)&m_piEmployeeRecordSet) );
```

This is raw COM programming. `CoInitialize` sets up the OLE system for creating COM interfaces. Then, `CoCreateInstance` attempts to create an actual object representing a COM interface. Which interface is determined by `CLSID_CADOConnection` and `IID_IADOConnection`. The former value is used to determine which overall COM object is being referenced, whereas the latter is the actual interface requested. If the connection is successful, this interface's pointer will return in `&m_piADOConnection`. A similar process takes place to get the `RecordSet` object through the `ADOConnection` interface. This is where the actual database login occurs, via the call to `Open`. If the call is successful, you can then set the `ADORecordset` interface (created after the call to open using the same technique) to connect with the database and return values from it.

```
THROW_ERR(m_piEmployeeRecordSet->putref_ActiveConnection(m_piADOConnection) );
THROW_ERR(m_piEmployeeRecordSet->put_Source(varSQL) );
vNull.vt = VT_ERROR;
vNull.scode = DISP_E_PARAMNOTFOUND;
THROW_ERR(m_piEmployeeRecordSet->Open(vNull, vNull,
        adOpenKeyset, adLockOptimistic, adCmdText) );
```

Here, the `ADOConnection` object is attached to the `ADORecordset` as its active connection. Then the SQL statement created earlier is placed as its source for getting records. With these items in place, a call is attempted to get the recordset via another `Open` method. This one takes parameters of the types of cursor and data lock as well as the way the data is returned.

This is enough to get started with ADO, but we'll dive more deeply into its powers in the coming How-To's!

Comments

Although all these How-To's demonstrate connections with an ODBC database, it is important to remember that ADO is specially designed to work with *any* datasource for which an OLD DB provider has been created, regardless of its format.

ADO-AXC

10.2 How do I... Allow user navigation in ADO with my C++ ActiveX control?

Problem

Our users need to be able to do user-interface–driven navigation in our ADO-supplied database. How much time is this going to cost us?

Technique

Less time than you think! ADO has a complete set of navigational methods, and this How-To will implement four of them to allow users to go to the first and last records in a database and move forward and backward in it. Although these directions create the project from scratch, the CD contains a completed file under `CH10\HT02\`.

Steps

1. Copy your project from How-To 10.1 to a new directory (or reuse the old one if you like). Open it in Visual C++ 5.0, bring up the `EMPLOYEEVIEWERCTL.H` file, and add the boldface code in Listing 10-11 to place four more MFC CommandButton controls on your ActiveX control's user interface.

Listing 10-11 `EMPLOYEEVIEWERCTL.H` **header file source code**

```
/////////////////////////////////////////////////////////////////////////////
// CEmployeeViewerCtrl : See EmployeeViewerCtl.cpp for implementation.

class CEmployeeViewerCtrl : public COleControl
{
      DECLARE_DYNCREATE(CEmployeeViewerCtrl)

// Constructor
public:
      CEmployeeViewerCtrl();
      CEdit m_FirstName;
      CEdit m_LastName;
      CEdit m_JobTitle;
      CEdit m_EmployeeID;
      CButton m_Connect;
      CButton m_Disconnect;
```

```
CButton m_MoveFirst;
CButton m_MovePrevious;
CButton m_MoveNext;
CButton m_MoveLast;
```

2. Move down to the Message Map section and enter the boldface code in Listing 10-12 to link the four button messages to their event handlers. Save the project.

Listing 10-12 EMPLOYEEVIEWERCTL.H header file message map source code

```
// Message maps
    //{{AFX_MSG(CEmployeeViewerCtrl)
    afx_msg int OnCreate(LPCREATESTRUCT lpCreateStruct);
    afx_msg void OnConnectClicked();
    afx_msg void OnDisconnectClicked();
    afx_msg void OnMoveFirst();
    afx_msg void OnMovePrevious();
    afx_msg void OnMoveNext();
    afx_msg void OnMoveLast();
    //}}AFX_MSG
    DECLARE_MESSAGE_MAP()
```

3. Change to the `EMPLOYEEVIEWERCTL.CPP` file in the text editor. Move to the Message Map section of this file and enter the boldface code in Listing 10-13 to link the event handlers from the `.H` file to the IDs of the MFC controls. Save the project.

Listing 10-13 EMPLOYEEVIEWERCTL.CPP message map source code

```
/////////////////////////////////////////////////////////////////////////////
// Message map

BEGIN_MESSAGE_MAP(CEmployeeViewerCtrl, COleControl)
    //{{AFX_MSG_MAP(CEmployeeViewerCtrl)
    ON_WM_CREATE()
    //}}AFX_MSG_MAP
    ON_OLEVERB(AFX_IDS_VERB_PROPERTIES, OnProperties)
    ON_BN_CLICKED(IDC_CONNECT, OnConnectClicked )
    ON_BN_CLICKED(IDC_DISCONNECT, OnDisconnectClicked )
    ON_BN_CLICKED(IDC_MOVEFIRST, OnMoveFirst )
    ON_BN_CLICKED(IDC_MOVEPREVIOUS, OnMovePrevious )
    ON_BN_CLICKED(IDC_MOVENEXT, OnMoveNext )
    ON_BN_CLICKED(IDC_MOVELAST, OnMoveLast )
END_MESSAGE_MAP()
```

4. Move down to the `OnCreate` event handler and enter the boldface code in Listing 10-14 to initialize the four MFC CommandButton controls. Save the project.

Listing 10-14 EMPLOYEEVIEWERCTL.CPP OnCreate source code

```
int CEmployeeViewerCtrl::OnCreate(LPCREATESTRUCT lpCreateStruct)
{
    if (COleControl::OnCreate(lpCreateStruct) == -1)
        return -1;

    // TODO: Add your specialized creation code here
    m_FirstName.Create( WS_CHILD¦ WS_VISIBLE ¦ WS_BORDER ¦ ES_AUTOHSCROLL ,
        CRect( 20 , 50 , 220 , 75 ), this , IDC_FIRSTNAME );
    m_LastName.Create( WS_CHILD¦ WS_VISIBLE ¦ WS_BORDER ¦ ES_AUTOHSCROLL ,
        CRect( 250 , 50 , 450 , 75 ), this , IDC_LASTNAME );
    m_JobTitle.Create( WS_CHILD¦ WS_VISIBLE ¦ WS_BORDER ¦ ES_AUTOHSCROLL ,
        CRect( 20 , 150 , 220 , 175 ), this , IDC_JOBTITLE );
    m_EmployeeID.Create( WS_CHILD¦ WS_VISIBLE ¦ WS_BORDER ¦ ES_AUTOHSCROLL ,
        CRect( 250 , 150 , 450 , 175 ), this , IDC_EMPLOYEEID );
     m_Connect.Create("Connect to Database",WS_CHILD ¦ WS_VISIBLE ¦ WS_BORDER⇐
                    ¦BS_PUSHBUTTON ,
        CRect( 20 , 200 , 300 , 240) , this , IDC_CONNECT );
    m_Disconnect.Create("Disconnect from Database",WS_CHILD ¦WS_VISIBLE ¦ ⇐
                    WS_BORDER ¦BS_PUSHBUTTON ,
        CRect( 20 , 250 , 300 , 290) , this , IDC_DISCONNECT );
    m_MoveFirst.Create("Move to First Record",WS_CHILD ¦ WS_VISIBLE ¦ ⇐
                    WS_BORDER ¦BS_PUSHBUTTON ,
        CRect( 320 , 200 , 600 , 240) , this , IDC_MOVEFIRST );
    m_MovePrevious.Create("Move to Previous Record",WS_CHILD ¦ WS_VISIBLE ¦ ⇐
                    WS_BORDER ¦BS_PUSHBUTTON ,
        CRect( 320 , 250 , 600 , 290) , this , IDC_MOVEPREVIOUS );
    m_MoveNext.Create("Move to Next Record",WS_CHILD ¦ WS_VISIBLE ¦ WS_BORDER ⇐
                    ¦BS_PUSHBUTTON ,
        CRect( 320 , 300 , 600 , 340) , this , IDC_MOVENEXT );
    m_MoveLast.Create("Move to Last Record",WS_CHILD ¦ WS_VISIBLE ¦ WS_BORDER ⇐
                    ¦BS_PUSHBUTTON ,
        CRect( 320 , 350 , 600 , 390) , this , IDC_MOVELAST );return 0;
}
```

5. Bring up the Resource Identifiers dialog and add the four new IDs for the navigation buttons, using the default values supplied by the system. Save the project.

6. Move to the end of the file and enter the code in Listing 10-15 to add handler code for the buttons. Save the project.

Listing 10-15 EMPLOYEEVIEWERCTL.CPP event handler source code

```
void CEmployeeViewerCtrl::OnMoveFirstClicked()
{
    try
    {
        if(m_pAdoWrapper->MoveFirst())
        {
        try
            {
        m_FirstName.SetWindowText( m_pAdoWrapper->GetFirstName() );
          m_LastName.SetWindowText( m_pAdoWrapper->GetLastName() );
```

```
            m_JobTitle.SetWindowText( m_pAdoWrapper->GetTitle() );
              char idstring[5];
              wsprintf( idstring , "%d" , m_pAdoWrapper->GetEmployeeId() );
              m_EmployeeID.SetWindowText( idstring );
              }
          catch (HRESULT hr)
              {
                TCHAR szBuf[256];
                MessageBeep(0);
                wsprintf(szBuf, _T("Error: %X \n"), hr);
                AfxMessageBox(szBuf);
                    return;
              }
              Refresh();
        }
        else
              MessageBeep(0);
  }
  catch( HRESULT hr )
  {
        TCHAR szBuf[256];
        wsprintf(szBuf, _T("Error: %X \n"), hr);
        AfxMessageBox(szBuf);
  }
}

void CEmployeeViewerCtrl::OnMovePreviousClicked()
{

  try
  {
        if(m_pAdoWrapper->MovePrevious())
        {
        try
              {
            m_FirstName.SetWindowText( m_pAdoWrapper->GetFirstName() );
              m_LastName.SetWindowText( m_pAdoWrapper->GetLastName() );
            m_JobTitle.SetWindowText( m_pAdoWrapper->GetTitle() );
              char idstring[5];
              wsprintf( idstring , "%d" , m_pAdoWrapper->GetEmployeeId() );
              m_EmployeeID.SetWindowText( idstring );
              }
          catch (HRESULT hr)
              {
                TCHAR szBuf[256];
                MessageBeep(0);
                wsprintf(szBuf, _T("Error: %X \n"), hr);
                AfxMessageBox(szBuf);
                    return;
              }
              Refresh();
        }
        else
              MessageBeep(0);
  }
```

continued on next page

continued from previous page

```
        catch( HRESULT hr )
        {
                TCHAR szBuf[256];
                wsprintf(szBuf, _T("Error: %X \n"), hr);
                AfxMessageBox(szBuf);
        }
}

void CEmployeeViewerCtrl::OnMoveNextClicked()
{
        try
        {
                if(m_pAdoWrapper->MoveNext())
                {
                try
                        {
                    m_FirstName.SetWindowText( m_pAdoWrapper->GetFirstName() );
                        m_LastName.SetWindowText( m_pAdoWrapper->GetLastName() );
                    m_JobTitle.SetWindowText( m_pAdoWrapper->GetTitle() );
                        char idstring[5];
                        wsprintf( idstring , "%d" , m_pAdoWrapper->GetEmployeeId() );
                        m_EmployeeID.SetWindowText( idstring );
                        }
                    catch (HRESULT hr)
                        {
                          TCHAR szBuf[256];
                          MessageBeep(0);
                          wsprintf(szBuf, _T("Error: %X \n"), hr);
                          AfxMessageBox(szBuf);
                              return;
                        }
                Refresh();
                }
                else
                        MessageBeep(0);
        }
        catch( HRESULT hr )
        {
                TCHAR szBuf[256];
                wsprintf(szBuf, _T("Error: %X \n"), hr);
                AfxMessageBox(szBuf);
        }
}

void CEmployeeViewerCtrl::OnMoveLastClicked()
{
        try
        {
                if(m_pAdoWrapper->MoveLast())
                {
                try
                        {
                    m_FirstName.SetWindowText( m_pAdoWrapper->GetFirstName() );
                        m_LastName.SetWindowText( m_pAdoWrapper->GetLastName() );
                    m_JobTitle.SetWindowText( m_pAdoWrapper->GetTitle() );
```

```
                  char idstring[5];
                  wsprintf( idstring , "%d" , m_pAdoWrapper->GetEmployeeId() );
                  m_EmployeeID.SetWindowText( idstring );
                  }
              catch (HRESULT hr)
                  {
                    TCHAR szBuf[256];
                    MessageBeep(0);
                    wsprintf(szBuf, _T("Error: %X \n"), hr);
                    AfxMessageBox(szBuf);
                        return;
                  }
                Refresh();
            }
            else
                  MessageBeep(0);
      }
      catch( HRESULT hr )
      {
            TCHAR szBuf[256];
            wsprintf(szBuf, _T("Error: %X \n"), hr);
            AfxMessageBox(szBuf);
      }
}
```

7. Now bring up the `ADOWRAPPER.H` file in the text editor. Enter the boldface code in Listing 10-16 to add the new methods for the navigation functionality to the `CAdoWrapper` object. Save the project.

Listing 10-16 `ADOWRAPPER.H` header file source code

```
// AdoWrapper.h : header file
//

/////////////////////////////////////////////////////////////////////////////
// CAdoWrapper dialog

class CAdoWrapper
{
// Construction
public:
      CAdoWrapper();        // standard constructor
      ~CAdoWrapper();

// Attributes
public:
      ADORecordset*    m_piEmpRecordSet;
      BOOL             m_fConnected;
      BOOL             m_fRecordsetEmpty;

protected:
      ADOConnection*    m_piConnection;
      COleVariant       m_varLastGoodRecord;
```

continued on next page

continued from previous page

```
// Operations
public:
      BOOL      ConnectToDatabase(); //Opens a database
      long      GetEmployeeId();
      CString GetFirstName();
      CString GetLastName();
      CString GetHomePhone() ;
      CString GetTitle() ;
      BOOL      MoveNext()       ;
      BOOL      MovePrevious();
      BOOL      MoveFirst() ;
      BOOL      MoveLast();
       void   ClearFilter();
};


#define EMP_EMPLOYEE_ID       L"EmployeeID"
#define EMP_LAST_NAME         L"LastName"
#define EMP_FIRST_NAME        L"FirstName"
#define EMP_TITLE             L"Title"
#define EMP_HOME_PHONE        L"HomePhone"
```

8. Bring up `ADOWRAPPER.CPP` in the text editor and enter the code in Listing 10-17 to add the navigation functionality to the object. Save the project.

Listing 10-17 `ADOWRAPPER.CPP` navigation methods source code

```
BOOL CAdoWrapper::MoveNext()
{
      // TODO: Add your control notification handler code here
      HRESULT            hr;
      VARIANT_BOOL vbEOF;

      if (!m_fConnected || m_fRecordsetEmpty)
            return FALSE;

      ClearFilter() ;

      THROW_ERR(      m_piEmpRecordSet->MoveNext() );

      //Watch for end of record set
      THROW_ERR(      m_piEmpRecordSet->get_EOF(&vbEOF) );
      if(vbEOF)
      {
            THROW_ERR(      m_piEmpRecordSet->MovePrevious() );
            return FALSE;
      }
      else
      {
```

```
            return TRUE;
        }
}


BOOL CAdoWrapper::MovePrevious()
{
        // TODO: Add your control notification handler code here
        HRESULT             hr;
        VARIANT_BOOL vbBOF;

        if (!m_fConnected || m_fRecordsetEmpty)
              return FALSE;

        ClearFilter() ;

        THROW_ERR(      m_piEmpRecordSet->MovePrevious() );

        //Watch for beginning of recordset
        THROW_ERR(      m_piEmpRecordSet->get_BOF(&vbBOF) );
        if(vbBOF)
        {
              THROW_ERR(      m_piEmpRecordSet->MoveNext() );
              return FALSE;
        }
        else
        {
              return TRUE;
        }
}


BOOL CAdoWrapper::MoveFirst()
{
        // TODO: Add your control notification handler code here
        HRESULT             hr;
        VARIANT_BOOL vbBOF;

        if (!m_fConnected || m_fRecordsetEmpty)
              return FALSE;

        ClearFilter() ;

        THROW_ERR(      m_piEmpRecordSet->MoveFirst() );

        //Watch for beginning of recordset
        THROW_ERR(      m_piEmpRecordSet->get_BOF(&vbBOF) );
        if(vbBOF)
        {
              return FALSE;
        }
```

continued on next page

continued from previous page

```
        else
        {
                return TRUE;
        }
}


BOOL CAdoWrapper::MoveLast()
{
        // TODO: Add your control notification handler code here
        HRESULT         hr;
        VARIANT_BOOL vbEOF;

        if (!m_fConnected || m_fRecordsetEmpty)
                return FALSE;

        ClearFilter() ;

        THROW_ERR(      m_piEmpRecordSet->MoveLast() );

        //Watch for beginning of recordset
        THROW_ERR(      m_piEmpRecordSet->get_BOF(&vbEOF) );
        if(vbEOF)
        {
                return FALSE;
        }
        else
        {
                return TRUE;
        }
}

void CAdoWrapper::ClearFilter()
{
        HRESULT         hr;
        VARIANT         v;

        if ( !m_fRecordsetEmpty)
        {
                v.vt = VT_I2;
                v.iVal = adFilterNone;
                THROW_ERR(      m_piEmpRecordSet->put_Filter(v) );
        }
}
```

9. Build the OCX. You should not encounter errors; if you do, make sure you used `INITGUID.H`. Also make sure the OCX is registered on the `C:` drive.

10. You can reuse ASPHT1001.HTM to redisplay the new ActiveX control or create a new file, but it will need the same functionality. Once the control is displayed, click the Connect button, then the Next button. As shown in Figure 10-13, the control will immediately display the second record in the database. Experiment with the other buttons and you will find they take you where you want to go! You have learned to add full user database navigation via ADO to your custom ActiveX control.

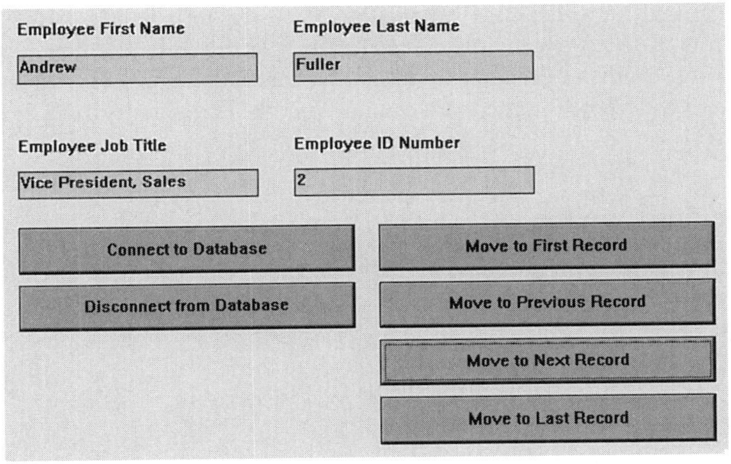

Employee First Name
Andrew
Employee Last Name
Fuller
Employee Job Title
Vice President, Sales
Employee ID Number
2
Connect to Database
Disconnect from Database
Move to First Record
Move to Previous Record
Move to Next Record
Move to Last Record

Figure 10-13 Navigating in the database via ADO

How It Works

This How-To begins to focus on *using* ADO, rather than doing all the grunt work to make it available. Let's look at the three issues needed for all ADO database navigation: testing for connection and data, clearing the filter, and watching for the end or beginning of the database.

First, notice these checks (I'll use the MoveNext method as the example, but the technique applies to all the methods):

```
if (!m_fConnected || m_fRecordsetEmpty)
    return FALSE;
```

The m_fConnected and m_fRecordsetEmpty member variables are both set at creation and database initialization. If the database isn't successfully connected, m_fConnected will always be false, avoiding GPF and other fun events when trying to reference a nonexistent COM pointer. However, even if the database exists and has been successfully connected, it may have no data! This is the province of the m_fRecordsetEmpty variable. It starts out false, but if both BOF and EOF are true on connection, then it is set to true to indicate no available data. In either case, the method aborts gracefully.

Directly after the status check comes a call to the `ClearFilter` method. Here's its relevant code:

```
if ( !m_fRecordsetEmpty)
{
     v.vt = VT_I2;
     v.iVal = adFilterNone;
     THROW_ERR(      m_piEmpRecordSet->put_Filter(v) );
}
```

Right now, this code doesn't make any difference because no filter has been applied to the database connection. However, in a few How-To's you'll add a `Find` method, which will use a filter. By placing this code now, you make sure that even after a `find` operation, normal navigation will work properly.

Finally, note the check for running past the end of data in the database.

```
ClearFilter() ;

THROW_ERR(      m_piEmpRecordSet->MoveNext() );

//Watch for end of record set
THROW_ERR(      m_piEmpRecordSet->get_EOF(&vbEOF) );
if(vbEOF)
{
      THROW_ERR(      m_piEmpRecordSet->MovePrevious() );
return FALSE;
}
else
{
      return TRUE;
}
```

After the `MoveNext` `COM` method is invoked, a check must be made using `get_EOF`. This method returns a value in its variant parameter (remember, COM methods return `HRESULTS` rather than actual results). If this parameter is set to `TRUE`, then the forward move has run past the end of data and a move back is needed, as well as a signal not to try that again (the `FALSE` return value).

Comments

It's important to remember that there are many more methods and properties of the ADO objects than can be covered here. This code will get you started with a good solid foundation you can build on, but to unlock the full power of ADOs in C++, you can do plenty more.

ADO-AXC

COMPLEXITY
ADVANCED

10.3 How do I… Allow user updates in ADO with my C++ ActiveX control?

Problem

We need to update our database directly from the user interface. Can ADO let our ActiveX control do this?

Technique

Information updates are an important part of ADO. This How-To will demonstrate adding user update capability to the developing EmployeeViewer ActiveX control. Although these directions create the project from scratch, the CD contains a completed file under `CH010\HT03\`.

Steps

1. Copy your project from How-To 10.2 to a new directory (or reuse the old one if you like). Open it in Visual C++ 5.0, bring up the `EMPLOYEEVIEWERCTL.H` file, and add the boldface code in Listing 10-18 to add the `update` method to the control's class definition.

Listing 10-18 `EMPLOYEEVIEWERCTL.H` header file source code

```
class CEmployeeViewerCtrl : public COleControl
{
      DECLARE_DYNCREATE(CEmployeeViewerCtrl)

// Constructor
public:
      CEmployeeViewerCtrl();
      CEdit m_FirstName;
      CEdit m_LastName;
      CEdit m_JobTitle;
      CEdit m_EmployeeID;
      CButton m_Connect;
      CButton m_Disconnect;
      CButton m_MoveFirst;
      CButton m_MovePrevious;
      CButton m_MoveNext;
      CButton m_MoveLast;
      CAdoWrapper*  m_pAdoWrapper;
      BOOL CommitAlteredEmpRec();
```

2. Bring up the `EMPLOYEEVIEWERCTL.CPP` file in the text editor and locate each of the four navigation methods. Enter the boldface code in Listing 10-19 to add updating to the behavior of the control. Save the project.

Listing 10-19 EMPLOYEEVIEWERCTL.CPP event handler source code

```
void CEmployeeViewerCtrl::OnMoveFirstClicked()
{
      if(!CommitAlteredEmpRec())
            return;

      try
      {
            if(m_pAdoWrapper->MoveFirst())
            {
            try
                  {
                m_FirstName.SetWindowText( m_pAdoWrapper->GetFirstName() );
                  m_LastName.SetWindowText( m_pAdoWrapper->GetLastName() );
                m_JobTitle.SetWindowText( m_pAdoWrapper->GetTitle() );
                  char idstring[5];
                  wsprintf( idstring , "%d" , m_pAdoWrapper->GetEmployeeId() );
                  m_EmployeeID.SetWindowText( idstring );
                  }
              catch (HRESULT hr)
                  {
                    TCHAR szBuf[256];
                    MessageBeep(0);
                    wsprintf(szBuf, _T("Error: %X \n"), hr);
                    AfxMessageBox(szBuf);
                        return;
                  }
                  Refresh();
            }
            else
                  MessageBeep(0);
      }
      catch( HRESULT hr )
      {
            TCHAR szBuf[256];
            wsprintf(szBuf, _T("Error: %X \n"), hr);
            AfxMessageBox(szBuf);
      }
}

void CEmployeeViewerCtrl::OnMovePreviousClicked()
{
      if(!CommitAlteredEmpRec())
            return;

      try
      {
            if(m_pAdoWrapper->MovePrevious())
            {
```

```
            try
                {
              m_FirstName.SetWindowText( m_pAdoWrapper->GetFirstName() );
                m_LastName.SetWindowText( m_pAdoWrapper->GetLastName() );
              m_JobTitle.SetWindowText( m_pAdoWrapper->GetTitle() );
                char idstring[5];
                wsprintf( idstring , "%d" , m_pAdoWrapper->GetEmployeeId() );
                m_EmployeeID.SetWindowText( idstring );
                }
             catch (HRESULT hr)
                {
                  TCHAR szBuf[256];
                  MessageBeep(0);
                  wsprintf(szBuf, _T("Error: %X \n"), hr);
                  AfxMessageBox(szBuf);
                      return;
                }
                Refresh();
            }
            else
                MessageBeep(0);
        }
        catch( HRESULT hr )
        {
            TCHAR szBuf[256];
            wsprintf(szBuf, _T("Error: %X \n"), hr);
            AfxMessageBox(szBuf);
        }
}

void CEmployeeViewerCtrl::OnMoveNextClicked()
{
        if(!CommitAlteredEmpRec())
            return;

        try
        {
            if(m_pAdoWrapper->MoveNext())
            {
            try
                {
              m_FirstName.SetWindowText( m_pAdoWrapper->GetFirstName() );
                m_LastName.SetWindowText( m_pAdoWrapper->GetLastName() );
              m_JobTitle.SetWindowText( m_pAdoWrapper->GetTitle() );
                char idstring[5];
                wsprintf( idstring , "%d" , m_pAdoWrapper->GetEmployeeId() );
                m_EmployeeID.SetWindowText( idstring );
                }
             catch (HRESULT hr)
                {
                  TCHAR szBuf[256];
                  MessageBeep(0);
                  wsprintf(szBuf, _T("Error: %X \n"), hr);
                  AfxMessageBox(szBuf);
```

continued on next page

continued from previous page

```
                        return;
                    }
            Refresh();
            }
            else
                MessageBeep(0);
        }
        catch( HRESULT hr )
        {
            TCHAR szBuf[256];
            wsprintf(szBuf, _T("Error: %X \n"), hr);
            AfxMessageBox(szBuf);
        }
}

void CEmployeeViewerCtrl::OnMoveLastClicked()
{
        if(!CommitAlteredEmpRec())
            return;

        try
        {
            if(m_pAdoWrapper->MoveLast())
            {
            try
                {
                m_FirstName.SetWindowText( m_pAdoWrapper->GetFirstName() );
                  m_LastName.SetWindowText( m_pAdoWrapper->GetLastName() );
                m_JobTitle.SetWindowText( m_pAdoWrapper->GetTitle() );
                  char idstring[5];
                  wsprintf( idstring , "%d" , m_pAdoWrapper->GetEmployeeId() );
                  m_EmployeeID.SetWindowText( idstring );
                }
              catch (HRESULT hr)
                {
                  TCHAR szBuf[256];
                  MessageBeep(0);
                  wsprintf(szBuf, _T("Error: %X \n"), hr);
                  AfxMessageBox(szBuf);
                      return;
                }
                Refresh();
            }
            else
                MessageBeep(0);
        }
        catch( HRESULT hr )
        {
            TCHAR szBuf[256];
            wsprintf(szBuf, _T("Error: %X \n"), hr);
            AfxMessageBox(szBuf);
        }
}
```

3. Move to the end of the file and enter the code in Listing 10-20 to handle the new method that actually updates the data. Save the project.

Listing 10-20 EMPLOYEEVIEWERCTL.CPP update handler source code

```
BOOL CEmployeeViewerCtrl::CommitAlteredEmpRec()
{
      CString       strOldFirstName, strOldHomePhone, strOldLastName, strOldTitle;
      COleVariant   vFirstName, vHomePhone, vLastName, vTitle, vID;

      if (!m_pAdoWrapper->m_fConnected)
            return FALSE;

      //Get current record string values
      try
      {
            strOldFirstName = m_pAdoWrapper->GetFirstName();
            strOldLastName = m_pAdoWrapper->GetLastName();
            strOldHomePhone = "237-2675";
            strOldTitle = m_pAdoWrapper->GetTitle();
      }
      catch(HRESULT  hr )
      {
            TCHAR szBuf[256];
            wsprintf(szBuf, _T("Error: %X \n"), hr);
            AfxMessageBox(szBuf);
            return FALSE;
      }

      //Force DDX to update member values
      UpdateData();
      CString      strCriteria = "";
    CString strFirstName = "";
      CString strLastName = "";
      CString strJobTitle = "";

    m_FirstName.GetWindowText( strFirstName );
      m_LastName.GetWindowText( strLastName );
      m_JobTitle.GetWindowText( strJobTitle );

      // Did any fields change value?
      if(
      (strFirstName      == strOldFirstName       ) &&
      (strLastName       == strOldLastName        ) &&
      (strJobTitle       == strOldTitle           ) && !m_pAdoWrapper->IsAddMode() )
            return TRUE;

      //Save it, dump it or stay on it?
      switch (AfxMessageBox(IDS_PROMPT_COMMIT_EMPREC, MB_YESNOCANCEL))
      {
            case IDYES:
            {
                  try
                  {
```

continued on next page

continued from previous page

```
                    m_pAdoWrapper ->UpdateEmpRec(strFirstName,
                                                 strOldHomePhone,
                                                 strLastName,
                                                 strJobTitle);
                }
                catch (CMemoryException &memx)
                {
                    TCHAR szBuf[256];
                    memx.GetErrorMessage(szBuf, sizeof(szBuf), NULL);
                    AfxMessageBox(szBuf);
                    return FALSE;
                }
                catch(HRESULT  hr )
                {
                    TCHAR szBuf[256];
                    wsprintf(szBuf, _T("Error: %X \n"), hr);
                    AfxMessageBox(szBuf);
                    return FALSE;
                }

                return TRUE;
            }

            case IDNO:
            {
                return TRUE;
            }

            default:
            {
                return TRUE;
            }
        }
            return TRUE;
}
```

4. Now bring up the `ADOWRAPPER.H` file in the text editor. Enter the boldface code in Listing 10-21 to add the new methods for update functionality to the `CAdoWrapper` object. Save the project.

Listing 10-21 `ADOWRAPPER.H` header file source code

```
// AdoWrapper.h : header file
//

/////////////////////////////////////////////////////////////////////////////
// CAdoWrapper dialog

class CAdoWrapper
{
// Construction
public:
    CAdoWrapper();      // standard constructor
```

```
    ~CAdoWrapper();

// Attributes
public:
    ADORecordset*       m_piEmpRecordSet;
    BOOL                m_fConnected;
    BOOL                m_fRecordsetEmpty;

protected:
    ADOConnection*              m_piConnection;
    COleVariant               m_varLastGoodRecord;

// Operations
public:
    BOOL      ConnectToDatabase(); //Opens a database
    long      GetEmployeeId();
    CString GetFirstName();
    CString GetLastName();
    CString GetHomePhone() ;
    CString GetTitle() ;
    BOOL      MoveNext()       ;
    BOOL      MovePrevious();
    BOOL      MoveFirst() ;
    BOOL      MoveLast();
    void      ClearFilter();
    BOOL      IsAddMode();
    void      UpdateEmpRec(CString &strFirstName,
                  CString &strHomePhone, CString &strLastName,
                  CString &strTitle);
};


#define EMP_EMPLOYEE_ID       L"EmployeeID"
#define EMP_LAST_NAME         L"LastName"
#define EMP_FIRST_NAME        L"FirstName"
#define EMP_TITLE             L"Title"
#define EMP_HOME_PHONE        L"HomePhone"
```

5. Bring up `ADOWRAPPER.CPP` in the text editor and enter the code in Listing 10-22 to add the update functionality to the object. Save the project.

Listing 10-22 `ADOWRAPPER.CPP` `Update` method source code

```
BOOL CAdoWrapper::IsAddMode()
{
    HRESULT                hr;
    EditModeEnum       lEditMode;

    THROW_ERR(      m_piEmpRecordSet->get_EditMode(&lEditMode) );

    return lEditMode == adEditAdd ;
}
```

continued on next page

continued from previous page

```
void CAdoWrapper::UpdateEmpRec(CString &strFirstName,
                  CString &strHomePhone, CString &strLastName,
                  CString &strTitle)
{
      HRESULT            hr;
      VARIANT            varFields;
      VARIANT            varValues;
      WCHAR            *columnNames[4] = { L"firstName", L"Lastname", L"title", ⇐
                                           L"homePhone"};
      ADOFields      *pFields = NULL;
      ADOField      *pField = NULL;
      CVar            varIndex(VT_BSTR);
      COleVariant      varFieldVal;

      if  (m_fRecordsetEmpty)
            return;

      varFields.vt = VT_ERROR;
      varFields.scode = DISP_E_PARAMNOTFOUND;
      varValues.vt = VT_ERROR;
      varValues.scode = DISP_E_PARAMNOTFOUND;

      try
      {
            // get the fields interface
            THROW_ERR(       m_piEmpRecordSet->get_Fields(&pFields) );

            varIndex = SysAllocString(columnNames[0]) ;
            THROW_ERR(       pFields->get_Item(varIndex, &pField) );
            varFieldVal.vt = VT_BSTR;
            varFieldVal.bstrVal = strFirstName.AllocSysString();
            THROW_ERR(       pField->put_Value(varFieldVal) );
            varFieldVal.Clear();

            varIndex = SysAllocString(columnNames[1]) ;
            THROW_ERR(       pFields->get_Item(varIndex, &pField) );
            varFieldVal.vt = VT_BSTR;
            varFieldVal.bstrVal = strLastName.AllocSysString();
            THROW_ERR(       pField->put_Value(varFieldVal) );
            varFieldVal.Clear();

            varIndex = SysAllocString(columnNames[2]) ;
            THROW_ERR(       pFields->get_Item(varIndex, &pField) );
            varFieldVal.vt = VT_BSTR;
            varFieldVal.bstrVal = strTitle.AllocSysString();
            THROW_ERR(       pField->put_Value(varFieldVal) );
            varFieldVal.Clear();

            varIndex = SysAllocString(columnNames[3]) ;
            THROW_ERR(       pFields->get_Item(varIndex, &pField) );
            varFieldVal.vt = VT_BSTR;
            varFieldVal.bstrVal = strHomePhone.AllocSysString();
            THROW_ERR(       pField->put_Value(varFieldVal) );
            varFieldVal.Clear();

            //Commit the changes
```

```
        THROW_ERR(      m_piEmpRecordSet->Update(varFields, varValues) );

        pField->Release();
        pFields->Release();

        //Return to the edited record
        //CADOBookmark cBookmark = m_piEmpRecordSet->GetLastModified();
        //m_piEmpRecordSet->SetBookmark(cBookmark);
    }
    catch (HRESULT hr)
    {
        if (pField)
            pField->Release();
        if (pFields)
            pFields->Release();
        throw hr;
    }
    return ;
}
```

6. Build the OCX. You should not encounter errors; if you do, make sure you used `INITGUID.H`. Also make sure the OCX is registered on the `C:` drive.

7. You can reuse `ASPHT1001.HTM` to redisplay the new ActiveX control or create a new file, but it will need the same functionality. When the control is displayed, click the Connect button, then the Next button four times. Alter the information on the display; then navigate backward or forward. A confirmation dialog will appear; press OK to commit your changes. Move back to record 5 and, as shown in Figure 10-14, the control will now display the changed record in the database. Your ADO war chest in C++ now includes updating records from user input.

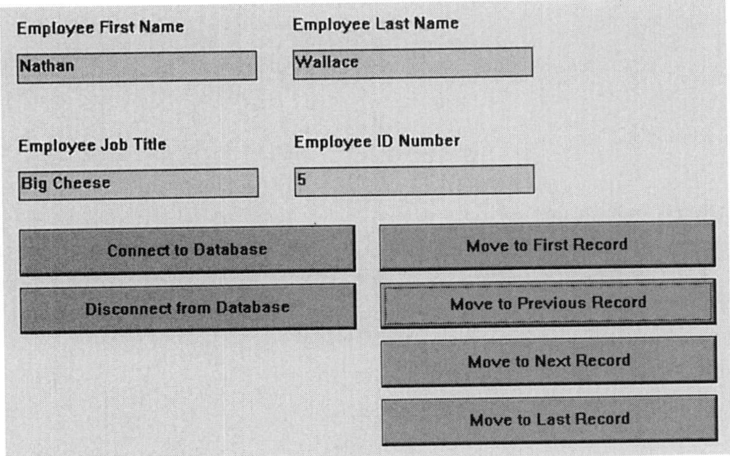

Figure 10-14 Updating in the database via ADO

How It Works

This is an unusually powerful How-To, and so it has more than its share of complexity, all of which lives in the **UpdateEmpRec** method of the **AdoWrapper** object. Let's examine its code in careful detail, starting with the code to obtain the Fields interface to the record being edited.

```
THROW_ERR(    m_piEmpRecordSet->get_Fields(&pFields) );
```

This object holds a pointer to the interface that accesses the individual fields of the record. Once it has been obtained, you can access a specific field.

```
varIndex = SysAllocString(columnNames[0]) ;
THROW_ERR(        pFields->get_Item(varIndex, &pField) );
```

Note that the **columnnames** array is preset to the four known fields of the record. A system string is created via **SysAllocString** for export across the OLE system. Then the **get_Item** method of the Fields interface is called, with the name of the field to get from the array and a pointer that will be filled with the **field** object if successful.

Once the **field** object is retrieved, its value needs to be reset.

```
varFieldVal.vt = VT_BSTR;
varFieldVal.bstrVal = strFirstName.AllocSysString();
THROW_ERR(        pField->put_Value(varFieldVal) );
varFieldVal.Clear();
```

The variant that will be needed to communicate with the ADO system has its type set to **BSTR**; then the first data field sends its information into the variant via another **AllocSysString** call. Next comes the actual placement of the data into the field via calling the **put_Value** method of the **field** object. The reusable **varFieldVal** is then cleared prior to its next use.

Once all four data fields have been set up, the actual change to the database must be made.

```
THROW_ERR(        m_piEmpRecordSet->Update(varFields, varValues) );

pField->Release();
pFields->Release();
```

Here, the **Update** method of the recordset is called with the two variants needed to handle any data it may send back. (The actual field data has already been written to the **pField** object, which is part of the current recordset and so doesn't need to be passed as a parameter.) Once the update has been successful, the two **Field** objects are released. (Remember, they are COM interfaces and so must be released rather than just deleted!)

We aren't quite done, though! Next, the database needs to be reset after the update operation to where it was.

```
//CADOBookmark cBookmark = m_piEmpRecordSet->GetLastModified();
//m_piEmpRecordSet->SetBookmark(cBookmark);
```

This code makes use of the bookmark capability of the ODBC database provider (not all providers support bookmarks). By obtaining the last modified record (which by definition is the one where we just were) and setting it as a bookmark, you automatically return the display is there.

Comments

Variants are a crucial part of COM, and ADO makes heavy use of them. Some time spent reading the documentation on `COleVariant` and its cousins would be a good investment for any prospective ADO developer.

ADO-AXC

10.4 How do I... Find records in the database with ADO in my C++ ActiveX control?

Problem

Our users often need to locate database records on one or two keys. Can ADO handle this kind of searching?

Technique

Absolutely! The ADO system supports several types of find operations via filters (special field groups used to locate matching records). This How-To will demonstrate adding a forward find capability to the developing ActiveX control project from previous How-To's. Although these directions create the project from scratch, the CD contains a completed file under `CH010\HT04\`.

Steps

1. Copy your project from How-To 10.1 to a new directory (or reuse the old one). Open it in Visual C++ 5.0, bring up the `EMPLOYEEVIEWERCTL.H` file, and add the boldface code in Listing 10-23 to place another MFC CommandButton control on your ActiveX control's user interface and add a needed support function for the finding procedure.

Listing 10-23 EMPLOYEEVIEWERCTL.H header file source code

```
// EmployeeViewerCtl.h : Declaration of the CEmployeeViewerCtrl ActiveX Control
// class.


/////////////////////////////////////////////////////////////////////////////
// CEmployeeViewerCtrl : See EmployeeViewerCtl.cpp for implementation.

class CEmployeeViewerCtrl : public COleControl
{
      DECLARE_DYNCREATE(CEmployeeViewerCtrl)

// Constructor
public:
      CEmployeeViewerCtrl();
    CEdit m_FirstName;
      CEdit m_LastName;
      CEdit m_JobTitle;
      CEdit m_EmployeeID;
      CButton m_Connect;
      CButton m_Disconnect;
      CButton m_MoveFirst;
      CButton m_MovePrevious;
      CButton m_MoveNext;
      CButton m_MoveLast;
      CButton m_Find;
      CAdoWrapper*      m_pAdoWrapper;
      BOOL CommitAlteredEmpRec();
      CString PrepareCriteria();

    // Overrides
      // ClassWizard generated virtual function overrides
```

2. Move down to the Message Map section and enter the boldface code in Listing 10-24 to link the new button's messages to its event handler. Save the project.

Listing 10-24 EMPLOYEEVIEWERCTL.H header file message map source code

```
// Message maps
      //{{AFX_MSG(CEmployeeViewerCtrl)
      afx_msg int OnCreate(LPCREATESTRUCT lpCreateStruct);
      afx_msg void OnConnectClicked();
      afx_msg void OnDisconnectClicked();
      afx_msg void OnMoveFirstClicked();
      afx_msg void OnMovePreviousClicked();
      afx_msg void OnMoveNextClicked();
      afx_msg void OnMoveLastClicked();
        afx_msg void OnFindClicked();
      //}}AFX_MSG
      DECLARE_MESSAGE_MAP()
```

3. Change to the `EMPLOYEEVIEWERCTL.CPP` file in the text editor. Move to the Message Map section of this file and enter the boldface code in Listing 10-25 to link the event handler from the `.H` file to the ID of the MFC control. Save the project.

Listing 10-25 EMPLOYEEVIEWERCTL.CPP message map source code

```
/////////////////////////////////////////////////////////////////////////////
// Message map

BEGIN_MESSAGE_MAP(CEmployeeViewerCtrl, COleControl)
    //{{AFX_MSG_MAP(CEmployeeViewerCtrl)
    ON_WM_CREATE()
    //}}AFX_MSG_MAP
    ON_OLEVERB(AFX_IDS_VERB_PROPERTIES, OnProperties)
     ON_BN_CLICKED(IDC_CONNECT, OnConnectClicked )
     ON_BN_CLICKED(IDC_DISCONNECT, OnDisconnectClicked )
     ON_BN_CLICKED(IDC_MOVEFIRST , OnMoveFirstClicked )
     ON_BN_CLICKED(IDC_MOVEPREVIOUS , OnMovePreviousClicked )
     ON_BN_CLICKED(IDC_MOVENEXT, OnMoveNextClicked )
     ON_BN_CLICKED(IDC_MOVELAST , OnMoveLastClicked )
     ON_BN_CLICKED(IDC_FIND , OnFindClicked )
END_MESSAGE_MAP()
```

4. Move down to the `OnCreate` event handler and enter the boldface code in Listing 10-26 to initialize the MFC CommandButton control. Save the project.

Listing 10-26 EMPLOYEEVIEWERCTL.CPP OnCreate source code

```
/////////////////////////////////////////////////////////////////////////////
// CEmployeeViewerCtrl message handlers

int CEmployeeViewerCtrl::OnCreate(LPCREATESTRUCT lpCreateStruct)
{
    if (COleControl::OnCreate(lpCreateStruct) == -1)
         return -1;

    // TODO: Add your specialized creation code here
    m_FirstName.Create( WS_CHILD¦ WS_VISIBLE ¦ WS_BORDER ¦ ES_AUTOHSCROLL ,
         CRect( 20 , 50 , 220 , 75 ), this , IDC_FIRSTNAME );
    m_LastName.Create( WS_CHILD¦ WS_VISIBLE ¦ WS_BORDER ¦ ES_AUTOHSCROLL ,
         CRect( 250 , 50 , 450 , 75 ), this , IDC_LASTNAME );
    m_JobTitle.Create( WS_CHILD¦ WS_VISIBLE ¦ WS_BORDER ¦ ES_AUTOHSCROLL ,
         CRect( 20 , 150 , 220 , 175 ), this , IDC_JOBTITLE );
    m_EmployeeID.Create( WS_CHILD¦ WS_VISIBLE ¦ WS_BORDER ¦ ES_AUTOHSCROLL ,
         CRect( 250 , 150 , 450 , 175 ), this , IDC_EMPLOYEEID );
    m_Connect.Create("Connect to Database",WS_CHILD ¦ WS_VISIBLE ¦ WS_BORDER ⇐
         ¦BS_PUSHBUTTON ,
         CRect( 20 , 200 , 300 , 240) , this , IDC_CONNECT );
    m_Disconnect.Create("Disconnect from Database",WS_CHILD ¦ WS_VISIBLE ¦ ⇐
         WS_BORDER ¦BS_PUSHBUTTON ,
         CRect( 20 , 250 , 300 , 290) , this , IDC_DISCONNECT );
```

continued on next page

continued from previous page

```
        m_MoveFirst.Create("Move to First Record",WS_CHILD ¦ WS_VISIBLE ¦ ⇐
              WS_BORDER ¦BS_PUSHBUTTON ,
              CRect( 320 , 200 , 600 , 240) , this , IDC_MOVEFIRST );
        m_MovePrevious.Create("Move to Previous Record",WS_CHILD ¦ WS_VISIBLE ¦ ⇐
              WS_BORDER ¦BS_PUSHBUTTON ,
              CRect( 320 , 250 , 600 , 290) , this , IDC_MOVEPREVIOUS );
        m_MoveNext.Create("Move to Next Record",WS_CHILD ¦ WS_VISIBLE ¦ WS_BORDER ⇐
              ¦BS_PUSHBUTTON ,
              CRect( 320 , 300 , 600 , 340) , this , IDC_MOVENEXT );
        m_MoveLast.Create("Move to Last Record",WS_CHILD ¦ WS_VISIBLE ¦ WS_BORDER ⇐
              ¦BS_PUSHBUTTON ,
              CRect( 320 , 350 , 600 , 390) , this , IDC_MOVELAST );
        m_Find.Create("Find Matching Record",WS_CHILD ¦ WS_VISIBLE ¦ WS_BORDER ⇐
              ¦BS_PUSHBUTTON ,
              CRect( 620 , 200 , 900 , 240) , this , IDC_FIND );
return 0;
}
```

5. Bring up the Resource Identifiers dialog and add the new ID for the find buttons, using the default value supplied by the system. Save the project.

6. Move to the end of the file and enter the code in Listing 10-27 to add handler code for the button. Save the project.

Listing 10-27 EMPLOYEEVIEWERCTL.CPP event handler source code

```
void CEmployeeViewerCtrl::OnFindClicked()
{
      try
      {
            if(m_pAdoWrapper->FindForward(PrepareCriteria()))
            {
            try
                  {
                m_FirstName.SetWindowText( m_pAdoWrapper->GetFirstName() );
                  m_LastName.SetWindowText( m_pAdoWrapper->GetLastName() );
                m_JobTitle.SetWindowText( m_pAdoWrapper->GetTitle() );
                  char idstring[5];
                  wsprintf( idstring , "%d" , m_pAdoWrapper->GetEmployeeId() );
                  m_EmployeeID.SetWindowText( idstring );
                  }
              catch (HRESULT hr)
                  {
                    TCHAR szBuf[256];
                    MessageBeep(0);
                    wsprintf(szBuf, _T("Error: %X \n"), hr);
                    AfxMessageBox(szBuf);
                        return;
                  }
```

```
                Refresh();
            }
            else
            {       //not found.
                MessageBeep(0);
                //.. Should return to the last visited record.
            }
        }
        catch( HRESULT hr )
        {
            TCHAR szBuf[256];
            MessageBeep(0);
            wsprintf(szBuf, _T("Error: %X \n"), hr);
            AfxMessageBox(szBuf);
        }
}
```

7. Move below the event handler and add the code in Listing 10-28 to provide the `PrepareCriteria` support function that checks for non-null data and prepares the `find` string. Save the project.

Listing 10-28 EMPLOYEEVIEWERCTL.CPP support function source code

```
CString CEmployeeViewerCtrl::PrepareCriteria()
{
    CString     strCriteria = "";
    CString strFirstName = "";
    CString strLastName = "";
    CString strPhoneNumber = "";
    CString strJobTitle = "";

    m_FirstName.GetWindowText( strFirstName );
    m_LastName.GetWindowText( strLastName );
    m_JobTitle.GetWindowText( strJobTitle );

    if(strFirstName != "") strCriteria = "FirstName = '" + strFirstName +"'";
    if(strLastName != "") strCriteria = strCriteria + ( strCriteria == "" ? "⇐
      ":" AND ") + "LastName = '" + strLastName +"'";
    if(strJobTitle != "") strCriteria = strCriteria + ( strCriteria == "" ? "⇐
      ":" AND ") + "Title = '" + strJobTitle +"'";

    return strCriteria;
}
```

8. Now bring up the `ADOWRAPPER.H` file in the text editor. Enter the boldface lines of code in Listing 10-29 to add the new method for the find functionality to the `CAdoWrapper` object. Save the project.

Listing 10-29 ADOWRAPPER.H header file source code

```
// AdoWrapper.h : header file
//

/////////////////////////////////////////////////////////////////////////////
// CAdoWrapper dialog

class CAdoWrapper
{
// Construction
public:
	CAdoWrapper();		// standard constructor
	~CAdoWrapper();

// Attributes
public:
	ADORecordset*		m_piEmpRecordSet;
	BOOL				m_fConnected;
	BOOL				m_fRecordsetEmpty;

protected:
	ADOConnection*			m_piConnection;
	COleVariant				m_varLastGoodRecord;

// Operations
public:
	BOOL	ConnectToDatabase(); //Opens a database
	long	GetEmployeeId();
	CString	GetFirstName();
	CString	GetLastName();
	CString	GetHomePhone() ;
	CString	GetTitle() ;
	BOOL	MoveNext()	;
	BOOL	MovePrevious();
	BOOL	MoveFirst() ;
	BOOL	MoveLast();
	BOOL	FindForward(CString strCriteria) ;
	void	ClearFilter();
	BOOL	IsAddMode();
	void	UpdateEmpRec(CString &strFirstName,
			CString &strHomePhone, CString &strLastName,
			CString &strTitle);
};


#define EMP_EMPLOYEE_ID		L"EmployeeID"
#define EMP_LAST_NAME		L"LastName"
#define EMP_FIRST_NAME		L"FirstName"
#define EMP_TITLE		L"Title"
#define EMP_HOME_PHONE		L"HomePhone"
```

9. Bring up **ADOWRAPPER.CPP** in the text editor and enter the code in Listing 10-30 to add the find functionality to the object. Save the project.

Listing 10-30 ADOWRAPPER.CPP Find method source code

```
BOOL CAdoWrapper::FindForward(CString strCriteria)
{
	HRESULT			hr;
	VARIANT_BOOL		vbEOF;
	COleVariant		v;

	if (!m_fConnected || m_fRecordsetEmpty)
		return FALSE;

	THROW_ERR(	m_piEmpRecordSet->get_Filter(&v) );
	if ( v.vt != VT_BSTR || strCriteria !=	v.bstrVal )
	{
		v.vt = VT_BSTR;
		v.bstrVal = strCriteria.AllocSysString();
		THROW_ERR(  m_piEmpRecordSet->put_Filter(v) );
	}
	else
	{
		THROW_ERR( m_piEmpRecordSet->MoveNext() );
	}

	//Watch for ending of recordset
	THROW_ERR(	m_piEmpRecordSet->get_EOF(&vbEOF));
	if(vbEOF)
	{
		ClearFilter() ;
		THROW_ERR( m_piEmpRecordSet->MoveLast() );

		return FALSE;
	}
	else
	{
		return TRUE;
	}
}
```

10. Build the OCX. You should not encounter errors; if you do, make sure you used **INITGUID.H**. Also make sure the OCX is registered on the **C:** drive.

11. You can reuse **ASPHT1001.HTM** to redisplay the new ActiveX control or create a new file, but it will need the same functionality. When the control is displayed, click the Connect button. Clear all the data in the fields, then enter **Robert** in the first name box and press the Find button. As shown in Figure 10-15, the control will immediately display the seventh record, Robert King, in the database. Experiment with other find combinations, and you will get either a valid record or a warning beep. You have learned to employ forward searching of a database via ADO in your custom ActiveX control.

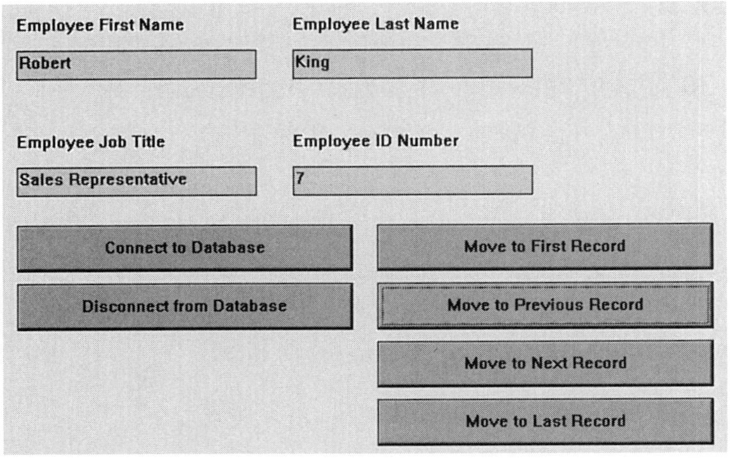

Figure 10-15 Finding in the database via ADO

How It Works

There are two separate pieces to this How-To: finding out what to search for and then searching for it. First, notice this code in the `PrepareCriteria` function:

```
m_FirstName.GetWindowText( strFirstName );
m_LastName.GetWindowText( strLastName );
m_JobTitle.GetWindowText( strJobTitle );
```

First, three important data items are acquired from their controls via `GetWindowText`. (Because you are not using member variables and DDX, a call to `UpdateData` is not needed.) Then, the actual comparison for null values is made.

```
if(strFirstName != "") strCriteria = "FirstName = '" + strFirstName +"'";
if(strLastName != "") strCriteria = strCriteria + ( strCriteria == "" ? "⇐
  ":" AND ") + "LastName = '" + strLastName +"'";
if(strJobTitle != "") strCriteria = strCriteria + ( strCriteria == "" ? "⇐
  ":" AND ") + "Title = '" + strJobTitle +"'";
```

If a value is null (`""`), then it is not added as a search parameter. Otherwise, it is appended to a string containing its field name, and if another field has been prepended, a `:` character is added.

Once the search criteria string has been built, the actual find routine must be called by the button's event handler.

```
try
{
      if(m_pAdoWrapper->FindForward(PrepareCriteria()))
      {
      try
```

It is important to notice that no call is made to add an altered record. Otherwise, clearing the fields to set the search criteria would prompt an invalid update call. Inside the `find` method itself, note this code:

```
THROW_ERR(      m_piEmpRecordSet->get_Filter(&v) );
if ( v.vt != VT_BSTR || strCriteria !=      v.bstrVal )
{
        v.vt = VT_BSTR;
        v.bstrVal = strCriteria.AllocSysString();
        THROW_ERR(  m_piEmpRecordSet->put_Filter(v) );
}
```

Here, the existing filter string is obtained via `get_Filter`. Its string value is tested against the imported string of search criteria. If the two values are different, the new search criteria are set as the filter value. (The filter controls what data is seen by the database methods in response to queries.) Next, the actual find is called.

```
{
        THROW_ERR( m_piEmpRecordSet->MoveNext() );
}
```

Wait a minute! Where's the find call? Surprise! Due to the control of the filter, only matching records will be seen now, so `MoveNext` is the same as `FindNext`. (Also remember that filters don't stick around; as noted in How-To 10.2, you put in a call to `ClearFilter` before every navigation call.)

Finally, you need to make sure the database hasn't run off its end because of not finding a match.

```
THROW_ERR(      m_piEmpRecordSet->get_EOF(&vbEOF));
if(vbEOF)
{
        ClearFilter() ;
        THROW_ERR( m_piEmpRecordSet->MoveLast() );
```

By clearing the filter and moving to the last record, a nonmatching find doesn't introduce an error condition.

Comments

Filters are rather sophisticated things, and can contain wildcards and other fun elements. Read up on filters in the ODBC documentation and you'll be amazed at all they can do.

ADO-AXC

COMPLEXITY
ADVANCED

10.5 How do I...
Add and delete records in the database with ADO in my C++ ActiveX control?

Problem

In addition to altering existing data, our users sometimes need to add and delete records online. Does ADO support this level of functionality?

Technique

Yes, although some care is needed to use add and delete functionality with ADO. This How-To will demonstrate using Add and Delete in combination with the update capabilities of the developing ActiveX control project from previous How-To's. Although these directions create the project from scratch, the CD contains a completed file under `CH10\HT05\`.

Steps

1. Copy your project from How-To 10.1 to a new directory (or reuse the old one). Open it in Visual C++ 5.0, bring up the `EMPLOYEEVIEWERCTL.H` file, and add the boldface code in Listing 10-31 to place two more MFC CommandButton controls on your ActiveX control's user interface.

Listing 10-31 `EMPLOYEEVIEWERCTL.H` header file source code

```
#if
!defined(AFX_EMPLOYEEVIEWERCTL_H__A7BAC253_FDCA_11D0_B7DF_444553540000__INCLUDED_)
#define AFX_EMPLOYEEVIEWERCTL_H__A7BAC253_FDCA_11D0_B7DF_444553540000__INCLUDED_

#if _MSC_VER >= 1000
#pragma once
#endif // _MSC_VER >= 1000

#include "AdoWrapper.h"

// EmployeeViewerCtl.h : Declaration of the CEmployeeViewerCtrl ActiveX Control
// class.
```

```
/////////////////////////////////////////////////////////////////////////////
// CEmployeeViewerCtrl  : See EmployeeViewerCtl.cpp for implementation.

class CEmployeeViewerCtrl : public COleControl
{
      DECLARE_DYNCREATE(CEmployeeViewerCtrl)

// Constructor
public:
      CEmployeeViewerCtrl();
    CEdit m_FirstName;
      CEdit m_LastName;
      CEdit m_JobTitle;
      CEdit m_EmployeeID;
      CButton m_Connect;
      CButton m_Disconnect;
      CButton m_MoveFirst;
      CButton m_MovePrevious;
      CButton m_MoveNext;
      CButton m_MoveLast;
      CButton m_Find;
      CButton m_Add;
      CButton m_Delete;
      CAdoWrapper*      m_pAdoWrapper;
      BOOL CommitAlteredEmpRec();
      CString PrepareCriteria();
```

2. Move down to the Message Map section and enter the boldface code in Listing 10-32 to link the two button messages to their event handlers. Save the project.

Listing 10-32 `EMPLOYEEVIEWERCTL.H` header file message map source code

```
// Message maps
      //{{AFX_MSG(CEmployeeViewerCtrl)
      afx_msg int OnCreate(LPCREATESTRUCT lpCreateStruct);
      afx_msg void OnConnectClicked();
      afx_msg void OnDisconnectClicked();
      afx_msg void OnMoveFirstClicked();
      afx_msg void OnMovePreviousClicked();
      afx_msg void OnMoveNextClicked();
      afx_msg void OnMoveLastClicked();
        afx_msg void OnFindClicked();
      afx_msg void OnAddClicked();
      afx_msg void OnDeleteClicked();
      //}}AFX_MSG
      DECLARE_MESSAGE_MAP()D
```

3. Change to the `EMPLOYEEVIEWERCTL.CPP` file in the text editor. Move to the Message Map section of this file and enter the boldface code in Listing 10-33 to link the event handlers from the `.H` file to the IDs of the MFC controls. Save the project.

Listing 10-33 EMPLOYEEVIEWERCTL.CPP message map source code

```
/////////////////////////////////////////////////////////////////////////////
// Message map

BEGIN_MESSAGE_MAP(CEmployeeViewerCtrl, COleControl)
	//{{AFX_MSG_MAP(CEmployeeViewerCtrl)
	ON_WM_CREATE()
	//}}AFX_MSG_MAP
	ON_OLEVERB(AFX_IDS_VERB_PROPERTIES, OnProperties)
	 ON_BN_CLICKED(IDC_CONNECT, OnConnectClicked )
	 ON_BN_CLICKED(IDC_DISCONNECT, OnDisconnectClicked )
	 ON_BN_CLICKED(IDC_MOVEFIRST , OnMoveFirstClicked )
	 ON_BN_CLICKED(IDC_MOVEPREVIOUS , OnMovePreviousClicked )
	 ON_BN_CLICKED(IDC_MOVENEXT, OnMoveNextClicked )
	 ON_BN_CLICKED(IDC_MOVELAST , OnMoveLastClicked )
	 ON_BN_CLICKED(IDC_FIND , OnFindClicked )
	 ON_BN_CLICKED(IDC_ADD , OnAddClicked )
	 ON_BN_CLICKED(IDC_DELETE , OnDeleteClicked )
END_MESSAGE_MAP()
```

4. Move down to the `OnCreate` event handler and enter the boldface code in Listing 10-34 to initialize the two MFC CommandButton controls. Save the project.

Listing 10-34 EMPLOYEEVIEWERCTL.CPP OnCreate source code

```
/////////////////////////////////////////////////////////////////////////////
// CEmployeeViewerCtrl message handlers

int CEmployeeViewerCtrl::OnCreate(LPCREATESTRUCT lpCreateStruct)
{
	if (COleControl::OnCreate(lpCreateStruct) == -1)
		return -1;

	// TODO: Add your specialized creation code here
	m_FirstName.Create( WS_CHILD| WS_VISIBLE | WS_BORDER | ES_AUTOHSCROLL ,
		CRect( 20 , 50 , 220 , 75 ), this , IDC_FIRSTNAME );
	m_LastName.Create( WS_CHILD| WS_VISIBLE | WS_BORDER | ES_AUTOHSCROLL ,
		CRect( 250 , 50 , 450 , 75 ), this , IDC_LASTNAME );
	m_JobTitle.Create( WS_CHILD| WS_VISIBLE | WS_BORDER | ES_AUTOHSCROLL ,
		CRect( 20 , 150 , 220 , 175 ), this , IDC_JOBTITLE );
	m_EmployeeID.Create( WS_CHILD| WS_VISIBLE | WS_BORDER | ES_AUTOHSCROLL ,
		CRect( 250 , 150 , 450 , 175 ), this , IDC_EMPLOYEEID );
	m_Connect.Create("Connect to Database",WS_CHILD | WS_VISIBLE | WS_BORDER ⇐
		|BS_PUSHBUTTON ,
		CRect( 20 , 200 , 300 , 240) , this , IDC_CONNECT );
	m_Disconnect.Create("Disconnect from Database",WS_CHILD | WS_VISIBLE | ⇐
		WS_BORDER |BS_PUSHBUTTON ,
		CRect( 20 , 250 , 300 , 290) , this , IDC_DISCONNECT );
	m_MoveFirst.Create("Move to First Record",WS_CHILD | WS_VISIBLE | ⇐
		WS_BORDER |BS_PUSHBUTTON ,
		CRect( 320 , 200 , 600 , 240) , this , IDC_MOVEFIRST );
	m_MovePrevious.Create("Move to Previous Record",WS_CHILD | WS_VISIBLE | ⇐
		WS_BORDER |BS_PUSHBUTTON ,
```

```
        CRect( 320  , 250 , 600 , 290) , this , IDC_MOVEPREVIOUS );
    m_MoveNext.Create("Move to Next Record",WS_CHILD ¦ WS_VISIBLE ¦ WS_BORDER ⇐
        ¦BS_PUSHBUTTON ,
        CRect( 320 , 300 , 600 , 340) , this , IDC_MOVENEXT );
    m_MoveLast.Create("Move to Last Record",WS_CHILD ¦ WS_VISIBLE ¦ WS_BORDER ⇐
        ¦BS_PUSHBUTTON ,
        CRect( 320 , 350 , 600 , 390) , this , IDC_MOVELAST );
    m_Find.Create("Find Matching Record",WS_CHILD ¦ WS_VISIBLE ¦ WS_BORDER ⇐
        ¦BS_PUSHBUTTON ,
        CRect( 620 , 200 , 900 , 240) , this , IDC_FIND );
    m_Add.Create("New Record (Fill In After)",WS_CHILD ¦ WS_VISIBLE ¦ ⇐
        WS_BORDER ¦BS_PUSHBUTTON ,
        CRect( 620 , 250 , 900 , 290) , this , IDC_ADD );
    m_Delete.Create("Delete Current Record",WS_CHILD ¦ WS_VISIBLE ¦ WS_BORDER ⇐
        ¦BS_PUSHBUTTON ,
        CRect( 620 , 300 , 900 , 340) , this , IDC_DELETE );
return 0;
}
```

5. Bring up the Resource Identifiers dialog and add the two new IDs for the navigation buttons, using the default values supplied by the system. Save the project.

6. Move to the end of the file and enter the code in Listing 10-35 to add handler code for the buttons. Save the project.

Listing 10-35 EMPLOYEEVIEWERCTL.CPP event handler source code

```
void CEmployeeViewerCtrl::OnAddClicked()
{
      try
      {
            if(!CommitAlteredEmpRec())
                  return;

            m_pAdoWrapper->AddRecord();
        try
            {
            m_FirstName.SetWindowText( m_pAdoWrapper->GetFirstName() );
              m_LastName.SetWindowText( m_pAdoWrapper->GetLastName() );
            m_JobTitle.SetWindowText( m_pAdoWrapper->GetTitle() );
              char idstring[5];
              wsprintf( idstring , "%d" , m_pAdoWrapper->GetEmployeeId() );
              m_EmployeeID.SetWindowText( idstring );
            }
          catch (HRESULT hr)
            {
                TCHAR szBuf[256];
                MessageBeep(0);
                wsprintf(szBuf, _T("Error: %X \n"), hr);
                AfxMessageBox(szBuf);
                return;
            }
          Refresh();
```

continued on next page

continued from previous page

```
        }
        catch( HRESULT hr )
        {
                TCHAR szBuf[256];
                MessageBeep(0);
                wsprintf(szBuf, _T("Error: %X \n"), hr);
                AfxMessageBox(szBuf);
        }
        return ;
}

void CEmployeeViewerCtrl::OnDeleteClicked()
{
        try
        {
                //Delete method depends on current mode
                m_pAdoWrapper->DeleteRecord();
           try
                {
                m_FirstName.SetWindowText( m_pAdoWrapper->GetFirstName() );
                  m_LastName.SetWindowText( m_pAdoWrapper->GetLastName() );
                m_JobTitle.SetWindowText( m_pAdoWrapper->GetTitle() );
                  char idstring[5];
                  wsprintf( idstring , "%d" , m_pAdoWrapper->GetEmployeeId() );
                  m_EmployeeID.SetWindowText( idstring );
                }
              catch (HRESULT hr)
                {
                    TCHAR szBuf[256];
                    MessageBeep(0);
                    wsprintf(szBuf, _T("Error: %X \n"), hr);
                    AfxMessageBox(szBuf);
                    return;
                }
              Refresh();
        }
        catch( HRESULT hr )
        {
                TCHAR szBuf[256];
                MessageBeep(0);
                wsprintf(szBuf, _T("Error: %X \n"), hr);
                AfxMessageBox(szBuf);
        }
        return ;
}
```

7. Now bring up the `ADOWRAPPER.H` file in the text editor. Enter the boldface code in Listing 10-36 to add the new methods for the add and delete functionality to the `CAdoWrapper` object. Save the project.

Listing 10-36 ADOWRAPPER.H header file source code

```
// AdoWrapper.h : header file
//

/////////////////////////////////////////////////////////////////////////////
// CAdoWrapper dialog

class CAdoWrapper
{
// Construction
public:
      CAdoWrapper();      // standard constructor
      ~CAdoWrapper();

// Attributes
public:
      ADORecordset*      m_piEmpRecordSet;
      BOOL                  m_fConnected;
      BOOL                  m_fRecordsetEmpty;

protected:
      ADOConnection*            m_piConnection;
      COleVariant                  m_varLastGoodRecord;

// Operations
public:
      BOOL      ConnectToDatabase(); //Opens a database
      long      GetEmployeeId();
      CString GetFirstName();
      CString GetLastName();
      CString GetHomePhone() ;
      CString GetTitle() ;
      void      AddRecord() ;
      void      DeleteRecord();
      BOOL      MoveNext()       ;
      BOOL      MovePrevious();
      BOOL      MoveFirst() ;
      BOOL      MoveLast();
      BOOL      FindForward(CString strCriteria) ;
      void      ClearFilter();
      BOOL      IsAddMode();
      void      UpdateEmpRec(CString &strFirstName,
                        CString &strHomePhone, CString &strLastName,
                        CString &strTitle);
};


#define EMP_EMPLOYEE_ID      L"EmployeeID"
#define EMP_LAST_NAME        L"LastName"
#define EMP_FIRST_NAME       L"FirstName"
#define EMP_TITLE            L"Title"
#define EMP_HOME_PHONE       L"HomePhone"
```

8. Bring up `ADOWRAPPER.CPP` in the text editor and enter the code in Listing 10-37 to add the navigation functionality to the object. Save the project.

Listing 10-37 `ADOWRAPPER.CPP` `Add` and `Delete` methods source code

```
void CAdoWrapper::AddRecord()
{
	// TODO: Add your control notification handler code here
	HRESULT			hr;
	VARIANT			rgvFields;
	VARIANT			rgvValues;

	if (!m_fConnected)
		return;

	ClearFilter() ;

	//Watch for empty recordset
	if(!m_fRecordsetEmpty && !IsAddMode() )
	{
		//Remember where we were before adding in case the user
		//cancels and we have to return
		THROW_ERR(	m_piEmpRecordSet->get_Bookmark(m_varLastGoodRecord) );
	}

	rgvFields.vt = VT_ERROR;
	rgvFields.scode = DISP_E_PARAMNOTFOUND;

	rgvValues.vt = VT_ERROR;
	rgvValues.scode = DISP_E_PARAMNOTFOUND;

	THROW_ERR(	m_piEmpRecordSet->AddNew(rgvFields, rgvValues) );

	m_fRecordsetEmpty = FALSE;
	return ;
}


void CAdoWrapper::DeleteRecord()
{
	// TODO: Add your control notification handler code here
	HRESULT			hr;
	 EditModeEnum		lEditMode;
	VARIANT_BOOL		vbEOF, vbBOF;

	//Watch for empty recordset
	if (!m_fConnected || m_fRecordsetEmpty)
		return;

	ClearFilter() ;

	//Delete method depends on current mode
	THROW_ERR(	m_piEmpRecordSet->get_EditMode(&lEditMode) );

		switch (lEditMode)
		{
```

```
                case adEditNone : // Just delete it
                {
                        THROW_ERR(    m_piEmpRecordSet->Delete(adAffectCurrent) );
                        THROW_ERR(    m_piEmpRecordSet->MoveNext() );
                        //Watch for end of record set
                        THROW_ERR(    m_piEmpRecordSet->get_EOF(&vbEOF) );
                        if(vbEOF)
                        {
                                THROW_ERR(    m_piEmpRecordSet->MovePrevious() );
                                //Check for empty record set.
                                THROW_ERR(    m_piEmpRecordSet->get_BOF(&vbBOF) );
                                if(vbBOF)
                                        m_fRecordsetEmpty  = TRUE;
                        }
                        break;
                }

                case adEditInProgress: //Forget changes
                {
                        THROW_ERR(    m_piEmpRecordSet->CancelUpdate() );
                        THROW_ERR(    m_piEmpRecordSet->Delete(adAffectCurrent) );
                        THROW_ERR(    m_piEmpRecordSet->MoveFirst() );
                        break;
                }

                case adEditAdd: //If new record, go back to last known
                {
                        THROW_ERR(    m_piEmpRecordSet->CancelUpdate() );
                        THROW_ER      m_piEmpRecordSet->put_Bookmark⇐
                                        (m_varLastGoodRecord) );
                }
        }

    return ;
}
```

9. Build the OCX. You should not encounter errors; if you do, make sure you used `INITGUID.H`. Also make sure the OCX is registered on the `C:` drive.

10. You can reuse `ASPHT1001.HTM` to redisplay the new ActiveX control or create a new file, but it will need the same functionality. Once the control is displayed, click the Connect button. At this point, you need to pay careful attention to how this works. First, click the Add button. An empty record appears with `0` as its employee ID. Enter new values for all fields *except* the employee ID. Then press any navigation button. A dialog appears, asking you to confirm adding the new data. Press Yes, and the new data will be added, BUT YOU WILL NOT SEE IT! Navigate to the place your navigation command would normally take you. Next, press the

Move Last button. As shown in Figure 10-16, *now* you will see the new record, added to the end of the database. Now press the Delete key, and the new record you added will disappear forever. Your ADO skills set is now complete, with addition and deletion under your belt.

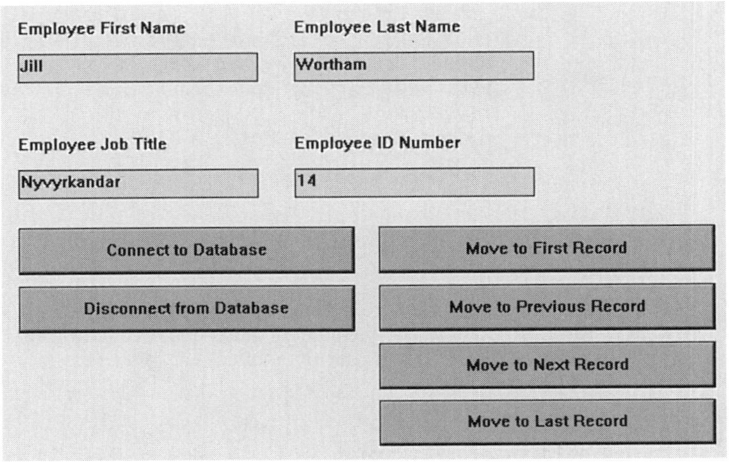

Employee First Name
Jill
Employee Last Name
Wortham
Employee Job Title
Nyvyrkandar
Employee ID Number
14
Connect to Database
Disconnect from Database
Move to First Record
Move to Previous Record
Move to Next Record
Move to Last Record

Figure 10-16 Adding a new database record via ADO

How It Works

As explained in step 10, subtraction using ADO is somewhat complex. The addition part is fairly simple.

```
try
{
      if(!CommitAlteredEmpRec())
            return;

      m_pAdoWrapper->AddRecord();
```

First, a check is made to see whether the current record has been altered (it might be a new one, after all); if so, it is updated. Then the `Add` method itself is called. Inside the `Add` method proper, this bit of code takes over:

```
//Watch for empty recordset
if(!m_fRecordsetEmpty && !IsAddMode() )
{
      //Remember where we were before adding in case the user
      //cancels and we have to return
      THROW_ERR(      m_piEmpRecordSet->get_Bookmark(m_varLastGoodRecord) );
}
```

If the database was previously empty, then this code doesn't execute, nor if a record has already been added but not updated. Otherwise, the current record is bookmarked in case the user cancels the update and a return is needed. Then the actual addition code is called.

```
THROW_ERR(      m_piEmpRecordSet->AddNew(rgvFields, rgvValues) );

m_fRecordsetEmpty = FALSE;
```

The `AddNew` method adds the new blank record to the end of the database. Note that the empty recordset flag is now cleared, because at least one record appears in the database.

Deletion is more complex! Note this important code fragment:

```
//Delete method depends on current mode
THROW_ERR(      m_piEmpRecordSet->get_EditMode(&lEditMode) );

      switch (lEditMode)
      {
```

The database may be in several different modes, depending on the last transaction. Thus, this call gets the current mode via the `get_EditMode` method. Once the mode is obtained, a `switch` statement checks the various possibilities. The easiest is if no edit mode is in force.

```
case adEditNone: // Just delete it
{
      THROW_ERR(      m_piEmpRecordSet->Delete(adAffectCurrent) );
      THROW_ERR(      m_piEmpRecordSet->MoveNext() );
```

The `Delete` method is simply invoked with a parameter to use the current record, and a call is made to move to the next one (remember, deletion in databases doesn't really remove anything due to consistency issues; instead it marks the record as deleted internally). If this runs off the end of the data, backup code is invoked. The more messy case is if an edit is in progress.

```
case adEditInProgress: //Forget changes
{
      THROW_ERR(      m_piEmpRecordSet->CancelUpdate() );
      THROW_ERR(      m_piEmpRecordSet->Delete(adAffectCurrent) );
      THROW_ERR(      m_piEmpRecordSet->MoveFirst() );
```

First, the update must be canceled so that consistency is maintained. Then the current record is deleted. For safety, to signal something different from a normal deletion, the cursor is moved to the start of the database. Finally, this is what happens if an add is in progress:

```
case adEditAdd: //If new record, go back to last known
{
      THROW_ERR(      m_piEmpRecordSet->CancelUpdate() );
      THROW_ERR(      m_piEmpRecordSet->put_Bookmark⇐
                        (m_varLastGoodRecord) );
```

The update is also canceled (removing the added record), and thus no actual deletion needs to take place. Here, `m_varLastGoodRecord` is put to use by jumping to a signal that an add was aborted.

Comments

You are now pretty much up to speed with the basic functionality of ADO. Although there are many more features to the system, these five How-To's have given you all the skills you need to manage a fully functional interactive database system using ActiveX and ADO.

ADO-AXC

COMPLEXITY
ADVANCED

10.6 How do I… Make ADO functionality available to ActiveX Scripting in my C++ ActiveX control?

Problem

We need to have our users interact with HTML forms and other client-side capabilities on the Web pages showing our ADO ActiveX control. How do we hook our ActiveX ADO control into the ActiveX Scripting system?

Technique

The key to connecting an ActiveX control into ActiveX Scripting is the use of properties and methods. This How-To will expose the Phone Number data field of the database to client-side scripting and make the find functionality available. Although these directions create the project from scratch, the CD contains a completed file under `CH10\HT06\`.

Steps

1. Copy your project from How-To 10.1 to a new directory (or reuse the old one). Open it in Visual C++ 5.0 and bring up the Class Wizard. As shown in Figure 10-17, add a property called `EmployeePhoneNumber` to the control, with a return type of `CString` using a member variable. Save the project.

2. Staying in the Class Wizard, add a method to the control named `FindEmployee`, with a return type of `void` and no parameters, as shown in Figure 10-18. Save the project.

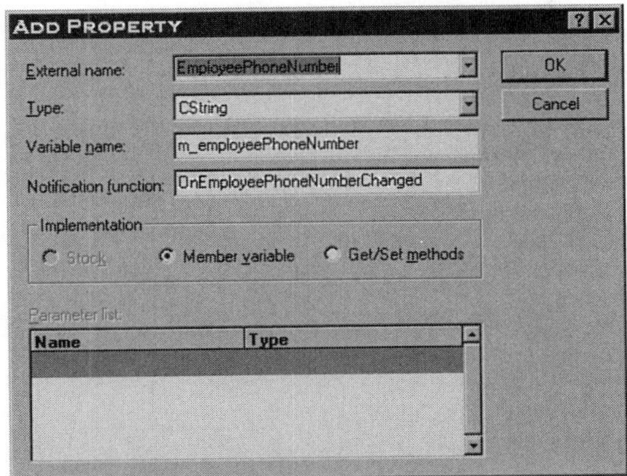

Figure 10-17 Adding the `EmployeePhoneNumber` property to the control

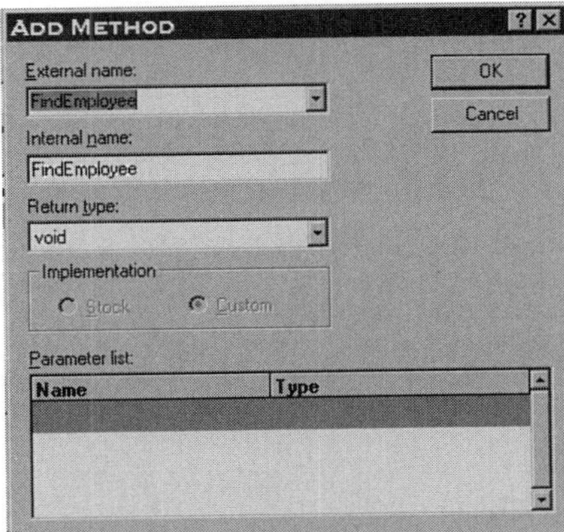

Figure 10-18 Adding the `FindEmployee` method to the control

3. Still staying in the Class Wizard, add an event named `DataChanged` to the control, with no parameters, as shown in Figure 10-19. Save the project.

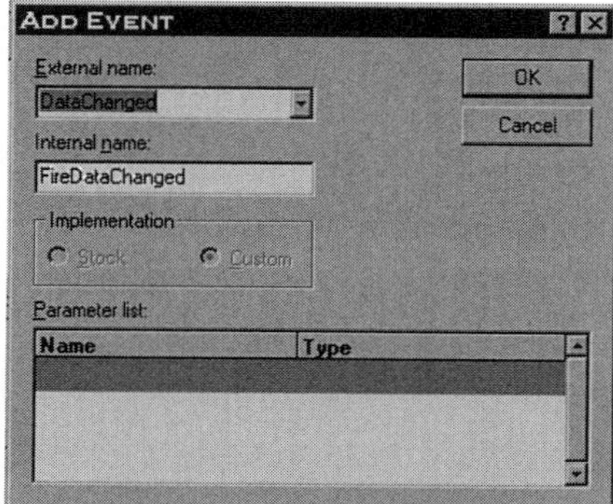

Figure 10-19 Adding the `DataChanged` event to the control

4. Bring up `EMPLOYEEVIEWERCTL.CPP` in the text editor. Move to the end of the file and add the code in Listing 10-38 to respond to the `FindEmployee` method invocation. Save the project.

Listing 10-38 `EMPLOYEEVIEWERCTL.CPP FindEmployee` method source code

```
void CEmployeeViewerCtrl::FindEmployee()
{
        // TODO: Add your dispatch handler code here
    OnFindClicked();
        FireDataChanged();
}
```

5. Move back up to the `PrepareCriteria` method and make the boldface changes in Listing 10-39 to integrate support for the `EmployeePhone-Number` property into the database system. Save the project.

Listing 10-39 `EMPLOYEEVIEWERCTL.CPP PrepareCriteria` method source code

```
CString CEmployeeViewerCtrl::PrepareCriteria()
{
        CString      strCriteria = "";
          CString strFirstName = "";
        CString strLastName = "";
        CString strPhoneNumber = m_employeePhoneNumber;
        CString strJobTitle = "";

          m_FirstName.GetWindowText( strFirstName );
        m_LastName.GetWindowText( strLastName );
        m_JobTitle.GetWindowText( strJobTitle );

        if(strFirstName != "")
```

```
            strCriteria =  "FirstName = '" + strFirstName +"'";
        if(strLastName != "")
            strCriteria = strCriteria + ( strCriteria == "" ? "":" AND ") + ⇐
                          "LastName = '" + strLastName +"'";
        if(strPhoneNumber != "")
            strCriteria = strCriteria + ( strCriteria == "" ? "":" AND ") + ⇐
                          "HomePhone = '" + strPhoneNumber +"'";
        if(strJobTitle != "")
            strCriteria = strCriteria + ( strCriteria == "" ? "":" AND ") + ⇐
                          "Title = '" + strJobTitle +"'";

        return strCriteria;
}
```

6. Move back up to the `CommitAlteredEmpRec` method and make the boldface changes in Listing 10-40 to integrate support for the `EmployeePhoneNumber` property into the database system. Save the project.

Listing 10-40 EMPLOYEEVIEWERCTL.CPP UpdateAlteredEmpRec method source code

```
BOOL CEmployeeViewerCtrl::CommitAlteredEmpRec()
{
        CString                 strOldFirstName, strOldHomePhone, strOldLastName,⇐
                                strOldTitle;
        COleVariant             vFirstName, vHomePhone, vLastName, vTitle, vID;

        if (!m_pAdoWrapper->m_fConnected)
            return FALSE;

        //Get current record string values
        try
        {
            strOldFirstName = m_pAdoWrapper->GetFirstName();
            strOldLastName = m_pAdoWrapper->GetLastName();
            strOldHomePhone = m_pAdoWrapper->GetHomePhone();
            strOldTitle = m_pAdoWrapper->GetTitle();
        }
        catch(HRESULT  hr )
        {
            TCHAR szBuf[256];
            wsprintf(szBuf, _T("Error: %X \n"), hr);
            AfxMessageBox(szBuf);
            return FALSE;
        }

        //Force DDX to update member values
        UpdateData();
        CString      strCriteria = "";
          CString strFirstName = "";
        CString strLastName = "";
        CString strPhoneNumber = m_employeePhoneNumber;
        CString strJobTitle = "";
```

continued on next page

continued from previous page

```
    m_FirstName. GetWindowText( strFirstName );
      m_LastName.GetWindowText( strLastName );
      m_JobTitle.GetWindowText( strJobTitle );

      // Did any fields change value?
      if(
      (strFirstName      == strOldFirstName      ) &&
      (strLastName       == strOldLastName      ) &&
      (strPhoneNumber == strOldHomePhone ) &&
      (strJobTitle       == strOldTitle          ) && !m_pAdoWrapper->IsAddMode() )
            return TRUE;

      //Save it, dump it or stay on it?
      switch (AfxMessageBox(IDS_PROMPT_COMMIT_EMPREC, MB_YESNOCANCEL))
      {
            case IDYES:
            {
                  try
                  {
                        m_pAdoWrapper->UpdateEmpRec(strFirstName,
                                          strPhoneNumber,
                                          strLastName,
                                          strJobTitle);
                  }
                  catch (CMemoryException &memx)
                  {
                        TCHAR szBuf[256];
                        memx.GetErrorMessage(szBuf, sizeof(szBuf), NULL);
                        AfxMessageBox(szBuf);
                        return FALSE;
                  }
                  catch(HRESULT  hr )
                  {
                        TCHAR szBuf[256];
                        wsprintf(szBuf, _T("Error: %X \n"), hr);
                        AfxMessageBox(szBuf);
                        return FALSE;
                  }

                  return TRUE;
            }

            case IDNO:
            {
                  return TRUE;
            }

            default:
            {
                  return TRUE;
            }
      }
            return TRUE;
}
```

7. Move back up through the remaining navigation and manipulation methods and make the boldface changes in Listing 10-41 to integrate support for the `EmployeePhoneNumber` property and `FireDataChanged` event calls into the database system. Save the project.

Listing 10-41 EMPLOYEEVIEWERCTL.CPP navigation methods source code

```
void CEmployeeViewerCtrl::OnConnectClicked()
{
      m_pAdoWrapper = new CAdoWrapper;

      if(!m_pAdoWrapper->ConnectToDatabase())
      {
            m_pAdoWrapper->m_fConnected = FALSE;
            return;
      }

      m_pAdoWrapper->m_fConnected = TRUE;

    m_FirstName.SetWindowText( m_pAdoWrapper->GetFirstName() );
      m_LastName.SetWindowText( m_pAdoWrapper->GetLastName() );
      m_JobTitle.SetWindowText( m_pAdoWrapper->GetTitle() );
      char idstring[5];
      wsprintf( idstring , "%d" , m_pAdoWrapper->GetEmployeeId() );
      m_EmployeeID.SetWindowText( idstring );
    m_employeePhoneNumber = m_pAdoWrapper->GetHomePhone();
      FireDataChanged();
}

void CEmployeeViewerCtrl::OnMoveFirstClicked()
{
      if(!CommitAlteredEmpRec())
            return;

      try
      {
            if(m_pAdoWrapper->MoveFirst())
            {
            try
                  {
                m_FirstName.SetWindowText( m_pAdoWrapper->GetFirstName() );
                  m_LastName.SetWindowText( m_pAdoWrapper->GetLastName() );
                m_JobTitle.SetWindowText( m_pAdoWrapper->GetTitle() );
                  char idstring[5];
                  wsprintf( idstring , "%d" , m_pAdoWrapper->GetEmployeeId() );
                  m_EmployeeID.SetWindowText( idstring );
                    m_employeePhoneNumber = m_pAdoWrapper->GetHomePhone();
                  FireDataChanged();
                  }
              catch (HRESULT hr)
                  {
                    TCHAR szBuf[256];
                    MessageBeep(0);
                    wsprintf(szBuf, _T("Error: %X \n"), hr);
```

continued on next page

continued from previous page

```
                    AfxMessageBox(szBuf);
                        return;
                    }
                    Refresh();
            }
            else
                    MessageBeep(0);
    }
    catch( HRESULT hr )
    {
            TCHAR szBuf[256];
            wsprintf(szBuf, _T("Error: %X \n"), hr);
            AfxMessageBox(szBuf);
    }
}

void CEmployeeViewerCtrl::OnMovePreviousClicked()
{
    if(!CommitAlteredEmpRec())
            return;

    try
    {
            if(m_pAdoWrapper->MovePrevious())
            {
            try
                    {
                m_FirstName.SetWindowText( m_pAdoWrapper->GetFirstName() );
                  m_LastName.SetWindowText( m_pAdoWrapper->GetLastName() );
                m_JobTitle.SetWindowText( m_pAdoWrapper->GetTitle() );
                  char idstring[5];
                  wsprintf( idstring , "%d" , m_pAdoWrapper->GetEmployeeId() );
                  m_EmployeeID.SetWindowText( idstring );
                    m_employeePhoneNumber = m_pAdoWrapper->GetHomePhone();
                  FireDataChanged();
                    }
              catch (HRESULT hr)
                    {
                    TCHAR szBuf[256];
                    MessageBeep(0);
                    wsprintf(szBuf, _T("Error: %X \n"), hr);
                    AfxMessageBox(szBuf);
                        return;
                    }
                    Refresh();
            }
            else
                    MessageBeep(0);
    }
    catch( HRESULT hr )
    {
            TCHAR szBuf[256];
            wsprintf(szBuf, _T("Error: %X \n"), hr);
            AfxMessageBox(szBuf);
    }
}
```

```
void CEmployeeViewerCtrl::OnMoveNextClicked()
{
      if(!CommitAlteredEmpRec())
            return;

      try
      {
            if(m_pAdoWrapper->MoveNext())
            {
            try
                  {
                m_FirstName.SetWindowText( m_pAdoWrapper->GetFirstName() );
                  m_LastName.SetWindowText( m_pAdoWrapper->GetLastName() );
                m_JobTitle.SetWindowText( m_pAdoWrapper->GetTitle() );
                  char idstring[5];
                  wsprintf( idstring , "%d" , m_pAdoWrapper->GetEmployeeId() );
                  m_EmployeeID.SetWindowText( idstring );
                    m_employeePhoneNumber = m_pAdoWrapper->GetHomePhone();
                  FireDataChanged();
                  }
              catch (HRESULT hr)
                  {
                    TCHAR szBuf[256];
                    MessageBeep(0);
                    wsprintf(szBuf, _T("Error: %X \n"), hr);
                    AfxMessageBox(szBuf);
                        return;
                  }
            Refresh();
            }
            else
                  MessageBeep(0);
      }
      catch( HRESULT hr )
      {
            TCHAR szBuf[256];
            wsprintf(szBuf, _T("Error: %X \n"), hr);
            AfxMessageBox(szBuf);
      }
}

void CEmployeeViewerCtrl::OnMoveLastClicked()
{
      if(!CommitAlteredEmpRec())
            return;

      try
      {
            if(m_pAdoWrapper->MoveLast())
            {
            try
                  {
                m_FirstName.SetWindowText( m_pAdoWrapper->GetFirstName() );
                  m_LastName.SetWindowText( m_pAdoWrapper->GetLastName() );
                m_JobTitle.SetWindowText( m_pAdoWrapper->GetTitle() );
                  char idstring[5];
```

continued on next page

continued from previous page

```
                    wsprintf( idstring ,  "%d" , m_pAdoWrapper->GetEmployeeId() );
                    m_EmployeeID.SetWindowText( idstring );
                      m_employeePhoneNumber = m_pAdoWrapper->GetHomePhone();
                    FireDataChanged();
                    }
                catch (HRESULT hr)
                    {
                      TCHAR szBuf[256];
                      MessageBeep(0);
                      wsprintf(szBuf, _T("Error: %X \n"), hr);
                      AfxMessageBox(szBuf);
                           return;
                    }
                  Refresh();
            }
            else
                    MessageBeep(0);
    }
    catch( HRESULT hr )
    {
            TCHAR szBuf[256];
            wsprintf(szBuf, _T("Error: %X \n"), hr);
            AfxMessageBox(szBuf);
    }
}

void CEmployeeViewerCtrl::OnFindClicked()
{
    try
    {
            if(m_pAdoWrapper->FindForward(PrepareCriteria()))
            {
            try
                    {
                 m_FirstName.SetWindowText( m_pAdoWrapper->GetFirstName() );
                   m_LastName.SetWindowText( m_pAdoWrapper->GetLastName() );
                 m_JobTitle.SetWindowText( m_pAdoWrapper->GetTitle() );
                   char idstring[5];
                   wsprintf( idstring , "%d" , m_pAdoWrapper->GetEmployeeId() );
                   m_EmployeeID.SetWindowText( idstring );
                     m_employeePhoneNumber = m_pAdoWrapper->GetHomePhone();
                   FireDataChanged();
                   }
               catch (HRESULT hr)
                   {
                     TCHAR szBuf[256];
                     MessageBeep(0);
                     wsprintf(szBuf, _T("Error: %X \n"), hr);
                     AfxMessageBox(szBuf);
                          return;
                   }
                   Refresh();
            }
            else
            {      //not found.
```

```
                MessageBeep(0);
                //.. Should return to the last visited record.
            }
        }
        catch( HRESULT hr )
        {
            TCHAR szBuf[256];
            MessageBeep(0);
            wsprintf(szBuf, _T("Error: %X \n"), hr);
            AfxMessageBox(szBuf);
        }
}

void CEmployeeViewerCtrl::OnAddClicked()
{
        try
        {
            if(!CommitAlteredEmpRec())
                return;

            m_pAdoWrapper->AddRecord();
          try
            {
            m_FirstName.SetWindowText( m_pAdoWrapper->GetFirstName() );
              m_LastName.SetWindowText( m_pAdoWrapper->GetLastName() );
            m_JobTitle.SetWindowText( m_pAdoWrapper->GetTitle() );
              char idstring[5];
              wsprintf( idstring , "%d" , m_pAdoWrapper->GetEmployeeId() );
              m_EmployeeID.SetWindowText( idstring );
                m_employeePhoneNumber = m_pAdoWrapper->GetHomePhone();
              FireDataChanged();
            }
          catch (HRESULT hr)
            {
                TCHAR szBuf[256];
                MessageBeep(0);
                wsprintf(szBuf, _T("Error: %X \n"), hr);
                AfxMessageBox(szBuf);
                return;
            }
          Refresh();

        }
        catch( HRESULT hr )
        {
            TCHAR szBuf[256];
            MessageBeep(0);
            wsprintf(szBuf, _T("Error: %X \n"), hr);
            AfxMessageBox(szBuf);
        }
        return ;
}

void CEmployeeViewerCtrl::OnDeleteClicked()
{
        try
```

continued on next page

continued from previous page

```
        {
            //Delete method depends on current mode
            m_pAdoWrapper->DeleteRecord();
          try
            {
            m_FirstName.SetWindowText( m_pAdoWrapper->GetFirstName() );
              m_LastName.SetWindowText( m_pAdoWrapper->GetLastName() );
            m_JobTitle.SetWindowText( m_pAdoWrapper->GetTitle() );
              char idstring[5];
              wsprintf( idstring , "%d" , m_pAdoWrapper->GetEmployeeId() );
              m_EmployeeID.SetWindowText( idstring );
                m_employeePhoneNumber = m_pAdoWrapper->GetHomePhone();
              FireDataChanged();
            }
          catch (HRESULT hr)
            {
                TCHAR szBuf[256];
                MessageBeep(0);
                wsprintf(szBuf, _T("Error: %X \n"), hr);
                AfxMessageBox(szBuf);
                return;
            }
          Refresh();
        }
        catch( HRESULT hr )
        {
              TCHAR szBuf[256];
              MessageBeep(0);
              wsprintf(szBuf, _T("Error: %X \n"), hr);
              AfxMessageBox(szBuf);
        }
        return ;
}
```

8. Activate ActiveX Control Pad. Create a new HTML file with the source code in Listing 10-42. Save the file as **ASPHT1006.HTM**. Remember to replace the ActiveX control listing with one from your system via the Edit|Insert ActiveX Control menu option, but change its **ExtentX** and **ExtentY** properties to match the following:

Listing 10-42 ASPHT1006.HTM source code

```
<HTML>
<HEAD>
<TITLE>Active Server Pages How To Chapter Ten How To Six</TITLE>
</HEAD>
<BODY>
This is a demo of an ActiveX Control using an ActiveX Data Objects Database!<P>
    <FORM NAME="Form1">
Employee Phone Number <P>
        <INPUT LANGUAGE="VBScript" TYPE=Text
         ONCHANGE="EmployeeViewer1.EmployeePhoneNumber = Document.Form1.⇐
         Text1.value"
         NAME="Text1">
<P>
```

```
        <INPUT LANGUAGE="VBScript" TYPE=BUTTON VALUE="Press To Find Record"
         ONCLICK="call EmployeeViewer1.FindEmployee()" NAME="Button1">
<HR>
    </FORM>
    <SCRIPT LANGUAGE="VBScript">
<!--
Sub EmployeeViewer1_DataChanged()
Document.Form1.Text1.value = EmployeeViewer1.EmployeePhoneNumber
end sub
-->
    </SCRIPT>
    <OBJECT ID="EmployeeViewer1" WIDTH=924 HEIGHT=407
     CLASSID="CLSID:A7BAC245-FDCA-11D0-B7DF-444553540000">
        <PARAM NAME="_Version" VALUE="65536">
        <PARAM NAME="_ExtentX" VALUE="24448">
        <PARAM NAME="_ExtentY" VALUE="10769">
        <PARAM NAME="_StockProps" VALUE="0">
    </OBJECT>
<HR>
Press "Connect To Database" to see the first employee record.<P>
Press "Disconnect From Database" before navigating or closing IE!<P>
</BODY>
</HTML>
```

9. Bring up Internet Explorer and display the **ASPHT1006.HTM** file. Connect to the database, and you will see a display similar to that shown in Figure 10-20, as the client-side scripting updates the form control with the phone number from the employee database. Now clear all the fields, including the phone number form field, and enter **Laura** in the first name field, as shown in Figure 10-21. Press the Press To Find Record form button. As shown in Figure 10-22, the control immediately finds record 8 and displays it, including the new phone number. You have now learned to make ADO functionality available to ActiveX Scripting on the client computer.

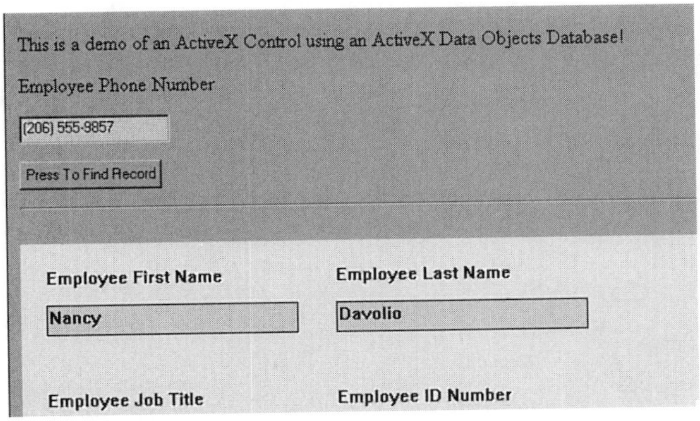

Figure 10-20 ASPHT1006 in IE showing ADO interacting with HTML forms via ActiveX Scripting

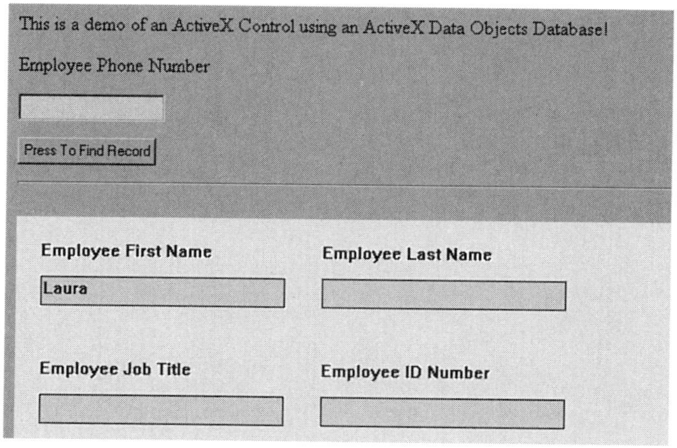

Figure 10-21 Clearing the fields for a find operation

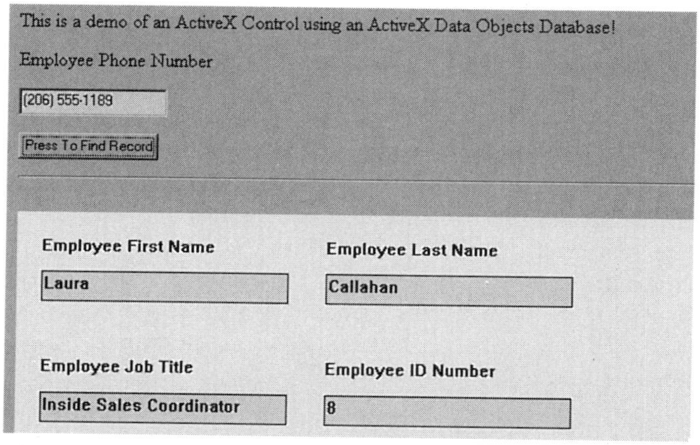

Figure 10-22 The results of a find operation using ActiveX scripting with ADO

How It Works

Three pieces of vital functionality are introduced in this How-To. The first is the use of an ActiveX property to get and set information. Notice how the get part works in the C++ code:

```
m_employeePhoneNumber = m_pAdoWrapper->GetHomePhone();
```

Yes, it's that simple! By merely connecting the member variable to the database field, the property always has the correct value. Now look at how it works on the HTML form:

```
Document.Form1.Text1.value = EmployeeViewer1.EmployeePhoneNumber
```

This is how the form's Text control always gets the employee's phone number, via a simple assignment from the property. Notice how setting the property works in reverse:

```
<INPUT LANGUAGE="VBScript" TYPE=Text ONCHANGE="EmployeeViewer1.⇐
       EmployeePhoneNumber = Document.Form1.Text1.value"
```

The **ONCHANGE** event fires every time anything changes in the Text control; this way, all changes made are guaranteed to be updated to the EmployeeViewer control's member variable.

You might think that is all there is to it, but unfortunately there's a catch. How does the HTML page know when the ActiveX control has updated its data? This does not happen automatically! Instead, here is where the `FireDataChanged` event comes into play.

```
m_employeePhoneNumber = m_pAdoWrapper->GetHomePhone();
 FireDataChanged();
```

Notice that everywhere the employee phone number is changed, a `FireDataChanged` method call is made next. This is vital to making ActiveX Scripting work effectively. Without an event to watch for, the HTML side of things cannot know when the control's state changes. By creating the event and then calling its `Fire` method internally, you permit watching and listening HTML pages to know when they should update their own states. This is how the event gets used on the HTML page:

```
Sub EmployeeViewer1_DataChanged()
Document.Form1.Text1.value = EmployeeViewer1.EmployeePhoneNumber
end sub
```

This linkage is the linchpin of ActiveX Scripting interaction. The `EmployeeViewer1_Datachanged` event is the client-side version of `FireDataChanged`; it will be called whenever `FireDataChanged` is invoked. The HTML form simply sets its text field to the desired value in response, and both sides are always in step.

Finally, notice how the find functionality is invoked.

```
<INPUT LANGUAGE="VBScript" TYPE=BUTTON VALUE="Press To Find Record"
        ONCLICK="call EmployeeViewer1.FindEmployee()" NAME="Button1">
```

The **ONCLICK** event will happen whenever the form button is pressed, and the EmployeeViewer control's ActiveX method will be invoked. Because the event simply calls the internal find routine, everything proceeds as if the Find button on the control were pushed.

Comments

The take-home message of this How-To is that *any* ADO functionality can be made available to client-side scripts via this methodology. Take a moment to consider the power this puts at your fingertips...

ADO-ASPC

COMPLEXITY
ADVANCED

10.7 How do I... Use ADO in a Visual C++ 5.0 ASP component?

Problem

We need to interact with users who don't use Internet Explorer or want ActiveX controls on their machines. How do we make the functionality of ADO available to these customers?

Technique

By shifting the ADO processing to the server computer via an ASP component! This How-To will show you how to port the completed ADO functionality from the ActiveX control environment to an ASP component project. These steps create the application from scratch, but for your convenience the complete project is on the CD under `CH10\HT07\`.

Steps

1. Activate Visual C++ 5.0. Bring up the New Projects dialog, and select an MFC AppWizard DLL, named `AdoAsp`, as shown in Figure 10-23. Press OK to start the wizard.

2. In the Wizard, leave the MFC DLL radio button where it is, as well as the source code comments radio button. Check the Automation button to allow the DLL to function as an ASP component. When you are done, the wizard dialog should look very similar to the one in Figure 10-24. Press Finish and accept the other dialogs to create the skeleton project.

3. Bring up the Class Wizard and move to the Automation tab. There, as shown in Figure 10-25, select Add Class and New Class from the options. Then, on the dialog that appears, create the `EmployeeViewer` class. Make it a descendant of `CCmdTarget` and make it creatable by `TypeID`. When you are done, the dialog should look very similar to Figure 10-26. Press OK twice to add the new class to your project.

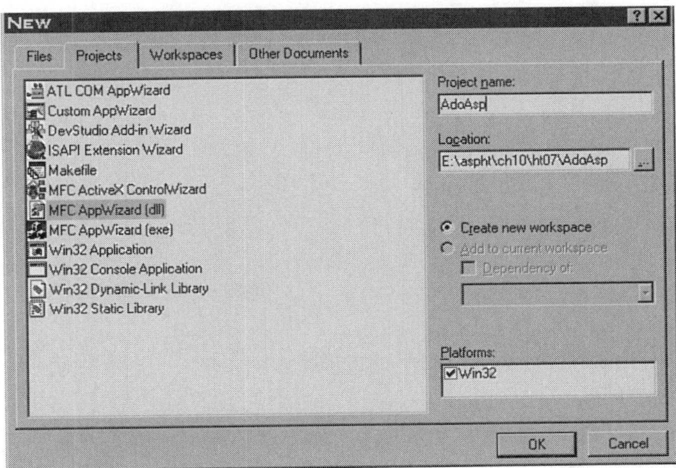

Figure 10-23 Creating the ASP component with MFC

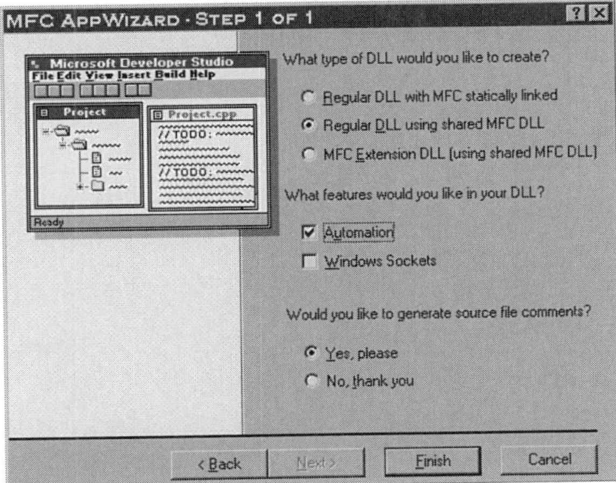

Figure 10-24 Adding automation support to the DLL

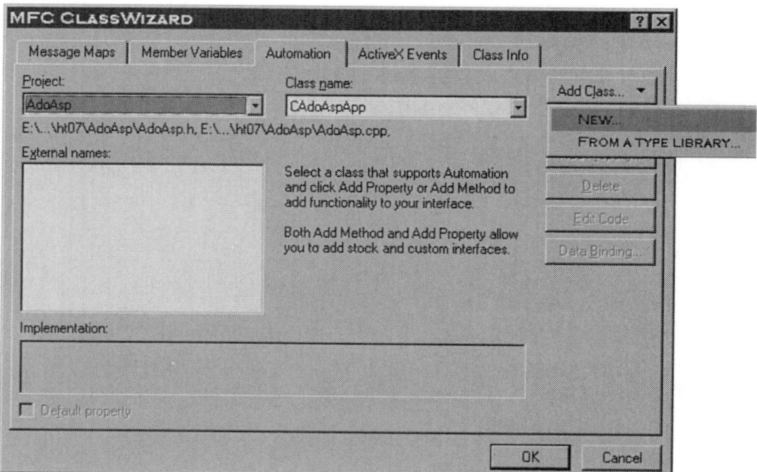

Figure 10-25 Adding a new class to support automation

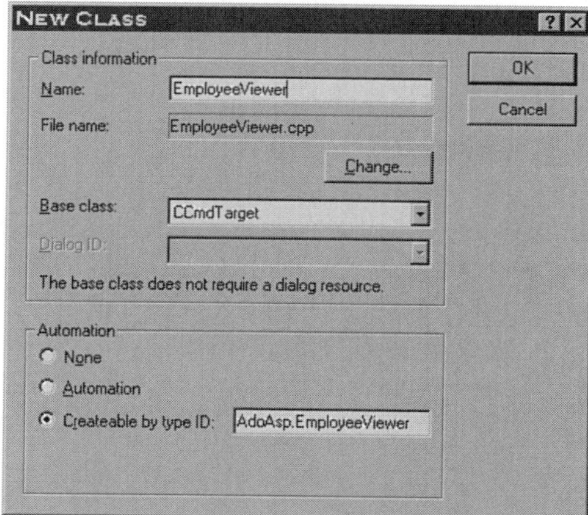

Figure 10-26 Creating the new automation class

4. Still in the Class Wizard, select the `EmployeeViewer` class and choose Add Property. Add five properties, all member variables of type `CString`, named `EmployeeFirstName`, `EmployeeLastName`, `EmployeeIDNumber`, `EmployeeJobTitle`, and `EmployeePhoneNumber`. Figure 10-27 shows a typical add dialog for these properties.

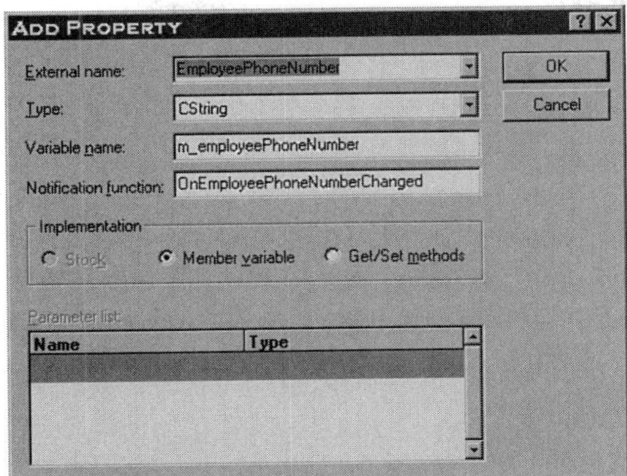

Figure 10-27 Adding automation properties to the DLL

5. Still in the Class Wizard, select the `EmployeeViewer` class and choose Add Method. Add one method, returning type `BSTR`, named `FindEmployee`. Figure 10-28 shows the add dialog for this method. Press OK twice to add all these changes to your project.

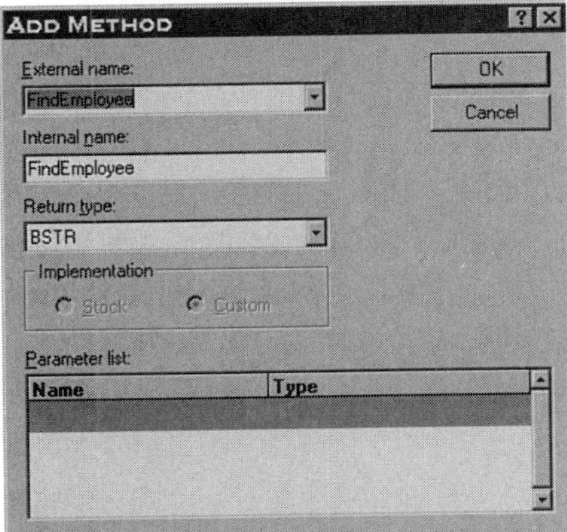

Figure 10-28 Adding an automation method to the DLL

6. To save considerable typing, copy the `ADOWRAPPER.H`, `ADOHEADERS.H`, and `ADOWRAPPER.CPP` files into the project directory. Then, as shown in Figure 10-29, right-click on the project viewer page and select Add Files to

Project. Add the files in their appropriate section to make the `CAdoWrapper` class available to the ASP component.

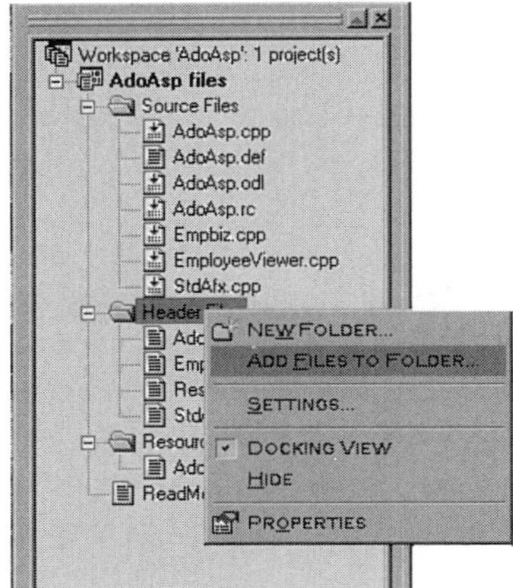

Figure 10-29 Adding files to the project

7. Bring up the `EMPLOYEEVIEWER.H` file in the text editor. Add the boldface code in Listing 10-43 to include support for the `AdoWrapper` class. Save the project.

Listing 10-43 EMPLOYEEVIEWER.H header file source code

```
#if
!defined(AFX_EMPLOYEEVIEWER_H__4483E7F4_001A_11D1_B7DF_444553540000__INCLUDED_)
#define AFX_EMPLOYEEVIEWER_H__4483E7F4_001A_11D1_B7DF_444553540000__INCLUDED_

#if _MSC_VER >= 1000
#pragma once
#endif // _MSC_VER >= 1000
// EmployeeViewer.h : header file
//
#include "AdoWrapper.h"


/////////////////////////////////////////////////////////////////////////////
// EmployeeViewer command target

class EmployeeViewer : public CCmdTarget
{
      DECLARE_DYNCREATE(EmployeeViewer)

      EmployeeViewer();           // protected constructor used by dynamic
                                  // creation
```

```
// Attributes
public:
      CAdoWrapper*      m_pAdoWrapper;

// Operations
public:
      BOOL CommitAlteredEmpRec();
      CString PrepareCriteria();

// Overrides
      // ClassWizard generated virtual function overrides
      //{{AFX_VIRTUAL(EmployeeViewer)
      public:
      virtual void OnFinalRelease();
      //}}AFX_VIRTUAL

// Implementation
protected:
      virtual ~EmployeeViewer();

      // Generated message map functions
      //{{AFX_MSG(EmployeeViewer)
            // NOTE - the ClassWizard will add and remove member functions here.
      //}}AFX_MSG

      DECLARE_MESSAGE_MAP()
      DECLARE_OLECREATE(EmployeeViewer)

      // Generated OLE dispatch map functions
      //{{AFX_DISPATCH(EmployeeViewer)
      CString m_employeeFirstName;
      afx_msg void OnEmployeeFirstNameChanged();
      CString m_employeeLastName;
      afx_msg void OnEmployeeLastNameChanged();
      CString m_employeeJobTitle;
      afx_msg void OnEmployeeJobTitleChanged();
      CString m_employeePhoneNumber;
      afx_msg void OnEmployeePhoneNumberChanged();
      long m_employeeIDNumber;
      afx_msg void OnEmployeeIDNumberChanged();
      afx_msg BSTR GetDatabaseRecord();
      //}}AFX_DISPATCH
      DECLARE_DISPATCH_MAP()
      DECLARE_INTERFACE_MAP()
};

/////////////////////////////////////////////////////////////////////////////

//{{AFX_INSERT_LOCATION}}
// Microsoft Developer Studio will insert additional declarations immediately
// before the previous line.

#endif //
!defined(AFX_EMPLOYEEVIEWER_H__4483E7F4_001A_11D1_B7DF_444553540000__INCLUDED_)
```

8. Now bring up the EMPLOYEEVIEWER.CPP file in the text editor. Add the boldface code in Listing 10-44 to provide code for the properties and method exported by automation. Save the project.

Listing 10-44 EMPLOYEEVIEWER.CPP **properties and methods source code**

```
// EmployeeViewer.cpp : implementation file
//

#include "stdafx.h"
#include "aspado.h"
#include "EmployeeViewer.h"

#ifdef _DEBUG
#define new DEBUG_NEW
#undef THIS_FILE
static char THIS_FILE[] = __FILE__;
#endif

/////////////////////////////////////////////////////////////////////////////
// EmployeeViewer

IMPLEMENT_DYNCREATE(EmployeeViewer, CCmdTarget)

EmployeeViewer::EmployeeViewer()
{
        EnableAutomation();

        // To keep the application running as long as an OLE automation
        //      object is active, the constructor calls AfxOleLockApp.

        AfxOleLockApp();
        m_pAdoWrapper = new CAdoWrapper;

        if(!m_pAdoWrapper->ConnectToDatabase())
        {
                m_pAdoWrapper->m_fConnected = FALSE;
                return;
        }

        m_pAdoWrapper->m_fConnected = TRUE;
}

EmployeeViewer::~EmployeeViewer()
{
        // To terminate the application when all objects created with
        // OLE automation, the destructor calls AfxOleUnlockApp.

        if (m_pAdoWrapper != NULL)
            delete m_pAdoWrapper;
        AfxOleUnlockApp();
}
```

```
BSTR EmployeeViewer::FindEmployee()
{
      CString strResult;
      // TODO: Add your dispatch handler code here
    if (( m_employeeFirstName == "" ) &&
              ( m_employeeLastName == "" ) &&
              ( m_employeeJobTitle == "" ) &&
              ( m_employeePhoneNumber == "" ))
      {
             strResult = "<TABLE WIDTH=600 COLSPAN=5 BORDER=5 CELLSPACING=5";
             strResult += "CELLPADDING=5 ALIGN=""CENTER"" VALIGN=""MIDDLE"" ⇐
                           BGCOLOR=""Teal"">";
             strResult += "<TR><TD COLSPAN=4 ALIGN=""CENTER"">Employee ⇐
                           Record</TD></TR><TR>";
             strResult += "<TD>Employee ID</TD><TD>First Name</TD><TD>Last ⇐
                           Name</TD><TD>Job Title</TD><TD>Home Phone</TD>⇐
                           </TR><TR>";
             strResult += "<TD>No Search Data Entered!</TD>";
             strResult += "<TD>No Search Data Entered!</TD>";
             strResult += "<TD>No Search Data Entered!</TD>";
             strResult += "<TD>No Search Data Entered!</TD>";
             strResult += "<TD>No Search Data Entered!</TD>";
             strResult += "</TR></TABLE>";
      }
      else
      {
          try
            {
                if(m_pAdoWrapper->FindForward(PrepareCriteria()))
                  {
                try
                       {
                    m_employeeFirstName = m_pAdoWrapper->GetFirstName();
                      m_employeeLastName = m_pAdoWrapper->GetLastName();
                    m_employeeJobTitle = m_pAdoWrapper->GetTitle();
                              m_employeePhoneNumber = m_pAdoWrapper- ⇐
                                                      >GetHomePhone();
                      m_employeeIDNumber = m_pAdoWrapper->GetEmployeeId();
                        strResult = "<TABLE WIDTH=600 COLSPAN=5 BORDER=5 ⇐
                                     CELLSPACING=5";
                        strResult += "CELLPADDING=5 ALIGN=""CENTER"" ⇐
                                     VALIGN=""MIDDLE"" BGCOLOR=""Teal"">";
                        strResult += "<TR><TD COLSPAN=5 ALIGN=""CENTER""> ⇐
                                      Employee Record</TD></TR><TR>";
                        strResult += "<TD>Employee ID</TD><TD>First ⇐
                                      Name</TD><TD>Last Name</TD><TD>Job Title ⇐
                                      </TD><TD>Home Phone</TD></TR><TR>";
                        char szbuf[ 5 ];
                       wsprintf( szbuf , "%d" , m_employeeIDNumber );
                       strResult += "<TD>"+ CString( szbuf , strlen( szbuf )) ⇐
                                    +"</TD>";
                        strResult += "<TD>"+ m_employeeFirstName +"</TD>";
                        strResult += "<TD>"+ m_employeeLastName +"</TD>";
                        strResult += "<TD>"+ m_employeeJobTitle +"</TD>";
                        strResult += "<TD>"+ m_employeePhoneNumber +"</TD>";
                        strResult += "</TR></TABLE>";
```

continued on next page

continued from previous page

```
                }
            catch (HRESULT hr)
                {
                TCHAR szBuf[256];
                wsprintf(szBuf, _T("%X"), hr);
                strResult = "<TABLE WIDTH=600 COLSPAN=5 BORDER=5 ⇐
                             CELLSPACING=5";
                strResult += "CELLPADDING=5 ALIGN=""CENTER"" ⇐
                             VALIGN=""MIDDLE"" BGCOLOR=""Red"">";
                strResult += "<TR><TD COLSPAN=5 ALIGN=""CENTER""> ⇐
                              Employee Record</TD></TR><TR>";
                strResult += "<TD>Employee ID </TD><TD>First ⇐
                              Name</TD><TD>Last Name</TD><TD>Job Title⇐
                              </TD><TD>Home Phone</TD></TR><TR>";
                strResult += "<TD>Error!</TD>";
                strResult += "<TD>HRESULT returned False!</TD>";
                strResult += "<TD>Error Code is</TD>";
                strResult += "<TD>" + CString(szBuf , strlen( szBuf )) ⇐
                              +"</TD>";
                strResult += "<TD>Please Try Again!</TD>";
                strResult += "</TR></TABLE>";
                }
            }
          else
            {
             strResult = "<TABLE WIDTH=600 COLSPAN=5 BORDER=5 ⇐
                          CELLSPACING=5";
             strResult += "CELLPADDING=5 ALIGN=""CENTER"" VALIGN="⇐
                          "MIDDLE"" BGCOLOR=""Yellow"">";
             strResult += "<TR><TD COLSPAN=5 ALIGN=""CENTER"">Employee ⇐
                           Record</TD></TR><TR>";
             strResult += "<TD>Employee ID</TD><TD>First Name</TD>⇐
                           <TD>Last Name</TD><TD>Job Title</TD><TD>⇐
                           Home Phone</TD></TR><TR>";
             strResult += "<TD>No Matching Record Found!</TD>";
             strResult += "<TD>No Matching Record Found!</TD>";
             strResult += "<TD>No Matching Record Found!</TD>";
             strResult += "<TD>No Matching Record Found!</TD>";
             strResult += "<TD>No Matching Record Found!</TD>";
             strResult += "</TR></TABLE>";
            }
      }
    catch( HRESULT hr )
      {
                TCHAR szBuf[256];
                wsprintf(szBuf, _T("%X"), hr);
                strResult = "<TABLE WIDTH=600 COLSPAN=5 BORDER=5 ⇐
                             CELLSPACING=5";
                strResult += "CELLPADDING=5 ALIGN=""CENTER"" ⇐
                             VALIGN=""MIDDLE"" BGCOLOR=""Red"">";
                strResult += "<TR><TD COLSPAN=5 ALIGN=""CENTER"">⇐
                              Employee Record</TD></TR><TR>";
                strResult += "<TD>Employee ID </TD><TD>First ⇐
                              Name</TD><TD>Last Name</TD><TD>Job Title⇐
                              </TD><TD>Home Phone</TD></TR><TR>";
                strResult += "<TD>Error!</TD>";
                strResult += "<TD>HRESULT returned False!</TD>";
```

```
                        strResult += "<TD>Error Code is</TD>";
                        strResult +=  "<TD>" + CString(szBuf , strlen( szBuf )) ⇐
                                +"</TD>";
                        strResult += "<TD>Please Try Again!</TD>";
                        strResult += "</TR></TABLE>";
                }
        }
        return strResult.AllocSysString();
}

BOOL EmployeeViewer::CommitAlteredEmpRec()
{
        CString                 strOldFirstName, strOldHomePhone, strOldLastName,⇐
                                strOldTitle;
        COleVariant             vFirstName, vHomePhone, vLastName, vTitle, vID;

        if (!m_pAdoWrapper->m_fConnected)
                return FALSE;

        //Get current record string values
        try
        {
                strOldFirstName = m_pAdoWrapper->GetFirstName();
                strOldLastName = m_pAdoWrapper->GetLastName();
                strOldHomePhone = m_pAdoWrapper->GetHomePhone();
                strOldTitle = m_pAdoWrapper->GetTitle();
        }
        catch(HRESULT  hr )
        {
        TCHAR szBuf[256];
      wsprintf(szBuf, _T("Error: %X \n"), hr);
        return FALSE;
        }

      CString strFirstName = m_employeeFirstName;
        CString strLastName =  m_employeeLastName;
        CString strPhoneNumber = m_employeePhoneNumber;
        CString strJobTitle = m_employeeJobTitle;

        // Did any fields change value?
        if(
        (strFirstName      == strOldFirstName      ) &&
        (strLastName      == strOldLastName      ) &&
        (strPhoneNumber == strOldHomePhone  ) &&
        (strJobTitle      == strOldTitle              ) && !m_pAdoWrapper->IsAddMode()
)
                return TRUE;

        try
        {
                m_pAdoWrapper->UpdateEmpRec(strFirstName,
                                        strPhoneNumber,
                                        strLastName,
                                        strJobTitle);
        }
        catch (CMemoryException &memx)
        {
```

continued on next page

continued from previous page

```
        TCHAR szBuf[256];
        memx.GetErrorMessage(szBuf, sizeof(szBuf), NULL);
        return FALSE;
    }
    catch(HRESULT hr )
    {
        TCHAR szBuf[256];
        wsprintf(szBuf, _T("Error: %X \n"), hr);
        return FALSE;
    }

    return TRUE;
}


CString EmployeeViewer::PrepareCriteria()
{
    CString     strCriteria = "";
     CString strFirstName = m_employeeFirstName;
    CString strLastName =  m_employeeLastName;
    CString strPhoneNumber = m_employeePhoneNumber;
    CString strJobTitle = m_employeeJobTitle;

    if(strFirstName != "")
        strCriteria = "FirstName = '" + strFirstName +"'";
    if(strLastName != "")
        strCriteria = strCriteria + ( strCriteria == "" ? "":" AND ") + ⇐
                     "LastName = '" + strLastName +"'";
    if(strPhoneNumber != "")
        strCriteria = strCriteria + ( strCriteria == "" ? "":" AND ") + ⇐
                     "Title = '" + strPhoneNumber +"'";
    if(strJobTitle != "")
        strCriteria = strCriteria + ( strCriteria == "" ? "":" AND ") + ⇐
                     "Title = '" + strJobTitle +"'";

    return strCriteria;
}
```

9. Build the DLL. Again, make sure the target directory is on drive `C:` to avoid the bug in ADO. Then activate ActiveX Control Pad. Create a new ASP file and enter the source code in Listing 10-45 to interface with the ASP component. Save the file as `ASPHT1007.ASP`. Create another file, named `ASPHT1007A.ASP`, with the code in Listing 10-46 and save it as well. Copy both files to the `ASPEXEC` directory.

Listing 10-45 `ASPHT1007.ASP` source code

```
<HTML>
<HEAD>
<TITLE>Active Server Pages How To Chapter 10 How To Seven</TITLE>
</HEAD>
```

```
<BODY>
This is a demonstration of the ASPADO Active Server Pages component!<P>
The following data is supplied by the component from the database on the FirstName
field of "Laura"<P>
<HR>
<%  Set AspAdoObj = Server.CreateObject("AspAdo.EmployeeViewer")
     AspAdoObj.EmployeeFirstName = "Laura"%>
<%= AspAdoObj.GetDatabaseRecord %>
<% Set AspAdoObj = Nothing %>
<HR>
</BODY>
</HTML>
```

Listing 10-46 ASPHT1007A.ASP source code

```
<HTML>
<HEAD>
<TITLE>Active Server Pages How To Chapter 10 How To Seven</TITLE>
</HEAD>
<BODY>
This is a demonstration of the ASPADO Active Server Pages component!<P>
The following data is supplied by the component from the database on the FirstName
field of "Cleopatra"<P>
(Cleopatra -- Asp -- I have no shame!)<P>
<HR>
<%  Set AspAdoObj = Server.CreateObject("AspAdo.EmployeeViewer")
     AspAdoObj.EmployeeFirstName = "Cleopatra"%>
<%= AspAdoObj.GetDatabaseRecord %>
<% Set AspAdoObj = Nothing %>
<HR>
</BODY>
</HTML>
```

10. Use the Start|Run menu option from the Windows 95/NT 4.0 task bar (or equivalent functionality on NT Server) to run **REGSVR32.EXE** on the DLL, giving its full path. Figure 10-30 shows how the Run dialog should appear.

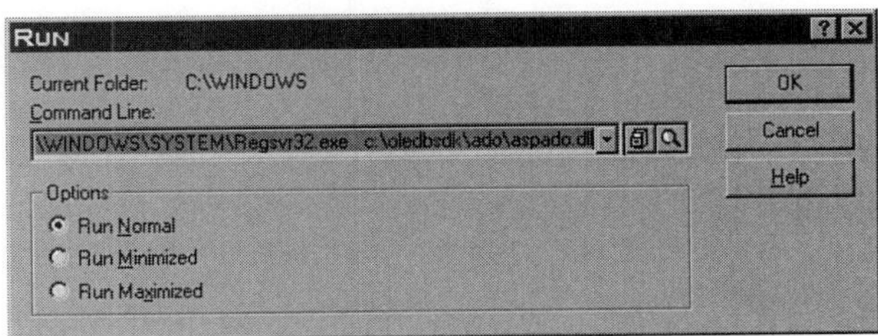

Figure 10-30 Registering the DLL

11. Using a non-IE browser such as Netscape Communicator, type in `HTTP://DEFAULT/ASPEXEC/ASPHT1007.ASP`. After a moment or two while ASP loads the DLL, you will see a display similar to Figure 10-31, showing the database record for the person with the first name of Laura. Now type in `HTTP://DEFAULT/ASPEXEC/ASPHT1007A.ASP` in the address bar. You will see a display similar to Figure 10-32 as the error display table is returned by the ASP component because there is no database record for anyone named Cleopatra. You have now learned how to add ADO functionality to ASP components using C++.

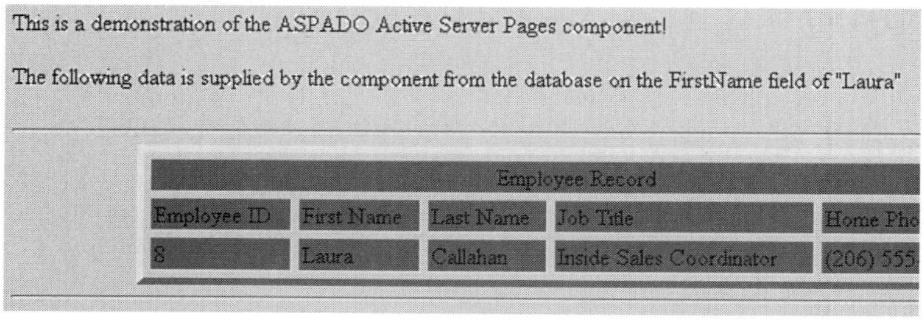

This is a demonstration of the ASPADO Active Server Pages component!

The following data is supplied by the component from the database on the FirstName field of "Laura"

Employee Record				
Employee ID	First Name	Last Name	Job Title	Home Pho
8	Laura	Callahan	Inside Sales Coordinator	(206) 555-

Figure 10-31 ASPHT1007.ASP in Netscape Communicator showing the database record for Laura

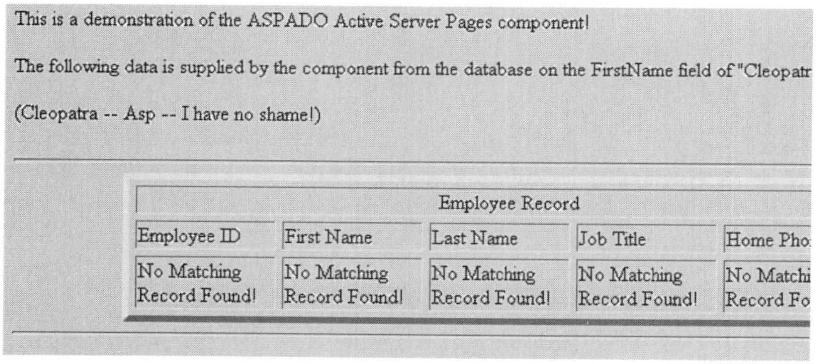

This is a demonstration of the ASPADO Active Server Pages component!

The following data is supplied by the component from the database on the FirstName field of "Cleopatr

(Cleopatra -- Asp -- I have no shame!)

Employee Record				
Employee ID	First Name	Last Name	Job Title	Home Pho
No Matching Record Found!	No Matching Record Found!	No Matching Record Found!	No Matching Record Found!	No Matchi Record Fo

Figure 10-32 ASPHT1007A.ASP in Netscape Communicator showing no database record for Cleopatra

How It Works

Aside from the mechanics of setting up the automation part of the DLL, the key aspect of using ADO with ASP components is linking member variables to properties.

```
CString      strCriteria = "";
CString strFirstName = m_employeeFirstName;
CString strLastName =  m_employeeLastName;
CString strPhoneNumber = m_employeePhoneNumber;
CString strJobTitle = m_employeeJobTitle;
```

By linking the member variables to the external properties, setting the external property makes its value available to the C++ code through the member variables. Thus, the find criteria can be prepared just by interrogating the values of the member variables, and a normal `FindForward` method call can be invoked.

The other half of the job concerns output. First, the normal output is formatted.

```
 char szbuf[ 5 ];
wsprintf( szbuf , "%d" , m_employeeIDNumber );
strResult += "<TD>"+ CString( szbuf , strlen( szbuf ))  +"</TD>";
strResult += "<TD>"+ m_employeeFirstName +"</TD>";
strResult += "<TD>"+ m_employeeLastName +"</TD>";
strResult += "<TD>"+ m_employeeJobTitle +"</TD>";
strResult += "<TD>"+ m_employeePhoneNumber +"</TD>";
strResult += "</TR></TABLE>";
```

The mixing of HTML syntax and the output from the database is how this particular bit of magic works! The other half of the problem is how to handle bad data or errors.

```
strResult += "<TD>No Matching Record Found!</TD>";
strResult += "<TD>No Matching Record Found!</TD>";
strResult += "<TD>No Matching Record Found!</TD>";
strResult += "<TD>No Matching Record Found!</TD>";
strResult += "<TD>No Matching Record Found!</TD>";
strResult += "</TR></TABLE>";
```

By sending back a nice table rather than a dumpy error message, the ASP component adds a bit of class!

Comments

Notice also that the normal table has a different background color than the error table. This type of visual feedback can be very user-friendly in a Web environment.

ADO-ASPC

COMPLEXITY
ADVANCED

10.8 How do I... Make ADO functionality available to ASP scripting in my C++ ASP component?

Problem

Although ADO is available as ASP code, we don't want to expose our company's data formats in a script. Is there a way to connect ADO in C++ with ASP scripts?

Technique

As with client-side scripting, all you need to do to make an ASP component's capabilities available to ASP scripts is export properties and methods. This How-To illustrates adding four navigation methods to the previously created ASP component. These steps create the application from scratch, but for your convenience the complete project is on the CD under `CH10\HT08\`.

Steps

1. Copy the files from the previous How-To to a new directory or continue to use the same directory. Bring up Visual C++ 5.0 and activate the Class Wizard. Enter four new methods, all returning `void`, with no parameters, named `MoveToFirstRecord`, `MoveToNextRecord`, `MoveToPreviousRecord`, and `MoveToLastRecord`. Figure 10-33 shows a typical creation dialog for the methods. Press OK twice to add them to the project.

2. Now bring up the `EMPLOYEEVIEWER.CPP` file in the text editor and move to the end of the file. Add the code in Listing 10-47 to provide code for the four new methods. Save the project.

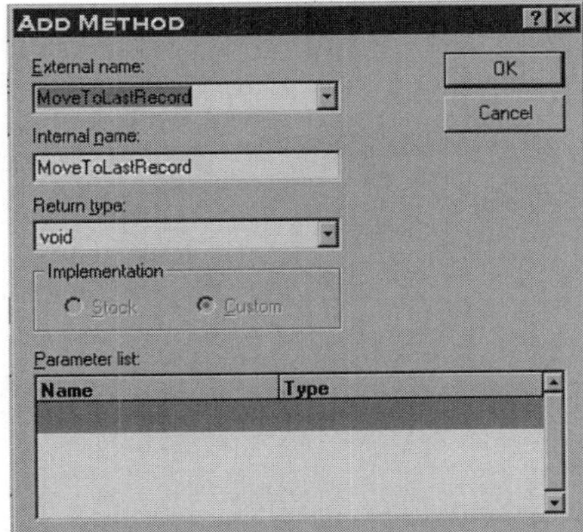

Figure 10-33 Adding four navigation methods to the ASP component project

Listing 10-47 EMPLOYEEVIEWER.CPP navigation methods source code

```
void EmployeeViewer::MoveToNextRecord()
{
	// TODO: Add your dispatch handler code here

    if(m_pAdoWrapper->MoveNext())
      {
       try
         {
           m_employeeFirstName = m_pAdoWrapper->GetFirstName();
             m_employeeLastName = m_pAdoWrapper->GetLastName();
           m_employeeJobTitle = m_pAdoWrapper->GetTitle();
               m_employeePhoneNumber = m_pAdoWrapper->GetHomePhone();
             m_employeeIDNumber = m_pAdoWrapper->GetEmployeeId();
           }
          catch (HRESULT hr)
            {
                TCHAR szBuf[256];
                wsprintf(szBuf, _T("%X"), hr);
            }
      }
}

void EmployeeViewer::MoveToFirstRecord()
{
	// TODO: Add your dispatch handler code here
    if(m_pAdoWrapper->MoveFirst())
      {
       try
         {
           m_employeeFirstName = m_pAdoWrapper->GetFirstName();
             m_employeeLastName = m_pAdoWrapper->GetLastName();
           m_employeeJobTitle = m_pAdoWrapper->GetTitle();
```

continued on next page

continued from previous page

```
                m_employeePhoneNumber = m_pAdoWrapper->GetHomePhone();
              m_employeeIDNumber = m_pAdoWrapper->GetEmployeeId();
             }
           catch (HRESULT hr)
             {
                 TCHAR szBuf[256];
                 wsprintf(szBuf, _T("%X"), hr);
             }
      }

}

void EmployeeViewer::MoveToPreviousRecord()
{
      // TODO: Add your dispatch handler code here
    if(m_pAdoWrapper->MovePrevious())
      {
       try
         {
           m_employeeFirstName = m_pAdoWrapper->GetFirstName();
             m_employeeLastName = m_pAdoWrapper->GetLastName();
           m_employeeJobTitle = m_pAdoWrapper->GetTitle();
               m_employeePhoneNumber = m_pAdoWrapper->GetHomePhone();
             m_employeeIDNumber = m_pAdoWrapper->GetEmployeeId();
            }
          catch (HRESULT hr)
            {
                TCHAR szBuf[256];
                wsprintf(szBuf, _T("%X"), hr);
            }
      }

}

void EmployeeViewer::MoveToLastRecord()
{
      // TODO: Add your dispatch handler code here
    if(m_pAdoWrapper->MoveLast())
      {
       try
         {
           m_employeeFirstName = m_pAdoWrapper->GetFirstName();
          m_employeeLastName = m_pAdoWrapper->GetLastName();
           m_employeeJobTitle = m_pAdoWrapper->GetTitle();
           m_employeePhoneNumber = m_pAdoWrapper->GetHomePhone();
          m_employeeIDNumber = m_pAdoWrapper->GetEmployeeId();
            }
          catch (HRESULT hr)
            {
                TCHAR szBuf[256];
                wsprintf(szBuf, _T("%X"), hr);
            }
      }

}
```

3. Build the DLL. Make sure the target directory is on drive `C:` to avoid the bug in ADO. Then run `REGSVR32.EXE` again (you don't need to unregister it, and in fact you can't) to update the registry with the new methods.

4. Activate ActiveX Control Pad. Create a new ASP file and enter the source code in Listing 10-48 to interface with the ASP component's new capabilities. Save the file as `ASPHT1008.ASP`. Copy the file to the `ASPEXEC` directory.

Listing 10-48 ASPHT1008.ASP source code

```
<HTML>
<HEAD>
<TITLE>Active Server Pages How To Chapter 10 How To 8</TITLE>
</HEAD>
<BODY>

<% if Request.Form("NavigationInstruction") <> "" then
        Set AspAdoObj = Server.CreateObject("AspAdo.EmployeeViewer")
        AspAdoObjRecord = Session("AspObjectRecord")
        Call AspAdoObj.MoveToFirstRecord
        for Counter1 = 1 to AspAdoObjRecord - 1
          Call AspAdoObj.MoveToNextRecord
        next
       if Ucase( Request.Form("NavigationInstruction")) = "FIRST" then
           call AspAdoObj.MoveToFirstRecord
        elseif Ucase( Request.Form("NavigationInstruction")) = "PREVIOUS" then
           call AspAdoObj.MoveToPreviousRecord
        elseif Ucase( Request.Form("NavigationInstruction")) = "NEXT" then
            call AspAdoObj.MoveToNextRecord
         elseif Ucase( Request.Form("NavigationInstruction")) = "LAST" then
            call AspAdoObj.MoveToLastRecord
          End if
        Session("AspObjectRecord") = AspAdoObj.EmployeeIDNumber
    else
      Set AspAdoObj = Server.CreateObject("AspAdo.EmployeeViewer")
      call AspAdoObj.MoveToFirstRecord
      Session("AspObjectRecord") = 1
end if
%>
<TABLE WIDTH=600 COLSPAN=5 BORDER=5 CELLSPACING=5
CELLPADDING=5 ALIGN="CENTER" VALIGN="MIDDLE" BGCOLOR="Teal">
<FORM NAME=Form1 ACTION="http://default/aspexec/aspht1008a.asp" METHOD="POST">
<TR><TD COLSPAN=3 ALIGN="CENTER">Navigation Command:</TD>
<TD ALIGN="CENTER">
<INPUT TYPE=Text Name="NavigationInstruction" VALUE="NEXT"></TD>
<TD ALIGN="CENTER">
<INPUT TYPE=SUBMIT NAME=Submit1 VALUE="Navigate!">
<TR>
</FORM>
<TD COLSPAN=5 ALIGN="CENTER">Employee Record</TD></TR><TR>
<TD>Employee ID</TD><TD>First Name</TD><TD>Last Name</TD><TD>Job
Title</TD><TD>Home Phone</TD></TR><TR>
<TD><%= AspAdoObj.EmployeeIDNumber%></TD>
```

continued on next page

continued from previous page

```
<TD><%= AspAdoObj.EmployeeLastName%></TD>
<TD><%= AspAdoObj.EmployeeFirstName%></TD>
<TD><%= AspAdoObj.EmployeeJobTitle%></TD>
<TD><%= AspAdoObj.EmployeePhoneNumber%></TD>
</TR></TABLE>
</BODY>
</HTML>
```

5. Bring up Netscape Navigator or some other non-IE browser, and enter the following address: `HTTP://DEFAULT/ASPEXEC/ASPHT1008.ASP`. As shown in Figure 10-34, the display comes up with the first database record. Enter `NEXT` in the text control and press the Navigate button to submit the form. In a moment, the second database record will appear in the display, as shown in Figure 10-35. Experiment with the `PREVIOUS`, `FIRST`, and `LAST` commands and you will find they all work as well. You now can expose ADO functionality through an ASP component to ASP scripts.

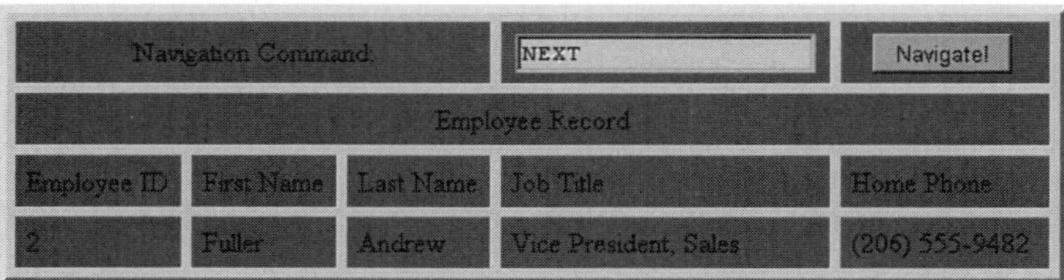

Figure 10-34 `ASPHT1008.ASP` **in Netscape Communicator showing the initial display from the ASP component**

Navigation Command:			NEXT	Navigate!
Employee Record				
Employee ID	First Name	Last Name	Job Title	Home Phone
14	Wortham	Jill	Nyvyrkandar	237-2675

Figure 10-35 `ASPHT1008.ASP` **in Netscape Communicator showing the next display from the ASP component after entering** `NEXT`

How It Works

At first glance, this seems to be like taking coal to Newcastle, as they used to say in Merry Olde England (that is, doing an unnecessary job). In fact, though, this How-To illustrates a very important point: Just because you can do something in

ADO directly from a script doesn't mean you should. ASP scripts are just text files, and on some systems they can easily be compromised and read by users or other nonauthorized folks. Thus, there can be a need to encapsulate sensitive information inside compiled C++ wrapper, but also a need to manipulate it via ASP scripts.

This How-To offloads the work of showing the data to the script, simply supporting internal database updates.

```
if(m_pAdoWrapper->MoveLast())
      {
       try
         {
           m_employeeFirstName = m_pAdoWrapper->GetFirstName();
           m_employeeLastName = m_pAdoWrapper->GetLastName();
           m_employeeJobTitle = m_pAdoWrapper->GetTitle();
           m_employeePhoneNumber = m_pAdoWrapper->GetHomePhone();
           m_employeeIDNumber = m_pAdoWrapper->GetEmployeeId();
```

If a successful navigation operation is performed, then the member variables are updated so that the ASP script can get them. This is done very easily.

```
<TD><%= AspAdoObj.EmployeeIDNumber%></TD>
<TD><%= AspAdoObj.EmployeeLastName%></TD>
<TD><%= AspAdoObj.EmployeeFirstName%></TD>
<TD><%= AspAdoObj.EmployeeJobTitle%></TD>
<TD><%= AspAdoObj.EmployeePhoneNumber%></TD>
```

What isn't so easy is keeping track of where you are. Because connection pooling is very useful with ADO behavior, it is best to connect and disconnect each time the page is loaded and unloaded. The problem is how to remember where you were with storing the connection record.

```
Set AspAdoObj = Server.CreateObject("AspAdo.EmployeeViewer")
AspAdoObjRecord = Session("AspObjectRecord")
Call AspAdoObj.MoveToFirstRecord
for Counter1 = 1 to AspAdoObjRecord - 1
  Call AspAdoObj.MoveToNextRecord
next
```

The key lies in retrieving the `AspAdoObjRecord` value. If it isn't stored, it will be `0`, so it can safely be used in a loop to move forward even the first time through. Notice that the counter is moved one less than the actual record count because it is one-based.

The other half of the solution is storing where you are each time.

```
if Ucase( Request.Form("NavigationInstruction")) = "FIRST" then
   call AspAdoObj.MoveToFirstRecord
elseif Ucase( Request.Form("NavigationInstruction")) = "PREVIOUS" then
   call AspAdoObj.MoveToPreviousRecord
elseif Ucase( Request.Form("NavigationInstruction")) = "NEXT" then
   call AspAdoObj.MoveToNextRecord
elseif Ucase( Request.Form("NavigationInstruction")) = "LAST" then
   call AspAdoObj.MoveToLastRecord
  End if
Session("AspObjectRecord") = AspAdoObj.EmployeeIDNumber
```

This way, after each navigation request, the current ID number is stored. Of course, if the database has ID numbers out of sync, this won't work as well, but it serves as a starting point.

Comments

Another solution—one that isn't vulnerable to ID number mismatches—is to store the object itself as a session variable and reload it each time through.

ADO-IEXT

10.9 How do I… Use ADO in a Visual C++ 5.0 ISAPI extension?

Problem

We have several ISAPI extensions that need ADO functionality. How can we make ADO available directly to a C++ ISAPI extension?

Technique

Via the same techniques as used in previous How-To's, except for several "gotchas." This How-To creates an ISAPI extension that matches a form input name and phone number and sends out either a URL for a valid match or an error message. The directions here create the project from scratch, but for your convenience a copy of the project is on the book CD under `\CH10\HT09\`.

Steps

1. Activate Visual C++ 5.0. Create a new MFC ISAPI extension project named `ISAPIXADO`, as shown in Figure 10-36. Select an `Extension` object only, with MFC as a shared DLL, as shown in Figure 10-37. Press Finish and accept the remaining dialog boxes to create the skeleton project.

2. Copy the `ADOHEADERS.H`, `ADOWRAPPER.H`, and `ADOWRAPPER.CPP` files into the project directory. Use the shortcut menus of the Project pane to add these files to the project.

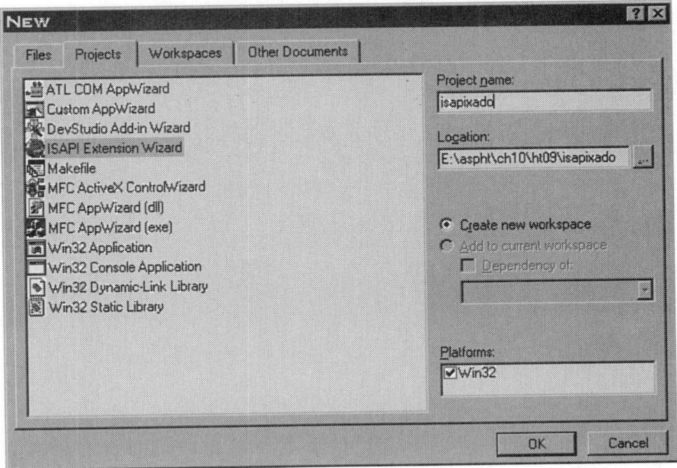

Figure 10-36 Creating a new ISAPI extension in MFC

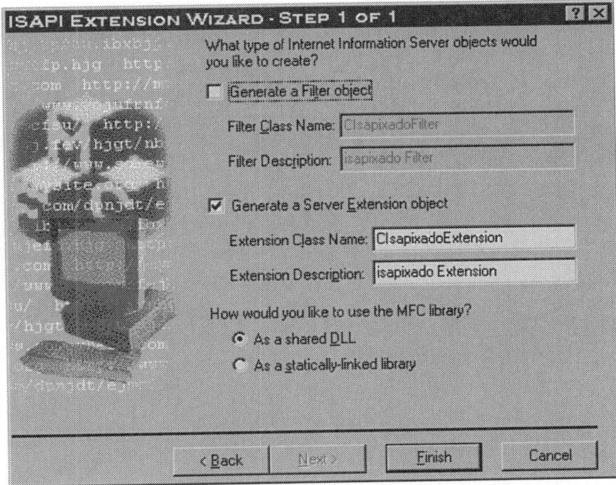

Figure 10-37 Setting an `Extension` object with a shared MFC DLL

3. Bring up `ISAPIXADO.H` in the text editor. Enter the boldface code in Listing 10-49 to add ADO support in the extension. Save the project.

Listing 10-49 ISAPIXADO.H source code

```
#if !defined(AFX_ISAPIXADO_H__4483E7F9_001A_11D1_B7DF_444553540000__INCLUDED_)
#define AFX_ISAPIXADO_H__4483E7F9_001A_11D1_B7DF_444553540000__INCLUDED_

// ISAPIXADO.H - Header file for your Internet Server
//    isapixado Extension

#include "resource.h"
#include "AdoWrapper.h"

class CIsapixadoExtension : public CHttpServer
{
public:
      CIsapixadoExtension();
      ~CIsapixadoExtension();
      CAdoWrapper*      m_pAdoWrapper;
// Operations
public:
      BOOL CommitAlteredEmpRec();
      CString PrepareCriteria();
    void HandleFormData(CHttpServerContext* pCtxt, LPCTSTR FirstNameTarget, ⇐
                        LPCTSTR PhoneNumberToTest );

// Overrides
      // ClassWizard generated virtual function overrides
            // NOTE - the ClassWizard will add and remove member functions here.
            //    DO NOT EDIT what you see in these blocks of generated code !
      //{{AFX_VIRTUAL(CIsapixadoExtension)
      virtual BOOL GetExtensionVersion(HSE_VERSION_INFO* pVer);
      //}}AFX_VIRTUAL

      // TODO: Add handlers for your commands here.
      // For example:

      void Default(CHttpServerContext* pCtxt);

      DECLARE_PARSE_MAP()

      //{{AFX_MSG(CIsapixadoExtension)
      //}}AFX_MSG
};


//{{AFX_INSERT_LOCATION}}
// Microsoft Developer Studio will insert additional declarations immediately
// before the previous line.

#endif //
!defined(AFX_ISAPIXADO_H__4483E7F9_001A_11D1_B7DF_444553540000__INCLUDED)
```

4. Now bring up `ISAPIXADO.CPP` in the text editor. Enter the boldface code in Listing 10-50 to add ADO support in the extension body. Save the project.

Listing 10-50 ISAPIXADO.CPP ADO support source code

```
// ISAPIXADO.CPP - Implementation file for your Internet Server
//    isapixado Extension

#include "stdafx.h"
#include "isapixado.h"

///////////////////////////////////////////////////////////////////////
// The one and only CWinApp object
// NOTE: You may remove this object if you alter your project to no
// longer use MFC in a DLL.

CWinApp theApp;

///////////////////////////////////////////////////////////////////////
// command-parsing map

BEGIN_PARSE_MAP(CIsapixadoExtension, CHttpServer)
      // TODO: insert your ON_PARSE_COMMAND() and
      // ON_PARSE_COMMAND_PARAMS() here to hook up your commands.
      // For example:

      ON_PARSE_COMMAND(Default, CIsapixadoExtension, ITS_EMPTY)
      DEFAULT_PARSE_COMMAND(Default, CIsapixadoExtension)
      ON_PARSE_COMMAND(HandleFormData, CIsapixadoExtension, ITS_PSTR ITS_PSTR)
      ON_PARSE_COMMAND_PARAMS("FirstNameHolder PhoneNumberHolder")
END_PARSE_MAP(CIsapixadoExtension)


///////////////////////////////////////////////////////////////////////
// The one and only CIsapixadoExtension object

CIsapixadoExtension theExtension;


///////////////////////////////////////////////////////////////////////
// CIsapixadoExtension implementation

CIsapixadoExtension::CIsapixadoExtension()
{
      m_pAdoWrapper = new CAdoWrapper;

      if(!m_pAdoWrapper->ConnectToDatabase())
      {
            m_pAdoWrapper->m_fConnected = FALSE;
            return;
      }

      m_pAdoWrapper->m_fConnected = TRUE;
}

CIsapixadoExtension::~CIsapixadoExtension()
{
      if (m_pAdoWrapper != NULL)
```

continued on next page

continued from previous page

```
        delete m_pAdoWrapper;
}

BOOL CIsapixadoExtension::GetExtensionVersion(HSE_VERSION_INFO* pVer)
{
      // Call default implementation for initialization
      CHttpServer::GetExtensionVersion(pVer);

      // Load description string
      TCHAR sz[HSE_MAX_EXT_DLL_NAME_LEN+1];
      ISAPIVERIFY(::LoadString(AfxGetResourceHandle(),
                  IDS_SERVER, sz, HSE_MAX_EXT_DLL_NAME_LEN));
      _tcscpy(pVer->lpszExtensionDesc, sz);
      return TRUE;
}

void CIsapixadoExtension::HandleFormData(CHttpServerContext* pCtxt, LPCTSTR ⇐
                              FirstNameTarget, LPCTSTR PhoneNumberToTest )
{
    CString      strCriteria = "";
    CString strFirstName = FirstNameTarget;
      CString strPhoneNumber = PhoneNumberToTest;

      if(strFirstName != "")
           strCriteria = "FirstName = '" + strFirstName +"'";
      if(strPhoneNumber != "")
          strCriteria = strCriteria + ( strCriteria == "" ? "":" AND ") + ⇐
                    "HomePhone = '" + strPhoneNumber +"'";
    if(strCriteria == "" )
      {
        StartContent(pCtxt);
          CString TheMessage = "<TITLE>Invalid Login!</TITLE></HEAD><BODY>";
          TheMessage += "<H1>No First Name or Phone Number entered!</H1>";
          *pCtxt << _T(TheMessage);
        EndContent(pCtxt);
      }
      else
      {
          if(m_pAdoWrapper->FindForward(strCriteria.AllocSysString()))
            {
            try
                  {
              StartContent(pCtxt);
                CString TheMessage = "<TITLE>Successful ⇐
                                  Login!</TITLE></HEAD><BODY>";
                TheMessage += "<H1>Your Login Is Accepted!</H1><P>";
                TheMessage += "Please click <A HREF=""http://default/aspexec/";
                    TheMessage += strFirstName;
                    TheMessage += ".asp>here</A> for your restricted URL ⇐
                                 information!";
                *pCtxt << _T(TheMessage);
              EndContent(pCtxt);
                  }
            catch (HRESULT hr)
                  {
```

```
            TCHAR szBuf[256];
            wsprintf(szBuf, _T("%X"), hr);
          StartContent(pCtxt);
            CString TheMessage = "<TITLE>Invalid ⇐
                                  Login!</TITLE></HEAD><BODY>";
            TheMessage += "<H1>HRESULT Returned an Error!</H1>";
            *pCtxt << _T(TheMessage);
          EndContent(pCtxt);
            }
      }
    else
      {
      StartContent(pCtxt);
        CString TheMessage = "<TITLE>Invalid Login!</TITLE></HEAD><BODY>";
        TheMessage += "<H1>The First Name and Phone Number entered do not ⇐
                       match our records!</H1>";
        *pCtxt << _T(TheMessage);
      EndContent(pCtxt);
      }
  }

}
```

5. Build the DLL and copy it to the ASPEXEC directory. Then activate ActiveX Control Pad and create a new HTML file. Enter the code in Listing 10-51 to invoke the ISAPI extension. Save it as LAURA.HTM in the ASPEXEC directory. Then create a new ASP file and enter the code in Listing 10-52. Save it in the ASPEXEC directory as LAURA.ASP.

Listing 10-51 LAURA.HTM HTML source code

```
<HTML>
<HEAD>
<TITLE>Laura's Restricted URL Login Page</TITLE>
</HEAD>
<BODY>
<FORM NAME=Form1 ACTION="http://default/aspexec/isapixado.dll?HandleFormData"
METHOD="Post">
<TABLE WIDTH=600 COLSPAN=2 BORDER=5 CELLSPACING=5
CELLPADDING=5 ALIGN="CENTER" VALIGN="MIDDLE" BGCOLOR="Teal">
<TR><TD ALIGN="CENTER">Hello</TD>
<TD ALIGN="CENTER">
<INPUT NAME=FirstNameHolder TYPE=TEXT VALUE="Laura"></TD>
</TR>
<TR>
<TD ALIGN="CENTER">
Please Enter your Phone Number to verify access to your restricted URL!</TD>
<TD ALIGN="CENTER">
<INPUT NAME=PhoneNumberHolder TYPE=TEXT VALUE=""></TD>
</TR>
<TR>
<TD ALIGN="CENTER">
Press VERIFY to log in!
</TD>
<TD ALIGN="CENTER">
```

continued on next page

continued from previous page

```
<INPUT TYPE=SUBMIT NAME=Submit1 VALUE="Verify"></TD>
</FORM>
</TR></TABLE>
</BODY>
</HTML>
```

Listing 10-52 LAURA.ASP ASP source code

```
<HTML>
<HEAD>
<TITLE>Active Server Pages How To Chapter 10 How To 9 -- Laura's Data</TITLE>
</HEAD>
<BODY>
<% Set AspAdoObj = Server.CreateObject("AspAdo.EmployeeViewer")
   AspAdoObj.EmployeeFirstName="Laura" %>
<%= AspAdoObj.GetDatabaseRecord %>
<% Set AspAdoObj = Nothing %>
</BODY>
</HTML>
```

6. Bring up LAURA.HTM in Internet Explorer or any other browser you like. You should see a display similar to Figure 10-38, with an HTML form containing two text controls, one of which contains the name **Laura** and the other of which is blank. Fill in **(206) 555-1189** in the phone number Text control (don't forget the space, the parentheses, and the -; the extension expects an exact match). Then press the Verify button. If you did the login right, you should see a display similar to Figure 10-39, with a simple HTML page confirming your login and redirecting you to another page. Press the link and you should see a display similar to Figure 10-40, as you are sent to the display created via the ASP component for Laura out of the database. You have now learned to link ISAPI extensions with ADO databases in C++ and use them in ASP and HTML.

Figure 10-38 The LAURA.HTM page in IE

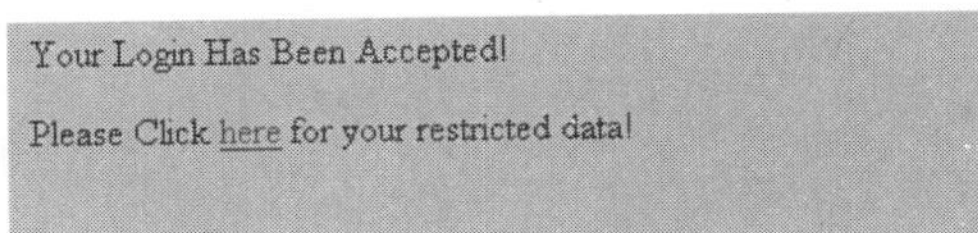

Figure 10-39 The response page from ISAPIXADO.DLL's analysis of the login data indicating a successful login

Employee Record				
Employee ID	First Name	Last Name	Job Title	Home Phone
8	Laura	Callahan	Inside Sales Coordinator	(206) 555-1189

Figure 10-40 The LAURA.ASP page in IE after jumping from the response page

How It Works

The connection used by this extension is its parse maps.

```
    ON_PARSE_COMMAND(Default, CIsapixadoExtension, ITS_EMPTY)
    DEFAULT_PARSE_COMMAND(Default, CIsapixadoExtension)
    ON_PARSE_COMMAND(HandleFormData, CIsapixadoExtension, ITS_PSTR ITS_PSTR)
    ON_PARSE_COMMAND_PARAMS("FirstNameHolder PhoneNumberHolder")
END_PARSE_MAP(CIsapixadoExtension)
```

These macros add the `HandleFormData` method and its two string parameters, `FirstNameHolder` and `PhoneNumberHolder`, to the incoming data stream from the HTTP server. They are then redirected to the part of the code where the actual lookup takes place.

```
CString      strCriteria = "";
CString strFirstName = FirstNameTarget;
CString strPhoneNumber = PhoneNumberToTest;

  if(strFirstName != "")
       strCriteria = "FirstName = '" + strFirstName +"'";
  if(strPhoneNumber != "")
  strCriteria = strCriteria + ( strCriteria == "" ? "":" AND ") + "HomePhone = ⇐
              '" + strPhoneNumber +"'";
```

Here, the two parameters are checked for empty values and placed in a search filter string. Then, assuming they aren't empty, the find routine is called and a result is returned based on its returned values.

```
if(m_pAdoWrapper->FindForward(strCriteria.AllocSysString()))
  {
  try
        {
```

continued on next page

continued from previous page

```
StartContent(pCtxt);
  CString TheMessage = "<TITLE>Successful Login!</TITLE></HEAD><BODY>";
  TheMessage += "<H1>Your Login Is Accepted!</H1><P>";
  TheMessage += "Please click <A HREF=""http://default/aspexec/";
  TheMessage += strFirstName;
  TheMessage += ".asp>here</A> for your restricted URL information!";
  *pCtxt << _T(TheMessage);
    EndContent(pCtxt);
    }
```

The valid message is sent only if the find was successful. Otherwise, the error display is sent.

Comments

Notice that the URL is constructed with the `first name` parameter appended to an ASP suffix. This allows the extension to function as a generic login checker.

IFIL-ADO-ASP

COMPLEXITY
ADVANCED

10.10 How do I... Use ADO in a Visual C++ 5.0 ISAPI filter?

Problem

Our site setup is heavily dependent on CGI and custom database lookups to verify user access to the pages. How can we convert to ASP, ADO, and ISAPI?

Technique

ASP, ADO, and ISAPI can work together to solve this real-world problem. This How-To will link an ISAPI filter with the ISAPI extension created in How-To 10.9 to produce a complete restricted URL system. Although the directions here create the project from scratch, the completed ASP files are on the book CD under `\CH10\HT10\`.

Steps

1. Activate Visual C++ 5.0. Create a new ISAPI filter named `ISAPIFADO` with the wizard, as shown in Figure 10-41. As shown in Figure 10-42, create a filter DLL only, with MFC as a shared DLL. Set its notifications to Nonsecured port sessions and URL mapping requests only, as shown in Figure 10-43. Accept the wizard's results and create the skeleton project.

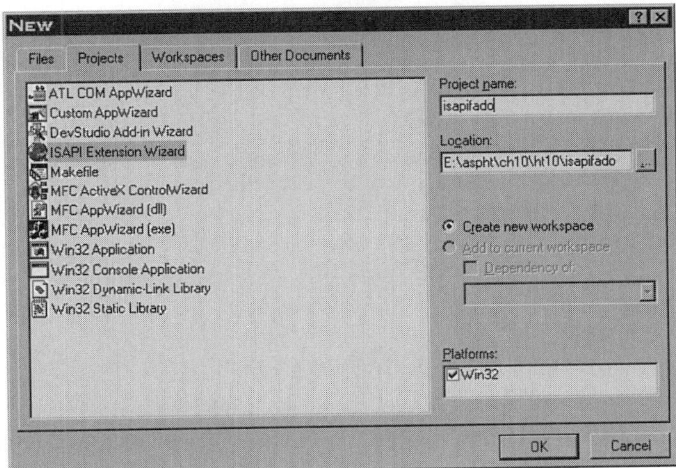

Figure 10-41 Creating an ISAPI filter named `ISAPIFADO`

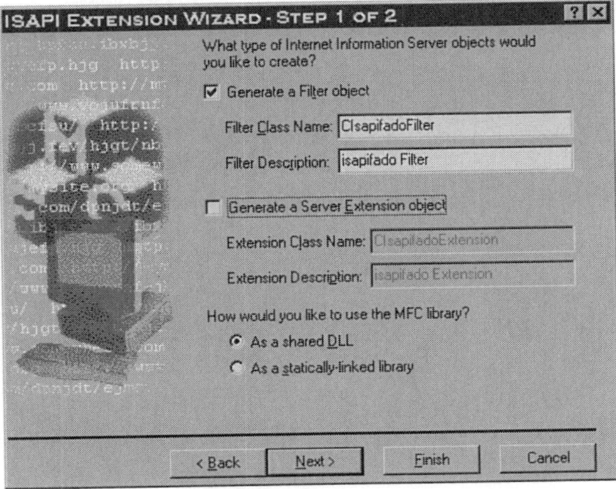

Figure 10-42 Creating a filter DLL with MFC as a shared DLL

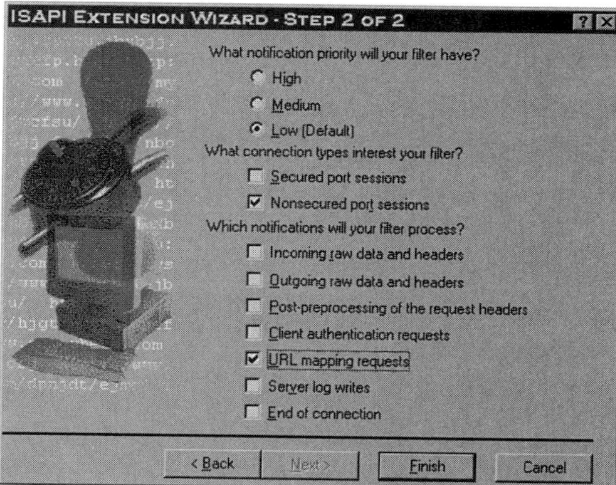

Figure 10-43 Setting URL mapping request notification for the ISAPIFADO filter

2. Copy the ADOHEADERS.H, ADOWRAPPER.H, and ADOWRAPPER.CPP files into the project directory. Use the shortcut menus of the Project pane to add these file to the project.

3. Bring up ISAPIFADO.H in the text editor. Enter the boldface code in Listing 10-53 to add ADO support in the filter. Save the project.

Listing 10-53 ISAPIFADO.H header file source code

```
#if !defined(AFX_ISAPIFADO_H__4483E804_001A_11D1_B7DF_444553540000__INCLUDED_)
#define AFX_ISAPIFADO_H__4483E804_001A_11D1_B7DF_444553540000__INCLUDED_

// ISAPIFADO.H - Header file for your Internet Server
//    isapifado Filter

#include "resource.h"
#include "Adoheaders.h"
#include "AdoWrapper.h"

class CIsapifadoFilter : public CHttpFilter
{
public:
      CIsapifadoFilter();
      ~CIsapifadoFilter();
      CAdoWrapper*      m_pAdoWrapper;

// Overrides
      // ClassWizard generated virtual function overrides
            // NOTE - the ClassWizard will add and remove member functions here.
            //    DO NOT EDIT what you see in these blocks of generated code !
      //{{AFX_VIRTUAL(CIsapifadoFilter)
      public:
```

```
    virtual BOOL GetFilterVersion(PHTTP_FILTER_VERSION pVer);
    virtual DWORD OnUrlMap(CHttpFilterContext* pCtxt, PHTTP_FILTER_URL_MAP ⇐
                    pMapInfo);
    //}}AFX_VIRTUAL

    //{{AFX_MSG(CIsapifadoFilter)
    //}}AFX_MSG
};

//{{AFX_INSERT_LOCATION}}
// Microsoft Developer Studio will insert additional declarations immediately
// before the previous line.

#endif //
!defined(AFX_ISAPIFADO_H__4483E804_001A_11D1_B7DF_444553540000__INCLUDED)
```

4. Bring up `ISAPIFADO.CPP` in the text editor. Enter the boldface code in Listing 10-54 to add ADO support code in the filter. Save the project. Then build the DLL and register the filter with IIS/PWS (see How-To 9.1, step 8, for directions if you are not clear on how to do this).

Listing 10-54 `ISAPIFADO.CPP` ADO support source code

```
// ISAPIFADO.CPP - Implementation file for your Internet Server
//    isapifado Filter

#include "stdafx.h"
#include "isapifado.h"

///////////////////////////////////////////////////////////////////////
// The one and only CWinApp object
// NOTE: You may remove this object if you alter your project to no
// longer use MFC in a DLL.

CWinApp theApp;



///////////////////////////////////////////////////////////////////////
// The one and only CIsapifadoFilter object

CIsapifadoFilter theFilter;


///////////////////////////////////////////////////////////////////////
// CIsapifadoFilter implementation

CIsapifadoFilter::CIsapifadoFilter()
{
        m_pAdoWrapper = new CAdoWrapper;

        if(!m_pAdoWrapper->ConnectToDatabase())
        {
                m_pAdoWrapper->m_fConnected = FALSE;
                return;
```

continued on next page

continued from previous page

```
        }

        m_pAdoWrapper->m_fConnected = TRUE;
}

CIsapifadoFilter::~CIsapifadoFilter()
{
        if (m_pAdoWrapper != NULL)
            delete m_pAdoWrapper;
}


BOOL CIsapifadoFilter::GetFilterVersion(PHTTP_FILTER_VERSION pVer)
{
        // Call default implementation for initialization
        CHttpFilter::GetFilterVersion(pVer);

        // Clear the flags set by base class
        pVer->dwFlags &= ~SF_NOTIFY_ORDER_MASK;

        // Set the flags we are interested in
        pVer->dwFlags |= SF_NOTIFY_ORDER_LOW | SF_NOTIFY_NONSECURE_PORT | ⇐
                         SF_NOTIFY_URL_MAP;

        // Load description string
        TCHAR sz[SF_MAX_FILTER_DESC_LEN+1];
        ISAPIVERIFY(::LoadString(AfxGetResourceHandle(),
                    IDS_FILTER, sz, SF_MAX_FILTER_DESC_LEN));
        _tcscpy(pVer->lpszFilterDesc, sz);
        return TRUE;
}

DWORD CIsapifadoFilter::OnUrlMap(CHttpFilterContext* pCtxt,
        PHTTP_FILTER_URL_MAP pMapInfo)
{
    CString strOutputPath;
    int nPosition = 0;

    strOutputPath = pMapInfo->pszPhysicalPath;

    nPosition = strOutputPath.Find("\\~~");
    if (nPosition != -1)
    {
        CString strHoldPath3 = strOutputPath.Left(nPosition + 1);
        CString strHoldPath = strOutputPath.Mid(nPosition + 3);

            nPosition = strHoldPath.Find("\\");

            if (nPosition != -1 )
            {
            CString strHoldName = strHoldPath.Left( nPosition - 1 );
                  CString      strCriteria = "FirstName = '" + strHoldName +"'";
            try
                  {
                  if(m_pAdoWrapper->FindForward(strCriteria.AllocSysString()))
```

```
                    {
                      strHoldName += ".htm";
                 strOutputPath = strHoldPath3 + "\\" + strHoldName;
                 strcpy (pMapInfo->pszPhysicalPath, (LPCTSTR)strOutputPath);
                    }
              }
          catch (HRESULT hr)
              {
               TCHAR szBuf[256];
               wsprintf(szBuf, _T("%X"), hr);
              }
        }

    }

    return SF_STATUS_REQ_NEXT_NOTIFICATION;
}
```

5. Bring up a browser and type in `HTTP://DEFAULT/ASPEXEC/~~LAURA/DEFAULT.HTM` as the URL. The filter will kick in, and instead of getting an error message that there is no such URL, you will see the `LAURA.HTM` file appear, as shown in Figure 10-44. Congratulations! You have created a complete restricted URL system using ISAPI filters, ISAPI extensions, ASP components and scripts, and C++ ADO. You now qualify as an ASP guru!

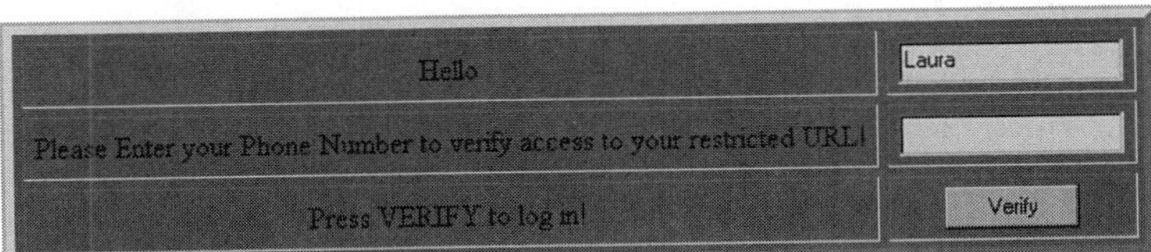

Figure 10-44 A ~~LAURA URL redirected to the LAURA.HTM file by the ISAPIFADO filter

How It Works

This How-To is a repeated version of the `TILDEFILTER` filter built in Chapter 9, "ISAPI Filters: Customizing Internet Information Server," with a twist.

```
nPosition = strOutputPath.Find("\\~~");
    if (nPosition != -1)
    {
        CString strHoldPath3 = strOutputPath.Left(nPosition + 1);
        CString strHoldPath = strOutputPath.Mid(nPosition + 3);

            nPosition = strHoldPath.Find("\\");

            if (nPosition != -1 )
            {
            CString strHoldName = strHoldPath.Left( nPosition - 1 );
                  CString      strCriteria = "FirstName = '" + strHoldName +"'";
```

First, a find is done on the input string to see if it has a double ~~. If so, the URL to that point is peeled off and stored in `strHoldPath3`. Then the rest of the string is sent to `strHoldPath`, where it is checked for a terminating backslash (remember the path has been turned into a Windows path, so it's a backslash and not a forward slash); if one is found, the URL's name portion is peeled off and set into a search criteria string. Then the find call is made.

```
if(m_pAdoWrapper->FindForward(strCriteria.AllocSysString()))
      {
       strHoldName += ".htm";
  strOutputPath = strHoldPath3 + "\\" + strHoldName;
  strcpy (pMapInfo->pszPhysicalPath, (LPCTSTR)strOutputPath);
      }
```

If the find matches, then the name is in the database and a possible restricted URL login is possible. The output path is then reconstructed using the original path, a dividing backslash, and the name, to which `.htm` has been appended. This value is then set into the physical path returned, and the HTTP transaction continues, but ends up at the proper file rather than a nonexistent URL.

Comments

That is the end of the book. I hope that you've learned more than enough from these 100 How-To's to justify the time and expense of this tome. Good luck, and happy coding!

INDEX

Symbols

A

D

F

G

H

I-J

K-L

M

N

P

Q-R

S

T

WAITE GROUP PRESS™

BORLAND® C++BUILDER HOW-TO

John Miano, Tom Cabanski, Harold Howe

Presents over 100 clear solutions to real-life C++Builder programming challenges. Popular "how-to" format covers ways to collect input and provide output, "spy" on other programs and their windows, create animated icons that report information while program is minimized, and create Windows user interfaces with simple point-and-click operations.

Available now • 750 pages
ISBN: 1-57169-109-X
U.S. $49.99 • 1 CD-ROM

HTML 4 HOW-TO

John Zakour, Jeff Foust, David Kerven

HTML 4 How-To explains how to create Web pages with links, sound, and graphics in the easy "How do I...?" format. It teaches how to format paragraphs, create bullets, add underlined and boldfaced characters and blinking text. It also covers the hottest new HTML 4 topics— Cascading Style Sheets, JavaScript Style Sheets, Dynamic HTML, and Dynamic Style Sheets including layers.

Available now • 680 pages
ISBN: 1-57169-050-6
U.S. $39.99 • 1 CD-ROM

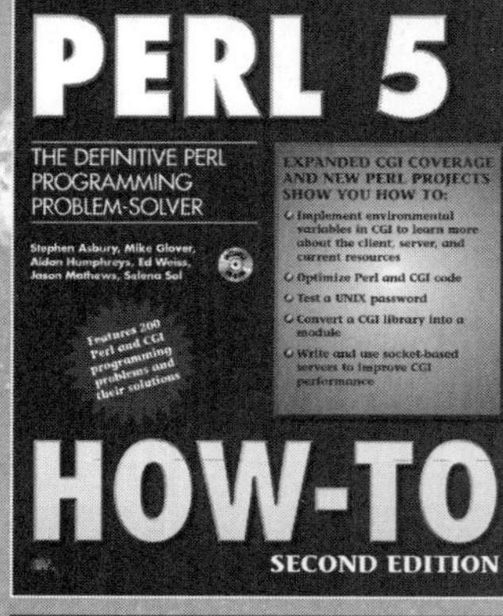

PERL 5 HOW-TO, SECOND EDITION

Stephen Asbury, Aiden Humphreys, Mike Glover, Ed Weiss, Selena Sol, Jason Mathews

Perl 5 How-To, 2nd Edition shows you how to use Perl to manipulate text, mark up pages for the Web, convert text pages to hypertext, parse files and process the resultant data, write scripts that locate and replace strings, or just write a quick and portable program. Includes extensive CGI coverage. The CD-ROM includes all the examples and a copy of Perl.

Available now • 800 pages
ISBN: 1-57169-118-9
U.S. $49.99 • 1 CD-ROM

Send for our unique catalog to get more information about these books as well as our other outstanding and award-winning titles.

VISUAL BASIC 5
DATABASE
THE DEFINITIVE VISUAL BASIC 5 DATABASE PROBLEM-SOLVER
COMPLETE COVERAGE OF VISUAL BASIC 5 DATABASE TOPICS. LEARN HOW TO:
Dennis Kennedy, Joe Garrick, Bill Harper, Jason T. Roff
HOW-TO

WAITE GROUP PRESS
VISUAL BASIC 5
INTERACTIVE COURSE
WEB-BASED LEARNING CENTER
www.waite.com/ezone

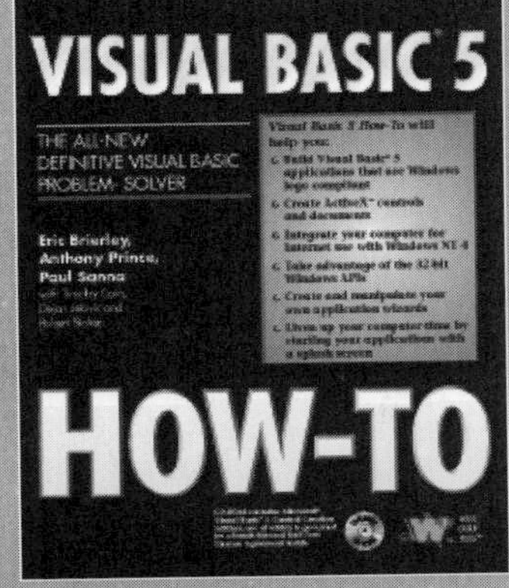
VISUAL BASIC 5
THE ALL-NEW DEFINITIVE VISUAL BASIC PROBLEM-SOLVER
Eric Brierley, Anthony Prince, Paul Sanna
HOW-TO

Message from the **Publisher**

Welcome to Our Nervous System

Some people say that the World Wide Web is a graphical extension of the information superhighway, just a network of humans and machines sending each other long lists of the equivalent of digital junk mail.

I think it is much more than that. To me, the Web is nothing less than the nervous system of the entire planet—not just a collection of computer brains connected together, but more like a billion silicon neurons entangled and recirculating electro-chemical signals of information and data, each contributing to the birth of another CPU and another Web site.

Think of each person's hard disk connected at once to every other hard disk on earth, driven by human navigators searching like Columbus for the New World. Seen this way the Web is more of a super entity, a growing, living thing, controlled by the universal human will to expand, to be more. Yet, unlike a purposeful business plan with rigid rules, the Web expands in a nonlinear, unpredictable, creative way that echoes natural evolution.

We created our Web site not just to extend the reach of our computer book products but to be part of this synaptic neural network, to experience, like a nerve in the body, the flow of ideas and then to pass those ideas up the food chain of the mind. Your mind. Even more, we wanted to pump some of our own creative juices into this rich wine of technology.

Taste Our Digital Wine

And so we ask you to taste our wine by visiting the body of our business. Begin by understanding the metaphor we have created for our Web site—a universal learning center, situated in outer space in the form of a space station. A place where you can journey to study any topic from the convenience of your own screen. Right now we are focusing on computer topics, but the stars are the limit on the Web.

If you are interested in discussing this Web site or finding out more about the Waite Group, please send me email with your comments, and I will be happy to respond. Being a programmer myself, I love to talk about technology and find out what our readers are looking for.

Sincerely,

Mitchell Waite, C.E.O. and Publisher

200 Tamal Plaza
Corte Madera, CA 94925
415-924-2575
415-924-2576 fax

Website:
http://www.waite.com/waite

Creating the Highest Quality Computer Books in the Industry

Waite Group Press

This is a legal agreement between you, the end user and purchaser, and The Waite Group®, Inc., and the authors of the programs contained in the disc. By opening the sealed disc package, you are agreeing to be bound by the terms of this Agreement. If you do not agree with the terms of this Agreement, promptly return the unopened disc package and the accompanying items (including the related book and other written material) to the place you obtained them for a refund.

SOFTWARE LICENSE

1. The Waite Group, Inc., grants you the right to use one copy of the enclosed software programs (the programs) on a single computer system (whether a single CPU, part of a licensed network, or a terminal connected to a single CPU). Each concurrent user of the program must have exclusive use of the related Waite Group, Inc., written materials.

2. The program, including the copyrights in each program, is owned by the respective author and the copyright in the entire work is owned by The Waite Group, Inc., and they are therefore protected under the copyright laws of the United States and other nations, under international treaties. You may make only one copy of the disc containing the programs exclusively for backup or archival purposes, or you may transfer the programs to one hard disk drive, using the original for backup or archival purposes. You may make no other copies of the programs, and you may make no copies of all or any part of the related Waite Group, Inc., written materials.

3. You may not rent or lease the programs, but you may transfer ownership of the programs and related written materials (including any and all updates and earlier versions) if you keep no copies of either, and if you make sure the transferee agrees to the terms of this license.

4. You may not decompile, reverse engineer, disassemble, copy, create a derivative work, or otherwise use the programs except as stated in this Agreement.

GOVERNING LAW

This Agreement is governed by the laws of the State of California.